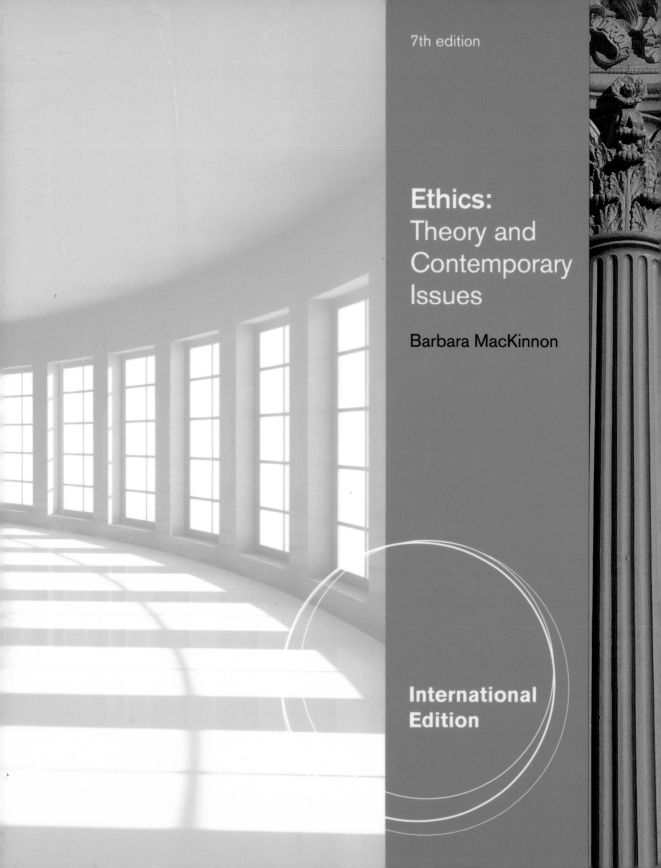

7th edition

Ethics:
Theory and Contemporary Issues

Barbara MacKinnon

International Edition

ETHICS

ETHICS

THEORY AND CONTEMPORARY ISSUES
SEVENTH EDITION

BARBARA MACKINNON
University of San Francisco, Professor Emerita

WADSWORTH
CENGAGE Learning™

Australia • Brazil • Japan • Korea • Mexico • Singapore • Spain • United Kingdom • United States

WADSWORTH
CENGAGE Learning™

Ethics: Theory and Contemporary Issues, **Seventh Edition**

Barbara MacKinnon

Publisher: Clark Baxter

Senior Sponsoring Editor: Joann Kozyrev

Development Editor: Ian Lague

Assistant Editor: Nathan Gamache

Editorial Assistant: Michaela Henry

Media Editor: Kimberly Apfelbaum

Marketing Manager: Mark T. Haynes

Marketing Coordinator: Josh Hendrick

Marketing Communications Manager: Laura Localio

Associate Content Project Manager: Sara Abbott

Senior Art Director: Jennifer Wahi

Senior Manufacturing Buyer: Karen Hunt

Senior Rights Acquisition Specialist: Katie Huha

Production Service/Compositor: KnowledgeWorks Global Limited

Text Designer: Norman Baugher

Cover Image: Courtesy of Jupiter Images (photos.com)

International Edition:
ISBN-13: 978-1-111-18590-9
ISBN-10: 1-111-18590-5

Cengage Learning International Offices

Asia
www.cengageasia.com
tel: (65) 6410 1200

Australia/New Zealand
www.cengage.com.au
tel: (61) 3 9685 4111

Brazil
www.cengage.com.br
tel: (55) 11 3665 9900

India
www.cengage.co.in
tel: (91) 11 4364 1111

Latin America
www.cengage.com.mx
tel: (52) 55 1500 6000

UK/Europe/Middle East/Africa
www.cengage.co.uk
tel: (44) 0 1264 332 424

Represented in Canada by Nelson Education, Ltd.
tel: (416) 752 9100 / (800) 668 0671
www.nelson.com

Cengage Learning is a leading provider of customized learning solutions with office locations around the globe, including Singapore, the United Kingdom, Australia, Mexico, Brazil, and Japan. Locate your local office at: **www.cengage.com/global**

For product information: **www.cengage.com/international**
Visit your local office: **www.cengage.com/global**
Visit our corporate website: **www.cengage.com**

AVAILABILITY OF RESOURCES MAY DIFFER BY REGION. Check with your local Cengage Learning representative for details.

Printed in the United States of America
1 2 3 4 5 6 7 14 13 12 11 10

For Edward, Jennifer, and Kathleen

Contents

Preface

This seventh edition of *Ethics: Theory and Contemporary Issues* provides increased coverage of ethical theory in Part I and a thorough introduction to contemporary ethical issues in Part II. As in past editions, each chapter begins with a detailed, accessible introduction by the author that prepares the student to read the accompanying selections from well-known philosophers. In this, it not only remains a comprehensive introduction to ethics, but also continues to emphasize pedagogy through examples that interest students and various study tools, such as the appendix on how to write an ethics paper.

ADDITIONS AND CHANGES

Although the basic elements remain the same, this edition has the following additions and changes from the sixth edition. All introductions have been updated, with special attention paid to the chapters in Part II. These updates include recent statistics, relevant cases, and contemporary examples. This seventh edition has two new chapters, one on Feminist Thought and the Ethics of Care and one on Contractarianism. It also includes several new readings, by C. L. Stevenson, Jean-Paul Sartre, Thomas Hobbes, T. M. Scanlon, Martin Luther King, Jr., and Amartya Sen. Perhaps the most obvious change is the attractive new page design, created to appeal to today's visually sophisticated student without detracting from the philosophical content.

Key Elements

The following are key elements of this edition:
Text Each chapter in both the theory and issues parts of the text contains an extended introduction.

These are somewhat more detailed than what might usually be found in a reader. As noted above, they have been thoroughly updated for relevant cases and current news items.

The theory chapters present moderately detailed summaries of the theories and major issues, positions, and arguments. The contemporary issues chapters present several different things, including summaries of:

> current social conditions and recent events that will interest the student in the topic and provide current information,

> conceptual issues, such as how to define key words and phrases (for example, cloning, terrorism, and distributive justice), and

> arguments and suggested ways to organize an ethical analysis of the particular topic.

The presentations in the text often ask questions and are usually followed by several different possible answers or explanations. The aim is to present more than one side of the issue so that students can decide for themselves what position they will take. This also allows instructors to put whatever emphases they wish on the material or direct the students' focus as they see fit.

Where possible throughout the text, the relation of ethical theory to the practical issues is indicated. For example, one pervasive distinction that is used throughout is the one between consequentialist and nonconsequentialist considerations and arguments. The idea is that if students are able to situate or categorize a kind of reason or argument, then they will be better able to evaluate it critically. References to treatments of related issues in other chapters are also given throughout the text.

Pedagogical Aids This text is designed to be "user-friendly." To aid both instructor and student, the following pedagogical aids are provided:

› clearly organized material in the textual sections by means of diagrams, subheadings, definitions, and key terms;
› a real-life event or hypothetical dialogue or updated empirical data at the beginning of each chapter to capture students' interest;
› study questions for each reading selection;
› review exercises at the end of each chapter that also can be used as test or exam questions;
› discussion cases that follow each chapter in Part II and provide opportunities for class or group discussions;
› topics and resources for written assignments in the discussion cases; and
› the popular appendix on how to write an ethics paper, which gives students helpful advice and brief examples of ethics papers.

The outline of the history of ethics on page xviii is admittedly sketchy. It makes only a limited attempt to include twentieth-century ethics and notes only a couple of non-Western figures. However, for those who are interested in history or in placing figures mentioned in this text into an historical context, it should be useful.

Gender and Racial Concerns Although this is primarily a general ethics text, it does make extra effort to include writings from female authors in the reading selections, and in the chapter on the ethics of care. Moreover, feminist issues are also treated throughout the text. These include questions of sex equality and sexual harassment, abortion, ecofeminism, and gender discrimination in the developing world. Racial concerns are stressed not only in the chapter on discrimination but also in the chapter on economic justice and throughout the text, where possible.

International Concerns References to international concerns are found throughout the text and are prominent in Chapter 20 on global issues. Chapter 19 on violence, terrorism, and war is also heavily international in scope.

IN SUMMARY

Ethics: Theory and Contemporary Issues continues to be the most comprehensive ethics text available. It combines theory and issues, text and readings. It aims to be flexible, user-friendly, current, pedagogically helpful, and balanced.

› It is flexible by allowing instructors to emphasize the theory or issues, or the textual material or readings as they choose.
› It is user-friendly while at the same time philosophically reliable. This book is not "pop ethics." (You cannot do that and at the same time be philosophically accurate and adequate.) On the other hand, it uses many pedagogical aids throughout and at the end of each chapter. This text often provides examples and up-to-date newsworthy events. The exposition provides stimulating questions throughout the textual presentations. It provides diagrams wherever I think they will help, along with helpful headings.
› The book is current not only on day-to-day developments that are in the news and in scientific journals but also on the issues as they are discussed by philosophers.
› It is pedagogically helpful by including online and textual tools that amplify its teachability.
› It is balanced in its collection of readings, including both the ethical theories and contemporary sources on the issues.

Web-Related Elements
Online Student and Instructor Resources Many student and instructor resources are available online at www.cengage.com/philosophy/mackinnon/ethics7e. The student companion website for this text includes test questions, quizzes, and web references for various topics treated in the text. The password-protected instructor website includes these items as well as an Instructor's Manual and PowerPoint® slides for lecture and review.

Instructor's Manual Online

The Instructor's Manual (IM) is available online at www.cengage.com/philosophy/mackinnon/ethics7e. It is available on the password-protected instructor companion site so that only instructors will have access to it. Interested instructors should contact their local Wadsworth sales representative or Wadsworth directly for a password.

Course-Management System

Wadsworth's comprehensive course-management system (CengageNow) includes step-by-step learning plans for each topic, pre- and post-reading questions, and tools to help professors create online assignments, tests, quizzes, and study units. The text will also be accompanied by Wadsworth's new interactive ethics learning modules. These modules prompt students to apply the ethical theories they have learned to challenging "real-world" situations by making a series of ethical choices in response to an unfolding story.

ACKNOWLEDGMENTS

I wish to thank the many people who have made valuable suggestions for improving the text, including Majid Behrouzi of Cuyahoga Community College, Jim Chesher of Santa Barbara City College, Brian Barnes of the University of Louisville, Michael Booker of Jefferson College, Louis Colombo of Bethune-Cookman University, Remy Debes of University of Memphis, Kai Draper of the University of Memphis, Lisa Fuller University of SUNY Albany, Dusan Galic of the College of DuPage, Susanne Goethais of Arizona Western College, Jennifer Harvey of Drake University, Travis Hreno of the University

of Akron, Leigh Johnson of Rhodes College, Jason Johnstone-Yellin of the University of Idaho, William Kallfelz of New Mexico State University, Sebastian Kaufmann of Triton College, Elizabeth Linehan of Saint Joseph's University, Alexander Miller of Northern Kentucky University, Lawrence Pasternack of Oklahoma State University, David Phillips of the University of Houston, Pam Sailors of Missouri State University, Ed Sherline of the University of Wyoming, Gerald Sullivan of Trinity Washington University, Phyllis Vanderberg of Grand Valley State University, and John Wadhams of Eastfield College.

The students in my classes at the University of San Francisco over the years also have contributed greatly to this text by challenging me to keep up with the times and to make things more clear and more interesting. I wish also to thank them here.

I wish to acknowledge the many professional people from Cengage Learning who have worked on this edition: Joann Kozyrev–Senior Sponsoring Editor, Ian Lague–Development Editor, Suzanne St. Clair–Production Manager, Sara Abbott–Associate Content Project Manager, Jennifer Wahi–Senior Art Director, Clark Baxter–Publisher, Nathan Gamache–Assistant Editor, Michaela Henry–Editorial Assistant, Kimberly Apfelbaum–Media Editor, Josh Hendrick–Marketing Coordinator, Mark Haynes–Marketing Manager, and Laura Localio–Marketing Communications Manager.

Finally, I greatly appreciate the support given me by my husband and fellow philosopher, Edward MacKinnon. To him and to our two wonderful daughters, Jennifer and Kathleen, this book is again dedicated.

Barbara MacKinnon
Oakland, California

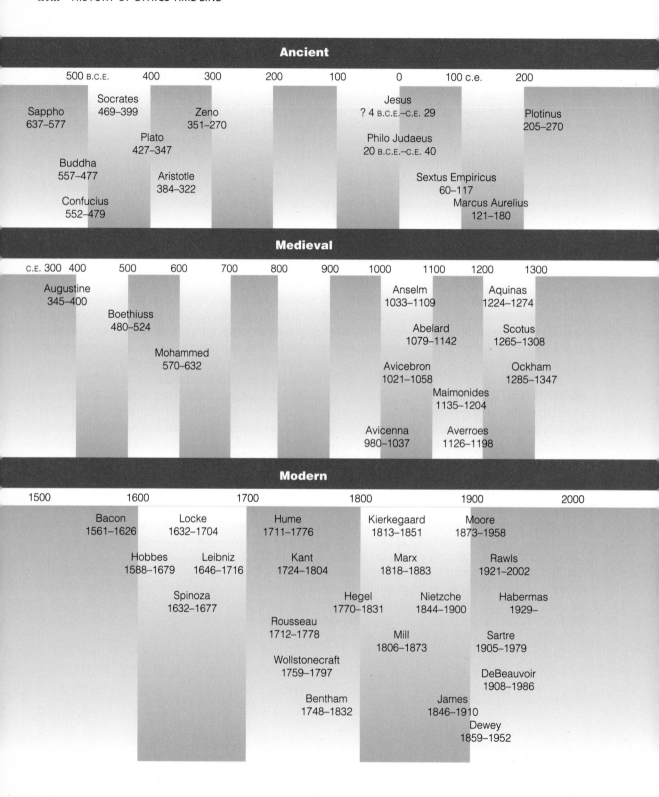

Ancient

| 500 B.C.E. | 400 | 300 | 200 | 100 | 0 | 100 C.E. | 200 |

Sappho
637–577

Socrates
469–399

Zeno
351–270

Jesus
? 4 B.C.E.–C.E. 29

Plotinus
205–270

Plato
427–347

Philo Judaeus
20 B.C.E.–C.E. 40

Buddha
557–477

Aristotle
384–322

Sextus Empiricus
60–117

Confucius
552–479

Marcus Aurelius
121–180

Medieval

| C.E. 300 | 400 | 500 | 600 | 700 | 800 | 900 | 1000 | 1100 | 1200 | 1300 |

Augustine
345–400

Anselm
1033–1109

Aquinas
1224–1274

Boethiuss
480–524

Abelard
1079–1142

Scotus
1265–1308

Mohammed
570–632

Avicebron
1021–1058

Ockham
1285–1347

Maimonides
1135–1204

Avicenna
980–1037

Averroes
1126–1198

Modern

| 1500 | 1600 | 1700 | 1800 | 1900 | 2000 |

Bacon
1561–1626

Locke
1632–1704

Hume
1711–1776

Kierkegaard
1813–1851

Moore
1873–1958

Hobbes
1588–1679

Leibniz
1646–1716

Kant
1724–1804

Marx
1818–1883

Rawls
1921–2002

Spinoza
1632–1677

Hegel
1770–1831

Nietzsche
1844–1900

Habermas
1929–

Rousseau
1712–1778

Mill
1806–1873

Sartre
1905–1979

Wollstonecraft
1759–1797

DeBeauvoir
1908–1986

Bentham
1748–1832

James
1846–1910

Dewey
1859–1952

1

Ethics and Ethical Reasoning

WHY STUDY ETHICS?

We live in a dangerous world. Whether it is more dangerous than in times past is an open question. One can think, for example, of the thirteenth century when Genghis Khan and his successors swept across Asia, Europe, and northern Africa and threatened to destroy all of Islamic civilization. We can also think of the bubonic plague in the mid-fourteenth century, which wiped out one-fourth of Western Europe's population and still reappeared in the following three centuries. On the other hand, today's threats may be even more powerful and have the capacity to affect many millions more people. For example, we have recently been made only too aware of the extent and capacity of terrorist networks around the world. Unstable nations and rulers possess powerful weapons of mass destruction. Individuals promoting a cause, acting out of revenge or in frustration, or for no clear reason at all can randomly kill people who are simply going about the business of life. We question what we may rightly do to lessen these dangers or prevent great possible harm. In some cases, the only way to do so seems to involve threats to other important values we hold—for example, rights to privacy and our basic civil liberties.

These are matters not only of practical and political bearing but also of moral rights and wrongs. They are also matters about which it is not easy to judge. We do not always know what is best to do, how to balance goods, or what reasons or principles we ought to follow.

For example, on October 24, 2001, six weeks after the terrorist attacks on the World Trade Center and the Pentagon, the U.S. Congress passed the Patriot Act. Among its provisions are "enhanced surveillance procedures." One of these is the "authority to intercept wire, oral, and electronic communications relating to terrorism." This act amended the 1978 Foreign Intelligence Surveillance Act (FISA) to include terrorism. Warrants to surveil were still required but could be delayed for a few days. Since that time, questions have been raised about whether such warrants are required. This is both a legal and an ethical matter. Whatever the legal conclusions, we can still ask whether the dangers are such that personal and private communications should be open to certain investigations without notification. How does one balance the supposed value of protection with the value of privacy? In February 2010, Congress voted to extend the act for one year as it was set to expire at the end of the month. However, they did so without adding any new privacy protections. Another example of a conflict between safety and privacy is exemplified by whole-body scanners at airport security.

Or consider academic cheating, such as buying and selling term papers or cutting and pasting pieces from Internet sites and passing them off as one's own work and ideas. One may admit that this is

Chip Somodevilla/Getty Images News/Getty Images

Images produced by a "millimeter wave" scanner at Ronald Reagan National Airport. Full-body scanners raise questions about the competing values of security and privacy.

clearly dishonest, yet one might argue that if professors make it easy to do so by the assignments they give or by their lack of oversight, then it should not be considered morally wrong.

In this text, we will examine some of the moral dilemmas we face as individuals and as peoples. Hopefully, by an explicit focus on such dilemmas, the decisions we must make will be more well-informed and, in fact, better decisions. At least that is the aim of this study of ethics.

METAETHICS

Questions about the nature of ethics are actually matters of metaethics. Metaethics seeks to understand the meaning of ethical terms and judgments. Thus this chapter as well as the following chapter on ethical relativism belong more properly to metaethics. The other chapters in part one are more properly designated as ethical theory.

WHAT IS ETHICS?

I have asked students on the first day of an ethics class to write one-paragraph answers to the question,

"What is ethics?" How would you answer? There have been significant differences of opinion among my students on this issue. Ethics is a highly personal thing, some wrote, a set of moral beliefs that develop over the years. Although the values may initially come from one's family upbringing, they later result from one's own convictions. Other students thought that ethics is a set of social principles, the codes of one's society or particular groups within it, such as medical or legal organizations. Some wrote that many people get their ethical beliefs from their religion.

One general conclusion can be drawn from these students' comments: We tend to think of ethics as the set of values or principles held by individuals or groups. I have my ethics and you have yours, and groups also have sets of values with which they tend to identify. We can think of ethics as a study of the various sets of values that people do have. This could be done historically and comparatively, for example, or with a psychological interest in determining how people form their values and when they tend to act on them. We can also think of ethics as a critical enterprise. We would then ask whether any particular set of values or beliefs is better than any other. We would compare and evaluate the sets of values and beliefs giving reasons for our evaluations. "Are there good reasons for preferring one set of ethics over another?" As we will pursue it in this text, ethics is this latter type of study. We will examine various ethical views and types of reasoning from a critical or evaluative standpoint. This examination will also help us come to a better understanding of our own and various societies' values.

Ethics is a branch of *philosophy*. It is also called *moral philosophy*. Although not everyone agrees on what philosophy is, let's think of it as a discipline or study in which we ask—and attempt to answer—basic questions about key areas or subject matters of human life and about pervasive and significant aspects of experience. Some philosophers, such as Plato and Kant, have tried to do this systematically by interrelating their philosophical views in many areas. According to Alfred North Whitehead, "Philosophy is the endeavor to frame a coherent, logical, necessary system of general ideas in terms of which every element of our experience can be interpreted."[1] Other people believe that philosophers today must work at problems piecemeal, focusing on one particular issue at a time. For instance, some might analyze the meaning of the phrase "to know," while others might work on the morality of lying. Furthermore, some philosophers are optimistic about our ability to answer these questions, while others are more skeptical because they think that the way we analyze the issues and the conclusions we draw will always be influenced by our background, culture, and ways of thinking. Most agree, however, that the questions are worth wondering about and caring about.

We can ask philosophical questions about many subjects. In aesthetics, or the philosophy of art, philosophers ask questions not about how to interpret a certain novel or painting, but about basic or foundational questions such as, What kinds of things do or should count as art (rocks arranged in a certain way, for example)? Is what makes something an object of aesthetic interest its emotional expressiveness, its peculiar formal nature, or its ability to show us certain truths that cannot be described? In the philosophy of science, philosophers ask not about the structure or composition of some chemical or biological material, but about such matters as whether scientific knowledge gives us a picture of reality as it is, whether progress exists in science, and whether it is meaningful to talk about the scientific method. Philosophers of law seek to understand the nature of law itself, the source of its authority, the nature of legal interpretation, and the basis of legal responsibility. In the philosophy of knowledge, called *epistemology*, we try to answer questions about what we can know of ourselves and our world and what it even is to know something rather than just to believe it. In each area, philosophers ask basic questions about the particular subject matter. This is also true of moral philosophy.

Ethics, or moral philosophy, asks basic questions about the good life, about what is better and worse, about whether there is any objective right and wrong, and how we know it if there is.

This definition of ethics assumes that its primary objective is to help us decide what is good or bad, better or worse, either in some general way or with regard to particular ethical issues. This is generally called *normative ethics*, to distinguish it from *metaethics*. Ethics, however, can be done in another way. From the mid-1930s until recently, metaethics predominated in English-speaking universities. Again, in doing metaethics, we would analyze the meaning of ethical language. Instead of asking whether the death penalty is morally justified, we would ask what we meant in calling something "morally justified" or "good" or "right." We would analyze ethical language, ethical terms, and ethical statements to determine what they mean. In doing this, we would be functioning at a level removed from that implied by our definition. It is for this reason that we call this other type of ethics *metaethics—meta* meaning "beyond." Some of the discussions in this chapter are metaethical discussions—for example, the analysis of various senses of "good." As you can see, much can be learned from such discussions. The various chapters of Part Two of this text do normative ethics, for they are concerned with particular concrete issues and how to evaluate or judge them.

ETHICS AND RELIGION

Many people get their ethical or moral views from their religion. Although religions include other elements, most do have explicit or implicit requirements or ideals for moral conduct. In some cases, they contain explicit rules or commandments: "Honor thy father and mother" and "Thou shalt not kill." Some religious morality is found in interpretations of religious books, lessons such as, "In this passage the Bible (or Koran or Bhagavad Gita) teaches us that we ought to…. " Some religions recognize and revere saints or holy people who provide models for us and exemplify virtues we should emulate.

Philosophers, however, believe that ethics does not necessarily require a religious grounding. Rather than relying on holy books or religious revelations, philosophical ethics uses reason and experience to determine what is good and bad, right and wrong, better and worse. In fact, even those people for whom morality is religiously based may want to examine some of these views using reason. They may want to know whether elements of their religious morality—some of its rules, for example—are good or valid ones given that other people have different views of what is right and wrong and given that that the problems of contemporary times are different from those of the past.

Moreover, if moral right and wrong were grounded only in religious beliefs, then nonbelievers could not be said to have moral views or make legitimate moral arguments. But even religious believers should want to be able to dialogue with such persons. In fact, even religious believers regularly make moral judgments that are not based strictly on their religious views but rather on reflection and common sense.

Thinking further about religious morality also raises challenges for it. A key element of many religious moralities is the view that certain things are good for us to do because this is what God wants. This conception is often referred to as the "divine command theory." The idea is that certain actions are right because they are what God wills for us. The reading at the end of this chapter from Plato's dialogue *Euthyphro* examines this view. In this dialogue, Socrates asks whether things are good because they are approved by the gods or whether the gods approve of them because they are good. To say that actions are good just because they are willed or approved by the gods or God seems to make morality arbitrary. God could decree anything to be good: lying or treachery, for example. It seems more reasonable to say that lying and treachery are bad, and for this reason the gods or God condemn or disapprove of them and that we should also. One implication of this view is that morality has a certain independence; if so, we should be able to determine whether certain actions are right or wrong in themselves and for some reason.

Religion, however, may still provide a motivation or inspiration to be moral for some people. They believe that if life has some eternal significance in relation to a supreme and most perfect being, then we ought to take life and morality extremely seriously. This would not be to say that the only reason religious persons have for being moral or trying to do the morally right thing is so that they will be rewarded in some life beyond this one. Rather, if something is morally right, then this is itself a reason for doing it. Thus, the good and conscientious person is the one who wants to do right just because it is right. However, questions about the meaning of life

may play a significant role in a person's thoughts about the moral life. Some people might even think that atheists have no reason to be moral or to be concerned with doing the morally right thing. However, this is not necessarily so. For example, a religious person may disvalue this life if he or she thinks of it as fleeting and less important than the things to come or what lies ahead in another world beyond this one. And atheists who believe that this life is all there is may in fact take this life more seriously and want to do well in it. Furthermore, the religious as well as the nonreligious should be able to think clearly and reason well about morality.

For at least three reasons, we all must be able to develop our natural moral reasoning skills. First, we should be able to evaluate critically our own or other views of what is thought to be good and bad or just and unjust, including religious views in some cases. Second, believers of various denominations as well as nonbelievers ought to be able to discuss moral matters together. Third, the fact that we live in organized secular communities, cities, states, and countries requires that we be able to develop and rely on widely shared reason-based views on issues of justice, fairness, and moral ideals. This is especially true in political communities with some separation of church and state, where no religion can be mandated, and where one has freedom within limits to practice a chosen religion or practice no religion at all. In these settings, it is important to have nonreligiously based ways of dealing with moral issues. This is one goal of philosophical ethics.

ETHICAL AND OTHER TYPES OF EVALUATION

"That's great!" "Now, this is what I call a delicious meal!" "That play was wonderful!" All of these statements express approval of something. They do not tell us much about the meal or the play, but they do imply that the speaker thought they were good. These are *evaluative* statements. Ethical statements or judgments are also evaluative. They tell us what the speaker believes is good or bad. They do not simply describe what the object of the judgment is like—for example, as an action that occurred at a certain time or that affected people in a certain way. They go further and express a positive or negative regard for it. However, factual matters are often relevant to our moral evaluations. For example, factual judgments about whether capital punishment has a deterrent effect might be quite relevant to our moral judgments about it. So also would we want to know whether violence can ever bring about peace; this would help us judge the morality of war and terrorism. Because ethical judgments often rely on such empirical or experientially based information, ethics is often indebted to other disciplines such as sociology, psychology, and history. Thus, we can distinguish between empirical or descriptive judgments, by which we state certain factual beliefs, and *evaluative judgments*, by which we make judgments about these matters. Evaluative judgments are also called *normative judgments*. Thus,

> Descriptive (empirical) judgment: Capital punishment acts (or does not act) as a deterrent.
> Normative (moral) judgment: Capital punishment is justifiable (or unjustifiable).

Moral judgments are evaluative because they "place a value," negative or positive, on some action or practice such as capital punishment. Because these evaluations also rely on beliefs in general about what is good or right—in other words, on *norms* or *standards* of good and bad or right and wrong—they are also *normative*. For example, the judgment that people ought to give their informed consent to participate as research subjects may rely on beliefs about the value of human autonomy. In this case, autonomy functions as a norm by which we judge the practice of using people as subjects of research. Thus, ethics of this sort is called *normative ethics*, both because it is evaluative and not simply descriptive and because it grounds its judgments in certain norms or values.

"That is a good knife" is an evaluative or normative statement. However, it does not mean that the knife is morally good. In making ethical judgments, we use terms such as *good*, *bad*, *right*, *wrong*, *obligatory*, and *permissible*. We talk about what we ought or ought not to do. These are evaluative terms. *But not all evaluations are moral in nature.* We speak of a good knife without attributing moral goodness to it. In so describing the knife, we are probably referring to its practical usefulness for

cutting or for impressing others. People tell us that we ought to pay this amount in taxes or stop at that corner before crossing because that is what the law requires. We read that two styles ought not to be worn or placed together because such a combination is distasteful. Here someone is making an aesthetic judgment. Religious leaders tell members of their communities what they ought to do because it is required by their religious beliefs. We may say that in some countries people ought to bow before the elders or use eating utensils in a certain way. This is a matter of custom. These normative or evaluative judgments appeal to practical, legal, aesthetic, religious, or customary norms for their justification.

How do other types of normative judgments differ from moral judgments? Some philosophers believe that it is a characteristic of moral "oughts" in particular that they override other "oughts" such as aesthetic ones. In other words, if we must choose between what is aesthetically pleasing and what is morally right, then we ought to do what is morally right. In this way, morality may also take precedence over the law and custom. The doctrine of civil disobedience relies on this belief, because it holds that we may disobey certain laws for moral reasons. Although moral evaluations are different from other normative evaluations, this is not to say that there is no relation between them. In fact, moral reasons often form the basis for certain laws. For example, consider copyright laws and the practice of downloading free music from the Internet. In 2005, the U.S. Supreme Court ruled unanimously that this is a form of illegal piracy and that file-sharing services are engaging in copyright infringement.[2] There may also be moral reasons supporting such opinions—considerations of basic justice, for example. Furthermore, the fit or harmony between forms and colors that ground some aesthetic judgments may be similar to the rightness or moral fit between certain actions and certain situations or beings. Moreover, in some ethical systems, actions are judged morally by their practical usefulness for producing valued ends. For now, however, note that ethics is not the only area in which we make normative judgments. Whether the artistic worth of an art object ought to be in any way judged by its moral value or influence poses another interesting question that may arise here.

Normative Judgments in					Descriptive Judgments in	
Ethics	Law	Aesthetics	Religion	Custom	Sociology	Psychology

Thus, we can distinguish various types of *normative* or evaluative judgments (and areas in which such judgments are made) from *descriptive* judgments about factual matters (and areas or disciplines that are in this sense descriptive).

Ethical Terms

You might have wondered what the difference is between calling something "right" and calling it "good." Consider the ethical meaning for these terms. *Right* and *wrong* usually apply to actions as in "You did the right thing" or "That is the wrong thing to do." These terms prescribe things for us to do or not to do. On the other hand, when we say that something is morally good, we are not explicitly recommending doing it. However, we do recommend that it be positively regarded. Thus, we say things such as "Peace is good, and distress is bad." It is also interesting that with "right" and "wrong" there seems to be no in-between; it is either one or the other. However, with "good" and "bad" there is room for degrees, and some things are thought to be better or worse than others.

We also use other ethical terms when we engage in moral evaluation and judgment. For example, we sometimes say that something "ought" or "ought not" to be done. There is the sense here of urgency. Thus, of these things we may talk in terms of an *obligation* to do or not do something. It is something about which there is morally no choice. We can refrain from doing what we ought to do, but the obligation is still there. On the other hand, there are certain actions that we think are permissible to do but we are not obligated to do them. Thus, one may think that there is no obligation to help someone in trouble, though it is "morally permissible" (i.e., not wrong) to do so and even "praiseworthy" to do so in some cases. Somewhat more specific ethical terms include *just* and *unjust* and *virtuous* and *vicious*.

To a certain extent, which set of terms we use depends on the particular overall ethical viewpoint or theory we adopt. (See the following discussion of types of ethical theory.) This will become clearer as we discuss and analyze the various ethical theories in this first part of the text.

ETHICS AND REASONS

When we evaluate an action as *right* or *wrong* or some condition as *good* or *bad*, we appeal to certain norms or reasons. Suppose, for example, I said that affirmative action is unjustified. I should give reasons for this conclusion; it will not be acceptable for me to respond that this is just the way I feel. If I have some intuitive negative response to preferential treatment forms of affirmative action, then I will be expected to delve deeper to determine whether there are reasons for this attitude. Perhaps I have experienced the bad results of such programs. Or I may believe that giving preference in hiring or school admissions on the basis of race or sex is unfair. In either case, I also will be expected to push the matter further and explain *why* it is unfair or even what constitutes fairness and unfairness.

To be required to give reasons to justify one's moral conclusions is essential to the moral enterprise and to doing ethics. However, this does not mean that making ethical judgments is and must be purely *rational*. We might be tempted to think that good moral judgments require us to be objective and not let our *feelings*, or *emotions*, enter into our decision making. Yet this assumes that feelings always get in the way of making good judgments. Sometimes this is surely true, as when we are overcome by anger, jealousy, or fear and cannot think clearly. Biases and prejudice may stem from such strong feelings. We think prejudice is wrong because it prevents us from judging rightly. But emotions can often aid good decision making. We may, for example, simply feel the injustice of a certain situation or the wrongness of someone's suffering. Furthermore, our caring about some issue or person may, in fact, direct us to think about the ethical issues involved. However, some explanation of why we hold a certain moral position is required. Not to give an explanation, but simply to say "X is just wrong," or simply to have strong feelings or convictions about "X," is not sufficient.

Alternate Theories: Intuitionism and Emotivism

Philosophers differ on how we know what is good. On one view, to say that something is good is very different from saying that something is yellow or heavy. The latter two qualities are empirical, known by our senses. However, "good" or "goodness" are held to be non-empirical properties, said by some to be knowable through intuition. One of the main proponents of this view is G. E. Moore.[3]

On another view, when we say something is good, we are showing our approval of it and recommending it to others rather than describing it. A main proponent of this view is Charles Stevenson, whose work "The Emotive Meaning of Ethical Terms" is excerpted in this chapter.

Both of these views differ from the more rationalistic view so far described in this chapter.

ETHICAL REASONING AND ARGUMENTS

We also should know how to *reason well* in thinking or speaking about ethical matters. This is helpful not only for trying to determine what to think about some questionable ethical matter but also for making a good case for something you believe is right as well as in critically evaluating positions held by other people.

The Structure of Ethical Reasoning and Argument

To be able to reason well in ethics you need to understand something about ethical arguments and argumentation, not in the sense of understanding why people get into arguments but rather in the sense of what constitutes a *good* argument. We can do this by looking at an argument's basic structure. This is the structure not only of ethical arguments about what is good or right but also of arguments about what is the case or what is true.

Suppose you are standing on the shore and a person in the water calls out for help. Should you try to rescue that person? You may or may not be able to swim. You may or may not be sure you could rescue the person. In this case, however, there is no time for reasoning, as you would have to act promptly. On the other hand, if this were an imaginary case, you would have to think through the reasons for and against trying to rescue the person. You might conclude that if you could actually rescue the person you ought to try to do it. Your reasoning might go as follows:

Every human life is valuable.
Whatever has a good chance of saving such a life should be attempted.
My swimming out to rescue this person has a good chance of saving his life.
Therefore, I ought to do so.

Or you might conclude that someone could not save this person, and your reasoning might go like this:

Every human life is valuable.
Whatever has a good chance of saving such a life should be attempted.
In this case, there is no chance of saving this life because I cannot swim.
Thus, I am not obligated to try to save him (although, if others are around who can help, I might be obligated to try to get them to help).

Some structure like this is implicit in any ethical argument, although some are longer and more complex chains than the simple form given here. One can recognize the *reasons* in an argument by their introduction through key words such as *since*, *because*, and *given that*. The conclusion often contains terms such as *thus* and *therefore*. The reasons supporting the conclusion are called premises. In a sound argument, the *premises* are true and the con-clusion follows from them. In this case, then, we want to know whether you can save this person and also whether his life is valuable. We also need to know whether the conclusion actually follows from the premises. In the case of the examples given above, it does: If you say you ought to do what will save a life and you can do it, then you ought to do it. However, there may be other principles that would need to be brought into the argument, such as whether and why, in fact, one is always obligated to save another when one can.

To know under what conditions a conclusion actually follows from the premises, we would need to analyze arguments with much greater detail than we can do here. Suffice it to say here, however, that the connection is a logical connection—in other words, it must make rational sense. You can improve your ability to reason well in ethics first by being able to pick out the reasons and the conclusion in an argument. Only then can you subject them to critical examination in ways we suggest below.

Evaluating and Making Good Arguments

Ethical reasoning can be done well or done poorly. Ethical arguments can be constructed well or con-structed poorly. A good argument is a *sound argu-ment*. It has a valid form in that the conclusion actually follows from the premises, and the premises or reasons given for the conclusion are true. An argument is poorly constructed when it is fallacious or when the reasons on which it is based are not true or are uncertain. This latter matter is of particular significance with ethical argumentation, because an ethical argument always involves some *value assumptions*—for example, that saving a life is good. These value matters are difficult to establish. Chapters 4 through 8 will help clarify how to analyze value assumptions. The discussion below of the relation between ethical theory and ethical judgments also suggests how thinking about values progresses.

However, in addition to such value assumptions or elements, ethical arguments also involve concep-tual and factual matters. *Conceptual matters* are those that relate to the meaning of terms or con-cepts. For example, in a case of *lying* we would want to know what lying actually is. Must it be verbal?

Must one have an intent to deceive? What is deceit itself? Other conceptual issues central to ethical arguments are questions such as, "What constitutes a 'person'?" (in arguments over abortion, for exam-ple) and "What is 'cruel and unusual punishment'?" (in death penalty arguments, for example). Sometimes, differences of opinion about an ethical issue are a matter of differences not in values but in the meaning of the terms used.

Ethical arguments often also rely on *factual assertions*. In our example, we might want to know whether it was actually true that you could save the person. In arguments about the death penalty, we may want to know whether such punishment is a deterrent. In such a case, we need to know what scientific studies have found and whether the studies themselves were well grounded. To have adequate factual grounding, we will want to seek out sources of information and be open-minded. Each chapter in Part Two of this book begins with or includes factual material that may be relevant to ethical decisions on the particular issue being treated. Even though they are limited, these discussions show the kinds of things one must consider to make good ethical decisions.

Notice that one can have an opinion about a matter of good and bad as well as an opinion about factual matters. For example, I might indicate that my opinion about whether random drug testing is a good thing is only an opinion because I do not feel adequately informed about the matter. This is an opinion about a moral matter. I can also have an opinion about the connection between passive smok-ing (inhaling others' tobacco smoke) and lung cancer. This would be an opinion about a factual matter. Because I can have an opinion about both values and matters of fact, I should not use this criterion as a basis for distinguishing values and facts. To do so would imply that moral matters are always matters of opinion and factual matters are never such.

Those who analyze good reasoning have catego-rized various ways in which reasoning can go wrong or be fallacious. We cannot go into detail on these here. However, one example that is often given is called the *ad hominem* fallacy. In this fallacy, people say something like, "That can't be right because just look who is saying it." They look at the source of the opinion rather than the reasons given for it. Another fallacy is called "begging the question" or arguing in a circle. Here you use the conclusion to support itself. An example of this would be something like "Lying in this case is wrong because lying is always wrong." You can find out more about these and other fallacies from almost any textbook in logic or critical thinking.

You also can improve your understanding of ethical arguments by being aware of a particular type of reasoning often used in ethics: *arguments from analogy*. In this type of argument, one compares familiar examples with the issue being disputed. If the two cases are similar in relevant ways, then whatever one concludes about the first familiar case one should also conclude about the disputed case. Thus, in a famous use of analogy that is included in Chapter 9 of this text, an argument about abortion by Judith Thomson, one is asked whether it would be ethically acceptable to unplug a violinist who had been attached to you and your kidney to save his life. She argues that if you say, as she thinks you should, that you are justified in unplugging the violinist, then a pregnant woman is also justified in "unplugging" her fetus. You would critically examine such an argument by asking whether or not the two cases were similar in relevant ways—that is, whether the analogy fits.

Finally, we should note that giving reasons to *justify* a conclusion is also not the same as giving an *explanation* for why one believes something. One might say that she does not support euthanasia because that was the way she was brought up or that she is opposed to the death penalty because she cannot stand to see someone die. To justify such beliefs, one would need rather to give reasons that show not why one does, in fact, believe something but why one *should* believe it. Nor are *rationalizations* justifying reasons. They are usually reasons given after the fact that are not one's true reasons. These false reasons are given to make us look better to others or ourselves. To argue well about ethical matters, we need to examine and give reasons that support the conclusions we draw.

ETHICAL THEORY

Good reasoning in ethics involves either implicit or explicit reference to an ethical theory. An *ethical theory* is a systematic exposition of a particular view about what is the nature and basis of good or right. The theory provides reasons or norms for judging acts to be right or wrong and attempts to give a justification for these norms. It provides ethical principles or guidelines that embody certain values. These can be used to decide in particular cases what action should be chosen and carried out. We can diagram the relationship between ethical theories and moral decision making as follows.

We can think of the diagram as a ladder. In practice, we can start at the ladder's top or bottom. At the top, at the level of theory, we can start by clarifying for ourselves what we think are basic ethical values. We then move downward to the level of principles generated from the theory. Moving next to conclusions about moral values in general, the bottom level, we use these principles to make concrete ethical judgments. Or we can start at the bottom of the ladder, facing a particular ethical choice or dilemma. We do not know what is best or what we ought to do. We work our way up the ladder by trying to think through our own values. Would it be better to realize this or that value, and why? Ultimately and ideally, we come to a basic justification, or the elements of what would be an ethical theory. If we look at the actual practice of thinking people as they develop their ethical views over time, the movement is probably in both directions. We use concrete cases to reform our basic ethical views, and we use the basic ethical views to throw light on concrete cases.

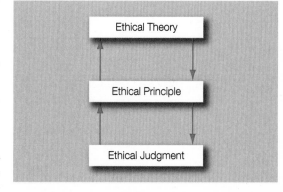

An example of this movement in both directions would be if we started with the belief that pleasure is the ultimate value and then found that applying this value in practice would lead us to do things that are contrary to common moral sense or that are repugnant to us and others. We may then be forced to look again and possibly alter our views about the moral significance of pleasure. Or we may change our views about the rightness or wrongness of some particular act or practice on the basis of our theoretical reflections. Obviously, this sketch of moral reasoning is quite simplified. Moreover, this model of ethical reasoning has been criticized by feminists and others, partly because it shows ethics to be governed by general principles that are supposedly applicable to all ethical situations. Does this form of reasoning give due consideration to the particularities of individual, concrete cases? Can we really make a general judgment about the value of truthfulness or courage that will help us know what to do in particular cases in which these issues play a role?

TYPES OF ETHICAL THEORY

In Part One of this text, we will consider the following types of moral theory: utilitarianism, Kant's moral theory, contractarianism, natural law, virtue ethics, and feminist ethics. These theories exemplify different approaches to doing ethics. Some of these theories differ in terms of what they say we should look at in making moral judgments about actions or practices. For example, does it matter morally that I tried to do the right thing or that I had a good motive? Surely it must make some moral difference, we think. But suppose that in acting sincerely I violate someone's rights. Does this make the action a bad action? We would probably be inclined to say yes. Suppose, however, that in violating someone's rights I am able to bring about a great good. Does this justify the violation of rights? Some theories judge actions in terms of their *motive*, some in terms of the character or nature of *the act itself*,

and others in terms of the *consequences* of the actions or practices.

We often appeal to one of these types of reason. Take a situation in which I strike a person, Jim. We can make the following judgments about this action. Note the different types of reasons given for the judgments.

That was good because you intended to do Jim good by awakening him—or it was bad because you meant to do him harm. (Motive)

That was good because it was an act of generosity—or it was bad because it violated the bodily integrity of another, Jim. (Act)

That was good because it helped form a sense of community—or it was bad because of the great suffering it caused Jim. (Consequences)

Although we generally think that a person's *motive* is relevant to the overall moral judgment about his or her *action*, we tend to think that it reflects primarily on our moral evaluation of the *person*. We also have good reasons to think that the results of actions matter morally. Those theories that base moral judgments on consequences are called *consequentialist* or sometimes *teleological* moral theories (from the Greek root *telos*, meaning "goal" or "end"). We also may think that what we actually do or how we act also counts morally. Those theories that hold that actions can be right or wrong regardless of their consequences are called *nonconsequentialist* or *deontological* theories (from the Greek root *deon*, meaning "duty"). One moral theory we will examine is *utilitarianism*. It provides us with an example of a consequentialist moral theory in which we judge whether an action is better than alternatives by its actual or expected results or consequences; actions are classically judged in terms of the promotion of human happiness. Kant's moral theory, which we will also examine, provides us with an example of a nonconsequentialist theory according to which acts are judged right or wrong independently of their consequences; in particular, acts are judged by whether they conform to requirements of rationality and human dignity. The naturalistic ethical theories that we will examine stress human nature as the source

Motive → Act → Consequences

of what is right and wrong. Some elements of these theories are deontological and some teleological. So, also, some goal-oriented or teleological theories are consequentialist in that they advise us to produce some good. But if the good is an ideal, such as self-realization, then such theories differ from consequentialist theories such as utilitarianism.[4] As anyone who has tried to put some order to the many ethical theories knows, no theory completely and easily fits one classification, even those given here. Feminist theories of care provide yet another way of determining what one ought to do (see Chapter 9). In Part Two of this text we will examine several concrete ethical issues. As we do so, we will note how these ethical theories analyze the problems from different perspectives and sometimes give different conclusions about what is morally right or wrong, better or worse.

CAN ETHICS BE TAUGHT?

It would be interesting to know just why some college and university programs require their students to take a course in ethics. Does this requirement rely on a belief that ethics or moral philosophy is designed to make people good and is capable of doing that?

On the question of whether ethics can be taught, my students have given a variety of answers. "If it can't be taught, then why are we taking this class?" one wondered. "Look at the behavior of certain corporate executives who have been found guilty of criminal conduct. They surely haven't learned proper ethical values," another responded. Still others disagreed. Although certain ideals or types of knowledge can be taught, ethical behavior cannot because it is a matter of individual choice, they said.

The ancient Greek philosopher Plato thought that ethics *could* be taught. He wrote, "All evil is ignorance." In other words, the only reason we do what is wrong is because we do not know or believe it is wrong. If we come to believe that something is right, however, it should then follow that we will necessarily do it. Now, we are free to disagree with Plato by appealing to our own experience. If I know that I should not have that second piece of pie, does this mean that I will not eat it? Never? Plato might

attempt to convince us that he is right by examining or clarifying what he means by the phrase "to know." If we were really convinced with our whole heart and mind, so to speak, that something is wrong, then we might be highly likely (if not determined) not to do it. However, whether ethics courses should attempt to convince students of such things is surely debatable.

Another aspect of the problem of teaching ethics concerns the problem of motivation. If one knows something to be the right thing to do, does there still remain the question of why we should do it? One way to teach ethics to youngsters, at least, and in the sense of motivating them, may be to show them that it is in their best interest to do the right thing.

With regard to teaching or taking a course in ethics, most, if not all, moral philosophers think that ethics, or a course on ethics, should do several other things. It should help students understand the nature of an ethical problem and help them think critically about ethical matters by providing certain conceptual tools and skills. It should enable them to form and critically analyze ethical arguments. It is up to the individual, however, to use these skills to reason about ethical matters. A study of ethics should also lead students to respect opposing views, because it requires them to analyze carefully the arguments that support views contrary to their own. It also provides opportunities to consider the reasonableness of at least some viewpoints that they may not have considered.

In this opening chapter, we have questioned the value of ethics and learned something about what ethics is and how it is different from other disciplines. We have considered the relationship between ethics and religion. We have provided a description of ethical reasoning and arguments and have examined briefly the nature of ethical theories and principles and the role they play in ethical reasoning. We will examine these theories more carefully in the chapters to come, and we will see how they might help us analyze and come to conclusions about particular ethical issues.

As noted, the reading selection for this chapter is from the writings of the ancient Greek philosopher

Plato. It is in the form of a dialogue and features Plato's mentor, Socrates. It treats one of the problems about ethics that we have noted in this chapter. In this reading from the *Euthyphro*, Socrates discusses the possible connection between ethics and religion.

NOTES

1. Alfred North Whitehead, *Process and Reality* (New York: Macmillan, 1929), 4.
2. *The New York Times*, June 28, 2005, p. A1.
3. G. E. Moore, *Principia Ethics* (Buffalo, NY: Prometheus, 1903).
4. I thank reviewer J. E. Chesher for this distinction.

R E A D I N G
Euthyphro
PLATO

Study Questions

1. What does Euthyphro first propose as a definition of piety?
2. How does Socrates suggest that those who have differences settle them?
3. What about the gods: Do they have different conceptions about what is good and evil, just and unjust? Why does this pose a problem for Euthyphro's first definition of piety (or goodness)?
4. What is it that people argue about when discussing whether the guilty, such as murderers, should be punished?
5. How does Socrates relate this to Euthyphro's situation?
6. To respond to Socrates, Euthyphro amends his definition of piety. How?
7. Socrates then asks another question of Euthyphro. What is it?
8. How does Socrates compare the question to the matter of what is carried or led or is in a state of suffering?
9. How does this help them to agree on which comes first: being pious or being loved by the gods?
10. What does Socrates suggest is yet needed to give a definition of piety or goodness?

Socrates and Euthyphro both have a practical interest in knowing what piety (or goodness) is— Socrates because he has been accused of impiety, and Euthyphro because he thinks he is doing the right thing in bringing a case against his father in court. His father had put a servant who killed another in chains and left him to die.

Euthyphro, 7a–11b. Trans. by B. Jowett.

Euthyphro. Piety ... is that which is dear to the gods, and impiety is that which is not dear to them.

Socrates. Very good, Euthyphro; you have now given me the sort of answer which I wanted. But whether what you say is true or not I cannot as yet tell, although I make no doubt that you will prove the truth of your words.

Euthyphro. Of course.

Socrates. Come, then, and let us examine what we are saying. That thing or person which is dear to the gods is pious, and that thing or person which is hateful to the gods is impious, these two being the extreme opposites of one another. Was not that said?

Euthyphro. It was.

Socrates. And well said?

Euthyphro. Yes, Socrates, I thought so; it was certainly said.

Socrates. And further, Euthyphro, the gods were admitted to have enmities and hatreds and differences?

Euthyphro. Yes, that was also said.

Socrates. And what sort of difference creates enmity and anger? Suppose for example that you and I, my good friend, differ about a number; do differences of this sort make us enemies and set us at variance with one another? Do we not go at once to arithmetic, and put an end to them by a sum?

Euthyphro. True.

Socrates. Or suppose that we differ about magnitudes, do we not quickly end the differences by measuring?

Euthyphro. Very true.

Socrates. And we end a controversy about heavy and light by resorting to a weighing machine?

Euthyphro. To be sure.

Socrates. But what differences are there which cannot be thus decided, and which therefore make us angry and set us at enmity with one another? I dare say the answer does not occur to you at the moment, and therefore I will suggest that these enmities arise when the matters of difference are the just and unjust, good and evil, honourable and dishonourable. Are not these the points about which men differ, and about which when we are unable satisfactorily to decide our differences, you and I and all of us quarrel, when we do quarrel?

Euthyphro. Yes, Socrates, the nature of the differences about which we quarrel is such as you describe.

Socrates. And the quarrels of the gods, noble Euthyphro, when they occur, are of a like nature?

Euthyphro. Certainly they are.

Socrates. They have differences of opinion, as you say, about good and evil, just and unjust, honourable and dishonourable: there would have been no quarrels among them, if there had been no such differences—would there now?

Euthyphro. You are quite right.

Socrates. Does not every man love that which he deems noble and just and good, and hate the opposite of them?

Euthyphro. Very true.

Socrates. But, as you say, people regard the same things, some as just and others as unjust—about these they dispute; and so there arise wars and fightings among them.

Euthyphro. Very true.

Socrates. Then the same things are hated by the gods and loved by the gods, and are both hateful and dear to them?

Euthyphro. True.

Socrates. And upon this view the same things, Euthyphro, will be pious and also impious?

Euthyphro. So I should suppose.

Socrates. Then, my friend, I remark with surprise that you have not answered the question which I asked. For I certainly did not ask you to tell me what action is both pious and impious: but now it would seem that what is loved by the gods is also hated by them. And therefore, Euthyphro, in thus chastising your father you may very likely be doing what is agreeable to Zeus but disagreeable to Cronos or Uranus, and what is acceptable to Hephaestus but unacceptable to Heré, and there may be other gods who have similar differences of opinion.

Euthyphro. But I believe, Socrates, that all the gods would be agreed as to the propriety of punishing a murderer: there would be no difference of opinion about that.

Socrates. Well, but speaking of men, Euthyphro, did you ever hear any one arguing that a murderer or any sort of evil-doer ought to be let off?

Euthyphro. I should rather say that these are the questions which they are always arguing, especially in courts of law: they commit all sorts of crimes, and there is nothing which they will not do or say in their own defence.

Socrates. But do they admit their guilt, Euthyphro, and yet say that they ought not to be punished?

Euthyphro. No; they do not.

Socrates. Then there are some things which they do not venture to say and do: for they do not venture to argue that the guilty are to be unpunished, but they deny their guilt, do they not?

Euthyphro. Yes.

Socrates. Then they do not argue that the evil-doer should not be punished, but they argue about the fact of who the evil-doer is, and what he did and when?

Euthyphro. True.

Socrates. And the gods are in the same case, if as you assert they quarrel about just and unjust, and some of them say while others deny that injustice is done among them. For surely neither God nor man will ever venture to say that the doer of injustice is not to be punished?

Euthyphro. That is true, Socrates, in the main.

Socrates. But they join issue about the particulars—gods and men alike; and, if they dispute at all, they dispute about some act which is called in question, and which by some is affirmed to be just, by others to be unjust. Is not that true?

Euthyphro. Quite true.

Socrates. Well then, my dear friend Euthyphro, do tell me, for my better instruction and information, what proof have you that in the opinion of all the gods a servant who is guilty of murder, and is put in chains by the master of the dead man, and dies because he is put in chains before he who bound him can learn from the interpreters of the gods what he ought to do with him, dies unjustly; and that on behalf of such a one a son ought to proceed against his father and accuse him of murder. How would you show that all the gods absolutely agree in approving of his act? Prove to me that they do, and I will applaud your wisdom as long as I live.

Euthyphro. It will be a difficult task; but I could make the matter very clear indeed to you.

Socrates. I understand; you mean to say that I am not so quick of apprehension as the judges: for to them you will be sure to prove that the act is unjust, and hateful to the gods.

Euthyphro. Yes indeed, Socrates; at least if they will listen to me.

Socrates. But they will be sure to listen if they find that you are a good speaker. There was a notion that came into my mind while you were speaking; I said to myself: "Well, and what if Euthyphro does prove to me that all the gods regarded the death of the serf as unjust, how do I know anything more of the nature of piety and impiety? For granting that this action may be hateful to the gods, still piety and impiety are not adequately defined by these distinctions, for that which is hateful to the gods has been shown to be also pleasing and dear to them." And therefore, Euthyphro, I do not ask you to prove this; I will suppose, if you like, that all the gods condemn and abominate such an action. But I will amend the definition so far as to say that what all the gods hate is impious, and what they love pious or holy; and what some of them love and others hate is both or neither. Shall this be our definition of piety and impiety?

Euthyphro. Why not, Socrates?

Socrates. Why not! Certainly, as far as I am concerned, Euthyphro, there is no reason why not. But whether this admission will greatly assist you in the task of instructing me as you promised, is a matter for you to consider.

Euthyphro. Yes, I should say that what all the gods love is pious and holy, and the opposite which they all hate, impious.

Socrates. Ought we to enquire into the truth of this, Euthyphro, or simply to accept the mere statement on our own authority and that of others? What do you say?

Euthyphro. We should enquire; and I believe that the statement will stand the test of enquiry.

Socrates. We shall know better, my good friend, in a little while. The point which I should first wish to understand is whether the pious or holy is beloved by the gods because it is holy, or holy because it is beloved of the gods.

Euthyphro. I do not understand your meaning, Socrates.

Socrates. I will endeavour to explain: we speak of carrying and we speak of being carried, of leading and being led, seeing and being seen. You know that in all such cases there is a difference, and you know also in what the difference lies?

Euthyphro. I think that I understand.

Socrates. And is not that which is beloved distinct from that which loves?

Euthyphro. Certainly.

Socrates. Well; and now tell me, is that which is carried in this state of carrying because it is carried, or for some other reason?

Euthyphro. No; that is the reason.

Socrates. And the same is true of what is led and of what is seen?

Euthyphro. True.

Socrates. And a thing is not seen because it is visible, but conversely, visible because it is seen; nor is a thing led because it is in the state of being led, or carried because it is in the state of being carried, but the converse of this. And now I think, Euthyphro, that my meaning will be intelligible; and my meaning is, that any state of action or passion implies previous action or passion. It does not become because it is becoming, but it is in a state of becoming because it becomes; neither does it suffer because it is in a state of suffering, but it is in a state of suffering because it suffers. Do you not agree?

Euthyphro. Yes.

Socrates. Is not that which is loved in some state either of becoming or suffering?

Euthyphro. Yes.

Socrates. And the same holds as in the previous instances; the state of being loved follows the act of being loved, and not the act the state.

Euthyphro. Certainly.

Socrates. And what do you say of piety, Euthyphro: is not piety, according to your definition, loved by all the gods?

Euthyphro. Yes.

Socrates. Because it is pious or holy, or for some other reason?

Euthyphro. No, that is the reason.

Socrates. It is loved because it is holy, not holy because it is loved?

Euthyphro. Yes.

Socrates. And that which is dear to the gods is loved by them, and is in a state to be loved of them because it is loved of them?

Euthyphro. Certainly.

Socrates. Then that which is dear to the gods, Euthyphro, is not holy, nor is that which is holy loved of God, as you affirm; but they are two different things.

Euthyphro. How do you mean, Socrates?

Socrates. I mean to say that the holy has been acknowledged by us to be loved of God because it is holy, not to be holy because it is loved.

Euthyphro. Yes.

Socrates. But that which is dear to the gods is dear to them because it is loved by them, not loved by them because it is dear to them.

Euthyphro. True.

Socrates. But, friend Euthyphro, if that which is holy is the same with that which is dear to God, and is loved because it is holy, then that which is dear to God would have been loved as being dear to God; but if that which is dear to God is dear to him because loved by him, then that which is holy would have been holy because loved by him. But now you see that the reverse is the case, and that they are quite different from one another. For one (qeojtlez) is of a kind to be loved because it is loved, and the other (oston) is loved because it is of a kind to be loved. Thus you appear to me, Euthyphro, when I ask you what is the essence of holiness, to offer an attribute only, and not the essence—the attribute of being loved by all the gods. But you still refuse to explain to me the nature of holiness. And therefore, if you please, I will ask you not to hide your treasure, but to tell me once more what holiness or piety really is, whether dear to the gods or not (for that is a matter about which we will not quarrel); and what is impiety?

Euthyphro. I really do not know, Socrates, how to express what I mean. For somehow or other our arguments, on whatever ground we rest them, seem to turn round and walk away from us.

R E A D I N G
The Emotive Meaning of Ethical Terms

C. L. STEVENSON

Study Questions

1. In seeking a substitute for the question, "Is X good?" must it be identical in meaning?
2. What is one way in which the substitute must be related to the original meaning? What must it be able to do?
3. What are some substitutes that other philosophers have used and why does Stevenson not accept them?
4. What does he mean by saying that ethical terms are not (or not simply) descriptive?
5. What meaning does he suggest instead, and how does the example of stealing illustrate this meaning?
6. What does he mean by saying that "ethical judgments propagate themselves"?
7. Finally, what does he mean by the "emotive meaning" of ethical terms?

I.

Ethical questions first arise in the form "Is so and so good?", or "Is this alternative better than that?" these questions are difficult partly because we don't quite know what we are seeking. We are asking, "Is there a needle in that haystack?" without even knowing just what a needle is. So the first thing to do is to examine the questions themselves. We must try to make them clearer, either by defining the terms in which they are expressed, or by any other method that is available.

From C.L. Stevenson, "The Emotive Meaning of Ethical Terms," *Mind*, Vol. 46, No. 181. (Jan., 1937), pp. 14-31. Reprinted by permission of Oxford University Press.

The present paper is concerned wholly with this preliminary step of making ethical questions clear. In order to help answer the question "Is X good?" we must *substitute* for it a question which is free from ambiguity and confusion.

It is obvious that in substituting a clearer question we must not introduce some utterly different kind of question. It won't do (to take an extreme instance of a prevalent fallacy) to substitute for "Is X good" the question "Is X pink with yellow trimmings" and then point out how easy the question really is. This would beg the original question, not help answer it. On the other hand, we must not expect the substituted question to be strictly "identical" with the original one. The original question may embody hypostatization, anthropomorphism, vagueness, and all the other ills to which our ordinary discourse is subject. If our substituted question is to be clearer, it must remove these ills. The questions will be identical only in the sense that a child is identical with the man he later becomes. Hence we must not demand that the substitution strike us, on immediate introspection, as making no change in meaning.

Just how, then, must the substituted question be related to the original? Let us assume (inaccurately) that it must result from replacing "good" by some set of terms which define it. The question then resolves itself to this: How must the defined meaning of "good" be related to its original meaning?

I answer that it must be *relevant*. A defined meaning will be called "relevant" to the original meaning under these circumstances: Those who have understood the definition must be able to say all that they then want to say by using the term in the defined way. They must never have occasion to use the term in the old, unclear sense. (If a person did have to go on using the term in the old sense, then to this extent his meaning would not be clarified, and the philosophical task would not be completed.) It frequently happens that a word is used so confusedly and ambiguously that we must give it several defined meanings, rather than one. In this case only the whole set of defined meanings will be called "relevant," and any one of them will be called "partially relevant". This is not a rigorous treatment of *relevance*, by any means; but it will serve for the present purposes.

Let us now turn to our particular task—that of giving a relevant definition of "good". Let us first examine some of the ways in which others have attempted to do this.

The word "good" has often been defined in terms of *approval*, or similar psychological attitudes. We may take as typical examples: "good" means *desired by me* (Hobbes); and "good" means *approved by most people* (Hume, in effect). It will be convenient to refer to definitions of this sort as "interest theories", following Mr. R. B. Perry, although neither "interest" nor "theory" is used in the most usual way.

Are definitions of this sort relevant ?

It is idle to deny their *partial* relevance. The most superficial inquiry will reveal that "good" is exceedingly ambiguous. To maintain that "good" is *never* used in Hobbes's sense, and never in Hume's, is only to manifest an insensitivity to the complexities of language. We must recognize, perhaps, not only these senses, but a variety of similar ones, differing both with regard to the kind of interest in question, and with regard to the people who are said to have the interest.

But this is a minor matter. The essential question is not whether interest theories are *partially* relevant, but whether they are *wholly* relevant. This is the only point for intelligent dispute. Briefly: Granted that some senses of "good" may relevantly be defined in terms of interest, is there some *other* sense which is *not* relevantly so defined? We must give this question careful attention. For it is quite possible that when philosophers (and many others) have found the question "Is X good?" so difficult, they have been grasping for this *other* sense of "good", and not any sense relevantly defined in terms of interest. If we insist on defining "good" in terms of interest, and answer the question when thus interpreted, we may be begging *their* question entirely. Of course this *other* sense of "good" may not exist, or it may be a complete confusion; but that is what we must discover.

Now many have maintained that interest theories are *far* from being completely relevant. They have argued that such theories neglect the very sense of "good" which is most vital. And certainly, their arguments are not without plausibility.

Only . . . what *is* this "vital" sense of "good"? The answers have been so vague, and so beset with difficulties, that one can scarcely determine.

There are certain requirements, however, with which this "vital" sense has been expected to comply—requirements which appeal strongly to our common sense. It will be helpful to summarize these, showing how they exclude the interest theories:

In the first place, we must be able sensibly to *disagree* about whether something is "good". This condition rules out Hobbes's definition. For consider the following argument: "This is good." "That isn't so; it's not good." As translated by Hobbes, this becomes: "I desire this." "That isn't so, for I don't." The speakers are not contradicting one another, and think they are, only because of an elementary confusion in the use of pronouns. The definition, "good" means d*esired by my community*, is also excluded, for how could people from different communities disagree?

In the second place, "goodness" must have, so to speak, a magnetism. A person who recognizes X to be "good" must *ipso facto* acquire a stronger tendency to act in its favour then he otherwise would have had. This rules out the Humian type of definition. For according to Hume, to recognize that something is "good" is simply to recognize that the majority approve of it. Clearly, a man may see that the majority approve of X without having, himself, a stronger tendency to favour it. This requirement excludes any attempt to define "good" in terms of the interest of people *other* than the speaker.

In the third place, the "goodness" of anything must not be verifiable solely by use of the scientific method. "Ethics must not be psychology." This restriction rules out all of the traditional interest theories, without exception. It is so sweeping a restriction that we must examine its plausibility...

II.

Let us now turn to my own analysis of ethical judgments. First let me present my position dogmatically, showing to what extent I vary from tradition.

I believe that the three requirements, given above, are perfectly sensible; that there is some *one* sense of "good" which satisfies all three requirements; and that no traditional interest theory satisfies them all. But this does not imply that "good"

must be explained in terms of a Platonic Idea, or of a Categorical Imperative, or of an unique, unanalyzable property. On the contrary, the three requirements can be met by a *kind* of interest theory. *But we must give up a presupposition which all the traditional interest theories have made.*

Traditional interest theories hold that ethical statements are *descriptive* of the existing state of interests—that they simply *give information* about interests. (More accurately, ethical judgments are said to describe what the state of interests is, was, or will be, or to indicate what the state of interests *would* be under specified circumstances.) It is this emphasis on description, on information, which leads to their incomplete relevance. Doubtless there is always *some* element of description in ethical judgments, but this is by no means all. Their major use is not to indicate facts, but to *create an influence*. Instead of merely describing people's interests, they *change* or *intensify* them. They recommend an interest in an object, rather than state that the interest already exists.

For instance: When you tell a man that he oughtn't to steal, your object isn't merely to let him know that people disapprove of stealing. You are attempting, rather, to get *him* to disapprove of it. Your ethical judgment has a quasi-imperative force which, operating through suggestion, and intensified by your tone of voice, readily permits you to begin to *influence*, to *modify*, his interests. If in the end you do not succeed in getting *him* to disapprove of stealing, you will feel that you've failed to convince him that stealing is wrong. You will continue to feel this, even though he fully acknowledges that you disapprove of it, and that almost everyone else does. When you point out to him the consequences of his actions—consequences which you suspect he already disapproves of—these *reasons* which support your ethical judgment are simply a means of facilitating your influence. If you think you can change his interests by making vivid to him how others will disapprove of him, you will do so; otherwise not. So the consideration about other people's interest is just an additional means you may employ, in order to move him, and is not a part of the ethical judgment itself. Your ethical judgment doesn't merely describe interests to him, it directs his very interests. The difference between the traditional interest theories and my view is like the difference between describing a desert and irrigating it...

Thus ethical terms are *instruments* used in the complicated interplay and readjustment of human interests. This can be seen plainly from more general observations. People from widely separated communities have different moral attitudes. Why? To a great extent because they have been subject to different social influences. Now clearly this influence doesn't operate through sticks and stones alone; words play a great part. People praise one another, to encourage certain inclinations, and blame one another, to discourage others. Those of forceful personalities issue commands which weaker people, for complicated instinctive reasons, find it difficult to disobey, quite apart from fears of consequences. Further influence is brought to bear by writers and orators. Thus social influence is exerted, to an enormous extent, by means that have nothing to do with physical force or material reward. The ethical terms facilitate such influence. Being suited for use in *suggestion*, they are a means by which men's attitudes may be led this way or that. The reason, then, that we find a greater similarity in the moral attitudes of one community than in those of different communities is largely this: ethical judgments propagate themselves. One man says "This is good"; this may influence the approval of another person, who then makes the same ethical judgment, which in turn influences another person, and so on. In the end, by a process of mutual influence, people take up more or less the same attitudes. Between people of widely separated communities, of course, the influence is less strong; hence different communities have different attitudes.

III.

I refer to "emotive" meaning (in a sense roughly like that employed by Ogden and Richards). The emotive meaning of a word is a tendency of a word, arising through the history of its usage, to produce (result from) *affective* responses in people. It is the immediate aura of feeling which hovers about a word. Such tendencies to produce affective responses cling to words very tenaciously. It would be difficult, for instance, to express merriment by using the interjection "alas". Because of the persistence of such affective tendencies (among other reasons) it becomes feasible to classify them as "meanings".

Just *what* is the relation between emotive meaning and the dynamic use of words? Let us take an example. Suppose that a man is talking with a group of people which includes Miss Jones, aged 59. He refers to her, without thinking, as an "old maid". Now even if his purposes are perfectly innocent—even if he is using the words purely descriptively—Miss Jones won't think so. She will think he is encouraging the others to have contempt for her, and will dram in her skirts, defensively. The man might have done better if instead of saying "old maid" he had said "elderly spinster". The latter words could have been put to the same descriptive use, and would not so readily have caused suspicions about the dynamic use.

"Old maid" and "elderly spinster" differ, to be sure, only in emotive meaning. From the example it will be clear that certain words, because of their emotive meaning, are suited to a certain kind of dynamic use—so well suited, in fact, that the hearer is likely to be misled when we use them in any other way. The more pronounced a word's emotive meaning is, the less likely people are to use it purely descriptively. Some words are suited to encourage people, some to discourage them, some to quiet them, and so on...

IV.

Let us now apply these remarks in defining "good". This word may be used morally or non-morally. I shall deal with the non-moral usage almost entirely, but only because it is simpler. The main points of the analysis will apply equally well to either usage...

For an example of a case where "We like this" is used in the dynamic way that "This is good" is used, consider the case of a mother who says to her several children, "One thing is certain, *we all like to be neat*". If she really believed this, she wouldn't bother to say so. But she is not using the words descriptively. She is *encouraging* the children to like neatness. By telling them that they like neatness, she will lead them to *make* her statement true, so to speak. If, instead of saying "We all like to be neat" in this way, she had said "It's a good thing to be neat", the effect would have been approximately the same...

Strictly speaking, then, it is impossible to define "good" in terms of favourable interest if emotive meaning is not to be distorted. Yet it is possible to say that "This is good" is *about* the favourable interest of the speaker and the hearer or hearers, and that it has a pleasing emotive meaning which fits the words for use in suggestion. This is a rough description of meaning, not a definition. But it serves the same clarifying function that a definition ordinarily does; and that, after all, is enough.

A word must be added about the moral use of "good". This differs from the above in that it is about a different kind of interest. Instead of being about what the hearer and speaker *like*, it is about a stronger sort of approval. When a person *likes* something, he is pleased when it prospers, and disappointed when it doesn't. When a person *morally approves* of something, he experiences a rich feeling of security when it prospers, and is indignant, or "shocked" when it doesn't. These are rough and inaccurate examples of the many factors which one would have to mention in distinguishing the two kinds of interest. In the moral usage, as well as in the non-moral, "good" has an emotive meaning which adapts it to suggestion.

REVIEW EXERCISES

1. Determine whether the following statements about the nature of ethics are true or false. Explain your answers.
   a. Ethics is the study of why people act in certain ways.
   b. To say that moral philosophy is *foundational* means that it asks questions about such things as the meaning of right and wrong and how we know what is good and bad.
   c. The statement "Most people believe that cheating is wrong" is an ethical evaluation of cheating.
2. What is meant by the "divine command theory"? How does Plato's *Euthyphro* treat this problem?
3. Label the following statements as either *normative* (N) or *descriptive* (D). If normative, label each as *ethics* (E), *aesthetics* (A), *law* (L), *religion* (R), or *custom* (C).
   a. One ought to respect one's elders because it is one of God's commandments.
   b. Twice as many people today, as compared to ten years ago, believe that the death penalty is morally justified in some cases.

   c. It would be wrong to put an antique chair in a modern room.
   d. People do not always do what they believe to be right.
   e. I ought not to turn left here because the sign says "No Left Turn."
   f. We ought to adopt a universal health insurance policy because everyone has a right to health care.
4. Discuss the relation between ethical theory and ethical reasons; between ethical theory and ethical reasoning.
5. As they occur in the following statements, label the reasons for the conclusion as appeals to the *motive* (M), the *act* (A), or the *consequences* (C).
   a. Although you intended well, what you did was bad because it caused more harm than good.
   b. We ought always to tell the truth to others because they have a right to know the truth.
   c. Although it did turn out badly, you did not want that, and thus you should not be judged harshly for what you caused.

2

Ethical Relativism

FOR DECADES, anthropologists and sociologists have collected information on the diverse mores of different cultures. Some societies hold bribery to be morally acceptable, but other societies condemn it. Views on appropriate sexual behavior and practices vary widely. Some societies believe that cannibalism, the eating of human flesh, is good because it ensures tribal fertility or increases manliness. Some Inuit groups, the native peoples of northern Canada and Alaska, believed that it was appropriate to abandon their elderly when they could no longer travel with the group, whereas other groups once practiced ritual strangulation of the old by their children. Ruth Benedict has documented the case of a Northwest Indian group that believed it was justified in killing an innocent person for each member of the group who had died. This was not a matter of revenge but a way of fighting death. In place of bereavement, the group felt relieved by the second killing.[1]

Some societies believe in female circumcision; in other societies, it not only is regarded as wrong but is also illegal. In some countries, it is acceptable for women to wear short skirts; in others, women are expected to cover their legs and hair. You should be able to think of many other examples of such differences.

Before we begin to examine some ethical theories, we ought to consider whether the very idea of applying ethical theories is misguided because it assumes that we can use these to determine what is morally right and wrong. We commonly hear people say, "What is right for one person is not necessarily right for another" and "What is right in some circumstances is not right in other circumstances." If this were true, then it would seem that we cannot make any general or objective moral assessments. "When in Rome," should we not then "do as the Romans do"? In other words, would not morality be either entirely a personal matter or a function of cultural values? These are questions about ethical relativism. In this chapter, we will examine ethical relativism and its two basic forms and then present reasons for and against it. The last sections on "Moral Realism" and "Moral Pluralism" are more technical and not necessary for a basic understanding of ethical relativism, but they do introduce two key related issues addressed by philosophers today.

WHAT IS ETHICAL RELATIVISM?

There are various views on what is the best way to understand ethical relativism or what the term essentially means. According to some philosophers, ethical relativism is a theory that holds that there are no universally accepted ethical standards. This is surely true, as one only needs to have a minimal understanding of various cultures to see this. But ethical relativism holds more than this. It is the view that there is no objective standard of right and wrong, even in principle. There are only different views of what is right and wrong. In saying they are "relative" to individuals or societies, we mean that they are a function of, or dependent on, what those individuals or societies do, in fact, believe. *According to ethical relativism, there is no objective right and wrong.* The opposite point of view, that there is an objective right and wrong, is often called *objectivism*, or sometimes *nonrelativism.*

We can understand more about ethical relativism by comparing our views of the status of ethics and ethical matters with our ordinary beliefs about science. Most people believe that the natural sciences (biology, chemistry, physics, geology, and their modern variants) tell us things about the natural world. Throughout the centuries, and modern times in particular, science seems to have made great progress in uncovering the nature and structure of our world. Moreover, science seems to have a universal validity. No matter what a person's individual temperament, background, or culture, the same natural world seems accessible to all who sincerely and openly investigate it. Modern science is thought to be governed by a generally accepted method and seems to produce a gradually evolving common body of knowledge. Although this is the popular view of science, philosophers hold that the situation regarding science is much more complex and problematic. Nevertheless, it is useful to compare this ordinary view of science with common understandings of morality.

Morality, in contrast to science, does not seem so objective. The few examples of diversity of moral beliefs noted at the beginning of this chapter could be multiplied many times over. Not only is there no general agreement about what is right and wrong, but also we often doubt that this is the kind of matter about which we can agree. We tend, then, to think of morality as a matter of subjective opinion. This is basically the conclusion of ethical relativism: Morality is simply a function of the moral beliefs that people have. There is nothing beyond this. Specifically, no realm of objective moral truth or reality exists that is comparable to that which we seem to find in the world of nature investigated by science.

TWO FORMS OF ETHICAL RELATIVISM

In further exploring the nature of ethical relativism, we should note that it has two basic and different forms.[2] According to one version, called *personal* or *individual ethical relativism*, ethical judgments and beliefs are the expressions of the moral outlook and attitudes of individual persons. I have my ethical views, and you have yours; neither my views nor

yours are better or more correct. I may believe that a particular war was unjust, and you may believe it was just. Someone else may believe that all war is wrong. According to this form of relativism, because no objective right or wrong exists, no *particular* war can be said to be really just or unjust, right or wrong, nor can *all* wars. We each have our individual histories that explain how we have come to hold our particular views or attitudes. But they are just that: our own individual views and attitudes. We cannot say that they are correct or incorrect, because to do so would assume some objective standard of right and wrong against which we could judge their correctness. Such a standard does not exist, according to ethical relativism.[3]

The second version of ethical relativism, called *social* or *cultural ethical relativism*, holds that ethical values vary from society to society and that the basis for moral judgments lies in these social or cultural views. For an individual to decide and do what is right, he or she must look to the norms of the society. People in a society may, in fact, believe that their views are the correct moral views. However, a cultural ethical relativist holds that no society's views are better than any other in a transcultural sense. Some may be different from others, and some may not be the views generally accepted by a wider group of societies, but that does not make these views worse, more backward, or incorrect in any objective sense.

STRONG VERSUS WEAK INTERPRETATIONS OF ETHICAL RELATIVISM

While it is obvious that different cultures or societies do in fact often have different views about what is morally right and wrong, ethical relativism goes farther. On the strong version, what is morally right for one just depends on what his or her society holds is right. There are no transcultural moral principles, even ideally. Louis Pojman has distinguished this strong "dependency thesis" from a weaker one. In the latter, the fact that the circumstances of various societies differ may require that ethical principles be applied differently from society to society.[4] On this view there would be objectively valid moral principles that flowed from the fact that "human nature is relatively similar in essential respects, having a common set of needs and interests."[5] Those moral principles that support or contribute to the satisfaction of these needs and interests would be objectively valid, even if in different circumstances they would need to be applied differently.

REASONS SUPPORTING ETHICAL RELATIVISM

There are many reasons for believing that what ethical relativism holds is true. We will first summarize three of the most commonly given of those reasons and then evaluate their related arguments.[6]

The Diversity of Moral Views

One reason most often given to support relativism is the existence of moral diversity among people and cultures. In fields such as science and history, investigation tends to result in general agreement despite the diversity among scientists. But we have not come to such agreement in ethics. Philosophers have been investigating questions about the basis of morality since ancient times. With sincere and capable thinkers pursuing such a topic for millennia, one would think that some agreement would have been reached. But this seems not to be the case. It is not only on particular issues such as abortion that sincere people disagree, but also on basic moral values or principles.

Moral Uncertainty

A second reason to believe that what relativism holds is true is the great difficulty we often have in knowing what is the morally right thing to believe or do. We don't know what is morally most important. For example, we do not know whether it is better to help one's friend or do the honest thing in a case in which we cannot do both. Perhaps helping the friend is best in some circumstances, but being honest is best in others. We are not sure which is best in a particular case. Furthermore, we cannot know for sure what will happen down the line if we choose one course over another. Each of us is also aware of our personal limitations and the subjective glance that we bring to moral judging. Thus, we distrust our own judgments. We then generalize and conclude that all moral judgments are simply personal and subjective viewpoints.

Situational Differences

Finally, people and situations, cultures and times differ in significant ways. The situations and living worlds of different people vary so much that it is difficult to believe that the same things that would be right for one would be right for another. In some places, overpopulation or drought is a problem; other places have too few people or too much water. In some places, people barely have access to the basic necessities of life; in other places, food is plentiful and the standard of living is high. Some individuals are more outgoing, and others are more reserved. How can the same things be right and wrong under such different circumstances and for such different individuals? It seems unlikely, then, that any moral theory or judgment can apply in a general or universal manner. We thus tend to conclude that they must be relative to the particular situation and circumstance and that no objective or universally valid moral good exists.

ARE THESE REASONS CONVINCING?

Let us consider possible responses by a nonrelativist or objectivist to the preceding three points.

The Diversity of Moral Views

We can consider the matter of diversity of moral views from two different perspectives. First, we can ask, how widespread and deep is the disagreement? Second, we may ask, what does the fact of disagreement prove?

How Widespread and Deep Is the Disagreement?

If two people disagree about a moral matter, does this always amount to a moral disagreement? For example, Bill says that we ought to cut down dramatically on carbon dioxide emissions, while Jane says that we do not have a moral obligation to do this. This looks like a basic moral disagreement, but it actually may result from differences in their factual beliefs. Bill may believe that the current rate of such emissions will result in dramatic and serious harmful global climate effects in the next decades, the so-called greenhouse effect. Jane may believe no such harmful consequences are likely, because she believes that the assessments and predictions are in error. If they did agree on the factual issues, then Bill and Jane would agree on the moral conclusion. They

David Parsons/iStockphoto.com

Arguments over moral matters often stem from factual disagreements, such as whether CO_2 emissions from cars and other sources are causing catastrophic climate change.

both agree on the basic moral obligation to do what we can to improve the current human condition and prevent serious harm to existing and future generations. The table below illustrates this.

It is an open question how many of our seeming moral disagreements are not basic moral disagreements at all but disagreements about factual or other beliefs. But suppose that at least some of them are about moral matters. Suppose that we do disagree about the relative value, for example, of health and peace, honesty and generosity, or about what rights people do and do not have. It is this type of disagreement that the moral relativist would need to make his or her point.

What Would Disagreement about Basic Moral Matters Prove?   I have asked students in my ethics class to tell me in what year George Washington died. A few brave souls venture a guess: 1801, or at least after 1790? No one is sure. Does this disagreement or lack of certitude prove that he did not die or that he died on no particular date? Belief that he did die and on a particular date is consistent with differences of opinion and with uncertainty. So also in ethics: People can disagree about what constitutes the right thing to do and yet believe that there is a right thing

to do. "Is it not because of this belief that we try to decide what is right and worry that we might miss it?" the nonrelativist would ask.

Or consider the supposed contrast between ethics and science. Although a body of knowledge exists on which those working in the physical sciences agree, those at the forefront of these sciences often profoundly disagree. Does such disagreement prove that no objectivity exists in such matters? If people disagree about whether the universe began with a "big bang" or about what happened in the first millisecond, then does this prove that no answer is to be found, even in principle, about the universe's beginning? Not necessarily.

Moral Uncertainty

Let us examine the point that moral matters are complex and difficult to determine. Because of this, we are often uncertain about what is the morally best thing to do. For example, those who "blow the whistle" on companies for which they work must find it difficult to know whether they are doing the right thing when they consider the possible cost of doing so to themselves and others around them. However, what is described here is not strictly relativism but *skepticism*. Skepticism is the view that it is difficult, if not impossible, to know something. However, does the fact that we are uncertain about the answer to some question, even a moral question, prove that it lacks an answer? One reason for skepticism might be the belief that we can only see things from our own perspective and thus can never know things, even in ethics, as they are. This is a form of *subjectivism*. The nonrelativist could argue that in our very dissatisfaction with not knowing and in our seeking to know what we ought to do, we behave as though we believe that a better choice can be made.

In contrast, matters of science and history often eventually get clarified and settled. We can now look up the date of George Washington's death (1799), and

Basic Moral Agreement	Factual Disagreement	Different Moral Conclusions
We ought not to harm.	CO_2 emissions harm.	We ought to reduce emissions.
We ought not to harm.	CO_2 emissions do not harm.	We need not reduce emissions.

scientists gradually improve our knowledge in various fields. "Why is there no similar progress in ethical matters?" relativists might respond. Or have we actually made some progress in resolving some moral matters?

Situational Differences

Do dramatic differences in people's life situations make it unlikely or impossible for them to have any common morality? A nonrelativist might suggest the following. Suppose that health is taken as an objective value. Is it not the case that what contributes to the health of some is different than what contributes to the health of others? Insulin injections are sometimes good for the diabetic but not for the nondiabetic. Even though the good in these specific cases differs, there is still a general value—health—that is the goal. Or is not justice an objective moral value? It involves "giving to each his or her due." Yet what is due people in justice is not the same. Those who work might well deserve something different from those who do not, and the guilty deserve punishment that the innocent do not. (See the table below.)

One reason situational differences may lead us to think that no objective moral value is possible is that we may be equating objectivism with what is sometimes called *absolutism*. Absolutism may be described as the view that moral rules or principles have no exceptions and are context-independent. One example of such a rule is "Stealing is always wrong." According to absolutism, situational differences such as whether or not a person is starving would make no difference to moral conclusions about whether they are justified in stealing food—if stealing is wrong. (See the table below.)

However, an objectivist who is not an absolutist holds that although there is some objective good—for example, health or justice—what is good in a concrete case may vary from person to person and

circumstance to circumstance. She or he could hold that stealing might be justified in some circumstances because it is necessary for life, an objective good, and a greater good than property. Opposing absolutism does not necessarily commit one to a similar opposition to objectivism.

One result of this clarification should be the realization that what is often taken as an expression of relativism is not necessarily so. Consider this statement: "What is right for one person is not necessarily right for another." If the term *for* means "in the view of," then the statement simply states the fact that people do disagree. It states that "What is right in the view of one person is not what is right in the view of the other." However, this is not yet relativism. Relativism goes beyond this in its belief that this is all there is. If *for* is used in the sense "Insulin injections are good for some people but not for others," then the original statement is also not necessarily relativistic. It could, in fact, imply that health is a true or objective good and that what leads to it is good and what diminishes it is bad. For ethical relativism, on the other hand, there is no such objective good.

FURTHER CONSIDERATIONS

The preceding should provide a basis for understanding and critically evaluating ethical relativism. However, each type of relativism and its opposite, nonrelativism, must overcome more problems.

One problem for the social or *cultural relativist* who holds that moral values are simply a reflection of society's views is to identify that society. With which group should my moral views coincide: my country, my state, my family, or myself and my peers? Different groups to which I belong have different moral views. Moreover, if a society changes its views, does this mean that morality changes? If 52 percent of its people once supported some war

Objective Value	Situational Differences	Different Moral Conclusions
Health	Diabetic.	Insulin injections are good.
Health	Nondiabetic.	Insulin injections are not good.
Justice	Works hard.	Deserves reward.
Justice	Does not work hard.	Does not deserve reward.

Absolute Value	Situational Differences	Same Moral Conclusions
Stealing is always wrong.	Person is starving.	Do not steal.
Stealing is always wrong.	Person is not starving.	Do not steal.

but later only 48 percent, does this mean that earlier the war was just but it became unjust when the people changed their minds about it?

One problem that the *individual relativist* faces is whether that view accords with personal experience. According to individual relativism, it seems that I should turn within and consult my moral feelings in order to solve a personal moral problem. This is often just the source of the difficulty, however, for when I look within I find conflicting feelings. I want to know not how I *do* feel but how I *ought* to feel and what I *ought* to believe. But the view that there is something I possibly ought to believe would not be relativism.

A problem for both types of relativist lies in the implied belief that relativism is a more tolerant position than objectivism. However, the cultural relativist can hold that people in a society should be tolerant only if tolerance is one of the dominant values of their society. He or she cannot hold that all people should be tolerant, because tolerance cannot be an objective or transcultural value, according to relativism. We can also question whether there is any reason for an individual relativist to be tolerant, especially if being tolerant means not just putting up with others who disagree with us but also listening to their positions and arguments. Why should I listen to another who disagrees with me? If ethical relativism is true, then it cannot be because the other person's moral views may be better than mine in an objective sense, for there is no objectively better position. Objectivists might insist that their position provides a better basis for both believing that tolerance is an objective and transcultural good and that we ought to be open to others' views because they may be closer to the truth than ours are.

Relativism, or expressions that seem to be relativistic, may sometimes manifest a kind of intellectual laziness or a lack of moral courage. Rather than attempt to give reasons or arguments for my own position, I may hide behind some statement such as, "What is good for some is not necessarily good for others." I may say this simply to excuse myself from having to think or be critical of various ethical positions. Those who hold that there is an objective right and wrong may also do so uncritically. They may simply adopt the views of their parents or peers without evaluating those views themselves. However, the major difficulty with an objectivist position is the problem it has in providing an alternative to the relativist position. The objectivist should give us reason to believe that there is an objective good. To pursue this problem in a little more detail, we will examine briefly two issues discussed by contemporary moral philosophers. One is the issue of the reality of moral value—*moral realism*; and the other concerns the problem of deciding between plural goods—*moral pluralism*.

MORAL REALISM

If there is an objective morality beyond the morality of cultures or individuals, then what is it like? Earlier in this chapter, we compared science and ethics. I suggested that natural science is generally regarded as the study of a reality independent of scientists—namely, nature. This view of the relation of science and nature can be called realism. Realism is the view that there exists a reality independent of those who know it. Most people are probably realists in this sense.

Now compare this to the situation regarding ethics. If I say that John's act of saving a drowning child was good, then what is the object of my moral judgment? Is there some real existing fact of goodness that I can somehow sense in this action? I can observe the actions of John to save the child, the characteristics of the child, John, the lake, and so forth. But in what sense, if any, do I observe the goodness itself? The British philosopher G. E. Moore held that goodness is a specific quality that attaches to people or acts.[7] Although we cannot observe it (we cannot hear, touch, taste, or see it), we intuit its presence. Philosophers such as Moore have had difficulty explaining both the nature of the quality and the particular intuitive or moral sense by which we are supposed to perceive it. (See the discussion of this in Chapter 1.)

Some moral philosophers who want to hold something of a realist view of morality try to argue that moral properties such as goodness are *supervenient*, or based on or flow from other qualities such as courage or generosity or honesty. Obviously, the exact relation between the moral and other qualities would need further explanation. Others attempt to explain moral reality as a relational matter: perhaps as a certain fit between actions and situations or actions and our innate sensibilities.[8] For example, because of innate human sensibilities, some say, we just would not be able to approve of torturing the innocent. The problems here are complex. However, the question is an important one. Are moral rights and wrongs, goods and bads something independent of particular people or cultures and their beliefs about what is right and wrong or good and bad? Or are they, as relativism holds, essentially a reflection or expression of individuals or cultures?

MORAL PLURALISM

Another problem nonrelativists or objectivists face is whether the good is one or many. According to some theories, there is one primary moral principle by which we can judge all actions. However, suppose this were not the case, that there were instead a variety of equally valid moral principles or equal moral values. For example, suppose that autonomy, justice, well-being, authenticity, and peace were all equally valuable. This would present a problem if we were ever forced to choose between the more just resolution of a conflict and that which promoted the well-being of more people. For example, we may be able to do more good overall with our health care resources if we spend them on treating diseases that affect more people. However, there is some element of unfairness in this proposal because people who have rare diseases did not choose to have them. In such cases when values conflict, we may be forced simply to choose one or the other for no reason or on the basis of something other than reason. Whether some rational and nonarbitrary way exists to make such decisions is an open question. Whether ultimate choices are thus subjective or can be grounded in an

assessment of what is objectively best is a question not only about how we do behave but also about what is possible in matters of moral judgment.

The issue of moral relativism is not easily digested or decided. The belief that guides this text, however, is that better and worse choices can be made, and that morality is not simply a matter of what we believe to be morally right or wrong. If this were not the case, then there would not seem to be much point in studying ethics. The purpose of studying ethics, as noted in Chapter 1, is to improve one's ability to make good ethical judgments. If ethical relativism were true, then this purpose could not be achieved.

The two major ethical theories that we will examine, utilitarianism and Kant's moral theory, are both objectivist or nonrelativist moral theories. Naturalist theories also tend to be objective because they have as their basis human nature and what perfects it. As you learn more about these views, consider what their reasons are for holding that the objective good they specify really exists.

In this chapter's reading selection, Mary Midgley describes her problems with a version of ethical relativism that she calls "moral isolationism." And Friedrich Nietzsche exemplifies a kind of moral relativism as he argues that one's morality, one's definition of good and bad, is a function of personality or mentality.

NOTES

1. Ruth Benedict, "Anthropology and the Abnormal," *Journal of General Psychology*, 10 (1934): 60–70.
2. We could also think of many forms of ethical relativism from the most individual or personal to the universal. Thus, we could think of individual relativism, or that based on family values, or local community or state or cultural values. The most universal, however, in which moral values are the same for all human beings, would probably no longer be a form of relativism.
3. According to some versions of individual ethical relativism, moral judgments are similar to expressions of taste. We each have our own individual tastes. I like certain styles or foods, and you like others. Just as no taste can be said to be correct or incorrect, so also no ethical view can be valued as better than any other. My saying that this war is or all wars are unjust is, in effect, my expression of my dislike of or aversion to war. An entire tradition in ethics, sometimes called

"emotivism," holds this view. For an example, see Charles Stevenson, *Ethics and Language* (New Haven, CT: Yale University Press, 1944).

4. Louis P. Pojman, "A Critique of Ethical Relativism," in Louis P. Pojman and James Fieser, *Ethical Theory*, 6th edition. (Boston: Wadsworth Cengage Learning, 2011), pp. 43–56.

5. Ibid, p. 52.

6. These are not necessarily complete and coherent arguments for relativism. Rather, they are more popular versions of why people generally are inclined toward what they believe is relativism.

7. G. E. Moore, *Principia Ethica* (Cambridge: Cambridge University Press, 1903).

8. Bruce W. Brower, "Dispositional Ethical Realism," *Ethics*, 103, no. 2 (Jan. 1993): 221–249.

READING
Trying Out One's New Sword

MARY MIDGLEY

Study Questions

1. What is "moral isolationism"?
2. Would "moral isolationism" make it impossible to praise or blame practices in other cultures, according to Midgley?
3. Does Midgley think that we could praise a culture if we could not criticize it? Why?
4. Why does she think that "moral isolationism" would make it impossible to judge even our own culture?
5. How does she believe the conversation over the Samurai practice of "trying out one's new sword" would go? Would it involve evaluations?
6. What are Midgley's views about distinct unmixed cultures?

ALL OF us are, more or less, in trouble today about trying to understand cultures strange to us. We hear constantly of alien customs. We see changes in our lifetime which would have astonished our parents. I want to discuss here one very short way of dealing with this difficulty, a drastic way which many people now theoretically favour. It consists in simply denying that we can ever understand any culture except our own well enough to make judgements about it. Those who recommend this hold that the world is sharply divided into separate societies, sealed units, each with its own system of thought. They feel that the respect and tolerance due from one system to another forbids us ever to

take up a critical position to any other culture. Moral judgement, they suggest, is a kind of coinage valid only in its country of origin.

I shall call this position "moral isolationism." I shall suggest that it is certainly not forced upon us, and indeed that it makes no sense at all. People usually take it up because they think it is a respectful attitude to other cultures. In fact, however, it is not respectful. Nobody can respect what is entirely unintelligible to them. To respect someone, we have to know enough about him to make a *favourable* judgement, however general and tentative. And we do understand people in other cultures to this extent. Otherwise a great mass of our most valuable thinking would be paralysed.

To show this, I shall take a remote example, because we shall probably find it easier to think calmly about it than we should with a contemporary one, such as female circumcision in Africa or the Chinese Cultural Revolution. The principles involved will still be the same. My example is this. There is, it seems, a verb in classical Japanese which means "to try out one's new sword on a chance wayfarer." (The word is *tsujigiri*, literally "crossroads-cut.") A Samurai sword had to be tried out because, if it was to work properly, it had to slice through someone at a single blow, from the shoulder to the opposite flank. Otherwise, the warrior bungled his stroke. This could injure his honour, offend his ancestors, and even let down his emperor. So tests were needed, and wayfarers had to be expended. Any wayfarer would do—provided, of course, that he was not another Samurai. Scientists will recognize a familiar problem about the rights of experimental subjects.

Now when we hear of a custom like this, we may well reflect that we simply do not understand it; and therefore are not qualified to criticize it at all, because we are not members of that culture. But we are not members of any other culture either, except our own. So we extend the principle to cover all extraneous cultures, and we seem therefore to be moral isolationists. But this is, as we shall see, an impossible position. Let us ask what it would involve.

We must ask first: Does the isolating barrier work both ways? Are people in other cultures equally unable to criticize us? This question struck me sharply when I read a remark in *The Guardian* by an anthropologist about a South American Indian who had been taken into a Brazilian town for an operation, which saved his life. When he came back to his village, he made several highly critical remarks about the white Brazilians' way of life. They may very well have been justified. But the interesting point was that the anthropologist called these remarks "a damning indictment of Western civilization." Now the Indian had been in that town about two weeks. Was he in a position to deliver a damning indictment? Would we ourselves be qualified to deliver such an indictment on the Samurai, provided we could spend two weeks in ancient Japan? What do we really think about this?

My own impression is that we believe that outsiders can, in principle, deliver perfectly good indictments—only, it usually takes more than two weeks to make them damning. Understanding has degrees. It is not a slapdash yes-or-no matter. Intelligent outsiders can progress in it, and in some ways will be at an advantage over the locals. But if this is so, it must clearly apply to ourselves as much as anybody else.

Our next question is this: Does the isolating barrier between cultures block praise as well as blame? If I want to say that the Samurai culture has many virtues, or to praise the South American Indians, am I prevented from doing *that* by my outside status? Now, we certainly do need to praise other societies in this way. But it is hardly possible that we could praise them effectively if we could not, in principle, criticize them. Our praise would be worthless if it rested on no definite grounds, if it did not flow from

some understanding. Certainly we may need to praise things which we do not *fully* understand. We say "there's something very good here, but I can't quite make out what it is yet." This happens when we want to learn from strangers. And we can learn from strangers. But to do this we have to distinguish between those strangers who are worth learning from and those who are not. Can we then judge which is which?

This brings us to our third question: What is involved in judging? Now plainly there is no question here of sitting on a bench in a red robe and sentencing people. Judging simply means forming an opinion, and expressing it if it is called for. Is there anything wrong about this? Naturally, we ought to avoid forming—and expressing—*crude* opinions, like that of a simple-minded missionary, who might dismiss the whole Samurai culture as entirely bad, because non-Christian. But this is a different objection. The trouble with crude opinions is that they are crude, whoever forms them, not that they are formed by the wrong people. Anthropologists, after all, are outsiders quite as much as missionaries. Moral isolationism forbids us to form any opinions on these matters. Its ground for doing so is that we don't understand them. But there is much that we don't understand in our own culture too. This brings us to our last question: If we can't judge other cultures, can we really judge our own? Our efforts to do so will be much damaged if we are really deprived of our opinions about other societies, because these provide the range of comparison, the spectrum of alternatives against which we set what we want to understand. We would have to stop using the mirror which anthropology so helpfully holds up to us.

In short, moral isolationism would lay down a general ban on moral reasoning. Essentially, this is the programme of immoralism, and it carries a distressing logical difficulty. Immoralists like Nietzsche are actually just a rather specialized sect of moralists. They can no more afford to put moralizing out of business than smugglers can afford to abolish customs regulations. The power of moral judgement is, in fact, not a luxury, not a perverse indulgence of the self-righteous. It is a necessity. When we judge something to be bad or good, better or worse than something else, we are taking it as an example to aim at or avoid. Without opinions of this sort, we would have no framework of comparison for our own policy, no chance of profiting by other people's insights or mistakes. In this vacuum, we could form no judgements on our own actions.

Now it would be odd if *Homo sapiens* had really got himself into a position as bad as this—a position where his main evolutionary asset, his brain, was so little use to him. None of us is going to accept this sceptical diagnosis. We cannot do so, because our involvement in moral isolationism does not flow from apathy, but from a rather acute concern about human hypocrisy and other forms of wickedness. But we polarize that concern around a few selected moral truths. We are rightly angry with those who despise, oppress or steamroll other cultures. We think that doing these things is actually *wrong*. But this is itself a moral judgement. We could not condemn oppression and insolence if we thought that all our condemnations were just a trivial local quirk of our own culture. We could still less do it if we tried to stop judging altogether.

Real moral scepticism, in fact, could lead only to inaction, to our losing all interest in moral questions, most of all in those which concern other societies. When we discuss these things, it becomes instantly clear how far we are from doing this. Suppose, for instance, that I criticize the bisecting Samurai, that I say his behaviour is brutal. What will usually happen next is that someone will protest, will say that I have no right to make criticisms like that of another culture. But it is most unlikely that he will use this move to end the discussion of the subject. Instead, he will justify the Samurai. He will try to fill in the background, to make me understand the custom, by explaining the exalted ideals of discipline and devotion which produced it. He will probably talk of the lower value which the ancient Japanese placed on individual life generally. He may well suggest that this is a healthier attitude than our own obsession with security. He may add, too, that the wayfarers did not seriously mind being bisected, that in principle they accepted the whole arrangement.

Now an objector who talks like this is implying that it is possible to understand alien customs. That is just what he is trying to make me do. And he implies, too, that if I do succeed in understanding

them, I shall do something better than giving up judging them. He expects me to change my present judgement to a truer one—namely, one that is favourable. And the standards I must use to do this cannot just be Samurai standards. They have to be ones current in my own culture. Ideals like discipline and devotion will not move anybody unless he himself accepts them. As it happens, neither discipline nor devotion is very popular in the West at present. Anyone who appeals to them may well have to do some more arguing to make *them* acceptable, before he can use them to explain the Samurai. But if he does succeed here, he will have persuaded us, not just that there was something to be said for them in ancient Japan, but that there would be here as well.

Isolating barriers simply cannot arise here. If we accept something as a serious moral truth about one culture, we can't refuse to apply it—in however different an outward form—to other cultures as well, wherever circumstances admit it. If we refuse to do this, we just are not taking the other culture seriously. This becomes clear if we look at the last argument used by my objector—that of justification by consent of the victim. It is suggested that sudden bisection is quite in order, *provided* that it takes place between consenting adults. I cannot now discuss how conclusive this justification is. What I am pointing out is simply that it can only work if we believe that *consent* can make such a transaction respectable—and this is a thoroughly modern and Western idea. It would probably never occur to a Samurai; if it did, it would surprise him very much. It is *our* standard. In applying it, too, we are likely to make another typically Western demand. We shall ask for good factual evidence that the wayfarers actually do have this rather surprising taste—that they are really willing to be bisected. In applying Western standards in this way, we are not being confused or irrelevant. We are asking the questions which arise *from where we stand*, questions which we can see the sense of. We do this because asking questions which you can't see the sense of is humbug. Certainly we can extend our questioning by imaginative effort. We can come to understand other societies better. By doing so, we may make their questions our own, or we may see that they are really forms of the questions which we are asking already. This is not impossible. It is just very hard work. The obstacles which often prevent it are simply those of ordinary ignorance, laziness and prejudice.

If there were really an isolating barrier, of course, our own culture could never have been formed. It is no sealed box, but a fertile jungle of different influences—Greek, Jewish, Roman, Norse, Celtic and so forth, into which further influences are still pouring—American, Indian, Japanese, Jamaican, you name it. The moral isolationist's picture of separate, unmixable cultures is quite unreal. People who talk about British history usually stress the value of this fertilizing mix, no doubt rightly. But this is not just an odd fact about Britain. Except for the very smallest and most remote, all cultures are formed out of many streams. All have the problem of digesting and assimilating things which, at the start, they do not understand. All have the choice of learning something from this challenge, or, alternatively, of refusing to learn, and fighting it mindlessly instead.

This universal predicament has been obscured by the fact that anthropologists used to concentrate largely on very small and remote cultures, which did not seem to have this problem. These tiny societies, which had often forgotten their own history, made neat, self-contained subjects for study. No doubt it was valuable to emphasize their remoteness, their extreme strangeness, their independence of our cultural tradition. This emphasis was, I think, the root of moral isolationism. But, as the tribal studies themselves showed, even there the anthropologists were able to interpret what they saw and make judgements—often favourable—about the tribesmen. And the tribesmen, too, were quite equal to making judgements about the anthropologists—and about the tourists and Coca-Cola salesmen who followed them. Both sets of judgements, no doubt, were somewhat hasty, and both have been refined in the light of further experience. A similar transaction between us and the Samurai might take even longer. But that is no reason at all for deeming it impossible. Morally as well as physically, there is only one world, and we all have to live in it.

Friedrich Nietzsche, *Beyond Good and Evil*, translated by Marion Farber, section 260, pp. 153–156. Oxford University Press, 1998.

READING

Master and Slave Moralities

FRIEDRICH NIETZSCHE

Study Questions

1. How does Nietzsche describe what he calls a "master morality"? How do persons adopting this define the concept of the good?
2. What do "good" and "bad" mean to one who adopts a master morality?
3. How does this person describe others?
4. What does Nietzsche mean in saying that this person "creates value"?
5. How does Nietzsche describe the other "slave" morality?
6. How do these two moralities differ in their notions of "good" and "bad"?

WHILE PERUSING the many subtler and cruder moral codes that have prevailed or still prevail on earth thus far, I found that certain traits regularly recurred in combination, linked to one another—until finally two basic types were revealed and a fundamental difference leapt out at me. There are *master moralities* and *slave moralities*. I would add at once that in all higher and more complex cultures, there are also apparent attempts to mediate between the two moralities, and even more often a confusion of the two and a mutual misunderstanding, indeed sometimes even their violent juxtaposition—even in the same person, within one single breast. Moral value distinctions have emerged either from among a masterful kind, pleasantly aware of how it differed from those whom it mastered, or else from among the mastered, those who were to varying degrees slaves or dependants. In the first case, when it is the masters who define the concept "good," it is the proud, exalted states of soul that are thought to distinguish and define the hierarchy. The noble person keeps away from those beings who express the opposite of these elevated, proud inner states: he despises them. Let us note immediately that in this first kind of morality the opposition "good" and "bad" means about the same thing as "noble" and "despicable"—the opposition "good" and "*evil*" has a different origin. The person who is cowardly or anxious or petty or concerned with narrow utility is despised; likewise the distrustful person with his constrained gaze, the self-disparager, the craven kind of person who endures maltreatment, the importunate flatterer, and above all the liar: all aristocrats hold the fundamental conviction that the common people are liars. "We truthful ones"—that is what the ancient Greek nobility called themselves. It is obvious that moral value distinctions everywhere are first attributed to *people* and only later and in a derivative fashion applied to *actions*: for that reason moral historians commit a crass error by starting with questions such as: "Why do we praise an empathetic action?" The noble type of person feels *himself* as determining value—he does not need approval, he judges that "what is harmful to me is harmful per se," he knows that he is the one who causes things to be revered in the first place, he *creates values*. Everything that he knows of himself he reveres: this kind of moral code is self-glorifying. In the foreground is a feeling of fullness, of overflowing power, of happiness in great tension, an awareness of a wealth that would like to bestow and share—the noble person will also help the unfortunate, but not, or not entirely, out of pity, but rather from the urgency created by an excess of power. The noble person reveres the power in himself, and also his power over himself, his ability to speak and to be silent, to enjoy the practice of severity and harshness towards himself and to respect everything that is severe and harsh. "Wotan placed a harsh heart within my breast," goes a line in an old Scandinavian saga: that is how it is written from the heart of a proud Viking—and rightly so. For this kind of a person is proud not to be made for pity; and so the hero of the saga adds a warning: "If your heart is not harsh when you are young, it will never become harsh." The noble and brave people who think like this are the most removed from that other moral code which sees the sign of morality in pity or altruistic behaviour or *désintéressement*; belief in

ourselves, pride in ourselves, a fundamental hostility and irony towards "selflessness"—these are as surely a part of a noble morality as caution and a slight disdain towards empathetic feelings and "warm hearts."

It is the powerful who *understand* how to revere, it is their art form, their realm of invention. Great reverence for old age and for origins (all law is based upon this twofold reverence), belief in ancestors and prejudice in their favour and to the disadvantage of the next generation—these are typical in the morality of the powerful; and if, conversely, people of "modern ideas" believe in progress and "the future," almost by instinct and show an increasing lack of respect for old age, that alone suffices to reveal the ignoble origin of these "ideas." Most of all, however, the master morality is foreign and embarrassing to current taste because of the severity of its fundamental principle: that we have duties only towards our peers, and that we may treat those of lower rank, anything foreign, as we think best or "as our heart dictates" or in any event "beyond good and evil"— pity and the like should be thought of in this context. The ability and duty to feel enduring gratitude or vengefulness (both only within a circle of equals), subtlety in the forms of retribution, a refined concept of friendship, a certain need for enemies (as drainage channels for the emotions of envy, combativeness, arrogance—in essence, in order to be a good *friend*): these are the typical signs of a noble morality, which, as we have suggested, is not the morality of "modern ideas" and is therefore difficult to sympathize with these days, also difficult to dig out and uncover.

It is different with the second type of morality, *slave morality*. Assuming that the raped, the oppressed, the suffering, the shackled, the weary, the insecure engage in moralizing, what will their moral value judgements have in common? They will probably express a pessimistic suspicion about the whole human condition, and they might condemn the human being along with his condition. The slave's eye does not readily apprehend the virtues of the powerful: he is sceptical and distrustful, he is *keenly* distrustful of everything that the powerful revere as "good"—he would like to convince himself that even their happiness is not genuine. Conversely, those qualities that serve to relieve the sufferers' existence are brought into relief and bathed in light: this is where pity, a kind, helpful hand, a warm heart, patience, diligence, humility, friendliness are revered—for in this context, these qualities are most useful and practically the only means of enduring an oppressive existence. Slave morality is essentially a morality of utility. It is upon this hearth that the famous opposition "good" and "*evil*" originates—power and dangerousness, a certain fear-inducing, subtle strength that keeps contempt from surfacing, are translated by experience into evil. According to slave morality, then, the "evil" person evokes fear; according to master morality, it is exactly the "good" person who evokes fear and wants to evoke it, while the "bad" person is felt to be despicable. The opposition comes to a head when, in terms of slave morality, a hint of condescension (it may be slight and well intentioned) clings even to those whom this morality designates as "good," since within a slave mentality a good person must in any event be *harmless*: he is good-natured, easily deceived, perhaps a bit stupid, a *banhomme*. Wherever slave morality gains the upper hand, language shows a tendency to make a closer association of the words "good" and "stupid."

A last fundamental difference: the longing for *freedom*, an instinct for the happiness and nuances of feeling free, is as necessarily a part of slave morals and morality as artistic, rapturous reverence and devotion invariably signal an aristocratic mentality and judgement.

From this we can immediately understand why *passionate love* (our European speciality) absolutely must have a noble origin: the Provençal poet-knights are acknowledged to have invented it, those splendid, inventive people of the "*gai saber*" to whom Europe owes so much—virtually its very self.

REVIEW EXERCISES

1. Explain the definition of ethical relativism given in the text: "the view that there is no objective standard of right and wrong, even in principle."
2. What is the difference between individual and social or cultural relativism?
3. What is the difference between the theory that people do differ in their moral beliefs and what the theory of ethical relativism holds?
4. What are the differences among the three reasons for supporting ethical relativism given in this chapter? In particular, what is the basic difference between the first and second? Between the first and third?
5. How would you know whether a moral disagreement was based on a basic difference in moral values or facts? As an example, use differences about the moral justifiability of capital punishment.
6. What is moral realism, and how does it differ from scientific realism? Is it similar in any way to scientific realism?

3
Egoism

IN THIS chapter, we will give thought to the issues raised by the following dialogue. Because the issues concern *egoism* and its opposite, *altruism*, our speakers are Edna Egoist and Alan Altruist.

Edna: I think that people are basically selfish. Everyone primarily looks out for number one.

Alan: That's not so. At least some people sometimes act unselfishly. Our parents made sacrifices for us. Remember the story in the news not long ago about Wesley Autrey, a New York City construction worker who became known as the "subway hero"? While Autrey was waiting on a subway platform with his two young daughters, a young man next to them suffered a seizure and fell onto the tracks. As an incoming train

Wesley Autrey, the New York construction worker who risked his life to save a stranger who had fallen on the subway tracks.

approached, Autrey jumped onto the tracks and held the young man down while the train passed inches above them. That was anything but selfish. And there are some people who dedicate their lives to service projects such as helping the poor or those in need of medical care.

Edna: But isn't it possible that the man who saved the other on the subway tracks did it without thinking? And don't those dedicated to helping others receive satisfaction from what they are doing?

Alan: I don't think that they help others because they receive satisfaction, though. And wouldn't it be disappointing if that were true? And wouldn't it be an awful world if everyone just looked out for themselves? For one thing, there would be no cooperation. Conflicts and wars would be everywhere.

Edna: I don't agree. Even if people are basically selfish, we do live together and we would need some rules. Otherwise, individuals would have no way to plan and get what they want.

Alan: If you were completely self-centered, then you would not be likely to have many friends.

Edna: I would want the satisfaction of having friends. I would help them when they were in need, because I would want help in return when I needed it. Isn't that what friends are for?

Alan: I don't think so. That's not true friendship. Also, I think what John Kennedy said is right. "Ask not what your country can do for you but what you can do for your country." We do want too much from others, including the government, without giving of ourselves. And that is not right.

Edna: But if people did not take care of themselves first, then they would have nothing to give to others. I think people should think of themselves first.

Notice in this dialogue that Edna and Alan first argue about whether people are basically self-centered or selfish. Then they move to talk about the implications or consequences of this type of behavior. Finally, they differ about whether such behavior would be a good or a bad thing. Notice that Edna and Alan disagree about two distinctly different issues. One is whether people are basically selfish; the second is whether being selfish is good or bad. These two issues illustrate two different versions or meanings of egoism. One is *descriptive*. According to this version, egoism is a theory that describes what people are like. Simply put, this theory holds that people are basically self-centered or selfish. It is a view about how people behave or why they do what they do. It is often referred to as *psychological egoism*. The other version of egoism is *normative*. It is a theory about how people ought to behave. Thus, it is an ethical theory and is called *ethical egoism*. We will examine each theory in turn, first attempting to understand it and what it holds. We will then try to evaluate it, asking whether it is reasonable or true. The final sections— "The Moral Point of View" and "Why Be Moral?"—are more technical. One can understand the basic philosophical concerns about egoism apart from these treatments. However, the issues are interesting, and the treatments of them do summarize key ideas from contemporary debates about egoism.

PSYCHOLOGICAL EGOISM

What Is Psychological Egoism?

In general, psychological egoism is a theory about what people are like, but we can understand what it asserts in several ways. One way to understand it is to say that people are basically selfish. This is what Edna says in the dialogue. The implication of this version is that people usually or always act for their own narrow and short-range self-interest. However, another formulation of this theory asserts that although people do act for their own self-interest, this self-interest is to be understood more broadly and as being more long-term. Thus, we might distinguish between acting selfishly and acting in our own self-interest.

On the broader view, many things are in a person's interest: good health, satisfaction in a career or work, prestige, self-respect, family, and friends. Moreover, if we really wanted to attain these things, we would need to avoid being shortsighted. For example, we would have to be self-disciplined in diet and lifestyle to be healthy. We would need to plan long-term for a career. And we would need to be concerned about others and not overbearing if we wanted to make and retain friends.

However, as some people have pointed out, we would not actually need to be concerned about others but only to appear to be concerned. Doing good to others, as Edna suggested, would be not for their sake but to enable one to call on those friends when they were needed. This would be helping a friend not for the friend's sake but for one's own sake.

Putting the matter in this way also raises another question about *how* to formulate this theory. Is psychological egoism a theory according to which people always act in their own best interest? Or does it hold that people are always motivated by the desire to attain their own best interest? The first version would be easily refuted; we notice that people do not always do what is best for them. They eat too much, choose the wrong careers, waste time, and so forth. This may be because they do not have sufficient knowledge to be good judges of what is in their best interest. It may be because of a phenomenon known as "weakness of will." For example, I may want to lose weight or get an A in a course but may not quite get myself to do what I have to do to achieve my goal. Philosophers have puzzled over how this can be so and how to explain it. It is a complex issue; to treat it adequately would take us beyond what we can do here.[1] On the other hand, it might well be true that people always do what they *think* is the best thing for them. This version of psychological egoism, which we will address next, asserts that human beings act for the sake of their own best interests. In this version, the idea is not that people sometimes or always act in their own interests, but that this is the only thing that ultimately does motivate people. If they sometimes act for others, it is only because they think that it is in their own best interests to do so. This is what Edna Egoist said in the dialogue about the subway hero.[2]

Is Psychological Egoism True?

Not long ago, a study was done in which people were asked whether they believed in or supported the jury system; that is, should people be proven guilty or not guilty by a group of peers? Most responded that they do support the jury system. However, when asked whether they would serve on a jury if called, significantly fewer said they would.[3] Those who answered the two questions differently might have wanted justice for themselves but were not willing to give it to others. Or consider the story about Abraham Lincoln.[4] It was reported that one day as he was riding in a coach over a bridge he heard a mother pig squealing. Her piglets had slipped into the water and she could not get them out. Lincoln supposedly asked the coachman to stop, got out, and rescued the piglets. When his companion cited this as an example of unselfishness, Lincoln responded that it was not for the sake of the pigs that he acted as he did. Rather, it was because he would have no peace later when he recalled the incident if he did not do something about it now. In other words, although it seemed unselfish, his action was quite self-centered.

Is the tendency to be self-oriented something that is innate to all of us, perhaps part of our survival instinct? Or are these traits learned? Developmental psychologists tell us about how children develop egoistic and altruistic tendencies. Are female children, for example, expected to be altruistic and caring while male children are taught to be independent and self-motivated? In the dialogue above, you may have noticed that these expectations have been deliberately turned around: Edna is the egoist and Alan the altruist. Although psychologists describe the incidence and development of these characteristics, philosophers speculate about how a person comes to be able to sympathize with another and take the other's point of view. These philosophical speculations and empirical descriptions attempt to tell us what the case is about: human development and motivation. Do they also make the case for or against psychological egoism?

How are we to evaluate the claims of psychological egoism? Note again that the view we will examine is a theory about human motivation. As such a theory, however, we will find it difficult, if not impossible, to prove. Suppose, for example, that Edna and Alan are trying to assess the motivations of particular people—say, their parents or the subway hero.

How are they to know what motivates these people? They cannot just assume that their parents or the subway hero are acting for the sake of the satisfaction they receive from what they do. Nor can we ask them, for people themselves are not always the best judge of what motivates them. We commonly hear or say to ourselves, "I don't know why I did that!"

Moreover, suppose that their parents and the subway hero do, in fact, get satisfaction from helping others. This is not the same thing as acting for the purpose of getting that satisfaction. What psychological egoism needs to show is not that people do get satisfaction from what they do, but that achieving such satisfaction is their aim. Now we can find at least some examples in our own actions to test this theory. Do we read the book to get satisfaction or to learn something? Do we pursue that career opportunity because of the satisfaction that we think it will bring or because of the nature of the opportunity? In addition, directly aiming at satisfaction may not be the best way to achieve it. We probably have a better chance of being happy if we do not aim at happiness itself but rather at the things that we enjoy doing.

Thus, we have seen that the most reasonable or common form of psychological egoism, a theory about human motivation, is especially difficult to prove. It also can't be disproved or falsified. Even if it were shown that we *often* act for the sake of our own interest, this is not enough to prove that psychological egoism is true. According to this theory, we must show that people *always* act to promote their own interests. We need next to consider whether this has any relevance to the normative question of how we *ought* to act.

ETHICAL EGOISM

What Is Ethical Egoism?

Ethical egoism is a normative theory. It is a theory about what we *ought* to do, how we *ought* to act. As with psychological egoism, we can formulate the normative theory called ethical egoism in different ways. One version is *individual ethical egoism*. According to this version, I ought to look out only for my own interests. I ought to be concerned about others only to the extent that this concern also contributes to my own interests. In the dialogue, Edna first said only that she would do what was in her own best interest. Her final comment also implied that she believed that others also ought to do what is in their own best interests. According to this formulation of ethical egoism, sometimes called *universal ethical egoism*, everyone ought to look out for and seek only their own best interests. As in the individual form, in this second version people ought to help others only when and to the extent that it is in their own best interest to do so.

Is Ethical Egoism a Good Theory?

We can evaluate ethical egoism in several ways. We will consider four: its grounding in psychological egoism, its consistency or coherence, its derivation from economic theory, and its conformity to commonsense moral views.

Grounding in Psychological Egoism   Let us consider first whether psychological egoism, if true, would provide a good basis for ethical egoism. If people were always motivated by their own interests, then would this be a good reason to hold that they ought to be so motivated? On the one hand, it seems superfluous to tell people that they ought to do what they always do anyway or will do no matter what. One would think that at least sometimes one of the functions of moral language is to try to motivate ourselves or others to do what we are not inclined to do. For example, I might tell myself that even though I could benefit by cheating on a test, it is wrong, and so I should not do it.[5]

On the other hand, the fact that we do behave in a certain way seems a poor reason for believing that we ought to do so. If people cheated or lied, we ask, would that in itself make these acts right? Thus, although it may at first seem reasonable to rely on a belief about people's basic selfishness to prove that people ought to look out for themselves alone, this seems far from convincing.

Consistency or Coherence   Universal ethical egoism in particular is possibly inconsistent or incoherent. According to this version of ethical egoism, everyone ought to seek their own best interests. However, could anyone consistently support such a view? Wouldn't this mean that we would want our own best interests served and at the same time be willing to allow that others serve their interests—even to our own detriment? If food were scarce, then I would want enough for myself, and yet at the same time would have to say that I should not have it for myself when another needs it to survive. This view seems to have an internal inconsistency. (We will return to this problem in our discussion of Kant's moral theory in Chapter 5.) We might compare it to playing a game in which I can say that the other player ought to block my move, even though at the same time I hope that she or he does not do so. These arguments are complex and difficult to fully evaluate. Philosophers disagree about whether universal ethical egoism is inconsistent on the grounds that no one can will it as a universal practice.[6]

Derivation from Economic Theory   One argument for ethical egoism is taken from economic theory—for example, that proposed by Adam Smith. He and other proponents of *laissez-faire* or government-hands-off capitalism believe that self-interest provides the best economic motivation. The idea is that when the profit motive or individual incentives are absent, people will either not work or not work as well. If it is my land or my business, then I will be more likely to take care of it than if the profits go to others or to the government. In addition, Smith believed that in a system in which each person looks out for his or her own economic interests, the general outcome will be best, as though an "invisible hand" were guiding things.[7]

Although this is not the place to go into an extended discussion of economic theory, it is enough to point out that not everyone agrees on the merits of *laissez-faire* capitalism. Much can be said for the competition that it supports, but it does raise questions about those who are unable to compete or unable to do so without help. Is care for these people a community responsibility? Recent community-oriented theories of social morality stress just this notion of responsibility and oppose *laissez-faire* capitalism's excessive emphasis on individual rights.[8] (Further discussion of capitalism can be found in Chapter 14.) In any case, a more basic question can be asked about the relevance of economics to morality. Even if an economic system worked well, would this prove that morality ought to be modeled on it? Is not the moral life broader than the economic life? For example, are all human relations economic relations?

Furthermore, the argument that everyone ought to seek his or her own best interest because this contributes to the general well-being is not ethical egoism at all. As we will come to see more clearly when we examine it, this is a form of utilitarianism. Thus, we can evaluate it in our discussion of utilitarianism in the next chapter.

Conformity to Commonsense Morality   Finally, is ethical egoism supported by commonsense morality? On the one hand, some elements of ethical egoism are contrary to commonsense morality. For example, doesn't it assume that anything is all right as long as it serves an individual's best interests? Torturing human beings or animals would be permitted so long as this served one's interests. When not useful to one's interests, traditional virtues of honesty, fidelity, and loyalty would have no value. Ethical egoists could argue on empirical or factual grounds that the torturing of others is never in one's best interests because this would make one less sensitive, and being sensitive is generally useful to people. Also, they might argue that the development of traditional virtues is often in one's own best interest because these traits are valued by the society. For example, my possessing these traits may enable me to get what I want more readily. Whether this is a good enough reason to value these virtues or condemn torture is something you must judge for yourself.

On the other hand, it may well be that people ought to take better care of themselves. By having a high regard for ourselves, we increase our self-esteem. We then depend less on others and more on ourselves. We might also be stronger and happier. These are surely desirable traits. The altruist, moreover, might be too self-effacing. He might be said to lack a proper regard for himself. There is also some truth in the view that unless one takes care of oneself, one is not of as much use to others. This view implies not ethical egoism but again a form of utilitarianism.

THE MORAL POINT OF VIEW

Finally, we will consider briefly two issues related to ethical egoism that have puzzled philosophers in recent times. One is whether one must take a particular point of view to view things morally and whether this is incompatible with egoism. The other, which is treated in the next section, is whether there are self-interested reasons to be moral.

Suppose that a person cares for no one but herself. Would you consider that person to be a moral person? This is not to ask whether she is a morally good person, but rather whether one can think of her as even operating in the moral realm, so to speak. In other words, the question concerns not whether the person's morality is a good one but whether she has any morals at all.

To take an example from W. D. Falk, suppose we want to know whether a person has been given a moral education.[9] Someone might answer that she had because she had been taught not to lie, to treat others kindly, not to drink to excess, and to work hard. When asked what reasons she had been given for behaving thus, suppose she responded that she was taught not to lie because others would not trust her if she did. She was taught to treat others well because then they would treat her well in return. She was taught to work hard because of the satisfaction this brought her or because she would then be better able to support herself. Would you consider her to have been given a moral education?

Falk thinks not. He suggests that she was given counsels of prudence, not morality. She was told what she probably should do to succeed in certain ways in life. She was taught the means that prudence would suggest she use to secure her own self-interest. According to Falk, only if she had been taught not to lie because it was wrong to do so, or because others had a right to know the truth, would she have been given a moral instruction. Only if she had been taught to treat others well because they deserved to be so treated, or that it would be wrong to do otherwise, would the counsel be a moral one. Similarly with working hard, if she had been told that she ought not to waste her talents or that she ought to contribute to society because it was the right thing to do, the teaching would have been a moral one. In summary, the education would not have been a moral one if it had been egoistically oriented. Do you agree?

Taking the moral point of view on this interpretation would then involve being able to see beyond ourselves and our own interests. It may also mean that we attempt to see things from another's point of view or to be impartial. Morality would then be thought of as providing rules for social living—ways, for example, of settling conflicts. The rules would apply equally to all, or one would have to give reasons why some persons would be treated differently than others. One reason might be that some persons had worked harder than others or their role demanded differential treatment.

In contrast, we do not think that we have to justify treating those close to us differently and more favorably than others. If we care more for our own children or our own friends than others, does this mean that we are not operating in the moral domain? Questions can be raised about the extent to which impartiality influences the moral domain or is required in order to be moral. Some feminists, for example, would rather define it in terms of sympathy and caring. See Chapter 9 for further treatment of this issue.

WHY BE MORAL?

Let us assume that morality does involve being able at least sometimes to take the other's point of view and at some level to treat people equally or impartially. Why should anyone do that, especially when it is not in her or his best interest to do so? In other words, are there any reasons that we can give to show why one should be moral? One reason is that doing what one ought to do is just what being moral means. One should not ask why one ought to do what one ought to do! However, perhaps something more can be said.

Notice that this is a question about why I as an individual ought to be moral. This is not the same as asking why everyone ought to be moral. We could argue that it is generally better for people to have and follow moral rules. Without such rules, our social lives would be pretty wretched. As Alan Altruist noted in the dialogue, and as Hobbes suggests in the second reading for this chapter, our life together would be one of constant conflict and wars. However, this does not answer the question concerning why I should be moral when it is not in my best interest to do so.

If you were trying to convince someone why he should be moral, how would you do it? You might appeal to his fear of reprisal if he did not generally follow moral rules. If he is not honest, then he will not be trusted. If he steals, he risks being punished. In *The Republic*, Glaucon tells the story of a shepherd named Gyges. Gyges comes into possession of a ring that he discovers makes him invisible when he turns it around on his finger. He proceeds to take advantage of his invisibility and take what he wants from others. Glaucon then asks whether we all would not do the same if we, like Gyges, could get away with it. He believes we would. But is he right? Is the only reason why people are just or do the right thing to avoid being punished for not doing so?

There are other more positive but still self-interested reasons you might offer someone to convince her that she ought to be moral. You might tell her that, as in Falk's moral education example, being virtuous is to one's own advantage. You might recall some of the advice from Benjamin Franklin's *Poor Richard's Almanac*.[10] "A stitch in time saves nine." "Observe all men, thyself most." "Spare and have is better than spend and crave." These are the self-interested counsels of a practical morality. Contemporary philosophers such as Philippa Foot also believe that most of the traditional virtues are in our own best interest.[11]

You might go even further in thinking about reasons to be moral. You might make the point that being moral is ennobling. Even when it involves sacrifice for a cause, being a moral person gives one a certain dignity, integrity, and self-respect. Only humans are capable of being moral, you might say, and human beings cannot flourish without being moral. You can give more thought to this question when you read about Kant's moral theory. For Kant, human dignity and worth is wholly bound up with being able to act for moral reasons.

Nevertheless, one can point to many examples in which people who break the moral rules seem to get away with it and fare better than those who keep them. "Nice guys [and gals?] finish last," baseball great Leo Durocher put it. If being moral seems too demanding, then some say this is too bad for morality. We ought to have a good life, even if it means sacrificing something of morality. In another view, if being moral involves sacrificing something of the personally fulfilling life and perhaps even "finishing last" sometimes, then this is what must be done. No one ever said being moral was going to be easy![12]

In the first reading for this chapter, Plato's characters in *The Republic* describe the view that was commonly accepted at the time that we always act in our own interest, one of the reasons given in support of an egoist theory. Next, Thomas Hobbes explains his views on why all human beings tend to pursue their own safety and interests and give up some control only for their own self-protection. Finally, the reading by Bishop Butler provides an argument against psychological egoism.

NOTES

1. For a discussion of "weakness of will," see Gwynneth Matthews, "Moral Weakness," *Mind*, 299 (July 1966): 405–419; Donald Davidson, "How Is Weakness of the Will Possible?" in *Moral Concepts*, Joel Feinberg (Ed.), 93–113 (New York: Oxford University Press, 1970).

2. A stronger version of psychological egoism asserts that people cannot do otherwise. According to this stronger version, people are such that they cannot do anything but act for the sake of their own interest. But how would we know this? We know how people do act, but how could we show that they cannot act otherwise? Perhaps we could appeal to certain views about human nature. We could argue that we always seek our own best interests because we are depraved by nature or perhaps by a religious "fall" such as the one described in the biblical book of Genesis.

3. Amitai Etzioni, a presentation at the University of San Francisco, December 1, 1992.

4. From the *Springfield Monitor* (ca. 1928), cited in Louis Pojman, *Ethics* (Belmont, CA: Wadsworth, 1990), 41.

5. However, we might by nature always act in our short-term interest. Morality might require, rather, that we act in our long-term interest. In this case, another problem arises. How could we be commanded by morality to do what we are not able to do? As we shall see in Chapter 5, according to Kant, "an ought implies a can."

6. We will return to this argument in looking at discussions on egoism by Kant. Other discussions of it can be found, for example, in James Sterba, "Justifying Morality: The Right and the Wrong Ways,"

Synthese, 72 (1987): 45–69; and James Rachels, "Egoism and Moral Skepticism," in *A New Introduction to Philosophy*, Steven M. Cahn (Ed.) (New York: Harper & Row, 1971).

7. See Adam Smith, *The Wealth of Nations* (New York: Edwin Cannan, 1904).

8. See the communitarian views in Robert Bellah, *Habits of the Heart* (Berkeley: University of California Press, 1985), and Amitai Etzioni, *The Spirit of Community: Rights, Responsibilities, and the Communitarian Agenda* (New York: Crown, 1993).

9. W. D. Falk, "Morality, Self, and Others," in *Morality and the Language of Conduct*, Hector-Neri Castaneda and George Nakhnikian (Eds.), 25–67 (Detroit: Wayne State University Press, 1963).

10. Benjamin Franklin, "Poor Richard's Almanac," in *American Philosophy: A Historical Anthology*, Barbara MacKinnon (Ed.), 46–47 (New York: State University of New York Press, 1985).

11. However, Foot has some problems fitting the virtue of justice into this generalization. Furthermore, she thinks of our best interest broadly—that is, as a kind of human flourishing. More discussion of this view can be found in Chapter 6 on natural law theory.

12. See Thomas Nagel's discussion of these different possibilities of the relation between the good life and the moral life in "Living Right and Living Well," in *The View from Nowhere* (New York: Oxford University Press, 1986), 189–207. Also see David Gauthier, "Morality and Advantage," *The Philosophical Review* (1967): 460–475.

R E A D I N G
The Ring of Gyges
PLATO

Study Questions

1. What view of the nature and origin of justice does Glaucon describe?
2. What does he try to show with the story of the ring of Gyges?
3. What does he want to demonstrate by giving two people such magic rings?
4. How does he attempt to show that a life of injustice is better than a life of justice?
5. How does he describe the difference between appearing just and being just?

6. According to the theory Glaucon and Socrates are explaining, what do parents teach their children?
7. What role do rewards in another life play in this account?
8. What do the prose writers say about justice and virtue? What of poets such as Hesiod and Homer?
9. What does Adeimantus request that Socrates tell them?
10. Why does Socrates lead them to a consideration of the state (something that is the focus of the rest of the dialogue)?

Glaucon (to Socrates). They say that to do injustice is, by nature, good; to suffer injustice, evil; but that the evil is greater than the good. And so when men have both done and suffered injustice and have had experience of both, not being able to avoid the one and obtain the other, they think that they had better agree among themselves to have neither; hence there arise laws and mutual covenants; and that which is ordained by law is termed by them lawful and just. This they affirm to be the origin and nature of justice;—it is a mean or compromise, between the best of all, which is to do injustice and not be punished, and the worst of all, which is to suffer injustice without the power of retaliation; and justice, being at a middle point between the two, is tolerated not as a good, but as the lesser evil, and honoured by reason of the inability of men to do injustice. For no man who is worthy to be called a man would ever submit to such an agreement if he were able to resist; he would be mad if he did. Such is the received account, Socrates, of the nature and origin of justice.

Now that those who practise justice do so involuntarily and because they have not the power to be unjust will best appear if we imagine something of this kind: having given both to the just and the unjust power to do what they will, let us watch and see whither desire will lead them; then we shall discover in the very act the just and unjust man to be proceeding along the same road, following their interest, which all natures deem to be their good, and are only diverted into the path of justice by the force of law. The liberty which we are supposing may be most completely given to them in the form of such a power as is said to have been possessed by Gyges the ancestor of Croesus the Lydian. According to the tradition, Gyges was a shepherd in the service of the king of Lydia; there was a great storm, and an earthquake made an opening in the earth at the place where he was feeding his flock. Amazed at the sight, he descended into the opening, where, among other marvels, he beheld a hollow brazen horse, having doors, at which he stooping and looking in saw a dead body of stature, as appeared to him, more than human, and having nothing on but a gold ring; this he took from the finger of the dead and reascended. Now the shepherds met together, according to custom,

that they might send their monthly report about the flocks to the king; into their assembly he came having the ring on his finger, and as he was sitting among them he chanced to turn the collet of the ring inside his hand, when instantly he became invisible to the rest of the company and they began to speak of him as if he were no longer present. He was astonished at this, and again touching the ring he turned the collet outwards and reappeared; he made several trials of the ring, and always with the same result—when he turned the collet inwards he became invisible, when outwards he reappeared. Whereupon he contrived to be chosen one of the messengers who were sent to the court; where as soon as he arrived he seduced the queen, and with her help conspired against the king and slew him, and took the kingdom. Suppose now that there were two such magic rings, and the just put on one of them and the unjust the other; no man can be imagined to be of such an iron nature that he would stand fast in justice. No man would keep his hands off what was not his own when he could safely take what he liked out of the market, or go into houses and lie with any one at his pleasure, or kill or release from prison whom he would, and in all respects be like a God among men. Then the actions of the just would be as the actions of the unjust; they would both come at last to the same point. And this we may truly affirm to be a great proof that a man is just, not willingly or because he thinks that justice is any good to him individually, but of necessity, for wherever any one thinks that he can safely be unjust, there he is unjust. For all men believe in their hearts that injustice is far more profitable to the individual than justice, and he who argues as I have been supposing, will say that they are right. If you could imagine any one obtaining this power of becoming invisible, and never doing any wrong or touching what was another's, he would be thought by the lookers-on to be a most wretched idiot, although they would praise him to one another's faces, and keep up appearances with one another from a fear that they too might suffer injustice. Enough of this.

Now, if we are to form a real judgment of the life of the just and unjust, we must isolate them; there is no other way; and how is the isolation to be effected? I answer: Let the unjust man be entirely unjust, and the just man entirely just; nothing is to be taken

---

Plato, *The Republic*, Bk. II, 357a–369. Trans. B. Jowett.

away from either of them, and both are to be perfectly furnished for the work of their respective lives. First, let the unjust be like other distinguished masters of craft; like the skilful pilot or physician, who knows intuitively his own powers and keeps within their limits, and who, if he fails at any point, is able to recover himself. So let the unjust make his unjust attempts in the right way, and lie hidden if he means to be great in his injustice (he who is found out is nobody): for the highest reach of injustice is, to be deemed just when you are not. Therefore I say that in the perfectly unjust man we must assume the most perfect injustice; there is to be no deduction, but we must allow him, while doing the most unjust acts, to have acquired the greatest reputation for justice. If he have taken a false step he must be able to recover himself; he must be one who can speak with effect, if any of his deeds come to light, and who can force his way where force is required by his courage and strength, and command of money and friends. And at his side let us place the just man in his nobleness and simplicity, wishing, as Aeschylus says, to be and not to seem good. There must be no seeming, for if he seem to be just he will be honoured and rewarded, and then we shall not know whether he is just for the sake of justice or for the sake of honours and rewards; therefore, let him be clothed in justice only, and have no other covering; and he must be imagined in a state of life the opposite of the former. Let him be the best of men, and let him be thought the worst; then he will have been put to the proof; and we shall see whether he will be affected by the fear of infamy and its consequences. And let him continue thus to the hour of death; being just and seeming to be unjust. When both have reached the uttermost extreme, the one of justice and the other of injustice, let judgment be given which of them is the happier of the two.

Socrates. Heavens! my dear Glaucon, I said, how energetically you polish them up for the decision, first one and then the other, as if they were two statues.

Glaucon. I do my best. And now that we know what they are like there is no difficulty in tracing out the sort of life which awaits either of them. This I will proceed to describe; but as you may think the description a little too coarse, I ask you to suppose, Socrates, that the words which follow are not mine.—Let me put them into the mouths of the eulogists of injustice: They will tell you that the just man who is thought unjust will be scourged, racked, bound—will have his eyes burnt out; and, at last, after suffering every kind of evil, he will be impaled: Then he will understand that he ought to seem only, and not to be, just; the words of Aeschylus may be more truly spoken of the unjust than of the just. For the unjust is pursuing a reality; he does not live with a view to appearances—he wants to be really unjust and not to seem only:—

> "His mind has a soil deep and fertile,
> Out of which spring his prudent counsels."

In the first place, he is thought just, and therefore bears rule in the city; he can marry whom he will, and give in marriage to whom he will; also he can trade and deal where he likes, and always to his own advantage, because he has no misgivings about injustice; and at every contest, whether in public or private, he gets the better of his antagonists, and gains at their expense, and is rich, and out of his gains he can benefit his friends, and harm his enemies; moreover, he can offer sacrifices, and dedicate gifts to the gods abundantly and magnificently, and can honour the gods or any man whom he wants to honour in a far better style than the just, and therefore he is likely to be dearer than they are to the gods. And thus, Socrates, gods and men are said to unite in making the life of the unjust better than the life of the just.

Adeimantus. Socrates, you do not suppose that there is nothing more to be urged?

Socrates. Why, what else is there?

Adeimantus. The strongest point of all has not been even mentioned.

Socrates. Well, then, according to the proverb, "Let brother help brother"—if he fails in any part do you assist him; although I must confess that Glaucon has already said quite enough to lay me in the dust, and take from me the power of helping justice.

Adeimantus. Nonsense. But let me add something more: There is another side to Glaucon's argument about the praise and censure of justice and injustice, which is equally required in order to bring out what I believe to be his meaning. Parents and tutors are always telling their sons and their wards that they are to be just; but why? not for the sake of justice, but for the sake of character and reputation; in the hope of obtaining for him who is reputed just some of those offices, marriages, and the like which Glaucon has enumerated among the advantages accruing to the unjust from the reputation of justice. More, however, is made of appearances by this class of persons than by the others; for they throw in the good opinion of the gods, and will tell you of a shower of benefits which the heavens, as they say, rain upon the pious; and this accords with the testimony of the noble Hesiod and Homer, the first of whom says, that the gods make the oaks of the just—

"To bear acorns at their summit, and bees in the middle; And the sheep are bowed down with the weight of their fleeces,"[1]

and many other blessings of a like kind are provided for them. And Homer has a very similar strain; for he speaks of one whose fame is—

"As the fame of some blameless king who, like a god, Maintains justice; to whom the black earth brings forth Wheat and barley, whose trees are bowed with fruit, And his sheep never fail to bear, and the sea gives him fish."[2]

Still grander are the gifts of heaven which Musaeus and his son[3] vouchsafe to the just; they take them down into the world below, where they have the saints lying on couches at a feast, everlastingly drunk, crowned with garlands; their idea seems to be that an immortality of drunkenness is the highest meed of virtue. Some extend their rewards yet further; the posterity, as they say, of the faithful and just shall survive to the third and fourth generation. This is the style in which they praise justice. But about the wicked there is another strain; they bury them in a slough in Hades, and make them carry water in a sieve; also while they are yet living they bring them to infamy, and inflict upon them the punishments which Glaucon described as the portion of the just who are reputed to be unjust; nothing else does their invention supply. Such is their manner of praising the one and censuring the other.

Once more, Socrates, I will ask you to consider another way of speaking about justice and injustice, which is not confined to the poets, but is found in prose writers. The universal voice of mankind is always declaring that justice and virtue are honourable, but grievous and toilsome; and that the pleasures of vice and injustice are easy of attainment, and are only censured by law and opinion. They say also that honesty is for the most part less profitable than dishonesty; and they are quite ready to call wicked men happy, and to honour them both in public and private when they are rich or in any other way influential, while they despise and overlook those who may be weak and poor, even though acknowledging them to be better than the others. But most extraordinary of all is their mode of speaking about virtue and the gods: they say that the gods apportion calamity and misery to many good men, and good and happiness to the wicked. And mendicant prophets go to rich men's doors and persuade them that they have a power committed to them by the gods of making an atonement for a man's own or his ancestor's sins by sacrifices or charms, with rejoicings and feasts; and they promise to harm an enemy, whether just or unjust, at a small cost; with magic arts and incantations binding heaven, as they say, to execute their will. And the poets are the authorities to whom they appeal, now smoothing the path of vice with the words of Hesiod:—

"Vice may be had in abundance without trouble; the way is smooth and her dwelling-place is near. But before virtue the gods have set toil,"[4]

and a tedious and uphill road: then citing Homer as a witness that the gods may be influenced by men; for he also says:—

"The gods, too, may be turned from their purpose; and men pray to them and avert their wrath by sacrifices and soothing entreaties, and by libations and the odour of fat, when they have sinned and transgressed."[5]

And they produce a host of books written by Musaeus and Orpheus, who were children of the Moon and the Muses—that is what they say— according to which they perform their ritual, and persuade not only individuals, but whole cities, that expiations and atonements for sin may be made by sacrifices and amusements which fill a vacant hour, and are equally at the service of the living and the dead; the latter sort they call mysteries, and they redeem us from the pains of hell, but if we neglect them no one knows what awaits us.

And now when the young hear all this said about virtue and vice, and the way in which gods and men regard them, how are their minds likely to be affected, my dear Socrates,—those of them, I mean, who are quickwitted, and, like bees on the wing, light on every flower, and from all that they hear are prone to draw conclusions as to what manner of persons they should be and in what way they should walk if they would make the best of life? Probably the youth will say to himself in the words of Pindar—

> "Can I by justice or by crooked ways of deceit ascend a loftier tower which may be a fortress to me all my days?"

For what men say is that, if I am really just and am not also thought just, profit there is none, but the pain and loss on the other hand are unmistakeable. But if, though unjust, I acquire the reputation of justice, a heavenly life is promised to me. Since then, as philosophers prove, appearance tyrannizes over truth and is lord of happiness, to appearance I must devote myself. I will describe around me a picture and shadow of virtue to be the vestibule and exterior of my house; behind I will trail the subtle and crafty fox, as Archilochus, greatest of sages, recommends. But I hear some one exclaiming that the concealment of wickedness is often difficult; to which I answer, Nothing great is easy. Nevertheless, the argument indicates this, if we would be happy, to be the path along which we should proceed. With a view to concealment we will establish secret brotherhoods and political clubs. And there are professors of rhetoric who teach the art of persuading courts and assemblies; and so, partly by persuasion and partly by force, I shall make unlawful gains and not be punished. Still I hear a voice saying that the gods cannot be deceived, neither can they be compelled. But what if there are no gods? or, suppose them to have no care of human things—why in either case should we mind about concealment? And even if there are gods, and they do care about us, yet we know of them only from tradition and the genealogies of the poets; and these are the very persons who say that they may be influenced and turned by "sacrifices and soothing entreaties and by offerings." Let us be consistent then, and believe both or neither. If the poets speak truly, why then we had better be unjust, and offer of the fruits of injustice; for if we are just, although we may escape the vengeance of heaven, we shall lose the gains of injustice; but, if we are unjust, we shall keep the gains, and by our sinning and praying, and praying and sinning, the gods will be propitiated, and we shall not be punished. "But there is a world below in which either we or our posterity will suffer for our unjust deeds." Yes, my friend, will be the reflection, but there are mysteries and atoning deities, and these have great power. That is what mighty cities declare; and the children of the gods, who were their poets and prophets, bear a like testimony.

On what principle, then, shall we any longer choose justice rather than the worst injustice? when, if we only unite the latter with a deceitful regard to appearance, we shall fare to our mind both with gods and men, in life and after death, as the most numerous and the highest authorities tell us. Knowing all this, Socrates, how can a man who has any superiority of mind or person or rank or wealth, be willing to honour justice; or indeed to refrain from laughing when he hears justice praised? And even if there should be some one who is able to disprove the truth of my words, and who is satisfied that justice is best, still he is not angry with the unjust, but is very ready to forgive them, because he also knows that men are not just of their own free will; unless, peradventure, there be some one whom the divinity within him may have inspired with a hatred of injustice, or who has attained knowledge of the truth—but no other man. He only blames injustice who, owing to cowardice or age or some weakness, has not the power of being unjust. And this is proved by the fact that when he obtains the power, he immediately becomes unjust as far as he can be.

The cause of all this, Socrates, was indicated by us at the beginning of the argument, when my brother and I told you how astonished we were to find that of all the professing panegyrists of justice—beginning with the ancient heroes of whom any memorial has been preserved to us, and ending with the men of our own time—no one has ever blamed injustice or praised justice except with a view to the glories, honours, and benefits which flow from them. No one has ever adequately described either in verse or prose the true essential nature of either of them abiding in the soul, and invisible to any human or divine eye; or shown that of all the things of a man's soul which he has within him, justice is the greatest good, and injustice the greatest evil. Had this been the universal strain, had you sought to persuade us of this from our youth upwards, we should not have been on the watch to keep one another from doing wrong, but every one would have been his own watchman, because afraid, if he did wrong, of harbouring in himself the greatest of evils. I dare say that Thrasymachus and others would seriously hold the language which I have been merely repeating, and words even stronger than these about justice and injustice, grossly, as I conceive, perverting their true nature. But I speak in this vehement manner, as I must frankly confess to you, because I want to hear from you the opposite side; and I would ask you to show not only the superiority which justice has over injustice, but what effect they have on the possessor of them which makes the one to be a good and the other an evil to him. And please, as Glaucon requested of you, to exclude reputations; for unless you take away from each of them his true reputation and add on the false, we shall say that you do not praise justice, but the appearance of it; we shall think that you are only exhorting us to keep injustice dark, and that you really agree with Thrasymachus in thinking that justice is another's good and the interest of the stronger, and that injustice is a man's own profit and interest, though injurious to the weaker. Now as you have admitted that justice is one of that highest class of goods which are desired indeed for their results, but in a far greater degree for their own sakes—like sight or hearing or knowledge or health, or any other real and natural and not merely conventional good—I would ask you in your praise of justice to regard one point only: I mean the essential good and evil which justice and injustice work in the possessors of them. Let others praise justice and censure injustice, magnifying the rewards and honours of the one and abusing the other; that is a manner of arguing which, coming from them, I am ready to tolerate, but from you who have spent your whole life in the consideration of this question, unless I hear the contrary from your own lips, I expect something better. And therefore, I say, not only prove to us that justice is better than injustice, but show what they either of them do to the possessor of them, which makes the one to be a good and the other an evil, whether seen or unseen by gods and men.

Socrates. Sons of an illustrious father, that was not a bad beginning of the Elegiac verses which the admirer of Glaucon made in honour of you after you had distinguished yourselves at the battle of Megara:—

> "'Sons of Ariston,' he sang, 'divine offspring of an illustrious hero.'"

The epithet is very appropriate, for there is something truly divine in being able to argue as you have done for the superiority of injustice, and remaining unconvinced by your own arguments. And I do believe that you are not convinced—this I infer from your general character, for had I judged only from your speeches I should have mistrusted you. But now, the greater my confidence in you, the greater is my difficulty in knowing what to say. For I am in a strait between two; on the one hand I feel that I am unequal to the task; and my inability is brought home to me by the fact that you were not satisfied with the answer which I made to Thrasymachus, proving, as I thought, the superiority which justice has over injustice. And yet I cannot refuse to help, while breath and speech remain to me; I am afraid that there would be an impiety in being present when justice is evil spoken of and not lifting up a hand in her defence. And therefore I had best give such help as I can.

Glaucon and the rest entreated me by all means not to let the question drop, but to proceed in the investigation. They wanted to arrive at the truth, first, about the nature of justice and injustice, and secondly, about their relative advantages. I told them, what I really thought, that the enquiry would be of a serious nature, and would require very good eyes. Seeing then, I said, that we are no great wits, I think that we had better adopt a method which I may illustrate thus; suppose that a short-sighted person had been asked by some one to read small letters from a distance; and it occurred to some one else that they might be found in another place which was larger and in which the letters were larger—if they were the same and he could read the larger letters first, and then proceed to the lesser—this would have been thought a rare piece of good fortune.

Adeimantus. Very true. But how does the illustration apply to our enquiry?

Socrates. I will tell you. Justice, which is the subject of our enquiry, is, as you know, sometimes spoken of as the virtue of an individual, and sometimes as the virtue of a state.

Adeimantus. True.

Socrates. And is not a State larger than an individual?

Adeimantus. It is.

Socrates. Then in the larger the quantity of justice is likely to be larger and more easily discernible. I propose therefore that we enquire into the nature of justice and injustice, first as they appear in the State, and secondly in the individual, proceeding from the greater to the lesser and comparing them.

Adeimantus. That is an excellent proposal.

NOTES

1. Hesiod, *Works and Days*, 230.
2. Homer, *Od*, xix. 109.
3. Eumolpus.
4. Hesiod, *Works and Days*, 287.
5. Homer, *Iliad*, ix. 493.

READING
Self Love*
THOMAS HOBBES

Study Questions

1. What are the two sorts of motion of which the body of animals, including humans, are capable, according to Hobbes?
2. What kinds of motions are appetite and aversion? How are these related to love and hate?
3. How are good and evil related to these bodily motions, according to Hobbes?
4. In what ways are men equal and unequal? Which is more significant?
5. What happens when people desire the same thing? How does one solve this problem for oneself, according to Hobbes?
6. Should power or dominion over others be allowed, according to Hobbes?
7. What does Hobbes mean when he says that nature has given everyone a right to all? What is the result of this?
8. Beyond society and its rules, is there any right or wrong, or just or unjust, according to Hobbes?

Thomas Hobbes, "Leviathan," in *The English Works of Thomas Hobbes*, Vol. II, ed. by Sir William Molesworth (London: John Bohn, 1839), pp. 38–41, 85.

*Title supplied by the editor.

THERE BE in animals, two sorts of *motions* peculiar to them: one called vital; begun in generation, and continued without interruption through their whole life; such as are the *course* of the *blood*, the *pulse*, the *breathing*, the *concoction*, *nutrition*, *excretion*, etc. to which motions there needs no help of imagination: the other is *animal motion*, otherwise called *voluntary motion*; as to *go*, to *speak*, to *move* any of our limbs, in such manner as is first fancied in our minds. That sense is motion in the organs and interior parts of man's body, caused by the action of the things we see, hear, etc.; and that fancy is but the relics of the same motion, remaining after sense. ... And because *going*, *speaking*, and the like *voluntary motions*, depend always upon a precedent thought of *whither*, *which way*, and *what*; it is evident, that the imagination is the first internal beginning of all voluntary motion. And although unstudied men do not conceive any motion at all to be there, where the thing moved is invisible; or the space it is moved in is, for the shortness of it, insensible; yet that doth not hinder, but that such motions are. For let a space be never so little, that which is moved over a greater space, whereof that little one is part, must first be moved over that. These small beginnings of motion, within the body of man, before they appear in walking, speaking, striking, and other visible actions, are commonly called ENDEAVOR.

This endeavor, when it is toward something which causes it, is called APPETITE, or DESIRE; the latter, being the general name; and the other oftentimes restrained to signify the desire of food, namely *hunger* and *thirst*. And when the endeavor is fromward something, it is generally called AVERSION. These words, *appetite* and *aversion*, we have from the Latins; and they both of them signify the motions, one of approaching, the other of retiring. … For nature itself does often press upon men those truths, which afterwards, when they look for somewhat beyond nature, they stumble at. For the schools find in mere appetite to go, or move, no actual motion at all: but because some motion they must acknowledge, they call it metaphorical motion; which is but an absurd speech: for though words may be called metaphorical; bodies and motions cannot.

That which men desire, they are also said to LOVE: and to HATE those things for which they have aversion. So that desire and love are the same thing; save that by desire, we always signify the absence of the object; by love, most commonly the presence of the same. So also by aversion, we signify the absence; and by hate, the presence of the object.

Of appetites and aversions, some are born with men; as appetite of food, appetite of excretion, and exoneration, which may also and more properly be called aversions, from somewhat they feel in their bodies; and some other appetites, not many. The rest, which are appetites of particular things, proceed from experience, and trial of their effects upon themselves or other men. For of things we know not at all, or believe not to be, we can have no further desire, than to taste and try. But aversion we have for things, not only which we know have hurt us, but also that we do not know whether they will hurt us, or not.

Those things which we neither desire, nor hate, we are said to *contemn*; CONTEMPT being nothing else but an immobility, or contumacy of the heart, in resisting the action of certain things; and proceeding from that the heart is already moved otherwise, by other more potent objects; or from want of experience of them.

And because the constitution of a man's body is in continual mutation, it is impossible that all the same things should always cause in him the same appetites, and aversions: much less can all men consent, in the desire of almost any one and the same object.

But whatsoever is the object of any man's appetite or desire, that is it which he for his part calleth *good*: and the object of his hate and aversion, *evil*; and of his *contempt*, *vile* and inconsiderable. For these words of good, evil, and contemptible, are ever used with relation to the person that useth them: there being nothing simply and absolutely so; nor any common rule of good and evil, to be taken from the nature of the objects themselves. …

Felicity of this life consisteth not in the repose of a mind satisfied. For there is no such finis *ultimus*, utmost aim, nor *summum bonum*, greatest good, as is spoken of in the books of the old moral philosophers. Nor can a man any more live, whose desires are at an end, than he, whose senses and imaginations are at a stand. Felicity is a continual progress of the desire, from one object to another; the attaining of the former, being still but the way to the latter. The cause whereof is, that the object of man's desire, is not to enjoy once only, and for one instant of time; but to assure for ever, the way of his future desire. …

So that in the first place, I put for a general inclination of all mankind, a perpetual and restless desire of power after power, that ceaseth only in death. And the cause of this, is … that a man … cannot assure the power and means to live well, which he hath present, without the acquisition of more. …

Nature hath made men so equal, in the faculties of the body, and mind; as that though there be found one man sometimes manifestly stronger in body, or of quicker mind than another; yet when all is reckoned together, the difference between man, and man, is not so considerable, as that one man can thereupon claim to himself any benefit, to which another may not pretend, as well as he. For as to the strength of body, the weakest has strength enough to kill the strongest, either by secret machination, or by confederacy with others, that are in the same danger with himself.

And as to the faculties of the mind, setting aside the arts grounded upon words, and especially that skill of proceeding upon general, and infallible rules, called science; which very few have, and but in few things; as being not native faculty, born with us; nor attained, as prudence, while we look after somewhat else, I find yet a greater equality amongst men, than that of strength. For prudence, is but experience; which equal time, equally bestows on all men, in those things they equally apply themselves unto. That which may perhaps make such equality incredible, is but a vain conceit of one's own wisdom, which almost all men think they have in a greater degree, than the vulgar; that is, than all men but themselves, and a few others, whom by fame, or for concurring with themselves, they approve. For such is the nature of men, that howsoever they may acknowledge many others to be more witty, or more eloquent, or more learned; yet they will hardly believe there be many so wise as themselves; for they see their own wit at hand, and other men's at a distance. But this proveth rather that men are in that point equal, than unequal. For there is not ordinarily a greater sign of the equal distribution of any thing, than that every man is contented with his share.

From this equality of ability, ariseth equality of hope in the attaining of our ends. And therefore if any two men desire the same thing, which nevertheless they cannot both enjoy, they become enemies; and in the way to their end, which is principally their own conservation, and sometimes their delectation only, endeavor to destroy, or subdue one another. And from hence it comes to pass, that where an invader hath no more to fear, than another man's single power; if one plant, sow, build, or possess a convenient seat, others may probably be expected to come prepared with forces united, to dispossess, and deprive him, not only of the fruit of his labor, but also of his life, or liberty. And the invader again is in the like danger of another.

And from this diffidence of one another, there is no way for any man to secure himself, so reasonable, as anticipation; that is, by force, or wiles, to master the persons of all men he can, so long, till he see no other power great enough to endanger him: and this is no more than his own conservation requireth, and generally allowed. Also because there be some, that taking pleasure in contemplating their own power in the acts of conquest, which they pursue farther than their security requires; if others, that otherwise would be glad to be at ease within modest bounds, should not by invasion increase their power, they would not be able, long time, by standing only on their defense, to subsist. And by consequence, such augmentation of dominion over men being necessary to a man's conservation, it ought to be allowed him.

Again, men have no pleasure, but on the contrary a great deal of grief, in keeping company, where there is no power able to overawe them all. For every man looketh that his companion should value him, at the same rate he sets upon himself: and upon all signs of contempt, or undervaluing, naturally endeavors, as far as he dares, (which amongst them that have no common power to keep them in quiet, is far enough to make them destroy each other), to extort a greater value from his contemners, by damage; and from others, by the example.

So that in the nature of man, we find three principal causes of quarrel. First, competition; secondly, diffidence; thirdly, glory.

The first, maketh men invade for gain; the second, for safety; and the third, for reputation. The first use violence, to make themselves masters of other men's persons, wives, children, and cattle; the second, to defend them; the third, for trifles, as a word, a smile, a different opinion, and any other sign of undervalue, either direct in their persons, or by reflection in their kindred, their friends, their nation, their profession, or their name.

Hereby it is manifest, that during the time men live without a common power to keep them all in awe, they are in that condition which is called war; and such a war, as is of every man, against every man. For WAR, consisteth not in battle only, or the act of fighting; but in a tract of time, wherein the will to contend by battle is sufficiently known: and therefore the notion of time, is to be considered in the nature of war; as it is in the nature of weather. For as the nature of foul weather, lieth not in a shower or two of rain; but in an inclination thereto of many days together: so the nature of war, consisteth not in actual fighting; but in the known disposition thereto, during all the time there is no assurance to the contrary. All other time is PEACE.

Whatsoever therefore is consequent to a time of war, where every man is enemy to every man; the same is consequent to the time, wherein men live without security, than what their own strength, and their own invention shall furnish them withal. In such condition, there is no place for industry; because the fruit thereof is uncertain: and consequently no culture of the earth; no navigation, nor use of the commodities that may be imported by sea; no commodious building; no instruments of moving, and removing, such things as require much force; no knowledge of the face of the earth; no account of time; no arts; no letters; no society; and which is worst of all, continual fear, and danger of violent death; and the life of man, solitary, poor, nasty, brutish, and short....

It may peradventure be thought, there was never such a time, nor condition of war as this; and I believe it was never generally so, over all the world: but there are many places, where they live so now. For the savage people in many places of America, except the government of small families, the concord whereof dependeth on natural lust, have no government at all;

and live at this day in that brutish manner, as I said before. Howsoever, it may be perceived what manner of life there would be, where there were no common power to fear, by the manner of life, which men that have formerly lived under a peaceful government, use to degenerate into, in a civil war.

But though there had never been any time, wherein particular men were in a condition of war one against another; yet in all times, kings, and persons of sovereign authority, because of their independency, are in continual jealousies, and in the state and posture of gladiators; having their weapons pointing, and their eyes fixed on one another; that is, their forts, garrisons, and guns upon the frontiers of their kingdoms; and continual spies upon their neighbors; which is a posture of war. But because they uphold thereby, the industry of their subjects; there does not follow from it, that misery, which accompanies the liberty of particular men....

R E A D I N G
Upon the Social Nature of Man

JOSEPH BUTLER

Study Questions

1. According to Butler, what is benevolence and how is it expressed?
2. How do self-love and benevolence promote each other?
3. According to Butler, how does Thomas Hobbes explain benevolence?
4. How is benevolence proven, according to Butler?
5. What are some other "appetites, passions, and particular affections quite distinct from both self-love and from benevolence"?
6. What is it by which we approve and disapprove our own actions? How does it function?

NATURAL PRINCIPLE OF BENEVOLENCE

First, there is a natural principle of *benevolence* in man, which is in some degree to *society* what *self-love* is to the *individual*. And if there be in mankind any disposition to friendship; if there be any such thing as compassion—for compassion is momentary love—if there be any such things as the paternal or filial affections; if

there be any affection in human nature, the object and end of which is the good of another, this is itself benevolence, or the love of another. Be it ever so short, be it in ever so low a degree, or ever so unhappily confined, it proves the assertion, and points out what we were designed for, as really as though it were in a higher degree and more extensive. I must, however, remind you that though benevolence and self-love are different, though the former tends most directly to public good, and the latter private, yet there are so perfectly coincident, that the greatest satisfactions to ourselves depend upon our having benevolence in a due degree; and that self-love is one chief security of our right behavior towards society. It may be added that their mutual coinciding, so that we can scarce promote one without the other, is equally a proof that we were made for both.

Adapted from Joseph Butler, *Fifteen Sermons* (1726), Sermon 1, "Upon the Social Nature of Man." Taken from "Against Egoism" by Louis Pojman and James Fieser, *Ethical Theory*, 6th ed. (Boston: Wadsworth, 2011), pp. 70–74.

Suppose a man of learning to be writing a grave book upon *human nature* [i.e., Thomas Hobbes], and to show in several parts of it that he had an insight into the subject he was considering, amongst other things, the following one would require to be accounted for—the appearance of benevolence or good-will in men towards each other in the instances of natural relation, and in others (Hobbes, *Of Human Nature*, Ch. 9, Sect. 13). Cautious of being deceived with outward show, he retires within himself to see exactly what that is in the mind of man from whence this appearance proceeds; and, upon deep reflection, asserts the principle in the mind to be only the love of power, and delight in the exercise of it. Would not every body think here was a mistake of one word for another—that the philosopher was contemplating and accounting for some other *human actions*, some other behavior of man to man? And could anyone be thoroughly satisfied that what is commonly called benevolence or good-will was really the affection meant, but only by being made to understand that this learned person had a general hypothesis, to which the appearance of good-will could not otherwise be reconciled? That what has this appearance is often nothing but ambition; that a delight in superiority often (suppose always) mixes itself with benevolence, only makes it more specious to call it ambition than hunger, of the two; but in reality that passion does no more account for the whole appearances of good-will than this appetite does. Is there not often the appearance of one man's wishing that good to another, which he knows himself unable to procure him; and rejoicing in it, though bestowed by a third person? And can love of power any way possibly come in to account for this desire or delight? Is there not often the appearance of men's distinguishing between two or more persons, preferring one before another, to do good to, in cases where love of power cannot in the least account for the distinction and preference? For this principle can no otherwise distinguish between objects than as it is a greater instance and exertion of power to do good to one rather than to another. Again, suppose good-will in the mind of man to be nothing but delight in the exercise of power: men might indeed be restrained by distant and accidental considerations; but these restraints being removed, they would have a disposition to, and delight in, mischief as an exercise and proof of power: and this disposition and delight would arise from, or be the same principle in the mind, as a disposition to and delight in charity. Thus cruelty, as distinct from envy and resentment, would be exactly the same in the mind of man as good-will: that one tends to the happiness, the other to the misery, of our fellow-creatures, is, it seems, merely an accidental circumstance, which the mind has not the least regard to. . . .

If any person can in earnest doubt whether there be such a thing as good-will in one man towards another (for the question is not concerning either the degree or extensiveness of it, but concerning the affection itself), let it be observed that *whether man be thus, or otherwise constituted, what is the inward frame in this particular* is a mere question of fact or natural history not provable immediately by reason. It is therefore to be judged of and determined in the same way other facts or matters of natural history are—by appealing to the external senses, or inward perceptions respectively, as the matter under consideration is cognizable by one or the other: by arguing from acknowledged facts and actions for a great number of actions of the same kind, in different circumstances, and on respecting different objects, will prove to a certainty what principles they do not, and to the greatest probability what principles they do, proceed from: and, lastly, by the testimony of mankind. Now that there is some degree of benevolence amongst men may be as of strongly and plainly proved in all these ways, as it could possibly be proved, supposing there was this affection in our nature. And should any one think fit to assert that resentment in the mind of man was of absolutely nothing but reasonable concern for our own safety, the falsity of this, and what is the real nature of that passion, could be shown in no other ways than those in which it may be shown that there is such a thing in *some degree* as real good-will in man towards man. . . .

EXISTENCE OF SEVERAL DISTINCT HUMAN MOTIVATIONS

Secondly, this will further appear, from observing that the *several passions* and *affections*, which are distinct both from benevolence and self-love, do in general contribute and lead us to *public good* as really as to *private*. It might be thought too minute and particular, and would carry us too great a length, to distinguish between and compare together the several passions or appetites distinct from benevolence, whose primary use and intention is the security and good of society, and the passions distinct from self-love, whose primary intention and design is the security and good of the individual. It is enough to the present argument that desire of esteem from others, contempt and esteem of them, love of society as distinct from affection to the good of it, indignation against successful vice—that these are public affections or passions, have an immediate respect to others, naturally lead us to regulate our behavior in such a manner as will be of service to our fellow-creatures. If any or all of these may be considered likewise as private affections, as tending to private good, this does not hinder them from being public affections too, or destroy the good influence of them upon society, and their tendency to public good. It may be added, that as persons without any conviction from reason of the desirableness of life would yet of course preserve it merely from the appetite of hunger, so, by acting merely from regard (suppose) to reputation, without any consideration of the good of others, men often contribute to public good. In both these instances they are plainly instruments in the hands of another, in the hands of Providence, to carry on ends—the preservation of the individual and good of society—which they themselves have not in their view or intention. The sum is, men have various appetites, passions, and particular affections, quite distinct both from self-love and from benevolence: all of these have a tendency to promote both public and private good, and may be considered as respecting others and ourselves equally and in common; but some of them seem most immediately to respect others, or tend to public good; others of them most immediately to respect self, or tend to private good: as the former are not benevolence, so the latter are not self-love: neither sort are instances of our love either to ourselves or others. ...

Everybody makes a distinction between self-love and the several particular passions, appetites, and affections; and yet they are often confounded again. That they are totally different, will be seen by anyone who will distinguish between the passions and appetites *themselves*, and *endeavoring* after the means of their gratification. Consider the appetite of hunger, and the desire of esteem: these being the occasion both of pleasure and pain, the coolest self-love, as well as the appetites and passions themselves, may put us upon making use of the *proper methods of obtaining* that pleasure, and avoiding that pain; but the *feelings* themselves, the pain of hunger and shame, and the delight from esteem, are no more self-love than they are any thing in the world. Though a man hated himself, he would as much feel the pain of hunger as he would that of the gout; and it is plainly supposable there may be creatures with self-love in them to the highest degree, who may be quite insensible and indifferent (as men in some cases are) to the contempt and esteem of those upon whom their happiness does not in some further respects depend. And as self-love and the several particular passions and appetites are in themselves totally different, so that some actions proceed from one and some from the other will be manifest to any who will observe the two following very supposable cases. One man rushes upon certain ruin for the gratification of a present desire: nobody will call the principle of this action self-love. Suppose another man to go through some laborious work upon promise of a great reward, without any distinct knowledge what the reward will be: this course of action cannot be ascribed to any particular passion. The former of these actions is plainly to be imputed to some particular passion or affection; the latter as plainly to the general affection or principle of self-love. That there are some particular pursuits or actions concerning which we cannot determine how far they are owing to one, and how far to the other, proceeds from this, that the two principles are frequently mixed together, and run up into each other. This distinction is further explained in the eleventh sermon.

If any desire to see this distinction and comparison made in a particular instance, the appetite and passion now mentioned may reward serve for one. Hunger is to be considered as a private appetite, because the end for which it was given us is the preservation of the individual. Desire of esteem is a public passion; because the end for which it was given us is to regulate our behavior towards society. The respect which this has to private good is as remote as the respect that has to public good; and the appetite is no more self-love than the passion is benevolence. The object and end of the former is merely food; the object and end of the latter is merely esteem: but the latter can no more be gratified without contributing to the good of society, than the former can be gratified without contributing to the preservation of the individual.

NATURAL FACULTY OF CONSCIENCE

Thirdly, there is a principle of reflection in men, by which they distinguish between, approve and disapprove their own actions. We are plainly constituted such sort of creatures as to reflect upon our own nature. The mind can take a view of what passes within itself, its propensions, aversions, passions, affections as respecting such objects, and in such degrees; and of the several actions consequent thereupon. In this survey it approves of one, disapproves of another, and towards a third is affected neither of these ways, but is quite indifferent. This principle in man, by which he approves or disapproves his heart, temper, and actions, is conscience; for this is the strict sense of the word, though sometimes it is used so as to take in more. And that this faculty tends to restrain men from doing mischief to each other, and leads them to do good, is too manifest to need being insisted upon. Thus, a parent has the affection of love to his children: this leads him to take care of, to educate, to make due provision for them—the natural affection leads to this: but the reflection that it is his proper business, what belongs to him, that it is right and commendable so to do—this, added to the affection, becomes a much more settled principle, and carries him on through more labor and difficulties for the sake of his children than he would undergo from that affection alone, if he thought it, and the course of action it led to, either indifferent or criminal. This indeed is impossible, to do that which is good, and not to approve of it; for which reason they are frequently not considered as distinct, though they really are: for men often approve of the actions of others which they will not imitate, and likewise do that which they approve not. It cannot possibly be denied that there is this principle of reflection or conscience in human nature. Suppose a man to relieve an innocent person in distress; suppose the same man afterwards, in the fury of anger, to do the greatest mischief to a person who had given no just cause of offence. To aggravate the injury, add the circumstances of former friendship and obligation from the injured person; let the man who is supposed to have done these two different actions coolly reflect upon them afterwards, without regard to their consequences to himself: to assert that any common man would be affected in the same way towards these different actions, that he would make no distinction between them, but approve or disapprove them equally, is too glaring a falsity to need being confuted. There is therefore this principle of reflection or conscience in mankind. It is needless to compare the respect it has to private good with the respect it has to public; since it plainly tends as much to the latter as to the former, and is commonly thought to tend chiefly to the latter. This faculty is now mentioned merely as another part in the inward frame of man, pointing out to us in some degree what we are intended for, and as what will naturally and of course have some influence. The particular place assigned to it by nature, what authority it has, and how great influence it ought to have, shall be hereafter considered.

REVIEW EXERCISES

1. Explain the basic difference between psychological egoism and ethical egoism.
2. Give two different formulations or versions of psychological egoism and ethical egoism.
3. To prove that the motivational version of psychological egoism is true, what must be shown?
4. How is psychological egoism supposed to provide support for an argument for ethical egoism? What is one problem for this argument?
5. Summarize the arguments regarding the consistency or inconsistency of ethical egoism.
6. In what sense does the argument for ethical egoism based on economics support not egoism but utilitarianism—in other words, the view that we ought to do what is in the best interest of all or the greatest number?
7. What is meant by taking the "moral point of view"?
8. How does the example of the "ring of Gyges" illustrate the question "Why be moral?"

4

Utilitarianism

IN 2010, the Environmental Protection Agency began considering a stricter standard for smog-causing pollutants, which would replace the one set by the Bush administration in 2008. The new rule would limit "ground level ozone" to "no more than 0.060 to 0.070 parts per million" and would be phased in over two decades. The cost to phase in this new standard was estimated to be $19 billion to $90 billion per year by 2020 and would be borne primarily by "manufacturers, oil refiners, and utilities." The costs, while high, were expected to yield $13 billion to $100 billion in health benefits per year.[1] This is an example of cost-benefit reasoning. One policy or action is better than another if the benefits outweigh the costs. One difficulty with this form of reasoning is attempting to put a dollar value on things such as health or lives saved. One way around this problem is to consider what people are willing to pay to reduce their risks to life or health. Another is to consider what increase in compensation people require to take on a job with increased risk.

Many people were horrified when the pictures of the abuse and humiliation of prisoners by American soldiers at Abu Ghraib prison in Iraq were made public. The prisoners were photographed naked, in embarrassing sexual positions, crawling on leashes, and being threatened by dogs. Questions were raised about whether higher-ups knew about the treatment, whether the soldiers involved were ordered to behave this way in order to "soften up" the prisoners for interrogation, or whether this was instead mere "entertainment" for the soldiers involved. Some of those soldiers were tried before military courts and sentenced to prison for their behavior.

Did this treatment constitute torture? And whether or not it did, would such tactics or torture ever be justified in order to obtain information that might prevent terrorist attacks? On the one hand, some assert that torture is never permissible because it violates the Geneva Conventions, which prohibit torture and partially define it as "any act by which severe pain or suffering, whether physical or mental, is intentionally inflicted on a person for such purposes as obtaining from him or a third person information or a confession."[2] On the other hand, suppose, for example, that torture could save many lives. Would it then be justified? A Pentagon study of "the ethics of troops on the front line" in Iraq found that 41 percent said that "torture should be allowed to save the life of a soldier or Marine," and about the same number said that it "should be allowed to gather important information from insurgents."[3] Does a good end justify otherwise objectionable means? What kind of moral reasoning would permit this? The theory treated in this chapter is meant to clarify this.

How should such matters be decided? One way is to compare the benefits and costs of each alternative. Whichever has the greater net benefit is the best alternative. Risk benefit reasoning is a type of reasoning similar to utilitarian reasoning. It begins with the belief that individuals can be made better and worse off. The idea is that actions are morally better or worse depending on how they affect human well-being. Another aspect of it is the belief that all count equally, no one counts for more than others. It is the totality of consequences of some policy or action that counts. What is urged is that we should do what maximizes human well-being. Forms of utilitarianism will differ depending how well-being is to be understood. There is no action or policy that is in itself good or bad, right or wrong. It is solely a function of its consequences. Thus even torture can be acceptable if it results in good such as valued information.

HISTORICAL BACKGROUND
Jeremy Bentham and John Stuart Mill

The classical formulation of utilitarian moral theory is found in the writings of Jeremy Bentham (1748–1832) and John Stuart Mill (1806–1873). Jeremy Bentham was an English-born student of law and the leader of a radical movement for social and legal reform based on utilitarian principles. His primary published work was *Introduction to the Principles of Morals and Legislation* (1789). The title itself indicates his aim—namely, to take the same principles that provide the basis for morals as a guide for the formation and revision of law. He believed that there are not two sets of principles, one for personal morality and another for social morality.

James Mill, the father of John Stuart Mill, was an associate of Bentham's and a supporter of his views. John Stuart was the eldest of his nine children. He was educated in the classics and history at home. By the time he was twenty, he had read Bentham and had become a devoted follower of his philosophy. The basic ideas of utilitarian moral theory are summarized in his short work, *Utilitarianism*, in which he sought to dispel misconceptions that morality has nothing to do with usefulness or utility or that morality is opposed to pleasure. According to one writer, John Stuart Mill "is generally held to be one of the most profound and effective spokesmen for the liberal view of man and society."[4] He was also a strong supporter of personal liberty, and in his pamphlet *On Liberty* he argued that the only reason for society to interfere in a person's life to force that person to behave in certain ways was to prevent him or her from doing harm to others. People might choose wrongly, but he believed that allowing bad choices was better than government coercion. Liberty to speak one's own opinion, he believed, would benefit all. However, it is not clear that utility is always served by promoting liberty. Nor is it clear what Mill would say in cases where liberty must be restricted to promote the general good. In his work *On the Subjection of Women*, Mill also emphasized the general good and criticized those social treatments of women that did not allow them to develop their talents and contribute to the good of society. Consistent with these views, he also supported the right of women to vote. Later in life he married his longtime companion and fellow liberal, Harriet Taylor. Mill also served in the British Parliament from 1865 to 1868.

The original utilitarians were democratic, progressive, empiricist, and optimistic. They were democratic in the sense that they believed that social policy ought to work for the good of all persons, not just the upper class. However, they also believed that when interests of various persons conflicted, the best choice was that which promoted the interests of the greater number. The utilitarians were progressive in that they questioned the status quo. They believed that if, for example, the contemporary punishment system was not working well, then it ought to be changed. Social programs should be judged by their usefulness in promoting what was deemed to be good. Observation would determine whether a project or practice promoted this good. Thus, utilitarianism is part of the empiricist tradition in philosophy, for we only know what is good by observation or by appeal to experience. Bentham and Mill were also optimists. They believed that human wisdom and science would improve the lot of humanity. Mill wrote in *Utilitarianism*, "All the grand sources of human suffering are in a great degree, many of them almost entirely, conquerable by human care and effort."[5]

In this chapter, you will learn about the basic principle of utilitarianism and how it is used to make moral judgments in individual cases. You will also learn something about different forms of utilitarianism. You can examine a few criticisms of the theory so as to judge for yourself whether it is a reasonable theory. Again, you will have the substance of utilitarianism in these sections. More detail about the theory can be found in the sections on act and rule utilitarianism, on Mill's proof of the theory, and on contemporary versions of utilitarianism.

THE PRINCIPLE OF UTILITY

The basic moral principle of utilitarianism is called the principle of *utility* or the *greatest happiness principle*. This principle has several formulations in Bentham and Mill as well as in utilitarianism after them. Here are two simplified formulations, one correlated with each title:

The morally best (or better) alternative is that which produces the greatest (or greater) net utility, where utility is defined in terms of happiness or pleasure.
We ought to do that which produces the greatest amount of happiness or pleasure for the greatest number of people.

A Consequentialist Principle

First, utilitarianism is *teleological* in orientation. In other words, it stresses the end or goal of actions. Second, it is also a *consequentialist* moral theory. Consider the diagram used to classify moral theories given in Chapter 1.

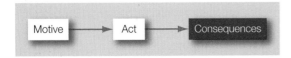

According to utilitarian moral theory, when we evaluate human acts or practices we consider neither the nature of the acts or practices nor the motive for which people do what they do. As Mill put it, "He who saves a fellow creature from drowning does what is morally right, whether his motive be duty or the hope of being paid for his trouble."[6] It is the result of one's action—that a life is saved—that matters morally. According to utilitarianism, we ought to decide which action or practice is best by considering the likely or actual consequences of each alternative. For example, over the years people have called for a suicide barrier on the Golden Gate Bridge to prevent people from using it to commit suicide. More than 1300 people have jumped from the bridge to their deaths. Building a suicide barrier on a bridge in itself is neither good nor bad. Nor is it sufficient that people supporting the building of such a barrier be well intentioned.

The Intrinsic Good: Pleasure or Happiness

It is not sufficient to say we ought to do that which has the best results or consequences because this in itself does not tell us which type of consequences are good. Any sort of consequences might be considered good—for example, power or fame or fortune. However, classical utilitarianism is a *pleasure* or *happiness* theory. It was not the first such theory to appear in the history of philosophy. Aristotle's ethics, as we shall see in Chapter 6, is a happiness theory although different from utilitarianism. Closer to utilitarianism is the classical theory that has come to be known as *hedonism* (from *hedon*, the Greek word for pleasure) or *Epicureanism* (named after Epicurus, 341 B.C.–270 B.C.). Epicurus held that the good life was the pleasant life. For him, this meant avoiding distress and desires for things beyond one's basic needs. Bodily pleasure and mental delight and peace were the goods to be sought in life.

Utilitarians also have believed that pleasure or happiness is the good to be produced. As Bentham put it, "Nature has placed mankind under the governance of two sovereign masters, *pain* and *pleasure*. It is for them alone to point out what we ought to do, as well as to determine what we shall do."[7] Things such as fame, fortune, education, and freedom may be good, but only to the extent that they produce pleasure or happiness. In philosophical terms, they are *instrumental* goods because they are useful for attaining the goals of happiness and pleasure. Happiness and pleasure are the only *intrinsic* goods—that is, the only things good in themselves.

In this explanation of utilitarianism, you may have noticed the seeming identification of pleasure and happiness. In classical utilitarianism, there is no difference between pleasure and happiness. Both terms refer to a kind of psychic state of satisfaction. However, there are different types of pleasure of which humans are capable. According to Mill, we experience a range of pleasures or satisfactions from the physical satisfaction of hunger to the personal satisfaction of a job well done. Aesthetic pleasures, such as the enjoyment of watching a beautiful sunset, are yet another type of pleasure. We also can experience intellectual pleasures such as the peculiar satisfaction of making sense out of something. We express this satisfaction in phrases such as "Ah, so that's it!" or "Now I see!" If this wider sense of pleasure is accepted, then it is easier to identify it with happiness.

We should consider the range of types of pleasure in our attempts to decide what the best action is. We also ought to consider other aspects of the pleasurable or happy experience. According to the greatest happiness or utility principle, we must measure, count, and compare the pleasurable experiences likely to be produced by various alternative actions in order to know which is best.

Calculating the Greatest Amount of Happiness

Utilitarianism is not an egoistic theory. As we noted in the previous chapter's presentation on egoism, those versions of egoism that said we ought to take care of ourselves because this works out better for all in the long run are actually versions of utilitarianism, not egoism. Some philosophers have called utilitarianism *universalistic* because it is the happiness or pleasure of all who are affected by an action or practice that is to be considered. We are not just to consider our own good, as in egoism, nor just the good of others, as in altruism. Sacrifice may be good, but not in itself. As Mill puts it, "A sacrifice which does not increase or tend to increase the sum total of happiness, [utilitarianism] considers as wasted."[8] Everyone affected by some action is to be counted equally. We ourselves hold no privileged place, so our own happiness counts no more than that of others. I may be required to do what displeases me but

pleases others. Thus, in the following scenario, Act B is a better choice than Act A:

Act A makes me happy and two other people happy.
Act B makes me unhappy but five others happy.

In addition to counting each person equally, these five elements are used to calculate the greatest amount of happiness: the net amount of pleasure or happiness, its intensity, its duration, its fruitfulness, and the likelihood of any act to produce it.[9] Note also that Jeremy Bentham, as well as J. S. Mill, held that the pleasures of *any* sentient being should be counted (see also Chapter 17, "Animal Rights").

Pleasure Minus Pain   Almost every alternative that we choose produces unhappiness or pain as well as happiness or pleasure for ourselves, if not for others. Pain is intrinsically bad, and pleasure is intrinsically good. Something that produces pain may be accepted, but only if it causes more pleasure overall. For instance, if the painfulness of a punishment deters an unwanted behavior, then we ought to punish but no more than is necessary or useful. When an act produces both pleasure or happiness and pain or unhappiness, we can think of each moment of unhappiness as canceling out a moment of happiness, so that what is left to evaluate is the remaining or *net* happiness or unhappiness. We are also to think of pleasure and pain as coming in bits or moments. We can then calculate this net amount by adding and subtracting units of pleasure and displeasure. This is a device for calculating the greatest amount of happiness even if we cannot make mathematically exact calculations. The following simplified equation indicates how the net utility for two acts, A and B, might be determined. Think of the units as either happy persons or days of happiness:

Act A produces twelve units of happiness and six of unhappiness ($12 - 6 = 6$ units of happiness).
Act B produces ten units of happiness and one of unhappiness ($10 - 1 = 9$ units of happiness).

On this measure, Act B is preferable because it produces a greater net amount of happiness—namely, nine units compared with six for Act A.

Intensity Moments of happiness or pleasure are not all alike. Some are more intense than others. The thrill of some exciting adventure—say, running river rapids—may produce a more intense pleasure than the serenity we feel in view of one of nature's wonders. All else being equal, the more intense the pleasure, the better. All other factors being equal, if I have an apple to give away and am deciding which of two friends to give it to I ought to give it to the friend who will enjoy it most. In calculations involving intensity of pleasure, a scale is sometimes useful. For example, we could use a positive scale of 1 to 10 degrees, from the least pleasurable to the most pleasurable. In the following scenario, then, Act B is better (all other things being equal) than Act A, even though Act A gives pleasure to thirty more people; this result is because of the greater intensity of pleasure produced by Act B:

Act A gives forty people each mild pleasure (40 × 2 = 80
  degrees of pleasure).
Act B gives ten people each intense pleasure (10 × 10
  = 100 degrees of pleasure).[10]

Duration Intensity is not all that matters regarding pleasure. The more serene pleasure may last longer. This also must be factored in our calculation. The longer lasting the pleasure the better, all else being equal. Thus, in the following scenario, Act A is better than Act B because it gives more total days of pleasure or happiness. This is so even though it affects fewer people (a fact that raises questions about how the number of people counts in comparison to the total amount of happiness):

Act A gives three people each eight days of happiness
  (3 × 8 = 24 days of happiness).
Act B gives six people each two days of happiness
  (6 × 2 = 12 days of happiness).

Fruitfulness A more serene pleasure from contemplating nature may or may not be more fruitful than an exciting pleasure such as that from running rapids. The fruitfulness of experiencing pleasure depends on whether it makes us more capable of experiencing similar or other pleasures. For example, the relaxing event may make one person more capable of experiencing other pleasures of friendship or understanding, whereas the thrilling event may do the same for another. The fruitfulness depends not only on the immediate pleasure but also on the long-term results. Indulging in immediate pleasure may bring pain later on, as we know only too well! So also the pain today may be the only way to prevent more pain tomorrow. The dentist's work on our teeth may be painful today, but it makes us feel better in the long run by providing us with pain-free meals and undistracted, enjoyable meal-time conversations.

Likelihood If before acting we are attempting to decide between two available alternative actions, we must estimate the likely results of each before we compare their net utility. If we are considering whether to go out for some competition, for example, we should consider the chances of doing well. We might have greater hope of success trying something else. It may turn out that we ought to choose an act with lesser rather than greater beneficial results if the chances of it happening are better. It is not only the chances that would count but also the size of the prize. In the following equation, A is preferable to B. In this case, "A bird in the hand is worth two in the bush," as the old saying goes:

Act A has a 90 percent chance of giving eight people
  each five days of pleasure (40 days × .90 = 36 days of
  pleasure).
Act B has a 40 percent chance of giving ten people each
  seven days of pleasure (70 days × .40 = 28 days of
  pleasure).

QUANTITY AND QUALITY OF PLEASURE

Bentham and Mill are in agreement that the more pleasure or happiness, the better. However, there is one significant difference between them. According to Bentham, we ought to consider only the *quantity* of pleasure or happiness brought about by various acts: how much pleasure, to how many people, how intense it is, how long-lasting, how fruitful, and how likely the desired outcome will occur. Consider Bentham's own comment on this point: The "quantity of pleasure being equal, pushpin [a game] is as good as poetry."[11] The aesthetic or intellectual pleasure that one might derive from reading and understanding a poem is no better in itself than the simple pleasures gained from playing a mindless game (which we suppose pushpin to be).

Although Mill agreed with Bentham that the greater amount of pleasure and happiness the better, he believed that the *quality* of the pleasure should also count. In his autobiography, Mill describes his experience of a mental crisis in which he realized that he had not found sufficient place in his life for aesthetic experiences; he realized that this side of the human personality also needed developing and that these pleasures were significantly different from others. This experience and his thoughts about it may have led him to focus on the quality of pleasures. Some are intrinsically better than others, he believed. Intellectual pleasures, for example, are more valuable in themselves than purely sensual pleasures. Although he does not tell us how much more valuable they are (twice as valuable?), he clearly believed this greater value ought to be factored into our calculation of the "greatest amount of happiness." Although I may not always be required to choose a book over food (for example, I may now need the food more than the book), the intellectual pleasures that might be derived from reading the book are of a higher quality than the pleasures gained from eating. Bentham, in contrast, would have asked how such pleasures can be more valuable except as they give us a greater amount of pleasure.

Mill attempts to prove or show that intellectual pleasures are better than sensual ones. We are to ask people who have experienced a range of pleasures whether they would prefer to live a life of a human, in spite of all its disappointments and pains, or the life of an animal, which is full of pleasures but only sensual pleasures. He believes that people generally would choose the former. They would prefer, as he puts it, "to be a human being dissatisfied than a pig satisfied; better to be Socrates dissatisfied than a fool satisfied."[12] Socrates, as you may know, was often frustrated in his attempt to know certain things. He did not know what was true beauty or justice. Because human beings have greater possibilities for knowledge and achievement, they also have greater potential for failure, pain, and frustration. The point

of the argument is that the only reason we would prefer a life of fewer net pleasures (the dissatisfactions subtracted from the total satisfactions of human life) to a life of a greater total amount of pleasures (the life of the pig) is that we value something other than the *amount* of pleasures; we value the *kind* of pleasures as well.[13] When considering this argument, you might ask yourself two questions. First, would people generally prefer to be Socrates than the pig? Second, if Mill is correct on his factual assessment, then what does this fact prove? If people do want a certain type of life with certain pleasures, does this fact make it a better life and the pleasures better pleasures? For that matter, this argument may introduce another independent criterion for what is good and perhaps create a quite different type of moral theory than utilitarianism.

EVALUATING UTILITARIANISM

The following are just some of the many considerations raised by those who wish to determine whether utilitarianism is a valid moral theory.

Application of the Principle

One reaction to calculating the greatest amount of happiness that students often have is that this theory is too complex. When we consider all of the variables concerning pleasure and happiness that are to be counted when trying to estimate the "greatest amount of pleasure or happiness," the task of doing so looks extremely difficult. We must consider how many people will be affected by alternative actions, whether they will be pleased or pained by them, how pleased or pained they will be and for how long, and the likelihood that what we estimate will happen will, in fact, come to be. In addition, if we want to follow Mill rather than Bentham, we must consider whether the pleasures will be the more lowly sensual pleasures, the higher types of more intellectual pleasures, or something in between. However, in reality we may at any one time only have to consider a couple of these variables because only they may be relevant.

The point of this criticism is that no one can consider all of the variables that utilitarianism requires us to consider: the probable consequences of our action to all affected in terms of duration, intensity, fruitfulness, likelihood, and type or quality of pleasure.[14] However, a utilitarian could respond that, although given this complexity no one is a perfect judge, we do make better judgments the better we are able to consider these variables. No moral theory is simple in its application. A more difficult problem in how to apply the principle of utility comes from Mill's own statements of it. It may well be that in some cases, at least, one cannot both maximize happiness and make the greatest number of people happy. Thus, one choice may produce 200 units of happiness—but for just one person. The other alternative might produce 150 units of happiness, 50 for each of three people. If the maximization overall is taken as primary, then we should go with the first choice; if the number of people is to take precedence, then we should go with the second choice. The best reading of Mill, however, seems to give preference to the maximization overall. In that case, how the happiness was distributed (to one or three) would not in itself count. This is one problem some people have with this theory.

Utilitarianism and Personal Integrity

A more substantive criticism of utilitarianism concerns its universalist and maximizing nature: that we should always do that which maximizes overall happiness. For one thing, this theory seems to allow us to consider neither our own happiness in some privileged place nor the happiness of those closer to us when to do so does not maximize happiness. I can give no more weight to my own projects or my own children in determining what to do than other peoples' similar projects or others' children. For some philosophers, that I must treat all persons equally is contrary to common sense. Utilitarians might respond that we should probably give more attention to our own projects and our own children, but only because this is likely to have better results overall. We know better how to promote our own projects and have more motivation to do so. Thus, giving preference to ourselves will probably be more effective. The objection remains that not to give some preference to ourselves is an affront to our personal integrity.[15] The idea is that utilitarianism seems to imply that I am not important from my own point of view. However, a utilitarian might respond that it is important that people regard themselves as unique and give due consideration for their own interests because this will probably have better consequences for both the society and themselves.

Ends and Means

A second criticism concerns utilitarianism's consequentialist nature. You may have heard the phrase "The end justifies the means." People often refer to it with a certain amount of disdain. Utilitarianism, as a consequentialist moral theory, holds that it is the consequences or ends of our actions that determine whether particular means to them are justified. This seems to lead to conclusions that are contrary to commonsense morality. For example, wouldn't it justify punishing an innocent person, a "scapegoat," in order to prevent a great evil or promote a great good? Or could we not justify on utilitarian grounds the killing of some for the sake of the good of a greater number? Or could I not make an exception for myself from obeying a law, alleging that it is for some greater long-term good? Utilitarians might respond by noting that such actions or practices will probably do more harm than good, especially if we take a long-range view. In particular, they might point out that practices that allow the punishment of those known to be innocent are not likely to deter as well as those that punish only the guilty or proven guilty.

The Trolley Problem

One particular problem for utilitarianism is exemplified by what has come to be called "the trolley problem."[16] According to one version of this scenario, you are beside a train track with a train headed down the track. However, on the track ahead are five people who will all be killed if the train continues. But you also have access to a switch, and if you pull it the train will be diverted onto another track where there is only one person. According to utilitarianism, if nothing else is relevant, you would not only be permitted but required to pull the switch. Now compare this scenario with another. In this case you are on a bridge and the train track with the five people on it is below. However, next to you on the bridge is a large fat man. The only way to stop the train in this case is to push the fat man over the bridge onto

One version of the "trolley problem."

the track. Would you be permitted to do this? In both cases five would be saved and one killed. But are the cases the same morally? It would seem that according to utilitarianism in which only the results matter, the cases would morally be the same. However, the intuition of most people would surely find the second case significantly different. You can't kill one person to save five. Just as in another example, a doctor who had five patients needing organs for transplant to save their lives would not be permitted to take these organs out of another patient, resulting in his death.

ACT AND RULE UTILITARIANISM

One criticism that is brought against utilitarianism described thus far is that it justifies any action just so long as it has better consequences than other available actions. Therefore, cheating, stealing, lying, and breaking promises may all seem to be justified, depending on whether they maximize happiness in some particular case. Whether as a response to this type of criticism or for other reasons, a slightly different version of utilitarianism has been developed in

the decades since Mill. Some people find evidence for it in Mill's own writings.[17] This second version is usually called *rule utilitarianism*, and it is contrasted with *act utilitarianism*, or what we have so far described.

Both are forms of utilitarianism. They are alike in requiring us to produce the greatest amount of happiness or pleasure (in all of the senses described) for the greatest number of people. They differ in what they believe we ought to consider in estimating the consequences. Act utilitarianism states that we ought to consider the consequences of *each act separately*. Rule utilitarianism states that we ought to consider the consequences of the act performed as a *general practice*.[18]

Take the following example. Sue is considering whether to keep or break her promise to go out with Ken. She believes that if she breaks this promise in order to do something else with other friends, Ken will be unhappy, but she and the other friends will be happier. According to act utilitarianism, if the consequences of her breaking the promise are better than keeping it, then that is what she ought to do. She may use handy "rules of thumb" to help her determine whether keeping the promise or breaking it is more likely to result in the better consequences. Mill called these "direction points along the way" that one can use.[19] "Honesty is the best policy" is one such guide. It is still the consequences of the act under consideration that determine what Sue ought to do.

Act utilitarianism: Consider the consequences of some particular act such as keeping or breaking one's promise.

A rule utilitarian, on the other hand, would tell Sue to consider what the results would be if everyone broke promises or broke them in similar situations. The question "What if everyone did that?" is familiar to us.[20] She should ask what the results would be if this were a general practice or a general rule that people followed. It is likely that trust in promises would be weakened. This would be bad, she might think, because the consequences would be that if we could not trust one another to keep our promises, then we would generally be less capable of making plans and relating to one another, two sources of human happiness. So, even if there would be no breakdown in that trust from just this one case of breaking a promise, Sue should still probably keep her promise according to rule utilitarian thinking.

Rule utilitarianism: Consider the consequences of some practice or rule of behavior—for example, the practice of promise keeping or promise breaking.

Another way to consider the method of reasoning used by the rule utilitarian is the following: I should ask what would be the best practice. For example, regarding promises, what rule would have the better results when people followed that rule? Would it be the rule or practice "Never break a promise made"? At the other extreme end of the spectrum would be a practice of keeping promises only if the results of doing so would be better than breaking them. (This actually amounts to act utilitarian reasoning.) However, there might be a better rule yet such as "Always keep your promise unless to do so would have very serious harmful consequences." If this rule were followed, then people would generally

have the benefits of being able to say, "I promise," and have people generally believe and trust them. The fact that the promise would not be kept in some limited circumstances would probably not do great harm to the practice of making promises.

Some philosophers go further and ask us to think about sets of rules. It is not only the practice of truthfulness but also of promise keeping and bravery and care for children that we must evaluate. Moreover, we should think of these rules as forming a system in which there are rules for priority and stringency. These rules would tell us which practices were more important and how important they were compared to the others. We should then do what the best system of moral rules would dictate, where *best* is still defined in terms of the maximization of happiness.[21]

Which form of utilitarianism is better is a matter of dispute. Act utilitarians can claim that we ought to consider only what will or is likely to happen if we act in certain ways, not what *would* happen if we acted in certain ways but will not happen because we are not going to so act. Rule utilitarians can claim that acts are similar to one another and so can be thought of as practices. My lying in one case to get myself out of a difficulty is similar to others' lying in other cases to get themselves out of difficulties. Because we should make the same judgments about similar cases (for consistency's sake), we should judge this act by comparing it with the results of the actions of everyone in similar circumstances. We can thus evaluate the general practice of "lying to get oneself out of a difficulty." You can be the judge of which reasoning is more persuasive.

"PROOF" OF THE THEORY

One of the best ways to evaluate a moral theory is to examine carefully the reasons that are given to support it. Being an empiricist theory, utilitarianism must draw its evidence from experience. This is what Mill does in his attempt to prove that the principle of utility is the correct moral principle. (Note, however, that Mill himself believes that the notion of "proof" is different for moral theory than perhaps for science.) His argument is as follows: Just as the only way in which we know that something is visible is its being seen, and the only way we can show that something is audible is if it can be heard, so also the only proof that we have that something is desirable is its being desired. Because we desire happiness, we thus know it is desirable or good. In addition, Mill holds that happiness is the only thing we desire for its own sake. All else we desire because we believe it will lead to happiness. Thus, happiness or pleasure is the only thing good in itself or the only intrinsic good. All other goods are instrumental goods; in other words, they are good in so far as they lead to happiness. For example, reading is not good in itself but only in so far as it brings us pleasure or understanding (which is either pleasurable in itself or leads to pleasure).

There are two main contentions here in this argument. One is that people's desiring something is a good basis for its being, or being thought to be, good. The other is that happiness in particular is the only thing desired for itself and thus it is the only intrinsic good. Critics have pointed out that Mill's analogy between what is visible, audible, and desirable does not hold up under analysis. In all three words, the suffix means "able to be," but in the case of *desirable*, Mill needs to prove not only that we can desire happiness (it is able to be desired) but also that it is *worth* being desired. Furthermore, just because we do desire something does not necessarily mean that we ought to desire it or that it is good. The moral philosopher David Hume put it succinctly: You cannot derive an "ought" from an "is."[22] However, Mill himself recognizes the difficulty of proving matters in ethics and that the proofs here will therefore be indirect rather than direct. On the second point, Mill adds a further comment to bolster his case about happiness in particular. He asserts that this desire for happiness is universal and that we are so constructed that we can desire nothing except what appears to us to be or to bring happiness. You may want to consider whether these latter assertions are consistent with his empiricism. Does he know these things from experience? In addition, Mill may be simply pointing to what we already know rather than giving a proof of the principle. You can find out what people believe is good by noticing what they do desire. In this case, they desire to be happy or they desire what they think will bring them happiness.[23]

Utilitarianism is a highly influential moral theory that also has had significant influence on a wide variety of policy assessment methods. It can be quite useful for evaluating alternative health care systems, for example. Whichever system brings the most benefit to the most people with the least cost is the system that we probably ought to support. Although Mill was quite optimistic about the ability and willingness of people to increase human happiness and reduce suffering, there is no doubt that the ideal is a good one. Nevertheless, utilitarianism has difficulties, some of which we have discussed here. You will know better how to evaluate this theory when you can compare it with those treated in the following chapters.

The reading selections in this chapter are from the classical works of Jeremy Bentham and John Stuart Mill.

NOTES

1. *The New York Times*, January 8, 2010, pp. A1 and A3.
2. Office of the United Nations High Commissioner for Human Rights. Convention Against Torture and Other Cruel, Inhuman, or Degrading Treatment or Punishment.
3. *San Francisco Examiner*, February 2, 1993, p. A4; *San Francisco Chronicle*, May 5, 2007, p. A5.
4. Sneewind in *The Encyclopedia of Philosophy*, Paul Edwards (Ed.), vol. 5 (New York: Macmillan, 1967), 314.
5. *Utilitarianism*, Oskar Priest (Ed.) (Indianapolis, IN: Bobbs-Merrill, 1957), 20.
6. Ibid., 24.
7. Jeremy Bentham, *An Introduction to the Principles of Morals and Legislation* (New York: Oxford University Press, 1789).
8. Priest, op. cit., 22.
9. These elements for calculation of the greatest amount of happiness are from Bentham's *Principles of Morals and Legislation*, op. cit.
10. You may have noticed some ambiguity in the formulation of the greatest happiness principle version just described and used so far in our explanation. In this example, Act A makes more people happy than Act B, but the overall amount of happiness when we consider degrees is greater in Act B. Thus, it is the greater amount of happiness that we have counted as more important than the greater number of

people. One must choose whether we shall count the greatest amount of happiness or the greatest number of people; we cannot always have both.

11. Bentham, *Principles of Morals and Legislation*, op. cit.

12. Priest, op. cit., 14.

13. Note that this is an empiricist argument: it is based on an appeal to purported facts. People's actual preferences for intellectual pleasures (if true) is the only source we have for believing them to be more valuable.

14. It also requires us to have a common unit of measurement of pleasure. Elementary units called hedons have been suggested. We must think of pleasures of all kinds, then, as variations on one basic type. Obviously, this is problematic.

15. J. J. C. Smart and Bernard Williams, *Utilitarianism: For and Against* (New York: Cambridge University Press, 1973). Also see Samuel Scheffler, *The Rejection of Consequentialism* (New York: Oxford University Press, 1984). In *The Limits of Morality* (New York: Oxford University Press, 1989), Shelley Kagan distinguishes the universalist element of utilitarianism—its demand that I treat all equally—from the maximizing element—that I must bring about the most good possible. The first element makes utilitarianism too demanding, whereas the second allows us to do anything as long as it maximizes happiness overall.

16. Philippa Foot, "The Problem of Abortion and the Doctrine of Double Effect, in *Virtues and Vices* (Oxford: Basil Blackwell, 1978); and Judith Jarvis Thomson, "Killing, Letting Die, and the Trolley Problem," *The Monist* (1976) 204–217.

17. One comment from *Utilitarianism* has a decidedly rule utilitarian ring: "In the case of abstinences indeed—of things which people forbear to do from moral considerations, though the consequences in the particular case might be beneficial—it would be unworthy of an intelligent agent not to be consciously aware that the action is of a class which, if practiced generally, would be generally injurious, and that this is the ground of the obligation to abstain from it" (p. 25). Other such examples can be found in the final chapter of Mill's work.

18. See, for example, the explanation of this difference in J. J. C. Smart, "Extreme and Restricted Utilitarianism," *Philosophical Quarterly*, (1956).

19. Ibid., 31.

20. Just how to formulate the "that," the practice or rule whose consequences we are to consider, is a significant problem for rule utilitarians—and one we will not develop here. Suffice it to note that it must have some degree of generality and not be something that applies just to us: "What if everyone named John Doe did that?" It would be more like, "What if everyone broke their promise to get themselves out of a difficulty?"

21. Richard Brandt, "Some Merits of One Form of Rule Utilitarianism," in *Morality and the Language of Conduct*, H. N. Castaneda and George Nakhnikian (Eds.) (Detroit: Wayne State University Press, 1970), 282–307.

22. David Hume, *Treatise on Human Nature* (London, 1739–1740).

23. This explanation is given by Mary Warnock in her introduction to the Fontana edition of Mill's *Utilitarianism*, 25–26.

An Introduction to the Principles of Morals and Legislation (1789)

JEREMY BENTHAM

Study Questions

1. According to Bentham, what is meant by the principle of utility? To what areas does this principle apply?

2. What is utility?

3. What is the interest of the community? Of the individual?

4. When is an action conformable to the principle of utility? What about a measure of government?

5. How does Bentham use the words *ought, right,* and *wrong*?

6. Does he believe that the principle of utility can be proven? Why or why not?

7. What is the principle of asceticism? According to Bentham, which two types of persons adopt this point of view?

8. What does Bentham think of this principle?

9. According to Bentham, what is meant by the principle of sympathy and antipathy?

10. What does he think of this principle?

11. According to Bentham, how are pleasures and pains to be measured? Describe what is meant by each of them.

12. Does it seem that Bentham requires this measurement to be taken on every occasion and to be strictly followed?

CHAPTER I: OF THE PRINCIPLE OF UTILITY

I. Nature has placed mankind under the governance of two sovereign masters, *pain* and *pleasure*. It is for them alone to point out what we ought to do, as well as to determine what we shall do. On the one hand the standard of right and wrong, on the other the chain of causes and effects, are fastened to their throne. They govern us in all we do, in all we say, in all we think: every effort we can make to throw off our subjection, will serve but to demonstrate and confirm it. In words a man may pretend to abjure their empire: but in reality he will remain subject to it all the while. The *principle of utility* recognizes this subjection, and assumes it for the foundation of that system, the object of which is to rear the fabric of felicity by the hands of reason and of law. Systems which attempt to question it, deal in sounds instead of sense, in caprice instead of reason, in darkness instead of light. But enough of metaphor and declamation: it is not by such means that moral science is to be improved.

II. The principle of utility is the foundation of the present work: it will be proper therefore at the outset to give an explicit and determinate account of what is meant by it. By the principle of utility is meant that principle which approves or disapproves of every action whatsoever, according to the tendency it appears to have to augment or diminish the happiness of the party whose interest is in question: or, what is the same thing in other words, to promote or to oppose that happiness. I say of every action whatsoever, and therefore not only of every action of a private individual, but of every measure of government.

From Jeremy Bentham, *An Introduction to the Principles of Morals and Legislation* (1789). Reprinted by Clarendon Press (Oxford), 1907.

III. By utility is meant that property in any object, whereby it tends to produce benefit, advantage, pleasure, good, or happiness, (all this in the present case comes to the same thing) or (what comes again to the same thing) to prevent the happening of mischief, pain, evil, or unhappiness to the party whose interest is considered: if that party be the community in general, then the happiness of the community: if a particular individual, then the happiness of that individual.

IV. The interest of the community is one of the most general expressions that can occur in the phraseology of morals: no wonder that the meaning of it is often lost. When it has a meaning, it is this. The community is a fictitious *body*, composed of the individual persons who are considered as constituting as it were its *members*. The interest of the community then is, what?—the sum of the interests of the several members who compose it.

V. It is in vain to talk of the interest of the community, without understanding what is the interest of the individual. A thing is said to promote the interest, or to be *for* the interest, of an individual, when it tends to add to the sum total of his pleasures: or, what comes to the same thing, to diminish the sum total of his pains.

VI. An action then may be said to be conformable to the principle of utility, or, for shortness sake, to utility, (meaning with respect to the community at large) when the tendency it has to augment the happiness of the community is greater than any it has to diminish it.

VII. A measure of government (which is but a particular kind of action, performed by a particular person or persons) may be said to be conformable to or dictated by the principle of utility, when in like manner the tendency which it has to augment the happiness of the community is greater than any which it has to diminish it.

VIII. When an action, or in particular a measure of government, is supposed by a man to be conformable to the principle of utility, it may be convenient, for the purposes of discourse, to imagine a kind of law or dictate, called a law or dictate of utility: and to speak of the action in question, as being conformable to such law or dictate.

IX. A man may be said to be a partisan of the principle of utility, when the approbation or disapprobation he annexes to any action, or to any measure, is determined by and proportioned to the tendency which he conceives it to have to augment or to diminish the happiness of the community: or in other words, to its conformity or unconformity to the laws or dictates of utility.

X. Of an action that is conformable to the principle of utility one may always say either that it is one that ought to be done, or at least that it is not one that ought not to be done. One may say also, that it is right it should be done; at least that it is not wrong it should be done: that it is a right action; at least that it is not a wrong action. When thus interpreted, the words *ought*, and *right* and *wrong* and others of that stamp, have a meaning: when otherwise, they have none.

XI. Has the rectitude of this principle been ever formally contested? It should seem that it had, by those who have not known what they have been meaning. Is it susceptible of any direct proof? it should seem not: for that which is used to prove every thing else, cannot itself be proved: a chain of proofs must have their commencement somewhere. To give such proof is as impossible as it is needless.

CHAPTER II: OF PRINCIPLES ADVERSE TO THAT OF UTILITY

I. If the principle of utility be a right principle to be governed by, and that in all cases, it follows from what has been just observed, that whatever principle differs from it in any case must necessarily be a wrong one. To prove any other principle, therefore, to be a wrong one, there needs no more than just to show it to be what it is, a principle of which the dictates are in some point or other different from those of the principle of utility: to state it is to confute it.

II. A principle may be different from that of utility in two ways—by being constantly opposed to it: this is the case with a principle which may be termed the principle of *asceticism*. By being sometimes opposed to it, and sometimes not, as it may happen: this is the case with another, which may be termed the principle of *sympathy* and *antipathy*.

III. By the principle of asceticism I mean that principle, which, like the principle of utility, approves or disapproves of any action, according to the tendency which it appears to have to augment or diminish the happiness of the party whose interest is in question; but in an inverse manner: approving of actions in as far as they tend to diminish his happiness; disapproving of them in as far as they tend to augment it.

IV. It is evident that any one who reprobates any the least particle of pleasure, as such, from whatever source derived, is *pro tanto* a partisan of the principle of asceticism. It is only upon that principle, and not from the principle of utility, that the most abominable pleasure which the vilest of malefactors ever reaped from his crime would be to be reprobated, if it stood alone. The case is, that it never does stand alone; but is necessarily followed by such a quantity of pain (or, what comes to the same thing, such a chance for a certain quantity of pain) that the pleasure in comparison of it, is as nothing: and this is the true and sole, but perfectly sufficient, reason for making it a ground for punishment.

V. There are two classes of men of very different complexions, by whom the principle of asceticism appears to have been embraced; the one a set of moralists, the other a set of religionists. Different accordingly have been the motives which appear to have recommended it to the notice of these different parties. Hope, that is the prospect of pleasure, seems to have animated the former: hope, the aliment of philosophic pride: the hope of honour and reputation at the hands of men. Fear, that is the prospect of pain, the latter: fear, the offspring of superstitious fancy: the fear of future punishment at the hands of a splenetic and revengeful Deity. I say in this case fear: for of the invisible future, fear is more powerful than hope. These circumstances characterize the two different parties among the partisans of the principle of asceticism; the parties and their motives different, the principle the same.

VI. The religious party, however, appear to have carried it farther than the philosophical: they have acted more consistently and less wisely. The philosophical party have scarcely gone farther than to reprobate pleasure: the religious party have frequently gone so far as to make it a matter of merit and of duty to court pain. The philosophical party have hardly gone farther than the making pain a matter of indifference. It is no evil, they have said: they have not said, it is a good. They have not so much as reprobated all pleasure in the lump. They have discarded only what they have called the gross; that is, such as are organical, or of which the origin is easily traced up to such as are organical: they have even cherished and magnified the refined. Yet this, however, not under the name of pleasure: to cleanse itself from the sordes of its impure original, it was necessary it should change its name: the honourable, the glorious, the reputable, the becoming, the *honestum*, the *decorum* it was to be called: in short, any thing but pleasure.

VII. From these two sources have flowed the doctrines from which the sentiments of the bulk of mankind have all along received a tincture of this principle; some from the philosophical, some from the religious, some from both. Men of education more frequently from the philosophical, as more suited to the elevation of their sentiments: the vulgar more frequently from the superstitious, as more suited to the narrowness of their intellect, undilated by knowledge: and to the abjectness of their condition, continually open to the attacks of fear. The tinctures, however, derived from the two sources, would naturally intermingle, insomuch that a man would not always know by which of them he was most influenced: and they would often serve to corroborate and enliven one another. It was this conformity that made a kind of alliance between parties of a complexion otherwise so dissimilar: and disposed them to unite upon various occasions against the common enemy, the partisan of the principle of utility, whom they joined in branding with the odious name of Epicurean.

VIII. The principle of asceticism, however, with whatever warmth it may have been embraced by its partisans as a rule of private conduct, seems not to have been carried to any considerable length, when applied to the business of government. . . .

XI. Among principles adverse to that of utility, that which at this day seems to have most influence in matters of government, is what may be called the principle of sympathy and antipathy. By the principle of sympathy and antipathy, I mean that principle which approves or disapproves of certain actions, not on account of their tending to augment the happiness, nor yet on account of their tending to diminish the happiness of the party whose interest is in question, but merely because a man finds himself disposed to approve or disapprove of them: holding up that approbation or disapprobation as a sufficient reason for itself, and disclaiming the necessity of looking out for any extrinsic ground. Thus far in the general department of morals: and in the particular department of politics, measuring out the quantum (as well as determining the ground) of punishment, by the degree of the disapprobation.

XII. It is manifest, that this is rather a principle in name than in reality: it is not a positive principle of itself, so much as a term employed to signify the negation of all principle. What one expects to find in a principle is something that points out some external consideration, as a means of warranting and guiding the internal sentiments of approbation and disapprobation: this expectation is but ill fulfilled by a proposition, which does neither more nor less than hold up each of those sentiments as a ground and standard for itself.

XIII. In looking over the catalogue of human actions (says a partisan of this principle) in order to determine which of them are to be marked with the seal of disapprobation, you need but to take counsel of your own feelings: whatever you find in yourself a propensity to condemn, is wrong for that very reason. For the same reason it is also meet for punishment: in what proportion it is adverse to utility, or whether it be adverse to utility at all, is a matter that makes no difference. In that same *proportion* also is it meet for punishment: if you hate much, punish much: if you hate little, punish little: punish as you hate. If you hate not at all, punish not at all: the fine feelings of the soul are not to be overborne and tyrannized by the harsh and rugged dictates of political utility. . . .

CHAPTER IV: VALUE OF A LOT OF PLEASURE OR PAIN, HOW TO BE MEASURED

I. Pleasures then, and the avoidance of pains, are the ends that the legislator has in view; it behoves him therefore to understand their *value*. Pleasures and pains are the *instruments* he has to work with: it behoves him therefore to understand their force, which is again, in other words, their value.

II. To a person considered by *himself*, the value of a pleasure or pain considered by *itself*, will be greater or less, according to the four following *circumstances*:

1. Its *intensity*.
2. Its *duration*.
3. Its *certainty* or *uncertainty*.
4. Its *propinquity* or *remoteness*.

III. These are the circumstances which are to be considered in estimating a pleasure or a pain considered each of them by itself. But when the value of any pleasure or pain is considered for the purpose of estimating the tendency of any *act* by which it is produced, there are two other circumstances to be taken into the account; these are,

5. Its *fecundity*, or the chance it has of being followed by sensations of the *same* kind: that is, pleasures, if it be a pleasure: pains, if it be a pain.
6. Its *purity*, or the chance it has of not being followed by sensations of the *opposite* kind: that is, pains, if it be a pleasure: pleasures, if it be a pain.

These two last, however, are in strictness scarcely to be deemed properties of the pleasure or the pain itself; they are not, therefore, in strictness to be taken into the account of the value of that pleasure or that pain. They are in strictness to be deemed properties only of the act, or other event, by which such pleasure or pain has been produced; and accordingly are only to be taken into the account of the tendency of such act or such event.

IV. To a *number* of persons, with reference to each of whom to the value of a pleasure or a pain is considered, it will be greater or less, according to seven circumstances: to wit, the six preceding ones; viz.

1. Its *intensity*.
2. Its *duration*.
3. Its *certainty* or *uncertainty*.
4. Its *propinquity* or *remoteness*.
5. Its *fecundity*.
6. Its *purity*.

And one other; to wit:

7. Its *extent*; that is, the number of persons to whom it *extends*; or (in other words) who are affected by it.

V. To take an exact account then of the general tendency of any act, by which the interests of a community are affected, proceed as follows. Begin with any one person of those whose interests seem most immediately to be affected by it: and take an account,

1. Of the value of each distinguishable *pleasure* which appears to be produced by it in the *first* instance.
2. Of the value of each *pain* which appears to be produced by it in the *first* instance.
3. Of the value of each pleasure which appears to be produced by it *after* the first. This constitutes the *fecundity* of the first *pleasure* and the *impurity* of the first *pain*.
4. Of the value of each *pain* which appears to be produced by it after the first. This constitutes the *fecundity* of the first *pain*, and the *impurity* of the first pleasure.
5. Sum up all the values of all the *pleasures* on the one side, and those of all the pains on the other. The balance, if it be on the side of pleasure, will give the *good* tendency of the act upon the whole, with respect to the interests of that *individual* person; if on the side of pain, the *bad* tendency of it upon the whole.
6. Take an account of the *number* of persons whose interests appear to be concerned; and repeat the above process with respect to each. *Sum up* the numbers expressive of the degrees of *good* tendency, which the act has, with respect to each individual, in regard to whom the tendency of it is *good* upon the whole: do this again with respect to each individual, in regard to whom the tendency of it is *good* upon the whole: do this again with respect to each individual, in regard to whom the tendency of it is *bad* upon the whole. Take the *balance* which if on the side of *pleasure*, will give the general *good tendency* of the act, with respect to the total number or community of individuals concerned; if on the side of

pain, the general *evil tendency*, with respect to the same community.

VI. It is not to be expected that this process should be strictly pursued previously to every moral judgment, or to every legislative or judicial operation. It may, however, be always kept in view: and as near as the process actually pursued on these occasions approaches to it, so near will such process approach to the character of an exact one.

READING
Utilitarianism
JOHN STUART MILL

Study Questions

1. How does Mill describe the basic moral standard of utilitarianism?
2. How does he defend himself against those who say that this is a crass pleasure theory?
3. What is the basis for knowing that some pleasures are better in quality than others? Which pleasures are these? How does Mill answer those who might say that people would not always prefer the life of a human being over the life of a fully satisfied animal such as a pig?
4. Whose happiness or pleasure, then, should we promote? Are animals included?
5. According to Mill, how are we to know whether anything is desirable or good?
6. How do we know that happiness is a good in itself or as an end?
7. How does Mill respond to the assertion that there are things other than happiness that people seem to desire for their own sakes?

WHAT UTILITARIANISM IS

The creed which accepts as the foundation of morals "utility" or the "greatest happiness principle" holds that actions are right in proportion as they tend to promote happiness; wrong as they tend to produce the reverse of happiness. By happiness is intended pleasure and the absence of pain; by unhappiness, pain and the privation of pleasure. To give a clear view of the moral standard set up by the theory, much more requires to be said; in particular, what things it includes in the ideas of pain and pleasure,

and to what extent this is left an open question. But these supplementary explanations do not affect the theory of life on which this theory of morality is grounded—namely, that pleasure and freedom from pain are the only things desirable as ends; and that all desirable things (which are as numerous in the utilitarian as in any other scheme) are desirable either for pleasure inherent in themselves or as means to the promotion of pleasure and the prevention of pain.

Now such a theory of life excites in many minds, and among them in some of the most estimable in feeling and purpose, inveterate dislike. To suppose that life has (as they express it) no higher end than pleasure—no better and nobler object of desire and pursuit—they designate as utterly mean and groveling, as a doctrine worthy only of swine, to whom the followers of Epicurus were, at a very early period, contemptuously likened; and modern holders of the doctrine are occasionally made the subject of equally polite comparisons by its German, French, and English assailants.

When thus attacked, the Epicureans have always answered that it is not they, but their accusers, who represent human nature in a degrading light, since the accusation supposes human beings to be capable of no pleasures except those of which swine are capable. If this supposition were true, the charge could not be gainsaid, but would then be no longer an imputation; for if the sources of pleasure were precisely the same to human beings and to swine, the rule of life which is good enough for the one would be good

Selections from *Utilitarianism*, Chapters 2 and 4 (London, 1863).

enough for the other. The comparison of the Epicurean life to that of beasts is felt as degrading, precisely because a beast's pleasures do not satisfy a human being's conceptions of happiness. Human beings have faculties more elevated than the animal appetites and, when once made conscious of them, do not regard anything as happiness which does not include their gratification. I do not, indeed, consider the Epicureans to have been by any means faultless in drawing out their scheme of consequences from the utilitarian principle. To do this in any sufficient manner, many Stoic, as well as Christian, elements require to be included. But there is no known Epicurean theory of life which does not assign to the pleasures of the intellect, of the feelings and imagination, and of the moral sentiments a much higher value as pleasures than to those of mere sensation. It must be admitted, however, that utilitarian writers in general have placed the superiority of mental over bodily pleasures chiefly in the greater permanency, safety, uncostliness, etc., of the former—that is, in their circumstantial advantages rather than in their intrinsic nature. And on all these points utilitarians have fully proved their case; but they might have taken the other and, as it may be called, higher ground with entire consistency. It is quite compatible with the principle of utility to recognize the fact that some kinds of pleasure are more desirable and more valuable than others. It would be absurd that, while in estimating all other things quality is considered as well as quantity, the estimation of pleasure should be supposed to depend on quantity alone.

Some Pleasures Are Better Than Others*

If I am asked what I mean by difference of quality in pleasures, or what makes one pleasure more valuable than another, merely as a pleasure, except its being greater in amount, there is but one possible answer. Of two pleasures, if there be one to which all or almost all who have experience of both give a decided preference, irrespective of any feeling of moral obligation to prefer it, that is the more desirable pleasure. If one of the two is, by those who are competently acquainted with both, placed so far above the other that they prefer it, even though

knowing it to be attended with a greater amount of discontent, and would not resign it for any quantity of the other pleasure which their nature is capable of, we are justified in ascribing to the preferred enjoyment a superiority in quality so far outweighing quantity as to render it, in comparison, of small account.

Now it is an unquestionable fact that those who are equally acquainted with and equally capable of appreciating and enjoying both do give a most marked preference to the manner of existence which employs their higher faculties. Few human creatures would consent to be changed into any of the lower animals for a promise of the fullest allowance of a beast's pleasures; no intelligent human being would consent to be a fool, no instructed person would be an ignoramus, no person of feeling and conscience would be selfish and base, even though they should be persuaded that the fool, the dunce, or the rascal is better satisfied with his lot than they are with theirs. They would not resign what they possess more than he for the most complete satisfaction of all the desires which they have in common with him. If they ever fancy they would, it is only in cases of unhappiness so extreme that to escape from it they would exchange their lot for almost any other, however undesirable in their own eyes. A being of higher faculties requires more to make him happy, is capable probably of more acute suffering, and certainly accessible to it at more points, than one of an inferior type; but in spite of these liabilities, he can never really wish to sink into what he feels to be a lower grade of existence. We may give what explanation we please of this unwillingness; we may attribute it to pride, a name which is given indiscriminately to some of the most and to some of the least estimable feelings of which mankind are capable; we may refer it to the love of liberty and personal independence, an appeal to which was with the Stoics one of the most effective means for the inculcation of it; to the love of power or to the love of excitement, both of which do really enter into and contribute to it; but its most appropriate appellation is a sense of dignity, which all human beings possess in one form or other, and in some, though by no means in exact, proportion to their higher faculties, and which is so essential a part of the happiness of those in whom it

---

*Headings added by the editor—.

is strong that nothing which conflicts with it could be otherwise than momentarily an object of desire to them. Whoever supposes that this preference takes place at a sacrifice of happiness—that the superior being, in anything like equal circumstances, is not happier than the inferior—confounds the two very different ideas of happiness and content. It is indisputable that the being whose capacities of enjoyment are low has the greatest chance of having them fully satisfied; and a highly endowed being will always feel that any happiness which he can look for, as the world is constituted, is imperfect. But he can learn to bear its imperfections, if they are at all bearable; and they will not make him envy the being who is indeed unconscious of the imperfections, but only because he feels not at all the good which those imperfections qualify. It is better to be a human being dissatisfied than a pig satisfied; better to be Socrates dissatisfied than a fool satisfied. And if the fool, or the pig, are of a different opinion, it is because they only know their own side of the question. The other party to the comparison knows both sides.

It may be objected that many who are capable of the higher pleasures occasionally, under the influence of temptation, postpone them to the lower. But this is quite compatible with a full appreciation of the intrinsic superiority of the higher. Men often, from infirmity of character, make their election for the nearer good, though they know it to be the less valuable; and this no less when the choice is between two bodily pleasures than when it is between bodily and mental. They pursue sensual indulgences to the injury of health, though perfectly aware that health is the greater good. It may be further objected that many who begin with youthful enthusiasm for everything noble, as they advance in years, sink into indolence and selfishness. But I do not believe that those who undergo this very common change voluntarily choose the lower description of pleasures in preference to the higher. I believe that, before they devote themselves exclusively to the one, they have already become incapable of the other. Capacity for the nobler feelings is in most natures a very tender plant, easily killed, not only by hostile influences, but by mere want of sustenance; and in the majority of young persons it speedily dies away if the occupations to which their position in life has devoted them,

and the society into which it has thrown them, are not favorable to keeping that higher capacity in exercise. Men lose their high aspirations as they lose their intellectual tastes, because they have not time or opportunity for indulging them; and they addict themselves to inferior pleasures, not because they deliberately prefer them, but because they are either the only ones to which they have access or the only ones which they are any longer capable of enjoying. It may be questioned whether anyone who has remained equally susceptible to both classes of pleasures ever knowingly and calmly preferred the lower, though many, in all ages, have broken down in an ineffectual attempt to combine both.

From this verdict of the only competent judges, I apprehend there can be no appeal. On a question which is the best worth having of two pleasures, or which of two modes of existence is the most grateful to the feelings, apart from its moral attributes and from its consequences, the judgment of those who are qualified by knowledge of both, or, if they differ, that of the majority among them, must be admitted as final. And there needs be the less hesitation to accept this judgment respecting the quality of pleasures, since there is no other tribunal to be referred to even on the question of quantity. What means are there of determining which is the acutest of two pains, or the intenser of two pleasurable sensations, except the general suffrage of those who are familiar with both? Neither pains nor pleasures are homogeneous, and pain is always heterogeneous with pleasure. What is there to decide whether a particular pleasure is worth purchasing at the cost of a particular pain, except the feelings and judgment of the experienced? When, therefore, those feelings and judgment declare the pleasures derived from the higher faculties to be preferable in kind, apart from the question of intensity, to those of which the animal nature, disjoined from the higher faculties, is susceptible, they are entitled on this subject to the same regard.

The Moral Standard
I have dwelt on this point as being a necessary part of a perfectly just conception of utility or happiness considered as the directive rule of human conduct. But it is by no means an indispensable condition to

the acceptance of the utilitarian standard; for that standard is not the agent's own greatest happiness, but the greatest amount of happiness altogether; and if it may possibly be doubted whether a noble character is always the happier for its nobleness, there can be no doubt that it makes other people happier, and that the world in general is immensely a gainer by it. Utilitarianism, therefore, could only attain its end by the general cultivation of nobleness of character, even if each individual were only benefited by the nobleness of others, and his own, so far as happiness is concerned, were a sheer deduction from the benefit. But the bare enunciation of such an absurdity as this last renders refutation superfluous.

According to the greatest happiness principle, as above explained, the ultimate end, with reference to and for the sake of which all other things are desirable—whether we are considering our own good or that of other people—is an existence exempt as far as possible from pain, and as rich as possible in enjoyments, both in point of quantity and quality; the test of quality and the rule for measuring it against quantity being the preference felt by those who, in their opportunities of experience, to which must be added their habits of self-consciousness and self-observation, are best furnished with the means of comparison. This, being according to the utilitarian opinion the end of human action, is necessarily also the standard of morality, which may accordingly be defined "the rules and precepts for human conduct," by the observance of which an existence such as has been described might be, to the greatest extent possible, secured to all mankind; and not to them only, but, so far as the nature of things admits, to the whole sentient creation. . . .

OF WHAT SORT OF PROOF THE PRINCIPLE OF UTILITY IS SUSCEPTIBLE

It has already been remarked that questions of ultimate ends do not admit of proof, in the ordinary acceptation of the term. To be incapable of proof by reasoning is common to all first principles, to the first premises of our knowledge, as well as to those of our conduct. But the former, being matters of fact, may be the subject of a direct appeal to the faculties which judge of fact—namely, our senses and our internal consciousness. Can an appeal be made to the same faculties on questions of practical ends? Or by what other faculty is cognizance taken of them?

Questions about ends are, in other words, questions [about] what things are desirable. The utilitarian doctrine is that happiness is desirable, and the only thing desirable, as an end; all other things being only desirable as means to that end. What ought to be required of this doctrine, what conditions is it requisite that the doctrine should fulfill—to make good its claim to be believed?

The only proof capable of being given that an object is visible is that people actually see it. The only proof that a sound is audible is that people hear it; and so of the other sources of our experience. In like manner, I apprehend, the sole evidence it is possible to produce that anything is desirable is that people do actually desire it. If the end which the utilitarian doctrine proposes to itself were not, in theory and in practice, acknowledged to be an end, nothing could ever convince any person that it was so. No reason can be given why the general happiness is desirable, except that each person, so far as he believes it to be attainable, desires his own happiness. This, however, being a fact, we have not only all the proof which the case admits of, but all which it is possible to require, that happiness is a good, that each person's happiness is a good to that person, and the general happiness, therefore, a good to the aggregate of all persons. Happiness has made out its title as one of the ends of conduct and, consequently, one of the criteria of morality.

But it has not, by this alone, proved itself to be the sole criterion. To do that, it would seem, by the same rule, necessary to show, not only that people desire happiness, but that they never desire anything else. Now it is palpable that they do desire things which, in common language, are decidedly distinguished from happiness. They desire, for example, virtue and the absence of vice no less really than pleasure and the absence of pain. The desire of virtue is not as universal, but it is as authentic a fact as the desire of happiness. And hence the opponents of the utilitarian standard deem that they have a right to infer that there are other ends of human action besides happiness, and that happiness is not the standard of approbation and disapprobation.

Happiness and Virtue

But does the utilitarian doctrine deny that people desire virtue, or maintain that virtue is not a thing to be desired? The very reverse. It maintains not only that virtue is to be desired, but that it is to be desired disinterestedly, for itself. Whatever may be the opinion of utilitarian moralists as to the original conditions by which virtue is made virtue, however they may believe (as they do) that actions and dispositions are only virtuous because they promote another end than virtue, yet this being granted, and it having been decided, from considerations of this description, what is virtuous, they not only place virtue at the very head of the things which are good as means to the ultimate end, but they also recognize as a psychological fact the possibility of its being, to the individual, a good in itself, without looking to any end beyond it; and hold that the mind is not in a right state, not in a state conformable to utility, not in the state most conducive to the general happiness, unless it does love virtue in this manner—as a thing desirable in itself, even although, in the individual instance, it should not produce those other desirable consequences which it tends to produce, and on account of which it is held to be virtue. This opinion is not, in the smallest degree, a departure from the happiness principle. The ingredients of happiness are very various, and each of them is desirable in itself, and not merely when considered as swelling an aggregate. The principle of utility does not mean that any given pleasure, as music, for instance, or any given exemption from pain, as for example health, is to be looked upon as means to a collective something termed happiness, and to be desired on that account. They are desired and desirable in and for themselves; besides being means, they are a part of the end. Virtue, according to the utilitarian doctrine, is not naturally and originally part of the end, but it is capable of becoming so; and in those who live it disinterestedly it has become so, and is desired and cherished, not as a means to happiness, but as a part of their happiness.

To illustrate this further, we may remember that virtue is not the only thing originally a means, and which if it were not a means to anything else would be and remain indifferent, but which by association with what it is a means to comes to be desired for itself, and that too with the utmost intensity. What, for example, shall we say of the love of money? There is nothing originally more desirable about money than about any heap of glittering pebbles. Its worth is solely that of the things which it will buy; the desires for other things than itself, which it is a means of gratifying. Yet the love of money is not only one of the strongest moving forces of human life, but money is, in many cases, desired in and for itself; the desire to possess it is often stronger than the desire to use it, and goes on increasing when all the desires which point to ends beyond it, to be compassed by it, are falling off. It may, then, be said truly that money is desired not for the sake of an end, but as part of the end. From being a means to happiness, it has come to be itself a principal ingredient of the individual's conception of happiness. The same may be said of the majority of the great objects of human life: power, for example, or fame, except that to each of these there is a certain amount of immediate pleasure annexed, which has at least the semblance of being naturally inherent in them—a thing which cannot be said of money. Still, however, the strongest natural attraction, both of power and of fame, is the immense aid they give to the attainment of our other wishes; and it is the strong association thus generated between them and all our objects of desire which gives to the direct desire of them the intensity it often assumes, so as in some characters to surpass in strength all other desires. In these cases the means have become a part of the end, and a more important part of it than any of the things which they are means to. What was once desired as an instrument for the attainment of happiness has come to be desired for its own sake. In being desired for its own sake it is, however, desired as part of happiness. The person is made, or thinks he would be made, happy by its mere possession; and is made unhappy by failure to obtain it. The desire of it is not a different thing from the desire of happiness any more than the love of music or the desire of health. They are included in happiness. They are some of the elements of which the desire of happiness is made up. Happiness is not an abstract idea but a concrete whole; and these are some of its parts. And the utilitarian standard sanctions and approves their being so. Life would be a poor thing, very ill provided with sources of happiness, if there were not this provision of nature by which things originally indifferent, but conducive to, or otherwise associated with, the satisfaction of our primitive desires, become in themselves sources of pleasure more valuable than the primitive pleasures, both in permanency, in the space of human existence that they are capable of covering, and even in intensity.

Virtue, according to the utilitarian conception, is a good of this description. There was no original desire of it, or motive to it, save its conduciveness to pleasure, and especially to protection from pain. But through the association thus formed it may be felt a good in itself, and desired as such with as great intensity as any other good; and with this difference between it and the love of money, of power, or of fame—that all of these may, and often do, render the individual noxious to the other members of the society to which he belongs, whereas there is nothing which makes him so much a blessing to them as the cultivation of the disinterested love of virtue. And consequently, the utilitarian standard, while it tolerates and approves those other acquired desires, up to the point beyond which they would be more injurious to the general happiness than promotive of it, enjoins and requires the cultivation of the love of virtue up to the greatest strength possible, as being above all things important to the general happiness.

Happiness the Only Intrinsic Good

It results from the preceding considerations that there is in reality nothing desired except happiness. Whatever is desired otherwise than as a means to some end beyond itself, and ultimately to happiness, is desired as itself a part of happiness, and is not desired for itself until it has become so. Those who desire virtue for its own sake desire it either because the consciousness of it is a pleasure, or because the consciousness of being without it is a pain, or for both reasons united; as in truth the pleasure and pain seldom exist separately, but almost always together—the same person feeling pleasure in the degree of virtue attained, and pain in not having attained more. If one of these gave him no pleasure, and the other no pain, he would not love or desire virtue, or would desire it only for the other benefits which it might produce to himself or to persons whom he cared for.

We have now, then, an answer to the question, of what sort of proof the principle of utility is susceptible. If the opinion which I have now stated is psychologically true—if human nature is so constituted as to desire nothing which is not either a part of happiness or a means of happiness—we can have no other proof, and we require no other, that these are the only things desirable. If so, happiness is the sole end of human action, and the promotion of it the test by which to judge all human conduct; from whence it necessarily follows that it must be the criterion of morality, since a part is included in the whole.

REVIEW EXERCISES

1. Give and explain the basic idea of the principle of utility or the greatest happiness principle.
2. What does it mean to speak of utilitarianism as a consequentialist moral theory? As a teleological moral theory?
3. What is the difference between intrinsic and instrumental good? Give examples of each.
4. Which of the following statements exemplify consequentialist reasonings? Can all of them be given consequentialist interpretations if expanded? Explain your answers.

   a. Honesty is the best policy.
   b. Sue has the right to know the truth.
   c. What good is going to come from giving money to a homeless person on the street?
   d. There is a symbolic value present in personally giving something to another person in need.
   e. It is only fair that you give him a chance to compete for the position.
   f. If I do not study for my ethics exam, it will hurt my GPA.
   g. If you are not honest with others, you cannot expect them to be honest with you.

5. Is utilitarianism a hedonist moral theory? Why or why not?

6. Using utilitarian calculation, which choice in each of the following pairs is better, X or Y?
   a. X makes four people happy and me unhappy. Y makes me and one other person happy and three people unhappy.
   b. X makes twenty people happy and five unhappy. Y makes ten people happy and no one unhappy.
   c. X will give five people each two hours of pleasure. Y will give three people each four hours of pleasure.
   d. X will make five people very happy and three people mildly unhappy. Y will make six people moderately happy and two people very unhappy.

7. What is Mill's argument for the difference in value between intellectual and sensual pleasures?

8. Which of the following is an example of act utilitarian reasoning and which rule utilitarian reasoning? Explain your answers.
   a. If I do not go to the meeting, then others will not go either. If that happens, then there would not be a quorum for the important vote, which would be bad. Thus, I ought to go to the meeting.
   b. If doctors generally lied to their patients about their diagnoses, then patients would lose trust in their doctors. Because that would be bad, I should tell this patient the truth.
   c. We ought to keep our promises because it is a valuable practice.
   d. If I cheat here, I will be more likely to cheat elsewhere. No one would trust me then. So I should not cheat on this test.

5

Kant's Moral Theory

BETWEEN 1932 and 1972, experiments were conducted in Tuskegee, Alabama, in which 390 poor and illiterate African American men who had syphilis were followed in order to determine the progress of the disease, whether it was always fatal, and how it was spread. The men were even denied penicillin treatment when it became available in the early 1940s. The study was ended in 1972 when it became public and people objected. The reasons were by now obvious: these men had not been treated with respect but had been used for the purpose of obtaining information. In the first place, they were not informed of the true purpose of the study.[1] They were used as guinea pigs in the same way those animals are used in experimentation. However, experimentation using human subjects through the years has led to important medical discoveries that benefited others. Moreover, it is necessary to test new techniques and drugs on actual human subjects before they become widely available. This is often done in controlled clinical trials, in which a control group is compared to the group receiving the treatment. Are these experiments morally unobjectionable? Ethicists distinguish therapeutic from nontherapeutic experimentation. In the case of therapeutic experimentation, the persons involved have some medical condition that the new therapy might help. They are informed and give their consent. In the case of nontherapeutic experimentation, the subjects are volunteers without the condition. The quality of the consent and the degree of risk compared to the potential benefit are also relevant.

According to utilitarian thinking, the Tuskegee experiment may well have been quite justifiable. If the psychological harm done to the participants was minimal and the study had no other negative effects, and if the knowledge gained was valuable, then the study would be justified.[2] It would have done more good than harm, and that is the basis for judging it to be morally praiseworthy. However, since the post–World War II trials of Nazi war criminals held in Nuremberg, Germany, other standards for treatment of human research subjects have become widely accepted. One of the most basic principles of the Nuremberg Code is this: "The voluntary consent of the human subject is absolutely essential."[3] Consent must be informed and uncoerced. Implied in this principle is the belief that persons are autonomous, and this autonomy ought to be respected and protected even if this means that we cannot do certain types of research and cannot thereby discover valuable information. This view of the significance of personal autonomy, and that people ought not to be simply used as they possibly were in this experiment, is also a central tenet of the moral philosophy of Immanuel Kant, which we will now examine.

Subjects in the infamous Tuskegee Syphillis Study.

HISTORICAL BACKGROUND: IMMANUEL KANT

Immanuel Kant (1724–1804) was a German philosophy professor who taught at the University of Königsberg in what is now the city of Kaliningrad in the westernmost section of Russia. He was such a popular lecturer that university students who wanted a seat had to arrive at his classroom at six in the morning, one hour before Kant was due to begin his lecture![4] After many years of financial and professional insecurity, he finally was appointed to a chair in philosophy. The writings that followed made him renowned even in his own time. Kant is now regarded as a central figure in the history of modern philosophy. Modern philosophy itself is sometimes divided into pre-Kantian and post-Kantian periods. In fact, some people regard him as the greatest modern philosopher. Although he is renowned for his philosophy, he wrote on a variety of matters including science, geography, beauty, and war and peace. He was a firm believer in the ideas of the Enlightenment, especially reason and freedom, and he also was a supporter of the American Revolution.

Two of the main questions that Kant believed philosophy should address were: "What can I know?" and "What ought I do?"[5] In answering the first question, he thought he was creating a new Copernican revolution.

Just as the astronomer Copernicus had argued in 1543 that we should no longer consider the Earth as the center of the solar system with heavenly bodies revolving around it, Kant asserted that we should no longer think of the human knower as revolving around objects known. Knowledge, he believed, was not the passive perception of things just as they are. Rather, he argued, the very nature of human perception and understanding determines the basic character of the world as we experience it. Forms within the mind determine the spatial and temporal nature of our world and give experience its basic structure.

In his moral philosophy, Kant addressed the other question, "What ought I do?" His answers can be found for the most part in two works. One is the *Fundamental Principles* (or *Foundations*) of the *Metaphysics of Morals* (1785), which one commentator described as "one of the most important ethical treatises ever written."[6] The other is the *Critique of Practical Reason* (1788). Selections from the first work are included in this chapter. You will be able to understand the basic elements of Kant's moral philosophy from the following sections on the basis of morality and the categorical imperative. You should benefit in your own reflections on this theory from the section on evaluating Kant's moral theory. The final sections on perfect and imperfect duties and contemporary versions of Kantian moral theory add further detail to this basic treatment.

WHAT GIVES AN ACT MORAL WORTH?

One way to begin your examination of Kant's moral theory is to think about how he would answer the question, What gives an act *moral* worth? It is not the consequences of the act, according to Kant. Suppose, for example, that I try to do what is right by complimenting someone on her achievements. Through no fault of my own, my action ends up hurting that person because she misunderstands my efforts. According to Kant, because I intended and tried to do what I thought was right, I ought not to be blamed for things having turned out badly. The idea is that we generally ought not to be blamed or praised for what is not in our control. The consequences of our acts are not always in our control, and things do not always turn out as we want. However, Kant believed that our motives are in our control. We are responsible for our motive to do good or bad, and thus it is for this that we are held morally accountable.

Kant also objected to basing morality on the consequences of our actions for another reason. To make morality a matter of producing certain states of affairs, such as happy experiences, puts matters backward, he might say. On such a view we could be thought of as having *use value*. We would be valued to the extent that we were instrumental in bringing about what itself was of greater value—namely, happy states or experiences. However, in Kant's view, we should not be used in this way for we are rational beings or *persons*. Persons have intrinsic or inherent value, according to Kant, not simply instrumental value. The belief that *people ought not to be used*, but ought to be regarded as having the highest intrinsic value, is central to Kant's ethics, as is the importance of *a motive to do what is right*. As we shall see in the next two sections, Kant uses this second idea to answer the question, What gives an act moral worth?

What Is the Right Motive?

Kant believed that an act has specifically moral worth only if it is done with a right intention or motive.[7] He referred to this as having a "good will." In his famous first lines of the first section of *Foundations*, Kant

writes that only such a will is good unconditionally. Everything else needs a good will to make it good. Without a right intention, such things as intelligence, wit, and control of emotions can be bad and used for evil purposes.[8] Having a right intention is to do what is right (or what one believes to be right) just because it is right. In Kant's words, it is to act "out of duty," out of a concern and respect for the moral law. Kant was not a relativist. He believed that there is a right and a wrong thing to do, whether or not we know or agree about it. This is the moral law.

To explain his views on the importance of a right motive or intention, Kant provides the example of a shopkeeper who does the right thing, who charges the customers a fair price and charges the same to all. But what is her motive? Kant discusses three possible motives. (1) The shopkeeper's motive or reason for acting might be because it is a good business practice to charge the same to all. It is in her own best interest that she do this. Although not necessarily wrong, this motive is not praiseworthy. (2) The shopkeeper might charge a fair and equal price because she is sympathetic toward her customers and is naturally inclined to do them good. Kant said that this motive is also not the highest. We do not have high moral esteem or praise for people who simply do what they feel like doing, even if we believe they are doing the right thing. (3) However, if the shopkeeper did the right thing just because she believed it was right, then this act would have the highest motive. We do have a special respect, or even a moral reverence, for people who act out of a will to do the right thing, especially when this is at great cost to themselves. Only when an act is motivated by this concern for morality, or for the moral law as Kant would say, does it have moral worth.

Now we do not always *know* when our acts are motivated by self-interest, inclination, or pure respect for morality. Also, we often act from mixed motives. We are more certain that the motive is pure, however, when we do what is right even when it is not in our best interest (when it costs us dearly) and when we do not feel like doing the right thing. In these cases, we can know that we are motivated by concern to do the right thing because the other two motives are missing. Moreover, this ability to act for moral reasons and resist the pushes and pulls of nature or natural inclination is one indication of and reason why Kant believes that it is persons that have a unique value and dignity. The person who says to himself, "I feel like being lazy (or mean or selfish), but I am going to try not to because it would not be right," is operating out of the motive of respect for morality itself. This ability to act for moral reasons or motives, Kant believes, is one part of what makes people possess particularly high and unique value.

What Is the Right Thing to Do?

For our action to have moral worth, according to Kant, we must not only act out of a right motivation but also do the right thing. Consider again the diagram that we used in the first chapter.

As noted earlier, Kant does not believe that morality is a function of producing good consequences. We may do what has good results, but if we do so for the wrong motive, then that act has no moral worth. However, it is not only the motive that counts for Kant. We must also do what is right. The act itself must be morally right. Both the act and the motive are morally relevant. In Kant's terms, we must not only act "out of duty" (have the right motive) but also "according to duty" or "as duty requires" (do what is right). How then are we to know what is the right thing to do? Once we know this, we can try to do it just because it is right.

To understand Kant's reasoning on this matter, we need to examine the difference between what he calls a *hypothetical imperative* and a *categorical imperative*. First of all, an imperative is simply a form of statement that tells us to do something, for example, "Stand up straight" and "Close the door" and also "You ought to close the door." Some, but only some, imperatives are moral imperatives. Other imperatives are hypothetical. For example, the statement "If I want to get there on time, I ought to leave early" does not embody a moral "ought" or imperative. What I ought to do in that case is a function of what I happen to want—to get there on time—and of the means necessary to achieve this— leave early. Moreover, I can avoid the obligation to leave early by changing my goals. I can decide that I do not need or want to get there on time. Then I need not leave early. These ends may be good or bad. Thus, the statement "If I want to harm someone, then I ought to use effective means" also expresses a hypothetical "ought." These "oughts" are avoidable, or, as Kant would say, contingent. They are contingent or dependent on what I happen to want or the desires I happen to have, such as to please others, to harm someone, to gain power, or to be punctual.

These "oughts" are also quite individualized. What I ought to do is contingent or dependent on my own individual goals or plans. These actions serve as means to whatever goals I happen to have or even goals that many or most of us do in fact have. Other people ought to do different things than I because they have different goals and plans. For example, I ought to take introduction to sociology because I want to be a sociology major, while you ought to take a course on the philosophy of Kant because you have chosen to be a philosophy major. These are obligations only for those who have these goals or desires. Think of them in this form: "If (or because) I want X, then I ought to do Y." Whether I ought to do Y is totally contingent or dependent on my wanting X.

Moral obligation, on the other hand, is quite different in nature. Kant believed that we experience moral obligation as something quite demanding. If there is something I morally ought to do, I ought to do it no matter what—whether or not I want to, and whether or not it fulfills my desires and goals or is approved by my society. Moral obligation is not contingent on what I or anyone happens to want or approve. Moral "oughts" are thus, in Kant's terminology, unconditional or necessary. Moreover, whereas hypothetical "oughts" relate to goals we each have as individuals, moral "oughts" stem from the ways in which we are alike as persons, for only persons are subject to morality. This is because persons are rational beings, and only persons can act from a reason or from principles. These "oughts" are thus not individualized but universal as they apply to all persons. Kant calls moral "oughts" categorical imperatives because they tell us what we ought to do no matter what, under all conditions, or categorically.

It is from the very nature of categorical or moral imperatives, their being unconditional and universally binding, that Kant derives his views about what it is that we ought to do. In fact, he calls the statement of his basic moral principle by which we determine what we ought and ought not to do simply the *categorical imperative*.

THE CATEGORICAL IMPERATIVE

The categorical imperative, Kant's basic moral principle, is comparable in importance for his moral philosophy to the principle of utility for utilitarians. It is Kant's test for right and wrong. Just as there are different ways to formulate the principle of utility, so also Kant had different formulations for his principle. Although at least four of them may be found in his writings, we will concentrate on just two and call them the first and second forms of the categorical imperative. The others, however, do add different elements to our understanding of his basic moral principle and will be mentioned briefly.

The First Form

Recall that moral obligation is categorical; that is, it is unconditional and applies to all persons as persons rather than to persons as individuals. It is in this sense universal. Moreover, because morality is not a matter of producing good consequences of any sort (be it happiness or knowledge or peace), the basic moral principle will be formal, without content. It will not include reference to any particular good. Knowing this, we are on the way to understanding the first form of the categorical imperative, which simply requires that we only do what we can accept or will that everyone do. Kant's own statement of it is basically the following:

Act only on that maxim that you can will as a universal law.

In other words, whatever I consider doing, it must be something that I can will or accept that all others do. To will something universally is similar to willing it as a law, for a law by its very nature has a degree of universality. By *maxim*, Kant means a description of the action or policy that I will put to the test. This is put in the form of a rule or principle. For example, I might want to know whether "being late for class" or "giving all my money to the homeless" describe morally permissible actions. I need only formulate some maxim or rule and ask whether I could will that

everyone follow that maxim. For example, I might ask whether I could will the maxim or general rule, "Whenever I have money to spare, I will give it to the homeless." However, this needs further clarification.[9]

How do I know what I can and cannot will as a universal practice? As a rational being, I can only will what is noncontradictory. What do we think of a person who says that it is both raining and not raining here now? It can be raining here and not there or now and not earlier. But it is either raining here or it is not. It cannot be both. So also we say that a person who wants to "have his cake and eat it, too" is not being rational. "Make up your mind," we say. "If you eat it, it is gone."

How I know if I can rationally, without contradiction, will something for all can best be explained by using one of Kant's own examples. He asks us to consider whether it is morally permissible for me to "make a lying or false promise in order to extricate myself from some difficulty." Thus, I would consider the maxim, "Whenever I am in some difficulty that I can get out of only by making a lying or false promise, I will do so." To know whether this would be morally acceptable, it must pass the test of the categorical imperative. If I were to use this test, I would ask whether I could will that sort of thing for all. I must ask whether I could will a general practice in which people who made promises—for example, to pay back some money—made the promises without intending to keep them. If people who generally made such promises did so falsely, then others would know this and would not believe the promises. Consider whether you would lend money to a person if she said she would pay you back but you knew she was lying. The reasoning is thus: if I tried to will a general practice of false promise-making, I would find that I could not do it because by willing that the promises could be false I would also will a situation in which it would be impossible to make a lying promise. No one could then make a promise, let alone a false promise, because no one would believe him or her. Part of being able to make a promise is to have it believed. This universal practice itself could not even exist. It is a self-destructive practice. If everyone made such lying promises, no one could!

Now consider the example at the beginning of this chapter: the experiment using people without their full knowing consent. Using Kant's categorical imperative to test this, one would see that if it were a general practice for researchers to lie to their subjects in order to get them into their experiments, they would not be able to get people to participate. They could not even lie because no one would believe them. The only way a particular researcher could lie would be if other researchers told the truth. Only then could she get her prospective subjects to believe her. But, on this interpretation of the case, this would be to make herself an exception to the universal rule. Because a universal practice in which researchers lied to their prospective subjects could not even exist, it is a morally impermissible action.[10]

The Second Form

The first form of Kant's categorical imperative requires universalizing one's contemplated action or policy. In the second form, we are asked to consider what constitutes proper treatment of persons as persons. According to Kant, one key characteristic of persons is their ability to set their own goals. Persons are autonomous (from *auto*, meaning "self," and *nomos*, meaning "rule" or "law"). They are literally self-ruled, or at least capable of being self-ruled. As persons, we choose our own life plans, what we want to be, our friends, our college courses, and so forth. We have our own reasons for doing so. We believe that although we are influenced in these choices and reasons by our situation and by others, we let ourselves be so influenced, and thus these choices are still our own choices.[11] In this way, persons are different from things. Things cannot choose what they wish to do. We decide how we shall use things. We impose our own goals on things, using the wood to build the house and the pen or computer to write our words and express our ideas. It is appropriate in this scheme of things to use things for our ends, but it is not appropriate to use persons as though they were things purely at our own disposal and without a will of their own. Kant's statement of this second form of the categorical imperative is as follows:

Always treat humanity, whether in your own person or
   that of another, never simply as a means but always at
   the same time as an end.

This formulation tells us several things. First, it tells us how we ought to treat ourselves as well as others, for we are persons as they are. Second, it tells us to treat ourselves and others as ends rather than merely as means. Kant believes that we should treat persons as having value in themselves and not just as having instrumental value. People are valuable in themselves, regardless of whether they are useful or loved or valued by others. However, this form also specifies that we should not simply use others or let ourselves be used. Although I may in some sense use someone—for example, to paint my house—I may not simply use them. The goal of getting my house painted must also be the goal of the painter, who is also a person and not just an object to be used by me for my own ends. She must know what is involved in the project. I cannot lie to her to manipulate her into doing something to which she otherwise would not agree. And she must agree to paint the house voluntarily rather than be coerced into doing it. This is to treat the person as an end rather than as a means to my ends or goals.

We can also use this second form to evaluate the examples considered for the first form of the categorical imperative. The moral conclusions should be the same whether we use the first or second form. Kant believes that in lying to another—for example, saying that we will pay back the money when we have no intention of doing so—we would be attempting to get that other to do what we want but which she or he presumably does not want to do—namely, just give us the money. This would violate the requirement not to use persons. So also in the experiment described at the beginning of this chapter, the researcher would be using deception to get people to "volunteer" for the study. One difficulty presented by this type of study, however, is that if the participants were to know the truth, it would undermine the study. Some people have argued that in such studies we can presume the voluntary consent of the subjects, judging that they would approve if they did know what was going on in the study. Do you think that presuming consent in this or similar cases would be sufficient?

We noted above that Kant had more than these two formulations of his categorical imperative. In another of these formulations, Kant relies on his views about nature as a system of everything that we experience because it is organized according to laws. Thus, he says that we ought always to ask whether some action we are contemplating could become a universal law of nature. The effect of this version is to stress the universality and rationality of morality, for nature necessarily operates according to coherent laws. Other formulations of the categorical imperative stress autonomy. We are to ask whether we could consider ourselves as the author of the moral practice that we are about to accept. We are both subject to the moral law and its author because it flows from our own nature as a rational being. Another formulation amplifies what we have here called the second form of the categorical imperative. This formulation points out that we are all alike as persons and together form a community of persons. He calls the community of rational persons a "kingdom of ends"—that is, a kingdom in which all persons are authors as well as subjects of the moral law. Thus, we ask whether the action we are contemplating would be fitting for and further or promote such a community. These formal actions of the categorical imperative involve other interesting elements of Kant's philosophy, but they also involve more than we can explore further here.

EVALUATING KANT'S MORAL THEORY

There is much that is appealing in Kant's moral philosophy, particularly its central aspects—fairness, consistency, and treating persons as autonomous and morally equal beings. They are also key elements of a particular tradition in morality, one that is quite different than that exemplified by utilitarianism with its emphasis on the maximization of happiness and the production of good consequences. To more fully evaluate Kant's theory, consider the following aspects of his thought.

The Nature of Moral Obligation

One of the bases on which Kant's moral philosophy rests is his view about the nature of moral obligation. He believes that moral obligation is real and strictly binding. According to Kant, this is how we generally think of moral obligation. If there is anything that we morally ought to do, then we simply ought to do it. Thus, this type of obligation is unlike

that which flows from what we ought to do because of the particular goals that we each have as individuals. To evaluate this aspect of Kant's moral philosophy, you must ask yourself whether this is also what you think about the nature of moral obligation. This is important for Kant's moral philosophy, because acting out of respect for the moral law is required for an action to have moral worth. Furthermore, being able to act out of such a regard for morality is also the source of human dignity, according to Kant.

The Application of the Categorical Imperative

Critics have pointed out problems with the universalizing form of the categorical imperative. For example, some have argued that when using the first form of the categorical imperative there are many things that I could will as universal practices that would hardly seem to be moral obligations. I could will that everyone write their name on the top of their test papers. If everyone did that, it would not prevent anyone from doing so. There would be no contradiction involved if this were a universal practice. Nevertheless, this would not mean that people have a moral obligation to write their names on their test papers. A Kantian might explain that to write your name on your test paper is an example of a hypothetical, not a categorical, imperative. I write my name on my paper because I want to be given credit for it. If I can will it as a universal practice, I then know it is a morally permissible action. If I cannot will it universally, then it is impermissible or wrong. Thus, the categorical imperative is actually a negative test—in other words, a test for what we should not do, more than a test for what we ought to do. Whether or not this is a satisfactory response, you should know that this is just one of several problems associated with Kant's universalizing test.

Note, too, that although both Kantians and rule utilitarians must universalize, how their reasoning proceeds from there is not identical. Rule utilitarians, on the one hand, require that we consider what the results would be if some act we are contemplating were to be a universal practice. Reasoning in this way, we ask what would be the results or consequences of some general practice, such as making false promises, or whether one practice would have better results than another. Although in some sense

Kant's theory requires that we consider the possible consequences when universalizing some action, the determinant of the action's morality is not whether its practice has good or bad consequences, but whether there would be anything contradictory in willing the practice as a universal law. Because we are rational beings, we must not will contradictory things.

The second form of the categorical imperative also has problems of application. In the concrete, it is not always easy to determine whether one is using a person, for example, what is coercion and what is simply influence, or what is deception and what is not. When I try to talk a friend into doing something for me, how do I know whether I am simply providing input for the person's own decision making or whether I am crossing the line and becoming coercive? Moreover, if I do not tell the whole truth or withhold information from another, should this count as deception on my part? (See further discussion of this issue in Chapter 12 on sexual morality.) Although these are real problems for anyone who tries to apply Kant's views about deceit and coercion, they are not unique to his moral philosophy. Theories vary in the ease of their use or application, but, as Kant puts it, "Ease of use and apparent adequacy of a principle are not any sure proof of its correctness."[12] The fact that a theory has a certain amount of ambiguity should not necessarily disqualify it. Difficulty of application is a problem for most, if not all, reasonable moral philosophies.

Duty

Some of the language and terminology found in Kant's moral theory can sound harsh to modern ears. Duty, obligation, law, and universality may not be the moral terms most commonly heard today. Yet if one considers what Kant meant by duty, the idea may not be so strange to us. He did not mean any particular moral code or set of duties that is held by any society or group. Rather, duty is whatever is the right thing to do. However, Kant might respond that there is a streak of absolutism in his philosophy. Recall from Chapter 2 that *absolutism* is distinguished from objectivism and usually refers to a morality that consists in a set of exceptionless rules. Kant does, at times, seem to favor such rules. He

provides examples in which it seems clear that he believes that it is always wrong to make a false promise or to lie deliberately. There is even one example in which Kant himself suggests that if a killer comes to the door asking for a friend of yours inside whom he intends to kill, you must tell the truth. But Kant's philosophy has only one exceptionless rule, and that is given in the categorical imperative. We are never permitted to do what we cannot will as a universal law or what violates the requirement to treat persons as persons. Even with these tests in hand, it is not always clear just how they apply. Furthermore, they may not give adequate help in deciding what to do when they seem to give us contradictory duties, as in the example both to tell the truth and preserve life. Kant believed that he was only setting basic principles of morality and establishing it on a firm basis. Nevertheless, it is reasonable to expect that a moral theory should go further.

Moral Equality and Impartiality

One positive feature of Kant's moral theory is its emphasis on the moral equality of all persons, which is implied in his view about the nature of moral obligation as universally binding. We should not make exceptions for ourselves but only do what we can will for all. Moral obligation and morality itself flow from our nature as persons as rational and autonomous. Morality is grounded in the ways in which we are alike as persons rather than the ways in which we are different as individuals. These views might provide a source for those who want to argue for moral equality and equal moral rights. (For other reflection on the nature of rights, refer to the discussion of it in Chapters 7 and 14.) Not to treat others as equal persons is, in a way, disrespecting them. Not to be willing to make the same judgment for cases similar to one's own, or not to be willing to have the same rules apply to all, could be viewed as a form of hypocrisy. When we criticize these behaviors, we act in the spirit of Kant.[13]

Another feature of Kant's moral philosophy is its spirit of impartiality. For an action to be morally permissible, we should be able to will it for all. However, persons do differ in significant ways. Among these are differences in gender, race, age, and talents. In what way does morality require that all persons be treated equally, and in what way does it perhaps require that different persons be treated differently? (Further discussion of this issue can be found in Chapter 13 on equality and discrimination.)[14]

Other people have wondered about Kant's stress on the nature of persons as rational beings. Some believe it is too male-oriented in its focus on reason rather than emotion. In Chapter 9, we will examine a type of morality that stresses the emotional and personal ties that we have to particular individuals. Kant might reply that we often have no control over how we feel and thus it should not be the key element of our moral lives. He might also point out that it is the common aspects of our existence as persons, and not the ways in which we are different and unique, that give us dignity and are the basis for the moral equality that we possess.

PERFECT AND IMPERFECT DUTIES

In his attempt to explain his views, Kant provides us with several examples. We have already considered one of these: making a false promise. His conclusion is that we should not make a false or lying promise, both because we could not consistently will it for all and because it violates our obligation to treat persons as persons and not to use them only for our own purposes. Kant calls such duties *perfect* or *necessary duties*. As the terms suggest, perfect duties are absolute. We can and should absolutely refrain from making false or lying promises. From the perspective of the first form of the categorical imperative, we have a perfect duty not to do those things that could not even exist and are inconceivable as universal practices. Using the second form of the categorical imperative, we have a perfect duty not to do what violates the requirement to treat persons as persons.

However, some duties are more flexible. Kant calls these duties *imperfect* or *meritorious duties*. Consider another example he provides us: egoism. Ethical egoism, you will recall, is the view that we may rightly seek only our own interest and help others only to the extent that this also benefits us. Is this a morally acceptable philosophy of life? Using the first form of Kant's categorical imperative to test the morality of this practice, we must ask whether we could will that everyone was an egoist. If I try to

do this, I would need to will that I was an egoist as well as others, even in those situations when I needed others' help. In those situations, I must allow that they not help me when it is not in their own best interest. But being an egoist myself, I would also want them to help me. In effect, I would be willing contradictories: that they help me (I being an egoist) and that they not help me (they being egoists). Although a society of egoists could indeed exist, Kant admits, no rational person could will it, for a rational person does not will contradictories. We have an imperfect or meritorious duty, then, not to be egoists but to help people for their own good and not just for ours. However, just when to help others and how much to help them is a matter of some choice. There is a certain flexibility here. One implication of this view is that there is no absolute duty to give one's whole life to helping others. We, too, are persons and thus have moral rights and also can at least sometimes act for our own interests.

The same conclusion regarding the wrongness of egoism results from the application of the second form of the categorical imperative. If I were an egoist and concerned only about myself, then no one could accuse me of using other people. I would simply leave them alone. According to Kant, such an attitude and practice would be inconsistent with the duty to treat others as persons. As persons, they also have interests and plans, and to recognize this I must at least sometimes and in some ways seek to promote their ends and goals. One implication of this distinction is in handling conflicts of duties. Perfect duties will take precedence over imperfect ones such that we cannot help some by violating the rights of others.

VARIATIONS ON KANTIAN MORAL THEORY

Just as there are contemporary versions of and developments within the utilitarian tradition, so also we can find many contemporary versions of Kantian moral philosophies. One is found in the moral philosophy of W. D. Ross (1877–1971), who also held that there are things that we ought and ought not do regardless of the consequences.[15] According to Ross, we not only have duties of beneficence, but we also have duties to keep promises, pay our debts, and be good friends and parents and children. (Refer to the discussion of moral pluralism in Chapter 2.) Contrary to Kant, Ross believed that we can know through moral intuition in any instance what we ought to do. Sometimes we are faced with a conflict of moral duties. It seems intuitively that we ought to be both loyal and honest but we cannot be both. We have *prima facie* or conditional duties of loyalty and honesty. Ross is the source of the phrase "prima facie," which is often used in ethical arguments. In such cases, according to Ross, we have to consider which duty is the stronger—that is, which has the greater balance of rightness over wrongness. In choosing honesty in some situation, however, one does not negate or forget that one also has a duty to be loyal. Obvious problems arise for such a theory. For example, how does one go about determining the amount of rightness or wrongness involved in some action? Don't people have different intuitions about the rightness or wrongness? This is a problem for anyone who holds that intuition is the basis for morality.

One of the most noted contemporary versions of Kant's moral philosophy is found in the political philosophy of John Rawls. In *A Theory of Justice*, Rawls applies some aspects of Kantian principles to issues of social justice. According to Rawls, justice is fairness.[16] To know what is fair, we must put ourselves imaginatively in the position of a group of free and equal rational beings who are choosing principles of justice for their society. In thinking of persons as free and equal rational beings in order to develop principles of justice, Rawls is securely in the Kantian tradition of moral philosophy. Kant has also stressed autonomy. It is this aspect of our nature that gives us our dignity as persons. Kant's categorical imperative also involved universalization. We must do only those things that we could will that everyone do. It is only a short move from these notions of autonomy and universalization to the Rawlsian requirement to choose those principles of justice that we could accept no matter whose position we were in. For details about the principles, see Chapter 14 on economic justice. Just as utilitarian moral theory is still being debated today and has many followers, so also Kantian types of philosophy continue to intrigue and interest moral thinkers. You will also be able to better evaluate this theory as you see aspects of it applied to issues in Part Two of this text.

The reading selection in this chapter from Kant's *Foundations of the Metaphysics of Morals* contains the key elements of his moral philosophy.

NOTES

1. See http://en.wikipedia.org/wiki/Tuskegee_ syphilis_study.
2. At least this might be true from an act utilitarian point of view. A rule utilitarian might want to know whether the results of the general practice of not fully informing research participants would be such that the good achieved would not be worth it.
3. From *The Trials of War Criminals before the Nuremberg Military Tribunals under Control Council Law*, No. 10, vol. 2 (Washington, DC: U.S. Government Printing Office, 1949), 181–182.
4. Reported by philosopher J. G. Hammann and noted in Roger Scruton's *Kant* (Oxford: Oxford University Press, 1982), 3–4.
5. Immanuel Kant, *Critique of Pure Reason*, Norman Kemp Smith (Trans.) (New York: St. Martin's, 1965), 635.
6. Lewis White Beck, introduction to his translation of Kant's *Foundations of the Metaphysics of Morals* (New York: Bobbs-Merrill, 1959), vii. The title is also sometimes translated as *Fundamental Principles of the Metaphysics of Morals*. For a readable interpretation of Kant's ethics, see Onora O'Neill's "A Simplified Account of Kant's Ethics," *Matters of Life and Death*, Tom Regan (Ed.) (New York: McGraw-Hill, 1986).
7. We will not distinguish here *motive* and *intention*, although the former usually signifies that out of which we act (a pusher) and the latter that for which we act (an aim).
8. Kant, *Foundations*, 9.
9. I thank Professor Joyce Mullan for suggestions regarding what Kant means by *maxim*.
10. In some ways, Kant's basic moral principle, the categorical imperative, is a principle of fairness. I cannot do what I am not able to will that everyone do. In the example, for me to make a lying promise, others must generally make truthful promises so that my lie will be believed. This would be to treat myself as an exception. But this is not fair. In some ways, the principle is similar to the so-called golden rule, which requires us only to do unto others what we would be willing for them to do unto us.

However, it is not quite the same, for Kant's principle requires our not willing self-defeating or self-canceling, contradictory practices, whereas the golden rule requires that we appeal in the final analysis to what we would or would not like to have done to us.

11. Kant does treat the whole issue of determinism versus freedom, but it is difficult to follow; to attempt explaining it would involve us deeply in his metaphysics. Although it is a serious issue, we will assume for purposes of understanding Kant that sometimes, at least, human choice is free.

12. Kant, *Foundations*, 8.

13. I would like to thank one of this book's reviewers for this suggestion.

14. See also the criticism of Kantian theories of justice in the treatment of gender and justice in Susan Moller Okin, *Justice, Gender, and the Family* (New York: Basic Books, 1989), 3–22. See also Marilyn Friedman, "The Social Self and the Partiality Debates," in *Feminist Ethics*, Claudia Card (Ed.) (Lawrence: University of Kansas Press, 1991).

15. W. D. Ross, *The Right and the Good* (Oxford: Oxford University Press, 1930).

16. John Rawls, *A Theory of Justice* (Cambridge, MA: Harvard University Press, 1971).

READING
Fundamental Principles of the Metaphysic of Morals
IMMANUEL KANT

Study Questions

1. What is meant by a "good will," and why is it the only thing good "without qualification"?
2. Out of what motives other than duty do people act?
3. If we do the right thing, such as not overcharging customers or preserving our life, do these actions always have full moral worth, according to Kant?
4. What does he mean when he says that some kinds of love cannot be commanded?
5. What does duty have to do with having respect for morality?
6. How does Kant state his basic moral principle?
7. What is the difference between how one would reason about whether it is prudent to make a false or lying promise and how one should determine whether it is the right thing to do?
8. How does Kant describe what it means to be under obligation or subject to an "ought"?
9. What is the difference between a rule of skill, a counsel of prudence, and a command of morality?
10. Explain how Kant uses the categorical imperative in his four examples.
11. What does Kant mean by an "end"? How does this notion relate to the second form of the moral imperative?
12. Explain how Kant uses the second formulation in the same four examples.

THE GOOD WILL*

Nothing can possibly be conceived in the world, or even out of it, which can be called good without qualification, except a Good Will. Intelligence, wit, judgment, and the other *talents* of the mind, however they may be named, or courage, resolution, perseverance, as qualities of temperament, are undoubtedly good and desirable in many respects; but these gifts of nature may also become extremely bad and mischievous if the will which is to make use of them, and which, therefore, constitutes what is called *character*, is not good. It is the same with the *gifts of fortune*. Power, riches, honour, even health, and the general well-being and contentment with one's condition which is called *happiness*, inspire pride, and often presumption, if there is not a good will to correct the influence of these on the mind, and with this also to rectify the whole principle of acting and adapt it to its end. The sight of a being who is not adorned with a single feature of a pure and good will, enjoying unbroken prosperity, can never give pleasure to an impartial rational spectator. Thus a good

---

Selections from Abbott translation, first and second sections (1879).

*Headings added by the editor.—ED.

will appears to constitute the indispensable condition even of being worthy of happiness.

There are even some qualities which are of service to this good will itself, and may facilitate its action, yet which have no intrinsic unconditional value, but always presuppose a good will, and this qualifies the esteem that we justly have for them, and does not permit us to regard them as absolutely good. Moderation in the affections and passions, self-control and calm deliberation are not only good in many respects, but even seem to constitute part of the intrinsic worth of the person; but they are far from deserving to be called good without qualification, although they have been so unconditionally praised by the ancients. For without the principles of a good will, they may become extremely bad, and the coolness of a villain not only makes him far more dangerous, but also immediately makes him more abominable in our eyes than he would have been without it.

A good will is good not because of what it performs or effects, not by its aptness for the attainment of some proposed end, but simply by virtue of the volition, that is, it is good in itself, and considered by itself is to be esteemed much higher than all that can be brought about by it in favour of any inclination, nay even of the sum total of all inclinations. Even if it should happen that, owing to special disfavour of fortune, or the niggardly provision of a step-motherly nature, this will should wholly lack power to accomplish its purpose, if with its greatest efforts it should yet achieve nothing, and there should remain only the good will (not, to be sure, a mere wish, but the summoning of all means in our power), then, like a jewel, it would still shine by its own light, as a thing which has its whole value in itself. Its usefulness or fruitlessness can neither add nor take away anything from this value. It would be, as it were, only the setting to enable us to handle it the more conveniently in common commerce, or to attract to it the attention of those who are not yet connoisseurs, but not to recommend it to true connoisseurs, or to determine its value. . . .

ACTING FROM DUTY

We have then to develop the notion of a will which deserves to be highly esteemed for itself, and is good without a view to anything further, a notion which exists already in the sound natural understanding,

requiring rather to be cleared up than to be taught, and which in estimating the value of our actions always takes the first place, and constitutes the condition of all the rest. In order to do this we will take the notion of duty, which includes that of a good will, although implying certain subjective restrictions and hindrances. These, however, far from concealing it, or rendering it unrecognizable, rather bring it out by contrast, and make it shine forth so much the brighter. I omit here all actions which are already recognized as inconsistent with duty, although they may be useful for this or that purpose, for with these the question whether they are done from duty cannot arise at all, since they even conflict with it. I also set aside those actions which really conform to duty, but to which men have no direct inclination, performing them because they are impelled thereto by some other inclination. For in this case we can readily distinguish whether the action which agrees with duty is done from duty, or from a selfish view. It is much harder to make this distinction when the action accords with duty, and the subject has besides a direct inclination to it. For example, it is always a matter of duty that a dealer should not overcharge an inexperienced purchaser, and wherever there is much commerce the prudent tradesman does not overcharge, but keeps a fixed price for every one, so that a child buys of him as well as any other. Men are thus honestly served; but this is not enough to make us believe that the tradesman has so acted from duty and from principles of honesty: his own advantage required it; it is out of the question in this case to suppose that he might besides have a direct inclination in favour of the buyers, so that, as it were, from love he should give no advantage to one over another. Accordingly the action was done neither from duty nor from direct inclination, but merely with a selfish view.

On the other hand, it is a duty to maintain one's life; and, in addition, every one has also a direct inclination to do so. But on this account the often anxious care which most men take for it has no intrinsic worth, and their maxim has no moral import. They preserve their life *as duty requires*, no doubt, but not *because duty requires*. On the other hand, if adversity and hopeless sorrow have completely taken away the relish for life; if the unfortunate one, strong in mind, indignant at his fate rather than desponding or dejected, wishes for death, and yet preserves his life without loving it—not from inclination or fear, but from duty—then his maxim has a moral worth.

To be beneficent when we can is a duty; and besides this, there are many minds so sympathetically constituted that without any other motive of vanity or self-interest, they find a pleasure in spreading joy around them, and can take delight in the satisfaction of others so far as it is their own work. But I maintain that in such a case an action of this kind, however proper, however amiable it may be, has nevertheless no true moral worth, but is on a level with other inclinations, e.g., the inclination to honour, which, if it is happily directed to that which is in fact of public utility and accordant with duty, and consequently honourable, deserves praise and encouragement, but not esteem. For the maxim wants the moral import, namely, that such actions be done *from duty*, not from inclination. Put the case that the mind of that philanthropist were clouded by sorrow of his own, extinguishing all sympathy with the lot of others, and that while he still has the power to benefit others in distress he is not touched by their trouble because he is absorbed with his own; and now suppose that he tears himself out of this dead insensibility, and performs the action without any inclination to it, but simply from duty, then first has his action its genuine moral worth. Further still; if nature has put little sympathy in the heart of this or that man; if he, supposed to be an upright man, is by temperament cold and indifferent to the sufferings of others, perhaps because in respect of his own he is provided with the special gift of patience and fortitude, and supposes, or even requires, that others should have the same—and such a man would certainly not be the meanest product of nature—but if nature had not specially framed him for a philanthropist, would he not still find in himself a source from whence to give himself a far higher worth than that of a good-natured temperament could be? Unquestionably. It is just in this that the moral worth of the character is brought out which is incomparably the highest of all, namely, that he is beneficent, not from inclination, but from duty.

To secure one's own happiness is a duty, at least indirectly; for discontent with one's condition under a pressure of many anxieties and amidst unsatisfied wants might easily become a great temptation to *transgression of duty*. . . .

It is in this manner, undoubtedly, that we are to understand those passages of Scripture also in which we are commanded to love our neighbour, even our enemy. For love, as an affection, cannot be commanded, but beneficence for duty's sake; even though we are not impelled to it by any inclination, nay, are even repelled by a natural and unconquerable aversion. This is *practical* love, and not *pathological*, a love which is seated in the will, and not in the propensions of sense, in principles of action and not of tender sympathy; and it is this love alone which can be commanded.

The second proposition[1] is: That an action done from duty derives its moral worth, *not from the purpose* which is to be attained by it, but from the maxim by which it is determined, and therefore does not depend on the realization of the object of the action, but merely on the *principle of volition* by which the action has taken place, without regard to any object of desire. It is clear from what precedes that the purposes which we may have in view in our actions, or their effects regarded as ends and springs of the will, cannot give to actions any unconditional or moral worth. In what then can their worth lie, if it is not to consist in the will and in reference to its expected effect? It cannot lie anywhere but in the *principle of the will* without regard to the ends which can be attained by the action. For the will stands between its *a priori* principle which is formal, and its *a posteriori* spring which is material, as between two roads, and as it must be determined by something, it follows that it must be determined by the formal principle of volition when an action is done from duty, in which case every material principle has been withdrawn from it.

RESPECT FOR THE MORAL LAW

The third proposition, which is a consequence of the two preceding, I would express thus: *Duty is the necessity of acting from respect for the law*. I may have inclination for an object as the effect of my proposed action, but I cannot have respect for it, just for this reason, that it is an effect and not an energy of will. Similarly, I cannot have respect for inclination, whether my own or another's; I can at most if my own, approve it; if another's, sometimes even love it; i.e., look on it as favorable to my own interest. It is only what is connected with my will as a principle, by no means as an effect—what does not subserve my inclination, but overpowers it, or at least in case of choice excludes it from its calculation—in other words, simply the law of itself, which can be an object of respect, and hence a command. Now an action done from duty must wholly exclude the influence of inclination, and with it every object of the will, so that nothing remains which can determine the will except objectively the *law*, and subjectively *pure respect* for this practical law, and consequently the maxim[2] to follow this law even to the thwarting of all my inclinations.

Thus the moral worth of an action does not lie in the effect expected from it, nor in any principle of action which requires to borrow its motive from this expected effect. For all these effects—agreeableness of one's condition, and even the promotion of the happiness of others—could have been also brought about by other causes, so that for this there would have been no need of the will of a rational being; it is in this, however, alone that the supreme and unconditional good can be found. The preeminent good which we call moral can therefore consist in nothing else *than the conception of law* in itself, *which certainly is only possible in a rational being*, in so far as this conception, and not the expected effect, determines the will. This is a good which is already present in the person who acts accordingly, and we have not to wait for it to appear first in the result.[3]

THE CATEGORICAL IMPERATIVE

But what sort of law can that be, the conception of which must determine the will, even without paying any regard to the effect expected from it, in order that this will may be called good absolutely and without qualification? As I have deprived the will of every impulse which could arise to it from obedience to any law, there remains nothing but the universal conformity of its actions to law in general, which alone is to serve the will as a principle, i.e., *I am never to act otherwise than so that I could also will*

that my maxim should become a universal law. Here now, it is the simple conformity to law in general, without assuming any particular law applicable to certain actions, that serves the will as its principle, and must so serve it, if duty is not to be a vain delusion and a chimerical notion. The common reason of men in its practical judgments perfectly coincides with this, and always has in view the principle here suggested. Let the question be, for example: May I when in distress make a promise with the intention not to keep it? I readily distinguish here between the two significations which the question may have: Whether it is prudent, or whether it is right, to make a false promise. The former may undoubtedly often be the case. I see clearly indeed that it is not enough to extricate myself from a present difficulty by means of this subterfuge, but it must be well considered whether there may not hereafter spring from this lie much greater inconvenience than that from which I now free myself, and as, with all my supposed cunning, the consequences cannot be so easily foreseen but that credit once lost may be much more injurious to me than any mischief which I seek to avoid at present, it should be considered whether it would not be more prudent to act herein according to a universal maxim, and to make it a habit to promise nothing except with the intention of keeping it. But it is soon clear to me that such a maxim will still only be based on the fear of consequences. Now it is a wholly different thing to be truthful from duty, and to be so from apprehension of injurious consequences. In the first case, the very notion of the action already implies a law for me; in the second case, I must first look about elsewhere to see what results may be combined with it which would affect myself. For to deviate from the principle of duty is beyond all doubt wicked; but to be unfaithful to my maxim of prudence may often be very advantageous to me, although to abide by it is certainly safer. The shortest way, however, and an unerring one, to discover the answer to this question whether a lying promise is consistent with duty, is to ask myself, Should I be content that my maxim (to extricate myself from difficulty by a false promise) should hold good as a universal law, for myself as well as for others? and should I be able to say to myself, "Every one may make a deceitful promise when he finds himself in a difficulty from which he cannot otherwise extricate himself"? Then I presently become aware that while I can will the lie, I can by no means will that lying should be a universal law. For with such a law there would be no promises at all, since it would be in vain to allege my intention in regard to my future actions to those who would not believe this allegation, or if they over hastily did so would pay me back in my own coin. Hence my maxim, as soon as it should be made a universal law, would necessarily destroy itself.

I do not therefore need any far-reaching penetration to discern what I have to do in order that my will may be morally good. Inexperienced in the course of the world, incapable of being prepared for all its contingencies, I only ask myself: Canst thou also will that thy maxim should be a universal law? If not, then it must be rejected, and that not because of a disadvantage accruing from it to myself or even to others, but because it cannot enter as a principle into a possible universal legislation, and reason extorts from me immediate respect for such legislation. I do not indeed as yet discern on what this respect is based (this the philosopher may inquire), but at least I understand this, that it is an estimation of the worth which far outweighs all worth of what is recommended by inclination, and that the necessity of acting from pure respect for the practical law is what constitutes duty, to which every other motive must give place, because it is the condition of a will being good in itself, and the worth of such a will is above everything.

Thus then, without quitting the moral knowledge of common human reason, we have arrived at its principle. And although no doubt common men do not conceive it in such an abstract and universal form, yet they always have it really before their eyes, and use it as the standard of their decision. . . .

MORAL AND NONMORAL IMPERATIVES

Everything in nature works according to laws. Rational beings alone have the faculty of acting according *to the conception of laws*, that is according to principles, i.e., have a will. Since the deduction of actions from principles requires *reason*, the will is nothing but practical reason. If reason infallibly determines the will, then the actions of such a

being which are recognised as objectively necessary are subjectively necessary also; i.e., the will is a faculty to choose *that only* which reason independent on inclination recognises as practically necessary, i.e., as good. But if reason of itself does not sufficiently determine the will, if the latter is subject also to subjective conditions (particular impulses) which do not always coincide with the objective conditions; in a word, if the will does not in itself completely accord with reason (which is actually the case with men), then the actions which objectively are recognised as necessary are subjectively contingent, and the determination of such a will according to objective laws is obligation, that is to say, the relation of the objective laws to a will that is not thoroughly good, is conceived as the determination of the will of a rational being by principles of reason, but which the will from its nature does not of necessity follow.

The conception of an objective principle, in so far as it is obligatory for a will, is called a command (of reason), and the formula of the command is called an Imperative.

All imperatives are expressed by the word *ought* [or *shall*], and thereby indicate the relation of an objective law of reason to a will, which from its subjective constitution is not necessarily determined by it (an obligation). They say that something would be good to do or to forbear, but they say it to a will which does not always do a thing because it is conceived to be good to do it. That is practically *good*, however, which determines the will by means of the conceptions of reason, and consequently not from subjective causes, but objectively, that is, on principles which are valid for every rational being as such. It is distinguished from the *pleasant*, as that which influences the will only by means of sensation from merely subjective causes, valid only for the sense of this or that one, and not as a principle of reason, which holds for every one.[4]

A perfectly good will would therefore be equally subject to objective laws (viz., of good), but could not be conceived as *obliged* thereby to act lawfully, because of itself from its subjective constitution it can only be determined by the conception of good. Therefore no imperatives hold for the Divine will, or in general for a *holy* will; *ought* is here out of place, because the volition is already of itself necessarily in unison with the law. Therefore imperatives are only formulae to express the relation of objective laws of all volition to the subjective imperfection of the will of this or that rational being, e.g., the human will.

Now all imperatives command either *hypothetically* or *categorically*. The former represent the practical necessity of a possible action as means to something else that is willed (or at least which one might possibly will). The categorical imperative would be that which represented an action as necessary of itself without reference to another end, that is, as objectively necessary.

Since every practical law represents a possible action as good, and on this account, for a subject who is practically determinable by reason as necessary, all imperatives are formulae determining an action which is necessary according to the principle of a will good in some respects. If now the action is good only as a *means to something else*, then the imperative is *hypothetical*; if it is conceived as good in itself and consequently as being necessarily the principle of a will which of itself conforms to reason, then it is *categorical*.

Thus the imperative declares what action possible by me would be good, and presents the practical rule in relation to a will which does not forthwith perform an action simply because it is good, whether because the subject does not always know that it is good, or because, even if it know this, yet its maxims might be opposed to the objective principles of practical reason.

Accordingly the hypothetical imperative only says that the action is good for some purpose, *possible* or *actual*. In the first case it is a *problematical*, in the second an *assertorical* practical principle. The categorical imperative which declares an action to be objectively necessary in itself without reference to any purpose, that is, without any other end, is valid as an *apodictic* (practical) principle.

Whatever is possible only by the power of some rational being may also be conceived as a possible purpose of some will; and therefore the principles of action as regards the means necessary to attain some possible purpose are in fact infinitely numerous. All sciences have a practical part consisting of problems expressing that some end is possible for us, and of imperatives directing how it may be attained.

These may, therefore, be called in general imperatives of skill. Here there is no question whether the end is rational and good, but only what one must do in order to attain it. The precepts for the physician to make his patient thoroughly healthy, and for a poisoner to ensure certain death, are of equal value in this respect, that each serves to effect its purpose perfectly. Since in early youth it cannot be known what ends are likely to occur to us in the course of life, parents seek to have their children taught a *great many things*, and provide for their skill in the use of means for all sorts of arbitrary ends, of none of which can they determine whether it may not perhaps hereafter be an object to their pupil, but which it is at all events possible that he might aim at; and this anxiety is so great that they commonly neglect to form and correct their judgment on the value of the things which may be chosen as ends.

There is *one* end, however, which may be assumed to be actually such to all rational beings (so far as imperatives apply to them, viz., as dependent beings), and, therefore, one purpose which they not merely may have, but which we may with certainty assume that they all actually have by a natural necessity, and this is *happiness*. The hypothetical imperative which expresses the practical necessity of an action as means to the advancement of happiness is *assertorical*. We are not to present it as necessary for an uncertain and merely possible purpose, but for a purpose which we may presuppose with certainty and *a priori* in every man, because it belongs to his being. Now skill in the choice of means to his own greatest well-being may be called *prudence*,[5] in the narrowest sense. And thus the imperative which refers to the choice of means to one's own happiness, that is, the precept of prudence, is still always *hypothetical*; the action is not commanded absolutely, but only as means to another purpose.

Finally, there is an imperative which commands a certain conduct immediately, without having as its condition any other purpose to be attained by it. This imperative is *categorical*. It concerns not the matter of the action, or its intended result, but its form and the principle of which it is itself a result; and what is essentially good in it consists in the mental disposition, let the consequence be what it may. This imperative may be called that of *morality*.

There is a marked distinction also between the volitions on these three sorts of principles in the dissimilarity of the obligation of the will. In order to mark this difference more clearly, I think they would be most suitably named in their order if we said they are either *rules* of skill, or *counsels* of prudence, or *commands* (laws) of morality. For it is law only that involves the conception of an unconditional and objective necessity, which is consequently universally valid; and commands are laws which must be obeyed, that is, must be followed, even in opposition to inclination. Counsels, indeed, involve necessity, but one which can only hold under a contingent subjective condition, viz., they depend on whether this or that man reckons this or that as part of his happiness; the categorical imperative, on the contrary, is not limited by any condition, and as being absolutely, although practically, necessary may be quite properly called a command. We might also call the first kind of imperatives *technical* (belonging to art), the second *pragmatic*[6] (belonging to welfare), the third moral (belonging to free conduct generally, that is, to morals).

Now arises the question, how are all these imperatives possible? This question does not seek to know how we can conceive the accomplishment of the action which the imperative ordains, but merely how we can conceive the obligation of the will which the imperative expresses. No special explanation is needed to show how an imperative of skill is possible. Whoever wills the end wills also (so far as reason decides his conduct) the means in his power which are indispensably necessary thereto. . . .

We shall therefore have to investigate *a priori* the possibility of a categorical imperative, as we have not in this case the advantage of its reality being given in experience, so that [the elucidation of] its possibility should be requisite only for its explanation, not for its establishment. In the meantime it may be discerned beforehand that the categorical imperative alone has the purport of a practical law; all the rest may indeed be called principles of the will but not laws, since whatever is only necessary for the attainment of some arbitrary purpose may be considered as in itself contingent, and we can at any time be free from the precept if we give up the purpose; on the contrary, the unconditional command

leaves the will no liberty to choose the opposite, consequently it alone carries with it that necessity which we require in a law. . . .

In this problem we will first inquire whether the mere conception of a categorical imperative may not perhaps supply us also with the formula of it, containing the proposition which alone can be a categorical imperative; for even if we know the tenor of such an absolute command, yet how it is possible will require further special and laborious study; which we postpone to the last section.

When I conceive a hypothetical imperative in general, I do not know before hand what it will contain, until I am given the condition. But when I conceive a categorical imperative I know at once what it contains. For as the imperative contains, besides the law, only the necessity of the maxim[7] conforming to this law, while the law contains no condition restricting it, there remains nothing but the general statement that the maxim of the action should conform to a universal law, and it is this conformity alone that the imperative properly represents as necessary.

There is therefore but one categorical imperative, namely this: *Act only on that maxim whereby thou canst at the same time will that it should become a universal law.*

Now if all imperatives of duty can be deduced from this one imperative as from their principle, then although it should remain undecided whether what is called duty is not merely a vain notion, yet at least we shall be able to show what we understand by it and what this notion means.

APPLYING THE CATEGORICAL IMPERATIVE

Since the universality of the law according to which effects are produced constitutes what is properly called *nature* in the most general sense (as to form), that is the existence of things so far as it is determined by general laws, the imperative of duty may be expressed thus: *Act as if the maxim of thy action were to become by thy will a Universal Law of Nature.*

We will now enumerate a few duties, adopting the usual division of them into duties to ourselves and to others, and into perfect and imperfect duties.[8]

1. A man reduced to despair by a series of misfortunes feels wearied of life, but is still so far in

possession of his reason that he can ask himself whether it would not be contrary to his duty to himself to take his own life. Now he inquires whether the maxim of his action could become a universal law of nature. His maxim is: From self-love I adopt it as a principle to shorten my life when its longer duration is likely to bring more evil than satisfaction. It is asked then simply whether this principle of self-love can become a universal law of nature. Now we see at once that a system of nature of which it should be a law to destroy life by the very feeling which is designed to impel to the maintenance of life would contradict itself, and therefore could not exist as a system of nature; hence that maxim cannot possibly exist as a universal law of nature and consequently would be wholly inconsistent with the supreme principle of all duty.

2. Another finds himself forced by necessity to borrow money. He knows that he will not be able to repay it, but sees also that nothing will be lent to him, unless he promises stoutly to repay it in a definite time. He desires to make this promise, but he has still so much conscience as to ask himself: Is it not unlawful and inconsistent with duty to get out of a difficulty in this way? Suppose however that he resolves to do so: then the maxim of his action would be expressed thus: When I think myself in want of money, I will borrow money and promise to repay it, although I know that I never can do so. Now this principle of self-love or of one's own advantage may perhaps be consistent with my whole future welfare; but the question now is, Is it right? I change then the suggestion of self-love into a universal law, and state the question thus: How would it be if my maxim were a universal law? Then I see at once that it could never hold as a universal law of nature, but would necessarily contradict itself. For supposing it to be a universal law that every one when he thinks himself in a difficulty should be able to promise whatever he pleases, with the purpose of not keeping his promise, the promise itself would become impossible, as well as the end that one might have in view in it, since no one would consider that anything was promised to him, and would ridicule all such statements as vain pretences.

3. A third finds in himself a talent which with the help of some culture might make him a useful man in many respects. But he finds himself in comfortable circumstances, and prefers to indulge in pleasure rather than to take pains in enlarging and improving his happy natural capacities. He asks, however, whether his maxim of neglect of his natural gifts, besides agreeing with his inclination to indulgence, agrees also with what is called duty. He sees then that a system of nature could indeed subsist with such a universal law, though men (like the South Sea islanders) should let their talents rust, and resolve to devote their lives merely to idleness, amusement, and propagation of their species, in a word to enjoyment; but he cannot possibly will that this should be a universal law of nature, or be implanted in us as such by a natural instinct. For, as a rational being, he necessarily wills that his faculties be developed, since they serve him for all sorts of possible purposes, and have been given him for this.

4. A fourth, who is in prosperity, while he sees that others have to contend with great wretchedness and that he could help them, thinks: What concern is it of mine? Let every one be as happy as heaven pleases or as he can make himself; I will take nothing from him nor even envy him, only I do not wish to contribute anything either to his welfare or to his assistance in distress! Now no doubt if such a mode of thinking were a universal law, the human race might very well subsist, and doubtless even better than in a state in which every one talks of sympathy and good will, or even takes care occasionally to put it into practice, but on the other side, also cheats when he can, betrays the rights of men or otherwise violates them. But although it is possible that a universal law of nature might exist in accordance with that maxim, it is impossible to will that such a principle should have the universal validity of a law of nature. For a will which resolved this would contradict itself, inasmuch as many cases might occur in which one would have need of the love and sympathy of others, and in which by such a law of nature, sprung from his own will, he would deprive himself of all hope of the aid he desires.

These are a few of the many actual duties, or at least what we regard as such, which obviously fall into two classes on the one principle that we have laid down. We must be *able to will* that a maxim of our action should be a universal law. This is the canon of the moral appreciation of the action generally. Some actions are of such a character, that their maxim cannot without contradiction be even *conceived* as a universal law of nature, far from it being possible that we should *will* that it should be so. In others this intrinsic impossibility is not found, but still it is impossible to *will* that their maxim should be raised to the universality of a law of nature, since such a will would contradict itself. It is easily seen that the former violate strict or rigorous (inflexible) duty; the latter only laxer (meritorious) duty. Thus it has been completely shown how all duties depend as regards the nature of the obligation (not the object of the action) on the same principle.

If now we attend to ourselves on occasion of any transgression of duty, we shall find that we in fact do not will that our maxim should be a universal law, for that it is impossible for us; on the contrary we will that the opposite should remain a universal law, only we assume the liberty of making an exception in our own favour or (just for this time only) in favour of our inclination. . . .

The will is conceived as a faculty of determining oneself to action *in accordance with the conception of certain laws*. And such a faculty can be found only in rational beings. Now that which serves the will as the objective ground of its self-determination is the *end*, and if this is assigned by reason alone, it must hold for all rational beings. On the other hand, that which merely contains the ground of possibility of the action of which the effect is the end, this is called the *means*. The subjective ground of the desire is the *spring*, the objective ground of the volition is the *motive*; hence the distinction between subjective ends which rest on springs, and objective ends which depend on motives that hold for every rational being. Practical principles are *formal* when they abstract from all subjective ends, they are *material* when they assume these, and therefore particular springs of action. The ends which a rational being proposes to himself at pleasure as *effects* of his actions (material ends) are all only relative, for it is only their relation to the particular desires of the subject that gives them their worth, which therefore cannot furnish principles universal and necessary for all rational beings and for every volition, that is to say practical

laws. Hence all these relative ends can give rise only to hypothetical imperatives.

PERSONS AS ENDS

Supposing, however, that there were something *whose existence has in itself* an absolute worth, something which being *an end in itself*, could be a source of definite laws, then in this and this alone would lie the source of a possible categorical imperative, i.e., a practical law. Now I say: man and generally any rational being exists as an end in himself, *not merely as a means* to be arbitrarily used by this or that will, but in all his actions, whether they concern himself or other rational beings, must always be regarded at the same time as an end. All objects of the inclinations have only a conditional worth, for if the inclinations and the wants founded on them did not exist, then their object would be without value. But the inclinations themselves being sources of want, are so far from having an absolute worth for which they should be desired, that on the contrary it must be the universal wish of every rational being to be wholly free from them. Thus the worth of any object which *is to be acquired* by our action is always conditional. Beings whose existence depends not on our will but on nature's, have nevertheless, if they are irrational beings, only a relative value as means, and are therefore called *things*; rational beings on the contrary, are called *persons*, because their very nature points them out as ends in themselves, that is as something which must not be used merely as means, and so far therefore restricts freedom of action (and is an object of respect). These, therefore, are not merely subjective ends whose existence has a worth for us as an effect of our action, but *objective ends*, that is things whose existence is an end in itself; an end moreover for which no other can be substituted, which they should subserve *merely* as means, for otherwise nothing whatever would possess *absolute worth*; but if all worth were conditioned and therefore contingent, then there would be no supreme practical principle of reason whatever.

If then there is a supreme practical principle or, in respect of the human will, a categorical imperative, it must be one which, drawn from the conception of that which is necessarily an end for every one because it is *an end in itself*, constitutes an objective principle of will, and can therefore serve as a universal practical law. The foundation of this principle is: *rational nature exists as an end in itself*. Man necessarily conceives his own existence as being so; so far then, this is a *subjective* principle of human actions. But every other rational being regards its existence similarly, just on the same rational principle that holds for me:[9] so that it is at the same time an objective principle, from which as a supreme practical law all laws of the will must be capable of being deduced. Accordingly the practical imperative will be as follows: *So act as to treat humanity, whether in thine own person or in that of any other, in every case as an end withal, never as a means only.* . . .

We will now inquire whether this can be practically carried out.

To abide by the previous examples:

First, under the head of necessary duty to oneself: He who contemplates suicide should ask himself whether his action can be consistent with the idea of humanity *as an end in itself*. If he destroys himself in order to escape from painful circumstances, he uses a person merely as a *means* to maintain a tolerable condition up to the end of life. But a man is not a thing, that is to say, something which can be used merely as means, but must in all his actions be always considered as an end in himself. I cannot, therefore, dispose in any way of a man in my own person so as to mutilate him, to damage or kill him. (It belongs to ethics proper to define this principle more precisely, so as to avoid all misunderstanding, for example, as to the amputation of the limbs in order to preserve myself; as to exposing my life to danger with a view to preserve it, etc. This question is therefore omitted here.)

Secondly, as regards necessary duties, or those of strict obligation, towards others: He who is thinking of making a lying promise to others will see at once that he would be using another *man merely as a means*, without the latter containing at the same time the end in himself. For he whom I propose by such a promise to use for my own purposes cannot possibly assent to my mode of acting towards him, and therefore cannot himself contain the end of this action. This violation of the principle of humanity in other men is more obvious if we take in examples of attacks on the freedom and property of others. For then it is clear that he who transgresses the rights of men intends to use the person of others merely as means, without considering that as rational beings they ought always to be esteemed also as ends, that is, as beings who must be capable of containing in themselves the end of the very same action.[10]

Thirdly, as regards contingent (meritorious) duties to oneself: It is not enough that the action does not violate humanity in our own person as an end in itself, it must also *harmonize with it*. . . . Now there are in humanity capacities of greater perfection which belong to the end that nature has in view in regard to humanity in ourselves as the subject; to neglect these might perhaps be consistent with the *maintenance* of humanity as an end in itself, but not with the advancement of this end.

Fourthly, as regards meritorious duties towards others: The natural end which all men have is their own happiness. Now humanity might indeed subsist although no one should contribute anything to the happiness of others, provided he did not intentionally withdraw anything from it; but after all, this would only harmonize negatively, not positively, with *humanity as an end in itself*, if everyone does not also endeavor, as far as in him lies, to forward the ends of others. For the ends of any subject which is an end in himself ought as far as possible to be my ends also, if that conception is to have its full effect with me.

NOTES[*]

1. The first proposition was that to have moral worth an action must be done from duty.

2. A *maxim* is the subjective principle of volition. The objective principle (*i.e.*, that which would also serve subjectively as a practical principle to all rational beings if reason had full power over the faculty of desire) is the practical *law*.

3. It might here be objected to me that I take refuge behind the word *respect* in an obscure feeling instead of giving a distinct solution of the question by a concept of the reason. But although respect is a feeling, it is not a feeling *received* through influence, but is *self-wrought* by a rational concept, and,

---

*Some notes have been deleted and the remaining ones renumbered.—ED.

therefore, is specially distinct from all feelings of the former kind, which may be referred either to inclination or fear. What I recognise immediately as a law for me, I recognise with respect. This merely signifies the consciousness that my will is *subordinate* to a law, without the intervention of other influences on my sense. The immediate determination of the will by the law, and the consciousness of this is called *respect*, so that this is regarded as an *effect* of the law on the subject, and not as the *cause* of it. Respect is properly the conception of a work which thwarts my self-love. Accordingly it is something which is considered neither as an object of inclination nor of fear, although it has something analogous to both. The *object* of respect is the *law* only, and that, the law which we impose on *ourselves*, and yet recognise as necessary in itself. As a law, we are subjected to it without consulting self-love; as imposed by us on ourselves, it is a result of our will. In the former respect it has an analogy to fear, in the latter to inclination. Respect for a person is properly only respect for the law (of honesty, & c.), of which he gives us an example. . . .

4. The dependence of the desires on sensations is called inclination, and this accordingly always indicates a *want*. The dependence of a contingently determinable will on principles of reason is called an *interest*. This, therefore, is found only in the case of a dependent will which does not always of itself conform to reason; in the Divine will we cannot conceive any interest. But the human will can also *take an interest* in a thing without therefore acting *from interest*. The former signifies the *practical* interest in the action, the latter the *pathological* in the object of the action. The former indicates only dependence of the will on principles of reason in themselves; the second, dependence on principles of reason for the sake of inclination, reason supplying only the practical rules how the requirement of the inclination may be satisfied. In the first case the action interests me; in the second the object of the action (because it is pleasant to me). We have seen in the first section that in an action done from duty we must look not to the interest in the object, but only to that in the action itself, and in its rational principle (viz., the law).

5. The word *prudence* is taken in two senses: in the one it may bear the name of knowledge of the world, in the other that of private prudence. The former is a man's ability to influence others so as to use them for his own purposes. The latter is the sagacity to combine all these purposes for his own lasting benefit. This latter is properly that to which the value even of the former is reduced, and when a man is prudent in the former sense, but not in the latter, we might better say of him that he is clever and cunning, but, on the whole, imprudent.

6. It seems to me that the proper signification of the word *pragmatic* may be most accurately defined in this way. For *sanctions* . . . are called pragmatic which flow properly, not from the law of the states as necessary enactments, but from *precaution* for the general welfare. A history is composed pragmatically when it teaches prudence, that is, instructs the world how it can provide for its interests better, or at least as well as the men of former time.

7. A MAXIM is a subjective principle of action . . . the principle on which the subject acts; but the law is the objective principle valid for every rational being, and is the principle on which it *ought to act* that is an imperative.

8. It must be noted here that I reserve the division of duties for a *future metaphysic of morals*; so that I give it here only as an arbitrary one (in order to arrange my examples). For the rest, I understand by a perfect duty, one that admits no exception in favour of inclination, and then I have not merely external but also internal perfect duties.

9. This proposition is here stated as a postulate. The ground of it will be found in the concluding section.

10. Let it not be thought that the common: *quod tibi non vis fieri, etc.*, could serve here as the rule or principle. For it is only a deduction from the former, though with several limitations; it cannot be a universal law, for it does not contain the principle of duties to oneself, nor of the duties of benevolence to others (for many a one would gladly consent that others should not benefit him, provided only that he might be excused from showing benevolence to them), nor finally that of duties of strict obligation to one another, for on this principle the criminal might argue against the judge who punishes him, and so on.

1. Give one of Kant's reasons for opposing the locating of an action's moral worth in its consequences.
2. Does Kant mean by "a good will" or "good intention" wishing others well? Explain.
3. What does Kant mean by "acting out of duty"? How does the shopkeeper exemplify this?
4. What is the basic difference between a categorical and a hypothetical imperative? In the following examples, which are hypothetical and which are categorical imperatives? Explain your answers.
   a. If you want others to be honest with you, then you ought to be honest with them.
   b. Whether or not you want to pay your share, you ought to do so.
   c. Because everyone wants to be happy, we ought to consider everyone's interests equally.
   d. I ought not to cheat on this test if I do not want to get caught.
5. How does the character of moral obligation lead to Kant's basic moral principle, the categorical imperative?
6. Explain Kant's use of the first form of the categorical imperative to argue that it is wrong to make a false promise. (Note that you do not appeal to the bad consequences as the basis of judging it wrong.)
7. According to the second form of Kant's categorical imperative, would it be morally permissible for me to agree to be someone's slave? Explain.
8. What is the practical difference between a perfect and an imperfect duty?

6

Contractarianism

THE VARIETY of theories going by the name of contractarianism or contractualism have in common the notion of a contract. In some cases a contract forms the basis of the political state. In others it is used to determine what justice requires. And in others, it forms the basis of morality itself.

One of the earliest versions of contractarianism is that given in the writings of Thomas Hobbes. Hobbes was a radical individualist; accordingly, he contended that individuals are prior to society.[1] Individuals are self interested; that is, they seek to fulfill their interests and desires and above all seek self-preservation. They exist in a "state of nature," however, where they are roughly equal to one another and "roughly similar in terms of strength and mental ability."[2] Conflict arises in cases where separate individuals seeks the same thing. One can try to gain it over the other through force. However, because they are similar in strength or wiles, this will be a problem. The individuals competing will thereby become enemies. Overall, then, the state of nature will be one of war, of all against all. As Hobbes describes it, they will each live "in continual fear and danger of violent death, and the life of man, solitary, poor, nasty, brutish, and short."[3] The solution is peace, in which one gives up so much liberty "as against other men, as he would allow other men against himself."[4] Hobbes says that such is a contract, an implicit agreement to give up certain things in order to better to secure one's own self-interest. Thus, individuals will agree to certain rules in society that would be in everyone's best interest to accept and obey. In order to secure

this peace and order and to see that these rules are obeyed, Hobbes also believed that an absolute sovereign was required. Many questions remain as to how

Title page of Thomas Hobbes's *Leviathan* 1651.

this sovereign is to be chosen and how permanent is to be the sovereign's position.

Hobbes' contractualism is based on a desire of each to achieve his own advantage while agreeing to social rules enforced by a sovereign; it is a view of how society should function and thus both a political and a moral position. Further, Hobbes' position is consonant with a form of utilitarian reasoning. Another major contractualist theory can be found in the works of John Rawls, whose views are treated in this text in chapter 14, "Economic Justice." Rawls' contentions are more closely related to Kantian ethics for they incorporate the notion of free and equal rational persons. Although Rawls' position is explained in more detail in that chapter, we will give a brief summary of it here. For Rawls, justice is fairness. How would we know if a distribution of goods in a society is fair? Some say if there is equal opportunity to obtain them, that is sufficient. Rawls does not believe that this is sufficient. Rather, he argues that to know if it is fair, we would need to ask what people would accept in a situation in which they were setting up principles to govern distribution in such a way that each would not know what position he or she would have in the society. Thus no one could bias distribution in their favor because they would not know who they would be. He calls this the original position. Thus it is a form of contractarianism, because it asks what people in the original position, equal and rational, would agree to.

A final version of contractarianism, more often called contractualism, is found in the work of T. M. Scanlon (which excerpted in this chapter). Scanlon writes, "An act is wrong if its performance under the circumstances would be disallowed by any system of rules for the general regulation of behavior which no one could reasonably reject as a basis for informed, unforced general agreement."[5] Scanlon attempts to explain the meaning of key terms in this definition. "Informed agreement" excludes false beliefs and superstition. The term "reasonably" is more difficult to explain, and some commentators assert that it is so vague that it amounts to a kind of intuition. Also, Scanlon's position is hypothetical, based on what people "would" agree to under certain conditions; further, it asks what no one could "reasonably reject" rather than a weaker "reasonably accept." This view is more Kantian in orientation, because it is based on equal and rational contractors. It is also the basis of a moral theory rather than a political one or a theory of justice. Examples in the reading should help clarify it for you.

This chapter is shorter than others we have included so far. As explained, one reason is that Rawls' views are treated in detail in chapter 14. The readings included here by Hobbes and Scanlon represent the two different versions of contractarianism (or contractualism) explained here.

NOTES

1. Jean Hampton, *Hobbes and the Social Contract Tradition* (Cambridge: Cambridge University Press, 1986), 6.
2. Ibid., 24.
3. Thomas Hobbes, "Leviathan," in *The English Works of Thomas Hobbes*, Vol. II, by Sir William Molesworth (London: John Bohn, 1839), pp. 38–41, 85.
4. Ibid., chapter 14.
5. T. M. Scanlon, "Contractarianism and Utilitarianism," *Utilitarianism and Beyond*, edited by Amartya Sen and Bernard Williams (New York: Cambridge University Press, 1981), II.

R E A D I N G
The Leviathan*
THOMAS HOBBES

Study Questions

1. How does Hobbes describe the equality of men (people)?
2. According to Hobbes, how do men become enemies?
3. What are the three principal causes of quarrel, according to Hobbes?
4. How does Hobbes describe "war" and thus the "life of man"?
5. According to Hobbes, what is necessary for there to be law?

*Title supplied by author.

6. According to Hobbes, why can there be no justice without a common power and law?
7. For Hobbes, what is a "law of nature"?
8. Why ought every man to "endeavor peace" according to Hobbes?
9. What must a man give up or renounce? Why?
10. What is a "contract"? What words express it?
11. What is required for people to keep their contracts?
12. What makes a commonwealth?

OF THE NATURAL CONDITION OF MANKIND AS CONCERNING THEIR FELICITY, AND MISERY

Nature hath made men so equal, in the faculties of body, and mind; as that though there be found one man sometimes manifestly stronger in body, or of quicker mind than another; yet when all is reckoned together, the difference between man, and man, is not so considerable, as that one man can thereupon claim to himself any benefit, to which another may not pretend, as well as he. For as to the strength of body, the weakest has strength enough to kill the strongest, either by secret machination, or by confederacy with others, that are in the same danger with himself.

And as to the faculties of the mind, setting aside the arts grounded upon words, and especially that skill of proceeding upon general, and infallible rules, called science; which very few have, and but in few things; as being not a native faculty, born with us; nor attained, as prudence, while we look after somewhat else, I find yet a greater equality amongst men, than that of strength. For prudence, is but experience; which equal time, equally bestows on all men, in those things they equally apply themselves unto. That which may perhaps make such equality incredible, is but a vain conceit of one's own wisdom, which almost all men think they have in a greater degree, than the vulgar; that is, than all men but themselves, and a few others, whom by fame, or for concurring with themselves, they approve. For such is the nature of men, that howsoever they may acknowledge many others to be more witty, or more eloquent, or more learned; yet they will hardly believe there be many so wise as themselves; for they see their own wit at

hand, and other men's at a distance. But this proveth rather that men are in that point equal, than unequal. For there is not ordinarily a greater sign of the equal distribution of any thing, than that every man is contented with his share.

From this equality of ability, ariseth equality of hope in the attaining of our ends. And therefore if any two men desire the same thing, which nevertheless they cannot both enjoy, they become enemies; and in the way to their end, which is principally their own conservation, and sometimes their delectation only, endeavour to destroy, or subdue one another. And from hence it comes to pass, that where an invader hath no more to fear, than another man's single power; if one plant, sow, build, or possess a convenient seat, others may probably be expected to come prepared with forces united, to dispossess, and deprive him, not only of the fruit of his labour, but also of his life, or liberty. And the invader again is in the like danger of another.

And from this diffidence of one another, there is no way for any man to secure himself, so reasonable, as anticipation; that is, by force, or wiles, to master the persons of all men he can, so long, till he see no other power great enough to endanger him: and this is no more than his own conservation requireth, and is generally allowed. Also because there be some, that taking pleasure in contemplating their own power in the acts of conquest, which they pursue farther than their security requires; if others, that otherwise would be glad to be at ease within modest bounds, should not by invasion increase their power, they would not be able, long time, by standing only on their defence, to subsist. And by consequence, such augmentation of dominion over men being necessary to a man's conservation, it ought to be allowed him.

Again, men have no pleasure, but on the contrary a great deal of grief, in keeping company, where there is no power able to over-awe them all. For every man looketh that his companion should value him, at the same rate he sets upon himself: and upon all signs of contempt, or undervaluing, naturally endeavours, as far as he dares (which amongst them that have no common power to keep them in quiet, is far enough to make them destroy each other), to extort a greater value from his condemners, by damage; and from others, by the example. So that in the nature of man,

Thomas Hobbes, "Leviathan," in *The English Works of Thomas Hobbes*, Vol. II, by Sir William Molesworth (London: John Bohn, 1839), pp. 38–41, 85.

we find three principal causes of quarrel. First, competition; secondly, diffidence; thirdly, glory.

The first maketh men invade for gain; the second, for safety; and the third, for reputation. The first use violence, to make themselves masters of other men's persons, wives, children, and cattle; the second, to defend them; the third, for trifles, as a word, a smile, a different opinion, and any other sign of undervalue, either direct in their persons, or by reflection in their kindred, their friends, their nation, their profession, or their name.

Hereby it is manifest, that during the time men live without a common power to keep them all in awe, they are in that condition which is called war; and such a war, as is of every man, against every man. For WAR, consisteth not in battle only, or the act of fighting; but in a tract of time, wherein the will to contend by battle is sufficiently known: and therefore the notion of *time*, is to be considered in the nature of war, as it is in the nature of weather. For as the nature of foul weather, lieth not in a shower or two of rain; but in an inclination thereto of many days together: so the nature of war, consisteth not in actual fighting; but in the known disposition thereto, during all the time there is no assurance to the contrary. All other time is PEACE.

Whatsoever therefore is consequent to a time of war, where every man is enemy to every man; the same consequent to the time, wherein men live without other security, than what their own strength, and their own invention shall furnish them withal. In such condition, there is no place for industry; because the fruit thereof is uncertain: and consequently no culture of the earth; no navigation, nor use of the commodities that may be imported by sea; no commodious building; no instruments of moving, and removing, such things as require much force; no knowledge of the face of the earth; no account of time; no arts; no letters; no society; and which is worst of all, continual fear, and danger of violent death; and the life of man, solitary, poor, nasty, brutish, and short.

It may seem strange to some man, that has not well weighed these things; that nature should thus dissociate, and render men apt to invade, and destroy one another: and he may therefore, not trusting to this inference, made from the passions, desire perhaps to have the same confirmed by experience. Let him therefore consider with himself, when taking a journey, he arms himself, and seeks to go well accompanied; when going to sleep, he locks his doors; when even in his house he locks his chests; and this when he knows there be laws, and public officers, armed, to revenge all injuries shall be done him; what opinion he has of his fellow-subjects, when he rides armed; of his fellow citizens, when he locks his doors; and of his children, and servants, when he locks his chests. Does he not there as much accuse mankind by his actions, as I do by my words? But neither of us accuse man's nature in it. The desires, and other passions of man, are in themselves no sin. No more are the actions, that proceed from those passions, till they know a law that forbids them: which till laws be made they cannot know: nor can any law be made, till they have agreed upon the person that shall make it.

It may peradventure be thought, there was never such a time, nor condition of war as this; and I believe it was never generally so, over all the world: but there are many places, where they live so now. For the savage people in many places of America, except the government of small families, the concord whereof dependeth on natural lust, have no government at all; and live at this day in that brutish manner, as I said before. Howsoever, it may be perceived what manner of life there would be, where there were no common power to fear, by the manner of life, which men that have formerly lived under a peaceful government, use to degenerate into, in a civil war.

But though there had never been any time, wherein particular men were in a condition of war one against another; yet in all times, kings and persons of sovereign authority, because of their independency, are in continual jealousies, and in the state and posture of gladiators; having their weapons pointing, and their eyes fixed on one another; that is, their forts, garrisons, and guns upon the frontiers of their kingdoms; and continual spies upon their neighbours; which is a posture of war. But because they uphold thereby, the industry of their subjects, there does not follow from it, that misery, which accompanies the liberty of particular men.

To this war of every man, against every man, this also is consequent; that nothing can be unjust. The notions of right and wrong, justice and injustice have there no place. Where there is no common power, there is no law: where no law, no injustice. Force, and fraud, are in war the two cardinal virtues. Justice, and injustice are none of the faculties neither of the body, nor mind. If they were, they might be in a man that were alone in the world, as well as his senses, and passions. They are qualities, that relate to men in society, not in solitude. It is consequent also to the same condition, that there be no propriety, no dominion, no *mine* and *thine* distinct; but only that to be every man's, that he can get; and for so long, as he can keep it. And thus much for the ill condition, which man by mere nature is actually placed in; though with a possibility to come out of it, consisting partly in the passions, partly in his reason.

The passions that incline men to peace, are fear of death; desire of such things as are necessary to commodious living; and a hope by their industry to obtain them. And reason suggesteth convenient articles of peace, upon which men may be drawn to agreement. These articles, are they, which otherwise are called the Laws of Nature: whereof I shall speak more particularly, in the two following chapters.

OF THE FIRST AND SECOND NATURAL LAWS, AND OF CONTRACTS

The right of nature, which writers commonly call *jus naturale*, is the liberty each man hath, to use his own power, as he will himself, for the preservation of his own nature; that is to say, of his own life; and consequently, of doing anything, which in his own judgment, and reason, he shall conceive to be the aptest means thereunto.

By LIBERTY, is understood, according to the proper signification of the word, the absence of external impediments: which impediments, may oft take away part of a man's power to do what he would; but cannot hinder him from using the power left him, according as his judgment, and reason shall dictate to him.

A LAW OF NATURE, *lex naturalis*, is a precept or general rule, found out by reason, by which a man is forbidden to do that, which is destructive of his life, or taketh away the means of preserving the same; and to omit that, by which he thinketh it may be

best preserved. For though they that speak of this subject, use to confound *jus*, and *lex*, *right* and *law*: yet they ought to be distinguished; because RIGHT, consisteth in liberty to do, or to forbear; whereas LAW determineth, and bindeth to one of them: so that law, and right, differ as much, as obligation, and liberty, which in one and the same matter are inconsistent.

And because the condition of man, as hath been declared in the precedent chapter, is a condition of war of every one against every one; in which case every one is governed by his own reason; and there is nothing he can make use of, that may not be a help unto him, in preserving his life against his enemies; it followeth, that in such a condition, every man has a right to every thing; even to one another's body. And therefore, as long as this natural right of every man to every thing endureth, there can be no security to any man, how strong or wise soever he be, of living out the time, which nature ordinarily alloweth men to live. And consequently it is a precept, or general rule of reason, *that every man, ought to endeavour peace, as far as he has hope of obtaining it; and when he cannot obtain it, that he may seek, and use, all helps, and advantages of war*. The first branch of which rule, containeth the first, and fundamental law of nature; which is, *to seek peace, and follow it*. The second, the sum of the right of nature; which is, *by all means we can, to defend ourselves*.

From this fundamental law of nature, by which men are commanded to endeavour peace, is derived this second law; *that a man be willing, when others are so too, as far-forth, as for peace, and defence of himself he shall think it necessary, to lay down this right to all things; and be contented with so much liberty against other men, as he would allow other men against himself*. For as long as every man holdeth this right, of doing anything he liketh; so long are all men in the condition of war. But if other men will not lay down their right, as well as he; then there is no reason for anyone, to divest himself of his: for that were to expose himself to prey, which no man is bound to, rather than to dispose himself to peace. This is that law of the Gospel; *whatsoever you require that others should do to you, that do ye to them*. And that law of all men, *quod tibi fieri non vis, alteri ne feceris*.

To lay down a man's *right* to any thing, is to divest himself of the *liberty*, of hindering another of the benefit of his own right to the same. For he that renounceth, or passeth away his right, giveth not to any other man a right which he had not before; because there is nothing to which every man had not right by nature: but only standeth out of his way, that he may enjoy his own original right, without hindrance from him; not without hindrance from another. So that the effect which redoundeth to one man, by another man's defect of right, is but so much diminution of impediments to the use of his own right original.

Right is laid aside, either by simply renouncing it; or by transferring it to another. By *simply* RENOUNCING; when he cares not to whom the benefit thereof redoundeth. By transferring, when he intendeth the benefit thereof to some certain person, or persons. And when a man hath in either manner abandoned, or granted away his right; then is he said to be OBLIGED, or BOUND, not to hinder those, to whom such right is granted, or abandoned, from the benefit of it: and that he *ought*, and it is duty, not to make void that voluntary act of his own: and that such hindrance is INJUSTICE, and INJURY, as being *sine jure*. The right being before renounced, or transferred. So that *injury*, or *injustice*, in the controversies of the world, is somewhat like to that, which in the disputations of scholars is called *absurdity*. For as it is there called an absurdity, to contradict what one maintained in the beginning: so in the world, it is called injustice, and injury, voluntarily to undo that, which from the beginning he had voluntarily done. The way by which a man either simply renounceth, or transferreth his right, is a declaration, or signification, by some voluntary and sufficient sign, or signs, that he doth so renounce, or transfer; or hath so renounced, or transferred the same, to him that accepteth it. And these signs are either words only, or actions only; or, as it happeneth most often, both words, and actions. And the same are the BONDS, by which men are bound, and obliged: bonds that have their strength, not from their own nature, for nothing is more easily broken than a man's word, but from fear of some evil consequence upon the rupture.

Whensoever a man transferreth his right, or renounceth it; it is either in consideration of some right reciprocally transferred to himself; or for some other good he hopeth for thereby. For it is a voluntary act: and of the voluntary acts of every man, the object is some *good to himself*. And therefore there be some rights, which no man can be understood by any words, or other signs, to have abandoned, or transferred. At first a man cannot lay down the right of resisting them, that assault him by force, to take away his life; because he cannot be understood to aim thereby, at any good to himself. The same may be said of wounds, and chains, and imprisonment; both because there is no benefit consequent to such patience; as there is to the patience of suffering another to be wounded, or imprisoned: as also because a man cannot tell, when he seeth men proceed against him by violence, whether they intend his death or not. And lastly the motive, and end for which this renouncing, and transferring of right is introduced, is nothing else but the security of a man's person, in his life, and in the means of so preserving life, as not to be weary of it. And therefore if a man by words, or other signs, seem to despoil himself of the end, for which those signs were intended; he is not to be understood as if he meant it, or that it was his will; but that he was ignorant of how such words and actions were to be interpreted.

The mutual transferring of right, is that which men call CONTRACT.

There is difference between transferring of right to the thing; and transferring, or tradition, that is delivery of the thing itself. For the thing may be delivered together with the translation of the right; as in buying and selling with ready money; or exchange of goods, or lands; and it may be delivered some time after.

Again, one of the contractors, may deliver the thing contracted for on his part, and leave the other to perform his part at some determinate time after, and in the meantime be trusted; and then the contract on his part is called PACT, or COVENANT: or both parts may contract now, to perform hereafter: in which cases, he that is to perform in time to come, being trusted, his performance is called *keeping of promise*, or faith; and the failing of performance, if it be voluntary, *violation of faith*.

When the transferring of right, is not mutual; but one of the parties transferreth in hope to gain thereby friendship, or service from another, or from his friends; or in hope to gain the reputation of charity, or magnanimity; or to deliver his mind from the pain of compassion; or in hope of reward in heaven; this is not contract, but GIFT, FREE-GIFT, GRACE: which words signify one and the same thing.

Signs of contract, are either *express*, or by *inference*. Express, are words spoken with understanding of what they signify: and such words are either of the time *present* or *past*; as, *I give, I grant, I have given, I have granted, I will that this be yours*: or of the future; as, *I will give, I will grant*: which words of the future are called PROMISE. . .

If a covenant be made, wherein neither of the parties perform presently, but trust one another; in the condition of mere nature, which is a condition of war of every man against every man, upon any reasonable suspicion, it is void: but if there be a common power set over them both, with right and force sufficient to compel performance, it is not void. For he that performeth first, has no assurance the other will perform after; because the bonds of words are too weak to bridle men's ambition, avarice, anger, and other passions, without the fear of some coercive power; which in the condition of mere nature, where all men are equal, and judges of the justness of their own fears, cannot possibly be supposed. And therefore he which performeth first, does but betray himself to his enemy; contrary to the right, he can never abandon, of defending his life; and means of living.

But in a civil estate, where there a power set up to constrain those that would otherwise violate their faith, that fear is no more reasonable: and for that cause, he which by the covenant is to perform first, is obliged so to do.

The cause of fear, which maketh such a covenant invalid, must be always something arising after the covenant made; as some new fact, or other sign of the will not to perform: else it cannot make the covenant void. For that which could not hinder a man from promising, ought not to be admitted as a hindrance of performing. . .

The only way to erect such a common power, as may be able to defend them from the invasion of foreigners, and the injuries of one another, and thereby to secure them in such sort, as that by their own industry, and by the fruits of the earth, they may nourish themselves and live contentedly; is, to confer all their power and strength upon one man, or upon one assembly of men, that may reduce all their wills, by plurality of voices, unto one will: which is as much as to say, to appoint one man, or assembly of men, to bear their person; and every one to own, and acknowledge himself to be author of whatsoever he that so beareth their person, shall act, or cause to be acted, in those things which concern the common peace and safety; and therein to submit their wills, every one to his will, and their judgments, to his judgment. This is more than consent, or concord; it is a real unity of them all, in one and the same person, made by covenant of every man with every man, in such manner as if every man should say to every man, *I authorize and give up my right of governing myself, to this man, or to this assembly of men, on this condition, that thou give up thy right to him, and authorize all his actions in like manner*. This done, the multitude so united in one person, is called a COMMONWEALTH; in Latin CIVITAS. This is the generation of that great LEVIATHAN, or rather, to speak more reverently, of that *mortal god*, to which we owe under the *immortal God*, our peace and defence. For by this authority, given him by every particular man in the commonwealth, he hath the use of so much power and strength conferred on him, that by terror thereof, he is enabled to perform the wills of them all, to peace at home, and mutual aid against their enemies abroad. And in him consisteth the essence of the commonwealth; which, to define it, *is one person, of whose acts a great multitude, by mutual covenants one with another, have made themselves every one the author, to the end he may use the strength and means of them, all as he shall think expedient, for their peace and common defence.*

R E A D I N G
Contractualism and Utilitarianism

T. M. SCANLON

Study Questions

1. According to Scanlon, do people generally hold utilitarian views?
2. How does Scanlon describe utilitarian thinking?
3. What is his contractualist account of moral reasoning?
4. How does he seek to clarify the meaning of this account?
5. In what sense is Scanlon's account hypothetical?
6. Why does he use the reasonableness of rejecting some principles rather than accepting them?
7. How do conventions fit into his account?
8. To whom does the scope of morality apply, according to Scanlon? What is required of such beings? How is this different from being a trustee?
9. How does the capacity to feel pain count, according to Scanlon?

UTILITARIANISM OCCUPIES a central place in the moral philosophy of our time. It is not the view which most people hold; certainly there are very few who would claim to be act utilitarians. But for a much wider range of people it is the view towards which they find themselves pressed when they try to give a theoretical account of their moral beliefs. Within moral philosophy it represents a position one must struggle against if one wishes to avoid it. This is so in spite of the fact that the implications of act utilitarianism are wildly at variance with firmly held moral convictions, while rule utilitarianism, the most common alternative formulation, strikes most people as an unstable compromise.

The wide appeal of utilitarianism is due, I think, to philosophical considerations of a more or less sophisticated kind which pull us in a quite different direction than our first order moral beliefs. In particular, utilitarianism derives much of its appeal from alleged difficulties about the foundations of rival

views. What a successful alternative to utilitarianism must do, first and foremost, is to sap this source of strength by providing a clear account of the foundations of non-utilitarian moral reasoning. In what follows I will first describe the problem in more detail by setting out the questions which a philosophical account of the foundations of morality must answer. I will then put forward a version of contractualism which, I will argue, offers a better set of responses to these questions than that supplied by straightforward versions of utilitarianism. Finally I will explain why contractualism, as I understand it, does not lead back to some utilitarian formula as its normative outcome.

Contractualism has been proposed as the alternative to utilitarianism before, notably by John Rawls in *A Theory of Justice* (Rawls 1971). Despite the wide discussion which this book has received, however, I think that the appeal of contractualism as a foundational view has been underrated. In particular, it has not been sufficiently appreciated that contractualism offers a particularly plausible account of moral motivation. The version of contractualism that I shall present differs from Rawls' in a number of respects. In particular, it makes no use, or only a different and more limited kind of use, of his notion of choice from behind a veil of ignorance. One result of this difference is to make the contrast between contractualism and utilitarianism stand out more clearly. . .

I.

If philosophical utilitarianism is accepted then some form of utilitarianism appears to be forced upon us as a normative doctrine, but further argument is required to determine which form we should accept. If all that counts morally is the well-being of individuals, no one of whom is singled out as counting for more than the other, and if all that matters in the

T. M. Scanlon, "Contractualism and Utilitarianism" from *Utilitarianism and Beyond*, edited by Amartya Sen and Bernard Williams (New York: Cambridge University Press, 1981). Reprinted with permission of Cambridge University Press.

case each individual is the degree to which his or her well-being I affected, then it would seem to follow that the basis of moral appraisal is the goal of maximizing the *sum*[1] of individual well-being. Whether this standard is to applied to the criticism of individual action, or to the selection of rules or polices, or to the inculcation of habits and dispositions to act is a further question, as is the quest of how "well-being" itself is to be understood. Thus the hypothesis that much of the appeal of utilitarianism as a normative doctrine derives from the attractiveness of philosophical utilitarianism explains how people can be convinced that some form of utilitarianism must be correct while yet being quite uncertain as to which form it is, whether it is "direct" or "act" utilitarianism or some form of indirect "rule" or "motive" utilitarianism. What these views have in common, despite their differing normative consequences, is the identification of the same class of fundamental moral facts.

II.

If what I have said about the appeal of utilitarianism is correct, then what a rival theory must do is to provide an alternative to philosophical utilitarianism as a conception of the subject matter of morality. This is what the theory which I shall call contractualism seeks to do. Even if it succeeds in this, however, and is judged superior to philosophical utilitarianism as an account of the nature of morality, normative utilitarianism will not have been refuted. The possibility will remain that normative utilitarianism can be established on other grounds, for example as the normative outcome of contractualism itself. But one direct and, I think, influential argument for normative utilitarianism will have been set aside.

To give an example of what I mean by contractualism, a contractualist account of the nature of moral wrongness might be stated as follows.

> An act is wrong if its performance under the circumstances would be disallowed by any system of rules for the general regulation of behavior which no one could reasonably reject as a basis for informed, unforced general agreement

This is intended as a characterization of the kind of property which moral wrongness is. Like philosophical utilitarianism, it will have normative consequences, but it is not my present purpose to explore these in detail. As a contractualist account of one moral notion, what I have set out here is only an approximation, which may need to he modified considerably. Here I can offer a few remarks by way of clarification.

The idea of "informed agreement" is meant to exclude agreement based on superstition or false belief about the consequences of actions, even if these beliefs are ones which it would be reasonable for the person in question to have. The intended force of the qualification "reasonably," on the other hand, is to exclude rejections that would be unreasonable *given* the aim of finding principles which could be the basis of informed, unforced general agreement. Given this aim, it would be unreasonable, for example, to reject a principle because it imposed a burden on you when every alternative principle would impose much greater burdens others. I will have more lo say about grounds for rejection later in the paper.

The requirement that the hypothetical agreement which is the subject of moral argument be unforced is meant not only to rule out coercion, but also to exclude being forced to accept an agreement by being in a weak bargaining position, for example because others are able to hold out longer and hence to insist on better terms. Moral argument abstracts from such considerations. The only relevant pressure for agreement comes from the desire to find and agree on principles which no one who had this desire could reasonably reject. According to contractualism, moral argument concerns the possibility of agreement among persons who are all moved by this desire, and moved by it to the same degree. But this counter-factual assumption characterizes only the agreement with which morality is concerned, not the world to which moral principles are to apply. Those who are concerned with morality look for principles for application to their imperfect world which they could not reasonably reject, and which others in this world, who are not now moved by the desire for agreement, could not reasonably reject should they come to be so moved.[2]

The contractualist account of moral wrongness refers to principles "which no one could reasonably reject" rather than to principles "which everyone could reasonably accept" for the following reason.[3] Consider a principle under which some people will suffer severe hardships, and suppose that these hardships are avoidable. That is, there are alternative principles under which no one would have to bear comparable burdens. It might happen, however, that the people on whom these hardships fall are particularly self-sacrificing, and are willing to accept these burdens for the sake of what they see as the greater good of all. We would not say, I think, that it would be unreasonable of them to do this. On the other hand, it might not be unreasonable for them to refuse these burdens, and, hence, not unreasonable for someone to reject a principle requiring him to bear them. If this rejection would be reasonable, then the principle imposing these burdens is put in doubt, despite the fact that some particularly self-sacrificing people could (reasonably) accept it. Thus it is the reasonableness of rejecting a principle, rather than the reasonableness of accepting it, on which moral argument turns.

It seems likely that many non-equivalent sets of principles will pass the test of non-rejectability. This is suggested, for example, by the fact that there are many different ways of defining important duties, no one of which is more or less "rejectable" than the others. There are, for example, many different systems of agreement-making and many different ways of assigning responsibility to care for others. It does not follow, however, that any action allowed by at least one of these sets of principles cannot be morally wrong according to contractualism. If it is important for us to have *some* duty of a given kind (some duty of fidelity to agreements, or some duty of mutual aid) of which there are many morally acceptable forms, then one of these forms needs to be established by convention. In a setting in which one of these forms *is* conventionally established, acts allowed by it will be wrong in the sense of the definition given. For, given the need for such conventions, one thing that could not be generally agreed to would be a set of principles allowing one to disregard conventionally established (and morally acceptable) definitions of important duties. This dependence of convention introduces a degree of cultural relativity into contractualist morality. In addition, what a person can

reasonably reject will depend on the aims and conditions that are important in his life, and these will also depend on the society in which he lives. The definition given above allows for variation of both of these kinds by making the wrongness of an action depend on the circumstances in which it is performed.

The partial statement of contractualism which I have given has the abstract character appropriate in an account of the subject matter of morality. On its face, it involves no specific claim as to which principles could be agreed to or even whether there is a unique set of principles which could be the basis of agreement. One way, though not the only way, for a contractualist to arrive at substantive moral claims would be to give a technical definition of the relevant notion of agreement, e.g. by specifying the conditions under which agreement is to be reached, the parties to this agreement and the criteria of reasonableness to be employed. Different contractualists have don this in different ways. What must be claimed for such a definition is that (under the circumstances in which it is to apply) what it describes is indeed the kind of unforced, reasonable agreement at which moral argument aims. But contractualism can also be understood as an informal description of the subject matter of morality on the basis of which ordinary forms of moral reasoning can be understood and appraised without proceeding via a technical notion of agreement.

Who is to be included in the general agreement to which contractualism refers? The scope of morality is a difficult question of substantive morality, but a philosophical theory of the nature of morality should provide some basis for answering it. What an adequate theory should do is to provide a framework within which what seem to be relevant arguments for and against particular interpretations of the moral boundary can be carried out. It is often thought that contractualism can provide no plausible basis for an answer to this question. Critics charge either that contractualism provides no answer at all, because it must begin with some set of contracting parties taken as given, or that contractualism suggests an answer which is obviously too restrictive, since a contract requires parties who are able to make and keep agreements and who are each able to offer the others some benefit in return for their cooperation. Neither of these objections applies to the version of contractualism that I am defending. The general specification of the scope of morality which it implies seems to me to be this: morality applies to a being if the notion of justification to a being of that kind makes sense. What is required in order for this to be the case? Here I can only suggest some necessary conditions. The first is that the being have a good, that is, that there be a clear sense in which things can be said to go better or worse for that being. This gives partial sense to the idea of what it would be reasonable for a trustee to accept on the being's behalf. It would be reasonable for a trustee to accept at least those things that are good, or not bad, for the being in question. Using this idea of trusteeship we can extend the notion of acceptance to apply to beings that are incapable of literally agreeing to anything. But this minimal notion of trusteeship is too weak to provide a basis for morality, according to contractualism. Contractualist morality relies on notions of what it would be reasonable to accept, or reasonable to reject, which are essentially comparative. Whether it would be unreasonable for me to reject a certain principle, given the aim of finding principles which no one with this aim could reasonably reject, depends not only on how much actions allowed by that principle might hurt me in absolute terms but also on how that potential loss compares with other potential losses to others under this principle and alternatives to it. Thus, in order for a being to stand in moral relations with us it is not enough that it have a good, it is also necessary that its good be sufficiently similar to our own to provide a basis for some system of comparability. Only on the basis of such a system can we give the proper kind of sense to the notion of what a trustee could reasonably reject on a being's behalf.

But the range of possible trusteeship is broader than that of morality. One could act as a trustee for a tomato plant, a forest or an ant colony, and such entities are not included in morality. Perhaps this can be explained by appeal to the requirement of comparability: while these entities have a good, it is not comparable to our own in a way that provides a basis for moral argument. Beyond this,

however, there is in these cases insufficient foothold for the notion of justification *to* a being. One further minimum requirement for this notion is that the being constitute a point of view; that is, that there be such a thing as what it is like to be that being, such a thing as what the world seems like to it. Without this, we do not stand in a relation to the being that makes even hypothetical justification to *it* appropriate.

On the basis of what I have said so far contractualism can explain why the capacity to feel pain should have seemed to many to count in favor of moral status: a being which has this capacity seems also to satisfy the three conditions I have just mentioned as necessary for the idea of justification to it to make sense. If a being can feel pain, then it constitutes a center of consciousness to which justification can be addressed. Feeling pain is a clear way in which the being can be worse off; having its pain alleviated a way in which it can he benefited; and these are forms of weal and woe which seem directly comparable to our own.

It is not clear that the three conditions I have listed as necessary are also sufficient for the idea of justification to a being to make sense. Whether they are, and, if they are not, what more may be required, are difficult and disputed questions. Some would restrict the moral sphere to those to whom justifications could in principle be communicated, or to those who can actually agree to something, or to those who have capacity to understand moral argument. Contractualism as I have stated it does not settle these issues at once. All I claim is that it provides a basis for argument about them which is at least as plausible as that offered by rival accounts of the nature of morality. These proposed restrictions on the scope of morality are naturally understood as debatable claims about the conditions under which the relevant notion of justification makes sense, and the arguments commonly offered for and against them can also be plausibly understood on this basis.

Some other possible restrictions on the scope of morality are more evidently rejectable. Morality might be restricted to those who have the capacity to observe its constraints, or to those who are able to confer some reciprocal benefit on other participants.

But it is extremely implausible to suppose that the beings excluded by these requirements fall entirely outside the protection of morality. Contractualism as I have formulated it[4] can explain why this is so: the absence of these capacities alone does nothing to undermine the possibility of justification to a being. What it may do in some cases, however, is to alter the justifications which are relevant. I suggest that whatever importance the capacities for deliberative control and reciprocal benefit may have is as factors altering the duties which beings have and the duties others have towards them, not as conditions whose absence suspends the moral framework altogether.

NOTES

1. "Average Utilitarianism" is most plausibly arrived at through quite a different form of argument, one more akin to contractualism. I discuss one such argument in section IV below.

2. Here I am indebted to Gilbert Harman for comments which have helped me to clarify my statement of contractualism.

3. A point I owe to Derek Parfit.

4. On this view (as contrasted with some others in which the notion of a contract is employed) what is fundamental to morality is the desire for reasonable agreement, not the pursuit of mutual advantage. See section V below. It should be clear that this version of contractualism can account for the moral standing of future persons who will be better or worse off as a result of what we do now. It is less clear how it can deal with the problem presented by future people who would not have been born but for actions of ours which also made the conditions in which they live worse. Do such people have reason to reject principles allowing these actions to be performed? This difficult problem, which I cannot explore here, is raised by Derek Parfit in Parfit 1976.

REVIEW EXERCISES

1. How are Hobbes' views individualistic?
2. According to Hobbes, what is the state of nature like and why?
3. Why does he believe an absolute sovereign is necessary?
4. If Hobbes' views are more related to utilitarian thought, how are Rawls' views more Kantian?
5. According to Rawls, how should we determine whether some distribution of goods in a society is just? What is the "original position," and what role does it play here?
6. What is Scanlon's principle for determining what is wrong?
7. How is Scanlon's account hypothetical in nature?
8. How is Scanlon's position a moral theory rather than a political one or a theory of justice?

7

Morality and Human Nature

IN 1776, Thomas Jefferson wrote in the Declaration of Independence, "We hold these truths to be self-evident, that all men are created equal, that they are endowed by their Creator with certain inalienable rights, that among these are life, liberty and the pursuit of happiness."[1] Jefferson had read the work of English philosopher John Locke, who had written in his *Second Treatise on Government* that all human beings were of the same species, born with the same basic capacities.[2] Thus, Locke argued, because all humans had the same basic nature, they should be treated equally.

Following the 2001 terrorist attack on the World Trade Center and the Pentagon, and with the U.S. invasion of Afghanistan, the question arose about what to do with people captured by the United States and considered to be terrorists. Since 2004, they have been transferred to Guantanamo Bay in Cuba, a U.S. naval base on the southeastern side of the island (the United States still holds a lease to this land because of the 1903 Cuban–American Treaty). A prison was set up, and those who were thought to be members, supporters, or sympathizers of al Qaeda or the Taliban were transferred there. It was said that they were not part of any army of any state and thus not prisoners of war but "enemy combatants" and thus not covered by any of the protections of the Geneva Conventions. They also were not given the protections of U.S. laws, and they were denied such basic human rights as knowing the charges against them and being allowed to defend themselves in court. In recent years, many of the 500 or so

Detainees in a holding area at Camp X-Ray at Guantanamo Bay, Cuba.

detainees have been sent back to the countries of their origins. Some were finally allowed lawyers, although not of their own choice. U.S. courts have ruled that the detainees must be given trials, not in the United States, but in U.S. military courts.[3] As of January 2010, 193 prisoners still remain held in the Guantanamo detention facility. Some may be brought to trial and some held indefinitely, either there or in maximum security prisons in the United States. In this and many other contemporary situations, we may ask what is meant by "human rights"—and does every person possess such rights? This is one of the questions addressed in this chapter.

The Nuremberg trials were trials of Nazi war criminals held in Nuremberg, Germany, from 1945 to 1949. There were thirteen trials in all. In the first trial, Nazi leaders were found guilty of violating international law by starting an aggressive war. Nine of them, including Hermann Goering and Rudolf Hess, were sentenced to death. In other trials, defendants were accused of committing atrocities against civilians. Nazi doctors who had conducted medical experiments on those imprisoned in the death camps were among those tried. Their experiments maimed and killed many people, all of whom were unwilling subjects. For example, experiments for the German air force were conducted to determine how fast people would die in very thin air. Other experiments tested the effects of freezing water on the human body. The defense contended that the military personnel, judges, and doctors were only following orders. However, the prosecution argued successfully that even if the experimentation did not violate the defendants' own laws, they were still "crimes against humanity." The idea was that a law more basic than civil laws exists—a moral law—and these doctors and others should have known what this basic moral law required.

The idea that the basic moral law can be known by human reason and that we know what it requires by looking to human nature are two of the tenets of natural law theory. Some treatments of human rights also use human nature as a basis. According to this view, human rights are those things that we can validly claim because they are essential for functioning well as human beings. This chapter will present the essential elements of both of these theories.

NATURAL LAW THEORY

One of the first questions to ask concerns the kind of law that natural law is. After addressing this question, we will examine the origins of this theory. Then we will explain what the theory holds. Finally, we will suggest things to think about when evaluating the theory.

What Kind of Law Is Natural Law?

The *natural law*, as this term is used in discussions of natural law theory, should not be confused with those other "laws of nature" that are the generalizations of

natural science. The laws of natural science are descriptive laws. They tell us how scientists believe nature behaves. Gases, for example, expand with their containers and when heat is applied. Boyle's law about the behavior of gases does not tell gases how they *ought* to behave. In fact, if gases were found to behave differently from what we had so far observed, then the laws would be changed to match this new information. Simply put, scientific laws are descriptive generalizations of fact.

Moral laws, on the other hand, are prescriptive laws. They tell us how we *ought* to behave. The natural law is the moral law written into nature itself. What we ought to do, according to this theory, is determined by considering certain aspects of nature. In particular, we ought to examine our nature as human beings to see what is essential for us to function well as members of our species. We look to certain aspects of our nature to know what is our good and what we ought to do.

Civil law is also prescriptive. As the moral law, however, natural law is supposed to be more basic or higher than the laws of any particular society. Although laws of particular societies vary and change over time, the natural law is supposed to be universal and stable. In an ancient Greek tragedy by Sophocles, the protagonist Antigone disobeys the king and buries her brother. She does so because she believes that she must follow a higher law that requires her to do this. In the story, she loses her life for obeying this law. In the Nuremberg trials, prosecutors had also argued that there was a higher law that all humans should recognize—one that takes precedence over national laws. People today sometimes appeal to this moral law in order to argue which civil laws ought to be instituted or changed.[4]

HISTORICAL ORIGINS: ARISTOTLE

The tradition of natural law ethics is a long one. Although one may find examples of the view that certain actions are right or wrong because they are suited to or go against human nature before Aristotle wrote about them, he was the first to develop a complex ethical philosophy based on this view.

Aristotle was born in 384 B.C. in Stagira in northern Greece. His father was a physician for King Philip of Macedonia. Around age seventeen, he went to study at Plato's Academy in Athens. Historians of philosophy have traced the influence of Plato's philosophy on Aristotle, but they have also noted significant differences between the two philosophers. Putting one difference somewhat simply, Plato's philosophy stresses the reality of the general and abstract, this reality being his famous forms or ideas which exist apart from the things that imitate them or participate in them. Aristotle was more interested in the individual and the concrete manifestations of the forms. After Plato's death, Aristotle traveled for several years and then for two or three years was the tutor to Alexander, the young son of King Philip, who later became known as Alexander the Great. In 335 B.C., Aristotle returned to Athens and organized his own school called the Lyceum. There he taught and wrote almost until his death thirteen years later in 322 B.C.[5] Aristotle is known not only for his moral theory but also for writings in logic, biology, physics, metaphysics, art, and politics. The basic notions of his moral theory can be found in his *Nicomachean Ethics*, named for his son Nicomachus.[6]

Nature, Human Nature, and the Human Good

Aristotle was a close observer of nature. In fact, in his writings he mentions some 500 different kinds of animals.[7] He noticed that seeds of the same sort always grew to the same mature form. He opened developing eggs of various species and noticed that these organisms manifested a pattern in their development even before birth. Tadpoles, he might have said, always follow the same path and become frogs, not turtles. So also with other living things. Acorns always become oak trees, not elms. He concluded that there was an order in nature. It was as if natural beings such as plants and animals had a principle of order within them that directed them toward their goal—their mature final form. This view can be called a *teleological* view, from the Greek word for goal, *telos*, because of its emphasis on a goal embedded in natural things. It was from this conclusion that Aristotle developed his notion of the good.

According to Aristotle, "the good is that at which all things aim."[8] We are to look at the purpose or end or goal of some activity or being to see what is its good. Thus, the good of the shipbuilder is to build ships. The good of the lyre player is to play well. Aristotle asks whether there is anything that is the good of the human being—not as shipbuilder or lyre

player, but simply as human. To answer this question, we must first think about what it is to be human. According to Aristotle, natural beings come in kinds or species. From their species flow their essential characteristics and certain key tendencies or capacities. A squirrel, for example, is a kind of animal that is, first of all, a living being, an animal. It develops from a young form to a mature form. It is a mammal and therefore has other characteristics of mammals. It is bushy-tailed, can run along telephone wires, and gathers and stores nuts for its food. From the characteristics that define a squirrel, we also can know what a *good* squirrel is. A good specimen of a squirrel is one that is effective, successful, and functions well. It follows the pattern of development and growth it has by nature. It does, in fact, have a bushy tail and good balance, and it knows how to find and store its food. It would be a bad example of a squirrel or a poor one that had no balance, couldn't find its food, or had no fur and was sickly. It would have been better for the squirrel if its inherent natural tendencies to grow and develop and live as a healthy squirrel had been realized.

According to the natural law tradition from Aristotle on, human beings are also thought to be natural beings with a specific human nature. They have certain specific characteristics and abilities that they share as humans. Unlike squirrels and acorns, human beings can choose to do what is their good or act against it. Just what is their good? Aristotle recognized that a good eye is a healthy eye that sees well. A good horse is a well-functioning horse, one that is healthy and able to run and do what horses do. What about human beings? Is there something comparable for the human being as human? Is there some good for humans as humans?

Just as we can tell what the good squirrel is from its own characteristics and abilities as a squirrel, according to natural law theory, the same should be true for the human being. For human beings to function well or flourish, they should perfect their human capacities. If they do this, they will be functioning well as human beings. They will also be happy, for a being is happy to the extent that it is functioning well. Aristotle believed that the ultimate good of humans is happiness, blessedness, or prosperity: *eudaimonia*.

But in what does happiness consist? To know what happiness is, we need to know what is the function of the human being.

Human beings have much in common with lower forms of beings. We are living, for example, just as plants are. Thus, we take in material from outside us for nourishment, and we grow from an immature to a mature form. We have senses of sight and hearing and so forth, as do the higher animals. But is there anything unique to humans? Aristotle believed that it is our "rational element" that is peculiar to us. The good for humans, then, should consist in their functioning in a way consistent with and guided by this rational element. Our rational element has two different functions: One is to know, and the other is to guide choice and action. We must develop our ability to know the world and the truth. We must also choose wisely. In doing this, we will be functioning well specifically as humans. Yet what is it to choose wisely? In partial answer to this, Aristotle developed ideas about prudential choice and suggested that we choose as a prudent person would choose.

One of the most well known interpreters of Aristotle's philosophy was Thomas Aquinas (1224–1274). Aquinas was a Dominican friar who taught at the University of Paris. He was also a theologian who held that the natural law is part of the divine law or plan for the universe. The record of much of what he taught can be found in his work the *Summa Theologica*.[9] In accord with Aristotle, Aquinas held that the moral good consists in following the innate tendencies of our nature. We are by nature biological beings. Because we tend by nature to grow and mature, we ought to preserve our being and our health by avoiding undue risks and doing what will make us healthy. Furthermore, like sentient animals, we can know our world through physical sense capacities. We ought to use our senses of touch, taste, hearing, and sight; we ought to develop and make use of these senses for appreciating those aspects of existence that they reveal to us. We ought not to do, or do deliberately, what injures these senses. Like many animals we reproduce our kind not asexually but sexually and heterosexually. This is what nature means for us to do, according to this version of natural law theory. (See further discussion of this issue in Chapter 12 on sexual morality.)

Unique to persons are the specific capacities of knowing and choosing freely. Thus, we ought to treat ourselves and others as beings capable of understanding and free choice. Those things that help us pursue the truth, such as education and freedom of public expression, are good. Those things that hinder pursuit of the truth are bad. Deceit and lack of access to the sources of knowledge are morally objectionable simply because they prevent us from fulfilling our innate natural drive or orientation to know the way things are.[10] Moreover, whatever enhances our ability to choose freely is good. A certain amount of self-discipline, options from which to choose, and reflection on what we ought to choose are among the things that enhance freedom. To coerce people and to limit their possibilities of choosing freely are examples of what is inherently bad or wrong. We also ought to find ways to live well together, for this is a theory according to which "no man—or woman—is an island." We are social creatures by nature. Thus, the essence of natural law theory is that we ought to further the inherent ends of human nature and not do what frustrates human fulfillment or flourishing.

Evaluating Natural Law Theory

Natural law theory has many appealing characteristics. Among them are its belief in the objectivity of moral values and the notion of the good as human flourishing. Various criticisms of the theory have also been advanced, including the following two.

First, according to natural law theory, we are to determine what we ought to do from deciphering the moral law as it is written into nature—specifically, human nature. One problem that natural law theory must address concerns our ability to read nature. The moral law is supposedly knowable by natural human reason. However, throughout the history of philosophy various thinkers have read nature differently. Even Aristotle, for example, thought that slavery could be justified in that it was in accord with nature.[11] Today people argue against slavery on just such natural law grounds. Philosopher Thomas Hobbes defended the absolutist rule of despots and John Locke criticized it, both doing so on natural law grounds. Moreover, traditional natural law theory has picked out highly positive traits: the desire to know the truth, to choose the good, and to develop as healthy mature beings. Not all views of the essential characteristics of human nature have been so positive, however. Some philosophers have depicted human nature as deceitful, evil, and uncontrolled. This is why Hobbes argued that we need a strong government. Without it, he wrote, life in a state of nature would be "nasty, brutish, and short."[12]

Moreover, if nature is taken in the broader sense—meaning *all* of nature—and if a natural law as a moral law were based on this, then the general approach might even cover such theories as Social Darwinism. This view holds that because the most fit organisms in nature are the ones that survive, so also the most fit should endure in human society and the weaker ought to perish. When combined with a belief in capitalism, this led to notions such as that it was only right and according to nature that wealthy industrialists at the end of the nineteenth century were rich and powerful. It also implied that the poor were so by the designs of nature and thus we ought not interfere with this situation.

A second question raised for natural law theory is the following. Can the way things are by nature provide the basis for knowing how they ought to be? On the face of it, this may not seem right. Just because something exists in a certain way does not necessarily mean that it is good. Floods, famine, and disease all exist, but that does not make them good. According to David Hume, as noted in our discussion of Mill's proof of the principle of utility in Chapter 4, you cannot derive an "ought" from an "is."[13] Evaluations cannot simply be derived from factual matters. Other moral philosophers have agreed. When we know something to be a fact, that things exist in a certain way, it still remains an open question whether it is good. However, the natural law assumes that nature is teleological, that it has a certain directedness. In Aristotle's terms, it moves toward its natural goal, its final purpose. Yet from the time of the scientific revolution of the seventeenth century, such final purposes have become suspect. One could not always observe nature's directedness, and it came to be associated with the notion of nonobservable spirits directing things from within. If natural law theory does depend on there being purposes in nature, it must be able to explain how this can be so.

Consider one possible explanation of the source of whatever purposes there might be in nature. Christian philosophers from Augustine on believed that nature manifests God's plan for the universe. For Aristotle, however, the universe is eternal; it always existed and was not created by God. His concept of God was that of a most perfect being toward which the universe is in some way directed. According to Aristotle, there is an order in nature, but it did not come from the mind of God. For Augustine and Thomas Aquinas, however, the reason why nature has the order that it does is because God, so to speak, put it there. Because the universe was created after a divine plan, nature not only is intelligible but also existed for a purpose that was built into it. Some natural law theorists follow Thomas Aquinas on this, whereas others either follow Aristotle or abstain from judgments about the source of the order (*telos*) in nature. But can we conceive of an order in nature without an orderer? This depends on what we mean by order in nature. If it is taken in the sense of a plan, then this implies that it has an author. However, natural beings may simply develop in certain ways as if they were directed there by some plan—but there is no plan. This may just be our way of reading or speaking about nature.[14]

Evolutionary theory also may present a challenge to natural law theory. If the way that things have come to be is the result of many chance variations, then how can this resulting form be other than arbitrary? Theists often interpret evolution itself as part of a divine plan. There is no necessary conflict between belief in God and evolution. *Chance*, then, would not mean *without direction*. Even a nontheist such as mid–nineteenth century American philosopher Chauncey Wright had an explanation of Darwin's assertion that chance evolutionary variations accounted for the fact that some species were better suited to survive than others. Wright said that "chance" does not mean "uncaused"; it means only that the causes are unknown to us.[15]

Natural Rights

A second theory according to which moral requirements may be grounded in human nature is the theory of natural rights. John Locke provided a good example that Jefferson used in the Declaration of

Independence, as noted at the beginning of this chapter. Certain things are essential for us if we are to function well as persons. Among these are life itself and then also liberty and the ability to pursue those things that bring happiness. These are said to be rights not because they are granted by some state but because of the fact that they are important for us as human beings or persons. They are thus moral rights first, though they may also need the enforcement power of the law.

There is a long tradition of natural rights in Western philosophy. For example, we find a variant of the natural rights tradition in the writings of the first- and second-century A.D. Stoics. Their key moral principle was to "follow nature." For them, this meant that we should follow reason rather than human emotion. They also believed that there are laws to which all people are subject no matter what their local customs or conventions. Early Roman jurists believed that a common element existed in the codes of various peoples: a *jus gentium*. For example, the jurist Grotius held that the moral law was determined by right reason. These views can be considered variations on natural law theory because of their reliance on human nature and human reason to ground a basic moral law that is common to all peoples.[16]

Throughout the eighteenth century, political philosophers often referred to the laws of nature in discussions of natural rights. For example, Voltaire wrote that morality has a universal source. It is the "natural law . . . which nature teaches all men" what we should do.[17] The Declaration of Independence was influenced by the writings of jurists and philosophers who believed that a moral law is built into nature. Thus, in the first section it asserts that the colonists were called on "to assume among the powers of the earth, the separate and equal station, to which the laws of nature and of nature's God entitle them."[18]

Today various international codes of human rights, such as the United Nations' Declaration of Human Rights and the Geneva Convention's principles for the conduct of war, contain elements of a natural rights tradition. These attempt to specify rights that all people have simply as a virtue of their being human, regardless of their country of origin, race, or religion.

Evaluating Natural Rights Theory

One problem for a natural rights theory is that not everyone agrees on what human nature requires or which human natural rights are central. In the 1948 U.N. Declaration of Human Rights, the list of rights includes welfare rights and rights to food, clothing, shelter, and basic security. Just what kinds of things can we validly claim as human rights? Freedom of speech? Freedom of assembly? Housing? Clean air? Friends? Work? Income? Many of these are listed in various documents that nations have signed that provide lists of human rights. However, more is needed than lists. A rationale for what is to be included in those lists of human rights is called for. This is also something that a natural rights theory should provide. Some contemporary philosophers argue that the basic rights that society ought to protect are not welfare rights such as rights to food, clothing, and shelter, but liberty rights such as the right not to be interfered with in our daily lives.[19] (See further discussion of negative and positive rights in Chapter 14, the section on socialism.) How are such differences to be settled? Moreover, women historically have not been given equal rights with men. In the United States, for example, women were not all granted the right to vote until 1920 on grounds that they were by nature not fully rational or that they were closer in nature to animals than males! The women of Kuwait only gained the right to vote in 2005. How is it possible that there could be such different views of what are our rights if morality is supposed to be knowable by natural human reason?

A second challenge for a natural rights theory concerns what it must prove to justify its holdings. First, it must show that human nature as it is ought to be furthered and that certain things ought to be granted to us in order to further our nature. These things we then speak of as rights. Basic to this demonstration would be to show why human beings are so valuable that what is essential for their full function can be claimed as a right. For example, do human beings have a higher value than other beings and, if so, why? Is a reference to something beyond this world—a creator God, for example—necessary to give value to humans or is there something about their nature itself that is the reason why they have such a high value? Second, a natural rights theorist has the job of detailing just what things are essential for the good functioning of human nature.

Finally, not all discussions of human rights have been of the sort described here. For example, Norman Daniels claims that the reason why people have a right to basic health care is because of the demands of justice; that is, justice demands that there be equal opportunity to life's goods, and whether people have equal opportunity depends, among other things, on their health.[20] Another example is found in the writings of Walter Lippmann, a political commentator more than half a century ago. He held a rather utilitarian view that we ought to agree that there are certain rights because these provide the basis for a democratic society, and it is precisely such a society that works best. It is not that we can prove that such rights as freedom of speech or assembly exist, we simply accept them for pragmatic reasons because they provide the basis for democracy.[21]

The notion of rights can be and has been discussed in many different contexts. Among those treated in this book are issues of animal rights (Chapter 17), economic rights (Chapter 14), fetal and women's rights (Chapters 11 and 9), equal rights and discrimination (Chapter 13), and war crimes and universal human rights (Chapter 19).

Is There a Human Nature

Not all philosophers believe that there is such a thing as human nature. Jean-Paul Sartre is one philosopher who does not believe that there is. The reading by Sartre in this chapter explains why he and some other existentialists hold that there is not such a thing as human nature.

In the reading selections here from Thomas Aquinas and John Locke, you will find discussions of the grounding of morality and rights in human nature. As noted, the reading by Jean-Paul Sartre contradicts the views of others in this chapter who are supporters of natural law and natural rights.

NOTES

1. Thomas Jefferson, "The Declaration of Independence," in Philip S. Foner (Ed.), *Basic Writings of Thomas Jefferson* (New York: Wiley, 1944), 551.
2. John Locke, *Two Treatises of Government* (London, 1690), Peter Laslett (Ed.) (Cambridge: Cambridge University Press, 1960).
3. http://en.wikipedia.org/wiki/Guantanamo_Bay_detention_camp.
4. This is the basic idea behind the theory of civil disobedience as outlined and practiced by Henry David Thoreau, Mahatma Gandhi, and Martin Luther King, Jr. When Thoreau was imprisoned for not paying taxes that he thought were used for unjust purposes, he wrote his famous essay, "Civil Disobedience." In it he writes, "Must the citizen ever for a moment, or in the least degree, resign his conscience to the legislator? Why has every man a conscience, then? I think that we should be men first, and subjects afterward. It is not desirable to cultivate a respect for the law, so much as for the right." Henry David Thoreau, "Civil Disobedience," in *Miscellanies* (Boston: Houghton Mifflin, 1983), 136–137.
5. W. T. Jones, *A History of Western Philosophy: The Classical Mind*, 2nd ed. (New York: Harcourt, Brace, & World, 1969), 214–216.
6. This was asserted by the neo-Platonist Porphyry (ca. A.D. 232). However, others believe that the work got its name because it was edited by Nicomachus. See Alasdair MacIntyre, *After Virtue* (Notre Dame, IN: Notre Dame University Press, 1984), 147.
7. W. T. Jones, op. cit., 233.
8. See the selection in Chapter 8 from *The Nicomachean Ethics*.
9. Thomas Aquinas, "Summa Theologica," in Anton Pegis (Ed.), *Basic Writings of Saint Thomas Aquinas* (New York: Random House, 1948).
10. This is obviously an incomplete presentation of the moral philosophy of Thomas Aquinas. We should at least note that he was as much a theologian as a philosopher, if not more so. True and complete happiness, he believed, would be achieved only in knowledge or contemplation of God.
11. Aristotle, *Politics*, Chap. V, VI.
12. Thomas Hobbes, *Leviathan*, Michael Oakeshott (Ed.) (New York: Oxford University Press, 1962).
13. David Hume, *Treatise on Human Nature* (London, 1739–1740).
14. Such a view can be found in Kant's work *The Critique of Judgment*.
15. See Chauncey Wright, "Evolution by Natural Selection," *The North American Review* (July 1872) 6–7.
16. See Roscoe Pound, *Jurisprudence* (St. Paul, MN: West, 1959).
17. Voltaire, *Ouvres*, XXV, 39; XI, 443, quoted in Carl L. Becker, *The Heavenly City of the Eighteenth-Century Philosophers* (Yale, 2003), 52; Becker's translation.
18. Thomas Jefferson, Declaration of Independence
19. On negative or liberty rights see, for example, the work of Robert Nozick, *State, Anarchy and Utopia*

(New York: Basic Books, 1974). See further discussion on welfare and liberty rights in Chapter 14, "Economic Justice."

20. Norman Daniels, "Health-Care Needs and Distributive Justice," *Philosophy and Public Affairs*, *10*, 2 (Spring 1981): 146–179.

21. The term *pragmatic* concerns what "works." Thus, to accept something on pragmatic grounds means to accept it because it works for us in some way. For Walter Lippmann's views, see *Essays in the Public Philosophy* (Boston: Little, Brown, 1955).

R E A D I N G
On Natural Law

THOMAS AQUINAS

Study Questions

1. What is the chief characteristic of first principles, both of demonstration and of practical reason?
2. What is the difference between something being self-evident in itself and self-evident to us?
3. What is the first principle of demonstration and on what is it founded?
4. What is the first thing that falls under the apprehension of practical reason? And thus what is its first principle on which all the principles of natural law are based?
5. How does one determine whether something is good or evil, according to Aquinas? Give some of his examples.
6. What is the natural function of the human as human? How is this related to natural law? To virtue?
7. What is the key difference in terms of certitude between principles of speculative and of practical reason? Is there a difference here between principles and conclusions?
8. Give Aquinas's example of this difference related to restoring the belongings of someone.
9. What types of things prevent people from agreeing in their moral judgments about particulars?
10. What does Aquinas want to show by the examples of murder as opposed to punishment?
11. How does Aquinas believe that we should decide which laws are just?

QUESTION 94

Article 2, Whether Natural Law Contains Many Precepts or Only One

In the human context, the precepts of natural law relate to activities in a way similar to first principles in demonstrations. But there are many indemonstrable first principles. Therefore there are many precepts of natural law.

As was previously stated, precepts of natural law relate to practical reason just as the first principles of demonstration relate to speculative reason, both being self-evident. However, something is said to be self-evident in two ways: one intrinsically self-evident, the other evident to us. A particular proposition is said to be intrinsically self-evident when the predicate is implicit in the subject, although this proposition would not be self-evident to someone ignorant of the definition of the subject. For instance, this proposition "man is rational" is self-evident by its very nature since saying "human" entails saying "rational." Nevertheless this proposition is not self-evident to one who does not know what a man is. . . .

(Now) that which is primary in apprehension is being, the understanding of which is included in anything whatsoever that is apprehended. Accordingly, the first indemonstrable principle is that one cannot simultaneously affirm and deny something. This is founded in the understanding of being and non-being and in this principle all others are founded, as stated in *Metaphysics IV*. Just as being is the first thing that falls under simple apprehension, so also the good is the first thing that falls under the apprehension of practical reason which is ordered to action. Every agent acts for an end, which is understood as a good. Accordingly, the first principle of practical reason is the one based on the concept of the good: Good is

From *Summa Theologiae*, 1265–1272. Translated from the Latin by Edward MacKinnon.

what everything desires. This, accordingly, is the first principle of law: Good is to be done and evil avoided. All the other precepts of natural law are based on this. All concern what is to be done or avoided, because practical reason naturally apprehends what is the human good.

Good has the nature of an end while evil has a contrary nature. Accordingly, every thing for which a man has a natural inclination is naturally apprehended as a good and consequently something to be pursued, while anything contrary to this is to be avoided as evil. Therefore the ordering of the precepts of natural law stems from the order of natural inclinations. In the first place, there is the inclination of man towards natural good, an inclination shared by all substances inasmuch as they naturally desire self-preservation. The consequence of this inclination is that whatever preserves human life and avoids obstacles is a matter of natural law. Secondly, there is in man a more specialized inclination following the natural bent he shares with other animals. Accordingly these things are said to pertain to natural law that "nature has taught to all animals," such as the mating of male and female, education of children, and similar things. Thirdly, there is in man an inclination toward good based on reason, something proper only to man. Thus man has a natural inclination to know the truth about God, and that he should live in society. On this ground, those things that stem from this inclination are also a matter of natural law. Thus, man should overcome ignorance and should not offend fellow members of society, and similar considerations.

Article 3, Whether All Acts of Virtue Are Prescribed by Natural Law

. . . All those things to which man is inclined by nature pertain to natural law. Everything naturally inclines to operations that are appropriate to its form, as fire toward heating. Since a rational soul is the proper form of humans the natural inclination of a man is to act according to reason. And this is acting virtuously. In this respect, all virtuous acts pertain to natural law. Each person's reason naturally tells him to act virtuously. However, if we speak of virtuous acts in themselves, or according to their proper spe-

cies, then not all virtuous acts are matters of natural law. For many things accord with virtue, though nature lacks an initial inclination. It is through rational inquisition that men come to know which things conduce to living well.

Article 4, Whether There Is One Natural Law for All

As was said previously, those things towards which man is naturally inclined pertain to natural law. Among such things it is distinctively human for a man to act in accord with reason. Reason inclines us to proceed from the common to the particular (as shown in *Physics I*). In this regard there is a difference between speculative and practical reason. Speculative reason is concerned in the first instance with things that are necessary, or could not be otherwise. Thus truth is easily found in proper conclusions just as in common principles. But practical reason is concerned with contingent matters involving human activity. Therefore, if there is some necessity in common principles, there is increasing error the further we descend to particular conclusions. In speculative reason, there is the same degree of truth in principles and conclusions, although the truth of the conclusion may not be as well known to many as the principles are, for they are common conceptions. In activities, however, there is not the same degree of truth or practical rectitude, among all people concerning conclusions, but only concerning principles. Even those people who share the same rectitude concerning conclusions do not share the same knowledge. . . . With regard to the proper conclusions of practical reason, all do not share the same truth or rectitude. Even those that do share equal truth are not equally known. For everyone, it is right and true to act in accord with reason. From this principle follows a quasi-proper conclusion, that debts should be paid. This is true as a general rule. However, it may happen to be harmful in a particular case, and consequently unreasonable to give goods back, if for example someone is intending to attack the homeland. Thus, uncertainty increases the more we descend to particulars. Thus if it is claimed that goods are to be restored with certain precautions, or under certain conditions, then the more detailed the conditions are, the more uncertainty increases, even to the degree that it is not clear whether or not they should be restored.

Accordingly, we claim that first principles of natural law are the same for all, but in rectitude and knowledge. However, the quasi conclusions from these principles are for the most part the same for all both in rectitude and knowledge, though in a few cases there can be a deficit both with respect to rectitude because of some particular impediments (just as things naturally generated and corrupted are deficient in a few cases because of obstacles) and there can also be a deficit in knowledge. The reason for this is that some people have their reason perverted by passion, which may be due to bad customs or to a defective natural disposition. . . .

QUESTION 95

Article 2, Whether Every Law Fashioned by Humans Is Derived from Natural Law

But it should be recognized that something can be deviant from natural law in two ways. The first is as a conclusion from principles; the other as a determination of some common generalities. The first mode is similar to the practice of the sciences, where conclusions are produced by deduction from principles. The second mode, however, is more like what occurs in the arts, where common forms are tailored to special cases. A carpenter, for example, must determine the common form of a home to be this or that particular shape. Therefore, some things are derived from the common principle of natural law in the form of conclusions. Thus the prohibition of murder is derived from the general principle that evil should not be done. Other things, however, have the form of a determination. Natural law requires punishment for the evildoer, but whether he receives this or that penalty is a particular determination of natural law. Both forms, accordingly, are found in human law. However, determinations of the first mode are not only contained in human law, but they also have force through natural law. The second mode, however, derive their force only from human law. . . .

Article 3

In every being that is for an end it is necessary that its form has a determinate proportionality to the end, as the form of a saw is geared towards cutting as is clear in *Physics II*. Anything that is ruled and measured should have a form proportioned to its ruler and measure. Now human law has both, because it is something ordered to an end; and it has a rule or measure regulated or measured by a higher measure, which is both divine law and the law of nature, as previously explained. The end of human law is the well-being of humans . . . accordingly, . . . the first condition of law posits three things: That it accords with religion, inasmuch as it is proportioned to divine law; that it fosters discipline, inasmuch as it is proportional to natural law; and that it advances well-being inasmuch as it is proportional to human needs.

R E A D I N G
Second Treatise of Civil Government
JOHN LOCKE

Study Questions

1. What two things characterize human beings in their natural state, according to Locke?
2. On the second characteristic, why does Locke hold that human beings are equal?
3. Why is the natural state of human liberty not a state of license, according to Locke? What does he mean by that?
4. How does the "state of nature" provide a basis for a "law of nature," according to Locke?
5. According to Locke, how is it that some members of a society may have power over others in meting out punishment and taking reparations from them?
6. Why, according to Locke, do we need civil government?
7. According to Locke, was there ever really an existing state of nature as he describes it?

BOOK II

Chapter II Of the State of Nature

4. To understand political power aright, and derive it from its original, we must consider what estate all men are naturally in, and that is, a state of perfect freedom to order their actions, and dispose of their possessions and persons as they think fit, within the bounds of the law of Nature, without asking leave or depending upon the will of any other man.

A state also of equality, wherein all the power and jurisdiction is reciprocal, no one having more than another, there being nothing more evident than that creatures of the same species and rank, promiscuously born to all the same advantages of Nature, and the use of the same faculties, should also be equal one amongst another, without subordination or subjection, unless the lord and master of them all should, by a manifest declaration of his will, set one above another, and confer on him, by an evident and clear appointment, an undoubted right to dominion and sovereignty. . . .

6. But though this be a state of liberty, yet it is not a state of license; though man in that state have an uncontrollable liberty to dispose of his person or possessions, yet he has not liberty to destroy himself, or so much as any creature in his possession, but where some nobler use than its bare preservation calls for it. The state of Nature has a law of Nature to govern it, which obliges every one, and reason, which is that law, teaches all mankind who will but consult it, that being all equal and independent, no one ought to harm another in his life, health, liberty or possessions; for men being all the workmanship of one omnipotent and infinitely wise Maker; all the servants of one sovereign Master, sent into the world by His order and about His business; they are His property, whose workmanship they are made to last during His, not one another's pleasure. And, being furnished with like faculties, sharing all in one community of Nature, there cannot be supposed any such subordination among us that may authorize us to destroy one another, as if we were made for one

another's uses, as the inferior ranks of creatures are for ours. Every one as he is bound to preserve himself, and not to quit his station wilfully, so by the like reason, when his own preservation comes not in competition, ought he as much as he can to preserve the rest of mankind, and not unless it be to do justice on an offender, take away, or impair the life, or what tends to the preservation of the life, the liberty, health, limb, or goods of another.

7. And that all men may be restrained from invading other's rights, and from doing hurt to one another, and the law of Nature be observed, which willeth the peace and preservation of all mankind, the execution of the law of Nature is in that state put into every man's hands, whereby every one has a right to punish the transgressors of that law to such a degree as may hinder its violation. For the law of Nature would, as all other laws that concern men in this world, be in vain if there were nobody that in the state of Nature had a power to execute that law, and thereby preserve the innocent and restrain offenders; and if any one in the state of Nature may punish another for any evil he has done, every one may do so. For in that state of perfect equality, where naturally there is no superiority or jurisdiction of one over another, what any may do in prosecution of that law, every one must needs have a right to do.

8. And thus, in the state of Nature, one man comes by a power over another, but yet no absolute or arbitrary power to use a criminal when he has got him in his hands, according to the passionate heats, or boundless extravagancy of his own will, but only to retribute to him so far as calm reason and conscience dictate, what is proportionate to his transgression, which is so much as may serve for reparation and restraint. For these two are the only reasons why one man may lawfully do harm to another, which is that we call punishment. In transgressing the law of Nature, the offender declares himself to live by another rule than that of reason and common equity, which is that measure God has set to the actions of men for their mutual security, and so he becomes dangerous to mankind; the tie which is to secure them from injury and violence being slighted and broken by him, which being a trespass against the whole species, and the peace

Selection from John Locke, *Second Treatise of Civil Government* (London Routledge and Sons, 1887).

and safety of it, provided for by the law of Nature, every man upon this score, by the right he hath to preserve mankind in general, may restrain, or where it is necessary, destroy things noxious to them, and so may bring such evil on any one who hath transgressed that law, as may make him repent the doing of it, and thereby deter him, and, by his example, others from doing the like mischief. And in this case, and upon this ground, every man hath a right to punish the offender, and be executioner of the law of Nature. . . .

11. From these two distinct rights (the one of punishing the crime, for restraint and preventing the like offence, which right of punishing is in everybody, the other of taking reparation, which belongs only to the injured party) comes it to pass that the magistrate, who by being magistrate hath the common right of punishing put into his hands, can often, where the public good demands not the execution of the law, remit the punishment of criminal offences by his own authority, but yet cannot remit the satisfaction due to any private man for the damage he has received. That he who hath suffered the damage has a right to demand in his own name, and he alone can remit. The damnified person has this power of appropriating to himself the goods or service of the offender by right of self-preservation, as every man has a power to punish the crime to prevent its being committed again, by the right he has of preserving all mankind, and doing all reasonable things he can in order to that end. And thus it is that every man in the state of Nature has a power to kill a murderer, both to deter others from doing the like injury (which no reparation can compensate) by the example of the punishment that attends it from everybody, and also to secure men from the attempts of a criminal who, having renounced reason, the common rule and measure God hath given to mankind, hath, by the unjust violence and slaughter he hath committed upon one, declared war against all mankind, and therefore may be destroyed as a lion or a tiger, one of those wild savage beasts with whom men can have no society nor security. And upon this is grounded that great law of Nature, "Whoso sheddeth man's blood by man shall his blood be shed." And Cain was so fully convinced that every one had a right to destroy

such a criminal, that, after the murder of his brother, he cried out, "Every one that findeth me shall slay me," so plain was it writ in the hearts of all mankind.

12. By the same reason may a man in the state of Nature punish the lesser breaches of that law, it will, perhaps, be demanded, with death? I answer: Each transgression may be punished to that degree, and with so much severity, as will suffice to make it an ill bargain to the offender, give him cause to repent, and terrify others from doing the like. Every offence that can be committed in the state of Nature may, in the state of Nature, be also punished equally, and as far forth, as it may, in a commonwealth. For though it would be beside my present purpose to enter here into the particulars of the law of Nature, or its measures of punishment; yet it is certain there is such a law, and that too as intelligible and plain to a rational creature and a studier of that law as the positive laws of commonwealths, nay, possibly plainer; as much as reason is easier to be understood than the fancies and intricate contrivances of men, following contrary and hidden interests put into words; for truly so are apart of the municipal laws of countries, which are only so far right as they are founded on the law of Nature, by which they are to be regulated and interpreted.

13. To this strange doctrine—viz., That in the state of Nature every one has the executive power of the law of Nature, I doubt not but it will be objected that it is unreasonable for men to be judges in their own cases, that self-love will make men partial to themselves and their friends; and, on the other side, ill-nature, passion, and revenge will carry them too far in punishing others, and hence nothing but confusion and disorder will follow, and that therefore God hath certainly appointed government to restrain the partiality and violence of men. I easily grant that civil government is the proper remedy for the inconveniencies of the state of Nature, which must certainly be great where men may be judges in their own case, since it is easy to be imagined that he who was so unjust as to do his brother an injury will scarce be so just as to condemn himself for it. But I shall desire those who make this objection to remember that absolute monarchs are but men; and if government is to be the remedy of those evils which

necessarily follow from men being judges in their own cases, and the state of Nature is therefore not to be endured, I desire to know what kind of government that is, and how much better it is than the state of Nature, where one man commanding a multitude has the liberty to be judge in his own case, and may do to all his subjects whatever he pleases without the least question or control of those who execute his pleasure? and in whatsoever he doth, whether led by reason, mistake, or passion, must be submitted to? which men in the state of Nature are not bound to do one to another. And if he that judges, judges amiss in his own or any other case, he is answerable for it to the rest of mankind.

14. It is often asked as a might objection, where are, or ever were, there any men in such a state of Nature? To which it may suffice as an answer at present, that since all princes and rulers of "independent" governments all through the world are in a state of Nature, it is plain the world never was, nor never will be, without numbers of men in that state. I have named all governors of "independent" communities, whether they are, or are not, in league with others; for it is not every compact that puts an end to the state of Nature between men, but only this one of agreeing together mutually to enter into one community, and make one body politic; other promises and compacts men may make one with another, and yet still be in the state of Nature. The promises and bargains for truck, &c., between the two men in Soldania, or between a Swiss and an Indian, in the woods of America, are binding to them, though they are perfectly in a state of Nature in reference to one another for truth, and keeping of faith belongs to men as men, and not as members of society. . . .

R E A D I N G
Existentialism Is a Humanism
JEAN-PAUL SATRE

1. Sartre says that French existentialists (himself included) believe that "existence precedes essence." What does he mean by this?
2. How does the example of the paper-cutter help him explain this contention?
3. How does his disbelief in the existence of God play a role in his views?
4. What two meanings does "subjectivism" have, according to Sartre?
5. How does he believe that his view makes us more responsible for ourselves?
6. What does he mean by "anguish," and what role does it play in his views?

WHAT IS meant by the term existentialism? . . . Actually, it is the least scandalous, the most austere of doctrines. It is intended strictly for specialists and philosophers. Yet it can be defined easily.

What complicates matters is that there are two kinds of existentialist; first, those who are Christian, among whom I would include Jaspers and Gabriel Marcel, both Catholic; and on the other hand the atheist existentialist, among whom I class Heidegger, and then the French existentialists and myself. What they have in common is that they think that existence precedes essence, or, if you prefer, that subjectivity must be the starting point.

Just what does that mean? Let us consider some object that is manufactured, for example, a book or a paper-cutter: here is an object which has been made by an artisan whose inspiration came from a concept. He referred to the concept of what a paper-cutter is and likewise to a known method of production, which is part of the concept, something which is, by and large, a routine. Thus, the paper-cutter is at once an object produced in a certain way and, on the other hand, one having a specific use; and one can not postulate a man who produces a paper-cutter but does not know what it is used for.

Therefore, let us say that, for the paper-cutter, essence—that is, the ensemble of both the production routines and the properties which enable it to be both produced and defined—precedes existence. Thus, the presence of a paper-cutter or book in front of me is determined. Therefore, we have here a technical view of the world whereby it can be said that production precedes existence.

When we conceive God as the Creator, He is generally thought of as a superior sort of artisan. Whatever doctrine we may be considering, whether one like that of Descartes or that of Leibnitz, we always grant that will more or less follows understanding or, at the very least, accompanies it, and that when God creates He knows exactly what He is creating. Thus, the concept of man in the mind of God is comparable to the concept of paper-cutter in the mind of the manufacturer, and, following certain techniques and a conception, God produces man, just as the artisan, following a definition and a technique, makes a paper-cutter. Thus, the individual man is the realization of a certain concept in the divine intelligence.

Atheistic existentialism, which I represent, . . . states that if God does not exist, there is at least one being in whom existence precedes essence, a being who exists before he can be defined by any concept and that this being is man, or, as Heidegger says, human reality. What is meant here by saying that existence precedes essence? It means that, first of all, man exists, turns up, appears on the scene, and, only afterwards, defines himself. If man, as the existentialist conceives him, is indefinable, it is because at first he is nothing. Only afterward will he be something, and he himself will have made what he will be. Thus, there is no human nature, since there is no God to conceive it. Nor only is man what he conceives himself to be, but he is also only what he wills himself to be after this thrust toward existence.

Man is nothing else but what he makes of himself. Such is the first principle of existentialism. It is also what is called subjectivity, the name we are labeled when charges are brought against us. But what do we mean by this, if not that man has a greater dignity than a stone or table? For we mean that man first exists, that is, that man first of all is the being who hurls himself toward a future and who is conscious of imagining himself as being in the Future. Man is at the start a plan which is aware of itself, rather than a patch of moss, a piece of garbage, or a cauliflower; nothing exists prior to this plan; there is nothing in heaven; man will be what he will have planned to be. Not what he will want to be. Because by the word "will" we generally mean a conscious decision, which is subsequent to what we have already made of ourselves. I may want to belong to a political party, write a book, get married; but all that is only a manifestation of an earlier, more spontaneous choice that is called "will." But if existence really does precede essence, man is responsible for what he is. Thus, existentialism's first move is to make every man aware of what he is and to make the full responsibility of his existence rest on him. And when we say that a man is responsible for himself, we do not only mean that he is responsible for his own individuality, but that he is responsible for all men.

The word subjectivism has two meanings, and our opponents play on the two. Subjectivism means, on the one hand, that an individual chooses and makes himself; and, on the other, that it is impossible for man to transcend human subjectivity. The second of these is the essential meaning of existentialism. When we say that man chooses his own self, we mean that every one of us does likewise; but we also mean by that that in making this choice he also chooses all men. In fact, in creating the man that we want to be, there is not a single one of our acts which does not at the same time create an image of man as we think he ought to be. To choose to be this or that is to affirm at the same time the value of what we choose, because we can never choose evil. We always choose the good, and nothing can be good for us without being good for all.

If, on the other hand, existence precedes essence, and if we grant that we exist and fashion our image at one and the same time, the image is valid for everybody and for our whole age. Thus, our responsibility is much greater than we might have supposed, because it involves all mankind. If I am a workingman and choose to join a Christian trade-union rather than be a communist, and if by being a member I want to show that the best thing for man is resignation, that the kingdom of man is not of this world, I am not only involving my own case—I want to be resigned for everyone. As a result, my action has involved all humanity. To take a more individual matter, if I want to marry, to have children; even if this marriage depends solely on my own circumstances or passion or wish, I am involving all humanity in monogamy and not merely myself. Therefore, I am responsible for myself and for everyone else. I am creating a certain image of man of my own choosing. In choosing myself, I choose man.

This helps us understand what the actual content is of such rather grandiloquent words as anguish, forlornness, despair. As you will see, it's all quite simple.

First, what is meant by anguish? The existentialists say at once that man is anguish. What that means is this: the man who involves himself and who realizes that he is not only the person he chooses to be, but also a lawmaker who is, at the same time, choosing all mankind as well as himself, can not help escape the feeling of his total and deep responsibility. Of course, there are many people who are not anxious; but we claim that they are hiding their anxiety, that they are fleeing from it. Certainly, many people believe that when they do something, they themselves are the only ones involved, and when someone says to them, "What if everyone acted that way?" they shrug their shoulders and answer, "Everyone doesn't act that way." But really, one should always ask himself, "What would happen if everybody looked at things that way?" There is no escaping this disturbing thought except by a kind of double-dealing. A man who lies and makes excuses for himself by saying "not everybody does that," is someone with an uneasy conscience, because the act of lying implies that a universal value is conferred upon the lie.

Anguish is evident even when it conceals itself. This is the anguish that Kierkegaard called the anguish of Abraham. You know the story: an angel has order Abraham to sacrifice his son; if it really were an angel who has come and said, "You are Abraham, you shall sacrifice your son," everything would be all right. But everyone might first wonder, "Is it really an angel, and am I really Abraham? What proof do I have?" . . .

There is no question here of the kind of anguish which would lead to quietism, to inaction. It is a matter of a simple sort of anguish that anybody who has had responsibilities is familiar with. For example, when a military officer takes the responsibility for an attack and sends a certain number of men to death, he chooses to do so, an in the main he alone makes the choice. Doubtless, orders come from above, but they are too broad; he interprets them, and on this interpretation depend the lives of ten or fourteen or twenty men. In making a decision he can not help having a certain anguish. All leaders know this anguish. That doesn't keep them from acting; on the contrary, it is the very condition of their action. For it implies that they envisage a number of possibilities, and when they choose one, they realize that it has value only because it is chosen. We shall see that this kind of anguish, which is the kind that existentialism describes, is explained, in addition, by a direct responsibility to the other men whom it involves. It is not a curtain separating us from action, but is part of action itself.

When we speak of forlornness, a term Heidegger was fond of, we mean only that God does not exist and that we have to face the consequences of this. The existentialist is strongly opposed to a certain kind of secular ethics which would like to abolish God with the least possible expense. About 1880, some French teachers tried to set up a secular ethics which went something like this: God is a useless and costly hypothesis; we are discarding it; but, meanwhile, in order for there to be an ethics, a society, a civilization, it is essential that certain values be taken seriously and that they be considered as having an *a priori* existence. It must be obligatory, *a priori*, to be honest, not to lie, not to beat your wife, to have children, etc., etc. So we're going to try a little device which will make it possible to show that values exist all the same, inscribed in a heaven of ideas, though otherwise God does not exist. In other words—and this, I believe, is the tendency of everything called reformism in France—nothing will be changed if God does not exist. We shall find ourselves with the same norms of honesty, progress, and humanism, and we shall have made of God an outdated hypothesis which will peacefully die off by itself.

The existentialist, on the contrary, thinks it very distressing that God does not exist, because all possibility of finding values in a heaven of ideas disappears along with Him; there can no longer be an *a priori* Good, since there is no infinite and perfect consciousness to think it. Nowhere is it written that Good exists, that we must be honest, that we must no lie; because the fact is we are on a plane where there are only men. Dostoievsky said, "If God didn't exist, everything would be possible." That is the very starting point of existentialism. Indeed, everything is permissible if God does not exist, and as a result man is forlorn, because neither within him nor without does he find anything to cling to. He can't start making excuses for himself.

If existence really does precede essence, there is no explaining things away by reference to a fixed and given human nature. In other words, there is no determinism, man is free, man is freedom. On the other hand, if God does not exist, we find no values or commands to turn to which legitimize our conduct. So, in the bright realm of values, we have no excuse behind us, nor justification before us. We are alone, with no excuses.

REVIEW EXERCISES

1. Give a basic definition of natural law theory.
2. What is the difference between the scientific laws of nature and the natural law?
3. In what way is natural law theory teleological?
4. What specific natural or human species capacities are singled out by natural law theorists? How do these determine what we ought to do, according to the theory?
5. What is the difference between Aristotle and Aquinas on the theistic basis of natural law?
6. Explain one area of concern or criticism of natural law theory.
7. Describe the basis of rights according to natural rights theorists.
8. Give examples of a natural rights tradition.
9. Explain one of the things that a natural rights theorist must show to prove that we can ground rights in human nature.

8

Virtue Ethics

MANY OF us are familiar with at least some aspects of the biblical story of Abraham. In various versions, it is part of the heritage of three major religions: Christianity, Judaism, and Islam. According to one part of the story, to test Abraham's faith and obedience, God tells him to sacrifice his son, Isaac. Crushed by the order but dedicated to his God, Abraham brings Isaac to Mount Moriah. Just as Abraham is about to plunge his knife into Isaac, God stays his hand. Whatever you think about the story, and whether you think Abraham should have been willing to sacrifice his son, this story may be taken as an example of a person's being able to do something extremely difficult because of certain virtues or strengths he had.

When I have treated the topic of virtue in ethics classes, I have often begun by asking students about people whom they admire. Most often they name mothers, fathers, sisters, or brothers. At other times they name people in the public eye: athletes, inventors, artists. I then try to bring out the reasons, asking about the traits that are the basis for their admiration. The list of traits is instructive. It often includes perseverance, loving nature, generosity, independence, and standing up to others. These are among the traits of character traditionally known as *virtues*.

Abraham's Sacrifice by Rembrandt Harmensz Van Rijn

VIRTUES AND EVERYDAY LIFE

The theories that we have treated so far in this text are concerned with how we determine what is the right thing to do. In this chapter, we will examine a rather different approach to morality. It is focused on virtue or virtues. Rather than help us determine what we ought to *do*, virtue ethics asks how we ought to *be*. Virtue ethics is concerned with those traits of character that make one a good person. We can all think of persons whom we admire, and we can sometimes tell why we admire or look up to them. When we do so, we often say that they are generous, kind, patient, persevering, or loyal, for example. When these traits are unusually well developed, these persons may be regarded as heroes (such as the person who rescued someone on the tracks of the New York subway as described in Chapter 3) or even as saints. People can also exhibit bad character traits. For example, they can be tactless, careless, boorish, stingy, vindictive, disloyal, lazy, or egotistical. An ethics focused on virtue encourages us to develop the good traits and get rid of the bad ones.

The ethical issues that are treated in the second half of this text are generally controversial social issues: the death penalty, abortion, and terrorism, for example. Virtue ethics seems more personal. It involves not so much asking which side of some social issue one should support as what kind of person one wants to be. It is everyday life and how one lives it that matters: How to treat one's relatives, friends, or co-workers; how honest one should be; what is fair in various situations; or what should one teach one's children by both word and example.

In this chapter, we will ask basic questions about what virtue is, whether there are different kinds or classes of virtues, and whether a virtue ethics presents an adequate account of morality.

WHAT IS VIRTUE?

Let us begin by examining the very notion of virtue. Although we probably do not use the term *virtuous* as commonly today as in times past, we still understand the essence of its meaning. A virtuous person is a morally good person, and virtues are good traits. Loyalty is a virtue, and so is honesty. The opposite of virtue is vice. Stinginess is a vice. A moral philosophy that concentrates on the notion of virtue is called a *virtue ethics*. For virtue ethics, the moral life is about developing good *character*. The moral life is about determining what are the ideals for human life and trying to embody these ideals in one's own life. The virtues are then ways in which we embody these ideals. If we consider

honesty to be such an ideal, for example, then we ought to try to become honest persons.

As noted in the previous chapter, Aristotle was one of the earliest writers to ground morality in nature, and specifically in *human* nature. His ethics or moral theory also stressed the notion of virtue. For Aristotle, virtue was an excellence of some sort. Our word *virtue* originally came from the Latin *vir* and referred to strength or manliness.[1] In Aristotle's ethics, the term used for what we translate as virtue was *arete*. It referred to excellences of various types.

According to Aristotle, there are two basic types of excellence or virtues: intellectual virtues and moral virtues. Intellectual virtues are excellences of mind, such as the ability to understand and reason and judge well. Aristotle said that these traits are learned from teachers. Moral virtues, on the other hand, dispose us to act well. These virtues are learned not by being taught but by repetition. For instance, by practicing courage or honesty, we become more courageous and honest. Just as repetition in playing a musical instrument makes playing easier, so also repeated acts of honesty make it easier to be honest. The person who has the virtue of honesty finds it easier to be honest than the person who does not have the virtue. It has become habitual or second nature to him or her. The same thing applies to the opposite of virtue—namely, vice. The person who lies and lies again finds that lying is easier and telling the truth more difficult. One can have bad moral habits (vices) as well as good ones (virtues). Just like other bad habits, bad moral habits are difficult to change or break. Aristotle's list of virtues includes courage, temperance, justice, pride, and magnanimity.

However, Aristotle is probably most well known for his position that virtue is a mean between extremes. Thus, the virtue of courage is to be understood as a mean or middle between the two extremes of deficiency and excess. Too little courage is cowardice, and too much is foolhardiness. We should have neither too much fear when facing danger or challenges, which makes us unable to act; nor too little fear, which makes us throw all caution to the wind, as we say. Courage is having just the right amount of fear, depending on what is appropriate for us as individuals and for the circumstances we face.

So, also, the other virtues are means between extremes. Consider the examples from Aristotle's list below, and see if you could add any.

Our own list today might be both similar to and differ from Aristotle's. For example, we might include loyalty and honesty in our list. If loyalty is a virtue, then is it also a middle between two extremes? Can there be such a thing as too little or too much loyalty? What about honesty? Too much honesty might be seen as undisciplined openness, and too little as deceitfulness. Would the right amount of honesty be forthrightness? We could exemplify Aristotle's view of virtue as a mean with the childhood story of Goldilocks. When she entered the bears' house, she ate the porridge that was not too hot and not too cold, but "just right"![2] But not all virtues may be rightly thought of as means between extremes. For example, if justice is a virtue, then could there be such a thing as being too just or too little just?

Various contemporary moral philosophers have also stressed the importance of virtue.[3] Philippa Foot, for example, has developed a type of neonaturalistic virtue ethics. She believes that the virtues are "in some general way, beneficial. Human beings do not get on well without them."[4] According to Foot, it is both ourselves and our community that benefit from our having certain virtues, just as having certain vices harms both ourselves and our communities. Think of courage, temperance, and wisdom, for example, and ask yourself how persons having these virtues might benefit others as well as themselves. Some virtues such as charity, however, seem to benefit mostly others. She also wonders how we should determine which beneficial traits are to be thought of as moral virtues and which are not. Wit or powers of concentration benefit us, but we would probably not consider them to be *moral* virtues. Foot also asks whether the virtue is in the intention or the action. Think of generosity. Does the person who

intends to be generous but cannot seem to do what helps others really possess the virtue of generosity? Or rather is it the person who actually does help who has the virtue? She believes that possessing the virtue of generosity must be more than simply having a naturally outgoing personality. It is something we choose to develop and work at personifying. Furthermore, following Aristotle, Foot also agrees that the virtues are corrective.[5] They help us be and do things that are difficult for us. Courage, for example, helps us overcome natural fear. Temperance helps us control our desires. People differ in their natural inclinations and thus would also differ in what virtues would be most helpful for them to develop. This is just one example of how the notion of virtue continues to be discussed by moral philosophers.

EVALUATING VIRTUE ETHICS

One question that has been raised for virtue ethics concerns how we determine which traits are virtues. Are there any universally valuable traits, for example? Wherever friendship exists, loyalty would seem necessary, although the form it might take would vary according to time and place. So also would honesty seem necessary for human relations wherever they exist. We might think that Aristotle's own list of virtues reflected what were considered civic virtues of his day. Our lists today might more reflect aspects of our own times. Contemporary moral philosopher Alasdair MacIntyre believes that virtues depend at least partly on the practices that constitute a culture or society. A warlike society will value heroic virtues, whereas a peaceful and prosperous society might think of generosity as a particularly important virtue.[6] However, these must be virtues specific to human beings as humans, for otherwise one could not speak of "human excellences." But

	Deficit (Too Little)	Virtue (the Mean)	Excess (Too Much)
Fear	Cowardice	Courage	Foolhardiness
Giving	Illiberality	Liberality	Prodigality
Self-Regard	Humility	Pride	Vanity
Pleasures	[No Name Given]	Temperance	Profligacy

this is just the problem. What is it to live a full human life? Can one specify this apart from what it is to live such a life in a particular society or as a particular person? This problem is related to the issue regarding stereotypical masculine and feminine virtues. The problem here is not only how we know what excellences are human excellences but also whether there are any such traits that are ideal for all persons.

Another problem about virtue is raised by Philippa Foot. Who manifests the virtue of courage most—the person "who wants to run away but does not or the one who does not even want to run away"?[7] One reason why this question is difficult to answer is that we generally believe that we ought to be rewarded for our moral efforts, and thus the person who wants to run away but does not seems the more courageous. On the other hand, possession of the virtue of courage is supposed to make it easier to be brave. Part of Foot's own answer to this dilemma has to do with the distinction between those fears for which we are in some way responsible and those that we cannot help. Thus, the person who feels like running away because she has contributed by her own choices to being afraid is not the more virtuous person. In the reading from her essay on virtue included in this chapter, Foot also addresses the question of whether someone who does something morally wrong—say, robs a bank or commits a murder—and does so courageously, demonstrates the virtue of courage.

We can also ask whether virtue ethics is really a distinct type of ethics. Consider the other theories we have treated: utilitarianism and Kantianism. The concept of virtue is not foreign to Mill or Kant. However, for both of them it is secondary. Their moral theories tell us how we ought to decide what to *do*. Doing the right thing—and with Kant, for the right reason—is primary. However, if the development of certain habits of action or tendencies to act in a certain way will enable us to do good more easily, then they would surely be recognized by these philosophers as good. Utilitarians would encourage the development of those virtues that would be conducive to the maximization of happiness. If temperance in eating and drinking will help us avoid the suffering that can come from illness and

drunkenness, then this virtue ought to be encouraged and developed in the young. So also with other virtues. According to a Kant, it would be well to develop in ourselves and others habits that would make it more likely that we would be fair and treat people as ends rather than simply as means.

In virtue ethics, however, the primary goal is to be a good person. Now, some people argue that *being* good is only a function of being more inclined to *do* good. For every virtue, there is a corresponding good to be achieved or done. The just person acts justly and does what increases justice, for example. Is virtue then simply one aspect of these otherwise action-oriented moral philosophies? Perhaps so. However, virtue ethics still has a different emphasis. It is an ethics whose goal is to determine what is essential to be a well-functioning or flourishing human being or person. Virtue ethics stresses the ideal for humans or persons. As an ethics of ideals or excellences, it is an optimistic and positive type of ethics. One problem that virtue ethics may face is what to say about those of us who do not meet the ideal. If we fall short of the ideal, does this make us bad? As with all moral theories, many questions concerning virtue remain to engage and puzzle us.

The first reading is the classic selection on virtue from Aristotle's *The Nicomachean Ethics*. In the second selection, Philippa Foot addresses certain central questions about virtue.

NOTES
1. Milton Gonsalves, *Fagothy's Right and Reason*, 9th ed. (Columbus, OH: Merrill, 1989), 201.
2. I thank reviewer Robert P. Tucker of Florida Southern College for this example.
3. See, for example, the collection of articles in Christina Hoff Sommers, *Vice and Virtue in Everyday Life* (New York: Harcourt Brace Jovanovich, 1985).
4. Philippa Foot, *Virtues and Vices* (Oxford, England: Oxford University Press, 2002).
5. Ibid.
6. Alasdair MacIntyre, "The Virtue in Heroic Societies" and "The Virtues at Athens," in *After Virtue* (Notre Dame, IN: Notre Dame University Press, 1984), 121–145.
7. Foot, op. cit.

R E A D I N G
The Nicomachean Ethics
ARISTOTLE

Study Questions

1. According to Aristotle, what is meant by the "good"?
2. What is the function of a person?
3. What is virtue and how do we acquire it?
4. How is virtue a mean? Explain by using some of Aristotle's examples.
5. Why is it so difficult to be virtuous?

THE NATURE OF THE GOOD*

Every art and every scientific inquiry, and similarly every action and purpose, may be said to aim at some good. Hence the good has been well defined as that at which all things aim. But it is clear that there is a difference in the ends; for the ends are sometimes activities, and sometimes results beyond the mere activities. Also, where there are certain ends beyond the actions, the results are naturally superior to the activities.

As there are various actions, arts, and sciences, it follows that the ends are also various. Thus health is the end of medicine, a vessel of shipbuilding, victory of strategy, and wealth of domestic economy. It often happens that there are a number of such arts or sciences which fall under a single faculty, as the art of making bridles, and all such other arts as make the instruments of horsemanship, under horsemanship, and this again as well as every military action under strategy, and in the same way other arts or sciences under other faculties. But in all these cases the ends of the architectonic arts or sciences, whatever they may be, are more desirable than those of the subordinate arts or sciences, as it is for the sake of the former that the latter are themselves sought after. It makes no difference to the argument whether the activities themselves are the ends of the actions, or something else beyond the activities as in the above mentioned sciences.

Selections from *The Nicomachean Ethics*, Books 1 and 2. Translated by J. E. C. Welldon (London: Macmillan, 1892).

*Headings added by the editor.—ED.

If it is true that in the sphere of action there is an end which we wish for its own sake, and for the sake of which we wish everything else, and that we do not desire all things for the sake of something else (for, if that is so, the process will go on ad infinitum, and our desire will be idle and futile) it is clear that this will be the good or the supreme good. Does it not follow then that the knowledge of this supreme good is of great importance for the conduct of life, and that, if we know it, we shall be like archers who have a mark at which to aim, we shall have a better chance of attaining what we want? But, if this is the case, we must endeavour to comprehend, at least in outline, its nature, and the science or faculty to which it belongs. . . .

HAPPINESS: LIVING AND DOING WELL

As every knowledge and moral purpose aspires to some good, what is in our view the good at which the political science aims, and what is the highest of all practical goods? As to its name there is, I may say, a general agreement. The masses and the cultured classes agree in calling it happiness, and conceive that "to live well" or "to do well" is the same thing as "to be happy." But as to the nature of happiness they do not agree, nor do the masses give the same account of it as the philosophers. The former define it as something visible and palpable, e.g. pleasure, wealth, or honour; different people give different definitions of it, and often the same person gives different definitions at different times; for when a person has been ill, it is health, when he is poor, it is wealth, and, if he is conscious of his own ignorance, he envies people who use grand language above his own comprehension. Some philosophers[1] on the other hand have held that, besides these various goods, there is an absolute good which is the cause of goodness in them all. . . .

THE FUNCTION OF A PERSON

Perhaps, however, it seems a truth which is generally admitted, that happiness is the supreme good; what is wanted is to define its nature a little more clearly. The best way of arriving at such a definition will probably be to ascertain the function of Man. For, as with a flute-player, a statuary, or any artisan, or in fact anybody who has a definite function and action, his goodness, or excellence seems to lie in his function, so it would seem to be with Man, if indeed he has a definite function. Can it be said then that, while a carpenter and a cobbler have definite functions and actions, Man, unlike them, is naturally functionless? The reasonable view is that, as the eye, the hand, the foot, and similarly each several part of the body has a definite function, so Man may be regarded as having a definite function apart from all these. What then, can this function be? It is not life; for life is apparently something which man shares with the plants; and it is something peculiar to him that we are looking for. We must exclude therefore the life of nutrition and increase. There is next what may be called the life of sensation. But this too, is apparently shared by Man with horses, cattle, and all other animals. There remains what I may call the practical life of the rational part of Man's being. But the rational part is twofold; it is rational partly in the sense of being obedient to reason, and partly in the sense of possessing reason and intelligence. The practical life too may be conceived of in two ways,[2] viz., either as a moral state, or as a moral activity: but we must understand by it the life of activity, as this seems to be the truer form of the conception.

The function of Man then is an activity of soul in accordance with reason, or not independently of reason. Again the functions of a person of a certain kind, and of such a person who is good of his kind e.g. of a harpist and a good harpist, are in our view generically the same, and this view is true of people of all kinds without exception, the superior excellence being only an addition to the function; for it is the function of a harpist to play the harp, and of a good harpist to play the harp well. This being so, if we define the function of Man as a kind of life, and this life as an activity of soul, or a course of action in conformity with reason, if the function of a good man is such activity or action of a good and noble kind, and if everything is successfully performed when it is performed in accordance with its proper excellence, it

follows that the good of Man is an activity of soul in accordance with virtue or, if there are more virtues than one, in accordance with the best and most complete virtue. But it is necessary to add the words "in a complete life." For as one swallow or one day does not make a spring, so one day or a short time does not make a fortunate or happy man. . . .

VIRTUE

Virtue or excellence being twofold, partly intellectual and partly moral, intellectual virtue is both originated and fostered mainly by teaching; it therefore demands experience and time. Moral[3] virtue on the other hand is the outcome of habit. . . . From this fact it is clear that no moral virtue is implanted in us by nature; a law of nature cannot be altered by habituation. Thus a stone naturally tends to fall downwards, and it cannot be habituated or trained to rise upwards, even if we were to habituate it by throwing it upwards ten thousand times; not again can fire be trained to sink downwards, nor anything else that follows one natural law be habituated or trained to follow another. It is neither by nature then nor in defiance of nature that virtues are implanted in us. Nature gives us the capacity of receiving them, and that capacity is perfected by habit.

Again, if we take the various natural powers which belong to us, we first acquire the proper faculties and afterwards display the activities. It is clearly so with the senses. It was not by seeing frequently or hearing frequently that we acquired the senses of seeing or hearing; on the contrary it was because we possessed the senses that we made use of them, not by making use of them that we obtained them. But the virtues we acquire by first exercising them, as is the case with all the arts, for it is by doing what we ought to do when we have learnt the arts that we learn the arts themselves; we become e.g. builders by building and harpists by playing the harp. Similarly it is by doing just acts that we become just, by doing temperate acts that we become temperate, by doing courageous acts that we become courageous. The experience of states is a witness to this truth, for it is by training the habits that legislators make the citizens good. This is the object which all legislators have at heart; if a legislator does not succeed in it, he fails of his purpose, and it constitutes the distinction between a good polity and a bad one.

Again, the causes and means by which any virtue is produced and by which it is destroyed are the same; and it is equally so with any art; for it is by playing the harp that both good and bad harpists are produced and the case of builders and all other artisans is similar, as it is by building well that they will be good builders and by building badly that they will be bad builders. If it were not so, there would be no need of anybody to teach them; they would all be born good or bad in their several trades. The case of the virtues is the same. It is by acting in such transactions as take place between man and man that we become either just or unjust. It is by acting in the face of danger and by habituating ourselves to fear or courage that we become either cowardly or courageous. It is much the same with our desires and angry passions. Some people become temperate and gentle, others become licentious and passionate, according as they conduct themselves in one way or another way in particular circumstances. In a word moral states are the results of activities corresponding to the moral states themselves. It is our duty therefore to give a certain character to the activities, as the moral states depend upon the differences of the activities. Accordingly the difference between one training of the habits and another from early days is not a light matter, but is serious or rather all-important.

DEFICIENCY AND EXCESS

The first point to be observed then is that in such matters as we are considering deficiency and excess are equally fatal. It is so, as we observe, in regard to health and strength; for we must judge of what we cannot see by the evidence of what we do see. Excess or deficiency of gymnastic exercise is fatal to strength. Similarly an excess or deficiency of meat and drink is fatal to health, whereas a suitable amount produces, augments and sustains it. It is the same then with temperance, courage, and the other virtues. A person who avoids and is afraid of everything and faces nothing becomes a coward; a person who is not afraid of anything but is ready to face everything becomes foolhardy. Similarly he who enjoys every pleasure and never abstains from any pleasure is licentious; he who eschews all pleasures like a boor is an insensible sort of person. For temperance and courage are destroyed by excess and deficiency but preserved by the mean state.

Again, not only are the causes and the agencies of production, increase and destruction in the moral states the same, but the sphere of their activity will be proved to be the same also. It is so in other instances which are more conspicuous, e.g. in strength; for strength is produced by taking a great deal of food and undergoing a great deal of labour, and it is the strong man who is able to take most food and to undergo most labour. The same is the case with the virtues. It is by abstinence from pleasures that we become temperate, and, when we have become temperate, we are best able to abstain from them. So too with courage; it is by habituating ourselves to despise and face alarms that we become courageous, and, when we have become courageous, we shall be best able to face them.

THE NATURE OF VIRTUE

We have next to consider the nature of virtue.

Now, as the qualities of the soul are three, viz. emotions, faculties and moral states, it follows that virtue must be one of the three. By the emotions I mean desire, anger, fear, courage, envy, joy, love, hatred, regret, emulation, pity, in a word whatever is attended by pleasure or pain. I call those faculties in respect of which we are said to be capable of experiencing these emotions, e.g. capable of getting angry or being pained or feeling pity. And I call those moral states in respect of which we are well or ill-disposed towards the emotions, ill-disposed e.g. towards the passion of anger, if our anger be too violent or too feeble, and well-disposed, if it be duly moderated, and similarly towards the other emotions.

Now neither the virtues nor the vices are emotions; for we are not called good or evil in respect of our emotions but in respect of our virtues or vices. Again, we are not praised or blamed in respect of our emotions; a person is not praised for being afraid or being angry, nor blamed for being angry in an absolute sense, but only for being angry in a certain way; but we are praised or blamed in respect of our virtues or vices. Again, whereas we are angry or afraid without deliberate purpose, the virtues are in some sense deliberate purposes, or do not exist in the absence of deliberate purpose. It may be added that while we are said to be moved in respect of our emotions, in respect of our virtues or vices we are not said to be moved but to have a certain disposition.

These reasons also prove that the virtues are not faculties. For we are not called either good or bad, nor are we praised or blamed, as having an abstract capacity for emotion. Also while Nature gives us our faculties, it is not Nature that makes us good or bad, but this is a point which we have already discussed. If then the virtues are neither emotions nor faculties, it remains that they must be moral states.

The nature of virtue has been now generically described. But it is not enough to state merely that virtue is a moral state, we must also describe the character of that moral state.

It must be laid down then that every virtue or excellence has the effect of producing a good condition of that of which it is a virtue or excellence, and of enabling it to perform its function well. Thus the excellence of the eye makes the eye good and its function good, as it is by the excellence of the eye that we see well. Similarly, the excellence of the horse makes a horse excellent and good at racing, at carrying its rider and at facing the enemy.

If then this is universally true, the virtue or excellence of man will be such a moral state as makes a man good and able to perform his proper function well. We have already explained how this will be the case, but another way of making it clear will be to study the nature or character of this virtue.

VIRTUE AS A MEAN

Now in everything, whether it be continuous or discrete,[4] it is possible to take a greater, a smaller, or an equal amount, and this either absolutely or in relation to ourselves, the equal being a mean between excess and deficiency. By the mean in respect of the thing itself, or the absolute mean, I understand that which is equally distinct from both extremes; and this is one and the same thing for everybody. By the mean considered relatively to ourselves I understand that which is neither too much nor too little; but this is not one thing, nor is it the same for everybody.

Thus if 10 be too much and 2 too little we take 6 as a mean in respect of the thing itself; for 6 is as much greater than 2 as it is less than 10, and this is a mean in arithmetical proportion. But the mean considered relatively to ourselves must not be ascertained in this way. It does not follow that if 10 pounds of meat be too much and 2 be too little for a man to eat, a trainer will order him 6 pounds, as this may itself be too much or too little for the person who is to take it; it will be too little e.g. for Milo,[5] but too much for a beginner in gymnastics. It will be the same with running and wrestling; the right amount will vary with the individual. This being so, everybody who understands his business avoids alike excess and deficiency; he seeks and chooses the mean, not the absolute mean, but the mean considered relatively to ourselves.

Every science then performs its function well, if it regards the mean and refers the works which it produces to the mean. This is the reason why it is usually said of successful works that it is impossible to take anything from them or to add anything to them, which implies that excess or deficiency is fatal to excellence but that the mean state ensures it. Good . . . artists too, as we say, have an eye to the mean in their works. But virtue, like Nature herself, is more accurate and better than any art; virtue therefore will aim at the mean;—I speak of moral virtue, as it is moral virtue which is concerned with emotions and actions, and it is these which admit of excess and deficiency and the mean. Thus it is possible to go too far, or not to go far enough, in respect of fear, courage, desire, anger, pity, and pleasure and pain generally, and the excess and the deficiency are alike wrong; but to experience these emotions at the right times and on the right occasions and towards the right persons and for the right causes and in the right manner is the mean or the supreme good, which is characteristic of virtue. Similarly there may be excess, deficiency, or the mean, in regard to actions. But virtue is concerned with emotions and actions, and here excess is an error and deficiency a fault, whereas the mean is successful and laudable, and success and merit are both characteristics of virtue.

It appears then that virtue is a mean state, so far at least as it aims at the mean. Again, there are many different ways of going wrong; for evil is in its nature infinite, to use the Pythagorean[6] figure, but good is finite. But there is only one possible way of going right. Accordingly the former is easy and the latter difficult; it is easy to miss the mark but difficult to hit it. This again is a reason why excess and deficiency are characteristics of vice and the mean state a characteristic of virtue.

"For good is simple, evil manifold."[7]

Virtue then is a state of deliberate moral purpose consisting in a mean that is relative to ourselves, the mean being determined . . . by reason, or as a prudent man would determine it.

It is a mean state *firstly as lying* between two vices, the vice of excess on the one hand, and the vice of deficiency on the other, and secondly because, whereas the vices either fall short of or go beyond what is proper in the emotions and actions, virtue not only discovers but embraces that mean.

Accordingly, virtue, if regarded in its essence or theoretical conception, is a mean state, but, if regarded from the point of view of the highest good, or of excellence, it is an extreme.

But it is not every action or every emotion that admits of a mean state. There are some whose very name implies wickedness, as e.g. malice, shamelessness, and envy, among emotions, or adultery, theft, and murder, among actions. All these, and others like them, are censured as being intrinsically wicked, not merely the excesses or deficiencies of them. It is never possible then to be right in respect of them; they are always sinful.

Right or wrong in such actions as adultery does not depend on our committing them with the right person, at the right time or in the right manner; on the contrary it is sinful to do anything of the kind at all. It would be equally wrong then to suppose that there can be a mean state or an excess or deficiency in unjust, cowardly, or licentious conduct; for, if it were so, there would be a mean state of an excess or of a deficiency, an excess of an excess and a deficiency of a deficiency. But as in temperance and courage there can be no excess or deficiency because the mean is, in a sense, an extreme, so too in these cases there cannot be a mean or an excess or deficiency, but, however the acts may be done, they are wrong. For it is a general rule that an excess or

deficiency does not admit of a mean state, nor a mean state of an excess or deficiency.

But it is not enough to lay down this as a general rule; it is necessary to apply it to particular cases, as in reasonings upon actions, general statements, although they are broader . . . , are less exact than particular statements. For all action refers to particulars, and it is essential that our theories should harmonize with the particular cases to which they apply.

SOME VIRTUES

We must take particular virtues then from the catalogue[8] *of virtues*.

In regard to feelings of fear and confidence, courage is a mean state. On the side of excess, he whose fearlessness is excessive has no name, as often happens, but he whose confidence is excessive is foolhardy, while he whose timidity is excessive and whose confidence is deficient is a coward.

In respect of pleasures and pains, although not indeed of all pleasures and pains, and to a less extent in respect of pains than of pleasures, the mean state is temperance . . . , the excess is licentiousness. We never find people who are deficient in regard to pleasures; accordingly such people again have not received a name, but we may call them insensible.

As regards the giving and taking of money, the mean state is liberality, the excess and deficiency are prodigality and illiberality. Here the excess and deficiency take opposite forms; for while the prodigal man is excessive in spending and deficient in taking, the illiberal man is excessive in taking and deficient in spending.

(For the present we are giving only a rough and summary account *of the virtues*, and that is sufficient for our purpose; we will hereafter determine their character more exactly.[9])

In respect of money there are other dispositions as well. There is the mean state which is magnificence; for the magnificent man, as having to do with large sums of money, differs from the liberal man who has to do only with small sums; and the excess corresponding to it is bad taste or vulgarity, the deficiency is meanness. These are different from the excess and deficiency of liberality; what the difference is will be explained hereafter.

In respect of honour and dishonour the mean state is highmindedness, the excess is what is called vanity, the deficiency littlemindedness. Corresponding to liberality, which, as we said, differs from magnificence as having to do *not with great but* with small sums of money, there is a moral state which has to do with petty honour and is related to highmindedness which has to do with great honour; for it is possible to aspire to honour in the right way, or in a way which is excessive or insufficient, and if a person's aspirations are excessive, he is called ambitious, if they are deficient, he is called unambitious, while if they are between the two, he has no name. The dispositions too are nameless, except that the disposition of the ambitious person is called ambition. The consequence is that the extremes lay claim to the mean or intermediate place. We ourselves speak of one who observes the mean sometimes as ambitious, and at other times as unambitious; we sometimes praise an ambitious, and at other times an unambitious person. The reason for our doing so will be stated in due course, but let us now discuss the other virtues in accordance with the method which we have followed hitherto.

Anger, like other emotions, has its excess, its deficiency, and its mean state. It may be said that they have no names, but as we call one who observes the mean gentle, we will call the mean state gentleness. Among the extremes, if a person errs on the side of excess, he may be called passionate and his vice passionateness, if on that of deficiency, he may be called impassive and his deficiency impassivity.

There are also three other mean states with a certain resemblance to each other, and yet with a difference. For while they are all concerned with intercourse in speech and action, they are different in that one of them is concerned with truth in such intercourse, and the others with pleasantness, one with pleasantness in amusement and the other with pleasantness in the various circumstances of life. We must therefore discuss these states in order to make it clear that in all cases it is the mean state which is an object of praise, and the extremes are neither right nor laudable but censurable. It is true that these mean and extreme states are generally nameless, but we must do our best here as elsewhere to give them a name, so that our argument may be clear and easy to follow. . . .

WHY IT IS SO DIFFICULT TO BE VIRTUOUS

That is the reason why it is so hard to be virtuous; for it is always hard work to find the mean in anything, e.g. it is not everybody, but only a man of science[10] who can find the mean or centre of a circle. So too anybody can get angry—that is an easy matter—and anybody can give or spend money, but to give it to the right persons, to give the right amount of it and to give it at the right time and for the right cause and in the right way, this is not what anybody can do, nor is it easy. That is the reason why it is rare and laudable and noble to do well. Accordingly one who aims at the mean must begin by departing from that extreme which is the more contrary to the mean; he must act in the spirit of Calypso's[11] advice,

"Far from this smoke and swell keep thou thy bark,"

for of the two extremes one is more sinful than the other. As it is difficult then to hit the mean exactly, we must take the second best course,[12] as the saying is, and choose the lesser of two evils, and this we shall best do in the way that we have described, *i.e. by steering clear of the evil which is further from the mean.* We must also observe the things to which we are ourselves particularly prone, as different natures have different inclinations, and we may ascertain what these are by a consideration of our feelings of pleasure and pain. And then we must drag ourselves in the direction opposite to them; for it is by removing ourselves as far as possible from what is wrong that we shall arrive at the mean, as we do when we pull a crooked stick straight.

But in all cases we must especially be on our guard against what is pleasant and against pleasure, as we are not impartial judges of pleasure. Hence our attitude towards pleasure must be like that of the elders of the people in the Iliad towards Helen, and we must never be afraid of applying the words they use; for if we dismiss pleasure as they dismissed Helen, we shall be less likely to go wrong. It is by action of this kind, to put it summarily, that we shall best succeed in hitting the mean.

NOTES*

1. Aristotle is thinking of the Platonic "ideas."
2. In other words life may be taken to mean either the mere possession of certain faculties or their active exercise.
3. The student of Aristotle must familiarize himself with the conception of intellectual as well as of moral virtues, although it is not the rule in modern philosophy to speak of the "virtues" of the intellect.
4. In Aristotelian language, as Mr. Peters says, a straight line is a "continuous quantity" but a rouleau of sovereigns a "discrete quantity."
5. The famous Crotoniate wrestler.
6. The Pythagoreans, starting from the mystical significance of number, took the opposite principles of "the finite" . . . and "the infinite" . . . to represent good and evil.
7. A line—perhaps Pythagorean—of unknown authorship.
8. It would seem that a catalogue of virtues . . . must have been recognized in the Aristotelian school. Cp. *Eud. Eth*. ii. ch. 3.
9. I have placed this sentence in a parenthesis, as it interrupts the argument respecting the right use of money.
10. Aristotle does not seem to be aware that the centre . . . of a circle is not really comparable to the mean . . . between the vices.
11. *Odyssey*, xii. 219, 200; but it is Odysseus who speaks there, and the advice has been given him not by Calypso but by Circe (ibid. 101–110).
12. The Greek proverb means properly "we must take to the oars, if sailing is impossible."

*Some notes omitted; the remaining notes renumbered.—ED.

READING
Virtues and Vices
PHILIPPA FOOT

Study Questions

1. What does Foot mean by saying that one cannot get on well without the virtues?
2. What is meant by saying that virtue is a perfection of the will rather than of body or mind?
3. What is the problem in attempting to decide whether virtue is a matter of intention rather than performance, or attitudes rather than actions?
4. What two things belong to the nature of wisdom, according to Foot, and how does she describe each?
5. What difference does she cite between virtue and skill or art?
6. What does she mean by saying that the virtues are corrective, and what examples of this does she give?
7. How are justice and charity different in this regard, according to Foot?
8. How do individual circumstances and obstacles to virtue play a role in deciding whether doing something right but difficult is more or less virtuous?
9. How does this relate to Kant's contention that some acts are in accordance with virtue yet have no positive moral worth?
10. What does Foot say about whether virtue can be displayed in bad actions? How does she use the example of poison to explain her view?

I

. . .[I]t seems that virtues are, in some general way, beneficial. Human beings do not get on well without them. Nobody can get on well if he lacks courage, and does not have some measure of temperance and wisdom, while communities where justice and charity are lacking are apt to be wretched places to live, as Russia was under the Stalinist terror, or Sicily under the Mafia. But now we must ask to whom the benefit goes, whether to the man who has the virtue or rather to those who have to do with him? In the case of some of the virtues the answer seems clear.

Courage, temperance and wisdom benefit both the man who has these dispositions and other people as well; and moral failings such as pride, vanity, worldliness, and avarice harm both their possessor and others, though chiefly perhaps the former. But what about the virtues of charity and justice? These are directly concerned with the welfare of others, and with what is owed to them; and since each may require sacrifice of interest on the part of the virtuous man both may seem to be deleterious to their possessor and beneficial to others. Whether in fact it is so has, of course, been a matter of controversy since Plato's time or earlier. It is a reasonable opinion that on the whole a man is better off for being charitable and just, but this is not to say that circumstances may not arise in which he will have to sacrifice everything for charity or justice.

Nor is this the only problem about the relation between virtue and human good. For one very difficult question concerns the relation between justice and the common good. Justice, in the wide sense in which it is understood in discussions of the cardinal virtues, and in this paper, has to do with that to which someone has a right—that which he is owed in respect of non-interference and positive service—and rights may stand in the way of the pursuit of the common good. Or so at least it seems to those who reject utilitarian doctrines. This dispute cannot be settled here, but I shall treat justice as a virtue independent of charity, and standing as a possible limit on the scope of that virtue.

Let us say then, leaving unsolved problems behind us, that virtues are in general beneficial characteristics, and indeed ones that a human being needs to have, for his own sake and that of his fellows. This will not, however, take us far towards a definition of a virtue, since there are many other qualities of a man that may be similarly beneficial, as for instance bodily characteristics such as health and physical strength, and mental powers such as those of memory and concentration. What is it, we must ask, that differentiates virtues from such things?

As a first approximation to an answer we might say that while health and strength are excellences of the body, and memory and concentration of the mind, it is the will that is good in a man of virtue. But this suggestion is worth only as much as the

explanation that follows it. What might we mean by saying that virtue belongs to the will?

In the first place we observe that it is primarily by his intentions that a man's moral dispositions are judged. If he does something unintentionally, this is usually irrelevant to our estimate of his virtue. But of course this thesis must be qualified, because failures in performance rather than intention may show a lack of virtue. This will be so when, for instance, one man brings harm to another without realizing he is doing it, but where his ignorance is itself culpable. Sometimes in such cases there will be a previous act or omission to which we can point as the source of the ignorance. Charity requires that we take care to find out how to render assistance where we are likely to be called on to do so, and thus, for example, it is contrary to charity to fail to find out about elementary first aid. But in an interesting class of cases in which it seems again to be performance rather than intention that counts in judging a man's virtue there is no possibility of shifting the judgement to previous intention. For sometimes one man succeeds where another fails not because there is some specific difference in their previous conduct but rather because his heart lies in a different place; and the disposition of the heart is part of virtue.

Thus it seems right to attribute a kind of moral failing to some deeply discouraging and debilitating people who say, without lying, that they mean to be helpful; and on the other side to see virtue *par excellence* in one who is prompt and resourceful in doing good. In his novel *A Single Pebble* John Hersey describes such a man, speaking of a rescue in a swift flowing river:

> It was the head tracker's marvelous swift response that captured my admiration at first, his split second solicitousness when he heard a cry of pain, his finding in mid-air, as it were, the only way to save the injured boy. But there was more to it than that. His action, which could not have been mulled over in his mind, showed a deep, instinctive love of life, a compassion, an optimism, which made me feel very good. . . .

What this suggests is that a man's virtue may be judged by his innermost desires as well as by his intentions; and this fits with our idea that a virtue such as generosity lies as much in someone's attitudes as in his actions. Pleasure in the good fortune of others is, one thinks, the sign of a generous spirit; and small reactions of pleasure and displeasure often the surest of signs of a man's moral disposition.

None of this shows that it is wrong to think of virtues as belonging to the will; what it does show is that 'will' must here be understood in its widest sense, to cover what is wished for as well as what is sought.

A different set of considerations will, however, force us to give up any simple statement about the relation between virtue and will, and these considerations have to do with the virtue of wisdom. Practical wisdom, we said, was counted by Aristotle among the intellectual virtues, and while our *wisdom* is not quite the same as *phronèsis* or *prudentia* it too might seem to belong to the intellect rather than the will. Is not wisdom a matter of knowledge, and how can knowledge be a matter of intention or desire? The answer is that it isn't, so that there is good reason for thinking of wisdom as an intellectual virtue. But on the other hand wisdom has special connexions with the will, meeting it at more than one point.

In order to get this rather complex picture in focus we must pause for a little and ask what it is that we ourselves understand by wisdom: what the wise man knows and what he does. Wisdom, as I see it, has two parts. In the first place the wise man knows the means to certain good ends; and secondly he knows how much particular ends are worth. Wisdom in its first part is relatively easy to understand. It seems that there are some ends belonging to human life in general rather than to particular skills such as medicine or boatbuilding, ends having to do with such matters as friendship, marriage, the bringing up of children, or the choice of ways of life; and it seems that knowledge of how to act well in these matters belongs to some people but not to others. We call those who have this knowledge wise, while those who do not have it are seen as lacking wisdom. So, as both Aristotle and Aquinas insisted, wisdom is to be contrasted with cleverness because cleverness is the ability to take the right steps to any end, whereas wisdom is related only to good ends and to human life in general rather than to the ends of particular arts.

Moreover, we should add, there belongs to wisdom only that part of knowledge which is within the reach of any ordinary adult human being; knowledge that can be acquired only by someone who is clever or who has access to special training is not counted as part of wisdom, and would not be so counted even if it could serve the ends that wisdom serves. It is therefore quite wrong to suggest that wisdom cannot be a moral virtue because virtue must be within the reach of anyone who really wants it and some people are too stupid to be anything but ignorant even about the most fundamental matters of human life. Some people are wise without being at all clever or well informed: they make good decisions and they know, as we say, "what's what."

In short wisdom, in what we called its first part, is connected with the will in the following ways. To begin with it presupposes good ends: the man who is wise does not merely know *how* to do good things such as looking after his children well, or strengthening someone in trouble, but must also want to do them. And then wisdom, in so far as it consists of knowledge which anyone can gain in the course of an ordinary life, is available to anyone who really wants it. As Aquinas put it, it belongs "to a power under the direction of the will."[1]

The second part of wisdom, which has to do with values, is much harder to describe, because here we meet ideas which are curiously elusive, such as the thought that some pursuits are more worthwhile than others, and some matters trivial and some important in human life. Since it makes good sense to say that most men waste a lot of their lives in ardent pursuit of what is trivial and unimportant it is not possible to explain the important and the trivial in terms of the amount of attention given to different subjects by the average man. But I have never seen, or been able to think out, a true account of this matter, and I believe that a complete account of wisdom, and of certain other virtues and vices must wait until this gap can be filled. What we can see is that one of the things a wise man knows and a foolish man does not is that such things as social position, and wealth, and the good opinion of the world, are too dearly bought at the cost of health or friendship or family ties. So we may say that a man who lacks wisdom "has false values," and that vices such as vanity and worldliness and avarice are contrary to wisdom in a special way. There is always an element of false judgement about these vices, since the man who is vain for instance sees admiration as more important than it is, while the worldly man is apt to see the good life as one of wealth and power. Adapting Aristotle's distinction between the weak-willed man (the akrat) who follows pleasure though he knows, in some sense, that he should not, and the licentious man (the akolastos) who sees the life of pleasure as the good life,[2] we may say that moral failings such as these are never purely "akratic." It is true that a man may criticize himself for his worldliness or vanity or love of money, but then it is his values that are the subject of his criticism.

Wisdom in this second part is, therefore, partly to be described in terms of apprehension, and even judgement, but since it has to do with a man's attachments it also characterizes his will.

The idea that virtues belong to the will, and that this helps to distinguish them from such things as bodily strength or intellectual ability has, then, survived the consideration of the virtue of wisdom, albeit in a fairly complex and slightly attenuated form. And we shall find this idea useful again if we turn to another important distinction that must be made, namely that between virtues and other practical excellences such as arts and skills.

Aristotle has sometimes been accused, for instance by von Wright, of failing to see how different virtues are from arts or skills,[3] but in fact one finds, among the many things that Aristotle and Aquinas say about this difference, the observation that seems to go to the heart of the matter. In the matter of arts and skills, they say, voluntary error is preferable to involuntary error, while in the matter of virtues (what we call virtues) it is the reverse.[4] The last part of the thesis is actually rather hard to interpret, because it is not clear what is meant by the idea of involuntary viciousness. But we can leave this aside and still have all we need in order to distinguish arts or skills from virtues. If we think, for instance, of someone who deliberately makes a spelling mistake (perhaps when writing on the blackboard in order to explain this particular point) we see that this does not in any way count against his skill as a speller: "I did it deliberately" rebuts an accusation of this kind. And what we can say without running into any difficulties is that there is no comparable rebuttal in the case of an accusation

relating to lack of virtue. If a man acts unjustly or uncharitably, or in a cowardly or intemperate manner, "I did it deliberately" cannot on any interpretation lead to exculpation. So, we may say, a virtue is not, like a skill or an art, a mere capacity: it must actually engage the will.

II

I shall now turn to another thesis about the virtues, which I might express by saying that they are *corrective*, each one standing at a point at which there is some temptation to be resisted or deficiency of motivation to be made good. As Aristotle put it, virtues are about what is difficult for men, and I want to see in what sense this is true, and then to consider a problem in Kant's moral philosophy in the light of what has been said.

Let us first think about courage and temperance. Aquinas contrasted these virtues with justice in the following respect. Justice was concerned with operation, and courage and temperance with passions.[5] What he meant by this seems to have been, primarily, that the man of courage does not fear immoderately nor the man of temperance have immoderate desires for pleasure, and that there was no corresponding moderation of a passion implied in the idea of justice. This particular account of courage and temperance might be disputed on the ground that a man's courage is measured by his action and not by anything as uncontrollable as fear; and similarly that the temperate man who must on occasion refuse pleasures need not *desire* them any less than the intemperate man. Be that as it may (and something will be said about it later) it is obviously true that courage and temperance have to do with particular springs of action as justice does not. Almost any desire can lead a man to act unjustly, not even excluding the desire to help a friend or to save a life, whereas a cowardly act must be motivated by fear or a desire for safety, an act of intemperance by a desire for pleasure, perhaps even for a particular range of pleasures such as those of eating or drinking or sex. And now, going back to the idea of virtues as correctives, one may say that it is only because fear and the desire for pleasure often operate as temptations that courage and temperance exist as virtues at all.

As things are we often want to run away not only where that is the right thing to do, but also where we should stand firm; and we want pleasure not only where we should seek pleasure but also where we should not. If human nature had been different there would have been no need of a corrective disposition in either place, as fear and pleasure would have been good guides to conduct throughout life. So Aquinas says, about the passions:

> They may incite us to something against reason, and so we need a curb, which we name *temperance*. Or they may make us shirk a course of action dictated by reason, through fear of dangers or hardships. Then a person needs to be steadfast and not run away from what is right; and for this *courage* is named.[6]

As with courage and temperance so with many other virtues: there is, for instance, a virtue of industriousness only because idleness is a temptation; and of humility only because men tend to think too well of themselves. Hope is a virtue because despair too is a temptation; it might have been that no one cried that all was lost except where he could really see it to be so, and in this case, there would have been no virtue of hope.

With virtues such as justice and charity it is a little different, because they correspond not to any particular desire or tendency that has to be kept in check but rather to a deficiency of motivation; and it is this that they must make good. If people were as much attached to the good of others as they are to their own good there would no more be a general virtue of benevolence than there is a general virtue of self-love. And if people cared about the rights of others as they care about their own rights no virtue of justice would be needed to look after the matter, and rules about such things as contracts and promises would only need to be made public, like the rules of a game that everyone was eager to play.

On this view of the virtues and vices everything is seen to depend on what human nature is like, and the traditional catalogue of the two kinds of dispositions is not hard to understand. Nevertheless it may be defective, and anyone who accepts the thesis that I am putting forward will feel free to ask himself where the temptations and deficiencies that need correcting are really to be found. It is possible, for example, that the theory of human nature lying behind the traditional list of the virtues and vices puts too much emphasis on hedonistic and sensual impulses, and does not sufficiently take account of less straightforward inclinations such as the desire to be put upon and dissatisfied, or the unwillingness to accept good things as they come along.

It should now be clear why I said that virtues should be seen as correctives; and part of what is meant by saying that virtue is about things that are difficult for men should also have appeared. The further application of this idea is, however, controversial, and the following difficulty presents itself: that we both are and are not inclined to think that the harder a man finds it to act virtuously the more virtue he shows if he does act well. For on the one hand great virtue is needed where it is particularly hard to act virtuously; yet on the other it could be argued that difficulty in acting virtuously shows that the agent is imperfect in virtue: according to Aristotle, to take pleasure in virtuous action is the mark of true virtue, with the self-mastery of the one who finds virtue difficult only a second best. How then is this conflict to be decided? Who shows most courage, the one who wants to run away but does not, or the one who does not even want to run away? Who shows most charity, the one who finds it easy to make the good of others his object, or the one who finds it hard?

What is certain is that the thought that virtues are corrective does not constrain us to relate virtue to difficulty in each individual man. Since men in general find it hard to face great dangers or evils, and even small ones, we may count as courageous those few who without blindness or indifference are nevertheless fearless even in terrible circumstances. And when someone has a natural charity or generosity it is at least part of the virtue that he has; if natural virtue cannot be the whole of virtue this is because a kindly or fearless disposition could be disastrous without justice and wisdom, and because these virtues have to be learned, not because natural virtue is too easily acquired. I have argued that the virtues can be seen as correctives in relation to human nature in general but not that each virtue must present a difficulty to each and every man.

Nevertheless many people feel strongly inclined to say that it is for moral effort that moral praise is to be bestowed, and that in proportion as a man finds it easy to be virtuous so much the less is he to be morally admired for his good actions. The dilemma can be resolved only when we stop talking about difficulties standing in the way of virtuous action as if they were of only one kind. The fact is that some kinds of difficulties do indeed provide an occasion for much virtue, but that others rather show that virtue is incomplete.

To illustrate this point I shall first consider an example of honest action. We may suppose for instance that a man has an opportunity to steal, in circumstances where stealing is not morally permissible, but that he refrains. And now let us ask our old question. For one man it is hard to refrain from stealing and for another man it is not: which shows the greater virtue in acting as he should? It is not difficult to see in this case that it makes all the difference whether the difficulty comes from circumstances, as that a man is poor, or that his theft is unlikely to be detected, or whether it comes from something that belongs to his own character. The fact that a man is *tempted* to steal is something about him that shows a certain lack of honesty: of the thoroughly honest man we say that it "never entered his head," meaning that it was never a real possibility for him. But the fact that he is poor is something that makes the occasion more *tempting*, and difficulties of this kind make honest action all the more virtuous.

A similar distinction can be made between different obstacles standing in the way of charitable action. Some circumstances, as that great sacrifice is needed, or that the one to be helped is a rival, give an occasion on which a man's charity is severely tested. Yet in given circumstances of this kind it is the man who acts easily rather than the one who finds it hard who shows the most charity. Charity is a virtue of attachment, and that sympathy for others which makes it easier to help them is part of the virtue itself.

These are fairly simple cases, but I am not supposing that it is always easy to say where the relevant distinction is to be drawn. What, for instance, should we say about the emotion of fear as an obstacle to action? Is a man more courageous if he fears much and nevertheless acts, or if he is relatively fearless? Several things must be said about this. In the first place it seems that the emotion of fear is not a necessary condition for the display of courage; in face of a great evil such as death or injury a man may show courage even if he does not tremble. On the other hand even irrational fears may give an occasion for courage: if someone suffers from claustrophobia or a dread of heights he may require courage to do that which would not be a courageous action for others. But not all fears belong from this point of view to the circumstances rather than to a man's character. For while we do not think of claustrophobia or a dread of heights as features of character, a general timorousness may be. Thus, although pathological fears are not a result of a man's choices and values some fears may be. The fears that count against a man's courage are those that we think he could overcome, and among them, in a special class, those that reflect the fact that he values safety too much.

In spite of problems such as these, which have certainly not all been solved, both the distinction between different kinds of obstacles to virtuous action the general idea that virtues are correctives will be useful in resolving a difficulty in Kant's moral philosophy closely related to the issues discussed in the preceding paragraphs. In a passage in the first section of the *Groundwork of the Metaphysics of Morals* Kant notoriously tied himself into a knot in trying to give an account of those actions which have as he put it "positive moral worth." Arguing that only actions done out of a sense of duty have this worth he contrasts a philanthropist who "takes pleasure in spreading happiness around him" with one who acts out of respect for duty, saying that the actions of the latter but not the former have moral worth. Much scorn has been poured on Kant for this curious doctrine, and indeed it does seem that something has gone wrong, but perhaps we are not in a position to scoff unless we can give our own account of the idea on which Kant is working. After all it does seem that he is right in saying that some actions are in accordance with duty, and even required by duty, without being the subjects of moral praise, like those of the honest trader who deals honestly in a situation in which it is in his interest to do so.

It was this kind of example that drove Kant to his strange conclusion. He added another example, however, in discussing acts of self-preservation;

these he said, while they normally have no positive moral worth, may have it when a man preserves his life not from inclination but without inclination and from a sense of duty. Is he not right in saying that acts of self-preservation normally have no moral significance but that they may have it, and how do we ourselves explain this fact?

To anyone who approaches this topic from a consideration of the virtues the solution readily suggests itself. Some actions are in accordance with virtue without requiring virtue for their performance, whereas others are both in accordance with virtue and such as to show possession of a virtue. So Kant's trader was dealing honestly in a situation in which the virtue of honesty is not required for honest dealing, and it is for this reason that his action did not have "positive moral worth." Similarly, the care that one ordinarily takes for one's life, as for instance on some ordinary morning in eating one's breakfast and keeping out of the way of a car on the road, is something for which no virtue is required. As we said earlier, there is no general virtue of self-love as there is a virtue of benevolence or charity, because men are generally attached sufficiently to their own good. Nevertheless in special circumstances virtues such as temperance, courage, fortitude, and hope may be needed if someone is to preserve his life. Are these circumstances in which the preservation of one's own life is a duty? Sometimes it is so, for sometimes it is what is owed to others that should keep a man from destroying himself, and then he may act out of a sense of duty. But not all cases in which acts of self-preservation show virtue are like this. For a man may display each of the virtues just listed even where he does not do any harm to others if he kills himself or fails to preserve his life. And it is this that explains why there may be a moral aspect to suicide which does not depend on possible injury to other people. It is not that suicide is "always wrong," whatever that would mean, but that suicide is *sometimes* contrary to virtues such as courage and hope.

Let us now return to Kant's philanthropists, with the thought that it is action that is in accordance with virtue and also displays a virtue that has moral worth. We see at once that Kant's difficulties are avoided, and the happy philanthropist reinstated in the position which belongs to him. For charity is, as

we said, a virtue of attachment as well as action, and the sympathy that makes it easier to act with charity is part of the virtue. The man who acts charitably out of a sense of duty is not to be undervalued, but it is the other who most shows virtue and therefore to the other that most moral worth is attributed. Only a detail of Kant's presentation of the case of the dutiful philanthropist tells on the other side. For what he actually said was that his man felt no sympathy and took no pleasure in the good of others because "his mind was clouded by some sorrow of his own," and this is the kind of circumstance that increases the virtue that is needed if a man is to act well.

III

It was suggested above that an action with "positive moral worth," or as we might say a positively good action, was to be seen as one which was in accordance with virtue, by which I mean contrary to no virtue, and moreover one for which a virtue was required. Nothing has so far been said about another case, excluded by the formula, in which it might seem that an act displaying one virtue was nevertheless contrary to another. In giving this last description I am thinking not of two virtues with competing claims, as if what were required by justice could nevertheless be demanded by charity, or something of that kind, but rather of the possibility that a virtue such as courage or temperance or industry which overcomes a special temptation, might be displayed in an act of folly or villainy. Is this something that we must allow for, or is it only good or innocent actions which can be acts of these virtues? Aquinas, in his definition of virtue, said that virtues can produce only good actions, and that they are dispositions "of which no one can make bad use,"[7] except when they are treated as objects, as in being the subject of hatred or pride. The common opinion nowadays is, however, quite different. With the notable exception of Peter Geach hardly anyone sees any difficulty in the thought that virtues may sometimes be displayed in bad actions. Von Wright, for instance, speaks of the courage of the villain as if this were a quite unproblematic idea, and most people take it for granted that the virtues of courage and temperance may aid a bad man in his evil work. It is also supposed that charity may lead a man to act badly, as when someone does what he has no right to do, but does it for the sake of a friend.

There are, however, reasons for thinking that the matter is not so simple as this. If a man who is willing to do an act of injustice to help a friend, or for the common good, is supposed to act out of charity, and he so acts where a just man will not, it should be said that the unjust man has more charity than the just man. But do we not think that someone not ready to act unjustly may yet be perfect in charity, the virtue having done its whole work in promoting him to do the acts that are permissible? And is there not more difficulty than might appear in the idea of an act of injustice which is nevertheless an act of courage? Suppose for instance that a sordid murder were in question, say a murder done for gain or to get an inconvenient person out of the way, but that this murder had to be done in alarming circumstances or in the face of real danger; should we be happy to say that such an action was an act of courage or a courageous act? Did the murderer, who certainly acted boldly, or with intrepidity, if he did the murder, also act courageously? Some people insist that they are ready to say this, but I have noticed that they like to move over to a murder for the sake of conscience, or to some other act done in the course of a villainous enterprise but whose immediate end is innocent or positively good. On their hypothesis, which is that bad acts can easily be seen as courageous acts or acts of courage, my original example should be just as good.

What are we to say about this difficult matter? There is no doubt that the murderer who murdered for gain was *not a coward*: he did not have a second moral defect which another villain might have had. There is no difficulty about this because it is clear that one defect may neutralize another. As Aquinas remarked, it is better for a blind horse if it is slow.[8] It does not follow, however, that an act of villainy can be courageous; we are inclined to say that it "took courage," and yet it seems wrong to think of courage as equally connected with good action and bad.

One way out of this difficulty might be to say that the man who is ready to pursue bad ends does indeed have courage, and shows courage in his action, but that in him courage is not a virtue. Later I shall consider some cases in which this might be

the right thing to say, but in this instance it does not seem to be. For unless the murderer consistently pursues bad ends his courage will often result in good; it may enable him to do many innocent or positively good things for himself or for his family and friends. On the strength of an individual bad action we can hardly say that in him courage is not a virtue. Nevertheless there is something to be said even about the individual action to distinguish it from one that would readily be called an act of courage or a courageous act. Perhaps the following analogy may help us to see what it is. We might think of words such as "courage" as naming characteristics of human beings in respect of a certain power, as words such as "poison" and "solvent" and "corrosive" so name the properties of physical things. The power to which virtue-words are so related is the power of producing good action, and good desires. But just as poisons, solvents and corrosives do not always operate characteristically, so it could be with virtues. If P (say arsenic) is a poison it does not follow that P acts as a poison wherever it is found. It is quite natural to say on occasion "P does not act as a poison here" though P is a poison and it is P that is acting here. Similarly courage is not operating as a virtue when the murderer turns his courage, which is a virtue, to bad ends. Not surprisingly the resistance that some of us registered was not to the expression "the courage of the murderer" or to the assertion that what he did "took courage" but rather to the description of that action as an act of courage or a courageous act. It is not that the action *could* not be so described, but that the fact that courage does not here have its characteristic operation is a reason for finding the description strange.

In this example we were considering an action in which courage was not operating as a virtue, without suggesting that in that agent it generally failed to do so. But the latter is also a possibility. If someone is both wicked and foolhardy this may be the case with courage, and it is even easier to find examples of a general connexion with evil rather than good in the case of some other virtues. Suppose, for instance, that we think of someone who is over-industrious, or too ready to refuse pleasure, and this is characteristic of him rather than something we find on one particular occasion. In this case the virtue of industry, or the virtue of temperance, has a systematic connexion with defective action rather than good action; and it might be said in either case that the virtue did not operate as a virtue in this man. Just as we might say in a certain setting "P is not a poison here" though P is a poison and P is here, so we might say that industriousness, or temperance, is not a virtue in some. Similarly in a man habitually given to wishful thinking, who clings to false hopes, hope does not operate as a virtue and we may say that it is not a virtue in him.

The thought developed in the last paragraph, to the effect that not every man who has a virtue has something that is a virtue in him, may help to explain a certain discomfort that one may feel when discussing the virtues. It is not easy to put one's finger on what is wrong, but it has something to do with a disparity between the moral ideals that may seem to be implied in our talk about the virtues, and the moral judgements that we actually make. Someone reading the foregoing pages might, for instance, think that the author of this paper always admired most those people who had all the virtues, being wise and temperate as well as courageous, charitable and just. And indeed it is sometimes so. There are some people who do possess all these virtues and who are loved and admired by all the world, as Pope John XXIII was loved and admired. Yet the fact is that many of us look up to some people whose chaotic lives contain rather little of wisdom or temperance, rather than to some others who possess these virtues. And while it may be that this is just romantic nonsense I suspect that it is not. For while wisdom always operates as a virtue, its close relation prudence does not, and it is prudence rather than wisdom that inspires many a careful life. Prudence is not a virtue in everyone, any more than industriousness is, for in some it is rather an over-anxious concern for safety and propriety, and a determination to keep away from people or situations which are apt to bring trouble with them; and by such defensiveness much good is lost. It is the same with temperance. Intemperance can be an appalling thing, as it was with Henry VIII of whom Wolsey remarked that

> rather than he will either miss or want any part of his will or appetite, he will put the loss of one half of his realm in danger.

Nevertheless in some people temperance is not a virtue, but is rather connected with timidity or with a grudging attitude to the acceptance of good things. Of course what is best is to live boldly yet without imprudence or intemperance, but the fact is that rather few can manage that.

POSTSCRIPT, JANUARY 2003

Since this paper first appeared, a great deal has been written under the heading of "Virtue Ethics," and by some philosophers, such as Rosalind Hursthouse, Christine Swanton, and Michael Slote, it has been suggested that agents' dispositions, motives, and other "internal" elements are the primary subjects and determinants of moral goodness and badness. But I myself have never been a "virtue ethicist" *in this sense*, and in my recent book, *Natural Goodness*, it is clearly acts (as for instance acts of justice and injustice) that appear in this position.

NOTES*

I am indebted to friends in many universities for their help in forming my views on this subject; and particularly to John Guiliano of UCLA, whose unpublished work on the unity of the virtues I have consulted with profit, and to Rosalind Hursthouse who commented on a draft of the middle period.

1. Aquinas, *Summa Theologica*, 1a2ae Q.56 a.3.
2. Aristotle, *Nicomachean Ethics*, especially bk. VII.
3. von Wright, *The Varieties of Goodness* (London, 1963). Chapter VIII.
4. Aristotle op. cit. 1140 b 22–25. Aquinas op. cit. 1a2ae Q.57 a.4.
5. Aristotle op. cit. 1106 b.15 and 1129 a.4 have this implication; but Aquinas is more explicit in op. cit. 1a–2ae Q.60 a.2.
6. Aquinas op. cit. 1a2ae Q.61 a.3.
7. Aquinas op. cit. 1a2ae Q.56 a.5.
8. Aquinas op. cit. 1a2ae Q.58 a.4.

*Some notes omitted; the remaining notes renumbered.—ED.

1. What is the basic difference between a virtue ethics and other types of ethics we have studied?
2. According to Aristotle, what is the difference between intellectual and moral virtues?
3. In what sense are virtues habits?
4. Give a list of some traits that have been thought to be virtues, according to Aristotle and other virtue theorists.
5. According to Aristotle, how is virtue a mean between extremes? Give some examples.
6. Explain the problem of whether virtues are human perfections or excellences or socially valuable traits.
7. Explain the problem raised by Philippa Foot as to who most exemplifies the virtue of, say, courage: the person who finds it difficult or easy to be courageous.

9

Feminist Thought and the Ethics of Care

IN A FAMOUS study conducted in the 1970s, a moral question about the following hypothetical situation was posed to two eleven-year-old children, Jake and Amy.[1] A man's wife was extremely ill and in danger of dying. A certain drug might save her life, but the man could not afford it, in part because the druggist had set an unreasonably high price for it. The question was whether the man should steal the drug. Jake answered by trying to figure out the relative value of the woman's life and the druggist's right to his property. He concluded that the man should steal the drug because he calculated that the woman's life was worth more. Amy was not so sure. She wondered what would happen to both the man and his wife if he stole the drug. "If he stole the drug, he might save his wife then, but if he did, he might have to go to jail, and then his wife might get sicker again." She said that if the husband and wife talked about this they might be able to think of some other way out of the dilemma.

One interesting thing about this case is the very different ways in which the two children tried to determine the right thing to do in this situation. The boy used a rational calculation in which he weighed and compared values from a neutral standpoint. The girl spoke about the possible effects of the proposed action on the two individuals and their relationship. Her method did not give the kind of definitive answer that is apparent in the boy's method. Perhaps the difference in their moral reasoning is the result of their sex or gender.[2]

Another example also seems to show a gender difference in moral reasoning.[3] In explaining how they would respond to a moral dilemma about maintaining one's moral principles in the light of peer or family pressure, two teens responded quite differently. The case was one in which the religious views of the teens differed from their parents. The male said that he had a right to his own opinions, though he respected his parents' views. The female said that she was concerned about how her parents would react to her views. "I understand their fear of my new religious ideas." However, she added, "they really ought to listen to me and try to understand my beliefs."[4] Although their conclusions were similar, their reasoning was not. They seemed to have two decidedly different orientations or perspectives. The male spoke in terms of an individual's right to his own opinions, while the female talked of the need for the particular people involved to talk with and come to understand one another. These two cases raise questions about whether a gender difference actually exists in the way people reason about moral matters.

AN ETHICS OF CARE

Debate about sex or gender differences in moral perspectives and moral reasoning has been sparked by the work of psychologist Carol Gilligan.[5] She interviewed both male and female subjects about various moral dilemmas and found that the women she interviewed had a different view than the men of what was morally required of them. They used a different moral language to explain themselves, and their reasoning involved a different moral logic. They talked in terms of hurting and benefiting others, and they reasoned that they ought to do that which helped the people involved in a particular case at hand. She concluded that males and females have different kinds of ethics. Since then, other observers have noted a variety of qualities that characterize male and female ethics. The ensuing debate, which will be discussed here, has focused on whether there is a specifically feminine morality, an *ethics of caring* or *care*. First, we will examine the supposed characteristics of feminine morality. Then we will summarize various explanations that have been given for these characteristics. Finally, we will suggest some things to consider in evaluating the theory that a feminine ethics of care does indeed exist.

Several contrasting pairs of terms are associated with or can be used to describe the two types of ethical perspective. These are listed in the table below.

The various characteristics or notions in this list may need explanation. First, consider the supposed typical *female moral perspective*. The context for women's moral decision-making is said to be one of *relatedness*. Women think about particular people and their relations and how they will be affected by some action. Women's morality is highly personal. They are partial to their particular loved ones and think that one's primary moral responsibility is to these people. It is the private and personal natural relations of family and friends that are the model for other relations. Women stress the concrete experiences of this or that

Female Ethical Perspective	Male Ethical Perspective
Personal	Impersonal
Partial	Impartial
Private	Public
Natural	Contractual
Feeling	Reason
Compassionate	Fair
Concrete	Universal
Responsibility	Rights
Relationship	Individual
Solidarity	Autonomy

event and are concerned about the real harm that might befall a particular person or persons. The primary moral obligation is to prevent harm and to help people. Women are able to empathize with others and are concerned about how they might feel if certain things were to happen to them. They believe that moral problems can be solved by talking about them and by trying to understand others' perspectives. Caring and compassion are key virtues. The primary moral obligation is not to turn away from those in need. Nel Noddings's work *Caring: A Feminine Approach to Ethics and Moral Education* provides a good example and further description of the ethics of care.[6] (See the selection from this work in this chapter.)

The supposed typical *male moral perspective* contrasts sharply with a feminine ethics of care. Supposedly, men take a more universal and more impartial standpoint in reasoning about what is morally good and bad. Men are more inclined to talk in terms of fairness and justice and rights. They ask about the overall effects of some action and whether the good effects, when all are considered, outweigh the bad. It is as though they think moral decisions ought to be made impersonally or from some unbiased and detached point of view. The moral realm would then in many ways be similar to the public domain of law and contract. The law must not be biased and must treat everyone equally. Moral thinking, on this view, involves a type of universalism that recognizes the equal moral worth of all as persons both in themselves and before the law. People ought to keep their promises because this is the just thing to do and helps create a reliable social order. Morality is a matter of doing one's duty, keeping one's agreements, and respecting other people's rights. Impartiality and respectfulness are key virtues. The primary obligation is not to act unfairly.

What are we to make of the view that two very different sets of characteristics describe male and female morality? In suggesting a difference between men's and women's morality, Carol Gilligan was taking aim at one of the dominant points of view about moral development—namely, that of Lawrence Kohlberg.[7] According to Kohlberg, the highest stage of moral development was supposed to be the stage in which an adult can be governed not by social pressure but by personal moral principles and a sense of justice. The principles regarded people as moral equals. They manifested an impartial and universal perspective. In his own research, Kohlberg found that women did not often reach this stage of development. He thus judged them to be morally underdeveloped or morally deficient. Of course, his conclusions were not totally surprising, because he had used an all-male sample in working out his theory.[8] After deriving his principles from male subjects, he then used them to judge both male and female moral development.

Gilligan and Kohlberg were not the first psychologists to believe a difference existed between men's and women's morality. Freud had also held that women "show less sense of justice than men, that they are less ready to submit to the great exigencies of life, that they are more often influenced in their judgments by feelings of affection or hostility. . . ."[9] According to Freud, women were morally inferior to men. Instead of being able to establish themselves as separate people living in society and adapting to its rules, girls remained in the home attached to their mothers. Thus, girls developed a capacity for personal relations and intimacy while their male counterparts developed a sense of separateness and personal autonomy. The idea was that women base their morality on concerns about personal relations while men base their morality on rules that can reconcile the separate competing individuals in society.[10] Believing that a focus on personal relations rather than a sense of justice was a lesser form of morality, Freud and others thought that women are inferior to men morally.

Three questions ought to be asked about the theory that women and men exhibit a different type of moral perspective and moral reasoning. First, is this contention true? Is it an empirical fact that men and women manifest a different type of moral thinking? Second, if it is a fact, then how are we to explain it? What may be the source or cause of this difference? Third, if there is a difference, is one type of moral thinking higher or more developed or better than the other?

Is There a Gender Difference in Morality?

To determine whether there is, in fact, a difference between the moral language and logic of males and females, we need to rely on empirical surveys and studies. What do people find who have examined this supposed phenomena? We have already described some of the earlier findings of Carol Gilligan. Her conclusions in more recent studies have varied somewhat.[11] For example, her later research finds some variation in moral reasoning among both men and women. According to these findings, while both men and women sometimes think in terms of a justice perspective, few men think in terms of a care perspective. Being able to take one perspective rather than the other, she wrote, is much like being able to see the well-known line drawing figure as a rabbit or as a duck. The perspective that one has affects how one sees the figure. If one has a justice perspective, one will see that "the *self* as moral agent stands as the figure against a ground of social relationships, judging the conflicting claims of self and others against a standard of equality or equal respect." If one has a care perspective, then one will see that "the *relationship* becomes the figure, defining self and others. Within the context of relationship, the self as a moral agent perceives and responds to the perception of need."[12] In these more recent studies, Gilligan used "educationally advantaged North American adolescents and adults" and found that two-thirds had one or the other orientation as their primary focus. Still she found sex differences in the focus. "With one exception, all of the men who focused, focused on justice. The women divided, with roughly one-third focusing on justice and one-third on care."[13] In this study, women did not always have the care perspective as their focus—but without the women in the study, the care focus would have been almost absent.

Other theorists are not so sure about what the data show. For example, Catherine Greeno and Eleanor Maccoby believe that any difference between men's and women's morality can be accounted for by social status and experience rather than gender. Using other studies, they point out that in many cases those who exhibit so-called feminine morality have been housewives and women who were less well educated. They found that career women showed types of moral reasoning similar to men.[14] The question of whether women do exhibit a unique type of moral language and logic will need to be decided by those who study the empirical data. And, of course, you can examine your own experience to see whether the males and females you know seem to reason differently when discussing moral issues.

The Source of Feminine Morality

At least three distinct types of explanation address a possible difference between male and female morality: One proposes differences in the psychosexual development of the two sexes, a second points to biological differences, and a third gives a social, cultural, or educational explanation.

We have already described something of the Freudian account of the effects of psychosexual development on male and female moral thinking. A few more points may be added. According to this view, males and females have different concepts of the self and their gender identities; this concept is influenced by their development in relation to their mothers and fathers. As they grow up, females develop a sense of being connected with their mothers, whereas males find themselves being different from their mothers. According to Nancy Chodorow, who amplifies Freud's theory, development of the self and one's sense of individuality depends on being able to separate oneself from others. Thus males, who tend to separate themselves from their mothers, come to have a sense of self as independent, whereas females do not develop the sense of separate selves and rather see themselves as attached or connected to others. From this developmental situation, males and females supposedly develop different senses of morality: males a morality associated with separation and autonomy, and females a morality with relationships and interdependence. According to a traditional view, mature moral thinking involves being able to be detached and see things from some impartial perspective. Judging from a care perspective means that one cannot judge dispassionately or without bias, as was noted above, and this was judged to be a moral defect. However, we will consider the opposite position about the value of these perspectives shortly.

A second account of the source of the difference, one exemplified by the writings of Caroline Whitbeck, locates it at least in part in women's and men's biology—that is, in the difference in their reproductive capacities and experiences. In pregnancy, labor, and childbirth, women experience certain feelings of dependency and contingency.[15] They do not have full control of their bodies. They experience weakness and pain. They feel themselves participating in species life at its most primitive level. Because of their own feelings during this time, they can sympathize more readily with the infant's or child's feelings of helplessness and dependency. Caring and nurturing are said to spring naturally from the intimate and sympathetic relation to the child.

Other people believe that mothering is not only a biological phenomenon but also a social and cultural one. Although some women bear children, it is not necessary that they rear them. Still, because they do give birth to and nurse infants, women have generally come to be the primary child rearers. It is from the elements of so-called maternal practice that women's morality arises, according to this third view.[16] To Sara Ruddick, for example, maternal practice results in "maternal thinking," which is the "vocabulary and logic of connections" that arises from "acting in response to demands of their children."[17] She believes that maternal thinking is not simply a kind of feeling that comes naturally to women, but a way of thinking and acting. It involves finding ways to preserve and develop and promote one's children. Infants are extremely vulnerable and will not survive if they do not have the basics of food, clothing, and shelter. Children must be safeguarded from the many dangers of life. They need help in growing—physically, socially, and morally. Particular virtues are needed for a mother to be able to satisfy the needs of her children. Among those described by Ruddick are humility (for one cannot do everything), cheerfulness combined with realism, and love and affection. Mothers also need to guard against certain negative traits and feelings—for example, feelings of hopelessness and possessiveness. According to this view, it is because they spend much of their lives mothering that women develop a morality consistent with this experience. This morality stresses relationships and the virtues that are necessary for mothering. One does not necessarily have to be a biological mother, however, both to engage in mothering and develop maternal ethics, according to this viewpoint. Just because men and some women do not give birth does not mean that they cannot be parents and develop the outlook required for this practice. Until now, it has been a social phenomenon that maternal practice has been principally women's work.

Feminine versus Masculine Morality

Many questions remain concerning these three hypotheses. Some are factual or *empirical questions*, for they ask whether something is or is not the case. Do women in fact think thus and so? Are they more likely to do so than men? Does giving birth or rearing children cause those involved in these practices to think in a certain way and to have a certain moral perspective? Much of what we say here is quite speculative in that we are making guesses that cannot strictly be proven to be true. Nevertheless, there is a great deal of appeal and suggestiveness in the theory of the ethics of care. In particular, we should compare this type of morality with more traditional theories such as utilitarianism and Kantianism to see how different the perspectives are as exemplified by the theories.

Whether one way of judging morally is *better* than the other is also an open question. As we have seen, there has been a tradition of thought that says that the so-called feminine morality, an ethics of care and relations and particularity and partiality, is a lower-level morality. When we consider the sources of this tradition, we find many reasons to criticize it. Perhaps, on the contrary, it is the ethics of care that provides a better moral orientation. For example, instead of judging war in terms of whether the overall benefits outweigh the costs, we may do well to think about the particular people involved—that every soldier, for example, is someone's daughter or son or sister or brother or mother or father. Or perhaps the two orientations are complementary. Perhaps a justice orientation is the minimum that morality requires. We could then build on this minimum and, for example, temper justice with care and mercy. On the other hand, the care orientation may be the more basic one, and justice concerns could then be brought in to determine how best to care.

If specific female and male virtues parallel these orientations, then another question arises. Would it not be possible and good for both men and women to develop both sets of virtues? If these virtues are described in a positive way—say, caring and not subservience—would they not be traits that all should strive to possess? These traits might be simply different aspects of the human personality, rather than the male or female personality. They would then be human virtues and human perspectives rather than male or female virtues and perspectives. On this view, an ethics of fidelity and care and sympathy would be just as important for human flourishing as an ethics of duty and justice and acting on principle. While there would be certain moral virtues that all people should develop, other psychological traits could also vary according to temperament and choice. Individuals would be free to choose to manifest, according to their own personalities, any combination of characteristics. These sets of characteristics and virtues would be various forms of androgyny, or the manifestation of both stereotypical masculine and feminine traits.[18]

FEMINIST THOUGHT

Not all feminist writers support some version of an ethics of care. While most would agree that one can describe a particular type of morality that exhibits the characteristics said to belong to an ethics of care, these writers question whether all aspects of such an ethics of care are good. For example, care ethics seems to be based on relations between unequals. The mother–child relation is such a relation. The dependency in the relation goes only one way. One does all (or most of) the giving and the other all (or most of) the receiving. This may tend to reinforce or promote a one-sided morality of self-sacrifice and subjugation. It may reinforce the view that women ought to be the ones who sacrifice and help and support others, chiefly children and men. Feminist writers, as we have described the orientation here, would have us rather focus on the social status of women. One of their main ethical concerns is the historical and present-day continuing oppression of women: their status in many cases and ways as second-class citizens.

According to Seyla Benhabib, there are two "premises" of feminist thinking:

> First, for feminist theory, the gender–sex system is not a contingent but an essential way in which social

reality is organized, symbolically divided, and experienced. By the "gender–sex" system, I mean the social-historical, symbolic constitution, and interpretation of the differences of the sexes. The gender–sex system is the context in which the self develops an embodied identity. . . .

Benhabib here points out how powerful and pervasive are the ways in which we are perceived and exist as males and females. It is not just a biological difference but a difference resulting from behavioral and social expectations. One might conclude from this picture of the situation of females (and males) that there are these two different types of gender-based morality. However, Benhabib describes another premise of feminist thinking.

> Second, the historically known gender-sex systems have contributed to the oppression and exploitation of women. The task of feminist critical theory is to uncover this fact, and to develop a theory that is emancipatory and reflective, and which can aid women in their struggles to overcome oppression and exploitation.[19]

Women need not be thought of as the opposite of men—as not autonomous or independent, not competitive, not public.[20] They can define their own positions and identities.

These feminist views are only some examples of what has been one of the goals of the so-called women's movement, which began in earnest in the West in the late nineteenth century. The history of the women's movement includes both those women primarily concerned with promoting women's equality with men and those who wanted to raise the value of women's unique characteristics. However, the most well-known writers and activists of this movement have been those who have stressed women's rights. Among the earliest examples is Mary Wollstonecraft, who wrote in *A Vindication of the Rights of Women* (1792)[21] that women were not by nature weak and emotional, but that their social situation had in many ways made them so. It was society that taught women negative moral traits such as cunning and vanity, she insisted. The suffragettes who sought political equality and the right to vote followed in her footsteps. Many years later, Simone de Beauvoir's work *The Second Sex* (1949) became a classic text for what has been called a "second wave" of feminists (the "first wave" being

the nineteenth-century women's rights advocates).[22] According to de Beauvoir, women are a second sex because they are regarded always in terms of being an "other" to the primary male sex. In an existentialist vein, she stressed the need for women to be independent selves and free to establish their own goals and projects. Various other writers in the history of the women's movement stressed the importance of raising women's consciousness, of helping women be aware of their second-class status and the various ways in which they were subject to oppression and subordination in their lives. The movement's aim was not only to raise consciousness, but also to act politically to bring about the equality of women. Thus, for example, they sought the passage of the Equal Rights Amendment to the U.S. Constitution.

Today, feminist moral thought is sometimes simply called *feminist ethics* and is distinguished from an ethics of care that is sometimes called *feminine ethics*.[23] Writers who explore the former focus on bringing out the causes of women's subordination

French philosopher Simone de Beauvoir (1908–1986).

and oppression and suggesting ways to eliminate these causes and their results. They also have a political orientation. At the international level, women have worked together to raise the status of women around the world and seek ways to better the conditions under which they live. International conferences have brought women from all nations together to discuss their problems and lend each other support.

Among the causes of women's oppression, some feminists point out, has been philosophy itself. Traditional moral philosophy has not been favorable to women. It has tended to support the view that women should develop women's virtues, and these are often to the detriment of women. For example, Aristotle seems to have held that women are inferior to men not only because of certain biological phenomena having to do with heat in the body, but also because they lack certain elements in their rationality. According to Aristotle, free adult males could rule over both slaves and women and children because of the weakness in their "deliberative" faculty. In the case of woman, while she has such a faculty, he said, it is "without authority."[24] Rousseau, in his work on the education of the young, described a quite different type of ideal education for Emile than for Sophie. Because morality is different for men and women, the young of each sex ought to be trained in different virtues, according to Rousseau. Emile is to be trained in virtues such as justice and fortitude, while Sophie is to be taught to be docile and patient.[25]

Even contemporary moral philosophers have not given women and women's concerns their due, according to many feminist writers. They have not been interested in matters of the home and domesticity. They have tended to ignore issues such as the "feminization of poverty," the use of reproductive technologies, sexual harassment, and violence against and sexual abuse of women. It is mainly with women writing on these topics in contemporary ethics that they have gained some respectability as topics of genuine philosophical interest. So also have the issues of female domination and oppression and subordination become topics of a wider philosophical interest. Lesbian feminists, in particular, have written about patriarchal practices that prevent women from flourishing. They believe that other feminist treatments sometimes do not go far enough, because they continue to see women in terms of their relation to men. Instead, they exhort women to become independent creative beings in their own right.[26]

EVALUATION OF FEMINIST THOUGHT AND THE ETHICS OF CARE

We have already pointed out some questions that have been raised about the ethics of care. There are others as well. First, some writers point out that mothering does not always come naturally to women, and not all women are good mothers or caring and nurturing. However, supporters of the ethics of care may reply that this is not the issue, but rather that there exists an ethics of care as a viable and valuable alternative morality. Second, critics contend that to promote the view that women should manifest these feminine traits may not be of benefit to women, for doing this can be used to continue women's subservient position in society, especially if its virtues include obedience, self-sacrifice, silence, and service. Supporters might respond that it is not these virtues that define an ethics of care. Rather, such an ethics tells us from what perspective we are to judge morally—namely, from the perspective of concrete people in relation to one another who can individually be harmed and benefited in particular ways. However, can an ethics of care free itself from the more negative aspects that these critics point out? Can feminist ethicists support an ethics of care while also seeking to promote women's equality? It is clear at least that women cannot be restricted to the role of those who serve others if they are to be treated equally and fairly in both the public social realm and in the realm of the home and family.

What these discussions have also suggested is that we can no longer maintain that one ethics exists for the home and the private realm (an ethics of care and relationships) and another ethics for work or the public realm (an ethics of justice and fairness and impartiality). "Neither the realm of domestic, personal life, nor that of non-domestic, economic and political life, can be understood or interpreted in isolation from the other," wrote feminist political philosopher Susan Moller Okin.[27] These two realms not only overlap and interpenetrate each other, but also each should exemplify the values and virtues of the other. Elements of altruism and concern for particular concrete individuals have a place in the political as well as the domestic realm. Furthermore, when feminists say that "the personal is political" they mean that "what happens in the personal life, particularly in relations between the sexes, is not immune from the dynamic of *power*, which has typically been seen as a distinguishing feature of the political."[28] These relations should thus also be restrained by considerations of fairness and justice.

One further question arises about the ethics of care. While such an ethics describes an ideal context for ethical decision making, it does not tell us how we are to determine what will help or harm particular individuals. It does not in itself say what constitutes benefit or harm. It gives no rules for what we are to do in cases of conflict of interest even among those to whom we are partial or what to do when we cannot benefit all. It seems to give little definitive help for knowing what to do in cases where we must harm some to benefit others. Supporters may respond that it is in setting the context for decision making that an ethics of care has already done something valuable, for it thus provides a balance for the otherwise one-sided traditional ethics of the impersonal and universal. Perhaps this is a valuable minimum. Or, even further, it may be that today we are more than ever in need of something such as this type of ethic, which promotes the connectedness of humans. As Gilligan notes:

> By rendering a care perspective more coherent and making its terms explicit, moral theory may facilitate women's ability to speak about their experiences and perceptions and may foster the ability of others to listen and to understand. At the same time, the evidence of care focus in women's moral thinking suggests that the study of women's development may provide a natural history of moral development in which care is ascendant, revealing the ways in which creating and sustaining responsive connection with others becomes or remains a central moral concern. The promise in joining women and moral theory lies in the fact that human survival, in the late twentieth century, may depend less on formal agreement than on human connection.[29]

If this was true for the late twentieth century, then it may even be more true for the early twenty-first century. Further thoughts on how these various perspectives might be reconciled can be found in this chapter's reading selections by Nel Noddings and Annette Baier. Other discussions of women's issues also occur throughout this text.

NOTES

1. This is a summary of a question that was posed by researchers for Lawrence Kohlberg. In Carol Gilligan, *In a Different Voice* (Cambridge, MA: Harvard University Press, 1982), 28, 173.
2. We use the term *sex* to refer to the biological male or female. The term *gender* includes psychological feminine and masculine traits as well as social roles assigned to the two sexes.
3. From Carol Gilligan, "Moral Orientation and Moral Development," in Eva Kittay and Diana Meyers (Eds.), *Women and Moral Theory* (Totowa, NJ: Rowman & Littlefield, 1987), 23.
4. Ibid.
5. Carol Gilligan, "Concepts of the Self and of Morality," *Harvard Educational Review* (Nov. 1977): 481–517.
6. Nel Noddings, *Caring: A Feminine Approach to Ethics and Moral Education* (Berkeley: University of California Press, 1984).
7. Lawrence Kohlberg, *The Psychology of Moral Development* (San Francisco: Harper & Row, 1984).
8. Gilligan, "Moral Orientation and Moral Development," 22.
9. Cited in Gilligan, op. cit.
10. See also Nancy Chodorow, *The Reproduction of Mothering* (Berkeley: University of California Press, 1978).
11. See, for example, Gilligan, "Adolescent Development Reconsidered," in Carol Gilligan, Janie Victoria Ward, and Jill McLean Taylor (Eds.), *Mapping the Moral Domain* (Cambridge, MA: Harvard University Press, 1988).
12. Gilligan, "Moral Orientation and Moral Development," 22–23. Emphasis added.
13. Ibid., 25.
14. Catherine G. Greeno and Eleanor E. Maccoby, "How Different Is the Different Voice?" in "On *In a Different Voice*: An Interdisciplinary Forum," *Signs: Journal of Women in Culture and Society*, *11*, no. 2 (Winter 1986): 211–220.
15. See, for example, Caroline Whitbeck, "The Maternal Instinct," in Joyce Treblicot (Ed.), *Mothering: Essays in Feminist Theory* (Totowa, NJ: Rowman & Allanheld, 1984).

16. See, for example, Sara Ruddick *Maternal Thinking: Toward a Politics of Peace* (Boston: Beacon, 1989).
17. Ibid., 214.
18. See Joyce Treblicot, "Two Forms of Androgynism," in *Journal of Social Philosophy*, no. 1 (Jan. 1977): 4–8.
19. Seyla Benhabib, "The Generalized and the Concrete Other," in *Women and Moral Theory*, 156–157.
20. Ibid., 162.
21. Mary Wollstonecraft, *A Vindication of the Rights of Women*, Miriam Brody (Ed.) (London: Penguin, 1988).
22. Simone de Beauvoir, *The Second Sex*, H. M. Parshley (Trans.) (New York: Knopf, 1953).
23. This terminology is from Rosemary Tong's *Feminine and Feminist Ethics* (Belmont, CA: Wadsworth, 1993). As a source of this terminology, Tong also cites Betty A. Sichel, "Different Strains and Strands: Feminist Contributions to Ethical Theory," *Newsletter on Feminism*, *90*, no. 2 (Winter 1991) 90; and Susan Sherwin, *No Longer Patient:*

24. *Feminist Ethics and Health Care* (Philadelphia: Temple University Press, 1992), 42.
24. Aristotle, *Politics*, as quoted in "Theories of Sex Difference," by Caroline Whitbeck in *Women and Moral Theory*, 35.
25. Jean-Jacques Rousseau, *Emile*, Allan Bloom (Trans.) (New York: Basic Books, 1979). Also see Nancy Tuana, *Woman and the History of Philosophy* (New York: Paragon House, 1992).
26. See, for example, Sarah Lucia Hoagland, *Lesbian Ethics* (Palo Alto, CA: Institute of Lesbian Studies, 1989).
27. Susan Moller Okin, "Gender, the Public and the Private," in David Held (Ed.), *Political Theory Today* (Stanford, CA: Stanford University Press, 1991), 77.
28. Ibid.
29. Gilligan, "Moral Orientation and Moral Development," 32.

READING
Caring
NEL NODDINGS

Study Questions

1. What kind of language has been the language of ethics, according to Noddings?
2. Is the approach she wants to describe one for women only?
3. How does she describe the "odd" approach of women to a moral question?
4. What is a "relation"? What are the two parties to the relation of caring?
5. According to Noddings, why do we want to be moral?
6. Why does she reject an ethics of principles and universality?

ETHICS, the philosophical study of morality, has concentrated for the most part on moral reasoning. Much current work, for example, focuses on the status of moral predicates and, in education, the dominant model presents a hierarchical picture of moral reasoning. This emphasis gives

ethics a contemporary, mathematical appearance, but it also moves discussion beyond the sphere of actual human activity and the feeling that pervades such activity. Even though careful philosophers have recognized the difference between "pure" or logical reason and "practical" or moral reason, ethical argumentation has frequently proceeded as if it were governed by the logical necessity characteristic of geometry. It has concentrated on the establishment of principles and that which can be logically derived from them. One might say that ethics has been discussed largely in the language of the father: in principles and propositions, in terms such as justification, fairness, justice. The mother's voice has been silent. Human caring and the memory of caring and being cared for, which I shall argue form the foundation of ethical response, have not received attention except as outcomes of ethical behavior. One is tempted to say that ethics has so far been guided by Logos, the masculine spirit, whereas the more natural and, perhaps, stronger approach would be through Eros, the feminine spirit. I hesitate to give way to this temptation, in part because the terms carry with them a Jungian baggage that I am unwilling to claim in its totality. In one sense, "Eros" does capture the flavor and spirit of what I am attempting here; the notion of psychic relatedness lies at the heart of the ethic I shall propose. In another sense, however, even "Eros" is masculine in its roots and fails to capture the receptive rationality of caring that is characteristic of the feminine approach.

When we look clear-eyed at the world today, we see it wracked with fighting, killing, vandalism, and psychic pain of all sorts. One of the saddest features of this picture of violence is that the deeds are so often done in the name of principle. When we establish a principle forbidding killing, we also establish principles describing the exceptions to the first principle. Supposing, then, that we are moral (we are principled, are we not?), we may tear into others whose beliefs or behaviors differ from ours with the promise of ultimate vindication.

This approach through law and principle is not, I suggest, the approach of the mother. It is the approach of the detached one, of the father. The view to be expressed here is a feminine view. This does not imply that all women will accept it or that men will reject it; indeed, there is no reason why men should not embrace it. It is feminine in the deep classical sense—rooted in receptivity, relatedness, and responsiveness. It does not imply either that logic is to be discarded or that logic is alien to women. It represents an alternative to present views, one that begins with the moral attitude or longing for goodness and not with moral reasoning. It may indeed be the case that such an approach is more typical of women than of men, but this is an empirical question I shall not attempt to answer.

. . . But we must realize, also, that one writing on philosophical/educational problems may be handicapped and even rejected in the attempt to bring a new voice to an old domain, particularly when entrance to that domain is gained by uttering the appropriate passwords. Whatever language is chosen, it must not be used as a cloak for sloppy thinking; that much is certain. This part of what I am doing, then, is not without risk.

Women, in general, face a similar problem when they enter the practical domain of moral action. They enter the domain through a different door, so to speak. It is not the case, certainly, that women cannot arrange principles hierarchically and derive conclusions logically. It is more likely that we see this process as peripheral to, or even alien to, many problems of moral action. Faced with a hypothetical moral dilemma, women often ask for more information. We want to know more, I think, in order to form a picture more nearly resembling real moral situations. Ideally, we need to talk to the participants, to see their eyes and facial expressions, to receive what they are feeling. Moral decisions are, after all, made in real situations; they are qualitatively different from the solution of geometry problems. Women can and do give reasons for their acts, but the reasons often point to feelings, needs, impressions, and a sense of personal ideal rather than to universal principles and their application. We shall see that, as a result of this "odd" approach, women have often been judged inferior to men in the moral domain.

Because I am entering the domain through a linguistic back door of sorts, much of what I say cannot be labeled "empirical" or "logical." (Some of it, of course, can be so labeled.) Well, what is it then? It is language that attempts to capture what Wittgenstein advised we "must pass over in silence." But if our language is extended to the expressive—and, after all, it is beautifully capable of such extension—perhaps we can say something in the realm of ethical feeling, and that something may at least achieve the status of conceptual aid or tool if not that of conceptual truth. We may present a coherent and enlightening picture without proving anything and, indeed, without claiming to present or to seek moral *knowledge* or moral *truth*. The hand that steadied us as we learned to ride our first bicycle did not provide propositional knowledge, but it guided and supported us all the same, and we finished up "knowing how."

. . . What does it mean to care and to be cared for? The analysis will occupy us at length, since relation will be taken as ontologically basic and the caring relation as ethically basic. For our purposes, "relation" may be thought of as a set of ordered pairs generated by some rule that describes the affect—or subjective experience—of the members.

In order to establish a firm conceptual foundation that will be free of equivocation, I have given names to the two parties of the relation: the first member is the "one-caring" and the second is the "cared-for." Regular readers of "existentialist" literature will recognize the need for such terminology—bothersome as it is. One may recall Sartre's use of for-itself and in-itself, Heidegger's being-in-the-world, and Buber's I-Thou and I-It. There are at least two good reasons for invoking this mechanism. First, it allows us to speak about our basic entities without explaining the entire conceptual apparatus repeatedly; second, it prevents us from smuggling in meanings through the use of synonyms. Hence, even though hyphenated entities offend the stylist, they represent in this case an attempt to achieve both economy and rigor. Another matter of style in connection with "one-caring" and "cared-for" should be mentioned here. In order to maintain balance and avoid confusion, I have consistently associated the generic "one-caring" with the universal feminine, "she," and "cared-for" with the masculine, "he." Clearly, however, when actual persons are substituted for "one-caring" and "cared-for" in the basic relation, they may be both male, both female, female-male, or male-female. Taking *relation* as ontologically basic simply means that we recognize human encounter and affective response as a basic fact of human existence. As we examine what it means to care and to be cared for, we shall see that both parties contribute to the relation; my caring must be somehow completed in the other if the relation is to be described as caring.

This suggests that the ethic to be developed is one of reciprocity, but our view of reciprocity will be different from that of "contract" theorists such as Plato and John Rawls. What the cared-for gives to the caring relation is not a promise to behave as the one-caring does, nor is it a form of "consideration." . . . When we see what it is that the cared-for contributes to the relation, we shall find it possible to separate human infants from nonhuman animals (a great problem for those who insist on some form of rationality in those we should treat ethically), and we shall do this without recourse to notions of God or some other external source of "sanctity" in human life.

The focus of our attention will be upon how to meet the other morally. Ethical caring, the relation in which we do meet the other morally, will be universal heart of the ethic, we must establish a convincing and comprehensive picture of caring at the outset.

Another outcome of our dependence on an ethical ideal is the emphasis upon moral education. Since we are dependent upon the strength and sensitivity of the ethical ideal—both our own and that of others—we must nurture that ideal in all of our educational encounters. I shall claim that we are dependent on each other even in the quest for personal goodness. How good *I* can be is party a function of how *you*—the other—receive and respond to me. Whatever virtue I exercise is completed, fulfilled, in you. The primary aim of all education must be nurturance of the ethical idea.

To accomplish the purposes set out above, I shall strike many contrasts between masculine and feminine approaches to ethics and education and, indeed, to living. These are not intended to divide men and women into opposing camps. They are meant, rather, to show how great the chasm is that already divides the masculine and feminine in each of us and to suggest that we enter a dialogue of genuine dialectical nature in order to achieve an ultimate transcendence of the masculine and feminine in moral matters. The reader must keep in mind, then, that I shall use the language of both father and mother; I shall have to argue for the positions I set out expressively.

An important difference between an ethic of caring and other ethics that give subjectivity its proper place is its foundation in relation. The philosopher who begins with a supremely free consciousness—an aloneness and emptiness at the heart of existence—identifies *anguish* as the basic human affect. But our view, rooted as it is in relation, identifies *joy* as a basic human affect. When I look at my child—even one of my grown children—and recognize the fundamental relation in which we are each defined, I often experience a deep and overwhelming joy. It is the recognition of and longing for relatedness that form the foundation of our ethic, and the joy that accompanies fulfillment of our caring enhances our commitment to the ethical ideal that sustains us as one-caring.

R E A D I N G
The Need for More Than Justice
ANNETTE BAIER

Study Questions

1. Who are the challengers to the supremacy of justice as a social virtue, and why does Baier suggest that this is surprising?
2. What kind of ethic or perspective (influenced by the work of Carol Gilligan) is contrasted with the ethics of justice?
3. According to Gilligan, what two evils of childhood parallel the two dimensions of moral development she describes?
4. What is the tradition contrasted with Gilligan's position, according to Baier? How do Kohlberg, Piaget, and Kant exemplify this tradition?
5. From her interview studies, what did Gilligan find about women's moral experience and moral maturity?
6. Why do some writers believe that it will not do to say that an ethic of care is an option that only some might choose?
7. How has the tradition of rights worked both against and for women?
8. According to Baier, what is wrong with the view that stresses relationships of equality?
9. What also does Baier believe is wrong with the stress this tradition places on free choice?
10. What is the fourth feature of the Gilligan challenge to liberal orthodoxy?
11. What, then, does Gilligan think is the best moral theory?

IN RECENT decades in North American social and moral philosophy, alongside the development and discussion of widely influential theories of justice, taken as Rawls takes it as the "first virtue of social institutions,"[1] there has been a counter-movement gathering strength, one coming from some interesting sources. For some of the most outspoken of the diverse group who have in a variety of ways been challenging the assumed supremacy of justice among the moral and

Annette Baier, "The Need for More Than Justice," *Canadian Journal of Philosophy*, supplementary vol. 13, Marshal Hanen and Kai Nielsen (Eds.), 41–56 (Calgary: University of Calgary Press, 1988). Reprinted with permission of the publisher.

social virtues are members of those sections of society whom one might have expected to be especially aware of the supreme importance of justice, namely blacks and women. Those who have only recently won recognition of their equal rights, who have only recently seen the correction or partial correction of long-standing racist and sexist injustices to their race and sex, are among the philosophers now suggesting that justice is only one virtue among many, and one that may need the presence of the others in order to deliver its own undenied value. Among these philosophers of the philosophical counterculture, as it were—but an increasingly large counterculture—I include Alasdair MacIntyre,[2] Michael Stocker,[3] Lawrence Blum,[4] Michael Slote,[5] Laurence Thomas,[6] Claudia Card,[7] Alison Jaggar,[8] Susan Wolf[9] and a whole group of men and women, myself included, who have been influenced by the writings of Harvard educational psychologist Carol Gilligan, whose book *In a Different Voice* (Harvard 1982; hereafter D.V.) caused a considerable stir both in the popular press and, more slowly, in the philosophical journals.[10]

Let me say quite clearly at this early point that there is little disagreement that justice is a social value of very great importance, and injustice an evil. Nor would those who have worked on theories of justice want to deny that other things matter besides justice. Rawls, for example, incorporates the value of freedom into his account of justice, so that denial of basic freedoms counts as injustice. Rawls also leaves room for a wider theory of right, of which the theory of justice is just a part. Still, he does claim that justice is the "first" virtue of social institutions, and it is only that claim about priority that I think has been challenged. It is easy to exaggerate the differences of view that exist, and I want to avoid that. The differences are as much in emphasis as in substance, or we can say that they are differences in tone of voice. But these differences do tend to make a difference in approaches to a wide range of topics not just in moral theory but in areas like medical ethics, where the discussion used to be conducted in terms of patients' rights, of informed consent, and so on, but now tends to get conducted in an enlarged moral vocabulary, which draws on what Gilligan calls the ethics of *care* as well as that of *justice*.

For "care" is the new buzz-word. It is not, as Shakespeare's Portia demanded, mercy that is to season justice, but a less authoritarian humanitarian supplement, a felt concern for the good of others and for community with them. The "cold jealous virtue of justice" (Hume) is found to be too cold, and it is "warmer" more communitarian virtues and social ideals that are being called in to supplement it. One might say that liberty and equality are being found inadequate without fraternity, except that "fraternity" will be quite the wrong word, if as Gilligan initially suggested, it is *women* who perceive this value most easily. ("Sorority" will do no better, since it is too exclusive, and English has no gender-neuter word for the mutual concern of siblings.) She has since modified this claim, allowing that there are two perspectives on moral and social issues that we all tend to alternate between, and which are not always easy to combine, one of them what she called the justice perspective, the other the care perspective. It is increasingly obvious that there are many male philosophical spokespersons for the care perspective (Laurence Thomas, Lawrence Blum, Michael Stocker) so that it cannot be the prerogative of women. Nevertheless Gilligan still wants to claim that women are most unlikely to take *only* the justice perspective, as some men are claimed to, at least until some mid-life crisis jolts them into "bifocal" moral vision (see D.V., ch. 6).

Gilligan in her book did not offer any explanatory theory of why there should be any difference between female and male moral outlook, but she did tend to link the naturalness to women of the care perspective with their role as primary caretakers of young children, that is with their parental and specifically maternal role. . . . Later, both in "The Conquistador and the Dark Continent: Reflections on the Nature of Love" (*Daedalus* Summer 1984), and "The Origins of Morality in Early Childhood" (in press), she develops this explanation. She postulates two evils that any infant may become aware of, the evil of detachment or isolation from others whose love one needs, and the evil of relative powerlessness and weakness. Two dimensions of moral development are thereby set—one aimed at achieving satisfying community with others, the other aiming at autonomy or equality of power. The relative predominance of one over the other development will depend both upon the relative salience of the two evils in early childhood, and on early and later reinforcement or discouragement in attempts made to guard against these two evils. This provides the germs of a theory about *why*, given current customs of childrearing, it should be mainly women who are not content with only the moral outlook that she calls the justice perspective, necessary though that was and is seen by them to have been to their hard won liberation from sexist oppression. They, like the blacks, used the language of rights and justice to change their own social position, but nevertheless see limitations in that language, according to Gilligan's findings as a moral psychologist. She reports their discontent with the individualist more or less Kantian moral framework that dominates Western moral theory and which influenced moral psychologists such as Lawrence Kohlberg,[11] to whose conception of moral maturity she seeks an alternative. Since the target of Gilligan's criticism is the dominant Kantian tradition, and since that has been the target also of moral philosophers as diverse in their own views as Bernard Williams,[12] Alasdair MacIntyre, Philippa Foot,[13] Susan Wolf, Claudia Card, her book is of interest as much for its attempt to articulate an alternative to the Kantian justice perspective as for its implicit raising of the question of male bias in Western moral theory, especially liberal democratic theory. For whether the supposed blind spots of that outlook are due to male bias, or to non-parental bias, or to early traumas of powerlessness or to early resignation to "detachment" from others, we need first to be persuaded that they are blind spots before we will have any interest in their cause and cure. Is justice blind to important social values, or at least only one-eyed? What is it that comes into view from the "care perspective" that is not seen from the "justice perspective"?

Gilligan's position here is most easily described by contrasting it with that of Kohlberg, against which she developed it. Kohlberg, influenced by Piaget and the Kantian philosophical tradition as developed by John Rawls, developed a theory about typical moral development which saw it to progress from a pre-conventional level, where what is seen to matter is pleasing or not offending parental authority-figures, through a conventional level in which the child tries to fit in with a group, such as a school community, and conform to its standards and rules, to a post-conventional critical level, in which such conventional rules are subjected to tests, and where those tests are of a utilitarian, or, eventually, a Kantian sort—namely ones that require respect for each person's individual rational will, or autonomy, and conformity to any implicit social contract such wills are deemed to have made, or to any hypothetical ones they would make if thinking clearly. What was found when Kohlberg's questionnaires (mostly by verbal response to verbally sketched moral dilemmas) were applied to female as well as male subjects, Gilligan reports, is that the girls and women not only scored generally lower than the boys and men, but tended to revert to the lower stage of the conventional level even after briefly (usually in adolescence) attaining the post-conventional level. Piaget's finding that girls were deficient in "the legal sense" was confirmed.

These results led Gilligan to wonder if there might not be a quite different pattern of development to be discerned, at least in female subjects. She therefore conducted interviews designed to elicit not just how far advanced the subjects were towards an appreciation of the nature and importance of Kantian autonomy, but also to find out what the subjects themselves saw as progress or lack of it, what conceptions of moral maturity they came to possess by the time they were adults. She found that although the Kohlberg version of moral maturity as respect for fellow persons, and for their rights as equals (rights including that of free association), did seem shared by many young men, the women tended to speak in a different voice about morality itself and about moral maturity. To quote Gilligan, "Since the reality of interconnexion is experienced by women as given rather than freely contracted, they arrive at an understanding of life that reflects the limits of autonomy and control. As a result, women's development

delineates the path not only to a less violent life but also to a maturity realized by interdependence and taking care" (D.V., 172). She writes that there is evidence that "women perceive and construe social reality differently from men, and that these differences center around experiences of attachment and separation . . . because women's sense of integrity appears to be intertwined with an ethics of care, so that to see themselves as women is to see themselves in a relationship of connexion, the major changes in women's lives would seem to involve changes in the understanding and activities of care" (D.V., 171). She contrasts this progressive understanding of care, from merely pleasing others to helping and nurturing, with the sort of progression that is involved in Kohlberg's stages, a progression in the understanding, not of mutual care, but of mutual respect, where this has its Kantian overtones of distance, even of some fear for the respected, and where personal autonomy and independence, rather than more satisfactory interdependence, are the paramount values.

This contrast, one cannot but feel, is one which Gilligan might have used the Marxist language of alienation to make. For the main complaint about the Kantian version of a society with its first virtue justice, construed as respect for equal rights to formal goods such as having contracts kept, due process, equal opportunity including opportunity to participate in political activities leading to policy and law-making, to basic liberties of speech, free association and assembly, religious worship, is that none of these goods do much to ensure that the people who have and mutually respect such rights will have any other relationships to one another than the minimal relationship needed to keep such a "civil society" going. They may well be lonely, driven to suicide, apathetic about their work and about participation in political processes, find their lives meaningless and have no wish to leave offspring to face the same meaningless existence. Their rights, and respect for rights, are quite compatible with very great misery, and misery whose causes are not just individual misfortunes and psychic sickness, but social and moral impoverishment. . . .

Let me try to summarize the main differences, as I see them, between on the one hand Gilligan's version of moral maturity and the sort of social structures that would encourage, express and protect it, and on the other the orthodoxy she sees herself to be challenging. I shall from now on be giving my own interpretation of the significance of her challenges, not merely reporting them.[14] The most obvious point is the challenge to the individualism of the Western tradition, to the fairly entrenched belief in the possibility and desirability of each person pursuing his own good in his own way, constrained only by a minimal formal common good, namely a working legal apparatus that enforces contracts and protects individuals from undue interference by others. Gilligan reminds us that noninterference can, especially for the relatively powerless, such as the very young, amount to neglect, and even between equals can be isolating and alienating. On her less individualist version of individuality, it becomes defined by responses to dependency and to patterns of interconnexion, both chosen and unchosen. It is not something a person has, and which she then chooses relationships to suit, but something that develops out of a series of dependencies and interdependencies, and responses to them. This conception of individuality is not flatly at odds with, say, Rawls' Kantian one, but there is at least a difference of tone of voice between speaking as Rawls does of each of us having our own rational life plan, which a just society's moral traffic rules will allow us to follow, and which may or may not include close association with other persons, and speaking as Gilligan does of a satisfactory life as involving "progress of affiliative relationship" (D.V., 170) where "the concept of identity expands to include the experience of interconnexion" (D.V., 173). Rawls can allow that progress to Gilligan-style moral maturity may be a rational life plan, but not a moral constraint on every life-pattern. The trouble is that it will not do just to say "let this version of morality be an optional extra. Let us agree on the essential minimum, that is on justice and rights, and let whoever wants to go further and cultivate this more demanding ideal of responsibility and care." For, first, it cannot be satisfactorily cultivated without closer cooperation from others than respect for rights and justice will ensure, and, second, the encouragement of some to cultivate it while others do not could easily lead to exploitation of those who do. It obviously *has* suited some in most societies well enough that others take on the responsibilities of care (for the sick, the helpless, the young) leaving them free to pursue their own less altruistic goods. Volunteer forces of those who accept an ethic of care, operating within a society where the power is exercised and the institutions designed, redesigned, or maintained by those who accept a less communal ethic of minimally constrained self-advancement, will not be the solution. The liberal individualists may be able to "tolerate" the more communally minded, if they keep the liberals' rules, but it is not so clear that the more communally minded can be content with just those rules, not be content to be tolerated and possibly exploited.

For the moral tradition which developed the concept of rights, autonomy and justice is the same tradition that provided "justifications" of the oppression of those whom the primary right-holders depended on to do the sort of work they themselves preferred not to do. The domestic work was left to women and slaves, and the liberal morality for right-holders was surreptitiously supplemented by a different set of demands made on domestic workers. As long as women could be got to assume responsibility for the care of home and children, and to train their children to continue the sexist system, the liberal morality could continue to be the official morality, by turning its eyes away from the contribution made by those it excluded. The long unnoticed moral proletariat were the domestic workers, mostly female. Rights have usually been for the privileged. Talking about laws, and the rights those laws recognize and protect, does not in itself ensure that the group of legislators and rights-holders will not be restricted to some elite. Bills of rights have usually been proclamations of the rights of some in-group, barons, landowners, males, whites, non-foreigners. The "justice perspective," and the legal sense that goes with it, are shadowed by their patriarchal past. What did Kant, the great prophet of autonomy, say in his moral theory about women? He said they were incapable of legislation, not fit to vote, that they needed the guidance of more "rational" males.[15] Autonomy was not for them, only for first class, really rational, persons. It is ironic that Gilligan's original findings in a way confirm Kant's views—it seems that autonomy really may not be for women. Many of them reject that ideal (D.V., 48), and have been found not as good at making rules as are men. But where

Kant concludes—"so much the worse for women," we can conclude—"so much the worse for the male fixation on the special skill of drafting legislation, for the bureaucratic mentality of rule worship, and for the male exaggeration of the importance of independence over mutual interdependence."

It is however also true that the moral theories that made the concept of a person's rights central were not just the instruments for excluding some persons, but also the instruments used by those who demanded that more and more persons be included in the favored group. Abolitionists, reformers, women, used the language of rights to assert their claims to inclusion in the group of full members of a community. The tradition of liberal moral theory has in fact developed so as to include the women it had for so long excluded, to include the poor as well as rich, blacks and whites, and so on. Women like Mary Wollstonecraft used the male moral theories to good purpose. So we should not be wholly ungrateful for those male moral theories, for all their objectionable earlier content. They were undoubtedly patriarchal, but they also contained the seeds of the challenge, or antidote, to this patriarchal poison.

But when we transcend the values of the Kantians, we should not forget the facts of history—that those values were the values of the oppressors of women. The Christian church, whose version of the moral law Aquinas codified, in his very legalistic moral theory, still insists on the maleness of the God it worships, and jealously reserves for males all the most powerful positions in its hierarchy. Its patriarchical prejudice is open and avowed. In the secular moral theories of men, the sexist patriarchal prejudice is today often less open, not as blatant as it is in Aquinas, in the later natural law tradition, and in Kant . . . , but is often still there. No moral theorist today would say that women are unfit to vote, to make laws, or to rule a nation without powerful male advisors (as most queens had), but the old doctrines die hard. . . . Traces of the old patriarchal poison still remain in even the best contemporary moral theorizing. Few may actually say that women's place is in the home, but there is much muttering, when unemployment figures rise, about how the relatively recent flood of women into the work force complicates the problem, as if it would be a good thing if women just went back home whenever unemployment rises, to leave the available jobs for the men. We still do not really have a wide acceptance of the equal right of women to employment outside the home. Nor do we have wide acceptance of the equal duty of men to perform those domestic tasks which in no way depend on special female anatomy, namely cooking, cleaning, and the care of weaned children. All sorts of stories (maybe true stories), about children's need for one "primary" parent, who must be the mother if the mother breast feeds the child, shore up the unequal division of domestic responsibility between mothers and fathers, wives and husbands. If we are really to transvalue the values of our patriarchal past, we need to rethink all of those assumptions, really test those psychological theories. And how will men ever develop an understanding of the "ethics of care" if they continue to be shielded or kept from that experience of caring for a dependent child, which complements the experience we all have had of being cared for as dependent children? These experiences form the natural background for the development of moral maturity as Gilligan's women.

Exploitation aside, why would women, once liberated, not be content to have their version of morality merely tolerated? Why should they not see themselves as voluntarily, for their own reasons, taking on more than the liberal rules demand, while having no quarrel with the content of those rules themselves, nor with their remaining the only ones that are expected to be generally obeyed? To see why, we need to move on to three more differences between the Kantian liberals (usually contractarians) and their critics. These concern the relative weight put on relationships between equals, and the relative weight put on freedom of choice, and on the authority of intellect over emotions. It is a typical feature of the dominant moral theories and traditions . . . that relationships between equals or those who are deemed equal in some important sense, have been the relations that morality is concerned primarily to regulate. Relationships between those who are clearly unequal in power, such as parents and children, earlier and later generations in relation to one another, states and citizens, doctors and patients, the well and the ill, large states and small states, have had to be shunted to the bottom of the agenda, and then dealt with by some sort of "promotion" of the weaker so that an appearance of virtual equality is achieved. Citizens collectively become equal to states, children are treated as adults-to-be, the ill and dying are treated as continuers of their earlier more potent selves, so that their "rights" could be seen as the rights of equals. This pretense of an equality that is in fact absent may often lead to desirable protection of the weaker, or more dependent. But it somewhat masks the question of what our moral relationships are to those who are our superiors or our inferiors in power. A more realistic acceptance of the fact that we begin as helpless children, that at almost every point of our lives we deal with both the more and the less helpless, that equality of power and interdependency, between two persons or groups, is rare and hard to recognize when it does occur, might lead us to a more direct approach to questions concerning the design of institutions structuring these relationships between unequals (families, schools, hospitals, armies) and of the morality of our dealings with the more and the less powerful. . . .

The recognition of the importance for all parties of relations between those who are and cannot but be unequal, both these relations in themselves and for their effect on personality formation and so on other relationships, goes along with a recognition of the plain fact that not all morally important relationships can or should be freely chosen. So far I have discussed three reasons women have not to be content to pursue their own values within the framework of the liberal morality. The first was its dubious record. The second was its inattention to relations of inequality or its pretence of equality. The third reason is its exaggeration of the scope of choice, or its inattention to unchosen relations. Showing up the partial myth of equality among actual members of a community, and of the undesirability of trying to pretend that we are treating all of them as equals, tends to go along with an exposure of the companion myth that moral obligations arise from freely *chosen* associations between such equals. Vulnerable future generations do not choose their dependence on earlier generations. The unequal infant does not choose its place in a family or nation, nor is it treated as free to do as it likes until some association is freely entered into. Nor do its parents always choose their parental role, or freely assume their parental responsibilities any more than we choose our

power to affect the conditions in which later generations will live. Gilligan's attention to the version of morality and moral maturity found in women, many of whom had faced a choice of whether or not to have an abortion, and who had at some point become mothers, is attention to the perceived inadequacy of the language of rights to help in such choices or to guide them in their parental role. It would not be much of an exaggeration to call the Gilligan "different voice" the voice of the potential parents. The emphasis on care goes with a recognition of the often unchosen nature of the responsibilities of those who give care, both of children who care for their aged or infirm parents, and of parents who care for the children they in fact have. Contract soon ceases to seem the paradigm source of moral obligation once we attend to parental responsibility, and justice as a virtue of social institutions will come to seem at best only first equal with the virtue, whatever its name, that ensures that each new generation is made appropriately welcome and prepared for their adult lives.

. . . The fourth feature of the Gilligan challenge to liberal orthodoxy is a challenge to its typical *rationalism*, or intellectualism, to its assumption that we need not worry what passions persons have, as long as their rational wills can control them. This Kantian picture of a controlling reason dictating to possibly unruly passions also tends to seem less useful when we are led to consider what sort of person we need to fill the role of parent, or indeed want in any close relationship. It might be important for father figures to have rational control over their violent urges to beat to death the children whose screams enrage them, but more than control of such nasty passions seems needed in the mother or primary parent, or parent-substitute, by most psychological theories. They need to love their children, not just to control their irritation. So the emphasis in Kantian theories on rational control of emotions, rather than on cultivating desirable forms of emotion, is challenged by Gilligan, along with the challenge to the assumption of the centrality of autonomy, or relations between equals, and of freely chosen relations. . . .

It is clear, I think, that the best moral theory has to be a cooperative product of women and men, has to harmonize justice and care. The morality it theorizes about is after all for all persons, for men and for women, and will need their combined insights. As Gilligan said (D.V., 174), what we need now is a "marriage" of the old male and the newly articulated female insights. If she is right about the special moral aptitudes of women, it will most likely be the women who propose the marriage, since they are the ones with more natural empathy, with the better diplomatic skills, the ones more likely to shoulder responsibility and take moral initiative, and the ones who find it easiest to empathize and care about how the other party feels. Then, once there is this union of male and female moral wisdom, we maybe can teach each other the moral skills each gender currently lacks, so that the gender difference in moral outlook that Gilligan found will slowly become less marked.

NOTES

1. John Rawls, *A Theory of Justice* (Harvard University Press).
2. Alasdair MacIntyre, *After Virtue* (Notre Dame: Notre Dame University Press).
3. Michael Stocker, "The Schizophrenia of Modern Ethical Theories," *Journal of Philosophy*, *73* (14), 453–466; and "Agent and Other: Against Ethical Universalism," *Australasian Journal of Philosophy*, *54*, 206–220.
4. Lawrence Blum, *Friendship, Altruism and Morality* (London: Routledge & Kegan Paul, 1980).
5. Michael Slote, *Goods and Virtues* (Oxford: Oxford University Press 1983).
6. Laurence Thomas, "Love and Morality," in James Fetzer (Ed.), *Epistemology and Sociobiology* (1985); and "Justice, Happiness and Self Knowledge," *Canadian Journal of Philosophy* (March 1986). Also "Beliefs and the Motivation to be Just," *American Philosophical Quarterly*, *22* (4), 347–352.
7. Claudia Card, "Mercy," *Philosophical Review*, *81*, 1; and "Gender and Moral Luck," forthcoming.
8. Alison Jaggar, *Feminist Politics and Human Nature* (London: Rowman & Allenheld, 1983).
9. Susan Wolf, "Moral Saints," *Journal of Philosophy*, *79* (August 1982), 419–439.
10. For a helpful survey article see Owen Flanagan and Kathryn Jackson, "Justice, Care & Gender: The Kohlberg-Gilligan Debate Revisited," *Ethics*, *97*, 3 (April 1987), 622–637.
11. Lawrence Kohlberg, *Essays in Moral Development*, vols. I & II (New York: Harper & Row, 1981, 1984).
12. Bernard Williams, *Ethics and the Limits of Philosophy* (Cambridge: Cambridge University Press 1985).
13. Philippa Foot, *Virtues and Vices* (Berkeley: University of California Press, 1978).
14. I have previously written about the significance of her findings for moral philosophy in "What Do Women Want in a Moral Theory?" *Nous*, *19* (March 1985); "Trust and Antitrust," *Ethics*, *96* (1986); and in "Hume the Women's Moral Theorist?" in *Women and Moral Theory*, Kittay and Meyers (Eds.).
15. Immanuel Kant, *Metaphysics of Morals*, sec. 46.

REVIEW EXERCISES

1. How do the two examples given of male and female reasoning exemplify the various supposed characteristics of female and male ethical perspectives?
2. Contrast the research findings of Carol Gilligan and Lawrence Kohlberg on male and female moral development.
3. According to Freud, why were women supposed to be morally deficient?
4. What three types of explanation for the male–female difference in morality have been given?
5. How does Gilligan's duck and rabbit example help explain the difference between the two moral perspectives?
6. Describe the psychosexual development explanation of female and male moral perspectives.
7. Summarize Caroline Whitbeck's biological explanation of the difference between female and male moral perspectives.
8. How has the difference been explained in terms of "maternal thinking"?
9. Describe the basic issues involved in trying to decide whether one type of moral perspective is better than another.
10. Describe some of the history and characteristics of feminist thought.

—10—

Euthanasia

IN MARCH, 2009, voters in Washington state passed an initiative, the "Death with Dignity Act," which made Washington the second state in the United States to have a law permitting physician-assisted suicide. The first was Oregon, whose voters passed their version in 1998.[1] According to both laws, a patient who has fewer than six months to live, according to the judgment of two independent doctors, may receive a prescription for a lethal dose of a drug to be taken orally. The patient must be competent, must have a clear and continuing request, made orally and in writing, and able to take the drug themselves. In Washington, since their law passed, 63 people have requested and received the drug, though only 36 of them took it and died. Since their law passed, 460 people in Oregon have used this method and died.[2] In the last couple of decades, voters in several states, including Michigan, Maine, and California, have rejected similar initiatives. Other states, including Montana, Connecticut, and Massachusetts, are considering similar proposals. In 2006 the U.S. Supreme Court rejected efforts of petitioners to stop this practice.[3]

Several questions suggest themselves regarding this matter. One is whether this is in fact "euthanasia." The other may be stated as follows: even if this is a form of euthanasia that is legally permitted in some states, is it a morally justifiable practice? This chapter addresses questions such as these.

Euthanasia has been a controversial topic for decades. The discussion of euthanasia involves issues of patient rights, life and death, the proper function of doctors, the ethics of suicide, and the overlap between law and morality. This chapter will address each of these issues. However, we begin with an issue that sometimes confuses discussions of euthanasia—namely, the issue of brain death.

BRAIN DEATH, COMA, AND PERSISTENT VEGETATIVE STATE

Years ago, an article in *The New York Times* reported on the case of a judge who was presiding over a disputed medical situation. The dispute concerned whether a woman's respirator could be disconnected. The judge was reported to have said, "This lady is dead, and has been dead, and they are keeping her alive artificially."[4] Did the judge believe that the woman was alive or dead? She could not be both. He said that she was dead but also that she was being kept alive by machines. If the woman was really dead, then machines may have been keeping some of her body functions going but could not have been keeping her alive. Perhaps the judge meant that, given her condition, she should be allowed to die. If so, then he should not have said she was dead. I note this item to make the point that people, even judges, confuse questions about whether someone is dead or ought to be considered dead with other questions about whether it is permissible to do things that might hasten death.

It is important to distinguish these two questions. Not doing so has practical consequences. For example, the judge's comment seems to imply that the only reason why the woman's respirator or other machine could be disconnected was because she was dead. However, we need not believe an individual to be dead in order to think it justifiable to disconnect her from a respirator and let her die. In fact, only if someone is not dead can we then sensibly ask whether we may let him die. It seems useful here to think briefly about *how* we do determine whether someone is dead so as to distinguish this issue from other questions that are properly euthanasia questions. Similar confusion and questions exist today.

Throughout history, people have used various means to determine whether someone is dead, and those means were a function of what they believed to be essential aspects of life. For example, if spirit was thought of as essential and was equated with a kind of thin air or breath, then the presence or absence of this life breath would indicate whether a person was living. When heart function was regarded as the key element of life, and the heart was thought to be like a furnace, then people would feel the body to see if it was warm in order to know whether the person was still living. Even today, with our better understanding of the function of the heart, other organs, and organ systems, we have great difficulty with this issue. One reason for this is that we now can use various machines to perform certain body functions such as respiration (oxygenation of the blood) and blood circulation. Sometimes, this is a temporary measure such as during a surgery. However, in other cases, the person may have lost significant brain function. In this latter sort of case, it is important to know whether the person is to be considered alive or dead.

Being able to give precise conditions and tests for determining whether or when an individual is dead became particularly problematic just three decades ago. It was problematic not only because of the arrival of new medical technologies, but also because surgeons had just begun doing human heart transplants. One could not take a heart for transplant from someone who was considered living, only from someone who had been declared dead. Was an individual whose heart function was being artificially maintained but who had no brain function considered living or dead? We still wonder about this today. In one odd case, a man accused of murder pleaded guilty to a lesser charge of assault and battery, claiming that even though the victim had lost all brain function his heart was still beating after the assault. The defendant argued that it was the doctor at Stanford Medical Center who removed the heart for transplant who had killed this individual![5]

In 1968, an *ad hoc* committee of the Harvard Medical School was set up to establish criteria for determining when someone is dead. This committee determined that someone should be considered dead if she or he has permanently lost all detectable brain function. This meant that if there was some nonconscious brain function, for example, or if the condition was temporary, then the individual would not be considered dead. Thus, various tests of reflexes and responsiveness were required to determine whether an individual had sustained a permanent and total loss of all brain function.[6] This condition is now known as *whole brain death* and is the primary criterion used for the legal determination of death. This is true even when other secondary criteria or tests such as loss of pulse are used, for it is assumed that lack of blood circulation for more than five to ten minutes results in brain cell death.

Whole brain death is distinguished from other conditions such as *persistent vegetative state* (PVS). In PVS, the individual has lost all cerebral cortex function but has retained some good brain stem function. Many nonconscious functions that are based in that area of the brain—respiratory and heart rate, facial reflexes and muscle control, and gag reflex and swallowing abilities—continue. Yet the individual in a permanent or persistent vegetative state has lost all conscious function. One reason for this condition is that the rate of oxygen use by the cerebral cortex is much higher than that of the brain stem, so these cells die much more quickly if deprived of oxygen for some time. The result is that the individual in this state will never regain consciousness but can often breathe naturally and needs no artificial aid to maintain circulation. Such an individual does not feel pain because he or she cannot interpret it as such. Because the gag reflex is good, individuals in this condition can clear their airways and thus may live for many years. They go through wake and sleep cycles in which they have their eyes open and then closed. This was the case with Terri Schiavo, a woman who's case became such a contentious political issue

This photograph of Terry Schaivo was used to support the argument for keeping her on life support.

in 2005. Schiavo was a twenty-six-year-old woman who suffered a cardiac arrest on the morning of February 25, 1990. Her husband called 911, and the emergency personnel who arrived shortly thereafter resuscitated her. However, Schiavo's brain had been deprived of oxygen for some time, and she remained in a coma for the next fifteen years. She was in a persistent vegetative state as described here. At that point, her husband wanted to remove her from the feeding tube on which she depended, but her parents objected. Her husband prevailed in court, her feeding tube was removed, and she died on March 31, 2005. An autopsy later revealed that her brain had shrunk to half its normal size, and thus she had not been conscious or aware. To some people, she seemed to follow their motions and to respond to their voices. However, we know from her autopsy as well as earlier brain scans that she had no conscious function and that these were autonomic or reflexive responses. Nevertheless, this is a disconcerting aspect of PVS. Patients in this state are unconscious but "awake." In contrast, someone who is not totally brain dead but who is in a coma is unconscious but "asleep." His or her brain stem functions poorly, and thus this person does not live as long as someone in a persistent vegetative state.[7] If we use whole brain death criteria to determine whether someone is dead, then neither a person in a persistent vegetative state nor a person in a coma is dead. In these cases, euthanasia questions about whether to let them die can be raised. On the other hand, if someone is dead by whole brain death criteria, then disconnecting equipment is not any form of euthanasia. We cannot let someone die who is already dead.

MEANING AND TYPES OF EUTHANASIA

The term *euthanasia* has Greek roots and literally means "good death." Although the term itself implies that there can be a good death, in itself it does not tell us when or under what conditions death is good. Is a good death one that comes suddenly or after some time to think about and prepare for it? Is it one that takes place at home and in familiar surroundings or one that occurs in a medical facility? Is it one that we know is coming and over which we have control or one that comes on us without notice? We usually think of life as a good, so the more of it the better. But we also know that in some conditions life is difficult and that some people have judged it too painful to continue.

Active and Passive Euthanasia

If you were approached by a pollster who asked whether you supported euthanasia, you would do well first to ask what she meant and to what kind of euthanasia she was referring. It is important to distinguish what is called *passive euthanasia* from what is called *active euthanasia*.

Passive euthanasia refers to withholding or withdrawing certain treatment and letting a patient die. Passive euthanasia is now a common practice and is not prohibited by law. In recent years, many doctors, as many as 96 percent, have withdrawn or withheld life-prolonging treatment for their patients. Most of the time this is done at the request of the patient or the patient's family. However, in some cases, doctors have done this unilaterally either without consulting patients or their families or even against their wishes.[8] The reasons given in either case were generally that such treatment would not extend the patient's life for long or that the patient's life would not be worth lengthening, such as when the patient was not expected to regain consciousness.

The landmark cases of Karen Quinlan in 1975 and Nancy Cruzan in 1990 brought this type of practice to public attention.[9] In Ms. Quinlan's case, the issue was whether a respirator that was keeping her alive could be disconnected. For some still unknown reason (some say it was a combination of barbiturates and alcohol), she had gone into a coma. When doctors assured them that she would not recover, her parents sought permission to retain legal guardianship (since by then she was twenty-one years old) and have her respirator disconnected. After several court hearings and final approval by the supreme court of the state of New Jersey, the Quinlans were finally permitted to disconnect her respirator. Although they expected she would die shortly after her respirator was removed, she continued to live in this comatose state for ten more years. One basic reason given by the court for its opinion in this case was that Quinlan did not lose her right of privacy by becoming incompetent and that she could thus refuse unwanted and useless interventions by others to keep her alive. None of the various state interests or social concerns that might override this right were found to be relevant in her case.

Nancy Cruzan was twenty-five years old in 1983 when an accident left her in a permanent vegetative state until her death eight years later. In her case, the issue brought to the courts was whether a feeding tube that was providing her with food and water could be withdrawn. This case eventually reached the U.S. Supreme Court, which ruled that such life-saving procedures could be withdrawn or withheld, but only if there was "clear and convincing evidence" that Nancy would have wanted that herself. Eventually, such evidence was brought forward. By that time, those who were protesting her case had withdrawn, and her feeding tube was removed and she was allowed to die.

Active euthanasia is using certain death-causing means to bring about or cause the death of a person. In the past, it used to be called "mercy killing." Drugs are the most common means. Rather than letting a person die, these means are used to actually kill the person. This is generally regarded as much more problematic and is generally legally prohibited.

On November 28, 2000, the lower house of the Dutch parliament approved the legalization of (active) euthanasia by a vote of 104 to 40; the upper house followed on April 10, 2001, by a vote of 46 to 28.[10] The Dutch euthanasia process involves injecting "a sedative and a muscle relaxant."[11] For decades, the country had informally accepted the practice, and

since 1993 rules have allowed doctors to carry out the procedure without fear of prosecution. The Netherlands has had a historical tradition of tolerance going back centuries, as evidenced by its provision of refuge for Jews, Catholics, and such controversial philosophers as Descartes and Spinoza.[12] The new law allowed physicians to medically end a patient's life if the following conditions were met:

1. The patient's request must be voluntary and clearly understood and repeatedly voiced.
2. The patient must be faced with unbearable and continuing suffering (although he or she need not be terminally ill, and the suffering need not be physical or physical only).
3. The patient must believe that no reasonable alternative is acceptable.
4. The doctor must consult with at least one other independent physician who also has examined the patient.
5. Physicians and not others must provide medically acceptable means to bring about the patient's death.
6. Children ages 12 to 16 who request it must also have parental consent, although not from age 16 onward.
7. Physicians are not to suggest this possibility to patients.
8. Euthanasia cases must be officially reported to authorities.[13]

It is difficult to get reliable statistics on how this practice has proceeded over the years when these guidelines were accepted but did not have the full force of law. However, it seems that not all of them have been fully complied with. For example, in 25 percent of the cases reported by physicians, not *current* suffering but fear of *future* suffering was the reason given for the requests.[14] The Dutch courts have said that if means to relieve suffering are available, even though the patient refuses them, this is not grounds for euthanasia; in 17 percent of cases, it was administered anyway. There have been difficulties in getting physicians to consult with other physicians who are independent and who actually will come to see the patient. In 2001, approximately 54 percent of euthanasia and assisted suicide deaths were not reported to the coroner as required by the guidelines; however, by 2005 the number of reported cases had risen to 80 percent.[15]

Approximately 8,400 people in Holland ask for either euthanasia or physician-assisted suicide each year. Out of this number, there are approximately 2,300 actual cases of euthanasia and 100 of physician-assisted suicide. "In 2005, 1.7 percent of all deaths in The Netherlands were the result of euthanasia and 0.1 percent were the result of physician-assisted suicide." This is down from 2.6 percent and 0.2 percent, respectively, in 2001. The decrease is thought to result from changing demographics and better pain control.[16]

It is difficult to know whether there are still cases of involuntary euthanasia—that is, doctors actively killing their patients without the patients' knowledge or consent. In 1990, a reported 1,040 people (an average of three per day) died from involuntary euthanasia. A 1997 study published in the British medical journal *The Lancet* reported that some 8 percent of all infants who die in The Netherlands are euthanized—approximately eighty per year.[17] In Holland, it is also the case that health care is a universal right, whereas it is not in the United States. Practices such as euthanasia or physician-assisted suicide might be particularly problematic in the United States in cases where physicians with HMOs are given bonuses for keeping costs down. In Holland, there may be less reason for people to request euthanasia because they do not have access to adequate health care. Another interesting fact is that the suicide rate in Holland has decreased since euthanasia has been available. Among people older than fifty, the number of suicides in the last two decades has fallen by one-third.

In October 2001, the Belgian senate voted by a ratio of 2 to 1 to allow doctors to provide assistance in dying to patients who request it. This law became effective on January 1, 2002. The Belgian law differs somewhat from the Dutch law by allowing advance directives (see the later discussion of this) and by promoting "the development of palliative care."[18] The Australian government had passed a similar measure but withdrew it when it was thought too open to abuse. With its own past history of Nazis gassing some 100,000 people who were deemed physically or mentally handicapped, Germany has criticized the Dutch approval as the dangerous breaching of a dike.[19] Still, 80 percent of Dutch citizens support the law as the best way to allow people to control their own lives. Assisted suicide is also legal in Switzerland, and people from countries where it is illegal often controversially go to Switzerland to participate in it.

Other arguments for and against euthanasia follow. It is sufficient here to give this as an example of what is called *active euthanasia*, which is distinguishable from *passive euthanasia*. These two ways of facing death may then be judged separately.

Passive euthanasia: Stopping (or not starting) some treatment, which allows the person to die. The person's condition causes his or her death.

Active euthanasia: Doing something such as administering a lethal drug or using other means that cause the person's death.

Physician-Assisted Suicide

Every year, some 30,000 people commit suicide in the United States, approximately 1.2 percent of all deaths. It is estimated that there are twenty-five nonfatal attempts for every actual suicide.[20] For every woman who completes a suicide attempt, four men do. Fifty-seven percent of suicides are by firearm; "suicide rates were increased four to ten times in adolescents if there was a gun in their household."[21] In the United States, every two hours or so, one young person between ages fifteen and twenty-four commits suicide. Suicide is the second leading cause of death for college students after accidents. "A 1999 survey reported that 20 percent of high-school students seriously contemplated suicide during the previous year."[22] On the other hand, the elderly attempt suicide less often than younger people but they succeed more often.

This issue is related to that of euthanasia because one form—physician-assisted suicide—is a form of suicide. In these cases, the physician does not actually inject a patient with a death-causing drug as in active euthanasia, but rather provides patients with drugs that they will take themselves. It is thus basically a form of suicide, with the doctor providing the means to carry it out. Just as questions can be raised about whether suicide is ever morally acceptable, so also can questions be raised about whether it is morally permissible for physicians (or others for that matter) to help someone commit suicide. What is also different about physician-assisted suicide is that it involves doctors. It thus jumps the barrier that prevents doctors from actually doing something that will cause the death of a person. In some ways, it looks like active euthanasia. In passive euthanasia, the doctor refrains from trying to do what saves or prolongs life, but in active euthanasia the doctor acts to bring about the death by some cause or means. However, the causation by the doctor in physician-assisted suicide is not immediate or direct but rather takes place through the action of the patient.

What moral difference there might or might not be between these forms of euthanasia we will consider later in this chapter. It is interesting however, to recount here a little of the recent history of the practice of physician-assisted suicide. The most well-known advocate and practitioner has been retired pathologist Jack Kevorkian. His activities in assisting suicides have been much publicized. For several years, he helped people who went to him to die by providing them with the means to kill themselves. His first method was a "suicide machine" that consisted of a metal pole to which bottles of three solutions were attached. First, a simple saline solution flowed through an intravenous needle that had been inserted into the person's vein. The patient then flipped a switch that started a flow of an anesthetic, thiopental, that caused the person to become unconscious. After sixty seconds, a solution of potassium chloride followed, causing death within minutes by heart seizure. In a later version of the machine, carbon monoxide was used. When a person pushed a control switch, carbon monoxide flowed through a tube to a bag placed over his or her head.[23] For eight years from 1990, he assisted more than 100 suicides (he claimed the number was 130), almost all of them in Michigan. To prevent these incidents from taking place in their state, Michigan legislators passed a law in 1993 against assisting a suicide. However, the law was struck down in the courts. Kevorkian was brought to trial in three separate cases, but the juries found him not guilty in each case. However, in November 1998, he himself administered a lethal injection to a fifty-two-year-old man who was suffering from Lou Gehrig's disease. He also provided the news media with a videotape of the injection and death. It was aired on CBS's *60 Minutes* on November 22, 1998. This was no longer a case of suicide, and after a brief trial, on April 13, 1999, Kevorkian was convicted of second-degree murder and sentenced to serve a 10- to 25-year prison term in a Michigan prison. He was paroled due to a severe (and possibly fatal) hepatitis C infection on June 1, 2007.[24]

Many families of people he has helped to die speak highly of Dr. Kevorkian. In the videotapes that he made before each death, the individuals who died were seen pleading to be allowed to die. His critics have a different view, however. They say that at least some of the people who wanted to die might not have done so if they had been helped—if their pain were adequately treated, for example. Some of the people were not terminally ill. One was in the early stages of Alzheimer's disease, and another had multiple sclerosis. The primary physician of another who claimed to have multiple sclerosis said the patient showed no evidence of this or any other disease; the patient had a history of depression, however. Another "patient" was determined by the medical examiner to have no trace of an earlier diagnosed cancer.[25] In one case, a woman had what has come to be called "chronic fatigue syndrome" and a history of abuse by her husband. Kevorkian's "patients" have been predominantly women who may have been worried about the impact of their disease on others as much as the difficulty of the disease itself or its prospects for them. In fact, three times as many women as men attempt suicide, though men succeed more often than do women.[26] Some critics suggest that their attempts are more of a cry for help. Death may also appear different to women. "If it is given a human face by a soothing physician/assister there is all the more reason why the super-altruistic woman with a life spent serving others would want to put down her burdens, and succumb."[27]

Although the American Medical Association continues to oppose physician-assisted suicide, federal appeals courts covering the states of Washington and New York have upheld the practice as constitutionally protected, one on grounds of privacy and the other on the assertion that physician-assisted suicide is the same as turning off a respirator.[28] In one analysis, the reason for the difference between the court and physicians may be that "members of the legal profession have a higher opinion of their colleagues in medicine than the doctors do of themselves. Or perhaps physicians simply have a better understanding of the pressures of contemporary medical practice than do judges."[29] Bills that have sought to legalize physician-assisted suicide have been rejected in some twenty states. In 1990, backers of a proposed California proposition sought to legalize active euthanasia for those with terminal illnesses who request it either at the time of illness or earlier through an advance directive; the backers failed to obtain the necessary signatures for a ballot measure. In Washington State in 1991, a similar ballot measure also failed. In 1997, the U.S. Supreme Court upheld court rulings regarding laws in New York and Washington State that made assisted suicide illegal. The Court based its findings on the conclusion that there was no constitutional "right to die." However, it said that individual states could make laws either permitting or prohibiting assisted suicide (see earlier discussion of the present day situation).

Thirty-six states have laws explicitly making it a crime to assist a suicide; in seven others, it is against common law. North Carolina, Utah, and Wyoming have no laws criminalizing assisted suicide. Four states (and Washington, D.C.) have no specific laws on assisted suicide. In 1997, the U.S. Supreme Court stated that there is no constitutional right to die with the help of a physician and "upheld state laws banning assisted suicide."[30]

Oregon voters narrowly approved the state's Death with Dignity Act in 1994 but reaffirmed it with a larger margin in 1997. When this law was challenged by the Bush administration in 2001, a federal appeals court judge ruled that the U.S. Attorney General "did not have legal authority to decide that doctors acting in compliance with Oregon's law were in violation of the federal Controlled Substances Act."[31]

Pain Medication That Causes Death

One type of action may be confused with active euthanasia but ought to be distinguished from it: giving pain medication to gravely ill and dying patients. Physicians are often hesitant to prescribe sufficient pain medication to such patients because they fear that the medication will actually cause their deaths. They fear that this would be considered comparable to mercy killing (or active euthanasia), which

is legally impermissible. Some philosophers believe that the *principle of double effect* may be of some help here.[32] According to this principle, it is one thing to intend and do something bad as a means to an end, and it is another to do something morally permissible for the purpose of achieving some good while knowing that it also may have a bad secondary effect.

The following diagram may be used to help understand the essence of this principle. It shows a morally permissible act with two effects: one intended main effect and one unintended side effect.

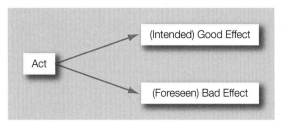

According to the principle of double effect, it may be morally permissible to administer a drug with the intention of relieving pain (a good effect) even though we know or foresee that our action also may have a bad effect (weakening the person and risking his death). Certain conditions must be met, however, for this to be permissible. *First*, the act must be morally permissible. One cannot do what is wrong to bring about a good end. *Second*, the person who acts must intend to bring about the good end rather than the harmful result. *Third*, the good results must outweigh the bad ones.

The idea behind the double effect principle is that there is a moral difference between intending to kill someone and intending to relieve pain. There is a moral difference between intending that someone die by *means of* one's actions (giving a drug overdose) and foreseeing that they will die *because of* one's actions (giving medication to relieve pain). Doing the latter is not, strictly speaking, active euthanasia. Active euthanasia would be the intentional giving of a drug with the purpose of bringing about a person's death. The difference is seen in the case of the dentist who foresees that she might pain her patient and the dentist who seeks to produce pain in her patient. The principle of double effect, nevertheless, continues to be an object of debate.[33]

In actual practice, it may be difficult to know what is going on—whether, for example, a person intends to use a prescribed drug just to relieve pain or actually bring about death. People may also have mixed or hidden motives for their actions. Yet it would seem helpful to use this principle so that doctors are permitted to give their patients sufficient pain medication without fear of being prosecuted for homicide. (The fact that they might cause addiction in their patients is another reason why some doctors hesitate to give narcotics for pain relief. This seems hardly a reasonable objection, especially if the patient is dying!) This principle may also help those who want patients to have good pain relief but are morally opposed to active euthanasia.

It is also interesting to note advances in the treatment of pain. For example, at a San Francisco meeting of members of the American Society of Anesthesiologists in October 2000, various new advances were described. For example, physicians described "pouches of anesthetics and narcotics that can be planted near the spine to give out steady bits of painkillers and muscle relaxants."[34] They also noted that "pacemaker-like devices" could be implanted near nerves to make buzzing sensations that would "drown out pain messages." One of the difficulties of some morphine-type pain medications is that they negatively affect consciousness. According to doctors at this meeting, one new drug being developed is "a highly diluted form of an exotic snail poison that blocks pain without being addictive or altering mental function."[35] New developments here may make it possible to treat pain without causing death, thereby keeping this issue separate from that of active euthanasia.

Ordinary and Extraordinary Measures

Philosophers have sometimes labeled those measures that are ineffective or excessively burdensome as *extraordinary*. They are often called *heroic* in the medical setting in the sense that using such measures is above and beyond what is required. A person's hospital medical chart might have the phrase "no heroics" on it, indicating that no such measures are to be used. There are other cases in which what is refused would actually be effective for curing or ameliorating a life-threatening condition. And yet decisions are made not to use these measures and to let the person die. These measures are called *ordinary*—not because they are common but because

they promise reasonable hope of benefit. With ordinary measures, the chances that the treatment will help are good, and the expected results are also good. One difficulty with determining whether a treatment would be considered ordinary or extraordinary is making an objective evaluation of the benefit and burden. It would be easier to do this if there were such a thing as a range for a normal life. Any measure that would not restore a life to that norm could then be considered extraordinary. However, if we were to set this standard very high, using it might also wrongly imply that the lives of disabled persons are of little or no benefit to them.

What would be considered an ordinary measure in the case of one person may be considered extraordinary in the case of another; a measure may effectively treat one person's condition, but another person will die shortly even if the measure were used (a blood transfusion, for example). Furthermore, the terminology can be misleading because many of the things that used to be experimental and risky are now common and quite beneficial. Drugs such as antibiotics and technologies such as respirators, which were once experimental and of questionable benefit, are now more effective and less expensive. In many cases, they would now be considered ordinary, whereas they once could have been considered extraordinary. It is their proven benefit in a time period and for particular individuals that makes them ordinary in our sense of the term, however, and not their commonness. (You will find use of the term *extraordinary* in the quote from the American Medical Association in the article by James Rachels. When reading that article, you also might consider whether one reason the cases of Smith and Jones are morally similar is because what was withheld from the child was an "ordinary" means of life support.)

The basic difference between ordinary and extraordinary measures of life support, then, is as follows:

Ordinary measures: Measures or treatments with reasonable hope of benefit, or the benefits outweigh the burdens to the patient.

Extraordinary measures: Measures or treatments with no reasonable hope of benefit, or the burdens outweigh the benefits to the patient.

One question that arises in relation to the Terri Schiavo case, as well as others, is how to view in this regard the withholding or withdrawing of artificial nutrition. It is instructive to know that Schiavo's family was Catholic; there has been a tradition in Catholic theology that provides the basis for much of the understanding of the distinctions between ordinary and extraordinary measures. Although the definitions are made in the context of making moral judgments about euthanasia, which we will discuss below, the key to the difference is whether that which is withheld or withdrawn offers "a reasonable hope of benefit" or not.[36] Although guidelines assert that "a person may forgo extraordinary or disproportionate means of preserving life. . .there should be a presumption in favor of providing nutrition and hydration to all patients, including patients who require medically assisted nutrition and hydration, as long as this is of sufficient benefit to outweigh the burdens involved to the patient."[37] In other words, in some cases this form of medical intervention would be deemed of insufficient benefit to a patient—for example, if it did not promise to return him or her to a conscious state.

Voluntary and Nonvoluntary Euthanasia

Before we move on to consider arguments regarding the morality of euthanasia, one more distinction needs to be made between what can be called *voluntary* and *nonvoluntary* euthanasia. In many cases, it is the person whose life is at issue who makes the decision about what is to be done. This is voluntary euthanasia. In other cases, people other than the one whose life is at issue decide what is to be done. These are cases of nonvoluntary euthanasia.[38] Nonvoluntary simply means not *through* the will of the individual. It does not mean *against* their will. Sometimes, others must make the decision because the person or patient is incapable of doing so. This is true of infants and small children and a person who is in a coma or permanent vegetative state. This is also true of people who are only minimally competent, as in cases of senility or certain psychiatric disorders. Deciding who is sufficiently competent to make decisions for themselves is clear in many but not all cases. What should we say, for example, of the mental competence of the eighty-year-old man who refuses an effective surgery that would save his life and at the same time says he does not want to die? Is such a person being rational?

In some cases, when a patient is not able to express his or her wishes, we can attempt to imagine what the person would want. We can rely, for example, on past personality or statements the person has made. Perhaps the person commented to friends or relatives as to what he or she would want if such and such a situation occurred.

In other cases, a person might have left a written expression of his or her wishes in the form of a *living will*. The living will may specify that one does not want extraordinary measures used to prolong life if one is dying and unable to communicate. However, it leaves it up to the physician—who may be a stranger—to determine what is extraordinary. A better directive is called a durable power of attorney. In this case, you appoint someone close to you who knows what you want under certain conditions if you are dying and unable to communicate this. This person need not be a lawyer but will be your legal representative to make medical decisions for you in the event that you are incapacitated. The form for *durable power of attorney* also provides for individualized expressions in writing about what you would want done or not done under certain conditions. The person you appoint will also be the only one to give permission for *do not resuscitate* (DNR) orders, or orders not to resuscitate under certain conditions. You should also have one or two alternates. Whether such orders are to be given is often a problem, especially if the physician believes that resuscitating will be futile or even make the patient worse off and some family members do not want to give up.[39] At the very least, these directives have moral force. They also have legal force in those states that have recognized them.[40] However, even then these directives are often not followed by physicians, especially if the patient is a woman. These measures can, if enforced or strengthened, give people some added control over what happens to them in their last days. To further ensure this, in December 1991 the Patient Self-Determination Act passed by the U.S. Congress went into effect. This act requires that health care institutions that participate in the Medicare and Medicaid programs have written policies for providing individuals in their care with information about and access to advance directives such as living wills.

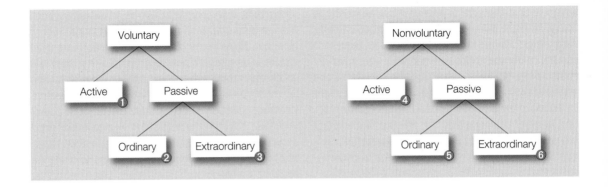

Again, the difference between voluntary and nonvoluntary cases can be specified as follows:

Voluntary euthanasia: The person whose life is at issue knowingly and freely decides what shall be done.
Nonvoluntary euthanasia: Persons other than the one whose life is at issue decide what shall be done.

Combining the Types of Euthanasia

We have noted the differences between various types of euthanasia: voluntary and nonvoluntary, active and passive, and (if passive) the withholding of ordinary and extraordinary measures. Combining the types of euthanasia gives six forms, as illustrated above.

There are three types of voluntary euthanasia.

1. Voluntary active euthanasia: The person who is dying says, "Give me the fatal dose."
2. Voluntary passive euthanasia, withholding ordinary measures: The person says, "Don't use lifesaving or life-prolonging medical measures even though the likely results of using them would be good and the costs or burdens minimal, because I want to die."
3. Voluntary passive euthanasia, withholding extraordinary measures: The person says, "Don't use those medical measures because the chances of benefit in terms of lifesaving or life extension would be small, the burdens too great, or both."

Likewise, there are three types of nonvoluntary euthanasia.

4. Nonvoluntary active euthanasia: Others decide to give the person a fatal drug overdose.

5. Nonvoluntary passive euthanasia, withholding ordinary measures: Others decide not to use lifesaving or life-prolonging medical measures even though the likely results of using them would be good and the costs or burdens minimal.
6. Nonvoluntary passive euthanasia, withholding extraordinary measures: Others decide not to use those medical measures because the chances of benefit—saving or extending life—are small, the burdens are too great, or both.

So far, we have attempted only to classify types of euthanasia. Our purpose has been to describe the various possible types so that we will then be better able to make appropriate distinctions in our moral judgments about these cases.

MORALITY AND THE LAW

Before we consider the moral arguments about euthanasia, we should first distinguish moral judgments from assertions about what the law should or should not be on this matter. Although we may sometimes have moral reasons for what we say the law should or should not do, *the two areas are distinct*. There are many things that are moral matters that ought not to be legislated or made subject to law and legal punishment. *Not everything that is immoral ought to be illegal*. For example, lying, while arguably a moral issue, is only sometimes subject to the law. In our thinking about euthanasia, it would be well to keep this distinction in mind. On the one hand, in some cases we might say that a person acted badly, though understandably, in giving up too easily on life. Yet we also may believe that the law should not force some action here if the person knows what he or she is doing, and the person's action does not seriously harm others. On the other hand, a person's request to end his or her life might be reasonable given his circumstances, but there might also be social reasons why the law should not permit it. These reasons might be related to the possible harmful effects of some practice on other persons or on the practice of medicine. *Just because some action (for example, euthanasia) might be morally permissible does not necessarily mean that it ought to be legally permissible.*

MAKING MORAL JUDGMENTS ABOUT EUTHANASIA

One way to get a handle on what to think about the morality of euthanasia is to look at its various types. We can then ask ourselves whether euthanasia of a certain type is morally justifiable. One way to help us answer these questions is to use the distinction made in our chapters on moral theory between *consequentialist* theories (such as utilitarianism) and *nonconsequentialist* theories (such as Kant's moral theory or natural law theory). If you think that it is the consequences rather than the nature of actions themselves that matter morally, then you can focus on those considerations. If you think that we should judge whether some action is right or wrong in itself for some reason, then you can focus on those considerations and reasons.

The Moral Significance of Voluntariness

Today, an individual's rights over his or her own life are highly valued. And yet the commonsense moral view is that there are limits to this right. It is limited, for example, when it conflicts with the interests or rights of others. Under what conditions and for what reasons should a person's own wishes prevail in euthanasia matters? How important is voluntary consent?

Consequentialist Considerations   From your study of utilitarianism, you know that one major method of deciding moral right and wrong appeals to the consequences of our actions (act utilitarianism) or practices (rule utilitarianism). From this perspective, voluntariness matters morally only to the extent that it affects human happiness and welfare. Respecting people's own choices about how they will die surely would have some beneficial consequences. For example, when people know that they will be allowed to make decisions

about their own lives and not be forced into things against their will, then they may gain a certain peace of mind. Thus, many of the persons who have used Oregon's assisted suicide law reported that they did so because they did not want to be dependent and felt better being in control over their lives. Moreover, knowing themselves better than others knew them, they also may be the ones best able to make good decisions in situations that primarily affect them. These are good consequentialist reasons to respect a person's wishes in euthanasia cases. But it is not just the person who is dying who will be affected by the decision. Thus, it also can be argued that the effects on others—on their feelings, for example—are also relevant to the moral decision making.

However, individual decisions are not always wise and do not always work for the greatest benefit of the person making them or for others. For example, critics of euthanasia worry that people who are ill or disabled would refuse certain lifesaving treatment because they lack or do not know about services, support, and money that are available to them. More than a decade ago, the Nevada supreme court ruled that people must receive information about care alternatives before they may refuse lifesaving treatment.[41] On consequentialist grounds, we should do what, in fact, is most likely to bring about the greatest happiness, not only to ourselves but also to all those affected by our actions. It does not in itself matter who makes the judgment. But it does matter insofar as one person rather than another is more likely to make a better judgment, one that would have better consequences overall, including consequences to the individual.

Moreover, from the perspective of rule utilitarian thinking, we ought to consider which policy would maximize happiness. (It is here that morality comes closer to concerns about what the law should be.) Would a policy that universally follows individual requests about dying be most likely to maximize happiness? Or would a policy that gives no special weight to individual desires, but which directs us to do whatever some panel decides, be more likely to have the best outcome? Or would some moderate policy be best, such as one that gives special but not absolute weight to what a person wants? An example of such a policy might be one in which the burden of proof not to do what a person wishes is placed on those who would refuse it. In other words, they must show some serious reason not to go along with what the person wanted.

Nonconsequentialist Considerations   To appeal to the value of personal autonomy in euthanasia decisions is to appeal to a nonconsequentialist reason or moral norm. The idea is that autonomy is a good in itself and therefore carries heavy moral weight. We like to think of ourselves, at least ideally, as masters of our own fate. A world of robots would probably be a lesser world than one populated by people who make their own decisions, even when those decisions are unwise. In fact, according to Kant, only in such a world is morality itself possible. His famous phrase, "an ought implies a can," indicates that if and only if we can or are *free* to act in certain ways can we be *commanded* to do so. According to a Kantian deontological position, persons are unique in being able to choose freely, and this capacity for choice ought to be respected.

However, in many euthanasia cases a person's mental competence and thus autonomy is compromised by fear and lack of understanding. Illness also makes a person more subject to undue influence or coercion. There is also a high correlation between suicide and depression. According to a 1998 study, it is not pain that makes one in ten terminally ill patients in the United States seriously consider suicide, it is depression and dependence on others.[42] "The most seriously depressed patients were twice as likely to have considered suicide as all terminally ill patients."[43] How, in such instances, do we know what the person really wants? Perhaps he or she primarily wants to talk to someone. These are practical problems that arise when attempting to respect autonomy. In addition, the issue raises theoretical problems. *Autonomy* literally means self-rule. But how often are we fully clear about who we are and what we want to be? Is the self whose decisions are to be respected the current self or one's ideal or authentic self? These issues of selfhood and personal identity are crucial to euthanasia arguments that focus on autonomy and personal decision making. It is also the case that they take us beyond ethics itself into philosophical notions of the self and freedom as well as into empirical psychology.

Note also here that although we have concentrated on pointing out the kinds of things that would be morally relevant from both consequentialist and nonconsequentialist points of view, the issues also may be analyzed from the perspective of an ethics of care. One would suppose that from this perspective both matters that relate to benefits and harms and those that relate to a person's autonomy would be relevant.

Active versus Passive Euthanasia

The distinction between active and passive euthanasia is a conceptual distinction, a matter of classification. Giving a patient a lethal drug to end her life is classified as active euthanasia. Stopping or not starting some life-lengthening treatment, knowing that a patient will die, is classified as passive euthanasia. For example, either not starting a respirator or disconnecting it is generally considered passive euthanasia because it is a matter of not providing life-prolonging aid for the person. In this case, the person's illness or weakness is the cause of his death if he dies. This does not mean that it is either justified or unjustified.

Let us pose the *moral* question about active and passive euthanasia like this: Is there any moral difference between them? This prompts the following questions: Is active euthanasia more morally problematic than passive euthanasia? Or are they on a moral par such that if passive euthanasia is morally permissible in some case, then so is active euthanasia? Is physician-assisted suicide (in which a physician only provides the means of death to the person) any more or less problematic than cases in which the physician actually administers the drug or uses other means to bring about death?

Consequentialist Concerns   Again, if we take the perspective of the consequentialist or act utilitarian, for example, we should only be concerned about our actions in terms of their consequences. The means by which the results come about do not matter in themselves. They matter only if they make a difference in the result. Generally, then, if a person's death is the *best outcome* in a difficult situation, it would not matter whether it came about through the administration of a lethal drug dose or from the discontinuance of some lifesaving treatment. Now, if one or the other means did make a difference in a person's experience (as when a person is relieved or pained more by one method than another), then this would count in favor of or against that method.

If we take the perspective of a rule utilitarian, we would be concerned about the consequences of this or that practice or policy. We would want to know which of the various alternative practices or policies would have the best results overall. Which would be the best policy: one that allowed those who are involved to choose active euthanasia, one that required active euthanasia in certain cases, one that permitted it only in rare cases, or one that prohibited it and attached legal penalties to it? Which policy would make more people happy and fewer people unhappy? One that prohibited active euthanasia would frustrate those who wished to use it, but it would prevent some abuses that might follow if it were permitted. Essential to this perspective are predictions about how a policy would work. Some people are concerned in particular about the effects of physician participation in the practice of euthanasia. It may have the positive results of being under the control of a profession known for its ethical concerns. Or it may have negative effects such as the lessening of patient trust in physicians. The disability advocacy group called Not Dead Yet has voiced its concerns about physician-assisted suicide and the plight of the disabled. Its members wonder whether people would be more inclined to think their lives were not worth living and whether there would be pressure on them to commit suicide.[44]

Even those who support physician-assisted suicide and in some cases actual active euthanasia worry about whether these practices would be open to abuse. The argument that there would be abuse has been given various names, depending on the particular metaphor of choice: the "domino effect," "slippery slope," "wedge," or "camel's nose" argument. The idea is that if we permit active euthanasia in a few reasonable cases, then we would slide and approve it in more and more cases until we were approving it in cases that were clearly unreasonable. In other words, if we permit euthanasia when a person is soon dying, in unrelievable pain, and has requested that his life be ended, then we will permit it when a person is not dying or has not requested to be killed. Evidence from The Netherlands cited above may or may not apply in the United States or elsewhere, but the questions to ask are: Would we slide down the slope? Is there something about us that would cause us to slide? Would we be so weak of mind that we could not see the difference between these cases? Would we be weak of will, not wanting to care for people whose care is costly and burdensome? This is an empirical and predictive matter. To know the force of the argument, we would need to show evidence for one or the other positions about the likelihood of sliding.[45]

Nonconsequentialist Concerns Many arguments and concerns about active and passive euthanasia are not based on appeals to good or bad results or consequences. Arguments about the right to die or to make one's own decisions about dying are nonconsequentialist arguments. On the one hand, some people argue that respecting personal autonomy is so important that it should override any concerns about bad results. Thus, we might conclude that people ought to be allowed to end their lives when they choose as an expression of their autonomy, and that this choice should be respected regardless of the consequences to others or even mistakes about their own cases.

On the other hand, some people believe that there is a significant moral difference between killing another person or themselves and letting a person die. Killing people except in self-defense is morally wrong, according to this view. Just why it is thought wrong is another matter. Some people rely on reasons like those purported by natural law, citing the innate drive toward living as a good in itself, however compromised—a good that should not be suppressed. Kant used reasoning similar to this. He argued that using the concern for life that usually promotes it to make a case for ending life was inherently contradictory and a violation of the categorical imperative.[46] Some people use religious reasons such as the belief that life-and-death decisions are for God and not ourselves to make. Some people use reasons that rely on concerns about the gravity of ending a life directly and intentionally, that in doing so we ally ourselves with what is at best a necessary evil.

We each need to consider what role consequentialist and nonconsequentialist reasons play in our own views about the morality of active and passive euthanasia. If consequentialist arguments have primacy, then one's argument for or against active euthanasia will depend on empirical judgments about the predicted consequences. If nonconsequentialist reasons have primacy, then these reasons must be evaluated. Are the nonconsequentialist reasons about autonomy, for example, stronger than the nonconsequentialist arguments about the morality of killing? This text does not intend to answer these questions for the student, but it does assume that a good start can be made in answering them if one is able to know whether an argument is based on consequentialist or nonconsequentialist considerations.

Ordinary versus Extraordinary Measures

There is considerable disagreement about the usefulness of the distinction between ordinary and extraordinary measures of life support. People disagree first of all about the definitions of the terms.[47] If the terms are defined primarily in terms of commonness and uncommonness, then surely it is difficult to see that this should make a moral difference. It would amount to saying that we ought to use those things that we commonly use and not use those we usually do not use. However, if the terms are defined in relation to benefit and burden, then they are by their nature morally relevant because these are value terms. The primary difficulty with using this distinction is that it is difficult to measure and compare benefits and burdens (as noted earlier). For instance, should financial cost to a family or society be part of the calculation? One danger with including the effect on others in the calculation, and not just the benefits and burdens to the patient herself, is that we might be inclined to say that some people should die because the burdens of caring for them are just too great.

If we could determine what are ordinary and extraordinary measures in a particular case, we would be on the way to deciding whether there is at least some good reason to provide the measures. If we judge them ordinary, then they probably ought to be provided. If we judge them extraordinary, then they probably need not be provided.

INFANT EUTHANASIA

Today, at least half of all live-born infants weighing less than 1,000 grams (2.2 pounds) survive, compared with less than 10 percent just twenty-five years ago. Survival rates for those who are born with congenital defects also have shown marked improvements.[48] However, some seriously ill newborns do not fare well. Some have low birth weight or severe defects and cannot survive for long, while others have serious impairments. Thus, improvements in medicine that have enabled us to save the lives of newborns also have given us new life-and-death decisions to make.

Every few years, a case of disputed life-and-death decisions regarding an infant seems to appear in the news. They are called Baby Doe cases to protect the families' privacy. Those that have drawn the most criticism are cases like the one in which an infant born with Down's syndrome was left untreated and died. Down's syndrome (also called trisomy 21) is a genetic anomaly that causes mental retardation and sometimes physical problems as well. In this case, the child had a repairable but life-threatening blockage between the stomach and the small intestines. The parents refused permission for surgery to repair the problem, and the doctors followed their wishes and let the infant die. Critics of this case protested that this surgery was simple and effective, and the infant, although retarded, could lead a generally happy life.

Not to treat in such cases has been interpreted as not using what would be considered ordinary means of life support—*ordinary* because the benefits to the patient would outweigh any burdens. Such cases have been criticized for their "buck-passing"—that is, shifting responsibility for the death to nature, as though in this situation but not elsewhere in medicine we should "let nature take its course."[49] Because the infant is not able to express his wishes, these will always be cases of nonvoluntary euthanasia. Although strong arguments can be made for treatment in such cases, in other cases knowing what is best is not so simple. Recently, a hospital in The Netherlands has proposed guidelines that allow for active euthanasia of some ill newborns. So far, the practice has officially been limited to those parents who themselves knowingly and freely requested it. The proposal, known as the Gronigen Protocol, allows doctors to "actively end the life of newborns deemed to be in similar pain (as adults) from incurable disease or extreme deformities."[50] The type of cases under consideration are of infants with a hopeless prognosis, as well as those with extremely poor quality of life. This latter designation specifically includes "severe cases of spina bifida," a birth defect in which the spinal column does not fully close in development; the most serious cases result in death or, if treated, may leave the person with "muscle weakness or paralysis below the area of the spine where the incomplete closure (or cleft) occurs, loss of sensation below the cleft, and loss of bowel and bladder control."[51] In some cases, spinal fluid builds up and can cause learning problems. In cases such as this, it is not clear whether medical assistance is in the infant's best interest. However, people have survived spina bifida and been able to enjoy life and contribute to their communities.[52] Moreover, some cases raise again the issue of determining when an individual is dead. In cases in Florida and California, for example, parents of a newborn with anencephaly, or no upper brain, wanted their child declared brain dead so that its organs could be used for transplant. However, such infants are not brain dead according to statutes in these states.

Two different types of moral questions can be raised about such cases. One is the question, *who* would be the best to decide whether to provide or deny certain treatments? The other is, what are the *reasons* to provide or deny care? Some people insist that the primary decision makers should be the parents because they not only are most likely to have the infant's best interests at heart, but also will be the ones to provide care for the child. Needless to say, we can imagine situations in which the parents would not be the most objective judges. They might be fearful, disappointed at the child's birth, or simply disagree about what is best to do. A presidential commission that was established to review medical ethical problems concluded that parents ought to make decisions for their seriously ill newborns, except in cases of decision-making incapacity, an unresolvable difference between them, or a choice that is clearly not in the infant's best interests. According to this commission, if a treatment is futile it is not advised. However, in other cases, the infant's best interests are said to be primary.

Permanent handicaps justify a decision not to provide life-sustaining treatment only when they are so severe that continued existence would not be a net benefit to the infant. Though inevitably somewhat subjective and imprecise in actual application, the concept of "benefit" excludes honoring idiosyncratic views that might be allowed if a person were deciding about his or her own treatment. Rather, net benefit is absent only if the burdens imposed on the patient by the disability or its treatment would lead a competent decision maker to choose to forgo the treatment. As in all surrogate decision making, the surrogate is obligated to try to evaluate benefits and burdens from the infant's own perspective.[53]

A society has an interest in protecting and providing for its children and thus is obligated to intervene in cases of parental neglect or abuse. However, just what constitutes neglect or abuse and what is reasonable parental decision making is far from clear. In addition, there are practical legal difficulties involved in treatment decisions for children. What would be the best policy regarding ill newborns? Should the federal government require state child-abuse agencies to monitor treatment of newborns and withhold funds if states do not comply? Critics of such a policy believe that this would be an unwarranted state interference in legitimate medical decision making. Obviously, more than medical decisions about diagnosis and prognosis are involved in such cases. These are judgments about what is best to do—these are value or moral judgments. Finding the best balance between the need to protect children and support parents in difficult and painful decision making remains a continuing problem.

In the readings in this chapter, J. Gay-Williams and James Rachels address the moral principles of euthanasia, and Carl Becker relates these to Buddhist views on the morality of suicide.

NOTES

1. *The New York Times*, March 5, 2010, p. A12
2. Ibid.
3. *The New York Times*, Oct. 31, 2008, p. A14
4. *The New York Times*, Dec. 5, 1976.
5. The case occurred in Oakland, California. The jury in the case found the defendant guilty even though California did not then have a "brain death" statute. See the *San Francisco Examiner* for May 1972.
6. Ad Hoc Committee of the Harvard Medical School to Examine the Definition of Brain Death, "A Definition of Irreversible Coma," *Journal of the American Medical Association, 205* (1968): 377.
7. Two types of cases are to be distinguished from both persistent vegetative state and coma. One is called *locked-in syndrome*, in which a person may be conscious but unable to respond. The other is *dementia*, or senility, in which the content of consciousness is impaired, as in Alzheimer's disease. Neither the person in a persistent vegetative state or coma nor the person with locked-in syndrome or dementia is considered dead by whole brain death criteria. We may say the person's life has a diminished value, but he or she

is not legally dead. However, some people argue that because the ability to think is what makes us persons, when someone loses this ability, as in the case of PVS, we ought to consider the person dead. Newborns with little or no upper brain or brain function also then and for the same reason could be considered dead. However, these are living, breathing beings, and it would be difficult to think of them as dead in the sense that we would bury them as they are. Rather than declare them dead, as some people have argued, others believe that it would be more practical and reasonable to judge these cases in terms of the kind of life they are living and to ask whether it would be morally permissible to bring about their deaths or allow them to die.

8. *San Francisco Chronicle*, Feb. 2, 1995, p. A4.
9. See *In re Quinlan*, 70 N.J. 10, 335 A. 2d 647 (1976); and *Cruzan* v. *Director, Missouri Department of Health*, United States Supreme Court, 110 S. Ct. 2841 (1990).
10. Raphael Cohen-Almagor, "Why The Netherlands?" *Journal of Law, Medicine & Ethics*, *30*, no.1 (Spring 2002): 95–116.
11. Yahoo News, Nov. 30, 2004.
12. Herbert Hendin, "The Dutch Experience," *Issues in Law & Medicine*, *17*, no. 3 (Spring 2002): 223–247.
13. *The New York Times*, Nov. 29, 2000, p. A3.
14. Ibid.
15. http://law.jrank.org/pages/1100/Euthanasia-Assisted-Suicide-Euthanasia-in-Netherlands.html; http://news.yahoo.com/s/hsn/20070510.
16. http://news.yahoo.com/s/hsn/20070510.
17. Ibid.; www.internationaltaskforce.org/fctholl.htm.
18. Richard H. Nicholson, "Death Is the Remedy?" *Hastings Center Report*, *32*, no. 1 (Jan–Feb. 2002): 9.
19. *The New York Times*, April 12, 2001, p. A6.
20. Ronald W. Maris, "Suicide," *The Lancet*, *360*, no. 9329 (July 27, 2002): 319.
21. Ibid.
22. *The Christian Century*, *119*, no. 6 (March 13, 2002): 5.
23. *The New York Times*, Dec. 4, 1990, describes the first publicized case in which Dr. Kevorkian's "suicide machine" was used, and the other two cases can be found, for example, in the *San Francisco Chronicle*, Oct. 29, 1991.
24. http://www.nytimes.com/2007/06/02/us/02 kevorkian.html?ref=jack_kevorkian
25. Stephanie Gutmann, "Death and the Maiden," *The New Republic* (June 24, 1996): 20–28.
26. Ibid.
27. Ibid.
28. *The New York Times*, July 15, 1996, p. A11. For a good analysis of these two court opinions, see "What Right to Die?" by Jeffrey Rosen in *The New Republic* (July 24, 1996): 28–31.
29. Ibid.
30. http://euthanasia.procon.org/view.resource .php?resourceID=000132; www.washingtonpost .com/wp-srv/national/ longterm/supcourt/1996-97/ assist96.htm.
31. Steve Perlstein, "Ruling Upholding Oregon Assisted Suicide Law Gets Mixed Reviews," *Family Practice News*, *32*, no. 10 (May 15, 2002): 31.
32. This principle was developed by the theologians of Salmance, in particular by John of St. Thomas in *De Bonitate et Malitia Actuum Humanorum*. See Antony Kenny, "The History of Intention in Ethics" in *Anatomy of the Soul* (London: Basil Blackwell, 1973), 140ff.
33. See, for example, Warren S. Quinn, "Actions, Intentions, and Consequences: The Doctrine of Double Effect," *Philosophy and Public Affairs*, *18*, no. 4 (Fall 1989): 334–351.
34. *San Francisco Chronicle*, Oct. 15, 2000, p. D3.
35. Ibid.
36. Directives 56 and 57 of the *Ethical and Religious Directives for Catholic Health Care Services*, approved by the U.S. bishops in 1995 and approved by the Vatican. See James Keenan, S. J., "A 400-year-old Logic," in *Boston College Magazine* Spring 2005: 41–42.
37. Ibid.
38. Some writers on this topic also list *involuntary* as a third type of euthanasia. Because it is a conceptual distinction rather than a moral one that is at issue here, I believe that the two-type classification system is preferable.
39. *The New York Times*, Oct. 10, 2006, pp. D1, D6.
40. However, what is requested in these documents may or may not be followed, depending on the circumstances and on what is requested. Medical staff may decide not to stop lifesaving treatments for a person who is not otherwise dying, even if she has stated this in writing. Staff members also may decide not to do certain things that they consider not medically appropriate or not legally permissible, even though these things have been requested in writing.
41. Reported in *Medical Ethics Advisor*, *7*, no. 4 (April 1991): 50–54.
42. *San Francisco Chronicle*, July 1, 1998, p. A5.
43. Ibid.
44. Debra Saunders, "Better Choice: Death with Longevity," *San Francisco Chronicle*, March 16, 1999, p. A19.

45. In an interesting version of this consequentialist argument, Susan Wolff writes that we ought to maintain a sharp dividing line between active and passive euthanasia, which allows a wide range of permissible cases of passive euthanasia but prohibits active euthanasia. The reason she gives is that if we do not have such a line and attempt to allow active euthanasia even in only a limited number of cases, then this will cause concern about the whole area of euthanasia and in the end work to limit acceptance of passive euthanasia as well. To retain freedom for passive euthanasia, she argues, we need to maintain the prohibition against active euthanasia. Again, this is an argument that relies on predictions of what would be likely to occur, and we would need some reason to believe that this would be so. From a presentation at a conference on "The Ethics and Economics of Death," the University of California at San Francisco Medical Center, November 1989.

46. Immanuel Kant, *Foundations of the Metaphysics of Morals*, second section, number 422.

47. Comments about the history of the distinction and the debate over its usefulness can be found in

48. Ibid.

49. From a comment made by a reviewer of this text, Robert P. Tucker of Florida Southern College, who has had hospital experience in this regard.

50. Toby Sterling, "Netherlands Hospital Euthanizes Babies," Yahoo News, Nov. 30, 2004.

51. Spina bifida fact sheet: www.nichcy.org/ubs/factshe/fs12txt.htm.

52. John Schwartz, "When Torment Is Baby's Destiny, Euthanasia Is Defended," *The New York Times*, March 10, 2005, p. A3.

53. *The President's Commission Report*, op. cit. For a perspective from a handicapped person, see "Unspeakable Conversations" by Harriet McBryde Johnson, *The New York Times Magazine*, Feb. 16, 2003. I thank Jennifer MacKinnon for this reference.

U.S. President's Commission for the Study of Ethical Problems in Medicine and Biomedical and Behavioral Research. Deciding to Forgo Life-Sustaining Treatment (Washington, DC: Government Printing Office, 1983).

R E A D I N G
The Wrongfulness of Euthanasia

J. GAY-WILLIAMS

Study Questions

1. What is Gay-Williams's definition of euthanasia? Why does he believe that it is misleading to speak of "passive euthanasia"?
2. How does he believe that euthanasia acts against our nature?
3. In what ways does he believe that euthanasia is not in our best interest?
4. How could euthanasia have a corrupting influence and lead to a "slippery slope"?

MY IMPRESSION is that euthanasia—the idea, if not the practice—is slowly gaining acceptance within our society. Cynics might attribute this to an increasing tendency to devalue human life, but I do not believe this is the major factor. The acceptance is much more likely to be the result of unthinking sympathy and benevolence. Well-publicized, tragic stories like that of Karen Quinlan elicit from us deep feelings of compassion. We think to ourselves, "She and her family would be better off if she were dead." It is an easy step from this very human response to the view that if someone (and others) would be better off dead, then it must be all right to kill that person.[1] Although I respect the compassion that leads to this conclusion, I believe the conclusion is wrong. I want to show that euthanasia is wrong. It is inherently wrong, but it is also wrong judged from the standpoints of self-interest and of practical effects.

Before presenting my arguments to support this claim, it would be well to define "euthanasia." An essential aspect of euthanasia is that it involves taking a human life, either one's own or that of another. Also, the person whose life is taken must be someone who is believed to be suffering from some disease or injury from which recovery cannot reasonably be expected. Finally, the action must be deliberate and intentional. Thus, euthanasia is intentionally taking the life of a presumably hopeless person. Whether the life is one's own or that of another, the taking of it is still euthanasia.

It is important to be clear about the deliberate and intentional aspect of the killing. If a hopeless person is given an injection of the wrong drug by mistake and this causes his death, this is wrongful killing but not euthanasia. The killing cannot be the result of accident. Furthermore, if the person is given an injection of a drug that is believed to be necessary to treat his disease or better his condition and the person dies as a result, then this is neither wrongful killing nor euthanasia. The intention was to make the patient well, not kill him. Similarly, when a patient's condition is such that it is not reasonable to hope that any medical procedures or treatments will save his life, a failure to implement the procedures or treatments is not euthanasia. If the person dies, this will be as a result of his injuries or disease and not because of his failure to receive treatment.

The failure to continue treatment after it has been realized that the patient has little chance of benefitting from it has been characterized by some as "passive euthanasia." This phrase is misleading and mistaken.[2] In such cases, the person involved is not killed (the first essential aspect of euthanasia), nor is the death of the person intended by the withholding of additional treatment (the third essential aspect of euthanasia). The aim may be to spare the person additional and unjustifiable pain, to save him from the indignities of hopeless manipulations, and to avoid increasing the financial and emotional burden on his family. When I buy a pencil it is so that I can use it to write, not to contribute to an increase in the gross national product. This may be the unintended consequence of my action, but it is not the aim of my action. So it is with failing to continue the treatment of a dying person. I intend his death no more than I intend to reduce the GNP by not using medical supplies. His is an unintended dying, and so-called "passive euthanasia" is not euthanasia at all.

1. THE ARGUMENT FROM NATURE

Every human being has a natural inclination to continue living. Our reflexes and responses fit us to fight attackers, flee wild animals, and dodge out of the way of trucks. In our daily lives we exercise the caution and care necessary to protect ourselves. Our bodies are similarly structured for survival right down to the molecular level. When we are cut, our capillaries seal shut, our blood clots, and fibrogen is produced to start the process of healing the wound. When we are invaded by bacteria, antibodies are produced to fight against the alien organisms, and their remains are swept out of the body by special cells designed for clean-up work.

Euthanasia does violence to this natural goal of survival. It is literally acting against nature because all the processes of nature are bent towards the end of bodily survival. Euthanasia defeats these subtle mechanisms in a way that, in a particular case, disease and injury might not.

It is possible, but not necessary, to make an appeal to revealed religion in this connection.[3] Man as trustee of his body acts against God, its rightful possessor, when he takes his own life. He also violates the commandment to hold life sacred and never to take it without just and compelling cause. But since this appeal will persuade only those who are prepared to accept that religion has access to revealed truths, I shall not employ this line of argument.

It is enough, I believe, to recognize that the organization of the human body and our patterns of behavioral responses make the continuation of life a natural goal. By reason alone, then, we can recognize that euthanasia sets us against our own nature.[4] Furthermore, in doing so, euthanasia does violence to our dignity. Our dignity comes from seeking our ends. When one of our goals is survival, and actions are taken that eliminate that goal, then our natural dignity suffers. Unlike animals, we are conscious through reason of our nature and our ends. Euthanasia involves acting as if this dual nature—inclination towards survival and awareness of this as an end—did not exist. Thus, euthanasia denies our basic human character and requires that we regard ourselves or others as something less than fully human.

2. THE ARGUMENT FROM SELF-INTEREST

The above arguments are, I believe, sufficient to show that euthanasia is inherently wrong. But there are reasons for considering it wrong when judged by standards other than reason. Because death is final and irreversible, euthanasia contains within it the possibility that we will work against our own interest if we practice it or allow it to be practiced on us.

Contemporary medicine has high standards of excellence and a proven record of accomplishment, but it does not possess perfect and complete knowledge. A mistaken diagnosis is possible, and so is a mistaken prognosis. Consequently, we may believe that we are dying of a disease when, as a matter of fact, we may not be. We may think that we have no hope of recovery when, as a matter of fact, our chances are quite good. In such circumstances, if euthanasia were permitted, we would die needlessly. Death is final and the chance of error too great to approve the practice of euthanasia.

Also, there is always the possibility that an experimental procedure or a hitherto untried technique will pull us through. We should at least keep this option open, but euthanasia closes it off. Furthermore, spontaneous remission does occur in many cases. For no apparent reason, a patient simply recovers when those all around him, including his physicians, expected him to die. Euthanasia would just guarantee their expectations and leave no room for the "miraculous" recoveries that frequently occur.

Finally, knowing that we can take our life at any time (or ask another to take it) might well incline us to give up too easily. The will to live is strong in all of us, but it can be weakened by pain and suffering and feelings of hopelessness. If during a bad time we allow ourselves to be killed, we never have a chance to reconsider. Recovery from a serious illness requires that we fight for it, and anything that weakens our determination by suggesting that there is an easy way out is ultimately against our own interest. Also, we may be inclined towards euthanasia because of our concern for others. If we see our sickness and suffering as an emotional and financial burden on our family, we may feel that to leave our life is to make their lives easier.[5] The very presence of the possibility of euthanasia may keep us from surviving when we might.

3. THE ARGUMENT FROM PRACTICAL EFFECTS

Doctors and nurses are, for the most part, totally committed to saving lives. A life lost is, for them, almost a personal failure, an insult to their skills and knowledge.

Euthanasia as a practice might well alter this. It could have a corrupting influence so that in any case that is severe doctors and nurses might not try hard enough to save the patient. They might decide that the patient would simply be "better off dead" and take the steps necessary to make that come about. This attitude could then carry over to their dealings with patients less seriously ill. The result would be an overall decline in the quality of medical care.

Finally, euthanasia as a policy is a slippery slope. A person apparently hopelessly ill may be allowed to take his own life. Then he may be permitted to deputize others to do it for him should he no longer be able to act. The judgment of others then becomes the ruling factor. Already at this point euthanasia is not personal and voluntary, for others are acting "on behalf of" the patient as they see fit. This may well incline them to act on behalf of other patients who have not authorized them to exercise their judgment. It is only a short step, then, from voluntary euthanasia (self-inflicted or authorized), to directed euthanasia administered to a patient who has given no authorization, to involuntary euthanasia conducted as part of a social policy.[6] Recently many psychiatrists and sociologists have argued that we define as "mental illness" those forms of behavior that we disapprove of.[7] This gives us license then to lock up those who display the behavior. The category of the "hopelessly ill" provides the possibility of even worse abuse.

Embedded in a social policy, it would give society or its representatives the authority to eliminate all those who might be considered too "ill" to function normally any longer. The dangers of euthanasia are too great to all to run the risk of approving it in any form. The first slippery step may well lead to a serious and harmful fall.

I hope that I have succeeded in showing why the benevolence that inclines us to give approval of euthanasia is misplaced. Euthanasia is inherently wrong because it violates the nature and dignity of human beings. But even those who are not convinced by this must be persuaded that the potential personal and social dangers inherent in euthanasia are sufficient to forbid our approving it either as a personal practice or as a public policy.

Suffering is surely a terrible thing, and we have a clear duty to comfort those in need and to ease their suffering when we can. But suffering is also a natural part of life with values for the individual and for others that we should not overlook. We may legitimately seek for others and for ourselves an easeful death, as Arthur Dyck has pointed out.[8] Euthanasia, however, is not just an easeful death. It is a wrongful death. Euthanasia is not just dying. It is killing.

NOTES

1. For a sophisticated defense of this position see Philippa Foot, "Euthanasia," *Philosophy and Public Affairs*, vol. 6 (1977), pp. 85–112. Foot does not endorse the radical conclusion that euthanasia, voluntary and involuntary, is always right.
2. James Rachels rejects the distinction between active and passive euthanasia as morally irrelevant in his "Active and Passive Euthanasia," *New England Journal of Medicine*, vol. 292, pp. 78–80. But see the criticism by Foot, pp. 100–103.
3. For a defense of this view see J. V. Sullivan, "The Immorality of Euthanasia," in *Beneficent Euthanasia*, ed. Marvin Kohl (Buffalo, NY: Prometheus Books, 1975), pp. 34–44.
4. This point is made by Ray V. McIntyre in "Voluntary Euthanasia: The Ultimate Perversion," *Medical Counterpoint*, vol. 2, 26–29.
5. See McIntyre, p. 28.
6. See Sullivan, "Immorality of Euthanasia," pp. 34–44, for a fuller argument in support of this view.
7. See, for example, Thomas S. Szasz, *The Myth of Mental Illness*, rev. ed. (New York: Harper & Row, 1974).
8. Arthur Dyck, "Beneficent Euthanasia and Benemortasia," in Kohl, op. cit., pp. 117–129.

READING
Active and Passive Euthanasia

JAMES RACHELS

Study Questions

1. What is the position of the American Medical Association on euthanasia as stated in its 1973 set of principles?
2. Why does Rachels believe that sometimes letting a person die is worse than bringing about their death, such as through a lethal injection?
3. Why does be believe that maintaining a moral distinction between active and passive euthanasia allows us to make life-and-death decisions on irrelevant grounds?
4. What is the example of Smith and Jones and their cousin supposed to show?
5. Does Rachels believe that an intentional cessation of treatment in which a patient dies can be equivalent to killing the patient?
6. Why does he believe that we usually think that killing is worse than letting die?
7. Does the doctor who lets a patient die do nothing?
8. What is Rachels's final conclusion?

THE DISTINCTION between active and passive euthanasia is thought to be crucial for medical ethics. The idea is that it is permissible, at least in some cases, to withhold treatment and allow a patient to die, but it is never permissible to take any direct action designed to kill the patient. This doctrine seems to be accepted by most doctors, and it is endorsed in a statement adopted by the House of Delegates of the American Medical Association on December 4, 1973:

> The intentional termination of the life of one human being by another—mercy killing—is contrary to that for which the medical profession stands and is contrary to the policy of the American Medical Association.
>
> The cessation of the employment of extraordinary means to prolong the life of the body when there is irrefutable evidence that biological death is imminent is the decision of the patient and/or his immediate family. The advice and judgment of the physician should be freely available to the patient and/or his immediate family.

From *The New England Journal of Medicine*, vol. 292, no. 2 (January 9, 1975): 78–80.

However, a strong case can be made against this doctrine. In what follows I will set out some of the relevant arguments, and urge doctors to reconsider their views on this matter.

To begin with a familiar type of situation, a patient who is dying of incurable cancer of the throat is in terrible pain, which can no longer be satisfactorily alleviated. He is certain to die within a few days, even if present treatment is continued, but he does not want to go on living for those days since the pain is unbearable. So he asks the doctor for an end to it, and his family joins in the request.

Suppose, the doctor agrees to withhold treatment, as the conventional doctrine says he may. The justification for his doing so is that the patient is in terrible agony, and since he is going to die anyway, it would be wrong to prolong his suffering needlessly. But now notice this. If one simply withholds treatment, it may take the patient longer to die, and so he may suffer more than he would if more direct action were taken and a lethal injection given. This fact provides strong reason for thinking that, once the initial decision not to prolong his agony has been made, active euthanasia is actually preferable to passive euthanasia, rather than the reverse. To say otherwise is to endorse the option that leads to more suffering rather than less, and is contrary to the humanitarian impulse that prompts the decision not to prolong his life in the first place.

Part of my point is that the process of being "allowed to die" can be relatively slow and painful, whereas being given a lethal injection is relatively quick and painless. Let me give a different sort of example. In the United States about one in 600 babies is born with Down's syndrome. Most of these babies are otherwise healthy—that is, with only the usual pediatric care, they will proceed to an otherwise normal infancy. Some, however, are born with congenital defects such as intestinal obstructions that require operations if they are to live. Sometimes, the parents and the doctor will decide not to operate, and let the infant die. Anthony Shaw describes what happens then:

> ...When surgery is denied [the doctor] must try to keep the infant from suffering while natural forces sap the baby's life away. As a surgeon whose natural inclination is to use the scalpel to fight off death, standing by and watching a salvageable baby die is the most emotionally exhausting experience I know. It is easy at a conference, in a theoretical discussion, to decide that such infants should be allowed to die. It is altogether different to stand in the nursery and watch as dehydration and infection wither a tiny being over hours and days. This is a terrible ordeal for me and the hospital staff—much more so than for the parents who never set foot in the nursery.[1]

I can understand why some people are opposed to all euthanasia, and insist that such infants must be allowed to live. I think I can also understand why other people favor destroying these babies quickly and painlessly. But why should anyone favor letting "dehydration and infection wither a tiny being over hours and days"? The doctrine that says that a baby may be allowed to dehydrate and wither, but may not be given an injection that would end its life without suffering, seems so patently cruel as to require no further refutation. The strong language is not intended to offend, but only to put the point in the clearest possible way.

My second argument is that the conventional doctrine leads to decisions concerning life and death made on irrelevant grounds.

Consider again the case of the infants with Down's syndrome who need operations for congenital defects unrelated to the syndrome to live. Sometimes, there is no operation, and the baby dies, but when there is no such defect, the baby lives on. Now, an operation such as that to remove an intestinal obstruction is not prohibitively difficult. The reason why such operations are not performed in these cases is, clearly, that the child has Down's syndrome and the parents and doctor judge that because of that fact it is better for the child to die.

But notice that this situation is absurd, no matter what view one takes of the lives and potentials of such babies. If the life of such an infant is worth preserving, what does it matter if it needs a simple operation? Or, if one thinks it better that such a baby should not live on, what difference does it make that it happens to have an unobstructed intestinal tract? In either case, the matter of life and death is being decided on irrelevant grounds. It is the Down's syndrome, and not the intestines, that is the issue. The matter should be decided, if at all, on that basis, and not be allowed to depend on the essentially irrelevant question of whether the intestinal tract is blocked.

What makes this situation possible, of course, is the idea that when there is an intestinal blockage, one can "let the baby die," but when there is no such defect there is nothing that can be done, for one must not "kill" it. The fact that this idea leads to such results as deciding life or death on irrelevant grounds is another good reason why the doctrine should be rejected.

One reason why so many people think that there is an important moral difference between active and passive euthanasia is that they think killing someone is morally worse than letting someone die. But is it? Is killing, in itself, worse than letting die? To investigate this issue, two cases may be considered that are exactly alike except that one involves killing whereas the other involves letting someone die. Then, it can be asked whether this difference makes any difference to the moral assessments. It is important that the cases be exactly alike, except for this one difference, since otherwise one cannot be confident that it is this difference and not some other that accounts for any variation in the assessments of the two cases. So, let us consider this pair of cases:

In the first, Smith stands to gain a large inheritance if anything should happen to his six-year-old cousin. One evening while the child is taking his bath, Smith sneaks into the bathroom and drowns the child, and then arranges things so that it will look like an accident.

In the second, Jones also stands to gain if anything should happen to his six-year-old cousin. Like Smith, Jones sneaks in planning to drown the child in his bath. However, just as he enters the bathroom Jones sees the child slip and hit his head, and fall face down in the water. Jones is delighted; he stands by, ready to push the child's head back under if it is necessary, but it is not necessary. With only a little thrashing about, the child drowns all by himself, "accidentally," as Jones watches and does nothing.

Now Smith killed the child, whereas Jones "merely" let the child die. That is the only difference between them. Did either man behave better, from a moral point of view? If the difference between killing and letting die were in itself a morally important matter, one should say that Jones's behavior was less reprehensible than Smith's. But does one really want to say that? I think not. In the first place, both men acted from the same motive, personal gain, and both had exactly the same end in view when they acted. It may be inferred from Smith's conduct that he is a bad man, although that judgment may be withdrawn or modified if certain further facts are learned about him—for example, that he is mentally deranged. But would not the very same thing be inferred about Jones from his conduct? And would not the same further considerations also be relevant to any modification of this judgment? Moreover, suppose Jones pleaded, in his own defense, "After all, I didn't do anything except stand there and watch the child drown. I didn't kill him; I only let him die." Again, if letting die were in itself less bad than killing, this defense should have at least some weight. But it does not. Such a "defense" can only be regarded as a grotesque perversion of moral reasoning. Morally speaking, it is no defense at all.

Now, it may be pointed out, quite properly, that the cases of euthanasia with which doctors are concerned are not like this at all. They do not involve personal gain or the destruction of normal healthy children. Doctors are concerned only with cases in which the patient's life is of no further use to him, or in which the patient's life has become or will soon become a terrible burden. However, the point is the same in these cases: the bare difference between killing and letting die does not, in itself, make a moral difference. If a doctor lets a patient die, for humane reasons, he is in the same moral position as if he had given the patient a lethal injection for humane reasons. If his decision was wrong—if, for example, the patient's illness was in fact curable—the decision would be equally regrettable no matter which method was used to carry it out. And if the doctor's decision was the right one, the method used is not in itself important.

The AMA policy statement isolates the crucial issue very well; the crucial issue is "the intentional termination of the life of one human being by another." But after identifying this issue, and forbidding "mercy killing," the statement goes on to deny that the cessation of treatment is the intentional termination of a life. This is where the mistake comes in, for what is the cessation of treatment, in these circumstances, if it is not "the intentional termination of the life of one human being by another"? Of course it is exactly that, and if it were not, there would be no point to it.

Many people will find this judgment hard to accept. One reason, I think, is that it is very easy to conflate the question of whether killing is, in itself, worse than letting die, with the very different question of whether most actual cases of killing are more reprehensible than most actual cases of letting die. Most actual cases of killing are clearly terrible (think, for example, of all the murders reported in the newspapers), and one hears of such cases every day. On the other hand, one hardly ever hears of a case of letting die, except for the actions of doctors who are motivated by humanitarian reasons. So one learns to think of killing in a much worse light than of letting die. But this does not mean that there is something about killing that makes it in itself worse than letting die, for it is not the bare difference between killing and letting die that makes the difference in these cases. Rather, the other factors—the murderer's motive of personal gain, for example, contrasted with the doctor's humanitarian motivation—account for different reactions to the different cases.

I have argued that killing is not in itself any worse than letting die; if my contention is right, it follows that active euthanasia is not any worse than passive euthanasia. What arguments can be given on the other side? The most common, I believe, is the following:

The important difference between active and passive euthanasia is that, in passive euthanasia, the doctor does not do anything to bring about the patient's death. The doctor does nothing, and the patient dies of whatever ills already afflict him. In active euthanasia, however, the doctor does something to bring about the patient's death: he kills him. The doctor who gives the patient with cancer a lethal injection has himself caused his patient's death; whereas if he merely ceases treatment, the cancer is the cause of the death.

A number of points need to be made here. The first is that it is not exactly correct to say that in passive euthanasia the doctor does nothing, for he does do one thing that is very important: he lets the patient die. "Letting someone die" is certainly different, in some respects, from other types of action—mainly in

that it is a kind of action that one may perform by way of not performing certain other actions. For example, one may let a patient die by way of not giving medication, just as one may insult someone by way of not shaking his hand. But for any purpose of moral assessment, it is a type of action nonetheless. The decision to let a patient die is subject to moral appraisal in the same way that a decision to kill him would be subject to moral appraisal: it may be assessed as wise or unwise, compassionate or sadistic, right or wrong. If a doctor deliberately let a patient die who was suffering from a routinely curable illness, the doctor would certainly be to blame for what he had done, just as he would be to blame if he had needlessly killed the patient. Charges against him would then be appropriate. If so, it would be no defense at all for him to insist that he didn't "do anything." He would have done something very serious indeed, for he let his patient die.

Fixing the cause of death may be very important from a legal point of view, for it may determine whether criminal charges are brought against the doctor. But I do not think that this notion can be used to show a moral difference between active and passive euthanasia. The reason why it is considered bad to be the cause of someone's death is that death is regarded as a great evil—and so it is. However, if it has been decided that euthanasia—even passive euthanasia—is desirable in a given case, it has also been decided that in this instance death is no greater an evil than the patient's continued existence. And if this is true, the usual reason for not wanting to be the cause of someone's death simply does not apply.

Finally, doctors may think that all of this is only of academic interest—the sort of thing that philosophers may worry about but that has no practical bearing on their own work. After all, doctors must be concerned about the legal consequences of what they do, and active euthanasia is clearly forbidden by the law. But even so, doctors should also be concerned with the fact that the law is forcing upon them a moral doctrine that may well be indefensible, and has a considerable effect on their practices. Of course, most doctors are not now in the position of being coerced in this matter, for they do not regard themselves as merely going along with what the law requires. Rather, in statements such as the AMA policy statement that I have quoted, they are endorsing this doctrine as a central point of medical ethics. In that statement, active euthanasia is condemned not merely as illegal but as "contrary to that for which the medical profession stands," whereas passive euthanasia is approved. However, the preceding considerations suggest that there is really no moral difference between the two, considered in themselves (there may be important moral differences in some cases in their consequences, but, as I pointed out, these differences may make

active euthanasia, and not passive euthanasia, the morally preferable option). So whereas doctors may have to discriminate between active and passive euthanasia to satisfy the law, they should not do any more than that. In particular, they should not give the distinction any added authority and weight by writing it into official statements of medical ethics.

NOTE

1. A. Shaw, "Doctor, Do We Have a Choice?" *The New York Times Magazine*, January 30, 1972, p. 54.

R E A D I N G
Buddhist Views of Suicide and Euthanasia

CARL B. BECKER

Study Questions

1. According to Becker, why do the Japanese oppose brain death criteria?
2. What problems does Becker describe for the view that a person is not an individual with rights but is instead one who is an object of attention by others?
3. Why was the moment of death important to Buddhists?
4. Did the Buddha approve of suicide?
5. What is required for suicide to result in rebirth in the Pure Land? How does the rope example dramatize this?
6. Would it be permissible for Buddhists to assist a suicide?
7. How does Becker use the example of the samurai to explain Buddhist views regarding euthanasia?

BIOETHICS AND BRAIN DEATH: THE RECENT DISCUSSION IN JAPAN

Japanese scholars of ethics and religions have been slow to come to grips with issues of bioethics, suicide, and death with dignity. Although the practical problems are frequently addressed in the popular press, and scattered citizen groups are beginning to

Carl B. Becker, "Buddhist Views of Suicide and Euthanasia," in *Philosophy East and West*, Vol. 40, No. 4 (October 1990): 543–556. Copyright © 1990 University of Hawaii Press. Reproduced by permission.

draw attention to the issues, few people outside of the medical community have seriously addressed these issues.[1] As one recent representative example of this situation, consider the 39th annual meeting of the Japan Ethics Association (the academic association of ethicists from the entire country) held at Waseda University in October of 1988. The title of the annual meeting, in deference to the late Emperor's ailing condition and growing urgency of bioethical issues, was "Life and Ethics." Ostensibly, this was a chance to further the discussion among medical, religious, and philosophical ethicists on topics such as euthanasia and death with dignity. In fact, more than half of the presentations discussed classical views of life, such as those of Hippocrates, Confucius, Vico, Kant, Nietzsche, and so forth. The periods planned for open discussion were entirely usurped by the panelists' overtime reading of such papers. To their credit, however, there were a few Japanese scholars who boldly attempted to establish some more-Japanese views on the topics in bioethics, particularly euthanasia and death with dignity. While not without their problems, these presentations displayed less a Buddhist than a popular Japanese approach to the issue. The majority agreed with Anzai Kazuhiro's early presentation that brain death should not be equated with human death.[2]

Anzai's reasoning runs as follows: If brain death implies human death, then, by contraposition, human life must imply conscious (brain) life. Now there are clearly segments of our lives in which we are alive but not always conscious. Therefore it is wrong to conclude that a human is dead because he or she lacks consciousness. Of course, this argument can be faulted for collapsing conscious life and brain life, and for failing to distinguish periods of unconsciousness with the expectation of future revival (like deep sleep) from periods of unconsciousness with no expectation of future revival (like irreversible coma). But it is representative of a widely seen Japanese rejection of brain death criteria.

This rejection comes partly from the Japanese association of brain-death criteria with organ transplantation. Many Japanese continue to manifest a distaste for organ transplantation, a distaste which dates back to Confucian teachings that the body, a gift from heaven and from one's parents, must be buried whole, and never cut. For this reason, dissections and autopsies were late in coming to Japan, not widely permitted until the nineteenth century. The modern Japanese practices of universal cremation, of surgical operations, and of flying to other countries to have organ transplants all have superseded the old Confucian prejudice against body-cutting. However, there remains a fear that if brain-death criteria were widely accepted, less conservative elements of society might abuse it for the sake of the "distasteful" practice of organ transplantation.

In his keynote address about Buddhist ethics, Tsukuba Professor Shinjo Kawasaki implied that this rejection of brain-death criteria may also be grounded in a Buddhist view of life and death.[3] He cited the *Visuddhimagga*, which indicates that life energy (*ayus*) is supported by body warmth and conscious faculties (broadly interpretable to include reflexes).[4] If either body heat or reflexes remain, then a person cannot be considered dead. Now Buddhism admits situations (such as meditative trances or hypothermia) in which neither body warmth nor reflexes are externally detectable, but the subject is not yet dead. So lack of warmth and reflexes is a necessary but not sufficient indicator of death; if either persists, it can be said that the body is not yet dead. In other words, Buddhism does not equate life with warmth and reflexes, but

holds that body heat and reflexes are the "supports" of life, and therefore life cannot be empirically measurable except through such variables. Kawasaki also reaffirms the widespread Japanese Buddhist view that death is not the end of life, but merely a brief transition to another state, commonly thought to last for forty-nine days, intermediate between life in this body and life in the next. The reluctance to dismiss a body as "dead" prior to its loss of warmth and reflexes is not based on a fear of personal extinction or annihilation, but rather on a Buddhist view of the basic components of the life system.[5]

Chiba's Iida Tsunesuke expands this view by arguing that "persons are not merely the meaningless 'subjects of rights,' but personalities, 'faces,' embodying the possibilities of fulfilling the dreams of their parents or loved ones. . .recipients of love, and therefore worthy of honoring."[6] This argument begs the question of "possibilities," since in the case of brain-dead victims, it is precisely such possibilities which are missing. Logically speaking, the "possibilities" argument has long ago been laid to rest by philosophers like Mary Anne Warren, who have demonstrated that we need not treat potential presidents as presidents, potential criminals as criminals, or potential humans as humans.[7] (Japanese society might differ in this respect; until recently, suspicion of crime or likelihood of committing crime were sufficient grounds for arrest, children of nobles [potential lords] were often honored or killed as real lords.)[8]

However, Iida's argument is important less for its logical persuasion than for its revelation of the Japanese attitude: that persons are not subjects with rights and individual free wills, but rather objects of the attention of others. (Japanese treatment of infants and children reinforces this view that Japanese children are not seen as persons but as possessions of their parents; this was the legal as well as philosophical status of women and servants as well as children prior to the twentieth century.)

This position is further developed by Ohara Nobuo, who argues that "although a body may be treated as a 'thing' or a corpse by physicians, it remains a body of value and meaning, and in that sense, a *person*, to members of its family. . . . In this sense, even vegetative humans and brain-dead corpses can give joy to other people."[9] Of course this point of view is pregnant with problems which Ohara himself seems loath to acknowledge. Only in the most metaphorical of senses can a corpse "give" anything to anyone; rather, it is the family who may *derive* some sense of joy by beholding the face of, one dear to them, even though that person is incapable of ever being conscious in that body again.

This attitude is akin to the Japanese reverence for pictures, sculptures, and myths; it provides no useful guidelines whatsoever to the medical faculty as to when to continue or desist from what kinds of treatment for the patient. To the question "When does a body stop being a person?" the Oharan answer, "It never stops being a person to those who love it," may be psychologically correct for some people, but is a dead end in medical ethics, for it fails to answer the question, "When should a body be treated not as a living person but as a dead body?"

Moreover, even if it were thought to have some utility in the case where relatives or "significant others" remain alive and concerned with the fate of the deceased, it values the person (or corpse) entirely in terms of his value *to others*. In cases where old people die alone and uncared for, the absence of concerned others leaves the medical practitioner utterly without guidelines. (This is consistent with the frequently noted proposition that Japanese without social contexts seem morally at a loss.)[10]

This position also presumes a wishful naïveté on the part of the parent of family, a failure to distinguish between a living human with a potential for interaction and a dead body with only the resemblance of a loved one. This may not bother many Japanese parents, for whom children are indeed "objects." In fact, there are "rehabilitation hospitals" in Japan in which anencephalic infants are cared for and raised for as many years as their parents' finances and interest dictate; they are propped up and made to "greet" their parents whenever their parents desire to visit.[11]

Such unwillingness to admit the finality of death or the fundamental suffering of the human condition runs counter to the basic tenets of Buddhism. We are reminded of the famous story of the woman who asked the Buddha to revive her baby. In response, the Buddha instructed her to ask for food from any house in which no one had died. In the process of asking around the entire village, the woman came to realize that all humans must die and deal with death. In this way she gained enlightenment, stopped grieving for her dead child, and became a follower of the Buddha. The relatives who refuse to pronounce dead a relative as long as he has a "face," or the parents who insist on artificially prolonging the appearance of life in an anencephalic infant, cannot claim to understand Buddhism.

A much larger misunderstanding lurks behind the whole discussion between "brain-death advocates" and "brain-dead opposers" in Japan. The real issue is not whether or not every body should immediately be scavenged for spare parts as soon as the brain is isoelectric, as some opponents would purport. Rather, the question is whether it is ever acceptable to desist from treatment after brain death (turning the hospital's valuable and limited resources to other waiting patients). In the absence of brain-death criteria, many otherwise hopeless bodies remain on artificial support systems almost indefinitely. Even if the brain-death criteria were accepted, nothing would prevent families from finding hospitals which would preserve the bodies of their beloved on artificial support systems indefinitely, nor would anything require organ donation if the patient and family did not desire it. Thus the issue, like that of suicide and euthanasia, is not, "Should everyone be forced to follow these criteria?" but rather, "May people who desire it be allowed to follow these criteria?" Groundless fears of widespread organ sales or piracy have made this issue into a much greater hobgoblin than it ever needed to become.

This is not merely to criticize the recently voiced opinions of Japanese ethicists. Rather, I introduce this body of evidence to demonstrate the slow growth of Japanese thought in bioethics, and particularly their concerns with *bodies of value to others* rather than with *subjects of value to themselves*. This concern finds no support either in Japanese Buddhism nor in samurai teaching, but in the level of popular belief, it may have serious ramifications for Japanese bioethics for many generations to come.

The World Federation of the Right to Die Society held an International Conference in Nice (France) in 1984. Although many Japanese attended this conference, apparently none of them contributed to the West's understanding of Buddhist views of euthanasia. When the President of the Society published a book on world attitudes on euthanasia the following year, only 2 percent (2.5 out of 150 pages) was about Buddhist attitudes, and those ideas were gained from California Buddhists, not from the Japanese Buddhists at Nice.[12]

Buddhists have a big contribution to make to the humanization and naturalization of medicine and bioethics. I may not speak for all of Japanese Buddhism, but I shall be happy if this article inspires further dialogue and contributions from the Japanese Buddhist side.

EARLY BUDDHIST VIEWS OF DEATH, SUICIDE, AND EUTHANASIA

Japan has long been more aware of and sensitive to the dying process than modern Western cultures. Moreover, Japan already has its own good philosophical and experiential background to deal effectively with "new" issues of bioethics, such as euthanasia. Japanese Buddhists have long recognized what Westerners are only recently rediscovering: that the manner of dying at the moment of death is very important. This fundamental premise probably predates Buddhism itself, but is made very explicit in the teachings of the Buddha.[13] In his meditations, the Buddha noticed that even people with good karma were sometimes born into bad situations, and even those with bad karma sometimes found inordinately pleasant rebirths. Buddha declared that the crucial variable governing rebirth was the nature of the consciousness at the moment of death. Thereafter, Buddhists placed high importance on holding the proper thoughts at the moment of death. Many examples of this idea can be found in two works of the Theravada canon, the *Petavatthu* and the *Vimanavatthu* ("Stories of the Departed"). Indeed, in many sutras, monks visit laymen on their deathbeds to ensure that their dying thoughts are wholesome,[14] and the Buddha recommends that lay followers similarly encourage each other on such occasions.[15]

Buddhism sees death as not the end of life, but simply a transition; suicide is therefore no escape from anything. Thus, in the early *sangha* (community of followers of the Buddha), suicide was in principle condemned as an inappropriate action.[16] But the early Buddhist texts include many cases of suicide which the Buddha himself accepted or condoned. For example, the suicides of Vakkali[17] and of Channa[18] were committed in the face of painful and irreversible sickness. It is significant, however, that the Buddha's praise of the suicides is *not* based on the fact that they were in terminal states, but rather that their minds were selfless, desireless, and enlightened at the moments of their passing.

This theme is more dramatically visible in the example of Godhika. This disciple repeatedly achieved an advanced level of *samadhi*, bordering on *parinirvana*, and then slipped out of the state of enlightenment into normal consciousness again. After this happened six times, Godhika at last vowed to pass on to the next realm while enlightened, and quietly committed suicide during his next period of enlightenment. While cautioning his other disciples against suicide, the Buddha nonetheless blessed and praised Godhika's steadiness of mind and purpose, and declared that he had passed on to *nirvana*. In short, the acceptability of suicide, even in the early Buddhist community, depended not on terminal illness alone, but upon the state of selfless equanimity with which one was able to pass away. It is interesting in passing that all these suicides were committed by the subject knifing himself, a technique which came to be standardized in later Japanese ritual suicide.

When asked about the morality of committing suicide to move on to the next world, the Buddha did not criticize it.[19] He emphasized that only the uncraving mind would be able to move on towards *nirvana*, and that, conversely, minds desiring to get free or flee something by their death might achieve nothing. Similarly, there are stories in the Jataka tales of the Buddha giving his own body (in former lives) to save other beings, both animals and humans. Thus death out of compassion for others is also lauded in the scriptures.[20] It is also well known that in the Jain tradition, saints were expected to fast until their deaths,[21] and thereafter there have been those both in China and Japan who have followed this tradition.[22]

In China, it is believed that a disciple of Zendo's jumped out of a tree in order to kill himself and reach the Pure Land. Zendo's response was not that the action of suicide was right or wrong in and of itself, but that the disciple who wanted so strongly to see the Pure Land was doubtless ready to reach it.[23] Other more recent examples may be found in the Buddhist suicides of the Vietnamese monks protesting against the Vietnam government.[24] Whether or not these stories are all historical fact is not at issue here. The point is that they demonstrate the consistent Buddhist position toward suicide: there is nothing intrinsically wrong with taking one's own life, if it is not done in hate, anger, or fear. Equanimity or preparedness of mind is the main issue.

In summary, Buddhism realizes that death is not the end of anything, but a transition. Buddhism has long recognized persons' rights to determine when they should move on from this existence to the next. The important consideration here is not whether the body lives or dies, but whether the mind can remain at peace and in harmony with itself. The Jodo (Pure Land) tradition tends to stress the continuity of life, while the Zen tradition tends to stress the importance of the time and manner of dying. Both of these ideas are deeply rooted in the Japanese consciousness.

RELIGIOUS SUICIDE AND DEATH WITH DIGNITY IN JAPAN

Japanese Buddhists demonstrated an unconcern with death even more than their neighbors. Japanese valued peace of mind and honor of life over length of life. While the samurai often committed suicide on the battlefield or in court to preserve their dignity in death, countless commoners chose to commit suicide in order to obtain a better future life in the Pure Land. On some occasions, whole masses of people committed suicide at the same time. In others, as in the situation depicted in Kurosawa's famous film "Red Beard," a poverty-stricken family would commit suicide in order to escape unbearable suffering in this life and find a better life in the world to come. Often parents would kill their children first, and then kill themselves; this kind of *shinju* can still be seen in Japan today. The issue for us today is:

how does Buddhism appraise such suicide in order to gain heavenly rebirth?

On a popular level, the desire to "leave this dirty world and approach the Pure Land" (*Enri edo, gongu jodo*) was fostered by wandering itinerant monks such as Kuya in the Heian period, and Ippen in the Kamakura period. The tradition of committing suicide by entering a river or west-facing seashore apparently began in the Kumano area, but rapidly spread throughout the nation along with the Pure Land faith upon which it was based. The common tradition was to enter the water with a rope tied around one's waist, held by one's retainers or horse.[25] If one's nerve and single-minded resolution failed, then one would not achieve rebirth in the Pure Land as desired. In such an instance, either the suicide himself, or his retainers (judging from his countenance), might pull him out of the water and save him from dying with inappropriate thoughts. However, if the suicide retained a peaceful and unperturbed mind and countenance throughout the drowning, the retainers were to let him die in peace, and simply retain the body for funeral purposes. Such situations clearly demonstrate that what is at stake here is not the individual's right to die, but rather his ability to die with peace of mind. If a death with a calm mind is possible, then it is not condemned.

A paradigmatic example of this situation can be found in the records of Saint Ippen.[26] Ajisaka Nyudo, a Pure Land aspirant possibly of noble descent, gave up his home and family to follow the teachings of Saint Ippen. For unclear reasons, Ippen refused admission to his band of itinerant mendicants, but advised him that the only way to enter the Pure Land was to die holding the Nembutsu (name and figure of Amida) in mind. Nyudo then committed suicide by drowning himself in the Fuji River.

The scene is vividly depicted in the scroll paintings.[27] Here, Ajisaka is seen with a rope around his waist. His attendants on the shore hold one end of the rope. As he bobs above the current, he is seen perfectly preserving the *gassho* position, at peace and in prayer. Music is heard from the purple clouds above him, a common sign of Ojo, or rebirth in the Pure Land.

When Ippen heard of this suicide, he praised Ajisaka's faith, interpreting the purple clouds and

Ajisaka's unruffled demeanor as proof of his attainment of rebirth in the Pure Land. At the same time, he warned his other disciples, repeating Ajisaka's last words (*nagori o oshimuna*), not to grieve over their master's passing.[28]

When Ippen himself died, six of his disciples also committed suicide in sympathy, hoping to accompany their master to the Pure Land. This occasioned some other debate about the propriety of "sympathy suicide." Shinkyo, Ippen's disciple and second patriarch of the Ji School, declared that the disciples had failed to obtain rebirth in the Pure Land, for their action was seen as "self-willed," and Pure Land faith relies entirely on the power and will of Amida Buddha. Assertion of self-will is seen as running counter to the reliance on other power demanded by the Amida faith.[29]

Several important points can be learned from these examples. First, suicide is never condemned per se. Rather it is the state of mind which determines the rightness or wrongness of the suicide situation. The dividing line between choosing one's own time and place of death with perfectly assured peace of mind, and self-willing one's own death at the time of one's master's death is perhaps a thin grey one, but this should not obscure the criteria involved: death with desire leads not to rebirth in the Pure Land, but death with calm assurance does. Even the method of water suicide, using a rope as a preventative backup, stresses the importance of the state of mind in this action.

Secondly, Ajisaka's famous phrase, "Nagori o oshimuna," means that Buddhists are not to kill themselves in "sympathy" when others die. A literal translation would be that we are not to cling to what remains of the name or person, but to let the deceased go freely on to the next world. In other words, when someone dies with an assured state of mind, it is not for those who remain either to criticize or to wish that he had not died in this situation. Those who are left behind are to respect and not resent, reject, or grieve for a death which might seem to them untimely.

It is not coincidental that the word for euthanasia in Japanese is *anrakushi*, a term with Buddhist meanings. In Buddhist terminology, *anrakukoku* is another name for the Pure Land, the next world of Amida Bodhisattva, to which each Japanese expects to go after death. German-educated doctor and historical novelist Mori Ogai's famous book *Takasebune* specifically deals with *anrakushi*; it is the story of Yoshisuke killing his sickly young brother who wants to die but lacks the strength to kill himself.[30] Many famous twentieth-century Japanese authors wrote of suicide, and some, such as Akutagawa, Dazai, Kawabata, and Mishima, actually committed suicide. Following the deaths of each emperor (Meiji, Taisho, and, last year, Showa), faithful retainers have also committed suicide in sympathy with their departed leaders. While some of these suicides are not Buddhistic (they show anger, pessimism, nihilism, and so forth), they are still reminders that the Japanese Buddhist world view does not condemn suicide.

Japanese law does not criminalize suicide, and European law is slowly beginning to follow the Japanese model in this regard. However, Japanese law does hold it to be a crime to assist or encourage a suicide. In normal situations, this is only wise and prudent, for healthy people should be encouraged to live and make the most of their lives. But in the situations where *songenshi* (death with dignity) is requested, it is precisely because the person is facing imminent death that it is morally acceptable to assist his suicide, particularly if the motive is mercy.

SAMURAI, *SEPPUKU*, AND EUTHANASIA

Among the warrior elite, who usually followed Zen Buddhism, suicide was considered an honorable alternative to being killed by others or continuing a life in shame or misery. Beginning with the famous *seppuku* of Minamoto no Tametomo and Minamoto no Yorimasi in 1170, *seppuku* became known as the way that a vanquished but proud Buddhist warrior would end his life.[31] Soon thereafter, headed by Taria Noritsune and tomomori, hundreds of Taira warriors and their families committed suicide in the battle of Dannoura of 1185. Famous suicides included that of Kusunoki Masahige in 1336, in the battle between Nitta and Hosokawa, and that of Hideyori Toyotomi, under siege by Tokugawa Ieyasu in 1615. In the Tokugawa period, love suicides were dramatized in a dozen plays by Chikamatsu Monzaemon including *Sonezaki shinju, Shinju ten no Amijima*, and *Shinju mannenso*.[32] The forty-seven Ako ronin, who committed suicide after avenging their master's death was another famous true story, dramatized in the *Chushingura* plays and films.[33] The samurai's creed, to be willing to die at any moment, was dramatically spelled out by the *Hagakure*.[34] According to the *Hagakure*, the important concern was not whether one lived or died, but (1) being pure, simple, single-minded, (2) taking full responsibility for doing one's duty, and (3) unconditionally serving one's master, without concern for oneself.

Although *seppuku* may seem like a violent death to the observer, it was designed to enable the samurai to die with the greatest dignity and peace.

It is particularly noteworthy that the samurai's code of suicide included a provision for euthanasia: the *kaishakunin* (attendant). Cutting of the hara alone was very painful, and would not lead to a swift death. After cutting their hara, few samurai had enough strength to cut their own necks or spines. Yet without cutting their necks, the pain of the opened hara would continue for minutes or even hours prior to death. Therefore, the samurai would make arrangements with one or more *kaishakunin* to assist his suicide. While the samurai steadied his mind and prepared to die in peace, the *kaishakunin* would wait by his side. If the samurai spoke to the *kaishakunin* before or during the *seppuku* ceremony, the standard response was "go anshin" (set your mind at peace). All of the interactions and conversations surrounding an officially ordered *seppuku* were also fixed by tradition, so that the suicide might die with the least tension and greatest peace of mind. After the samurai had finished cutting to the prearranged point, or gave some other signal, it was the duty of the *kaishakunin* to cut the neck of the samurai to terminate his pain by administering the coup de grace.[35]

Many samurai suicides were in fact the moral equivalent of euthanasia. The reasons for a samurai's suicide were either (1) to avoid an inevitable death at the hands of others, or (2) to escape a longer period of unbearable pain or psychological misery, without being an active, fruitful member of society. These are exactly the sorts of situations when euthanasia is desired today: (1) to avoid an inevitable death at the hands of others (including disease, cancer, or bacteria), (2) to escape a longer period of pain or misery without being a fruitful, active member of society.

In regard to (1), most Japanese are now cut down in their seventies by the enemies of cancer and other diseases, rather than in their youth on a battlefield. Regardless of whether the person is hopelessly surrounded by enemies on a battlefield, or hopelessly defeated by enemy organisms within his body, the morality of the situation is the same. In regard to (2), it might be argued that there is a difference between the pain or misery of the permanent incapacitation of a samurai, and the pain or misery of the permanent incapacitation of a hospital patient. But if anything, the hospital patient is in even less of a position to contribute to society or feel valued than is the samurai, so he has even more reason to be granted the option of leaving his arena (world) when he chooses. The samurai tradition shows that the important issue is not the level of physical pain, but the prospect for meaningful and productive interaction with other members of society. If there are no prospects for such interactions, the samurai society claimed no right to prevent the person from seeking more meaningful experiences in another world.

Now in both cases, there may be relatives or retainers in the area who do not wish to see their friend die. The issue in these cases is not whether or not the besieged person will die; it is only a question of how soon, and in what manner. From ancient times, Japanese have respected the right of the individual to choose the moment and manner of dying. The Buddhist principle ought to apply equally well to the modern medical battles against the enemies of the body. The argument that if a body still has a face, it is still a person to those around him, is a basically un-Buddhist failure to understand (a) the difference between body and life, (b) the importance of each person's determination of his own mental states, and (c) the importance of placing mercy over desire in Buddhism.

Of course there need to be safeguards in such situations, and those safeguards have already been spelled out by the decision of the Nagoya High Court. In case of euthanasia, the Nagoya High Court (22 December 1962) defined certain conditions under which euthanasia could be considered acceptable:

1. The disease is considered terminal and incurable by present medicine.
2. The pain is unbearable—both for the patient and those around him.
3. The death is for the purpose of his peaceful passing.
4. The person himself has requested the death, while conscious and sane.
5. The killing is done by a doctor.
6. The method of killing is humane.

If these safeguards are followed, it seems there is no moral reason that Buddhists should oppose euthanasia.

CONCLUSIONS

There are Japanese who hold that the Japanese lack the independent decision-making abilities of Western people, and that therefore doctors should make the decisions for their patients. This logic is backwards. The reason patients cannot make good independent judgments is because the doctors refuse them the information and freedom to do so, not because they lack the mental abilities or personal characteristics to make judgments.[36] Buddhism has always recognized the importance of individual choice, despite social pressures; examples range from the Buddha himself, through Kukai, Honen, Shinran, and Nagamatsu Nissen. The ability of Japanese to take personal responsibility for important decisions in times of stress, danger, or anguish has been repeatedly shown in the historical examples of these bold Buddhist reformers.

In order for the patient to make an intelligent decision about when and how he wants to die, he needs to know the facts about the nature of his disease, not only its real name, but the realistic prospects and alternative outcomes of all available forms of treatment. This means renouncing the paternalistic model held by present Japanese medicine, and granting substantial freedom to the patient in deciding his own case. Some Japanese doctors have argued that (1) patients do not really want to know the bad news about themselves, that (2) knowing the truth may harm their conditions, and that (3) the

physicians can judge more intelligently than the patient. However, studies in the West show that none of these claims is true. As Bok points out, "the attitude that what [the patient] doesn't know won't hurt him is proving unrealistic—it is rather what patients do not know but vaguely suspect that causes them corrosive (destructive) worry."[37] People recover faster from surgery and tolerate pain with less medication when they understand their own medical problems and what can and cannot be done about them.[38] In any case, doctors' withholding of information from patients is based not on statistical proof or ethical principles, but on the physician's desires to retain control over patients.[39] This is a situation that clear-thinking Buddhists naturally oppose. There is no reason to believe that these findings, long known and supported in Western medicine, should prove any different for the Japanese.

One important question for Buddhists today remains: what, if any, are the differences between suicide and euthanasia? Obviously one important difference is in the case where the person receiving euthanasia is unconscious. In this case, we have no way of knowing whether the patient genuinely desires euthanasia, unless he or she has previously made a declaration of wishes in a living will. On the other hand, once the consciousness has permanently disassociated itself from the body, there is no reason in Buddhism to continue to nourish or stimulate the body, for the body deprived of its *skandhas* is not a person. The Japan Songenshi Kyokai (Association for Death with Dignity) has done much to improve the ability of the individual Japanese to choose his time and manner of death.

Another issue is the relation of pain-killing to prolonging life and hastening death itself. The Japan Songenshi Kyokai proposes the administering of pain-killing drugs even if they hasten the death of the patient. Buddhists would agree that relief of pain is desirable, and whether the death is hastened or not is not the primary issue. However, consider a case where the pain is extreme and only very strong drugs will stop the pain. Here there may be a choice between: (a) no treatment at all, (b) pain-killing which only blurs or confuses the mind of the patient, and (c) treatment which hastens the end while keeping the mind clear. In such a situation, the Buddhist would first prefer the most natural way of (a) no treatment at all. But if his mind were unable to focus or be at peace because of the great pain, the Buddhist would choose (c) over (b), because clarity of consciousness at the moment of death is so important in Buddhism.

Doctors who do not like the idea of shortening a person's life would prefer to prolong the material life-processes, regardless of the mental quality of that life. This is where Buddhists disagree with materialistic Western medicine. But there need be no conflict between Buddhism and medicine. There is no reason to assign the doctor the "responsibility" for the death of the patient. Following the guidelines of the Nagoya court, patients potentially eligible for euthanasia are going to die soon anyway, so that is not the fault of the doctor. And the patient has the right to determine his own death. The fact that he is too weak to hold a sword or to cut short his own life is not morally significant. If his mind is clear, calm and ready for death, then the one who understands and compassionately assists that person is also following Buddhist morality. In summary, the important issue for Buddhists here is whether or not the person will be allowed responsibility for his own life and fate. The entire Buddhist tradition, and particularly that of suicide within Japan, argues that personal choice in time and manner of death is of extreme importance, and anything done by others to dim the mind or deprive the dying person of such choice is a violation of Buddhist principles. Japanese Buddhists may respect this decision more than Western cultures, and lead humanitarian bioethics in a different perspective towards dignified death.

NOTES

1. Morioka Masahiro, "Noshi to wa nan de atta ka" (What was brain death?), in *Nihon Rinri Gokkai kenkyu happyo yoshi* (Japanese Ethics Association outline of presentations) (Japan Ethics Association 39th Annual Conference, Waseda University, October 14–15, 1988, p. 7.

2. Anzai Kazuhiro, "No to sono ishiki" (Brain and its consciousness), in *Hihon Rinri Gakkai*, p. 6.

3. Kawasaki Shinjo, "Toyo kodai no seimei juyo" (The accepted understanding of life in the ancient Orient), in *Nibon Rinri Gakkai*, p. 26.

4. *Visuddhimagga*, pp. 229ff.

5. Kawasaki, "Toyo kodai no seimei juyo," p. 27.

6. Iida Tsunesuke, "Bioethics wa nani o nasu no ka" (What does bioethics accomplish?), in *Nibon Rinri Gakkai*, pp. 40ff.

7. Mary Anne Warren, "Do Potential People Have Moral Rights?" *Canadian Journal of Philosophy*, 7 no. 2 (1978): 275–289.

8. Carl Becker, "Old and New: Japan's Mechanisms for Crime Control and Social Justice," *Howard Journal of Criminal Justice* 27 no. 4 (November 1988): 284–285.

9. Ohara Nobuo, "Sei to shi no rinrigaku" (The ethics of life and death), in *Nibon Rinri Gakkai*, pp. 54–55.

10. Carl Becker, "Religion and Politics in Japan," chap. 13 of *Movements and Issues in World Religious*, ed. C. W-H. Fu and G. S. Spiegler (New York: Greenwood Press, 1987), 278.

11. Among the author's students are nurses at such hospitals.

12. Gerald A. Larue, *Euthanasia and Religion: A Survey of the Attitudes of World Religions to the Right-To-Die* (Los Angeles: The Hemlock Society, 1985).

13. Cf. *Hastings Encyclopedia of Religion*, Vol. 4, p. 448.

14. *Majhima Nikaya* II, 91; III, 258.

15. *Samyutta Nikaya* V, 408.

16. Tamaki Koshiro, "Shino oboegaki" (Memoranda on death), in *Bukkyo Shiso*, vol. 10, ed. Bukkyo Shiso Kenkyukai, Tokyo (September 1988), pp. 465–475.

17. *Sutta Vibhanga, Vinaya* III, 74; cf. *Samyutta Nikaya* III, 119–124.

18. *Majhima Nikaya* III, 263–266 (*Channovada-sutta*); *Samyutta Nikaya* IV, 55–60 (*Channavaga*).

19. *Samyutta Nikaya* I, 121.

20. *Jataka Suvarna Prabhasa* 206ff.

21. Acaranga Sutra I, 7, 6.

22. A mummified body of one such monk is preserved at the Myorenji temple, close to Tsukuba University.

23. Ogasawara Senshu, *Chugoku Jodokyo no kenkyu* (Researches in Chinese Pure Land Buddhism) (Kyoto: Heirakuji, 1951), pp. 60ff.

24. Thich Nhat Hanh, *The Lotus in the Sea of Fire* (London, 1967).

25. Kurita Isamu, *Ippen Shonin, tabi no shisakuska* (Saint Ippen, the meditative wayfarer) (Tokyo: Shinchosha, 1977), pp. 165–169.

26. Ohashi Shunno, *Ippen* (Tokyo: Yoshikawa Kobunkan, 1983), pp. 105ff.

27. *Ippen goroku*, scroll 6, stage 2 (maki o, dan 2).

28. Kurita, *Ippen Shonin*.

29. Ohashi, *Ippen*, pp. 107ff.

30. Mori Ogai, *Takasebune* (Tokyo: Iwanami Bunko, 1978).
31. Jack Seward, *Hara-Kiri: Japanese Ritual Suicide* (Tokyo: Charles E. Tuttle, 1968). Seward describes these and many other significant suicides in detail.
32. Donald Keene, trans., *Major Plays of Chikamatsu* (New York: Columbia University Press, 1961).
33. Fujino Yoshio, ed., *Kanatebon Chushingura: Kaisabaku to kenkyu* (Chushinguar) (Tokyo: Ofusha, 1975).
34. Watsuji Tetsuro, ed. *Hagakure* (Tokyo: Iwanami Bunko, 1970).
35. All condensed from Seward, *Hara-Kiri*.
36. Kimura Rihito, "In Japan, Parents Participate but Doctors Decide," *Hastings Center Report* 16, no. 4 (1986): 22–23.
37. Sisela Bok, "Lies to the Sick and Dying," in *Lying: Moral Choice in Public and Private Life* (New York: Pantheon Books, 1978).
38. Lawrence Egbert, George Batitt, et al., "Reduction of Post-operative Pain by Encouragement and Instruction of Patients," *New England Journal of Medicine* 270 (1964): 825–827; and Howard Waitskin and John Stoeckle, "The Communication of Information About Illness," *Advances in Psychosomatic Medicine* 8 (1972): 185–215.
39. Cf. Bernard Gert and Charles Culver, "Paternalistic Behavior," *Philosophy and Public Affairs* 6 (Summer 1976); and Allen Buchanan, "Medical Paternalism," ibid., vol. 7 (Summer 1978).

REVIEW EXERCISES

1. What is the difference between "whole brain death" and "persistent vegetative state"?
2. If a person has whole brain death, then what kind of euthanasia is possible? Explain.
3. What is the difference between active and passive euthanasia? Is physician-assisted suicide more like active or passive euthanasia? How so?
4. Where do advance directives such as living wills and durable powers of attorney fit into the distinction between voluntary and nonvoluntary euthanasia?
5. What is the difference between ordinary and extraordinary measures of life support? If some measure of life support were rather common and inexpensive, would this necessarily make it an ordinary means of life support? Explain.
6. Label the following as examples of voluntary or nonvoluntary and active or passive euthanasia; if passive, are the measures described more likely to be considered ordinary or extraordinary measures of life support?
    a. A person who is dying asks to be given a fatal drug dose to bring about his death.
    b. A dying patient asks that no more chemotherapy be administered because it is doing nothing but prolonging her time until death, which is inevitable in a short time anyway.
    c. Parents of a newborn whose condition involves moderate retardation refuse permission for a simple surgery that would repair a physical anomaly inconsistent with continued life, and they let the infant die.
    d. A husband gives his wife a lethal overdose of her pain medicine because he does not want to see her suffer anymore.
    e. Doctors decide not to try to start artificial feeding mechanisms for their patient because they believe that it will be futile—that is, ineffective given the condition of their patient.
7. List the consequentialist concerns that could be given in arguing about whether the actions proposed in three of the scenarios in Question 6 are justified.
8. What nonconsequentialist concerns could be given in arguing about these same three scenarios?

DISCUSSION CASES

1. Respirator Removal. Jim was an active person. He was a lawyer by profession. When he was forty-four years old, a routine physical revealed that he had a tumor on his right lung. After surgery to remove that lung, he returned to a normal life. However, four years later, a cancerous tumor was found in his other lung. He knew he had only months to live. Then came the last hospitalization. He was on a respirator. It was extremely uncomfortable for him, and he was frustrated by not being able to talk because of the tubes. After some thought, he decided that he did not want to live out his last few weeks like this and asked to have the respirator removed. Because he was no longer able to breathe on his own, he knew this meant he would die shortly after it was removed.

Did Jim or the doctors who removed the respirator and then watched Jim die as a result do anything wrong? Why or why not? Would there be any difference between this case and that of a person such as Terri Schiavo, who was in a persistent vegetative state, was not able to express her current wishes, and had left no written request? Would there be a difference in cases such as hers between removing a respirator (which she was not using) and removing a feeding tube? How would you tell whether either one would be considered an ordinary or extraordinary means of life support? Would it matter which one it would be labeled?

2. Pill Overdose. Mary Jones had a severe case of cerebral palsy. She now had spent twenty-eight years of life trying to cope with the varying disabilities it caused. She could get around somewhat in her motorized wheelchair. An aide fed her and took care of her small apartment. She had gone to junior college and earned a degree in sociology. She also had a mechanism whereby she could type on a computer. However, she had lately become weary with life. She saw no improvement ahead and wanted to die. She had been receiving pain pills from her doctor. Now she asked for several weeks' worth of prescriptions so that she would not have to return for more so often. Her doctor suspected that she might be suicidal.

Should Mary Jones's doctor continue giving her the pills? Why or why not? Would she be assisting in Mary's suicide if she did? Does Mary Jones have a right to end her life if she chooses? Why or why not? Should her physician actually be able to administer some death-causing drug and not just provide the pills? Why or why not?

3. Teen Euthanasia. Thirteen-year-old Samantha is in the last stages of cancer. She says she doesn't want any further treatment because she thinks that it is not going to make her well. Her parents want the doctors to try a new experimental therapy for which there is some hope. If they cannot convince Samantha to undergo this experimental procedure, should the doctors sedate Samantha and go ahead with it anyway or should they do what she asks and let her die? Do you think that the doctors should be allowed to end her life with a fatal dose of a drug if that is what she wishes, even though her parents object and they are still her legal guardians?

4. Baby John Doe. Sarah and Mike's baby boy was born with a defect called *spina bifida*, which consists of an opening in the spine. In his case, it was of the more severe kind in which the spinal cord also protruded through the hole. The opening was moderately high in the spine, and thus they were told that his neurological control below that level would be affected. He would have no bowel and bladder control and would not be able to walk unassisted. The cerebral spinal fluid had already started to back up into the cavity surrounding his brain, and his head was swelling. Doctors advised that they could have a shunt put in place to drain this fluid from the brain and prevent pressure on the brain. They could also have the spinal opening repaired. If they did not do so, however, the baby would probably die from the infection that would develop. Sarah and Mike are afraid of raising such a child and think that he also would have an extremely difficult life. In a few cases, however, children with this anomaly who do not have the surgery do not die, and then they are worse off than if the operation were done.

What should Sarah and Mike do? Why?

11

Abortion

IMAGINE THE case of a single young woman who believes she is pregnant but does not want to be a young single mother. She sees a billboard with the words "Pregnant and Scared" followed by a telephone number. She calls the number thinking that she can get information about how to obtain an abortion. The person answering the phone says that she can help and invites her to visit the Pregnancy Support Center. When the young woman arrives, she finds out that it is not at all what she expected. Rather than direct her to where she can obtain an abortion, a counselor offers her a free ultrasound test. When it reveals that the woman, is in fact, pregnant, the counselor hands her some hand-knit baby booties and says, "Congratulations, you are a mother." She is also shown little tiny rubber fetuses, about as big as a thumb. She also may be told that there is a "higher incidence of breast cancer, infertility, and depression and suicide in those who have had abortions."

Such clinics or centers are set up for the purpose of talking women out of having abortions and encouraging them to give birth. They are most often associated with Christian charities. Critics such as Planned Parenthood and prochoice groups argue that these centers take advantage of women at an emotionally difficult moment. They also point out that mistaken factual information is being given, such as the increased cancer and other risks from abortion. In fact, the National Cancer Institute in a 2003 study found no increased risk of breast cancer. Other studies note that "fewer than 0.3% of patients experience

Abortion opponents often employ billboards, hotlines, and specialized "clinics" to try to dissuade women from having abortions.

a complication serious enough to require hospitalization." Abortion, rather, is said to be "one of the most common surgical procedures" and especially in the first trimester is "extremely safe."[1]

Those who do provide abortion services are often harassed. On May 31, 2009, Dr. George Tiller was shot and killed in the back of his church. He was known to perform late-term abortions. Scott Roeder, an avid antiabortionist, was arrested shortly after for the killing; Roeder claimed he was preventing babies from being killed. He was tried and convicted for the killing of Dr. Tiller and sentenced to 50 years in prison.[2]

This was not the first time a doctor who performed abortions was shot and killed. In March 1993, a doctor who performed abortions was shot and killed by an antiabortion protester. More than five years later, in October 1998, Dr. Barnett Slepian was shot to death in his home by someone with a high-powered rifle. Like six other clinic workers before him, Dr. Slepian was killed for performing abortions. On July 18, 2005, Eric Rudolph was sentenced to life in prison in Alabama for placing a bomb at a women's health care clinic that also performed abortions. This bomb killed an off-duty police officer and seriously injured and blinded the director of nursing at the clinic. Rudolph was also responsible for bombs placed at another abortion clinic, a gay club, and the 1996 Olympics. In 2005, he was sentenced to several consecutive life terms and is presently serving out this sentence in a maximum security prison in Colorado.[3] At his latest sentencing, he continued to insist that he was justified in what he did. Some in the prolife movement, however, disagree with the tactics of more militant antiabortion individuals and groups. They believe that these tactics and the murders of physicians have hurt their cause. They preach nonviolence and urge respect for all persons, including the unborn.[4] In 2003, the only abortion provider in a small North Carolina town had her center's windows blown out by a shotgun, an event that caused the doctor to put a fence around the building and install cameras, alarms, and a security guard. At one point, flyers designed like wanted posters with her picture on them were circulated around the town. The director met with members of a local church where one of those responsible attended, and this helped.[5]

In 1994, the U.S. Supreme Court upheld a Florida statute that required a thirty-six-foot buffer zone around abortion clinics; the zone had been established to protect patients who were entering the clinics from antiabortion demonstrators and undue noise. Although the Court ruled that protesters could not enter this buffer zone, it overturned elements of the statute restricting them from displaying signs and talking to people beyond this thirty-six-foot zone.[6] Still, we continue to hear reports of such scenes as described here on the evening news and in newspapers. Why? Abortion is an issue about which people have extremely strong opinions. Expressions of their opinions are often highly emotionally charged. Among the probable reasons why it is such

a volatile issue is that it is a matter of life and death and involves beliefs about the very meaning of life itself. It is also a gender issue and touches our beliefs about the most intimate and powerful aspects of our lives as women and men and as mothers and fathers. Sometimes, people's views are based on religious beliefs, but this is not always or necessarily the case.

To complicate matters further, people do not always notice that there is a difference between asking about the morality of abortion and asking what the law ought or ought not to be in its regard. In fact, one could hold that the law ought to allow abortion and still believe that in many if not all cases abortion is morally objectionable. In addition, the language that is used in the debate over abortion often influences the conclusions people reach. What is meant by *prolife*? Do not both those who oppose and those who condone abortion act in support of life? What is meant by *prochoice*? The position supporting a woman's right to choose abortion is the usual meaning of *prochoice*. The terms *proabortion* and *antichoice* have significantly different overtones than the terms generally used. This shows the importance of language in how an ethical debate is couched. In this chapter, we try to avoid labels and analyze the issues and arguments in such a way as to help us focus more clearly on the alternative views and the reasons that support them.

What we say about the morality of abortion will depend on several issues. Some are strictly ethical matters and involve basic ethical perspectives, such as the nature and basis of moral rights. Others are factual matters, such as what happens at different stages of fetal development and what the likely consequences are of certain actions given particular social conditions. Others still are conceptual matters, such as the meaning of *abortion* or *a person* or *a human being*. We begin our analysis with certain factual matters about the stages of fetal development and contemporary methods of abortion.

STAGES OF FETAL DEVELOPMENT

When considering stages of fetal development, the label given to the developing fetus at particular stages is not likely to be relevant to any ethical argument because these are just names given for purposes of identification and communication; in fact, they are terms that are used throughout the biological sciences and pertain to most if not all vertebrates. The newly fertilized egg is called a *zygote*, which simply means "joining together." When the ball of cells reaches the uterus seven to ten days after fertilization, it is called a *blastocyst*—a *blastula* is a fluid-filled cavity surrounded by a single layer of cells. From the second to eighth week of gestation, the developing organism is called an *embryo*, as is any animal at this early stage of primitive tissue and organ development. From then until birth, it is called a *fetus*, which means "young unborn." We will simplify things and use the term *fetus* throughout development, but use of this term does not imply anything about its value or status. We can single out the following stages of fetal development (times are approximate).

› **Day 1**: Fertilization—An ovum, or egg (23 chromosomes), is penetrated by sperm (23 chromosomes), and one cell is formed that contains 46 chromosomes.
› **Days 2–3**: The fertilized ovum passes through the fallopian tube as cell division increases.
› **Days 7–10**: The blastocyst reaches the uterus; it has now become a "ball of cells."
› **Week 2**: The developing embryo becomes embedded in the uterine wall.
› **Weeks 2–8**: Organ systems such as the brain, spinal cord, heart, and digestive tube and certain structural features such as arm and leg buds begin and then continue to develop.
› **Weeks 12–16**: "Quickening" occurs, and the mother can feel the fetus's movements; the fetus is approximately 5½ inches long.
› **Weeks 20–24**: So-called brain waves become detectable as the human cortex begins to form. Nevertheless, they are not of the kind that is present much later in fetal development as the structure of the brain develops. Otherwise, electrical activity detected earlier is more like that detected in plants or other organs or skin.[7]
› **Weeks 20–28**: The process of "viability" takes place, and the fetus is able to live apart from its mother, depending on size and lung development.
› **Week 40**: Birth.

All changes during fetal development occur gradually. Even conception takes some time as the sperm penetrates the egg and together they come to form one cell. Any of these stages may or may not be morally relevant as we shall consider shortly.

METHODS OF ABORTION

From perhaps their earliest times, human beings have discovered and known various methods of abortion. The Hippocratic Oath of the fourth century B.C. mentions it. When we speak of abortion, we mean induced abortion. This is to be distinguished from spontaneous abortion or what we generally call "miscarriage." Among current methods of inducing abortion are the following.

› **Morning-after pill:** This chemical compound, which the Food and Drug Administration refers to as Plan B, prevents the blastocyst from embedding in the uterine wall (the intrauterine device—IUD—and some contraceptive pills operate in a similar way, causing the fertilized egg to be expelled by making the uterine wall inhospitable). Since August 2006, this pill has been available over the counter for customers eighteen years of age and older.
› **RU486 (mifepristone):** This drug was developed in France and induces uterine contractions and expulsion of the embryo. It must be used within seven weeks of a missed menstrual period.[8]
› **Uterine or vacuum aspiration:** In this procedure, the cervix (the opening of the uterus) is dilated, and the uterine contents are removed by suction tube.
› **Dilation and curettage (D&C):** This procedure also dilates the cervix so that the uterus can be scraped with a spoon-shaped curette. This method is similar to the vacuum method except that it is performed somewhat later and requires that the fetus be dismembered and then removed.
› **Saline solution:** A solution of salt and water is used to replace amniotic fluid and thus effect a miscarriage.
› **Prostaglandin drugs:** These pharmaceuticals induce early labor.
› **Hysterotomy:** This uncommon procedure is similar to a cesarean section but is used for later-term abortions.

> **Dilation and extraction (D&X) or Intact D&X or "Partial birth abortion":** In this uncommon second- and third-trimester procedure, forceps are used to deliver the torso of the fetus, its skull is punctured and the cranial contents suctioned out, and then delivery is completed.

In recent years there have been between 800,000 and one million abortions performed in the United States annually. Each year, two out of every 100 women aged 15–44 have an abortion. Forty-eight percent of them have had at least one previous abortion. Fifty-two percent of those having abortions are under 25 years of age, and 33 percent are between the ages of 20 and 24. According to the Guttmacher Institute, African American women are five times as likely as white women to have an abortion, and Hispanic women are twice as likely as whites to have the procedure.[9] One cause of this higher rate is likely to be the cuts for family planning funding over the last ten years, resulting in, among other things, reduced contraceptive use, especially among poor women.[10] The rate of abortions for women living below the federal poverty line is more than four times that of women with incomes 300 percent above that level. In terms of claimed religious affiliation, 43 percent were Protestant and 27 percent were Catholic. A 2004 study reported that among the reasons that women cite for choosing an abortion are the following:

> having a child would dramatically change their lives, their ability to continue with school or work, or their ability to care for others (74 percent);
> they could not afford children (73 percent);
> they were finished having children (38 percent); or
> they did not want to become single mothers (48 percent).

Few cited health problems of either fetus or mother (12 percent).[11] Around the world, abortions are permitted without restriction as to reason in 56 countries (40 percent of the world's population) and completely illegal in 68 countries (26 percent of the world's population). Another 72 countries (34 percent of the world's population) only allow abortion based on the health, mental health, or socioeconomic circumstances of the mother.[12] Seventy-eight percent of all abortions are obtained in developing countries, and 22 percent occur in developed countries.[13] There are approximately 42 millions abortions conducted each year around the world. Of these, 20 million are deemed unsafe, the vast majority in countries where abortion is illegal or highly restricted. According to the World Health Organization, "Every 8 minutes a woman in a developing country dies of complications of an unsafe abortion."[14]

In China, abortion has resulted in a demographic phenomenon. Because of Chinese parents' preferences for boys (who can care for their parents in their old age) and government fines for those who have more than one or two children, the ratio of boys to girls in some sections of China today is now 144 to 100. With the availability of ultrasound scanners since the 1990s, many potential parents choose to terminate pregnancy if the child is to be a girl. This practice is less prevalent in larger cities where women have a higher status.[15]

ABORTION AND THE LAW

Much of the contemporary debate about abortion is concerned with whether the law ought to permit abortion and, if so, what if any legal regulations ought to be placed on it. The relationship between morality and the law is often ignored in these debates. Sometimes, it is assumed that if abortion is immoral, it ought to be illegal just for that reason, or if it is morally permissible, it therefore ought to be legally permissible. As noted in the previous chapter on euthanasia, this equivalence between morality and the law is questionable. We can think of actions that are possibly immoral but that we would not want to be legally prohibited. For example, I may wrongly waste my talents, but I would not want the law to force me to develop and use them. However, many of our laws, such as civil rights laws, are grounded in moral reasons. What one believes the law should and should not do is bound up with an entire philosophy of law. Because this is an ethics text, we will not be able to explore this here. What we can do is note and be aware of the recent legislation about abortion. We can also note, as we summarize here, that some of the reasons given for these laws do nevertheless involve appeals to rights and other moral values.

Abortion has not always been condemned, even by churches now opposed to it.[16] Nor was it always illegal in the United States before the 1970s. In fact, according to U.S. Supreme Court Justice Blackmun, writing in 1973, "At the time of the adoption of our Constitution, and throughout the major portion of the 19th century, abortion was viewed with less disfavor than under most American statutes currently in effect."[17] In the first half of the twentieth century, most states passed laws regulating or making abortion illegal, except in certain cases such as a pregnancy resulting from rape or incest or when the pregnant woman's life or health was threatened. However, women continued to have abortions illegally and under dangerous conditions. In the early 1970s, a pregnant woman from Texas, who was given the fictitious name Jane Roe, appealed the denial of a legal abortion. This case finally made its way to the U.S. Supreme Court, which ruled in its 1973 decision known as *Roe* v. *Wade*. In this decision, the Court stated that no state may prohibit abortion before the time of fetal viability, based on a fundamental "right to privacy" grounded in the Constitution, chiefly in the liberty and due process clauses of the Fourteenth Amendment. The term *privacy* here does not refer to matters that must be kept secret or to what goes on in one's own home, but to a basic liberty, a freedom from restraint in decisions about how to live and enjoy one's life.[18] However, the Court noted that the state did have some interest in protecting what it called the "potential life" of the fetus as well as an interest in maternal health. (Note that the phrase *potential life* is not especially illuminating, because most people do not deny that the fetus is actually alive.) In the case of maternal health, this interest becomes "compelling" (1) from the end of the first trimester (or third month) of pregnancy on, and (2) in the case of the fetus's "potential life," beginning with viability. The right to privacy was said not to be absolute but limited when these compelling state or social interests were at stake. The decision divided pregnancy into three trimesters and ruled that

1. from the end of the first trimester on, states could make laws to ensure the medical safety of the abortion procedures;
2. before the time of viability, about the end of the second trimester (the sixth month), the abortion decision should be left up to the pregnant woman and her doctor; and

3. from the time of viability on, states could prohibit abortion except in those cases in which the continued pregnancy would endanger the life or health of the pregnant woman.[19]

Since *Roe* v. *Wade*, the U.S. Supreme Court has handed down several other abortion-related decisions. These have restricted Medicaid funding to cases in which the woman's life was at risk or the pregnancy resulted from rape or incest (*Harris* v. *McRae*, 1980), or they have put other restrictions on the timing of an abortion and on its procedure. In *Akron* v. *Center for Reproductive Health* (1983), a state law that required a twenty-four-hour waiting period and notification of risks was held to be unconstitutional,[20] and in *Webster* v. *Reproductive Health Services* (1989), a ban on the use of public facilities and employees for performing abortion and a test to determine fetal viability were found to be constitutional. In a 1992 opinion concerning a Pennsylvania case, *Planned Parenthood* v. *Casey*, the Court again found some state restrictions to be permissible while also affirming the basic decision in *Roe* v. *Wade*. Noting that there had been no significant factual or legal changes or developments since the 1973 decision, and that it was important that the Court not change significant opinions on which people had come to depend, the 1992 decision again supported the legal right to privacy and abortion. It commented on the relationship of abortion to the situation of equal opportunity for women. It also reiterated the state's interest in protecting life and argued that states could make regulations for such things as waiting periods to support this interest. However, the court argued that these restrictions should not place an *undue burden* on women in the exercise of their constitutional right to privacy. This means that state laws may not create "substantial obstacles" for women who wish abortions.[21] In the case of parental notification laws, for example, the Supreme Court has ruled that "minors must have an alternative, such as the ability to seek a court order authorizing the procedure."[22] On April 18, 2007, the U.S. Supreme Court upheld, by a vote of five to four, the law banning so-called partial birth abortion passed by Congress in 2003. It held that this law was not unconstitutional and did not impose "an undue burden on women's exercise of their right to end a pregnancy."[23] The reasoning of the majority opinion concluded that there were alternatives to this procedure, and that the law enacted by Congress reflected the government's "legitimate, substantial interest in preserving and promoting fetal life." It allowed exceptions to protect a woman's life but not her health. However, critics assert that this procedure is sometimes necessary to protect a woman's health because it is "often the safest to use late in the pregnancy because it minimizes the chances of injury to the uterus." Partial birth abortion was deemed appropriate for certain cases by the American College of Obstetricians and Gynecologists, the dissenting opinion noted. This ruling resulted in part from the recent appointment of two conservative justices and the retirement of Justice Sandra Day O'Connor.[24] States have tried to pass related statutes. However, one by Virginia was struck down in 2008. It had differed from the federal law in that it prohibited not only an intentional performance of this type of abortion but also one which was performed by mistake.[25]

Also controversial are state laws that require underage daughters to obtain parental or state permission to have legal abortions. One issue here is whether abortion should follow the rule for surgeries in general, needing permission from a legal guardian, or whether it is uniquely personal and thus a matter for private decision even by those under ages eighteen or twenty-one.

Questions have also been raised about so-called feticide laws that more than half the U.S. states now have. These are laws that make it a crime to cause harm to a fetus. Thus, someone who attacks a pregnant woman and kills the fetus that she wanted to carry to term can be found guilty of murder or manslaughter. States differ in how they classify the crime, whether as "feticide" or under general manslaughter or murder laws. It may seem contradictory that the woman can end her fetus's life through abortion but a third party who kills the fetus she wanted may be guilty of murder. Some have said that the difference is between one who exercises a "reproductive choice" and another person who does not. Further questions are raised by states who want to protect fetal life from harmful actions of the pregnant woman such as ingesting drugs. She could be punished if her fetus is

born harmed but not if she aborts the fetus. Should a state be able to prevent her from continuing drug use during pregnancy?

On April 13, 2010, the governor of Nebraska signed into law a statute "banning most abortions 20 weeks after conception or later on the theory that a fetus by that stage in pregnancy has the capacity to feel pain."[26] This law is sure to raise questions and debate.

Although recent Supreme Court decisions on abortion have not been unanimous, many seem to be attempts to balance concerns for the various moral values involved. In doing so, however, these decisions have made neither side in the abortion debate particularly happy. On the one hand, they stress the values of privacy, liberty, and equal opportunity; on the other hand, they conclude that some recognition ought to be given to the origins of human life. Because these are moral values reflected in the law, some of the issues about the morality of abortion will be relevant to what we think the law should or should not do here. In what follows, however, we will concentrate on the question of the morality of abortion.

ABORTION: THE MORAL QUESTION

Although the position that abortion ought to be a private matter and not a matter of law is debatable, it is much more difficult to make an argument that abortion is not a moral matter. After all, abortion involves issues of rights, happiness, and well-being, as well as the value of human life. If these things are morally relevant, then abortion is a moral matter. This is not to say that it is good or bad, simply that it is morally important.

What one says about abortion also may have relevance for what to think about fetal research. For example, promising studies have shown that tissue from aborted fetuses might be used to relieve the symptoms of some persons with Parkinson's disease, an incurable degenerative neurological condition.[27] And recent developments in cloning technology have shown possibilities for taking stem cells from the embryo at the blastocyst stage and programming them to produce organs such as kidneys for transplant.[28]

Rather than outlining so-called conservative, liberal, and moderate views on abortion, let us approach the issue somewhat differently. Then we can take a new look at it and not get caught up in labels. Suppose we consider two types of arguments both for and against abortion: arguments for which the moral status of the fetus is irrelevant and arguments for which it is relevant. We may suppose that all arguments regarding abortion hinge on this issue, but this is not the case. "Moral status of the fetus" is meant to cover questions about whether the fetus is a human being or whether it is a person, and whether the fetus has any value or any rights, including a right to life. We look first at arguments that do not concern themselves with the fetus's moral status. As you examine the arguments, you may find that one or another seems more valid or reasonable to you.

ARGUMENTS THAT DO NOT DEPEND ON THE MORAL STATUS OF THE FETUS

First, we will consider arguments for which the moral status of the fetus is irrelevant. These arguments are based on utilitarian reasoning and issues of persons' rights.

Utilitarian Reasoning

Many arguments that focus on something other than the moral status of the fetus are consequentialist in nature and broadly utilitarian. Arguments for abortion often cite the bad consequences that may result from a continued pregnancy—for example, the loss of a job or other opportunities for the pregnant woman, the suffering of the future child, the burden of caring for the child under particular circumstances, and so on. Some arguments against abortion also cite the loss of happiness and the future contributions of the being who is aborted.

According to act utilitarian reasoning, each case or action stands on its own, so to speak. Its own consequences determine whether it is good or bad, better or worse than other alternatives. Act utilitarians believe that the people making the abortion decision must consider the likely consequences of the alternative actions—in other words, having or not having an abortion (as well as such considerations as where and when). Among the kinds of consequences to consider are health risks and benefits, positive or negative mental or psychological consequences, and financial and social aspects of the alternative choices. For example, a pregnant woman should consider questions such as these: What

would be the effect on her of having the child versus ending the pregnancy? What are the consequences to any others affected? Would the child, if born, be likely to have a happy or unhappy life, and how would one determine this? How would an abortion or the child's birth affect her family, other children, the father, the grandparents, and so on?

Notice that the issue of whether the fetus (in the sense we are using it here) is a person or a human being is not among the things to consider when arguing from this type of consequentialist perspective. Abortion at a later stage of pregnancy might have different effects on people than at an earlier stage, and it might also have different effects on the fetus in terms of whether it might experience pain. It is the effects on the mother, child, and others that matter in utilitarian thinking, not the moral status of the fetus (what kind of value it has) or its ontological status (i.e., what kind of being we say it is) at that stage of development.[29] Also notice that on utilitarian or consequentialist grounds, abortion sometimes would be permissible (the morally right thing to do) and sometimes not: it would depend on the consequences of the various sorts noted earlier. Moral judgments about abortion will be better or worse, according to this view, depending on the adequacy of the prediction of consequences.

Critics of utilitarian reasoning generally object to its seeming disregard of rights. They may point out that if we do not take the right to life seriously, then utilitarian reasoning may condone the taking of any life if the overall consequences of doing so are good! Thus, some critics might argue that the moral status of the fetus, such as whether it is the kind of being that has a right to life, is quite relevant to moral decisions about abortion. Others would insist that we address the matter of the rights of the pregnant woman (or others) and the problem of conflicts of rights.

Some Rights Arguments

Some arguments about abortion *do* consider the rights of persons but still maintain that the moral status of the fetus is irrelevant. It is irrelevant in the sense that whether or not we think of the fetus as a person with full moral rights is not crucial for decisions about the morality of abortion. The article on abortion by Judith Jarvis Thomson in this chapter presents such an argument. She does assume for the purpose of argument that the fetus is a person from early on in pregnancy. But her conclusion is that abortion is still justified, even if the fetus is a person with a right to life (and she assumes it is also permissible if the fetus is not a person).[30] This is why the argument does not turn on what we say about the moral status of the fetus.

The question she poses is whether the pregnant woman has an obligation to sustain the life of the fetus through providing it with the means of life. To have us think about this, she asks us to consider an imaginary scenario. Suppose, she says, that you wake up one morning and find yourself attached through various medical tubings to a famous violinist. You find out that during the night you have been kidnapped and hooked up to this violinist. The violinist has severe kidney problems, and the only way that his life can be saved is through being hooked up to another person so that the other person's kidneys will do the job of purifying his blood for some period of time until his own kidneys have recovered. The question Thomson poses is this: Would you be morally permitted or justified in "unplugging" the violinist, even though to do so would result in his death? Thomson argues that you would be justified, in particular because you had not consented to save the violinist. The point of this example applies most obviously to cases of rape. However, Thomson means it to apply more widely, and she uses other analogies to help make her point. One would only have a responsibility to save the violinist (or nurture the fetus) if one had agreed to do so. The consent that Thomson has in mind is a deliberate and planned choice. She argues that although it would be generous of you to save the life of the violinist (or the fetus), you are not obligated to do so. Her point is that no one has a right to use your body, even to save his own life, unless you give him that right. Such views are consistent with a position that stresses that women are persons and have a right to bodily integrity as do other people, and that as people they ought not to be used against their will for whatever purposes by others, even noble purposes such as the nurturing of children. Critics of this argument point out that it may apply at most to cases of rape, for in some other cases one might be said to implicitly consent to a pregnancy if one did

what one knew might result in it. One response to this is that we do not always consider a person to have consented to chance consequences of their actions.

The persons' rights and utilitarian arguments are examples of arguments about abortion that do not depend on what we say about the moral status of the fetus, but other arguments hold this issue to be crucial. Some arguments for the moral permissibility of abortion as well as some against it rely in crucial ways on what is said about the fetus. We next consider some of these arguments.

ARGUMENTS THAT DEPEND ON THE MORAL STATUS OF THE FETUS

As we have just seen, not all arguments depend on what we say about the fetus; however, some abortion arguments turn on what is said about the moral status of the fetus. They ask such questions as: Is it a human being? A person? Alive? Let us for the moment focus not on these terms and what they might mean, but on the more general issue—that is, let us focus on the question of what kind of value or moral status the developing fetus has. Does it have a different status in various stages of development? If so, when does the status change, and why? (Further issues would include how to weigh its value or rights in comparison to other values or the rights of others.) I suggest that we examine a first approach and call it "Method I" and distinguish it from a broader approach that I will call "Method II." Briefly put, Method I focuses on the characteristics of the fetus and asks when it has what should be considered so significant that it is a person or has a new moral status from that point on. Method II asks a more general question. It asks us to think about what kind of beings of any sort, human or nonhuman, have some special moral status and possibly also rights such as a right to life. In this way it is also related to issues of animal rights (see Chapter 17).

Method I

In using this method, we focus on fetal development and ask three things about possibly significant stages: (1) *What* is present? (2) *When* is this present (at what stage)? and (3) *Why* is this significant—in other words, why does this give this being special moral status, if it does? By "special moral status" we might mean various things. Among the most important would be whether the status were such that the fetus would be thought to have something like a right to life. If this were the case, then abortion would become morally problematic.[31]

Suppose we try Method I on various stages in fetal development and see what the arguments would look like. In each case, let us consider the arguments for the position and then some criticisms of these arguments.

Conception or Fertilization Fertilization, or when sperm penetrate the ovum, is the time at which many opponents of abortion say that the fetus has full moral status. The reason usually given is that this is when the fetus has the full genetic makeup from the combining of sperm and egg. In times past, people held that the egg provided the entire substance and the sperm only gave it a charge or impetus to grow, or that the sperm was "the little man" and only needed a place to grow and obtain nourishment, which the egg provided! We now know about the contribution of both sperm and ovum to the zygote. The argument for taking this stage as the morally significant one supposes an ontological argument[32] something like this: If we say that the resulting being that is born is a human being or person, and if there is no significant change in its development from its initial form, then it is the same being all the way through the development period. Otherwise, we would be implying that different beings are succeeding one another during this process.

Critics of this position may point out that, although fetal development is continuous, the bare genetic basis present at conception is not enough to constitute a person at that point. In this early stage, the cells are *totipotent* and can become skin cells or heart cells or many other types of cells.[33] There is no structure or differentiation at this point, nothing that resembles a person in this initial form. There is not even an individual there. Consider, for example, what happens in the case of identical twinning. Before implantation, identical twins are formed by the splitting of cells in the early embryo. Each resulting twin has the same genetic makeup. Now what are we to think of the original embryo? Suppose conception is the time when we are supposed to have an individual being. We will call him John. The twins that develop and later are born are Jim and Joe. What happened to John,

if there was a John? Jim and Joe are two new individuals, genetically alike as twins, but also two different people. Is there a little of John in each of them? Or does the fact that there are two individuals after twinning mean that there was not any individual there before that time—that John never existed? Those who support conception as the crucial time at which we have a being with full moral status and rights must explain how there can be an individual at conception, at least in the case of identical twinning.

Detectable Brain Waves Another possibility for when a fetus might attain new moral status is that point at which brain waves begin to be detectable. The idea is reasonable given that the human brain is the locus of consciousness, language, and communication, and it is what makes us crucially different from other animals. Moreover, we now use the *cessation* of brain function as the determinant of death. Why should we not use the *beginning* of brain function as the beginning of an individual's life? We can detect brain activity between the sixth and eighth weeks of fetal development, which makes that point the significant time for this view.

Critics of this argument point out that brain activity develops gradually, and we can single out no one time during its development as unique. However, this may be only a practical problem. We might be satisfied with an approximation rather than a determinate time. Other questions about the type of brain function also might be raised. At six to eight weeks, the brain is quite simple; only much later do those parts develop that are the basis of conscious function. At earlier stages, the brain is arguably not that different from other animal brains in structure or function.

Quickening Usually, the pregnant woman can feel the fetus kick or move in approximately the fourth month of fetal development. This is what is meant by *quickening*. In former times, people may have thought there was no fetal movement before this time, and this would then be a more persuasive reason to consider this stage as crucial. Still, we could think of the movement present at this time as self-initiated movement because it now stems from a new level of brain development. This would make a better reason for considering this the beginning of the being's new life because it would now be moving about on its own.

Critics will raise the same issue for this point as for brain development—namely, that there is no dramatic break in development of the ability of the fetus to move. Moreover, they might also point out that other animals and even plants move on their own, and this does not give them special moral status or a right to life. Furthermore, those who argue for animal rights usually do so because of their sentience, their ability to feel pleasure and pain, and not their ability to move.

Viability   Viability is approximately the fifth month in fetal development, at which time the fetus is capable of existing apart from the pregnant woman or mother. All its organs and organ systems are sufficiently developed that it can function on its own. The last system to be functionally complete is the respiratory system. During previous stages of fetal development, the fetus "breathes" amniotic fluid. Before twenty-three or twenty-four weeks of gestation, "capillaries have not yet moved close enough to the air sacs to carry gases to and from the lung."[34] A lubricant, surfactant, can be administered to "help the lungs expand and take in air," but even then the chance of survival is slim. One practical problem with using viability as a criterion is its variability. When *Roe* v. *Wade* took effect, viability was considered to be approximately twenty-six weeks; the estimation has since been shortened by a couple of weeks. At twenty-three or twenty-four weeks, the "micropremie" weighs slightly less than a pound. Its prematurity is also a function of this weight and the mother's socioeconomic status; if she's poor, then the chances are that her nutrition is poor. Prematurity also varies by sex and race: girls are approximately one week ahead of boys in development, and blacks are approximately one week ahead of whites.[35]

Why is the stage of viability singled out as the stage at which the fetus may take on a new moral status? Some answer that it is the capacity for *independent* existence that is the basis for the new status. However, if it were delivered at this time and left on its own, no infant would be able to survive. Perhaps the notion of *separate* existence is what is intended. The idea would be that the fetus is more clearly distinct from the mother before birth at this

point. Or perhaps the notion of *completeness* is what is intended. Although the fetus is not fully formed at viability because much development takes place after birth, the argument might be that the viable fetus is sufficiently complete, enabling us to think of it as a new being.

Critics of viability can point again to the gradual nature of development and the seeming arbitrariness of picking out one stage of completeness as crucially different from the others. They also can point out that the viable fetus would still be dependent on others even if it were delivered at the point of viability. In addition, they can question the whole notion of making moral status a function of independence. We are all dependent on one another, and those who are more independent—just because of viability—have no greater value than those who are more dependent. Even someone dependent on machines is not for this reason less human, they might argue. Furthermore, the viable unborn fetus is still, in fact, dependent on the mother and does not have an existence separate from her. Birth, on these terms, would be a better time to pick than viability, they might argue, if it is separateness and independence that are crucial.

Each point in fetal development may provide a reasonable basis for concluding something about the moral status of the fetus. However, as we can clearly see, none are problem-free. In any case, the whole idea of grounding moral status and rights on the possession of certain characteristics also may be called into question. We might be able to get some help in thinking about this problem by looking at a second method.

Method II

If what we say about the fetus is crucial to a position about the morality of abortion, then we may do well to compare what we say here to what we say about beings other than human fetuses. Why, for example, do we believe that people generally have rights? Are we significantly different from other animals such that we have unique moral status simply because we are *human beings*? Or is the crucial determinant of special moral status or worth the ability to reason or think or imagine or dream? If so, then if there are other intelligent beings in the universe, would they have the same moral status as we do, even if they were not members of our species? Or suppose further that we consider cases in which human beings do not have the capacity for thought and reasoning and communication. Think, for example, of a newborn with anencephaly—that is, without a developed upper brain and thus no chance of consciousness or thought. In fact, such an infant does not usually live for long. But it is a human being biologically and not a member of some other species. Or take the case at the other end of life in which a person is in a permanent vegetative state. There is no doubt that the person is still human in the biological sense, but does this person lack human rights because he or she lacks some mental qualities that are the basis for rights? Finally, perhaps it is not actual ability to think or communicate but the potential for the development of these characteristics that grounds special moral worth and rights. A normal fetus would have this potentiality whereas a two-year-old dog would not. Of course, this depends on the level or type of thinking that is seen to be crucial, because dogs do have some type of mental capacity and some ability to communicate.

Taking each suggestion and giving it a name, we might have something like the following positions. Each gives an answer to this question: What kind of beings have special moral status, which may include something like a right to life?[36]

Being Human According to one point of view, it is being a human being that counts—being a member of the human species. Now, using this criterion, we can note that human fetuses are members of the human species and conclude that they have equal moral status with all other human beings. The argument for this position might include something about the moral advance we make when we recognize that all humans have equal moral worth. This has not always been the case, such as when children or women were considered more as property than as human beings with equal and full moral status as humans, or when African American slaves were each considered to be three-fifths of a person. Nevertheless, questions can be raised about why only members of the human species are included here. If some other species of being were sufficiently like us in the relevant respects, then should they not be considered to have the same worth as members of our own species? In considering this possibility, we may be better able to decide whether it is membership in a species or something else that grounds moral worth.

Being Like Human Beings Suppose that moral status (or personhood) depends on being a member of any species whose members have certain significant characteristics like human beings. But what characteristics are significant enough to ground high moral value and status, including rights? For example, consider the abilities to communicate, reason, and plan. Depending on how high a level of communicating, reasoning, and planning is required, perhaps other animals would qualify for the high moral status envisioned. Some chimpanzees and gorillas, for instance, can learn to communicate through sign language, according to some scientists. If there are beings elsewhere in the universe who are members of a different species but who can communicate, reason, and plan, then according to this criterion they too would have the same moral worth as humans. If a lower level of ability were used, then members of other animal species would also qualify.

These first two criteria are alike in that it is membership in a species that is the determinant of one's moral status. If any humans have this status, then they all do. If chimpanzees have this status, or Martians, then all members of their species also have this status. It does not matter what the individual member of the species is like or what individual capacities she or he possesses. On the other hand, perhaps it is not of what species you are a member but what individual characteristics you have that forms the basis of the special moral status we are concerned with here. If this were the case, then there would be at least three other possible positions about the basis of moral status. These are as follows.

Potentiality *Potentiality* literally means "power." According to this criterion, all beings that have the power to develop certain key characteristics have full moral worth. Thus, if a particular fetus had the potential for developing the requisite mental capacities, then this fetus would have full moral status. However, any fetus or other human being that does not have this potential (anencephalic infants or those in a permanent vegetative state, for example) does not have this status.

Yet how important is potential—and what, in fact, is it? Suppose that one had the potential to become a famous star or hold political office. Would one then have the same respect and rights due the actual star, say, or the legislator? Consider a fictitious story.[37] Suppose that we have a kitten that will grow into a mature cat if left alone. We also have a serum that if injected into the kitten will make it grow into a human being. After the injection, first the fur changes, then the tail goes, and so forth. Now if we ask whether the kitten had the potential to be a human being before the injection, we probably would say no, or that it had potential in only the weakest sense. But what would we say about the potential of the kitten to be a human being after it was injected? Only then, critics of the potentiality criterion might argue, would the potential for being a human being or person be relevant to treating the injected kitten differently than an ordinary kitten. In any case, the notion of potentiality may be morally significant, but supporters of this view must be able to address the issues raised by these criticisms.

Actuality   At the other end of the spectrum is the view according to which simple "potentiality" for developing certain characteristics counts for nothing (or at least does not give one the kind of moral status about which we are concerned). Only the actual possession of the requisite characteristics is sufficient for full moral status. Again, it makes a significant difference to one's position here whether the characteristics are high-level or low-level. For example, if a rather high level of reasoning is required before an individual has the requisite moral status, then newborns probably would not be included, as well as many others.[38] According to this view, although the fetus, newborn infant, and extremely young child are human beings biologically, they are not yet persons or beings with the requisite moral status. They are not yet members of the moral community. There may be good reasons to treat them well and with respect, but it is not because they are persons with rights.

Evolving Value   Finally, let us consider a position that is intermediate between the last two positions. Its underlying idea is that potential counts—but not as much as actual possession of the significant char-

acteristics. Furthermore, as the potential is gradually developed, the moral status of the being also grows. This position also could be described in terms of competing interests and claims. The stronger the claim, the more it should prevail. If this is my book, then I have a stronger claim over it than you who would like to have the book.

In applying this criterion to fetal development, the conclusion would be that the early term fetus has less moral value or moral status than the late-term fetus. Less of a claim or interest on the part of others is needed to override its claim to consideration. Moderately serious interests of the pregnant woman or of society could override the interests or claims of the early term fetus, but it would take more serious interests to override the claims of the late-term fetus. In the end, according to this view, when potentiality is sufficiently actualized, the fetus or infant has as much right as any other person. Although some people may view the evolving value position as a reasonable moral one, it would be more difficult to use it in a legal context in which claims and interests would need to be publicly weighed and compared.

We might note a variant view held by some feminists. Most feminists support a woman's legal right to abortion, but they are not all happy with the rationale for it provided in *Roe* v. *Wade*.[39] For example, some worry that the "right to privacy" could be interpreted in ways that are detrimental to women. If this right is taken to imply that everything done in the privacy of one's home is out of the law's reach, then this would include some abuse of women and children.[40] Some feminists also have misgivings about the implications of some abortion supporters' views of the moral status of the fetus. Like the last of the five positions in Method II, they argue that the fetus is surely human. It is both part and not part of the pregnant woman, but a separate being. Abortion is morally problematic, in some of these views, because the loss of an early form of human life is, in fact, loss of part of the mother's own life. However, this is not to imply that these views grant the fetus full moral status and rights. These critics do not necessarily conclude that abortion is morally impermissible.

These positions, as well as those summarized in Method I, focus on what to say about the status of the fetus. If the fetus does not have the requisite moral status, then abortion is probably morally permissible. If it does have that status, then abortion is morally problematic. If the fetus is said to have a somewhat in-between status, then the conclusion about abortion would be mixed. Again, these are positions that put the whole weight of the moral judgment about abortion on what status the fetus does or does not have. As the utilitarian and persons' rights arguments exemplified, however, there are other considerations about what counts in thinking about the morality of abortion. Finally, remember that unless you believe that everything that is immoral ought to be illegal, then even if abortion were in some case thought to be immoral, one would need to give further reasons about the purpose of law to conclude that it also ought to be illegal. So also if you believe that the only reason why something ought to be illegal is if it is immoral, then if abortion is morally permissible you should conclude that it ought to be legally permissible. From this point of view, there would be no other relevant legal considerations. Both views are problematic.

In the readings in this chapter, Judith Jarvis Thomson provides several analogies to help us think about the morality of abortion, and Don Marquis argues that abortion is immoral.

NOTES

1. *Time*, Feb. 26, 2007, p. 28.
2. http://en.wikipedia.org/wiki/Assassination_of_George_Tiller
3. http://en.wikipedia.org/wiki/Eric_Robert_Rudolph#Arrest_and_guilty_plea
4. Based on a report in *The New York Times*, March 7, 1993, p. B3, and March 11, 1993, p. A1. Also see Jennifer Gonnerma, "The Terrorist Campaign against Abortion," Nov. 3–9, 1998 (www.villagevoice.com/features/9845/abortion.shtml).
5. *Time*, Feb. 26, 2007, p. 30.
6. *Madsen* v. *Women's Health Ctr., Inc.*, U.S. (June 30, 1994).
7. Thanks to Charles Cardwell for calling this to my attention.
8. The drug has been used by 200,000 European women, and the U.S. Food and Drug Administration has determined that it is safe and effective. The FDA also noted that "safe" does not mean risk-free. The drug's administration requires a two-stage procedure. Patients first take 600 milligrams of mifepristone and then return two days later for 200 micrograms of misoprostol, which triggers contractions 95 percent of the time. In the remaining 5 percent of cases, a surgical abortion is recommended. See *The New York Times*, July 20, 1996, pp. A1, A11. Once this method became available, there was expectation that it would become a method of choice. However, because of the greater time and expense, surgical abortions have not been replaced by this method.
9. http://www.guttmacher.org/pubs/gpr/11/3/gpr110302.html
10. *The New York Times*, May 5, 2006, p. A19.
11. http://www.guttmacher.org/pubs/psrh/full/3711005.pdf
12. http://www.guttmacher.org/pubs/journals/3411008.html
13. www.abortiontv.com/Misc/AbortionStatistics.htm.
14. http://www.who.int/reproductivehealth/topics/unsafe_abortion/en/index.html; *The New York Times*, May 16, 2008, p. A23.
15. Stanley K. Henshaw, Sushelela Singh, and Taylor Haas, "Recent Trends in Abortion Rates Worldwide," *Family Planning Perspectives*, 25, no. 1 (March 1999). Also see *The New York Times*, June 21, 2002.
16. In fact, abortion also has not always been condemned or treated as equivalent to the killing of a human being by one of its strongest opponents—the Roman Catholic Church. Following the teachings of Thomas Aquinas, the Church held until perhaps the fifteenth and sixteenth centuries that the fetus was not human until sometime after conception when the matter was suitable for the reception of a human soul. See John Noonan, *The Morality of Abortion* (Cambridge, MA: Harvard University Press, 1970), 18ff.
17. Associate Justice Harry A. Blackmun, majority opinion in *Roe* v. *Wade*, United States Supreme Court, 410 U.S. 113 (1973).
18. See comments about this interpretation in Ronald Dworkin, "Feminists and Abortion," *New York Review of Books*, no. 11 (June 10, 1993): 27–29.
19. Blackmun, *Roe* v. *Wade*.
20. Thanks to Alan Preti of Montgomery County Community College for calling this aspect of the ruling to my attention.
21. Justices O'Connor, Kennedy, and Souter, majority opinion in *Planned Parenthood of Southeastern Pennsylvania v. Casey*, United States Supreme Court, 505 U.S. 833 (1992).
22. http://www.wpclinic.org/abortion/abortion-statistics/
23. *The New York Times*, April 18, 2007.
24. Ibid.

25. *The New York Times*, May 21, 2008, p. A19

26. *The New York Times*, April 14, 2010, p. A15

27. http://www.nytimes.com/1992/11/26/us/success-reported-using-fetal-tissue-to-repair-a-brain.html

28. See Shirley J. Wright, "Human Embryonic Stem-Cell Research: Science and Ethics," *American Scientist*, *87* (July–August, 1999): 352–361.

29. Recall that rule utilitarian reasoning about abortion would be somewhat different. A rule utilitarian must consider which practice regarding abortion would be best. Whatever she judged to be the best practice, she should follow. She should mentally survey various possible practices or rules. Would the rule "No one should have an abortion" be likely to maximize happiness? Would the rule "No one should have an abortion unless the pregnancy threatens the mother's health or well-being" have better consequences overall? What about a rule that says "Persons who are in situations *x, y*, or *z* should have abortions"? How would too easy access to abortion affect our regard for the very young? How would the practice of abortion when the fetus has certain abnormalities affect our treatment of the physically or mentally disabled in general? How would a restrictive abortion policy affect women's ability to participate as equal human beings, enjoying jobs and other opportunities? Whichever practice or rule is likely to have the better net results—that is, more good consequences and fewer bad ones—is the best practice.

30. Judith Jarvis Thomson, "A Defense of Abortion," *Philosophy and Public Affairs*, *1*, no. 1 (Fall 1971): 47–66.

31. Note that if the fetus had no right to life, then this would not automatically make abortion problem-free. See the comments in the last paragraph under "Method II."

32. An *ontological* argument is one that has to do with the nature and identity of beings; *ontos* means "being."

33. This issue has recently arisen with developments in stem cell research and cloning.

34. Sheryl Gay Stolberg, "Definition of Fetal Viability Is Focus of Debate in Senate," *The New York Times*, May 15, 1997, p. A13.

35. Ibid.

36. Compare this discussion with similar discussions in Chapters 16 and 17 on the environment and animal rights. In particular, note the possible distinction between having moral value and having rights.

37. This is taken from Michael Tooley's "Abortion and Infanticide," *Philosophy and Public Affairs*, *2*, no. 1 (1972): 37–65.

38. This is the position of Mary Ann Warren in "On the Moral and Legal Status of Abortion," *The Monist*, *57*, no. 1 (January 1973): 43–61.

39. See the summary of these views in Dworkin, "Feminists and Abortion," op. cit.

40. Note that this was not the interpretation of the "right to privacy" given earlier in this chapter. As based in the liberty clause of the Fourteenth Amendment, it was noted that it was a liberty right, the right or power to make one's own decisions about personal matters.

READING
A Defense of Abortion

JUDITH JARVIS THOMSON

Study Questions

1. What starting point for consideration of abortion does Thomson accept? Why?

2. Describe the violinist example. What argument could be made for keeping the violinist "plugged in"?

3. What is the so-called extreme position? How does it distinguish between directly killing and letting die?

4. How could the violinist case be a case of self-defense? How is abortion to save the mother's life similar to or different from this case?

5. What is the example of the child growing in the house supposed to show?

6. What is the example of Henry Fonda's cool hand supposed to show? The box of chocolates?

7. How does the peopleseeds example bring out the issue of consent or voluntariness?

8. What problems regarding the meaning of a right does Thomson's argument raise?

9. What is the Good Samaritan example's point?

10. What, finally, is Thomson arguing for, and what is she not claiming?

MOST OPPOSITION to abortion relies on the premise that the fetus is a human being, a person, from the moment of conception. The premise is argued for, but, as I think, not well. Take, for example, the most common argument. We are asked to notice that the development of a human being from conception through birth into childhood is continuous; then it is said that to draw a line, to choose a point in this development and say "before this point the thing is not a person, after this point it is a person" is to make an arbitrary choice, a choice for which in the nature of things no good reason can be given. It is concluded that the fetus is, or anyway that we had better say it is, a person from the moment of conception. But this conclusion does not follow. Similar things might be said about the development of an acorn into an oak tree, and it does not follow that acorns are oak trees, or that we had better say they are. Arguments of this form are sometimes called "slippery slope arguments"—the phrase is perhaps self-explanatory—and it is dismaying that opponents of abortion rely on them so heavily and uncritically.

I am inclined to agree, however, that the prospects for "drawing a line" in the development of the fetus look dim. I am inclined to think also that we shall probably have to agree that the fetus has already become a human person well before birth. Indeed, it comes as a surprise when one first learns how early in its life it begins to acquire human characteristics. By the tenth week, for example, it already has a face, arms and legs, fingers and toes; it has internal organs, and brain activity is detectable.[1] On the other hand, I think that the premise is false, that the fetus is not a person from the moment of conception. A newly fertilized ovum, a newly implanted clump of cells, is no more a person than an acorn is an oak tree. But I shall not discuss any of this. For it seems to me to be of great interest to ask what happens if, for the sake of argument, we allow the premise. How, precisely, are we supposed to get from there to the conclusion that abortion is morally impermissible? Opponents of abortion commonly spend most of their time establishing that the fetus is a person, and hardly any time explaining the step from there to the impermissibility of abortion. Perhaps they think the step too simple and obvious to require much comment. Or perhaps instead they are simply being economical in argument. Many of those who defend abortion rely on the premise that the fetus is not a person, but only a bit of tissue that will become a person at birth; and why pay out more arguments than you have to? Whatever the explanation, I suggest that the step they take is neither easy nor obvious, that it calls for closer examination than it is commonly given, and that when we do give it this closer examination we shall feel inclined to reject it.

I propose, then, that we grant that the fetus is a person from the moment of conception. How does the argument go from here? Something like this, I take it. Every person has a right to life. So the fetus has a right to life. No doubt the mother has a right to decide what shall happen in and to her body; everyone would grant that. But surely a person's right to life is stronger and more stringent than the mother's right to decide what happens in and to her body, and so outweighs it. So the fetus may not be killed; an abortion may not be performed.

It sounds plausible. But now let me ask you to imagine this. You wake up in the morning and find yourself back to back in bed with an unconscious violinist. A famous unconscious violinist. He has been found to have a fatal kidney ailment, and the Society of Music Lovers has canvassed all the available medical records and found that you alone have the right blood type to help. They have therefore kidnapped you, and last night the violinist's circulatory system was plugged into yours, so that your kidneys can be used to extract poisons from his blood as well as your own. The director of the hospital now tells you, "Look, we're sorry the Society of Music Lovers did this to you—we would never have permitted it if we had known. But still, they did it, and the violinist now is plugged into you. To unplug you would be to kill him. But never mind, it's only for nine months. By then he will have recovered from his ailment, and can safely be unplugged from you." Is it morally incumbent on you to accede to this situation? No doubt it would be very nice of you if you did, a great kindness. But do you *have* to accede to it? What if it were not nine months, but

Judith Jarvis Thomson, "A Defense of Abortion," From *Philosophy & Public Affairs*, vol. 1, no. 1 (Fall 1971): 47–66. Copyright © 1971 Wiley Periodicals, Inc. Reproduced by permission of Blackwell Publishing Ltd.

nine years? Or longer still? What if the director of the hospital says, "Tough luck, I agree, but you've now got to stay in bed, with the violinist plugged into you, for the rest of your life. Because remember this. All persons have a right to life, and violinists are persons. Granted you have a right to decide what happens in and to your body, but a person's right to life outweighs your right to decide what happens in and to your body. So you cannot ever be unplugged from him." I imagine you would regard this as outrageous, which suggests that something really is wrong with that plausible-sounding argument I mentioned a moment ago.

In this case, of course, you were kidnapped; you didn't volunteer for the operation that plugged the violinist into your kidneys. Can those who oppose abortion on the ground I mentioned make an exception for a pregnancy due to rape? Certainly. They can say that persons have a right to life only if they didn't come into existence because of rape; or they can say that all persons have a right to life, but that some have less of a right to life than others, in particular, that those who came into existence because of rape have less. But these statements have a rather unpleasant sound. Surely the question of whether you have a right to life at all, or how much of it you have, shouldn't turn on the question of whether or not you are the product of a rape. And in fact the people who oppose abortion on the ground I mentioned do not make this distinction, and hence do not make an exception in the case of rape.

Nor do they make an exception for a case in which the mother has to spend the nine months of her pregnancy in bed. They would agree that would be a great pity, and hard on the mother; but all the same, all persons have a right to life, the fetus is a person, and so on. I suspect, in fact, that they would not make an exception for a case in which, miraculously enough, the pregnancy went on for nine years, or even the rest of the mother's life.

Some won't even make an exception for a case in which continuation of the pregnancy is likely to shorten the mother's life; they regard abortion as impermissible even to save the mother's life. Such cases are nowadays very rare, and many opponents of abortion do not accept this extreme view. All the same, it is a good place to begin: A number of points of interest come out in respect to it.

1. Let us call the view that abortion is impermissible even to save the mother's life "the extreme view." I want to suggest first that it does not issue from the argument I mentioned earlier without the addition of some fairly powerful premises. Suppose a woman has become pregnant, and now learns that she has a cardiac condition such that she will die if she carries the baby to term. What may be done for her? The fetus, being a person, has a right to life, but as the mother is a person too, so has she a right to life. Presumably they have an equal right to life. How is it supposed to come out that an abortion may not be performed? If mother and child have an equal right to life, shouldn't we perhaps flip a coin? Or should we add to the mother's right to life her right to decide what happens in and to her body, which everybody seems to be ready to grant—the sum of her rights now outweighing the fetus's right to life?

The most familiar argument here is the following. We are told that performing the abortion would be directly killing[2] the child, whereas doing nothing would not be killing the mother, but only letting her die. Moreover, in killing the child, one would be killing an innocent person, for the child has committed no crime, and is not aiming at his mother's death. And then there are a variety of ways in which this might be continued. (1) But as directly killing an innocent person is always and absolutely impermissible, an abortion may not be performed. Or, (2) as directly killing an innocent person is murder, and murder is always and absolutely impermissible, an abortion may not be performed.[3] Or, (3) as one's duty to refrain from directly killing an innocent person is more stringent than one's duty to keep a person from dying, an abortion may not be performed. Or, (4) if one's only options are directly killing an innocent person or letting a person die, one must prefer letting the person die, and thus an abortion may not be performed.[4]

Some people seem to have thought that these are not further premises which must be added if the conclusion is to be reached, but that they follow from the very fact that an innocent person has a right to life.[5] But this seems to me to be a mistake, and perhaps the simplest way to show this is to bring out that while we must certainly grant that innocent persons have a right to life, the theses in (1) through (4) are all false. Take (2), for example. If directly killing an innocent person is murder, and thus is impermissible, then the mother's directly killing the innocent person inside her is murder, and thus is impermissible. But it cannot seriously be thought to be murder if the mother performs an abortion on herself to save her life. It cannot seriously be said that she *must* refrain, that she *must* sit passively by and wait for her death. Let us look again at the case of you and the violinist. There you are, in bed with the violinist, and the director of the hospital says to you, "It's all most distressing, and I deeply sympathize, but you see this is putting an additional strain on your kidneys, and you'll be dead within the month. But you *have* to stay where you are all the same. Because unplugging you would be directly killing an innocent violinist, and that's murder, and that's impermissible." If anything in the world is true, it is that you do not commit murder, you do not do what is impermissible, if you reach around to your back and unplug yourself from that violinist to save your life.

The main focus of attention in writings on abortion has been on what a third party may or may not do in answer to a request from a woman for an abortion. This is in a way understandable. Things being as they are, there isn't much a woman can safely do to abort herself. So the question asked is what a third party may do, and what the mother may do, if it is mentioned at all, is deduced, almost as an afterthought, from what it is concluded that third parties may do. But it seems to me that to treat the matter in this way is to refuse to grant to the mother that very status of person which is so firmly insisted on for the fetus. For we cannot simply read off what a person may do from what a third party may do. Suppose you find yourself trapped in a tiny house with a growing child. I mean a very tiny house, and a rapidly growing child—you are already up against the wall of the house and in a few minutes you'll be crushed to death. The child on the other hand won't be crushed to death; if nothing is done to stop him from growing he'll be hurt, but in the end he'll simply burst open the house and walk out a free man. Now I could well understand it if a bystander were to say, "There's nothing we can do for you. We cannot choose between your life and his, we cannot be the ones to decide who is to live, we cannot intervene." But it cannot be concluded that you too can do nothing, that you

cannot attack it to save your life. However innocent the child may be, you do not have to wait passively while it crushes you to death. Perhaps a pregnant woman is vaguely felt to have the status of a house, to which we don't allow the right of self-defense. But if the woman houses the child, it should be remembered that she is a person who houses it.

I should perhaps stop to say explicitly that I am not claiming that people have a right to do anything whatever to save their lives. I think, rather, that there are drastic limits to the right of self-defense. If someone threatens you with death unless you torture someone else to death, I think you have not the right, even to save your life, to do so. But the case under consideration here is very different. In our case there are only two people involved, one whose life is threatened, and one who threatens it. Both are innocent: The one who is threatened is not threatened because of any fault, the one who threatens does not threaten because of any fault. For this reason we may feel that we bystanders cannot intervene. But the person threatened can.

In sum, a woman surely can defend her life against the threat to it posed by the unborn child, even if doing so involves its death. And this shows not merely that the theses in (1) through (4) are false; it shows also that the extreme view of abortion is false, and so we need not canvass any other possible ways of arriving at it from the argument I mentioned at the outset.

2. The extreme view could of course be weakened to say that while abortion is permissible to save the mother's life, it may not be performed by a third party, but only by the mother herself. But this cannot be right either. For what we have to keep in mind is that the mother and the unborn child are not like two tenants in a small house which has, by an unfortunate mistake, been rented to both: The mother *owns* the house. The fact that she does adds to the offensiveness of deducing that the mother can do nothing from the supposition that third parties can do nothing. But it does more than this: It casts a bright light on the supposition that third parties can do nothing. Certainly it lets us see that a third party who says "I cannot choose between you" is fooling himself if he thinks this is impartiality. If Jones has found and fastened on a certain coat, which he needs to keep him from freezing, but which Smith also needs to keep

him from freezing, then it is not impartiality that says "I cannot choose between you" when Smith owns the coat. Women have said again and again "This body is *my* body!" and they have reason to feel angry, reason to feel that it has been like shouting into the wind. Smith, after all, is hardly likely to bless us if we say to him, "Of course it's your coat, anybody would grant that it is. But no one may choose between you and Jones who is to have it."

We should really ask what it is that says "no one may choose" in the face of the fact that the body that houses the child is the mother's body. It may be simply a failure to appreciate this fact. But it may be something more interesting, namely the sense that one has a right to refuse to lay hands on people, even where it would be just and fair to do so, even where justice seems to require that somebody do so. Thus justice might call for somebody to get Smith's coat back from Jones, and yet you have a right to refuse to be the one to lay hands on Jones, a right to refuse to do physical violence to him. This, I think, must be granted. But then what should be said is not "no one may choose," but only "*I* cannot choose," and indeed not even this, but "*I* will not *act*," leaving it open that somebody else can or should, and in particular that anyone in a position of authority, with the job of securing people's rights, both can and should. So this is no difficulty. I have not been arguing that any given third party must accede to the mother's request that he perform an abortion to save her life, but only that he may.

I suppose that in some views of human life the mother's body is only on loan to her, the loan not being one which gives her any prior claim to it. One who held this view might well think it impartiality to say "I cannot choose." But I shall simply ignore this possibility. My own view is that if a human being has any just, prior claim to anything at all, he has a just, prior claim to his own body. And perhaps this needn't be argued for here anyway, since, as I mentioned, the arguments against abortion we are looking at do grant that the woman has a right to decide what happens in and to her body.

But although they do grant it, I have tried to show that they do not take seriously what is done in granting it. I suggest the same thing will reappear even more clearly when we turn away from cases in which the mother's life is at stake, and

attend, as I propose we now do, to the vastly more common cases in which a woman wants an abortion for some less weighty reason than preserving her own life.

3. Where the mother's life is not at stake, the argument I mentioned at the outset seems to have a much stronger pull. "Everyone has a right to life, so the unborn person has a right to life." And isn't the child's right to life weightier than anything other than the mother's own right to life, which she might put forward as ground for an abortion?

This argument treats the right to life as if it were unproblematic. It is not, and this seems to me to be precisely the source of the mistake.

For we should now, at long last, ask what it comes to, to have a right to life. In some views having a right to life includes having a right to be given at least the bare minimum one needs for continued life. But suppose that what in fact is the bare minimum a man needs for continued life is something he has no right at all to be given. If I am sick unto death, and the only thing that will save my life is the touch of Henry Fonda's cool hand on my fevered brow, then all the same, I have no right to be given the touch of Henry Fonda's cool hand on my fevered brow. It would be frightfully nice of him to fly in from the West Coast to provide it. It would be less nice, though no doubt well meant, if my friends flew out to the West Coast and carried Henry Fonda back with them. But I have no right at all against anybody that he should do this for me. Or again, to return to the story I told earlier, the fact that for continued life that violinist needs the continued use of your kidneys does not establish that he has a right to be given the continued use of your kidneys. He certainly has no right against you that *you* should give him continued use of your kidneys. For nobody has any right to use your kidneys unless you give him such a right; and nobody has the right against you that you shall give him this right—if you do allow him to go on using your kidneys, this is a kindness on your part, and not something he can claim from you as his due. Nor has he any right against anybody else that *they* should give him continued use of your kidneys. Certainly he had no right against the Society of Music Lovers that they should plug him into you in the first place. And if you now start to unplug yourself, having learned that you will otherwise have to spend nine years in bed with him, there is nobody in the world who must try to prevent you, in order to see to it that he is given something he has a right to be given.

Some people are rather stricter about the right to life. In their view, it does not include the right to be given anything, but amounts to, and only to, the right not to be killed by anybody. But here a related difficulty arises. If everybody is to refrain from killing that violinist, then everybody must refrain from doing a great many different sorts of things. Everybody must refrain from slitting his throat, everybody must refrain from shooting him—and everybody must refrain from unplugging you from him. But does he have a right against everybody that they shall refrain from unplugging you from him? To refrain from doing this is to allow him to continue to use your kidneys. It could be argued that he has a right against us that *we* should allow him to continue to use your kidneys. That is, while he had no right against us that we should give him the use of your kidneys, it might be argued that he anyway has a right against us that we shall not now intervene and deprive him of the use of your kidneys. I shall come back to third-party interventions later. But certainly the violinist has no right against you that *you* shall allow him to continue to use your kidneys. As I said, if you do allow him to use them, it is a kindness on your part, and not something you owe him.

The difficulty I point to here is not peculiar to the right of life. It reappears in connection with all the other natural rights; and it is something which an adequate account of rights must deal with. For present purposes it is enough just to draw attention to it. But I would stress that I am not arguing that people do not have a right to life—quite to the contrary, it seems to me that the primary control we must place on the acceptability of an account of rights is that it should turn out in that account to be a truth that all persons have a right to life. I am arguing only that having a right to life does not guarantee having either a right to be given the use of or a right to be allowed continued use of another person's body— even if one needs it for life itself. So the right to life will not serve the opponents of abortion in the very simple and clear way in which they seem to have thought it would.

4. There is another way to bring out the difficulty. In the most ordinary sort of case, to deprive someone of what he has a right to is to treat him unjustly. Suppose a boy and his small brother are jointly given a box of chocolates for Christmas. If the older boy takes the box and refuses to give his brother any of the chocolates, he is unjust to him, for the brother has been given a right to half of them. But suppose that, having learned that otherwise it means nine years in bed with that violinist, you unplug yourself from him. You surely are not being unjust to him, for you gave him no right to use your kidneys, and no one else can have given him any such right. But we have to notice that in unplugging yourself, you are killing him; and violinists, like everybody else, have a right to life, and thus in the view we were considering just now, the right not to be killed. So here you do what he supposedly has a right you shall not do, but you do not act unjustly to him in doing it.

The emendation which may be made at this point is this: The right to life consists not in the right not to be killed, but rather in the right not to be killed unjustly. This runs a risk of circularity, but never mind: It would enable us to square the fact that the violinist has a right to life with the fact that you do not act unjustly toward him in unplugging yourself, thereby killing him. For if you do not kill him unjustly, you do not violate his right to life, and so it is no wonder you do him no injustice.

But if this emendation is accepted, the gap in the argument against abortion stares us plainly in the face: It is by no means enough to show that the fetus is a person, and to remind us that all persons have a right to life—we need to be shown also that killing the fetus violates its right to life, i.e., that abortion is unjust killing. And is it?

I suppose we may take it as a datum that in the case of pregnancy due to rape the mother has not given the unborn person a right to the use of her body for food and shelter. Indeed, in what pregnancy should it be supposed that the mother has given the unborn person such a right? It is not as if there were unborn persons drifting about the world, to whom a woman who wants a child says "I invite you in."

But it might be argued that there are other ways one can have acquired a right to the use of another person's body than by having been invited to use it by that person. Suppose a woman voluntarily indulges in intercourse, knowing of the chance it will issue in pregnancy, and then she does become pregnant; is she not in part responsible for the presence, in fact the very existence, of the unborn person inside? No doubt she did not invite it in. But doesn't her partial responsibility for its being there itself give it a right to the use of her body?[6] If so, then her aborting it would be more like the boy's taking away the chocolates, and less like your unplugging yourself from the violinist—doing so would be depriving it of what it does have a right to, and thus would be doing it an injustice.

And then, too, it might be asked whether or not she can kill it even to save her own life: If she voluntarily called it into existence, how can she now kill it, even in self-defense?

The first thing to be said about this is that it is something new. Opponents of abortion have been so concerned to make out the independence of the fetus, in order to establish that it has a right to life, just as its mother does, that they have tended to overlook the possible support they might gain from making out that the fetus is *dependent* on the mother, in order to establish that she has a special kind of responsibility for it, a responsibility that gives it rights against her which are not possessed by any independent person—such as an ailing violinist who is a stranger to her.

On the other hand, this argument would give the unborn person a right to its mother's body only if her pregnancy resulted from a voluntary act, undertaken in full knowledge of the chance a pregnancy might result from it. It would leave out entirely the unborn person whose existence is due to rape. Pending the availability of some further argument, then, we would be left with the conclusion that unborn persons whose existence is due to rape have no right to the use of their mothers' bodies, and thus that aborting them is not depriving them of anything they have a right to and hence is not unjust killing.

And we should also notice that it is not at all plain that this argument really does go even as far as it purports to. For there are cases and cases, and the details make a difference. If the room is stuffy, and I therefore open a window to air it, and a burglar climbs in, it would be absurd to say, "Ah, now he can stay, she's given him a right to the use of her house—for she is partially responsible for his presence there, having voluntarily done what enabled him to get in, in full knowledge that there are such things as burglars, and that burglars burgle." It would be still more absurd to say this if I had had bars installed outside my windows, precisely to prevent burglars from getting in, and a burglar got in only because of a defect in the bars. It remains equally absurd if we imagine it is not a burglar who climbs in, but an innocent person who blunders or falls in. Again, suppose it were like this: Peopleseeds drift about in the air like pollen, and if you open your windows, one may drift in and take root in your carpets or upholstery. You don't want children, so you fix up your windows with fine mesh screens, the very best you can buy. As can happen, however, and on very, very rare occasions does happen, one of the screens is defective; and a seed drifts in and takes root. Does the personplant who now develops have a right to the use of your house? Surely not—despite the fact that you voluntarily opened your windows, you knowingly kept carpets and upholstered furniture, and you knew that screens were sometimes defective. Someone may argue that you are responsible for its rooting, that it does have a right to your house, because after all you *could* have lived out your life with bare floors and furniture, or with sealed windows and doors. But this won't do—for by the same token anyone can avoid a pregnancy due to rape by having a hysterectomy, or anyway by never leaving home without a (reliable!) army.

It seems to me that the argument we are looking at can establish at most that there are *some* cases in which the unborn person has a right to the use of its mother's body, and therefore *some* cases in which abortion is unjust killing. There is room for much discussion and argument as to precisely which, if any. But I think we should sidestep this issue and leave it open, for at any rate the argument certainly does not establish that all abortion is unjust killing.

5. There is room for yet another argument here, however. We surely must grant that there may be cases in which it would be morally indecent to detach a person from your body at the cost of his life. Suppose you learn that what the violinist needs is not nine years of your life, but only one hour: All

you need do to save his life is spend one hour in that bed with him. Suppose also that letting him use your kidneys for that one hour would not affect your health in the slightest. Admittedly you were kidnapped. Admittedly you did not give anyone permission to plug him into you. Nevertheless it seems to me plain you *ought* to allow him to use your kidneys for that hour—it would be indecent to refuse.

Again, suppose pregnancy lasted only an hour, and constituted no threat to life or death [sic]. And suppose that a woman becomes pregnant as a result of rape. Admittedly she did not voluntarily do anything to bring about the existence of a child. Admittedly she did nothing at all which would give the unborn person a right to the use of her body. All the same it might well be said, as in the newly emended violinist story, that she *ought* to allow it to remain for that hour—that it would be indecent of her to refuse.

Now some people are inclined to use the term "right" in such a way that it follows from the fact that you ought to allow a person to use your body for the hour he needs, that he has a right to use your body for the hour he needs, even though he has not been given that right by any person or act. They may say that it follows also that if you refuse, you act unjustly toward him. This use of the term is perhaps so common that it cannot be called wrong; nevertheless it seems to me to be an unfortunate loosening of what we would do better to keep a tight rein on. Suppose that box of chocolates I mentioned earlier had not been given to both boys jointly, but was given only to the older boy. There he sits, stolidly eating his way through the box, his small brother watching enviously. Here we are likely to say "You ought not to be so mean. You ought to give your brother some of those chocolates." My own view is that it just does not follow from the truth of this that the brother has any right to any of the chocolates. If the boy refuses to give his brother any, he is greedy, stingy, callous—but not unjust. I suppose that the people I have in mind will say it does follow that the brother has a right to some of the chocolates, and thus that the boy does act unjustly if he refuses to give his brother any. But the effect of saying this is to obscure what we should keep distinct, namely the difference between the boy's refusal in this case and the boy's refusal in the earlier case, in which the box was given to both boys jointly, and in which the small brother thus had what was from any point of view clear title to half.

A further objection to so using the term "right" that from the fact that A ought to do a thing for B, it follows that B has a right against A that A do it for him, is that it is going to make the question of whether or not a man has a right to a thing turn on how easy it is to provide him with it; and this seems not merely unfortunate, but morally unacceptable. Take the case of Henry Fonda again. I said earlier that I had no right to the touch of his cool hand on my fevered brow, even though I needed it to save my life. I said it would be frightfully nice of him to fly in from the West Coast to provide me with it, but that I had no right against him that he should do so. But suppose he isn't on the West Coast. Suppose he has only to walk across the room, place a hand briefly on my brow—and lo, my life is saved. Then surely he ought to do it, it would be indecent to refuse. Is it to be said, "Ah, well, it follows that in this case she has a right to the touch of his hand on her brow, and so it would be an injustice to him to refuse"? So that I have a right to it when it is easy for him to provide it, though no right when it's hard? It's rather a shocking idea that anyone's rights should fade away and disappear as it gets harder and harder to accord them to him.

So my own view is that even though you ought to let the violinist use your kidneys for the one hour he needs, we should not conclude that he has a right to do so—we should say that if you refuse, you are, like the boy who owns all the chocolates and will give none away, self-centered and callous, indecent in fact, but not unjust. And similarly, that even supposing a case in which a woman pregnant due to rape ought to allow the unborn person to use her body for the hour he needs, we should not conclude that he has a right to do so; we should conclude that she is self-centered, callous, indecent, but not unjust, if she refuses. The complaints are no less grave; they are just different. However, there is no need to insist on this point. If anyone does wish to deduce "he has a right" from "you ought," then all the same he must surely grant that there are cases in which it is not morally required of you that you allow that violinist to use your kidneys, and in which he does not have a right to use them, and in which you do not do him an injustice if you refuse. And so also for mother and unborn child. Except in such cases as the unborn person has a right to demand it—and we were leaving open the possibility that there may be such cases—nobody is morally *required* to make large sacrifices, of health, of all other interests and concerns, of all other duties and commitments, for nine years, or even for nine months, in order to keep another person alive.

6. We have in fact to distinguish between the two kinds of Samaritan: the Good Samaritan and what we might call the Minimally Decent Samaritan. The story of the Good Samaritan, you will remember, goes like this:

> A certain man went down from Jerusalem to Jericho, and fell among thieves, which stripped him of his raiment, and wounded him, and departed, leaving him half dead.
> And by chance there came down a certain priest that way; and when he saw him, he passed by on the other side.
> And likewise a Levite, when he was at the place, came and looked on him, and passed by on the other side.
> But a certain Samaritan, as he journeyed, came where he was; and when he saw him he had compassion on him.
> And went to him, and bound up his wounds, pouring in oil and wine, and set him on his own beast, and brought him to an inn, and took care of him.
> And on the morrow, when he departed, he took out two pence, and gave them to the host, and said unto him, "Take care of him; and whatsoever thou spendest more, when I come again, I will repay thee." (Luke 10:30–35)

The Good Samaritan went out of his way, at some cost to himself, to help one in need of it. We are not told what the options were, that is, whether or not the priest and the Levite could have helped by doing less than the Good Samaritan did, but assuming they could have, then the fact they did nothing at all shows they were not even Minimally Decent Samaritans, not because they were not Samaritans, but because they were not even minimally decent.

These things are a matter of degree, of course, but there is a difference, and it comes out perhaps most clearly in the story of Kitty Genovese, who, as you will remember, was murdered while thirty-eight people watched or listened, and did nothing at all to help her. A Good Samaritan would have rushed out to give direct assistance against the murderer. Or perhaps we had better allow that it would have been a Splendid Samaritan who did this, on the ground that it would have involved a risk of death for himself. But the thirty-eight not only did not do this, they did not even trouble to pick up a phone to call the police. Minimally Decent Samaritanism would call for doing at least that, and their not having done it was monstrous.

After telling the story of the Good Samaritan, Jesus said, "Go, and do thou likewise." Perhaps he meant that we are morally required to act as the Good Samaritan did. Perhaps he was urging people to do more than is morally required of them. At all events it seems plain that it was not morally required of any of the thirty-eight that he rush out to give direct assistance at the risk of his own life, and that it is not morally required of anyone that he give long stretches of his life—nine years or nine months—to sustaining the life of a person who has no special right (we were leaving open the possibility of this) to demand it.

Indeed, with one rather striking class of exceptions, no one in any country in the world is *legally* required to do anywhere near as much as this for anyone else. The class of exceptions is obvious. My main concern here is not the state of the law in respect to abortion, but it is worth drawing attention to the fact that in no state in this country is any man compelled by law to be even a Minimally Decent Samaritan to any person; there is no law under which charges could be brought against the thirty-eight who stood by while Kitty Genovese died. By contrast, in most states in this country women are compelled by law to be not merely Minimally Decent Samaritans, but Good Samaritans to unborn persons inside them. This doesn't by itself settle anything one way or the other, because it may well be argued that there should be laws in this country—as there are in many European countries—compelling at least Minimally Decent Samaritanism.[7] But it does show that there is a gross injustice in the existing state of the law. And it shows also that the groups currently working against liberalization of abortion laws, in fact working toward having it declared unconstitutional for a state to permit abortion, had better start working for the adoption of Good Samaritan laws generally, or earn the charge that they are acting in bad faith.

I should think, myself, that Minimally Decent Samaritan laws would be one thing, Good Samaritan laws quite another, and in fact highly improper. But we are not here concerned with the law. What we should ask is not whether anybody should be compelled by law to be a Good Samaritan, but whether we must accede to a situation in which somebody is being compelled—by nature, perhaps—to be a Good Samaritan. We have, in other words, to look now at third-party interventions. I have been arguing that no person is morally required to make large sacrifices to sustain the life of another who has no right to demand them, and this even where the sacrifices do not include life itself; we are not morally required to be Good Samaritans or anyway Very Good Samaritans to one another. But what if a man cannot extricate himself from such a situation? What if he appeals to us to extricate him? It seems to me plain that there are cases in which we can, cases in which a Good Samaritan would extricate him. There you are, you were kidnapped, and nine years in bed with that violinist lie ahead of you. You have your own life to lead. You are sorry, but you simply cannot see giving up so much of your life to the sustaining of his. You cannot extricate yourself, and ask us to do so. I should have thought that—in light of his having no right to the use of your body—it was obvious that we do not have to accede to your being forced to give up so much. We can do what you ask. There is no injustice to the violinist in our doing so.

7. Following the lead of the opponents of abortion, I have throughout been speaking of the fetus merely as a person, and what I have been asking is whether or not the argument we began with, which proceeds only from the fetus's being a person, really does establish its conclusion. I have argued that it does not.

But of course there are arguments and arguments, and it may be said that I have simply fastened on the

wrong one. It may be said that what is important is not merely the fact that the fetus is a person, but that it is a person for whom the woman has a special kind of responsibility issuing from the fact that she is its mother. And it might be argued that all my analogies are therefore irrelevant—for you do not have that special kind of responsibility for that violinist, Henry Fonda does not have that special kind of responsibility for me. And our attention might be drawn to the fact that men and women both *are* compelled by law to provide support for their children.

I have in effect dealt (briefly) with this argument in section 4 above; but a (still briefer) recapitulation now may be in order. Surely we do not have any such "special responsibility" for a person unless we have assumed it, explicitly or implicitly. If a set of parents do not try to prevent pregnancy, do not obtain an abortion, but rather take it home with them, then they have assumed responsibility for it, they have given it rights, and they cannot *now* withdraw support from it at the cost of its life because they now find it difficult to go on providing for it. But if they have taken all reasonable precautions against having a child, they do not simply by virtue of their biological relationship to the child who comes into existence have a special responsibility for it. They may wish to assume responsibility for it, or they may not wish to. And I am suggesting that if assuming responsibility for it would require large sacrifices, then they may refuse. A Good Samaritan would not refuse—or anyway, a Splendid Samaritan, if the sacrifices that had to be made were enormous. But then so would a Good Samaritan assume responsibility for that violinist; so would Henry Fonda, if he is a Good Samaritan, fly in from the West Coast and assume responsibility for me.

8. My argument will be found unsatisfactory on two counts by many of those who want to regard abortion as morally permissible. First, while I do argue that abortion is not impermissible, I do not argue that it is always permissible. There may well be cases in which carrying the child to term required only Minimally Decent Samaritanism of the mother, and this is a standard we must not fall below. I am inclined to think it a merit of my account precisely that it does *not* give a general yes or a general no. It

allows for and supports our sense that, for example, a sick and desperately frightened fourteen-year-old schoolgirl, pregnant due to rape, may *of course* choose abortion, and that any law which rules this out is an insane law. And it also allows for and supports our sense that in other cases resort to abortion is even positively indecent. It would be indecent in the woman to request an abortion, and indecent in a doctor to perform it, if she is in her seventh month, and wants the abortion just to avoid the nuisance of postponing a trip abroad. The very fact that the arguments I have been drawing attention to treat all cases of abortion, or even all cases of abortion in which the mother's life is not at stake, as morally on a par ought to have made them suspect at the outset.

Secondly, while I am arguing for the permissibility of abortion in some cases, I am not arguing for the right to secure the death of the unborn child. It is easy to confuse these two things in that up to a certain point in the life of the fetus it is not able to survive outside the mother's body; hence removing it from her body guarantees its death. But they are importantly different. I have argued that you are not morally required to spend nine months in bed, sustaining the life of that violinist; but to say this is by no means to say that if, when you unplug yourself, there is a miracle and he survives, you then have a right to turn around and slit his throat. You may detach yourself even if this costs him his life; you have no right to be guaranteed his death, by some other means, if unplugging yourself does not kill him. There are some people who will feel dissatisfied by this feature of my argument. A woman may be utterly devastated by the thought of a child, a bit of herself, put out for adoption and never seen or heard of again. She may therefore want not merely that the child be detached from her, but more, that it die. Some opponents of abortion are inclined to regard this as beneath contempt—thereby showing insensitivity to what is surely a powerful source of despair. All the same, I agree that the desire for the child's death is not one which anybody may gratify, should it turn out to be possible to detach the child alive.

At this place, however, it should be remembered that we have only been pretending throughout that the fetus is a human being from the moment of conception. A very early abortion is surely not the killing of a person, and so is not dealt with by anything I have said here.

NOTES

1. Daniel Callahan, *Abortion: Law, Choice and Morality* (New York, 1970), p. 373. This book gives a fascinating survey of the available information on abortion. The Jewish tradition in David M. Feldman, *Birth Control in Jewish Law* (New York, 1963), part 5; the Catholic tradition in John T. Noonan, Jr., "An Almost Absolute Value in History," in *The Morality of Abortion*, ed. John T. Noonan, Jr. (Cambridge, Mass., 1970).

2. The term "direct" in the arguments I refer to is a technical one. Roughly, what is meant by "direct killing" is either killing as an end in itself, or killing as a means to some end, for example, the end of saving someone else's life. See note 5 on this page, for an example of its use.

3. Cf. *Encyclical Letter of Pope Pius XI on Christian Marriage*, St. Paul Editions (Boston, n.d.), p. 32: "However much we may pity the mother whose health and even life is gravely imperiled in the performance of the duty allotted to her by nature, nevertheless what could ever be a sufficient reason for excusing in any way the direct murder of the innocent? This is precisely what we are dealing with here." Noonan (*The Morality of Abortion*, p. 43) reads this as follows: "What cause can ever avail to excuse in any way the direct killing of the innocent? For it is a question of that."

4. The thesis in (4) is in an interesting way weaker than those in (1), (2), and (3): They rule out abortion even in cases in which both mother and child will die if the abortion is not performed. By contrast, one who held the view expressed in (4) could consistently say that one needn't prefer letting two persons die to killing one.

5. Cf. the following passage from Pius XII, Address to the Italian Catholic Society of Midwives: "The baby in the maternal breast has the right to life immediately from God.—Hence there is no man, no human authority, no science, no medical, eugenic, social, economic or moral 'indication' which can establish or grant a valid juridical ground for a direct deliberate disposition of an innocent human life, that is a disposition which looks to its destruction either as an end or as a means to another end perhaps in

itself not illicit.—The baby, still not born, is a man in the same degree and for the same reason as the mother" (quoted in Noonan, *The Morality of Abortion*, p. 45).

6. The need for a discussion of this argument was brought home to me by members of the Society of

Ethical and Legal Philosophy, to whom this paper was originally presented.

7. For a discussion of the difficulties involved, and a survey of the European experience with such laws, see *The Good Samaritan and the Law*, ed. James M. Ratcliffe (New York, 1966).

R E A D I N G

Why Abortion Is Immoral

DON MARQUIS

Study Questions

1. On what major assumptions is the argument by Marquis based?
2. What basic principles of antiabortionists and prochoicers does Marquis cite?
3. How do antiabortionists and prochoicers each attempt to refine their position? How does this reflect different definitions of *human being* or *person?*
4. With what unproblematic assumptions does Marquis believe we should begin and why?
5. Why is the loss of one's life the greatest loss one can suffer?
6. What, then, is it that makes killing a person wrong? Does this make euthanasia wrong?
7. Why does Marquis believe that this also makes killing a fetus wrong?
8. Why does it not follow, according to Marquis, that contraception is wrong?

THE VIEW that abortion is, with rare exceptions, seriously immoral has received little support in the recent philosophical literature. No doubt most philosophers affiliated with secular institutions of higher education believe that the anti-abortion position is either a symptom of irrational religious dogma or a conclusion generated by seriously confused philosophical argument. The purpose of this essay is to undermine this general belief. This essay sets out an argument that purports to show, as well as any argument in ethics can show, that abortion is, except

possibly in rare cases, seriously immoral, that it is in the same moral category as killing an innocent adult human being.

The argument is based on a major assumption. Many of the most insightful and careful writers on the ethics of abortion—such as Joel Feinberg, Michael Tooley, Mary Anne Warren, H. Tristram Engelhardt, Jr., L. W. Sumner, John T. Noonan, Jr., and Philip Devine[1]—believe that whether or not abortion is morally permissible stands or falls on whether or not a fetus is the sort of being whose life it is seriously wrong to end. The argument of this essay will assume, but not argue, that they are correct.

Also, this essay will neglect issues of great importance to a complete ethics of abortion. Some anti-abortionists will allow that certain abortions, such as abortion before implantation or abortion when the life of a woman is threatened by a pregnancy or abortion after rape, may be morally permissible. This essay will not explore the casuistry of these hard cases. The purpose of this essay is to develop a general argument for the claim that the overwhelming majority of deliberate abortions are seriously immoral.

I

A sketch of standard anti-abortion and pro-choice arguments exhibits how those arguments possess certain symmetries that explain why partisans of those positions are so convinced of the correctness of their own positions, why they are not successful in convincing their opponents, and why, to others, this issue seems to be unresolvable. An analysis of the nature of this standoff suggests a strategy for surmounting it.

Don Marquis, "Why Abortion is Immoral," from *The Journal of Philosophy*, vol. LXXXVI, no. 4 (April 1989) 183–185, 200–202. Reprinted by The Journal of Philosophy.

Consider the way a typical anti-abortionist argues. She will argue or assert that life is present from the moment of conception or that fetuses look like babies or that fetuses possess a characteristic such as a genetic code that is both necessary and sufficient for being human. Anti-abortionists seem to believe that (1) the truth of all of these claims is quite obvious, and (2) establishing any of these claims is sufficient to show that abortion is morally akin to murder.

A standard pro-choice strategy exhibits similarities. The pro-choicer will argue or assert that fetuses are not persons or that fetuses are not rational agents or that fetuses are not social beings. Pro-choicers seem to believe that (1) the truth of any of these claims is quite obvious, and (2) establishing any of these claims is sufficient to show that an abortion is not a wrongful killing.

In fact, both the pro-choice and the anti-abortion claims do seem to be true, although the "it looks like a baby" claim is more difficult to establish the earlier the pregnancy. We seem to have a standoff. How can it be resolved?

As everyone who has taken a bit of logic knows, if any of these arguments concerning abortion is a good argument, it requires not only some claim characterizing fetuses, but also some general moral principle that ties a characteristic of fetuses to having or not having the right to life or to some other moral characteristic that will generate the obligation or the lack of obligation not to end the life of a fetus. Accordingly, the arguments of the anti-abortionist and the pro-choicer need a bit of filling in to be regarded as adequate.

Note what each partisan will say. The anti-abortionist will claim that her position is supported by such generally accepted moral principles as "It is always prima facie seriously wrong to take a human life" or "It is always prima facie seriously wrong to end the life of a baby." Since these are generally accepted moral principles, her position is certainly not obviously wrong. The pro-choicer will claim that her position is supported by such plausible moral principles as "Being a person is what gives an individual intrinsic moral worth" or "It is only seriously prima facie wrong to take the life of a member of the human community." Since these are generally

accepted moral principles, the pro-choice position is certainly not obviously wrong. Unfortunately, we have again arrived at a standoff.

Now, how might one deal with this standoff? The standard approach is to try to show how the moral principles of one's opponent lose their plausibility under analysis. It is easy to see how this is possible. On the one hand, the anti-abortionist will defend a moral principle concerning the wrongness of killing which tends to be broad in scope in order that even fetuses at an early stage of pregnancy will fall under it. The problem with broad principles is that they often embrace too much. In this particular instance, the principle "It is always prima facie wrong to take a human life" seems to entail that it is wrong to end the existence of a living human cancer-cell culture, on the grounds that the culture is both living and human. Therefore, it seems that the anti-abortionist's favored principle is too broad.

On the other hand, the pro-choicer wants to find a moral principle concerning the wrongness of killing which tends to be narrow in scope in order that fetuses will *not* fall under it. The problem with narrow principles is that they often do not embrace enough. Hence, the needed principles such as "It is prima facie seriously wrong to kill only persons" or "It is prima facie wrong to kill only rational agents" do not explain why it is wrong to kill infants or young children or the severely retarded or even perhaps the severely mentally ill. Therefore, we seem again to have a standoff. The anti-abortionist charges, not unreasonably, that pro-choice principles concerning killing are too narrow to be acceptable; the pro-choicer charges, not unreasonably, that anti-abortionist principles concerning killing are too broad to be acceptable.

Attempts by both sides to patch up the difficulties in their positions run into further difficulties. The anti-abortionist will try to remove the problem in her position by reformulating her principle concerning killing in terms of human beings. Now we end up with: "It is always prima facie seriously wrong to end the life of a human being." This principle has the advantage of avoiding the problem of the human cancer-cell culture counterexample. But this advantage is purchased at a high price. For although it is clear that a fetus is both human and alive, it is not at all clear that a fetus is a human *being*. There is at least something to be said for the view that something becomes a human being only after a process of development, and that therefore first trimester fetuses and perhaps all fetuses are not yet human beings. Hence, the anti-abortionist, by this move, has merely exchanged one problem for another.[2]

The pro-choicer fares no better. She may attempt to find reasons why killing infants, young children, and the severely retarded is wrong which are independent of her major principle that is supposed to explain the wrongness of taking human life, but which will not also make abortion immoral. This is no easy task. Appeals to social utility will seem satisfactory only to those who resolve not to think of the enormous difficulties with a utilitarian account of the wrongness of killing and the significant social costs of preserving the lives of the unproductive.[3] A pro-choice strategy that extends the definition of "person" to infants or even to young children seems just as arbitrary as an anti-abortion strategy that extends the definition of "human being" to fetuses. Again, we find symmetries in the two positions and we arrive at a standoff.

There are even further problems that reflect symmetries in the two positions. In addition to counterexample problems, or the arbitrary application problems that can be exchanged for them, the standard anti-abortionist principle "It is prima facie seriously wrong to kill a human being," or one of its variants, can be objected to on the grounds of ambiguity. If "human being" is taken to be a *biological* category, then the anti-abortionist is left with the problem of explaining why a merely biological category should make a moral difference. Why, it is asked, is it any more reasonable to base a moral conclusion on the number of chromosomes in one's cells than on the color of one's skin?[4] If "human being," on the other hand, is taken to be a *moral* category, then the claim that a fetus is a human being cannot be taken to be a premise in the anti-abortion argument, for it is precisely what needs to be established. Hence, either the anti-abortionist's main category is a morally irrelevant, merely biological category, or it is of no use to the anti-abortionist in establishing (noncircularly, of course) that abortion is wrong.

Although this problem with the anti-abortionist position is often noticed, it is less often noticed that the pro-choice position suffers from an analogous problem. The principle "Only persons have the right to life" also suffers from an ambiguity. The term "person" is typically defined in terms of psychological characteristics, although there will certainly be disagreement concerning which characteristics are most important. Supposing that this matter can be settled, the pro-choicer is left with the problem of explaining why *psychological* characteristics should make a *moral* difference. If the pro-choicer should attempt to deal with this problem by claiming that an explanation is not necessary, that in fact we do treat such a cluster of psychological properties as having moral significance, the sharp-witted anti-abortionist should have a ready response. We do treat being both living and human as having moral significance. If it is legitimate for the pro-choicer to demand that the anti-abortionist provide an explanation of the connection between the biological character of being a human being and the wrongness of being killed (even though people accept this connection), then it is legitimate for the anti-abortionist to demand that the pro-choicer provide an explanation of the connection between psychological criteria for being a person and the wrongness of being killed (even though that connection is accepted).[5]

Feinberg has attempted to meet this objection (he calls psychological personhood "commonsense personhood"):

> The characteristics that confer commonsense personhood are not arbitrary bases for rights and duties, such as race, sex or species membership; rather they are traits that make sense out of rights and duties and without which those moral attributes would have no point or function. It is because people are conscious; have a sense of their personal identities; have plans, goals, and projects; experience emotions; are liable to pains, anxieties, and frustrations; can reason and bargain, and so on—it is because of these attributes that people have values and interests, desires and expectations of their own, including a stake in their own futures, and a personal well-being of a sort we cannot ascribe to unconscious or nonrational beings. Because of their developed capacities they can assume duties and responsibilities and can have and make claims on one another. Only because of their sense of self, their life plans, their value hierarchies, and their stakes in

their own futures can they be ascribed fundamental rights. There is nothing arbitrary about these linkages (op. cit., p. 270).

The plausible aspects of this attempt should not be taken to obscure its implausible features. There is a great deal to be said for the view that being a psychological person under some description is a necessary condition for having duties. One cannot have a duty unless one is capable of behaving morally, and a being's capability of behaving morally will require having a certain psychology. It is far from obvious, however, that having rights entails consciousness or rationality, as Feinberg suggests. We speak of the rights of the severely retarded or the severely mentally ill, yet some of these persons are not rational. We speak of the rights of the temporarily unconscious. The New Jersey Supreme Court based their decision in the Quinlan case on Karen Ann Quinlan's right to privacy, and she was known to be permanently unconscious at that time. Hence, Feinberg's claim that having rights entails being conscious is, on its face, obviously false.

Of course, it might not make sense to attribute rights to a being that would never in its natural history have certain psychological traits. This modest connection between psychological personhood and moral personhood will create a place for Karen Ann Quinlan and the temporarily unconscious. But then it makes a place for fetuses also. Hence, it does not serve Feinberg's pro-choice purposes. Accordingly, it seems that the pro-choicer will have as much difficulty bridging the gap between psychological personhood and personhood in the moral sense as the anti-abortionist has bridging the gap between being a biological human being and being a human being in the moral sense.

Furthermore, the pro-choicer cannot any more escape her problem by making person a purely moral category than the anti-abortionist could escape by the analogous move. For if person is a moral category, then the pro-choicer is left without the resources for establishing (noncircularly, of course) the claim that a fetus is not a person, which is an essential premise in her argument. Again, we have both a symmetry and a standoff between pro-choice and anti-abortion views.

Passions in the abortion debate run high. There are both plausibilities and difficulties with the standard

positions. Accordingly, it is hardly surprising that partisans of either side embrace with fervor the moral generalizations that support the conclusions they preanalytically favor, and reject with disdain the moral generalizations of their opponents as being subject to inescapable difficulties. It is easy to believe that the counterexamples to one's own moral principles are merely temporary difficulties that will dissolve in the wake of further philosophical research, and that the counterexamples to the principles of one's opponents are as straightforward as the contradiction between A and O propositions in traditional logic. This might suggest to an impartial observer (if there are any) that the abortion issue is unresolvable.

There is a way out of this apparent dialectical quandary. The moral generalizations of both sides are not quite correct. The generalizations hold for the most part, for the usual cases. This suggests that they are all *accidental* generalizations, that the moral claims made by those on both sides of the dispute do not touch on the *essence* of the matter.

This use of the distinction between essence and accident is not meant to invoke obscure metaphysical categories. Rather, it is intended to reflect the rather atheoretical nature of the abortion discussion. If the generalization a partisan in the abortion dispute adopts were derived from the reason why ending the life of a human being is wrong, then there could not be exceptions to that generalization unless some special case obtains in which there are even more powerful countervailing reasons. Such generalizations would not be merely accidental generalizations; they would point to, or be based upon, the essence of the wrongness of killing, what it is that makes killing wrong. All this suggests that a necessary condition of resolving the abortion controversy is a more theoretical account of the wrongness of killing. After all, if we merely believe, but do not understand, why killing adult human beings such as ourselves is wrong, how could we conceivably show that abortion is either immoral or permissible?

II

In order to develop such an account, we can start from the following unproblematic assumption concerning our own case: it is wrong to kill *us*. Why is it wrong? Some answers can be easily eliminated. It might be said that what makes killing us wrong is that a killing brutalizes the one who kills. But the brutalization consists of being inured to the performance of an act that is hideously immoral; hence, the brutalization does not explain the immorality. It might be said that what makes killing us wrong is the great loss others would experience due to our absence. Although such hubris is understandable, such an explanation does not account for the wrongness of killing hermits, or those whose lives are relatively independent and whose friends find it easy to make new friends.

A more obvious answer is better. What primarily makes killing wrong is neither its effect on the murderer nor its effect on the victim's friends and relatives, but its effect on the victim. The loss of one's life is one of the greatest losses one can suffer. The loss of one's life deprives one of all the experiences, activities, projects, and enjoyments that would otherwise have constituted one's future. Therefore, killing someone is wrong, primarily because the killing inflicts (one of) the greatest possible losses on the victim. To describe this as the loss of life can be misleading, however. The change in my biological state does not by itself make killing me wrong. The effect of the loss of my biological life is the loss to me of all those activities, projects, experiences, and enjoyments which would otherwise have constituted my future personal life. These activities, projects, experiences, and enjoyments are either valuable for their own sakes or are means to something else that is valuable for its own sake. Some parts of my future are not valued by me now, but will come to be valued by me as I grow older and as my values and capacities change. When I am killed, I am deprived both of what I now value which would have been part of my future personal life, but also what I would come to value. Therefore, when I die, I am deprived of all of the value of my future. Inflicting this loss on me is ultimately what makes killing me wrong. This being the case, it would seem that what makes killing any adult human being prima facie seriously wrong is the loss of his or her future.[6]

How should this rudimentary theory of the wrongness of killing be evaluated? It cannot be faulted for deriving an "ought" from an "is," for it does not. The analysis assumes that killing me (or you, reader) is prima facie seriously wrong. The point of the analysis is to establish which natural property ultimately explains the wrongness of the killing, given that it is wrong. A natural property will ultimately explain the wrongness of killing, only if (1) the explanation fits with our intuitions about the matter and (2) there is no other natural property that provides the basis for a better explanation of the wrongness of killing. This analysis rests on the intuition that what makes killing a particular human or animal wrong is what it does to that particular human or animal. What makes killing wrong is some natural effect or other of the killing. Some would deny this. For instance, a divine-command theorist in ethics would deny it. Surely this denial is, however, one of those features of divine-command theory which renders it so implausible.

The claim that what makes killing wrong is the loss of the victim's future is directly supported by two considerations. In the first place, this theory explains why we regard killing as one of the worst of crimes. Killing is especially wrong, because it deprives the victim of more than perhaps any other crime. In the second place, people with AIDS or cancer who know they are dying believe, of course, that dying is a very bad thing for them. They believe that the loss of a future to them that they would otherwise have experienced is what makes their premature death a very bad thing for them. A better theory of the wrongness of killing would require a different natural property associated with killing which better fits with the attitudes of the dying. What could it be?

The view that what makes killing wrong is the loss to the victim of the value of the victim's future gains additional support when some of its implications are examined. In the first place, it is incompatible with the view that it is wrong to kill only beings who are biologically human. It is possible that there exists a different species from another planet whose members have a future like ours. Since having a future like that is what makes killing someone wrong, this theory entails that it would be wrong to kill members of such a species. Hence, this theory is opposed to the claim that only life that is biologically human has great moral worth, a claim which many anti-abortionists have seemed to adopt. This opposition, which this theory has in common with personhood theories, seems to be a merit of the theory.

In the second place, the claim that the loss of one's future is the wrong-making feature of one's being killed entails the possibility that the futures of some actual nonhuman mammals on our own planet are sufficiently like ours that it is seriously wrong to kill them also. Whether some animals do have the same right to life as human beings depends on adding to the account of just what it is about my future or the futures of other adult human beings which makes it wrong to kill us. No such additional account will be offered in this essay. Undoubtedly, the provision of such an account would be a very difficult matter. Undoubtedly, any such account would be quite controversial. Hence, it surely should not reflect badly on this sketch of an elementary theory of the wrongness of killing that it is indeterminate with respect to some very difficult issues regarding animal rights.

In the third place, the claim that the loss of one's future is the wrong-making feature of one's being killed does not entail, as sanctity-of-human-life theories do, that active euthanasia is wrong. Persons who are severely and incurably ill, who face a future of pain and despair, and who wish to die will not have suffered a loss if they are killed. It is, strictly speaking, the value of a human's future which makes killing wrong in this theory. This being so, killing does not necessarily wrong some persons who are sick and dying. Of course, there may be other reasons for a prohibition of active euthanasia, but that is another matter. Sanctity-of-human-life theories seem to hold that active euthanasia is seriously wrong even in an individual case where there seems to be good reason for it independently of public policy considerations. This consequence is most implausible, and it is a plus for the claim that the loss of a future of value is what makes killing wrong that it does not share this consequence.

In the fourth place, the account of the wrongness of killing defended in this essay does straightforwardly entail that it is prima facie seriously wrong to kill children and infants, for we do presume that they have futures of value. Since we do believe that it is wrong to kill defenseless little babies, it is important that a theory of the wrongness of killing easily account for this. Personhood theories of the wrongness of killing, on the other hand, cannot straightforwardly account for the wrongness of killing infants and young children.[7] Hence, such theories must add special ad hoc accounts of the wrongness of killing the young. The plausibility of such ad hoc theories seems to be a function of how desperately one wants such theories to work. The claim that the primary wrong-making feature of a killing is the loss to the victim of the value of its future accounts for the wrongness of killing young children and infants directly; it makes the wrongness of such acts as obvious as we actually think it is. This is a further merit of this theory. Accordingly, it seems that this value of a future-like-ours theory of the wrongness of killing shares strengths of both sanctity-of-life and personhood accounts while avoiding weaknesses of both. In addition, it meshes with a central intuition concerning what makes killing wrong.

The claim that the primary wrong-making feature of a killing is the loss to the victim of the value of its future has obvious consequences for the ethics of abortion. The future of a standard fetus includes a set of experiences, projects, activities, and such which are identical with the futures of adult human beings and are identical with the futures of young children. Since the reason that is sufficient to explain why it is wrong to kill human beings after the time of birth is a reason that also applies to fetuses, it follows that abortion is prima facie seriously morally wrong.

This argument does not rely on the invalid inference that, since it is wrong to kill persons, it is wrong to kill potential persons also. The category that is morally central to this analysis is the category of having a valuable future like ours; it is not the category of personhood. The argument to the conclusion that abortion is prima facie seriously morally wrong proceeded independently of the notion of person or potential person or any equivalent. Someone may wish to start with this analysis in terms of the value of a human future, conclude that abortion is, except perhaps in rare circumstances, seriously morally wrong, infer that fetuses have the right to life, and then call fetuses "persons" as a result of their having the right to life. Clearly, in this case, the category of person is being used to state the *conclusion* of the analysis rather than to generate the *argument* of the analysis.

The structure of this anti-abortion argument can be both illuminated and defended by comparing it to what appears to be the best argument for the wrongness of the wanton infliction of pain on animals. This latter argument is based on the assumption that it is prima facie wrong to inflict pain on me (or you, reader). What is the natural property associated with the infliction of pain which makes such infliction wrong? The obvious answer seems to be that the infliction of pain causes suffering and that suffering is a misfortune. The suffering caused by the infliction of pain is what makes the wanton infliction of pain on me wrong. The wanton infliction of pain on other adult humans causes suffering. The wanton infliction of pain on animals causes suffering. Since causing suffering is what makes the wanton infliction of pain wrong and since the wanton infliction of pain on animals causes suffering, it follows that the wanton infliction of pain on animals is wrong.

This argument for the wrongness of the wanton infliction of pain on animals shares a number of structural features with the argument for the serious prima facie wrongness of abortion. Both arguments start with an obvious assumption concerning what it is wrong to do to me (or you, reader). Both then look for the characteristic or the consequence of the wrong action which makes the action wrong. Both recognize that the wrong-making feature of these immoral actions is a property of actions sometimes directed at individuals other than postnatal human beings. If the structure of the argument for the wrongness of the wanton infliction of pain on animals is sound, then the structure of the argument for the prima facie serious wrongness of abortion is also sound, for the structure of the two arguments is the same. The structure common to both is the key to the explanation of how the wrongness of abortion can be demonstrated without recourse to the category of person. In neither argument is that category crucial.

This defense of an argument for the wrongness of abortion in terms of a structurally similar argument for the wrongness of the wanton infliction of pain on animals succeeds only if the account regarding animals is the correct account. Is it? In the first place, it seems plausible. In the second place, its major competition is Kant's account. Kant believed that we do not have direct duties to animals at all, because they are not persons. Hence, Kant had to explain and justify the wrongness of inflicting pain on animals on the grounds that "he who is hard in his dealings with animals becomes hard also in his dealing with men."[8] The problem with Kant's account is that there seems to be no reason for accepting this latter claim unless Kant's account is rejected. If the alternative to Kant's account is accepted, then it is easy to understand why someone who is indifferent to inflicting pain on animals is also indifferent to inflicting pain on humans, for one is indifferent to what makes inflicting pain wrong in both cases. But, if Kant's account is accepted, there is no intelligible reason why one who is hard in his dealings with animals (or crabgrass or stones) should also be hard in his dealings with men. After all, men are persons: animals are no more persons than crabgrass or stones. Persons are Kant's crucial moral category. Why, in short, should a Kantian accept the basic claim in Kant's argument?

Hence, Kant's argument for the wrongness of inflicting pain on animals rests on a claim that, in a world of Kantian moral agents, is demonstrably false. Therefore, the alternative analysis, being more plausible anyway, should be accepted. Since this alternative analysis has the same structure as the anti-abortion argument being defended here, we have further support for the argument for the immorality of abortion being defended in this essay.

Of course, this value of a future-like-ours argument, if sound, shows only that abortion is prima facie wrong, not that it is wrong in any and all circumstances. Since the loss of the future to a standard fetus, if killed, is, however, at least as great a loss as the loss of the future to a standard adult human being who is killed, abortion, like ordinary killing, could be justified only by the most compelling reasons. The loss of one's life is almost the greatest misfortune that can happen to one. Presumably abortion could be justified in some circumstances, only if the loss consequent on failing to abort would be at least as great. Accordingly, morally permissible abortions will be rare indeed unless, perhaps, they occur so early in pregnancy that a fetus is not yet definitely an individual. Hence, this argument should be taken as showing that abortion is presumptively very seriously wrong, where the presumption is very strong—as strong as the presumption that killing another adult human being is wrong. . . .

V

In this essay, it has been argued that the correct ethic of the wrongness of killing can be extended to fetal life and used to show that there is a strong presumption that any abortion is morally impermissible. If the ethic of killing adopted here entails, however, that contraception is also seriously immoral, then there would appear to be a difficulty with the analysis of this essay.

But this analysis does not entail that contraception is wrong. Of course, contraception prevents the actualization of a possible future of value. Hence, it follows from the claim that futures of value should be maximized that contraception is prima facie immoral. This obligation to maximize does not exist, however; furthermore, nothing in the ethics of killing in this paper entails that it does. The ethics of killing in this essay would entail that contraception is wrong only if something were denied a human future of value by contraception. Nothing at all is denied such a future by contraception, however.

Candidates for a subject of harm by contraception fall into four categories: (1) some sperm or other, (2) some ovum or other, (3) a sperm and an ovum separately, and (4) a sperm and an ovum together. Assigning the harm to some sperm is utterly arbitrary, for no reason can be given for making a sperm the subject of harm rather than an ovum. Assigning the harm to some ovum is utterly arbitrary, for no reason can be given for making an ovum the subject of harm rather than a sperm. One might attempt to avoid these problems by insisting that contraception deprives both the sperm and the ovum separately of a valuable future like ours. On this alternative, too many futures are lost. Contraception was supposed to be wrong, because it deprives us of one future of value, not two. One might attempt to avoid this problem by holding that contraception deprives the combination of sperm and ovum of a valuable future like ours. But here the definite article misleads. At the time of contraception, there are hundreds of millions of sperm, one (released) ovum and millions of possible combinations of all of these. There is no actual combination at all. Is the subject of the loss to be a merely possible combination? Which one? This alternative does not yield an actual subject of harm either. Accordingly, the immorality of contraception is not entailed by the loss of a future-like-ours argument simply because there is no nonarbitrarily identifiable subject of the loss in the case of contraception.

VI

The purpose of this essay has been to set out an argument for the serious presumptive wrongness of abortion subject to the assumption that the moral permissibility of abortion stands or falls on the moral status of the fetus. Since a fetus possesses a property, the possession of which in adult human beings is sufficient to make killing an adult human being wrong, abortion is wrong. This way of dealing with the problem of abortion seems superior to other approaches to the ethics of abortion, because it rests on an ethics of killing which is close to self-evident, because the crucial morally relevant property clearly applies to fetuses, and because the argument avoids the usual equivocations on "human life," "human being," or "person." The argument rests neither on religious claims nor on Papal dogma. It is not subject to the objection of "speciesism." Its soundness is compatible with the moral permissibility of euthanasia and contraception. It deals with our intuitions concerning young children.

Finally, this analysis can be viewed as resolving a standard problem—indeed, *the* standard problem— concerning the ethics of abortion. Clearly, it is wrong to kill adult human beings. Clearly, it is not wrong to end the life of some arbitrarily chosen single human cell. Fetuses seem to be like arbitrarily chosen human cells in some respects and like adult humans in other respects. The problem of the ethics of abortion is the problem of determining the fetal property that settles this moral controversy. The thesis of this essay is that the problem of the ethics of abortion, so understood, is solvable.

NOTES

1. Feinberg, "Abortion," in *Matters of Life and Death: New Introductory Essays in Moral Philosophy*, Tom Regan, ed. (New York: Random House, 1986), pp. 256–293; Tooley, "Abortion and Infanticide," *Philosophy and Public Affairs*, *II*, 1 (1972): 37–65, Tooley, *Abortion and Infanticide* (New York: Oxford, 1984); Warren, "On the Moral and Legal Status of Abortion," *The Monist*, *LVII*, 1 (1973): 43–61; Engelhardt, "The Ontology of Abortion," *Ethics*, *LXXXIV*, 3 (1974): 217–234; Sumner, *Abortion and Moral Theory* (Princeton: University Press, 1981); Noonan, "An Almost Absolute Value in History," in *The Morality of Abortion: Legal and Historical Perspectives*, Noonan, ed. (Cambridge: Harvard, 1970); and Devine, *The Ethics of Homicide* (Ithaca: Cornell, 1978).
2. For interesting discussions of this issue, see Warren Quinn, "Abortion: Identity and Loss," *Philosophy*

and *Public Affairs*, *XIII*, 1 (1984): 24–54; and Lawrence C. Becker, "Human Being: The Boundaries of the Concept," *Philosophy and Public Affairs*, *IV*, 4 (1975): 334–359.

3. For example, see my "Ethics and the Elderly: Some Problems," in Stuart Spicker, Kathleen Woodward, and David Van Tassel, eds., *Aging and the Elderly: Humanistic Perspectives in Gerontology* (Atlantic Highlands, NJ: Humanities, 1978), pp. 341–355.

4. See Warren, op. cit., and Tooley, "Abortion and Infanticide."

5. This seems to be the fatal flaw in Warren's treatment of this issue.

6. I have been most influenced on this matter by Jonathan Glover, *Causing Death and Saving Lives* (New York: Penguin, 1977), ch. 3; and Robert Young, "What Is So Wrong with Killing People?" *Philosophy*, *LIV*, 210 (1979): 515–528.

7. Feinberg, Tooley, Warren, and Engelhardt have all dealt with this problem.

8. "Duties to Animals and Spirits," in *Lectures on Ethics*, Louis Infeld, trans. (New York: Harper, 1963), p. 239.

REVIEW EXERCISES

1. Outline the various stages of fetal development.
2. Explain the conclusions of *Roe* v. *Wade* and *Planned Parenthood* v. *Casey*.
3. Give a utilitarian argument for abortion. Give one against abortion. Are these act or rule utilitarian arguments? Explain.
4. Describe how Thomson uses the violinist analogy to make an argument about the moral permissibility of abortion.
5. Use Method I to make one argument for and one against abortion.
6. Which of the positions under Method II does each of the following statement exemplify?
   a. Because this fetus has all the potential to develop the abilities of a person, it has all the rights of a person.
   b. Only when a being can think and communicate does it have full moral status. Because a fetus does not have these abilities, it has neither moral rights nor claims.
   c. If it is a human being, then it has full moral status and rights.
   d. Its capacity to feel pain gives a being full moral status. The fetus has this capactity beginning in the fifth or sixth month, and so abortion is not morally justifiable beyond that stage.
   e. Early-term fetuses do not have as much moral significance as later-term fetuses because their potential is not as well developed as later.

DISCUSSION CASES

1. Abortion for Sex Selection. The sex of a child can now be determined before birth. In the waiting room of a local women's clinic, June has started a conversation with another woman, Ann. She finds out that each woman is there for an amniocentesis to determine the sex of her fetus. June reveals that she wants to know the sex because her husband and his family really want a boy. Because they plan to have only one child, they plan to end this pregnancy if it is a girl and try again. Ann tells her that her reason is different. She is a genetic carrier of a particular kind of muscular dystrophy. Duchenne muscular dystrophy is a sex-linked disease that is inherited through the mother. Only males develop the disease, and each male child has a 50 percent chance of having it. The disease causes muscle weakness and often some mental retardation. It also causes death through respiratory failure, usually in early adulthood. Ann does not want to risk having such a child, and this abnormality cannot yet be determined through prenatal testing. Thus, if the prenatal diagnosis reveals that her fetus is male, she plans to end this pregnancy.

What do you think of the use of prenatal diagnosis and abortion for purposes of sex selection in these or in other cases?

2. Father's Consent to Abortion. Jim and Sue had been planning to have a child for two years. Finally, she became pregnant. However, their marriage had been a rough one, and by the time she was in her third month of pregnancy they had decided to divorce. At that point, both parents were ambivalent about the pregnancy. They had both wanted the child, but now things were different. Sue finally decided that she did not want to raise a child alone and did not want to raise Jim's child. She wanted to get on with her life. However, Jim had long wanted a child, and he realized that the developing fetus was partly his own because he had provided half of its genetic makeup. He did not want Sue to end the pregnancy. He wanted to keep and raise the child. The case was currently being heard by the court.

Although the primary decision is a legal one, do you think that Jim had any moral rights in this case or should the decision be strictly Sue's? Why or why not?

3. Parental Consent to Abortion. Judy is a high-school sophomore and fifteen years old. She recently became sexually active with her boyfriend. She does not want to tell him that she is now pregnant, and she does not feel that she can talk to her parents. They have been quite strict with her and would condemn her recent behavior. They also oppose abortion. Judy would like simply to end this pregnancy and start over with her life. However, minors in her state must get parental consent for an abortion; it is a medical procedure, and parents must consent to other medical procedures for their children.

What should Judy do? Do you agree that states should require parental consent for abortion for their minor children? Why or why not?

4. Pregnant Woman Detained. In 1995, a woman who was pregnant and refused to discontinue her use of cocaine was reported by her obstetrician to child-abuse authorities, who obtained an order from the juvenile court to take custody of the unborn child. Obviously, this involved detaining the mother. The case was settled after the child was born. If the fetus was regarded as a child who was being abused, then would it be reasonable in your view to detain the mother? Would it also be reasonable for a pregnant woman to be able to use a car pool lane by counting her fetus as a second person in the car? (Reported by Tamar Lewin, "Detention of Pregnant Woman for Drug Use Is Struck Down," *The New York Times*, April 23, 1997, p. A10.)

YOU MAKE THE DECISION

Apply the theories and issues discussed in this chapter by accessing this animated simulation on the Ethics Resource Center.

Use the passkey that accompanies your book to gain access. If you do not have a passkey, visit cengagebrain.com to purchase instant access to additional study material.

12

Sexual Morality

IN A comprehensive study of data from fifty-nine nations on sexual behavior done by *The Lancet*, a British medical journal, many myths are dispelled. Although the study was conducted by asking people to self-report, and thus subject to some error, it was thought to be basically reliable. The survey found that sexual interaction is not starting earlier than it was a decade ago. The study found that the first sexual experience for both men and women was in the late teens, "from 15 to 19 years old—with generally younger ages for women than for men, especially in developing countries."[1] Whereas the first sexual experiences of men and women in Britain was sixteen and one-half and seventeen and one-half, respectively, in Indonesia it was twenty-four and one-half and eighteen and one-half. People in industrialized countries had higher numbers of partners than those in countries with higher rates for the human immunodeficiency virus (HIV) and acquired immune deficiency syndrome (AIDS). And there was some variation in this, as men and women in Western countries had equal numbers of sexual partners, whereas men in Cameroon and Kenya "had multiple partners while women had only one."[2] The study also found that married people had more sex than did singles. Among the reasons teenagers cited for not having had sex were having made a conscious decision to wait and concerns about sexually transmitted diseases (STDs) and pregnancy.[3]

Moreover, a recent study that explored teens' post-sex emotions found that many first-time experiences resulted in guilt or feeling manipulated, with girls more often reporting this than boys. Of the teens who had engaged in oral sex, 41 percent "said they felt bad about themselves later" and "nearly 20 percent felt guilty, and 25 percent felt used," while the figures were 42 percent and 38 percent for sexual intercourse.[4] Even though teenagers in the United States are not more sexually active than those in other Western countries, they have the highest birthrate. They are also more likely to become pregnant. "American girls are four times as likely as German girls to become pregnant, almost five times as likely as French girls to have a baby, and more than seven times as likely as Dutch girls to have an abortion."[5] Researchers believe this is because, contrary to other countries, "we don't educate about birth control in sex education classes, we don't discuss it at home, we don't give teens good access to it, and we don't advertise it in our media."[6] Some people believe that doing so would increase the rate of pregnancy, but studies have found that it does not. Furthermore, "abstinence-only" sex education that does not also include information about contraception has not led to decreased sexual activity, but it has increased the incidence of STDs. Although the birthrates for U.S. teens have been declining in the past decade, it still is the case that those who do give birth are more likely not to finish high school and to end up on welfare.[7]

The incidence of cohabitation, or living with one's partner before marriage, has also increased dramatically in recent years, nearly tripling between 1990 and

2000.[8] As of May 2009, there were more than five million cohabiting couples in the United States. Further, "the majority of cohabitants either break up or marry within five years."[9] With the rise in the practice of cohabitation comes the fact that people marry later, and those who marry after age twenty-five are less likely to divorce than those who marry in their teens. It is often assumed that cohabiting couples who marry are more likely to divorce than those who did not live together before they married, and there is some evidence for this.[10] "Couples who live together before they get married are less likely to stay married," a recent study has found.[11] However, this may also be because of the type of people who do this, being more liberal and less religious, for example. If they are engaged or committed or their relationship is based on love, then they are no less likely to later divorce.[12]

Still, people may actually be more conservative sexually than they are depicted in the media. Some 70 percent of Americans report having had only one sexual partner in the previous year, and 80 percent said they have never had an extramarital affair.[13] Several groups that promote sexual abstinence before marriage have formed. According to members of these groups, "having sex before achieving a level of intimacy is a hindrance to building a quality relationship."[14] Many people believe there should be no sex without love. However, there continues to be a gender difference concerning the importance of love to sex. More adolescent females than males think affection should be a precursor to sexual intimacy.[15]

Almost everywhere in the world, different sexual standards apply to men and to women. In some Arab countries, men and women may not even socialize together in public. A particularly extreme example of sexual practice is that of female genital mutilation or so-called female circumcision. Although many countries have outlawed it, the practice persists in more than twenty-eight African countries and several countries in Asia and the Middle East as well as some immigrant communities in the West. It is estimated that 135 million women and girls have been subjected to this practice, with 2 million girls every year, or 6,000 each day.[16] In rural Ethiopia, up to 90 percent of girls still undergo this practice. The practice involves degrees of severity, from excision of the skin surrounding the clitoris to removal of all or part of the clitoris and some of the surrounding tissues, to stitching the labia together so that only a small opening remains. Among the cultural and parental reasons given for these practices are to enable families to exercise control over reproduction, to keep women virgins until marriage, and to reduce or eliminate female sexual pleasure.[17] The procedure is usually done without even a local anesthetic and often with unclean and crude instruments. Often a reverse cutting is necessary later in marriage before intercourse can take place, which can be quite painful. It also causes problems in childbirth.[18] In fact, this procedure raises "by more than 50 percent the likelihood that the woman or her baby will die."[19] The more extensive forms of cutting resulted in higher rates of maternal and infant death during childbirth" and "even many years later." The incidence is thought actually to be higher because the study on which these figures were based was for women who delivered in hospitals, while many women, especially in Africa, deliver their babies at home.[20]

The 1996 U.S. Federal Criminalization of Female Genital Mutilation Act prohibited this practice for women under eighteen years of age. Human rights groups have lobbied internationally for an end to this practice, which in some countries is "routinely forced on girls as young as four or five years old, and . . . sustained through social coercion."[21] In Africa, between 60 percent and 90 percent of all women and girls in certain countries undergo the procedure, even in countries where it is illegal. Many Muslim critics argue that there is no basis for this practice in the Koran; in fact, they note that this holy book commands parents to protect their children from harm and regards people's anatomy as part of God's creation.[22]

Elsewhere in the world, many people believe that women as well as men have a right to benefit from sexual pleasure. Pharmaceutical companies in particular recognize this attitude and have been investing in research into drugs to improve sexual response and function in both women and men. Some of these pharmaceuticals, such as Viagra, are vasodilators that increase blood flow in the genitals. Testosterone pills and patches increase libido, particularly in males, but they may have negative side effects.[23]

Sexual behavior and moral judgments about it also should be influenced by considering related health risks, which include various STDs and HIV. The U.S.

Centers for Disease Control and Prevention estimates that "19 million STD infections occur annually, almost half of them among youth ages 15–24."[24] This includes chlamydia, gonorrhea, and syphilis but not the less reportable viral infections such as human papillomavirus and herpes. Yet, "few adolescent males are getting the information they need to protect themselves from H.I.V. and other sexually transmitted diseases, a new study reports."[25] Current figures show that the rate of HIV infection in the United States has remained approximately the same since the early 1990s, approximately 40,000 new cases each year. This is down from 150,000 new cases per year in the late 1980s. "More than 830,000 cases of AIDS have been reported in the United States since 1981", when it was first diagnosed. Nearly a million people in the United States now have the AIDS virus, and approximately one-quarter of these do not know it.[26] The World Health Organization estimates that approximately 40 million people around the world are living with AIDS or HIV. The mortality rate from AIDS is declining, but it is still high. In 2006, 2.9 million people died of AIDS-related illnesses. Thirty-two percent of the people infected with HIV live in sub-Saharan Africa, and thirty-four percent of AIDS-related deaths occur there. In some African countries, as many as one-quarter of the people are infected with HIV. Approximately 8.6 million people in Asia are HIV-positive. There are currently an estimated 700,000 people living with HIV in China, including about 75,000 AIDS patients. During 2007, around 39,000 people died from AIDS.[27]

Also relevant to moral judgments about sex is the issue of rape. Reliable statistics on the incidence of rape are difficult to establish. One reason is underreporting. Another reason is the incidence of acquaintance rape. This form of sexual assault is particularly prevalent among college students. "Eighty percent of all rapes are believed to be acquaintance rapes."[28] Among the factors that accompany acquaintance rape are "consumption of alcohol . . . , private date locations . . . , and misinterpretation of sexual intent."[29] Contributing to the uncertainty regarding the incidence of all types of rape is the way the statistics are determined. For example, surveys from random phone interviews give different numbers from the cases reported to police. One such survey in the United States, for example, showed the number of rapes in 1999 to be 141,070 but 92,440 in 2000.[30] Rape is not just a moral issue, but also a matter of law; so also is sex trafficking. It is estimated that around the world perhaps "two million women and children are sold into the sex trade every year." The women who are trafficked are often from poor backgrounds and are lured with the promise of jobs and better lives. However, when they arrive they find out that this is not the case. Often they have no way to get away or out of the control of those who have lured them. Sex tourism is also a problem. In this case, very young girls are sometimes sold by their parents to a pimp who keeps them as prisoners for the exploitation of tourists, who are often from the West. Effectively they are sex slaves. Governments and nongovernmental organizations are working to prevent these practices and to punish those responsible.[31]

Sex workers in Bangladesh waiting for customers.

Returning to the issue of morality itself, perhaps too much is made of the morality of sexual behavior, often as if it is the only moral issue. What are we to make of the various views and practices of sexual behavior? When we hear expressions such as "Doesn't he have any morals?" or "She has loose morals," the speakers most probably are referring to the person's sexual morals. But many other moral issues are arguably more important than sexual behavior.

Some of you might even be inclined to say that one's sexual behavior is not a moral matter at all. Is it not a private matter and too personal and individual to be a moral matter? To hold that it is not a moral matter, however, would seem to imply that our sexual lives are morally insignificant. Or it might imply that something has to be public or universal in order to have moral significance. However, most of us would not want to hold that personal matters *cannot* be moral matters. Furthermore, consider that sexual behavior lends itself to valuable experiences—those of personal relations, pleasure, fruitfulness and descendants, and self-esteem and enhancement. It also involves unusual opportunities for cruelty, deceit, unfairness, and selfishness. Because these are moral matters, sexual behavior must itself have moral significance.

CONCEPTUAL PROBLEMS: WHAT IS AND IS NOT SEXUAL

To discuss sexual morality, we might benefit from preliminary thinking about the subject of our discussion. Just what are we talking about when we speak of sexual pleasure, sexual desire, or sexual activity? Consider the meaning of the qualifier *sexual*. Suppose we said that behavior is sexual when it involves "pleasurable bodily contact with another." Will this do? This definition is quite broad. It includes passionate caresses and kisses as well as sexual intercourse. But it would not include activity that does not involve another individual such as masturbation or looking at sexually stimulating pictures. It would also not include erotic dancing or phone sex, because these activities do not involve physical contact with another. So the definition seems to be too narrow.

However, this definition is also too broad. It covers too much. Not all kisses or caresses are sexual, even though they are physical and can be pleasurable. And the contact sport of football is supposedly pleasurable for those who play it, but presumably not in a sexual way. It seems reasonable to think of sexual pleasure as pleasure that involves our so-called erogenous zones—those areas of the body that are sexually sensitive. Thus, only after a certain stage of biological development do we become capable of sexual passions or feelings. Could we then say that sexuality is necessarily bodily in nature? To answer this question, try the following thought experiment. Suppose we did not have bodies—in other words, suppose we were ghosts or spirits of some sort. Would we then be sexual beings? Could we experience sexual desire, for example? If we did, it would surely be different from that which we now experience. Moreover, it is not just that our own bodily existence seems required for us to experience sexual desire, but sexual desire for another would seem most properly to be for the embodied other. It cannot be simply the body of another that is desirable—or dead bodies generally would be sexually stimulating. It is an *embodied* person who is the normal object of sexual desire. This is not to say that bodily touching is necessary, as is clear from the fact that dancing can be sexy and phone sex can be heated. Finally, if the body is so important for sexuality, we also can wonder whether there are any significant differences between male and female sexuality in addition to, and based on, genital and reproductive differences.

Let us also note one more conceptual puzzle. Many people refer to sexual intercourse as "making love." Some people argue that sexual intercourse should be accompanied by or be an expression of love, while others do not believe that this is necessary. Probably we would do best to consult the poets about the meaning of love. Briefly consider what you would regard as the difference between being in love (or falling in love) and loving someone. To "be in love" seems to suggest passivity. Similarly, to "fall in love" seems to be something that happens to a person. Supposedly, one has little control over one's feelings and even some thoughts in such a state. One cannot get the other person out of one's mind. One is, so to speak, "head over heels in love" or "madly in love"; one has "fallen passionately in love." Yet compare these notions to those of loving someone.

To love someone is to be actively directed to that person's good. We want the best for him or her. In his essay on friendship in *The Nicomachean Ethics*, Aristotle wrote that true friendship is different from that which is based on the usefulness of the friend or the pleasure one obtains from being with the friend. The true friend cares about his friend for the friend's own sake. According to Aristotle, "Those who wish well to their friends for their sake are most truly friends."[32] This kind of friendship is less common, he believed, though more lasting. For Aristotle and the Greeks of his time, true friendship was more or less reserved for men. One contribution an ethics of care makes to this discussion is the importance to all of friendship and loving care. Moreover, we need not be in love with someone to love them. We can love our friends, or parents, or children, and yet we are not in love with them. So when considering what sex has to do with love, we would do well to consider the kind of love that is intended. We might also do well to ponder what happens when sexual feelings are joined with friendship.

RELEVANT FACTUAL MATTERS

In addition to conceptual clarification, certain factual matters may also be relevant to what we say about matters of sexual morality. For example, would it not be morally significant to know the effects of celibacy or of restraining sexual urges? It is well known that Freud thought that if we repressed our sexual desires we would either become neurotic or artists! Art, he argues, provides an emotional expressive outlet for repressed sexual feelings. Freudian theory about both sexual repression and the basis of art still has supporters—Camille Paglia, for example.[33] It also has not gone unchallenged. Knowing what the likely effects would be, both psychologically and physically, of sexual promiscuity might also be useful for thinking about sexual morality. Does separating sex and bodily pleasure from other aspects of oneself as a complete person have any effect on one's ability to have a more holistic and more fulfilling sexual experience? Furthermore, factual matters such as the likelihood of contracting a disease such as AIDS would be important for what we say about the moral character of some sexual encounters. Our conclusions about many factual or empirical matters would seem to influence greatly what we say about sexual morality—that is, the morality of sex, just like the morality of other human activities, is at least sometimes determined by the benefits and harms that result from it.

SEXUAL MORALITY AND ETHICAL THEORIES

Factual matters may be relevant only if we are judging the morality of actions on the basis of their consequences. If instead we adopt a nonconsequentialist moral theory such as Kant's, then our concerns will not be about the consequences of sexual behavior but about whether we are enhancing or using people, for example, or being fair or unfair. If we adopt a natural law position, our concerns will again be significantly different, or at least based on different reasons. We will want to know whether certain sexual behavior fits or is befitting human nature.

In fact, the moral theory that we hold will even determine how we pose the moral question about sex. For example, if we are guided by a consequentialist moral theory such as utilitarianism, then we will be likely to pose the moral question in terms of good or bad, better or worse sexual behavior. If we are governed by Kantian principles, then our questions will more likely be in terms of right or wrong, justifiable or unjustifiable sexual behavior. And if we judge from a natural law basis, then we will want to know whether a particular sexual behavior is natural or unnatural, proper or improper, or even perverted. Let us consider each of these three ways of posing moral questions about sexual matters and see some of the probable considerations appropriate to each type of reasoning.

Consequentialist or Utilitarian Considerations

If we were to take a consequentialist point of view—say, that of an act utilitarian—we would judge our actions or make our decisions about how to behave sexually one at a time. In each case, we would consider our alternatives and their likely consequences for all who would be affected by them. In each case, we would consider who would benefit or suffer as well as the type of benefit or suffering. In sexual relations, we would probably want to consider physical, psychological, and social consequences. Considerations such as these are necessary for arguments that are consequentialist in nature. According to this perspective, the sexual practice or relation that has better consequences than other possibilities is the preferred one. Any practice in which the bad consequences outweigh the good consequences would be morally problematic.

Among the negative consequences to be avoided are physical harms, including sexually transmitted diseases such as syphilis, gonorrhea, and HIV, which causes AIDS. Psychic sufferings are no less real. There is the embarrassment caused by an unwanted sexual advance and the trauma of forced sex. Also to be considered are possible feelings of disappointment and foolishness for having false expectations or of being deceived or used. Pregnancy, although regarded in some circumstances as a good or a benefit, may in other circumstances be unwanted and involve significant suffering. Some people might include as a negative consequence the effects on the family of certain sexual practices. In consequentialist reasoning, all of the consequences count, and short-term benefit or pleasure may be outweighed by long-term suffering or pain. However, the pain caused to one person also can be outweighed by the pleasure given to another or others, and this is a major problem for this type of moral theory.

Many positive consequences or benefits also may come from sexual relations or activity. First of all, there is sexual pleasure itself. Furthermore, we may benefit both physically and psychologically from having this outlet for sexual urges and desires. It is relaxing. It enables us to appreciate other sensual things and to be more passionate and perhaps even more compassionate. It may enhance our perceptions of the world. Colors can be brighter and individual differences more noticeable. For many people, intimate sexual relations supposedly improve personal relations by breaking down barriers. However, one would think that this is likely to be so only where a good relationship already exists between the persons involved.

What about sex in the context of marriage and children? Because children are people too, any possible effects on them of sexual activity also must play a role in consequentialist considerations. The availability of contraception now makes it easier to control these consequences, so offspring that result from sexual relations are presumably (but not necessarily) more likely to be wanted and well cared for. Abortion and its consequences also may play a role in determining whether a particular sexual relation is good from this perspective.

Finally, consequentialist thinking has room for judging not only what is good and bad, or better and worse, but also what is worst and best. This perspective is entirely open to talking about better and worse sex or the best and worst. On utilitarian grounds, the most pleasurable and most productive of overall happiness is the best. If one cannot have the ideal best, however, then one should choose the best that is available, provided that this choice does not negatively affect one's ability to have the best or cause problems in other aspects of one's life. It is consistent with a consequentialist perspective to judge sexual behavior not in terms of what we must avoid to do right but in terms of what we should hope and aim for as the best. Nevertheless, in classical utilitarianism, the ideal is always to be thought of in terms of happiness or pleasure.

Nonconsequentialist or Kantian Considerations

Nonconsequentialist moral theories, such as that of Kant, would direct us to judge sexual actions as well as other actions quite differently from consequentialist theories. Although the golden rule is not strictly the same thing as the categorical imperative, there are similarities between these two moral principles. According to both, as a person in a sexual relation, I should only do what would seem acceptable no matter whose shoes I were in or from whose perspective I judged. In the case of a couple, each person should consider what the sexual relation would look like from the other's point of view, and each should only proceed if a contemplated action or relation is also acceptable from that other viewpoint.

This looks like a position regarding sexual relations according to which anything is permissible sexually as long as it is agreed to by the participants. In some versions of Kantianism, this would probably be so. The primary concern would then be whether the agreement is real. For example, we would want to know whether the participants are fully informed and aware of what is involved. Lying would certainly be morally objectionable. So also would other forms of deceit and failure to inform. Not telling someone that one is married or that one has a communicable disease could also be forms of objectionable deceit, in particular when this information, if known, would make a difference to the other person's willingness to participate.

In addition, the relation would have to be freely entered into. Any form of coercion would be morally objectionable on Kantian grounds. This is one of the strongest reasons for prohibiting sex with children—namely, that they cannot fully consent to it. They have neither the experience nor understanding of it, and they are not independent enough to resist pressure or coercion. As with deceit, what counts as coercion is not always easy to say, both in general and in any concrete case. Certainly, physically forcing a person to engage in sexual intercourse against his or her will is coercion. We call it rape. However, some forms of "persuasion" may also be coercive. Threats to do what is harmful are coercive. For example, threatening to demote an employee or deny him promotion if he does not engage in a sexual relation, can be coercive. But more subtle forms of coercion also exist, including implied threats to withhold one's affection from the other or to break off a relationship. Perhaps even some offers or bribes are coercive, especially when what is promised is not only desirable but also something that one does not have and cannot get along without. Saying "I know that you are starving, and I will feed you if you have sex with me" is surely coercive.

Naturalness Considerations

Some naturalistic moral theories described in Chapter 7 hold that morality is grounded in human nature. That is good which furthers human nature or is fitting for it, and that is bad or morally objectionable which frustrates or violates or is inconsistent with human nature. How would such a theory be used to make moral judgments about sexual behavior? Obviously, the key is the description of human nature.

In any use of human nature as a basis for determining what is good, a key issue will be describing that nature. To see how crucial this is, suppose that we examine a version of natural law theory that stresses the biological aspects of human nature. How would this require us to think about sexual morality? It would probably require us to note that an essential aspect of human nature is the orientation of the genital and reproductive system toward reproducing young. The very nature of heterosexual sexual intercourse (unless changed by accident or human intervention by sterilization or contraception) is to release male sperm into a female vagina and uterus. The sperm naturally tend to seek and penetrate an egg, fertilizing it, and forming with the egg the beginning of a fetus, which develops naturally into a young member of the species. On this version of natural law theory, that which interferes with or seeks deliberately to frustrate this natural purpose of sexual intercourse as oriented toward reproduction would be morally objectionable. Thus, contraception, masturbation, and homosexual sexual relations would be contrary to nature. Further arguments would be needed to show that sexual relations should take place only in marriage. These arguments would possibly have to do with the relation of sex and commitment, with the biological relation of the child to the parents, and with the necessary or best setting for the raising of children.

We could also envision other natural law–like arguments about sexual morality that are based on somewhat different notions of human nature. For example, we could argue that the natural purpose of sexual relations is pleasure, because nature has so constructed the nerve components of the genital system. Furthermore, the intimacy and naturally uniting aspect of sexual intercourse may provide a basis for arguing that this is its natural tendency—to unite people, to express their unity, or to bring them closer together.

To believe that there is such a thing as sexual behavior that is consistent with human nature—or *natural*—also implies that there can be sexual behavior that is inconsistent with human nature or unnatural. Sometimes the term *perverted* has been used synonymously with *unnatural*. Thus, in the context of a discussion or analysis of natural law views about sexual morality, we also can consider the question of whether there is such a thing as sexual perversion. This is not to say that notions of sexual perversion are limited to natural law theory, however. *Perversion* literally means turned against or away from something—usually away from some norm. Perverted sexual behavior would then be sexual behavior that departs from some norm for such behavior. "That's not normal," we say. By *norm* here we mean not just the usual type of behavior, for this depends on what in fact people do. Rather, by *norm* or *normal* we mean what coincides with a moral standard. If most human beings in a particular famine-ridden society died before age thirty-five, then we could still say that this was abnormal because it was not the norm for human survival in most other societies.[34]

To consider whether there is a natural type of sexual behavior or desire, we might compare it with another appetite—namely, the appetite of hunger, whose natural object we might say is food. If a person were to eat pictures of food instead of food, this would generally be considered abnormal. Would we also say that a person who was satisfied with pictures of a sexually attractive person and used them as a substitute for a real person was in some sense abnormal or acting abnormally? This depends on whether there is such a thing as a normal sex drive and what its natural object would be. People have used the notion of normal sex drive and desire to say that things such as shoe fetishism (being sexually excited by shoes) and desire for sex with animals or dead bodies are abnormal. One suggestion is that sexual desire in its normal form is for another individual and not just for the other but for the other's mutual and embodied response.

These notions of perverted versus normal sexual desire and behavior can belong in some loose way to a tradition that considers human nature as a moral norm. Like the utilitarian and Kantian moral traditions, natural law theory has its own way of judging sexual and other types of behavior. These three ways of judging sexual behavior are not necessarily incompatible with one another, however. We might find that some forms of sexual behavior are not only ill-fit for human nature but also involve using another as a thing rather than treating her or him as a person, and that they also have bad consequences. Or we may find that what is most fitting for human nature is also what has the best consequences and treats persons with the respect that is due them. The more difficult cases will be those in which no harm comes to persons from a sexual relation, but they have nevertheless been used, or cases in which knowing consent is present but it is for activities that seem ill-fit for human nature or do not promise happiness, pleasure, or other benefits.[35]

HOMOSEXUALITY

When making moral judgments about homosexuality, the same considerations can be used as for sexual morality generally: conseqentialist and nonconsequentialist considerations, as well as naturalness. Some issues are conceptual, such as what is meant by *homosexual* as opposed to *heterosexual* and *bisexual*. In contemporary language, the source of one's gender or sexual identity, be it lesbian, gay, bisexual, or transsexual is an empirical matter, whether they are fixed orientations or chosen life styles. Arguments about the morality of these identities also depend on conceptual and empirical issues.

From a consequentialist point of view, there is nothing in the nature of sex itself that requires that it be heterosexual or occur only between married individuals or for reproductive purposes. In some cases, where the consequences would be better, sex should be reserved for a married relation. It would depend on the individual persons. If particular individuals find sex fulfilling only in the context of a long-term or married relationship and where it is part of a desire to have children together, then this is what would be best for them. But this is not always the case, for people vary in how they are affected by different experiences. The social context and rules of a society may well make a difference. This may be especially true for homosexuality. Social acceptability or stigma will make a difference in whether people can be happy doing what they do. But it is happiness or pleasure and unhappiness or displeasure alone, from a classical consequentialist point of view, that determines the morality. In homosexual as well as in heterosexual relations, questions about whether monogamy is the best practice will be raised. Gay men and lesbian women, for example, have been known to disagree on this issue. Likewise, when they have disagreed on whether disclosing one's sexual orientation is a good thing, the debate has often turned on a disagreement about the likely consequences of such action.

Nonconsequentialist considerations also may apply here. For example, as in other sexual relations, considerations of honesty or dishonesty and free choice or coercion are relevant. One of the most common nonconsequentialist arguments against homosexual sex is that it is unnatural, that it goes against nature. According to traditional natural law theory, although we differ individually in many ways, people share a common human nature. I may have individual inclinations—or things may be natural to me that are not natural to you, simply because of our differing talents, psychic traits, and other unique characteristics. Natural law theory tells us that certain things are right or wrong not because they further or frustrate our individual inclinations, but because they promote or work against our species' inclinations and aspects of our common human nature. When appealing to a traditional type of natural law theory to make judgments about homosexual behavior, we need to determine whether this is consistent with common human nature rather than individual natures. The argument that gay men or lesbian women find relating sexually to members of their own sex "natural" to them as individuals may or may not work as part of a natural law argument that supports that behavior. However, if one had a broader view of sexuality in its passionate, emotional, and social aspects, then one could make a reasonable natural law–type of argument that these are also aspects of a common human sexuality that is manifested in several ways, including homosexual sex. Historically, natural law arguments have not gone this way. But this is not to say that such an argument could not be reasonably put forth.

Recent legal issues concerning gay and lesbian rights also have highlighted issues of sexual morality. In May 1996, for example, the U.S. Supreme Court struck down a Colorado law that banned legal protection for homosexuals.[36] Supporters of the ban argued that the people of Colorado had a right to do what they could to preserve what they saw as traditional moral values. Those who sought to overturn the ban saw it as a matter of protection from discrimination and equal rights for all. The issue of legal recognition of same-sex marriage and "civil unions" has also been the subject of heated debate recently. It may be helpful to put this issue in a larger context. For example, African Americans in the United States were not allowed to marry until after the Civil War, and mixed race couples could not do so everywhere in the United States until a Supreme Court decision in 1967. Since the early 2000s, various countries around the world have legalized same-sex marriage, a group that now includes Belgium, Canada, Iceland, the Netherlands, Norway, Portugal, South Africa, Spain, and Sweden. At this time, five states—Connecticut, Iowa, Massachusetts, New Hampshire, and Vermont—along with the District of Columbia, permit same sex marriage in the United States. Elsewhere, legislators, voters, or state courts have held that "marriage is between a man and a woman." Such was the case in California, where voters in 2008 supported Proposition 8, "the Marriage Protection Act." The federal law, "The Defense of Marriage Act," was passed by the U.S. Congress in 1996. It held that no state needs to recognize gay marriage from another state and defined marriage as "a legal union exclusively between one man and one woman."[37]

More widely available are so-called civil unions or domestic partnerships that grant many of the same legal benefits as married couples have. On August 3, 2009, Wisconsin became the latest U.S. state to pass such legislation, despite having a constitutional amendment banning gay marriage.[38]

Also at issue is the so-called "don't ask, don't tell" rule for the military. It was passed by Congress in 1993 as part of a defense directive. It directs that gay and lesbian soldiers not disclose that this is their orientation and also restricts military personel from inquiring about the same. Obviously there are those who believe that soldiers ought to be able to be honest about themselves. And it also has had the effect that some 13,000 troops have been discharged for homosexual behavior.[39]

Laws that address issues of rights, whether in this area or others, are often grounded in questions of morality. Nevertheless, morality is a distinct realm, and we may ask whether certain actions or practices are morally good or bad apart from whether they ought to be regulated by law. So, in the realm of sexual matters, we can ask about the morality of certain actions or practices. Questions about sexual morality are obviously quite personal. Nevertheless, because this is one of the major drives and aspects of a fulfilling human life, it is important to think about what may be best and worst, and what may be right and wrong in these matters.

In this chapter's readings, Thomas Nagel attempts to describe essential characteristics of a sexual relation by focusing on the notion of "sexual perversion," and Richard Mohr gives various responses to criticisms of the view that homosexuality is morally objectionable.

NOTES

1. *San Francisco Chronicle*, Nov. 1, 2006, p. A12.
2. Ibid.
3. Ibid.
4. *San Francisco Chronicle*, Feb. 15, 2007, pp. B1, B5.
5. Nicholas D. Kristof, "Bush's Sex Scandal," *The New York Times*, Feb. 16, 2005, p. A27.
6. http://wiki.answers.com/Q/How_many_teens_get_pregnant_in_a_year
7. Ibid.
8. Dennie Hughes, "Is It So Wrong to Live Together?" *USA Weekend*, Jan. 16–18, 2004, p. 12.
9. *Time*, May 25, 2009, pp. 57–58
10. David Whitman, "Was It Good for Us?" *U.S. News & World Report*, *122*, no. 19 (May 19, 1997): 56.
11. *The New York Times*, March 3, 2010, p. A14
12. Hughes, op. cit.
13. E. D. Widmer, J. Treas, and R. Newcomb, "Attitudes toward Nonmarital Sex in 24 Countries," *Journal of Sex Research*, *35* (1998); 349–358.
14. "Insight on the News," *Washington Times*, May 20, 1996, p. 48.
15. Ronald Jay Werner-Wilson, "Gender Differences in Adolescent Sexual Attitudes," *Adolescence*, *33* (Fall 1998): 519.
16. See http://www.amnestyusa.org/violence-against-women/female-genital-mutilation--fgm/page.do?id=1108439
17. James Ciment, "Senegal Outlaws Female Genital Mutilation," *British Medical Journal*, *3* (Feb. 6, 1999): 348; and Joel E. Frader et al., "Female Genital Mutilation," *Pediatrics*, *102* (July 1998): 153.
18. Ibid.
19. *The New York Times*, June 2, 2006, p. A10.
20. Ibid.
21. Xiaorong Li, "Tolerating the Intolerable: The Case of Female Genital Mutilation," *Philosophy and Public Policy Quarterly*, *21*, no. 1 (Winter 2001): 4.
22. Ibid., p. 6.
23. Judith Newman, "Passion Pills," *Discover*, *20* (Sept. 1999): 66.
24. http://www.unlv.edu/centers/cdclv/healthnv/teensex.html
25. *The New York Times*, April 20, 2010, p. D6
26. http://www.cdc.gov/mmwr/preview/mmwrhtml/mm5521a1.htm
27. http://www.avert.org/aidschina.htm
28. See http://www.ncvc.org/ncvc/main.aspx?dbName=DocumentViewer&DocumentID=32306
29. See http://www.med.unc.edu/alcohol/prevention/rape
30. http://www.msmagazine.com/news/uswirestory.asp?id=5606
31. See en.wikipedia.org/wiki/Human_trafficking; http://archives.cnn.com/2001/WORLD/europe/03/08/women.trafficking/index.html.
32. Aristotle, *The Nicomachean Ethics*, Book VIII, Chap. 4.
33. Camille Paglia, *Sex, Art, and American Culture* (New York: Vintage Books, 1992).
34. Similar considerations, consequentialist, Kantian, and naturalness, can be used to judge the morality of prostitution, pornography, polygamy, and other sex-related issues.
35. There are obvious problems here with determining the norm because longevity is a function of nutrition and exercise as well as genetics. We also might be inclined to consider norms for sexual behavior as partly a function of the setting or cultural conditions.
36. *San Francisco Chronicle*, May 21, 1996, pp. A1, A13.
37. www.religioustolerance.org/hom_marr.htm.
38. http://en.wikipedia.org/wiki/Recognition_of_same-sex_unions_in_Wisconsin
39. http://en.wikipedia.org/wiki/Don't_ask,_don't_tell.

READING
Sexual Perversion

THOMAS NAGEL

Study Questions

1. According to Nagel, if something is a sexual perversion, what basic traits must it have?
2. Why does Nagel say that there is no connection between reproduction and sexual perversion?
3. Why is sexual perversion not a matter of what is disapproved of by society?
4. How does Nagel describe the "skeptical" position regarding sexual perversion?
5. According to Nagel, what would count as a perversion of the natural appetite of hunger?
6. How does he distinguish the various purposes sex may serve and its own content?
7. What is the object of a sexual attraction?
8. How does Nagel describe the interaction between Romeo and Juliet?
9. Why are the practices that he considers to be sexual perversion deviations from the normal sexual capacities?
10. Why does he not think that homosexuality is a perverted sexual relation?
11. Explain his contention that perverted sex is neither necessarily immoral sex nor bad sex.

THERE IS something to be learned about sex from the fact that we possess a concept of sexual perversion. I wish to examine the idea, defending it against the charge of unintelligibility and trying to say exactly what about human sexuality qualifies it to admit of perversions. These can be accepted without assuming any particular analysis.

First, if there are any sexual perversions, they will have to be sexual desires or practices that are in some sense unnatural, though the explanation of this natural/unnatural distinction is of course the main problem. Second, certain practices will be perversions if anything is, such as shoe fetishism, bestiality, and sadism; other practices, such as unadorned sexual intercourse, will not be; about still others there is controversy. Third, if there are perversions, they will be unnatural sexual *inclinations* rather

Thomas Nagel, "Sexual Perversion," *The Journal of Philosophy,* LXVI, 1, January 16, 1969, 5-17. Copyright © January 16, 1969 Columbia University. Reprinted by permission of the author and publisher.

than just unnatural practices adopted not from inclination but for other reasons. Thus contraception, even if it is thought to be a deliberate perversion of the sexual and reproductive functions, cannot be significantly described as a sexual perversion. A sexual perversion must reveal itself in conduct that expresses an unnatural *sexual* preference. And although there might be a form of fetishism focused on the employment of contraceptive devices, that is not the usual explanation for their use.

The connection between sex and reproduction has no bearing on sexual perversion. The latter is a concept of psychological, not physiological, interest, and it is a concept that we do not apply to the lower animals, let alone to plants, all of which have reproductive functions that can go astray in various ways. (Think of seedless oranges.) Insofar as we are prepared to regard higher animals as perverted, it is because of their psychological, not their anatomical, similarity to humans. Furthermore, we do not regard as a perversion every deviation from the reproductive function of sex in humans: sterility, miscarriage, contraception, abortion.

Nor can the concept of sexual perversion be defined in terms of social disapprobation or custom. Consider all the societies that have frowned upon adultery and fornication. These have not been regarded as unnatural practices, but have been thought objectionable in other ways. What is regarded as unnatural admittedly varies from culture to culture, but the classification is not a pure expression of disapproval or distaste. In fact it is often regarded as a *ground* for disapproval, and that suggests that the classification has independent content.

I shall offer a psychological account of sexual perversion that depends on a theory of sexual desire and human sexual interactions. To approach this solution I shall first consider a contrary position that would justify skepticism about the existence of any sexual perversions at all, and perhaps even about the significance of the term. The skeptical argument runs as follows:

"Sexual desire is simply one of the appetites, like hunger and thirst. As such it may have various objects, some more common than others perhaps, but none in any sense 'natural.' An appetite is identified as sexual by means of the organs and erogenous zones in which its satisfaction can be to some extent localized, and the special sensory pleasures which form the core of that satisfaction. This enables us to recognize widely divergent goals, activities, and desires as sexual, since it is conceivable in principle that anything should produce sexual pleasure and that a nondeliberate, sexually charged desire for it should arise (as a result of conditioning, if nothing else). We may fail to empathize with some of these desires, and some of them, like sadism, may be objectionable on extraneous grounds, but once we have observed that they meet the criteria for being sexual, there is nothing more to be said on that score. Either they are sexual or they are not: sexuality does not admit of imperfection, or perversion, or any other such qualification—it is not that sort of affection."

This is probably the received radical position. It suggests that the cost of defending a psychological account may be to deny that sexual desire is an appetite. But insofar as that line of defense is plausible, it should make us suspicious of the simple picture of appetites on which the skepticism depends. Perhaps the standard appetites, like hunger, cannot be classed as pure appetites in that sense either, at least in their human versions.

Can we imagine anything that would qualify as a gastronomical perversion? Hunger and eating, like sex, serve a biological function and also play a significant role in our inner lives. Note that there is little temptation to describe as perverted an appetite for substances that are not nourishing: we should probably not consider someone's appetites *perverted* if he liked to eat paper, sand, wood, or cotton. Those are merely rather odd and very unhealthy tastes: they lack the psychological complexity that we expect of perversions. (Coprophilia, being already a sexual perversion, may be disregarded.) If on the other hand someone liked to eat cookbooks, or magazines with pictures of food in them, and preferred these to ordinary food—or if when hungry he sought satisfaction by fondling a napkin or ashtray from his favorite restaurant—then the concept of perversion might seem appropriate (it would be natural to call it gastronomical fetishism). It would be natural to

describe as gastronomically perverted someone who could eat only by having food forced down his throat through a funnel, or only if the meal were a living animal. What helps is the peculiarity of the desire itself, rather than the in appropriateness of its object to the biological function that the desire serves. Even an appetite can have perversions if in addition to its biological function it has a significant psychological structure.

In the case of hunger, psychological complexity is provided by the activities that give it expression. Hunger is not merely a disturbing sensation that can be quelled by eating; it is an attitude toward edible portions of the external world, a desire to treat them in rather special ways. The method of ingestion: chewing, savoring, swallowing, appreciating the texture and smell, all are important components of the relation, as is the passivity and controllability of the food (the only animals we eat live are helpless mollusks). Our relation to food depends also on our size: we do not live upon it or burrow into it like aphids or worms. Some of these features are more central than others, but an adequate phenomenology of eating would have to treat it as a relation to the external world and a way of appropriating bits of that world, with characteristic affection. Dis-placements or serious restrictions of the desire to eat could then be described as perversions, if they undermined that direct relation between man and food which is the natural expression of hunger. This explains why it is easy to imagine gastronomical fetishism, voyeurism, exhibitionism, or even gastronomical sadism and masochism. Some of these perversions are fairly common.

If we can imagine perversions of an appetite like hunger, it should be possible to make sense of the concept of sexual perversion. I do not wish to imply that sexual desire is an appetite—only that being an appetite is no bar to admitting of perversions. Like hunger, sexual desire has as its characteristic object a certain relation with something in the external world; only in this case it is usually a person rather than an omelet, and the relation is considerably more complicated. This added complication allows scope for correspondingly complicated perversions.

The fact that sexual desire is a feeling about other persons may encourage a pious view of its psychological content—that it is properly the expression of some other attitude, like love, and that when it occurs by itself it is incomplete or subhuman. (The extreme Platonic version of such a view is that sexual practices are all vain attempts to express something they can not in principle achieve: this makes them all perversions, in a sense.) But sexual desire is complicated enough without having to be linked to anything else as a condition for phenomenological analysis. Sex may serve various functions—economic, social, altruistic—but it also has its own content as a relation between persons.

The object of sexual attraction is a particular individual who transcends the properties that make him attractive. When different persons are attracted to a single person for different reasons—eyes, hair, figure, laugh, intelligence—we nevertheless feel that the object of their desire is the same. There is even an inclination to feel that this is so if the lovers have different sexual aims, if they include both men and women, for example. Different specific attractive characteristics seem to provide enabling conditions for the operation of a single basic feeling, and the different aims all provide expressions of it. We approach the sexual attitude toward the person through the feature that we find attractive, but these features are not the objects of that attitude.

This is very different from the use of an omelet. Various people may desire it for different reasons, one for its fluffiness, another for its mushrooms, another for its unique combination of aroma and visual aspect; yet we do not enshrine the transcendental omelet as the true common object of their affections. Instead we might say that several desires have accidentally converged on the same object: any omelet with the crucial characteristics would do as well. It is not similarly true that any person with the same flesh distribution and way of smoking can be substituted as object for a particular sexual desire that has been elicited by those characteristics. It may be that they recur, but it will be a new sexual attraction with a new particular object, not merely a transfer of the old desire to someone else. (This is true even in cases where the new object is unconsciously identified with a former one.)

The importance of this point will emerge when we see how complex a psychological interchange constitutes the natural development of sexual attraction.

This would be incomprehensible if its object were not a particular person, but rather a person of a certain *kind*. Attraction is only the beginning, and fulfillment does not consist merely of behavior and contact expressing this attraction, but involves much more. . . .

Sexual desire involves a kind of perception, but not merely a single perception of its object, for in the paradigm case of mutual desire there is a complex system of superimposed mutual perceptions—not only perceptions of the sexual object, but perceptions of oneself. Moreover, sexual awareness of another involves considerable self-awareness to begin with—more than is involved in ordinary sensory perception. The experience is felt as an assault on oneself by the view (or touch, or whatever) of the sexual object.

Let us consider a case in which the elements can be separated. For clarity we will restrict ourselves initially to the somewhat artificial case of desire at a distance. Suppose a man and a woman, whom we may call Romeo and Juliet, are at opposite ends of a cocktail lounge, with many mirrors on the walls which permit unobserved observation, and even mutual unobserved observation. Each of them is sipping a martini and studying other people in the mirrors. At some point Romeo notices Juliet. He is moved, somehow, by the softness of her hair and the diffidence with which she sips her martini, and this arouses him sexually. Let us say that X senses Y whenever X regards Y with sexual desire. (Y need not be a person, and X's apprehension of Y can be visual, tactile, olfactory, etc., or purely imaginary; in the present example we shall concentrate on vision.) So Romeo senses Juliet, rather than merely noticing her. At this stage he is aroused by an unaroused object, so he is more in the sexual grip of his body than she of hers.

Let us suppose, however, that Juliet now senses Romeo in another mirror on the opposite wall, though neither of them yet knows that he is seen by the other (the mirror angles provide three-quarter views). Romeo then begins to notice in Juliet the subtle signs of sexual arousal, heavy-lidded stare, dilating pupils, faint flush, etc. This of course intensifies her bodily presence, and he not only notices but senses this as well. His arousal is nevertheless still solitary. But now, cleverly calculating the line of her stare without actually looking her in the eyes, he realizes that it is directed at him through the mirror on the opposite wall. That is, he notices, and moreover senses, Juliet sensing him. This is definitely a new development, for it gives him a sense of embodiment not only through his own reactions but through the eyes and reactions of another. Moreover, it is separable from the initial sensing of Juliet; for sexual arousal might begin with a person's sensing that he is sensed and being assailed by the perception of the other person's desire rather than merely by the perception of the person.

But there is a further step. Let us suppose that Juliet, who is a little slower than Romeo, now senses that he senses her. This puts Romeo in a position to notice, and be aroused by, her arousal at being sensed by him. He senses that she senses that he senses her. This is still another level of arousal, for he becomes conscious of his sexuality through his awareness of its effect on her and of her awareness that this effect is due to him. Once she takes the same step and senses that he senses her sensing him, it becomes difficult to state, let alone imagine, further iterations, though they may be logically distinct. If both are alone, they will presumably turn to look at each other directly, and the proceedings will continue on another plane. Physical contact and intercourse are natural extensions of this complicated visual exchange, and mutual touch can involve all the complexities of awareness present in the visual case, but with a far greater range of subtlety and acuteness.

Ordinarily, of course, things happen in a less orderly fashion—sometimes in a great rush—but I believe that some version of this overlapping system of distinct sexual perceptions and interactions is the basic framework of any full-fledged sexual relation and that relations involving only part of the complex are significantly incomplete. The account is only schematic, as it must be to achieve generality. Every real sexual act will be psychologically far more specific and detailed, in ways that depend not only on the physical techniques employed and on anatomical details, but also on countless features of the participants' conceptions of themselves and of each other, which become embodied in the act. (It is a familiar enough fact, for example, that people often take their social roles and the social roles of their partners to bed with them.)

The general schema is important, however, and the proliferation of levels of mutual awareness it involves is an example of a type of complexity that typifies human interactions. Consider aggression, for example. If I am angry with someone, I want to make him feel it, either to produce self-reproach by getting him to see himself through the eyes of my anger, and to dislike what he sees—or else to produce reciprocal anger or fear, by getting him to perceive my anger as a threat or attack. What I want will depend on the details of my anger, but in either case it will involve a desire that the object of that anger will be aroused. This accomplishment constitutes the fulfillment of my emotion, through domination of the object's feelings.

Another example of such reflexive mutual recognition is to be found in the phenomenon of meaning, which appears to involve an intention to produce a belief or other effect in another by bringing about his recognition of one's intention to produce that effect. . . . Sex has a related structure: it involves a desire that one's partner be aroused by the recognition of one's desire that he or she be aroused.

. . . Hunger leads to spontaneous interactions with food; sexual desire leads to spontaneous interactions with other persons, whose bodies are asserting their sovereignty in the same way, produc-ing in voluntary reactions and spontaneous impulses in *them*. These reactions are perceived, and the perception of them is perceived, and that percep-tion is in turn per-ceived; at each step the domination of the person by his body is reinforced, and the sex-ual partner becomes more possessible by physical contact, penetration, and envelopment.

Desire is therefore not merely the perception of a pre-existing embodiment of the other, but ideally a contribution to his further embodiment which in turn enhances the original subject's sense of himself. This explains why it is important that the partner be aroused, and not merely aroused, but aroused by the awareness of one's desire. It also explains the sense in which desire has unity and possession as its object: physical possession must eventuate in creation of the sexual object in the image of one's desire, and not merely in the object's recognition of that desire, or in his or her own private arousal.

Even if this is a correct model of the adult sexual capacity, it is not plausible to describe as perverted every deviation from it. For example, if the partners in heterosexual intercourse indulge in private heterosexual fantasies, thus avoiding recognition of the real partner, that would, on this model, constitute a defective sexual relation. It is not, however, generally regarded as a perversion. Such examples suggest that a simple dichotomy between perverted and unperverted sex is too crude to organize the phenomena adequately.

Still, various familiar deviations constitute truncated or incomplete versions of the complete configuration, and may be regarded as perversions of the central impulse. If sexual desire is prevented from taking its full interpersonal form, it is likely to find a different one. The concept of perversion implies that a normal sexual development has been turned aside by distorting influences. I have little to say about this causal condition. But if perversions are in some sense unnatural, they must result from interference with the development of a capacity that is there potentially.

It is difficult to apply this condition, because environmental factors play a role in determining the precise form of anyone's sexual impulse. Early experiences in particular seem to determine the choice of a sexual object. To describe some causal influences as distorting and others as merely formative is to imply that certain general aspects of human sexuality realize a definite potential whereas many of the details in which people differ realize an indeterminate potential, so that they cannot be called more or less natural. What is included in the definite potential is therefore very important, although the distinction between definite and indeterminate potential is obscure. Obviously a creature incapable of developing the levels of interpersonal sexual awareness I have described could not be deviant in virtue of the failure to do so. (Though even a chicken might be called perverted in an extended sense if it had been conditioned to develop a fetishistic attachment to a telephone.) But if humans will tend to develop some version of reciprocal interpersonal sexual awareness unless prevented, then cases of blockage can be called unnatural or perverted.

Some familiar deviations can be described in this way. Narcissistic practices and intercourse with animals, infants, and inanimate objects seem to be stuck at some primitive version of the first stage of sexual feeling. If the object is not alive, the experience is reduced entirely to an awareness of one's own sexual embodiment. Small children and animals permit awareness of the embodiment of the other, but present obstacles to reciprocity, to the recognition by the sexual object of the subject's desire as the source of his (the object's) sexual self-awareness. Voyeurism and exhibitionism are also incomplete relations. The exhibitionist wishes to display his desire without needing to be desired in return; he may even fear the sexual attentions of others. A voyeur, on the other hand, need not require any recognition by his object at all: certainly not a recognition of the voyeur's arousal.

On the other hand, if we apply our model to the various forms that may be taken by two-party heterosexual intercourse, none of them seem clearly to qualify as perversions. Hardly anyone can be found these days to inveigh against oral-genital contact, and the merits of buggery are urged by such respectable figures as D. H. Lawrence and Norman Mailer. In general, it would appear that any bodily contact between a man and a woman that gives them sexual pleasure is a possible vehicle for the system of multilevel interpersonal awareness that I have claimed is the basic psychological content of sexual interaction. Thus a liberal platitude about sex is upheld.

The really difficult cases are sadism, masochism, and homosexuality. The first two are widely regarded as perversions and the last is controversial. In all three cases the issue depends partly on causal factors: do these dispositions result only when normal development has been prevented? Even the form in which this question has been posed is circular, because of the word "normal." We appear to need an independent criterion for a distorting influence, and we do not have one.

It may be possible to class sadism and maso-chism as perversions because they fall short of interpersonal reciprocity. Sadism concentrates on the evocation of passive self-awareness in others, but the sadist's engagement is itself active and requires a retention of deliberate control which may impede awareness of himself as a bodily subject of passion in the required sense. De Sade claimed that the object of sexual desire was to evoke involuntary responses from one's partner, especially audible ones. The infliction of pain is no doubt the most efficient way to accomplish this, but it requires a certain abrogation of one's own exposed spontaneity. A masochist on the other hand imposes the same disability on his partner as the sadist imposes on himself. The masochist cannot find a satisfactory embodiment as the object of another's sexual desire, but only as the object of his control. He is passive not in relation to his partner's passion but in relation to his nonpassive agency. In addition, the subjection to one's body characteristic of pain and physical restraint is of a very different kind from that of sexual excitement: pain causes people to contract rather than dissolve. These descriptions may not be generally accurate. But to the extent that they are, sadism and masochism would be disorders of the second stage of awareness— the awareness of oneself as an object of desire.

Homosexuality cannot similarly be classed as a perversion on phenomenological grounds. Nothing rules out the full range of interpersonal perceptions between persons of the same sex. The issue then depends on whether homosexuality is produced by distorting influences that block or displace a natural tendency to heterosexual development. And the influences must be more distorting than those which lead to a taste for large breasts or fair hair or dark eyes. These also are contingencies of sexual preference in which people differ, without being perverted.

The question is whether heterosexuality is the natural expression of male and female sexual dispositions that have not been distorted. It is an unclear question, and I do not know how to approach it. There is much support for an aggressive-passive distinction between male and female sexuality. In our culture the male's arousal tends to initiate the perceptual exchange, he usually makes the sexual approach, largely controls the course of the act, and of course penetrates whereas the woman receives. When two men or two women engage in intercourse they cannot both adhere to these sexual roles. But a good deal of deviation from them occurs in heterosexual intercourse. Women can be sexually aggressive and men passive, and temporary reversals of role are not uncommon in heterosexual exchanges of reasonable length. For these reasons it seems to be doubtful that homosexuality must be a perversion, though like heterosexuality it has perverted forms.

Let me close with some remarks about the relation of perversion to good, bad, and morality. The concept of perversion can hardly fail to be evaluative in some sense, for it appears to involve the notion of an ideal or at least adequate sexuality which the perversions in some way fail to achieve. So, if the concept is viable, the judgment that a person or practice or desire is perverted will constitute a sexual evaluation, implying that better sex, or a better specimen of sex, is possible. This in itself is a very weak claim, since the evaluation might be in a dimension that is of little interest to us. (Though, if my account is correct, that will not be true.)

Whether it is a moral evaluation, however, is another question entirely—one whose answer would require more understanding of both morality and perversion than can be deployed here. Moral evaluation of acts and of persons is a rather special and very complicated matter, and by no means all our evaluations of persons and their activities are moral evaluations. We make judgments about people's beauty or health or intelligence which are evaluative without being moral. Assessments of their sexuality may be similar in that respect.

Furthermore, moral issues aside, it is not clear that unperverted sex is necessarily *preferable* to the perversions. It may be that sex which receives the highest marks for perfection as sex is less enjoyable than certain perversions; and if enjoyment is considered very important, that might outweigh considerations of sexual perfection in determining rational preference.

That raises the question of the relation between the evaluative content of judgments of perversion and the rather common *general* distinction between good and bad sex. The latter distinction is usually confined to sexual acts, and it would seem, within limits, to cut across the other: even someone who believed, for example, that homosexuality was a perversion could admit a distinction between better and worse homosexual sex, and might even allow that good homosexual sex could be better sex than not very good unperverted sex. If this is correct, it supports the position that, if judgments of perversion are viable at all, they represent only one aspect of the possible evaluation of sex, even *qua sex*. Moreover it is not the only important aspect: sexual deficiencies that evidently do not constitute perversions can be the object of great concern.

Finally, even if perverted sex is to that extent not so good as it might be, bad sex is generally better than none at all. This should not be controversial: it seems to hold for other important matters, like food, music, literature, and society. In the end, one must choose from among the available alternatives, whether their availability depends on the environment or on one's own constitution. And the alternatives have to be fairly grim before it becomes rational to opt for nothing.

R E A D I N G
Prejudice and Homosexuality

RICHARD D. MOHR

Study Questions

1. What kinds of discrimination do many gays and lesbians face?
2. Distinguish descriptive from normative or prescriptive morality. Which does Mohr believe we need to determine how gays ought to be treated?
3. How does Mohr evaluate certain religious opposition to homosexuality?
4. According to Mohr, is the claim that homosexuality is wrong because it is unnatural always a rationally based evaluation? Explain.
5. Does he believe that equating "unnatural" with "artificial" or "manmade" provides an adequate basis for condemning homosexuality? Explain.
6. What does he say of the argument that the "proper function" of sex is to produce children?
7. How does Mohr respond to the assertion that being homosexual is a matter of choice?
8. How does Mohr respond to the prediction that society would be harmed if it accepted homosexuality? How does he believe it might be benefited by such acceptance?

WHO ARE gays anyway? A 1993 *New York Times*–CBS poll found that only one-fifth of Americans suppose that they have a friend or family member who is gay or lesbian. This finding is extraordinary given the number of practicing homosexuals in America. In 1948, Alfred Kinsey published a study of the sex lives of 12,000 white males. Its method was so rigorous that it set the standard for subsequent statistical research across the social sciences, but its results shocked the nation: thirty-seven percent of the men had at least

one homosexual experience to orgasm in their adult lives; an additional thirteen percent had homosexual fantasies to orgasm; four percent were exclusively homosexual in their practices; another five percent had virtually no heterosexual experience; and nearly one-fifth had at least as many homosexual as heterosexual experiences. Kinsey's 1953 study of the sex lives of 8000 women found the occurrence of homosexual behavior at about half the rates for men. . . .

Gays are . . . subject to widespread discrimination in employment. Governments are leading offenders here. They do a lot of discriminating themselves, require that others do it, and set precedents favoring discrimination in the private sector. Lesbians and gay men are barred from serving in the armed forces. The federal government has also denied gays employment in the CIA, FBI, National Security Agency, and the state department. The government refuses to give security clearances to gays and so forces the country's considerable private sector military and aerospace contractors to fire employees known to be gay and to avoid hiring those perceived to be gay. State and local governments regularly fire gay teachers, policemen, firemen, social workers, and anyone who has contact with the public. Further, state licensing laws (though frequently honored only in the breach) officially bar gays from a vast array of occupations and professions—everything from doctors, lawyers, accountants, and nurses to hairdressers, morticians, even used car dealers.

Gays are subject to discrimination in a wide variety of other ways, including private-sector employment, public accommodations, housing, insurance of all types, custody, adoption, and zoning regulations that bar "singles" or "nonrelated" couples from living together. A 1988 study by the Congressional Office of Technology Assessment found that a third of America's insurance companies openly admit that they discriminate against lesbians and gay men. In nearly half the states, same-sex sexual behavior is illegal, so that the central role of sex to meaningful life is officially denied to lesbians and gay men.

Illegality, discrimination and the absorption by gays of society's hatred of them all interact to impede and, for some, block altogether the ability of gay men and lesbians to create and maintain significant personal relations with loved ones. Every facet of life is affected by discrimination. Only the most compelling reasons could justify it.

Many people think society's treatment of gays is justified because they think gays are extremely immoral. To evaluate this claim, different senses of "moral" must be distinguished. Sometimes by "morality" is meant the values generally held by members of a society—its mores, norms, and customs. On this understanding, gays certainly are not moral: lots of people hate them, and social customs are designed to register widespread disapproval of gays. The problem here is that this sense of morality is merely a descriptive one. On this understanding, every society has a morality—even Nazi society, which had racism and mob rule as central features of its "morality" understood in this sense. What is needed in order to use the notion of morality to praise or condemn behavior is a sense of morality that is prescriptive or normative.

As the Nazi example makes clear, that a belief or claim is descriptively moral does not entail that it is normatively moral. A lot of people in a society saying something is good, even over aeons, does not make it so. The rejection of the long history of socially approved and state-enforced slavery is another good example of this principle at work. Slavery would be wrong even if nearly everyone liked it. So consistency and fairness require that one abandon the belief that gays are immoral simply because most people dislike or disapprove of gays.

Furthermore, recent historical and anthropological research has shown that opinion about gays has been by no means universally negative. It has varied widely even within the larger part of the Christian era and even within the Church itself. There are even

societies—current ones—where homosexual behavior is not only tolerated but is a universal compulsory part of male social maturation. Within the last thirty years, American society has undergone a grand turnabout from deeply ingrained, near total condemnation to near total acceptance on two emotionally charged "moral" or "family" issues—contraception and divorce. Society holds its current descriptive morality of gays not because it has to, but because it chooses to.

If popular opinion and custom are not enough to ground moral condemnation of homosexuality, perhaps religion can. Such arguments usually proceed along two lines. One claims that the condemnation is a direct revelation of God, usually through the Bible. The other claims to be able to detect condemnation in God's plan as manifested in nature; homosexuality (it is claimed) is "contrary to nature."

One of the more remarkable discoveries of recent gay research is that the Bible may not be as univocal in its condemnation of homosexuality as many have believed. Christ never mentions homosexuality. Recent interpreters of the Old Testament have pointed out that the story of Lot at Sodom is probably intended to condemn inhospitality rather than homosexuality.

Further, some of the Old Testament condemnations of homosexuality seem simply to be ways of tarring those of the Israelites' opponents who happen to accept homosexual practices when the Israelites themselves did not. If so, the condemnation is merely a quirk of history and rhetoric rather than a moral precept.

What does seem clear is that those who regularly cite the Bible to condemn an activity like homosexuality do so by reading it selectively. Do ministers who cite what they take to be condemnations of homosexuality in Leviticus maintain in their lives all the hygienic and dietary laws of Leviticus? If they cite the story of Lot at Sodom to condemn homosexuality, do they also cite the story of Lot in the Cave to praise incestuous rape? It seems then not that the Bible is being used to ground condemnations of homosexuality as much as society's dislike of homosexuality is being used to interpret the Bible.

Even if a consistent portrait of condemnation could be gleaned from the Bible, what social significance should it be given? One of the guiding principles of society, enshrined in the Constitution as a check against the government, is that decisions affecting social policy are not made on religious grounds. The Religious Right has been successful in stymieing sodomy-law reform, in defunding gay safe-sex literature and gay art, and in blocking the introduction of gay materials into school curriculums. If the real ground of the alleged immorality invoked by governments to discriminate against gays is religious (as it seems to be in these cases), then one of the major commitments of our nation is violated. Religious belief is a fine guide around which a person might organize his own life, but an awful instrument around which to organize someone else's life.

People also try to justify society's treatment of gays by saying they are unnatural. Though the accusation of unnaturalness looks whimsical, when applied to homosexuality, it is usually delivered with venom of forethought. It carries a high emotional charge, usually expressing disgust and evincing queasiness. Probably it is nothing but an emotional charge. For people get equally disgusted and queasy at all sorts of things that are perfectly natural, yet that could hardly be fit subjects for moral condemnation. Two typical examples in current American culture are some people's responses to mothers' suckling in public and to women who do not shave body hair. Similarly people fling the term "unnatural" against gays in the same breath and with the same force as when they call gays "sick" and "gross." When people have strong emotional reactions, as they do in these cases, without being able to give good reasons for them, they are thought of not as operating morally, but as being obsessed and manic. So the feelings of disgust that some people have toward gays will hardly ground a charge of immorality.

When "nature" is taken in technical rather than ordinary usages, it also cannot ground a charge of homosexual immorality. When unnatural means "by artifice" or "made by humans," it can be pointed out that virtually everything that is good about life is unnatural in this sense. The chief feature that distinguishes people from other animals is people's very ability to make over the world to meet their needs and desires. Indeed people's well-being depends upon these departures from nature. On this understanding of human nature and the natural, homosexuality is

perfectly unobjectionable; it is simply a means by which some people adapt nature to fulfill their desires and needs.

Another technical sense of natural is that something is natural and so, good, if it fulfills some function in nature. On this view, homosexuality is unnatural because it violates the function of genitals, which is to produce babies. One problem with this view is that lots of bodily parts have lots of functions and just because some one activity can be fulfilled by only one organ (say, the mouth for eating), this activity does not condemn other functions of the organ to immorality (say, the mouth for talking, licking stamps, blowing bubbles, or having sex). So the possible use of the genitals to produce children does not, without more, condemn the use of the genitals for other purposes, say, achieving ecstasy and intimacy.

The functional view of nature will only provide a morally condemnatory sense to the unnatural if a thing which might have many uses has but one proper function to the exclusion of other possible functions. But whether this is so cannot be established simply by looking at the thing. For what is seen is all its possible functions. The notion of function seemed like it might ground moral authority, but instead it turns out that moral authority is needed to define proper function.

Some people try to fill in this moral authority by appeal to the "design" or "order" of an organ, saying, for instance, that the genitals are designed for the purpose of procreation. But these people cheat intellectually if they do not make explicit who the designer and orderer is. If the "who" is God, we are back to square one—holding others accountable to one's own religious beliefs.

Further, ordinary moral attitudes about childbearing will not provide the needed supplement which would produce a positive obligation to use the genitals for procreation. Though there are local exceptions, society's general attitude toward a childless couple is that of pity, not censure—even if the couple could have children. The pity may be an unsympathetic one, that is, not registering a course one would choose for oneself, but this does not make it a course one would require of others. The couple who discovers they cannot have children are viewed not as having thereby had a debt canceled, but rather as having to forgo some of the richness of life, just as a quadriplegic is viewed not as absolved from some moral obligation to hop, skip, and jump, but as missing some of the richness of life. Consistency requires then that, at most, gays who do not or cannot have children are to be pitied rather than condemned. What is immoral is the willful preventing of people from achieving the richness of life. Immorality in this regard lies with those social customs, regulations, and statutes that prevent lesbians and gay men from establishing blood or adoptive families, not with gays themselves.

Many gays would like to raise or foster children— perhaps those alarming number of gay kids who have been beaten up and thrown out of their "families" for being gay. And indeed many lesbian and gay male couples are now raising robust, happy families where children are the blessings of adoption, artificial insemination, or surrogacy. The country is experiencing something approaching a gay and lesbian baby boom.

Sometimes people attempt to establish authority for a moral obligation to use bodily parts in a certain fashion simply by claiming that moral laws are natural laws and vice versa. On this account, inanimate objects and plants are good in that they follow natural laws by necessity, animals follow them by instinct, and persons follow them by a rational will. People are special in that they must first discover the laws that govern them. Now, even if one believes the view—dubious in the post-Newtonian, post-Darwinian world—that natural laws in the usual sense ($e = mc^2$, for instance) have some moral content, it is not at all clear how one is to discover the laws in nature that apply to people.

On the one hand, if one looks to people themselves for a model—and looks hard enough—one finds amazing variety, including homosexual relations as a social ideal (as in upper-class fifth-century Athens) and even as socially mandatory (as in some Melanesian initiation rites today). When one looks to people, one is simply unable to strip away the layers of social custom, history, and taboo in order to see what's really there to any degree more specific than that people are the creatures that make over their world and are capable of abstract thought. That this is so should raise doubts that neutral principles

are to be found in human nature that will condemn homosexuality.

On the other hand, if one looks to nature apart from people for models, the possibilities are staggering. There are fish that change sex over their lifetimes: should we "follow nature" and be operative transsexuals? Orangutans, genetically our next of kin, live completely solitary lives without social organization of any kind among adults: ought we to "follow nature" and be hermits? There are many species where only two members per generation reproduce: shall we be bees? The search in nature for people's purpose far from finding sure models for action is likely to leave one morally rudderless.

But (it might also be asked) aren't gays willfully the way they are? It is generally conceded that if sexual orientation is something over which an individual—for whatever reason—has virtually no control, then discrimination against gays is presumptively wrong, as it is against racial and ethnic classes.

Attempts to answer the question whether or not sexual orientation is something that is reasonably thought to be within one's own control usually appeal simply to various claims of the biological or "mental" sciences. But the ensuing debate over genes, hormones, hypothalamuses, twins, early childhood development, and the like is as unnecessary as it is currently inconclusive. All that is needed to answer the question is to look at the actual experience of lesbians and gay men in current society and it becomes fairly clear that sexual orientation is not likely a matter of choice.

On the one hand, the "choice" of the gender of a sexual partner does not seem to express a trivial desire which might as easily be fulfilled by a simple substitution of the desired object. Picking the gender of a sex partner is decidedly dissimilar, that is, to such activities as picking a flavor of ice cream. If an ice cream parlor is out of one's flavor, one simply picks another. And if people were persecuted, threatened with jail terms, shattered careers, loss of family and housing and the like for eating, say, rocky road ice cream, no one would ever eat it. Everyone would pick another easily available flavor. That gay people abide in being gay even in the face of persecution suggests that being gay is not a matter of easy choice.

On the other hand, even if establishing a sexual orientation is not like making a relatively trivial choice, perhaps it is relevantly like making the central and serious life-choices by which individuals try to establish themselves as being of some type or having some occupation. Again, if one examines gay experience, this seems not to be the general case. For one virtually never sees anyone setting out to become a homosexual, in the way one does see people setting out to become doctors, lawyers, and bricklayers. One does not find gays-to-be picking some end—"At some point in the future, I want to become a homosexual"—and then set about planning and acquiring the ways and means to that end, in the way one does see people deciding that they want to become lawyers, and then sees them plan what courses to take and what sort of temperaments, habits, and skills to develop in order to become lawyers. Typically gays-to-be simply find themselves having homosexual encounters and yet, at least initially, resisting quite strongly the identification of being homosexual. Such a person even very likely resists having such encounters, but ends up having them anyway. Only with time, luck, and great personal effort, but sometimes never, does the person gradually come to accept her or his orientation, to view it as a given material condition of life, coming as materials do with certain capacities and limitations. The person begins to act in accordance with his or her orientation and its capacities, seeing its actualization as a requisite for an integrated personality and as a central component of personal well-being. As a result, the experience of coming out to oneself has for gays the basic structure of a discovery, not the structure of a choice. And far from signaling immorality, coming out to others affords one of the few remaining opportunities in ever more bureaucratic, technological, and socialistic societies to manifest courage.

How would society at large be changed if gays were socially accepted? Suggestions to change social policy with regard to gays are invariably met with claims that to do so would invite the destruction of civilization itself: after all isn't that what did Rome in? Actually, Rome's decay paralleled not the flourishing of homosexuality but its repression under the later Christianized emperors. Predictions of American civilization's imminent demise have been as premature as they have been frequent. Civilization has shown itself to be rather resilient here, in large part because of the country's traditional commitments to respect for privacy, to individual liberties, and especially to people minding their own business. These all give society an open texture and the flexibility to try out things to see what works. And because of this, one now need not speculate about what changes reforms in gay social policy might bring to society at large. For many reforms have already been tried.

Half the states have decriminalized lesbian and gay male sex acts. Can you guess which of the following states still have sodomy laws: Wisconsin, Minnesota; New Mexico, Arizona; Vermont, New Hampshire; Nebraska, Kansas. One from each pair does and one does not have sodomy laws. And yet one would be hard pressed to point out any substantial social differences between the members of each pair. (If you're interested: it is the second of each pair with them.) Empirical studies have shown that there is no increase in other crimes in states that have decriminalized.

Neither has the passage of legislation barring discrimination against gays ushered in the end of civilization. Nearly a hundred counties and municipalities, including some of the country's largest cities (like Chicago and New York City) have passed such statutes, as have eight states: Wisconsin, Connecticut, Massachusetts, Hawaii, New Jersey, Vermont, California, and Minnesota. Again, no more brimstone has fallen in these places than elsewhere. Staunchly anti-gay cities, like Miami and Houston, have not been spared the AIDS crisis.

Berkeley, California, followed by a couple dozen other cities including New York, has even passed "domestic partner" legislation giving gay couples at least some of the same rights to city benefits as are held by heterosexually married couples, and yet Berkeley has not become more weird than it already was. A number of major universities (like Stanford and the University of Chicago) and respected corporations (like Levi Strauss and Company, the Montefiore Medical Center of New York, and Apple Computer, Inc.) are also following Berkeley's lead.

Seemingly hysterical predictions that the American family would collapse if such reforms would pass proved false, just as the same dire predictions that the availability of divorce would lessen the ideal and desirability of marriage proved unfounded. Indeed if current discrimination, which drives gays into hiding and into anonymous relations, ended, far from seeing gays destroying American families, one would see gays forming them.

Virtually all gays express a desire to have a permanent lover. But currently society and its discriminatory impulse make gay coupling very difficult. It is difficult for people to live together as couples without having their sexual orientation perceived in the public realm and so becoming targets for discrimination. Life in hiding is a pressure-cooker existence not easily shared with another. Members of nongay couples are here asked to imagine what it would take to erase every trace of their own sexual orientation for even just one week.

Even against oppressive odds, gays have shown an amazing tendency to nest. And those gay couples who have survived the odds show that the structure of more usual couplings is not a matter of destiny, but of personal responsibility. The so-called basic unit of society turns out not to be a unique immutable atom, but can adopt different parts, be adapted to different needs, and even be improved. Gays might even have a thing or two to teach others about divisions of labor, the relation of sensuality and intimacy, and the stages of development in such relations.

If discrimination ceased, gay men and lesbians would enter the mainstream of the human community openly and with self-respect. The energies that the typical gay person wastes in the anxiety of leading a day-to-day existence of systematic disguise would be released for use in personal flourishing. From this release would be generated the many spin-off benefits that accrue to a society when its individual members thrive.

Society would be richer for acknowledging another aspect of human diversity. Families with gay members would develop relations based on truth and trust rather than lies and fear. And the heterosexual majority would be better off for knowing that they are no longer trampling their gay friends and neighbors.

Finally and perhaps paradoxically, in extending to gays the rights and benefits it has reserved for its dominant culture, America would confirm its deeply held vision of itself as a morally progressing nation, a nation itself advancing and serving as a beacon for others—especially with regard to human rights. The words with which our national pledge ends—"with liberty and justice for all"—are not a description of the present, but a call for the future. America is a nation given to a prophetic political rhetoric which acknowledges that morality is not arbitrary and that justice is not merely the expression of the current collective will. It is this vision that led the black civil rights movement to its successes. Those senators and representatives who opposed that movement and its centerpiece, the 1964 Civil Rights Act, on obscurantist grounds, but who lived long enough and were noble enough, came in time to express their heartfelt regret and shame at what they had done. It is to be hoped and someday to be expected that those who now grasp at anything to oppose the extension of that which is best about America to gays will one day feel the same.

REVIEW EXERCISES

1. Distinguish "conceptual" from "factual" matters with regard to sexual morality. What is the difference between them?
2. What are some factual matters that would be relevant for consequentialist arguments regarding sexual behavior?
3. According to a Kantian type of morality, we ought to treat persons as persons. Deceit and coercion violate this requirement. In this view, what kinds of things regarding sexual morality would be morally objectionable?
4. How would a natural law theory be used to judge sexual behavior? Explain.
5. What is meant by the term *perversion*? How would this notion be used to determine whether there was something called "sexual perversion"?

D I S C U S S I O N   C A S E S

1. Date Rape? The students at a local university had heard much about date rape, what it was, what could lead to it, and that it was morally wrong and legally a crime. However, they were not always so clear about what counted as true consent to a sexual relation or experience. John insisted that unless the other person clearly said "No," consent should be implied. Amy said it was not so easy as that. Sometimes the issue comes up too quickly for a person to realize what is happening. The person has voluntarily gone along up to a certain point but may be ambiguous about proceeding further. Bill insisted that he would want a clear expression of a positive desire to go on for him to consider there to be a real consent. He also said that guys also could be ambiguous and sometimes not actually want to get involved sexually but be talked into it against their will by their partners.

What do you think is required for true consent to a sexual involvement?

2. Defining Marriage. Several localities in recent years have been grappling with the issue of whether to broaden the definition of marriage as a union between a man and a woman. The issue is whether the state should recognize a commitment between members of the same sex. Those who argue for this broadening say that same-sex couples can be just as committed to one another as heterosexuals and they thus should have whatever rights marriage bestows on them. Those who argue against this cite religious or natural law–like sources and reasons. They say this would open up the definition of marriage also to include more than two people—polygamy. How would you go about deciding whether to vote for such an ordinance? Although the issue of defining marriage involves more than issues of sexual morality, your definition may depend partly on what you say on this issue.

YOU MAKE THE DECISION

Apply the theories and issues discussed in this chapter by accessing this animated simulation on the Ethics Resource Center.

Use the passkey that accompanies your book to gain access. If you do not have a passkey, visit cengagebrain.com to purchase instant access to additional study material.

Which of the following is closest to your main reason for declining to officiate?

Ethics Module 11 : Gay Marriage

© Cengage Learning

13

Equality and Discrimination

I N NOVEMBER 2006, six imams (Muslim religious leaders) returning from an Islamic conference boarded a US Airways flight in Minneapolis. Several other passengers complained that the imams' behavior was suspicious. They had knelt and prayed loudly at the boarding gate and had chanted "Allahu Akbar," a phrase that many Americans associate with Muslim terrorists, and they were complaining about U.S. foreign policy. When they got on the plane, they sat in different places throughout the plane, and a couple of them asked for seat belt extenders with heavy buckles on the ends, even though these passengers didn't seem to need the extenders. Security personnel were called, and they asked the six imams to leave the plane. When they refused, the police were called, and they were handcuffed and taken off the plane. After hours of questioning, they were allowed to take another flight to their destination of Phoenix.[1]

After they returned home, the imams complained to US Airways and the Muslim American Society. They argued that they had been humiliated and were the victims of religious or racial discrimination, or both. They noted that they had round-trip tickets and had carry-on luggage. They said that they had prayed at the boarding gate because that was the time of the day when prayers were supposed to be given. In March 2007, they filed a lawsuit against US Airways, the airport, and the passengers who had complained.[2]

Omar Shahin, one of six imams removed from a US Airways Phoenix-bound plane at the Minneapolis-St. Paul International Airport.

Now some of the details of what happened have been disputed. But if this account is basically correct, would you say that this was in fact unjust discrimination? Or did the airline act reasonably given the post-9/11 concerns about airline security?

Racial profiling has also sparked questions about discrimination in other areas. What exactly is it? According to the American Civil Liberties Union, "[r]acial profiling is any police or private security practice in which a person is treated as a suspect because of his or her race, ethnicity, nationality or religion." This could be drug searches or stopping drivers on the highway. There are cases, for example, of drivers allegedly being stopped simply because they were African Americans—the supposed crime of "driving while black." In 1992 in Orlando, Florida, for example, 5 percent of the drivers were black or Hispanic, but they accounted for 70 to 80 percent of those who were stopped and searched.[3] In 2006, Dallas police pulled over more than 267,000 motorists. The number of black motorists stopped (36 percent) was disproportionate to their numbers in the local population (26 percent).[4] More recent numbers are hard to come by, and negative publicity over this type of incident may have lessened its occurrence. Other racial profiling concerns relate to drug-enforcement practices. Operation Pipeline of the Federal Drug Enforcement Administration also has used racial profiles in its work. In one study, 95 percent of those who were stopped for suspicion of being drug couriers were minorities.[5] In April 2010, the Arizona legislature passed a bill that would give police "broad powers to enforce immigration law," by allowing officers to stop people suspected of being illegal immigrants and demand that the suspected individuals show proof of citizenship.[6]

Whether a policy counts as racial profiling and whether it always implies racial bias and discrimination is a matter of some debate. For example, when decisions to stop motorists are made primarily or solely on the basis of race, this is surely discriminatory. However, in other cases in which race is just one of many factors in selecting targets of investigation, the question of discrimination is not so clear. This is the difference between "hard" and "soft" profiling. In the former case, race is the only factor that is used to single out someone, whereas in the latter it is just one of many factors. An example of the latter is "questioning or detaining a person because of the confluence of a variety of factors—age (young), dress (hooded sweatshirt, baggy pants, etc.), time (late evening), geography (the person is walking through the 'wrong' neighborhood)—that include

race (black)."[7] Or consider the New Jersey highway patrolman who pulls over a black driver who is speeding in a Nissan Pathfinder because the police have intelligence that Jamaican drug rings favor this car as a means for their marijuana trade in the Northeast.[8] Is this an example of unjust discrimination or a reasonable procedure?

One might think, given the fact that the United States has elected its first African-American president, that racism is behind us. However, consider this: In 2010, the governor of Virginia, Robert F. McDonnell, called for April to be "Confederate History Month," following Black History Month, in February. The declaration makes no mention of slavery, one of the main causes of the civil war.[9]

A clearer expression of racial prejudice is that of *hate crimes*. During a speech in Paris on July 17, 2005, to mark the sixty-third anniversary of the roundup of French Jews in World War II, the French prime minister spoke against anti-Semitism and hate crimes committed in its name.[10] In the weeks after the attacks on the London subway trains and buses in July 2005, there were several attacks on mosques. These mosques were attacked in a case of misguided retaliation for the suicide bombings by men of Pakistani background.[11] In the summer of 2005, a group devoted to stopping hate crimes in Eugene, Oregon reported that it had recently seen an increase in such incidents. Volunteers from the group handed out fliers with the words "Hate-Free Zone" written large. The fliers informed people what to do if they witnessed any hate crimes taking place. As a result, there were reports of racist, anti-Semitic, and antigay activity by local Nazi skinheads in the area.[12]

It is difficult to get overall good numbers on the incidence of hate crimes. However, if anecdotal reports are indicative, the number seems to be increasing. For example, according to authorities, there was a significant jump of 32 percent in the number of antigay hate crimes in the city of New York in 2005.[13] Moreover, there were 514 hate crimes reported for L.A. County in 2006. Overall in California for 2006, 1,306 hate crimes were reported. Sixty-four percent of these were for race, ethnicity, or national origin; 15.7 percent by antireligion motives; 18.8 percent for sexual orientation; 0.2 percent for antidisability reasons; and 0.6 percent for antigender motives.[14] Just as there are more severe penalties for killing a police officer than a layperson, federal and state law sometimes imposes more severe penalties for crimes motivated by hatred. Critics of these policies respond that to do this is to punish people for the views they hold, and that no matter how objectionable these might be, such laws constitute a violation of free speech.

Discrimination in the application of *criminal laws* also has not been completely overcome. Some social critics cite this as one reason for the high incidence of AIDS among minorities. In 1992, for example, 30 percent of those who were diagnosed with AIDS were blacks, who formed only 12 percent of the population; Latinos constituted 17 percent of AIDS cases but only 9 percent of the population. Thus, Latinos and blacks together accounted for 46 percent of AIDS cases. In 1996, blacks and Latinos represented 66 percent of infected youths. Although the causes for such numbers may be many, not the least of which is the combination of historic patterns of discrimination and current patterns of drug use and promiscuity, some critics believe that it is also the product of racial bias in the war against drugs. For example, it may well be that "fear of arrest compels injection drug users to rely on syringes borrowed at the moment of injection," and "persistent police harassment has promoted the spread of underground shooting galleries." Also as a result, male drug users expose "women and their offspring who live in those neighborhoods to a much higher risk of infection from unprotected sex."[15]

Education has been the great equalizer and the hope of the less fortunate. However, here also problems remain. The dropout rate for African-American college students is higher than for white students. "Compared to white students, African Americans are 20 percent less likely to complete college within a six-year period."[16] A newly released study of high school drop out rates shows that 16 percent of those between the ages of 16 and 24 dropped out of school in 2007. Most of these were Latino or black.[17] The causes are many, but prominent to many observers are the stress and feelings of not belonging and the

disincentives that follow from racial discrimination. Officers at some of the nation's elite colleges have pointed out that few students who come from poor families attend their schools. Financial aid is insufficient to adequately increase their numbers. In 1995, of students entering the top nineteen schools, only "3.1 percent . . . were from lower-income families." Fewer of these students are fast-tracked at school from early on. For example, "wealthy students are six times more likely to take the SAT and score at least 1200 as students from poor homes."[18] And at the University of Michigan, there were more students entering the freshman class whose parents make more than $200,000 a year than those who make "less than the national median of about $53,000."[19]

Racial stereotypes also have been thought to be the cause of continuing discriminatory attitudes. Although news media have done much better in recent years in weeding out racial stereotypes, a 1997 survey found that many national news magazines and television shows continued to "show blacks in stories about poverty 62 percent to 65 percent of the time, yet only 29 percent of poor Americans are black."[20]

If we look at *employment statistics*, we also find problems. In 1985, "50 percent of all black men were chronically unemployed." In 2004, black men earned only 74.5 percent and Hispanic men only 63.2 percent of what white men earned. The income of all women compared to men has improved over the years, but in 2004 they still only earned 77 percent of what men earned. Furthermore, the wage gap "cuts across a wide spectrum of occupations. The Bureau of Labor Statistics reported that in 2005 female physicians and surgeons earned 60.9% of the median weekly wages of male physicians, and women in sales occupations earned just 63.4% of men's wages in equivalent positions."[21] A look at the professions also gives us reason to be concerned. The American Bar Association (ABA) is concerned that too few lawyers are members of ethnic minority groups. "Our Society is increasingly racially and ethnically diverse, but our profession is not," the ABA's head said in 1999. Although 30 percent of U.S. Americans are members of racial or ethnic minorities, they constitute less than 10 percent of lawyers.[22]

Asian Americans also face problems of misunderstanding and prejudice even though their academic achievements have been phenomenal. Further, figures for median income for Asian Americans, especially more recent immigrants, are often deceiving, particularly when family income is the focus, because three to five household workers may be contributing to that income.

Forty-three million Americans have one or more physical or mental disabilities. Although great efforts have been made to remove barriers and ensure that positions are open to such people, such individuals are still disadvantaged in many areas.[23] Stereotypes and prejudice remain. Older workers are also often the victims of discrimination, subjected to arbitrary age limits in employment, where age alone rather than judgments of individual job performance are used to dismiss someone.[24] By contrast, it has been reported that 85 percent of Americans surveyed "favor equal treatment in the workplace for homosexuals and heterosexuals." By 1996, 313 companies, thirty-six cities, twelve counties, and four states had extended health benefits to gay partners of their employees.[25]

Gender discrimination also continues to be a problem. For example, males continue to dominate the fields of science and engineering. One causal cultural factor appears to be that fewer girls are encouraged to succeed in math and science, and self-defeating attitudes and behaviors seem to be reinforced early in girls' lives. For several years, Barbie dolls, for example, were programmed to say, "Math class is tough." The line was discontinued in 1992 after the doll maker received complaints. It's not surprising that many girls believe that it is not cool to be smarter than boys. There continue to be fewer women in mathematics and science and engineering than in other fields. However, some progress is evidently being made. A 2004 report of the National Center for Education Statistics points out that from kindergarten through twelfth grade, "math and computer usage gender gaps have disappeared (though) a small science proficiency gap remains. . . . Males were more likely to take AP exams in science and

calculus but in terms of performance, there were no significant differences between girls' and boys' proficiency in mathematics."[26]

Progress is also being made by women in wages. Women now earn on average 80 percent of what men do, which is a significant increase from the 62 percent of twenty-five years ago.[27] However, the cause may be problematic: During recent recessionary times, men were laid off from their jobs, while women who were cheaper to hire retained theirs, thus raising the average rate. Moreover, more women were employed in recession-proof fields such as health care and education. More positive is the fact that women were reaching higher educational levels and thus obtaining higher-paying jobs.[28]

Still, sexual harassment incidents negatively affect women's status and functioning in the workplace. Between 1992 and 1996, 67,751 sexual harassment complaints were filed with the Equal Employment Opportunity Commission. Some 143,842 were filed between 1997 and 2006. Between 41 percent and 48 percent of these were found to have no reasonable cause, and between 5 percent and 10 percent were determined to have reasonable cause. Between 11 percent and 15 percent of the complaints were filed by males.[29] These incidents are also a reoccurring problem in education. Recently, the U.S. Supreme Court ruled that school districts can be held financially liable for sexual harassment of students by other students if school administrators know about the harassment and are "deliberately indifferent" to it. Even men who sexually harass other men can be sued for harassment.[30]

Discrimination is an international problem. For example, many European countries do not have effective antidiscrimination laws. Although their governments claim that workers have freedom of movement within the European Union, such movement is often caused by discrimination. For example, "in Germany, the driving force behind the European Union, racist violence rose by 25 percent in 1997, and the authorities recorded 11,720 offenses by far-right groups."[31] Cases of anti-Semitism have also been on the rise in recent years. In many countries, women and men do not have equal rights. In Afghanistan, for example, the insurgent Islamic fundamentalist Taliban groups attempt to ban women from working and have thrown acid on girls trying to attend schools. Migrant workers in the United States and Europe and other parts of the world continue to face discrimination. In Singapore, for example, "most working women are limited to low-paying jobs in both periphery and core industries"—partly, it is said, to protect male economic success.[32]

Numerous examples of sex discrimination continue to be documented internationally. According to studies by UNICEF, in 1997 India reported "more than 6,000 dowry deaths" and an equal number of bride burnings. "The women died because they did not bring what in-laws considered satisfactory dowries or, sometimes, because the grooms were not happy with brides chosen by their families."[33] Bangladesh also reported that in 1998 more than 200 women were disfigured in assaults, often by acid and most often by men or boys whom the women had rejected.[34] The U.N. Population Fund has estimated that some 5,000 females are killed each year by so-called honor killings. These are cases in which sexual misbehavior of a female family member, even when that behavior is only *suspected*, is thought to dishonor the family; the suspicion or the fact becomes grounds for their murder. These cases typically occur in Middle East countries or those with majority Muslim populations. However, many scholars suggest that it is rooted in pre-Islamic cultures rather than religious doctrine. Amnesty International blames an "interplay between discriminatory tribal traditions of justice and statutory law. . . [i]n some countries . . . exacerbated by inclusion of Shari'a, or Islamic law, or the concept of zina (sex outside of marriage) as a crime within statutory law."[35] A meeting of women's groups to review the progress of women's rights since the 1995 Beijing meeting focused on "honor killings," dowry deaths, female infanticide, and acid attacks. Even in countries where such killing is illegal, families who murder their daughters because they have brought shame to them often are not prosecuted. Another tragic example of gender discrimination is found in the AIDS epidemic in sub-Saharan Africa. Women there are three times more likely than men of the same age to be infected. Because women are dependent economically on men, they often "marry older men who have been sexually active for decades."[36]

Patterns of gender difference also exist in domestic violence and homicide statistics. For example, "on average, more than three women are murdered by their husbands or boyfriends in this country every day."[37]

Statistics on forced prostitution also exemplify discriminatory treatment of women. "Activists estimate that 2 million women and children are sent across borders into some form of prostitution each year, and the State Department believes that approximately 50,000 could be in the United States."[38]

Clearly, the ideal of equal treatment and equal respect for all people regardless of race, sex, national origin, age, sexual orientation, and ethnicity has not been fully realized. However, it is not clear just what is required of us and why. After a brief look at some important moments in the history of the civil rights movement, particularly in the United States, we will examine key ethical issues: What is discrimination? What is wrong with it and why? A second section deals with the related issue of affirmative action.

CIVIL RIGHTS LAWS: A BRIEF HISTORY

We like to think that civil rights laws enacted in the United States and other Western countries have lessened racial injustice and promoted equal treatment for all citizens. Consider, for example, the following highlights of U.S. civil rights–related legislation.

> **1868** The Fourteenth Amendment to the Constitution, the equal protection clause, declared that no state may "deny to any person within its jurisdiction the equal protection of the law." This followed the Thirteenth Amendment in 1865, which prohibited slavery.

> **1920** The Nineteenth Amendment to the Constitution gave women the right to vote. This followed efforts and demonstrations by the suffragettes and the enactment of state laws that gave this right to women. (This is also fifty years after blacks were given the right to vote.)

> **1954** The U.S. Supreme Court's ruling in *Brown* v. *Board of Education* overturned the "separate but equal" schooling decision of the Court's 1896 *Plessy* v. *Ferguson* ruling.

> **1959** Vice President Richard M. Nixon recommended preferential treatment for qualified blacks in jobs with government contractors. In an executive order in 1961, President John F. Kennedy instituted affirmative action in government hiring; and in 1965, President Lyndon B. Johnson issued enforcement procedures such as goals and timetables for hiring women and underrepresented minorities.

> **1963** The Equal Pay Act required equal pay for substantially equal work by companies that were engaged in production for commerce.

> **1964** The Civil Rights Act, Title VII, prohibited discrimination in employment by private employers, employment agencies, and unions with fifteen or more employees. It prohibited the sex segregation of jobs and required that there be a *bona fide occupational qualification* (BFOQ) to allow preferences for specific group members for certain jobs—for instance, for wet nurses and clothing models.

> **1978** The U.S. Supreme Court ruling *Bakke* v. *U.C. Davis Medical School* forbade the use of racial quotas in school admissions but allowed some consideration of race in admissions decisions. This decision was challenged by the 1995 decision *Adarand* v. *Pena*. According to this 5–4 decision, any race-conscious federal program must serve a "compelling state interest" and must be "narrowly tailored" to achieve its goal. However, in 2003, a less rigid standard for acceptance of a race-conscious program was appealed to by the U.S. Supreme Court in its decision regarding the affirmative action practices of the University of Michigan. In *Grutter* v. *Bollinger*, a 5–4 decision, the Court upheld the university's law school policy, which considers an applicant's race as one factor among others such as test scores, talent, and grade-point averages in admissions. The Court rejected the undergraduate school's more mechanical practice of giving set extra points for a particular race. The Court also gave added support to earlier rulings that there was a "compelling state interest" in racial diversity in education.[39] In another case, the 1979 *Weber* v. *Kaiser Aluminum* decision, the Court permitted a company to remedy its past discriminatory practices by using race as a criterion for admission to special training programs. These programs were aimed at ensuring that a percentage of black persons equal to that in the local labor force would be moved up to managerial positions in the company.

> **1991** The Civil Rights Act required that businesses that use employment practices with a discriminatory impact (even if unintentional) must show that the practices are business necessities; otherwise, the business must reform its practices to eliminate this impact.[40] Quotas were forbidden except when required by court order for rectifying wrongful past or present discrimination. Sexual harassment was also noted as a form of discrimination. Although cases of sexual harassment began to appear in court in the late 1970s, the concept is still being defined by the courts. Two forms of this harassment are generally recognized: One promises employment rewards for sexual favors, and the other creates a "hostile work environment."

These are just a few of the highlights of the last 150 years of civil rights laws as enacted by various government bodies. They have played a major role in the way we carry out our common social and economic life. We might also cite other laws and court decisions that concern housing, lending, and the busing of school students, as well as laws that have been designed to prevent discrimination on the basis of not only race and sex but also religion, age, disability, and sexual orientation.[41] Many of these laws rely on and are based on legal precedent. But they also are grounded in moral notions such as equality and justice and fairness. In this chapter, we will examine some of the moral notions and arguments that play a role in discussions about what a just society should be like.

RACISM AND SEXISM

Some time ago, I came across an article titled "What's Wrong with Racism?" It is an intriguing title. To answer the question, we ought first to ask, what is racism? Race, as a biological classification of humans, is based on a selection of common characteristics. These characteristics have included appearance, blood groups, geographic location, and gene frequency. Depending on which of these are the focus, anthropologists have classified the human species into anywhere from six to eighty races. One traditional division is into the following groups: "Caucasians, black Africans, Mongoloids, South Asian aborigines, Native Americans, Oceanians, and Australian Aborigines."[42] If we focus on genetic variation, then we find that only 8 to 10 percent of the differences between human individuals are associated with differences in race, whereas 85 percent accounts for individual differences and 15 percent for differences in local populations. Differences in skin color are not solely genetic, and so-called racial differences change over time with mobility and intermixing. For example, "differences between frequencies of West Africans and American blacks show that 20% to 25% of the genes of urban black Americans have come from European and American Indian ancestors. . . ."[43]

On the other hand, race has sometimes been thought also to involve cultural differences, either real or imagined. Examples include preferences for certain foods, dress, or music; religious affiliation; and certain psychological or even ethical traits. It is these supposed differences that have influenced racist views—as much as, or possibly more than, biological and geographical differences. Still, certain constructions of race are of some interest. For example, if people want to be or think of themselves as belonging to a particular racial or ethnic group, should this count in how they are classified? For example, a white person who wants to fit in with black friends may adopt certain mannerisms and preferences of the group. Does such behavior make this person black? Or perhaps a black person undergoes surgeries and medical procedures that make him look white. Do such measures make him white, or is he still black even though he no longer has that coloration?

A more controversial recent effort has been to investigate the genetic basis of race. Although most of us have mixed ancestry, genetic variations have been noted. In particular, they incline us to different disease susceptibilities. Some scientific studies aim to "catalogue and compare the genetics of people with African, Asian, and European ancestry."[44] One particular effort is known as the International

Haplotype Project and is financed by organizations and governments from Japan, the United Kingdom, Canada, China, Nigeria, and the United States. The Human Genome Project (see Chapter 18) completed in 2000 found that "humans as a species are 99.9 percent genetically identical." However, according to researchers now, this 0.1 percent difference is significant and is made up of genetic variations that may include racial differences. The purpose of the project is ultimately to find out why certain groups suffer differential rates of high blood pressure and heart attacks by finding, for example, the genetic variants or mutations that may be involved in these diseases. In so doing, the hope is that drugs and treatment can be tailor-made for people in these groups. The populations studied are 270 people from Yoruba in Ibadan, Nigeria; Japanese in Tokyo; Han Chinese in Beijing; and Utah residents with ancestry from northern and western Europe.[45]

Obviously, if other traits are included, such as athletic ability or intelligence, then the project becomes more controversial and could be used for racist purposes. However, simply to note certain genetic or phenotypic variations by race is not itself racism. First of all, racism involves making race a significant factor about the person—more important, say, than height or strength. Race becomes a key identifying factor. It sets people of one race apart from people of other races, leading to demarcations between "us" and "them" on the basis of this classification.

History has long provided examples of such insider–outsider phenomena. Sometimes, it is a matter of blood and kin that determines the border. Sometimes, the line is drawn based on religious beliefs. Those with different religions may have been tolerated in some cases but not given equal rights. Muslims tolerated Christians and Jews in the Middle East, and Muslims were tolerated in Christian Europe. With the rise of democracies around the world, however, tolerance was no longer enough. People demanded equality.[46] Racism involves not only making distinctions and grouping people but also denigration. It involves believing that all persons of a certain race are inferior to persons of other races in some way. Does this necessarily make racism wrong?

In the abstract, it would seem that believing that someone is shorter than another or less strong is not necessarily objectionable, especially if the belief is true. However, what we presume makes racism wrong is that it involves making false judgments about people. It also involves value judgments about their worth as people. A similar definition could be given of sexism—namely, having false beliefs about people because of their sex or devaluing them because of this. It also involves power and oppression, for those groups that are devalued by racism are also likely to be treated accordingly.

Furthermore, racism and sexism are not the same as prejudice. Prejudice is making judgments or forming beliefs before knowing the truth about something or someone. These prejudgments might accidentally be correct beliefs. However, the negative connotation of the term *prejudice* indicates that these beliefs or judgments are formed without adequate information and are also mistaken. Moreover, prejudice in this context also may be a matter of judging an individual on the basis of judgments about the characteristics of a group to which he or she belongs. They are supposedly false generalizations. Thus, if I think that all people of a certain race or sex like to drink warm beer because I have seen some of that group do so, then I am making a false generalization—one without adequate basis in the facts. Racism or sexism, although different from prejudice, may follow from prejudiced beliefs.

Knowing what racism is, we can then answer the question, what is wrong with it? We believe racism, like sexism, is wrong because it is unjust or unfair. It is also wrong because it is harmful to people. The racist or sexist individual treats people of a particular race or sex differently and less well simply because of their race or sex.

Yet we still have not gotten to the root of what is wrong with racism or sexism. Suppose that our views about members of a group are not based on prejudice but on an objective factual assessment about the group. For example, if men differ from women in significant ways—and surely they do—then is this not a sufficient reason to treat them differently? A moral principle can be used to help us think about this issue: the *principle of equality*. The general idea embodied in this principle is that we should treat equals equally and unequals unequally. In analyzing this principle, we will be able to clarify what is meant by discrimination, and whether or why it is morally objectionable. We also will be able to consider what is meant by affirmative action or reverse discrimination and analyze the arguments for and against them.

THE PRINCIPLE OF EQUALITY

The principle of equality can be formulated in various ways. Consider the following formulation:

It is unjust to treat people differently in ways that deny to some of them significant social benefits unless we can show that there is a difference between them that is relevant to the differential treatment.

To understand the meaning of this principle, we will focus on its emphasized parts.

Justice

First, we notice that the principle is a principle of *justice*. It tells us that certain actions or practices that treat people unequally are unjust, and others are presumably just. To understand this principle fully, we would need to further explore the concept of justice. Here we do so only briefly. (Further treatment of the nature of justice occurs in Chapter 14.) Consider, for instance, our symbols of justice. Outside the U.S. Supreme Court building in Washington, D.C. is a statue of a woman. She is blindfolded and holds a scale in one hand. The idea of the blindfold is that justice is blind—in other words, it is not biased. It does not favor one person over another on the basis of irrelevant characteristics. The same laws are supposed to apply to all. The scale indicates that justice may involve not strict equality but proportionality. It requires that treatment of persons be according to what is due them on some grounds. Therefore, it requires that there be valid reasons for differential treatment.

Social Benefits and Harms

We are not required to justify treating people differently from others in every case. For example, I may give personal favors to my friends or family and not to others without having to give a reason. However, sometimes social policy effectively treats people differently in ways that penalize or harm some and benefit others. This harm can be obvious or it can be subtle. In addition, there is a difference between primary racism or sexism and secondary racism or sexism.[47] In primary racism or sexism, a person is singled out and directly penalized simply because he or she is a member of a particular race or sex—as when denied school admissions or promotions just because of this characteristic. In secondary racism or sexism, criteria for benefit or harm are used that do not directly apply to members of particular groups and only indirectly affect them. Thus, the policy "last hired, first fired" is often likely to have a discriminatory effect. Such policies may be allowed in the workplace or other social settings, policies that may seem harmless but actually have a harmful effect on certain groups. What we now label "sexual harassment" is an example of harmful discriminatory practices. This aspect of the principle of equality, then, directs us to consider the ways in which social benefits and penalties or harms sometimes occur for reasons that are not justified.

Proof

The principle states that we must show or prove that certain differences exist that justify treating people differently in socially significant ways. The principle can be stronger or weaker depending on the kind of proof of differences required by it. It is not acceptable to treat people differently on the basis of differences that we only think or suspect exist. Scientific studies of sex differences, for example, must be provided to show that certain sex differences actually exist.

Real Differences

The principle of equality requires that we show or prove that actual differences exist between the people that we would treat differently. Many sex differences are obvious, and others that are not obvious have been confirmed by empirical studies—such as differences in metabolic rate, strength and size, hearing acuity, shoulder structure, and disease susceptibility. However, it is unlikely that these differences would be relevant for any differential social treatment. Those that would be relevant are differences such as type of intellectual ability, aggressiveness, or nurturing capacity.

We might look to scientific studies of sex differences to help us determine whether any such possibly relevant sex differences exist. Women have been found to do better on tests that measure verbal speed, and men to do better at being able to imagine what an object would look like if it were rotated in three-dimensional space. Recent discoveries have shown that men and women use different parts of their brains to do the same tasks. For example, to recognize whether nonsense words rhyme, men used a tiny area in the front left side of the brain, whereas women used a comparable section of the right side.[48] Whether this difference has a wider significance for different types of intelligence is a matter of some debate. So also are the studies of aggressiveness. Testosterone has been shown to increase size and strength, but whether it also makes males more aggressive than females is disputed. This dispute arises not only because of the difficulties we have in tracing physical causation, but also because of our uncertainty about just what we mean by aggressiveness.

However, most studies that examine supposed male and female differences also look at males and females after they have been socialized. Thus, it is not surprising that they do find differences. Suppose that a study found that little girls play with dolls and make block enclosures while little boys prefer trucks and use the blocks to build imaginary adventure settings. Would this necessarily mean that some innate difference causes this? If there were such differences and if they were innate, then this may be relevant to how we would structure education and some other aspects of society. We might prefer women for the job of nurse or early child-care provider, for example. We might provide women, but not men, with paid child-care leave.[49]

However, if we cannot prove that these or any such characteristics come from nature rather than by nurture, then we are left with the following type of problem. For many years, society thought that females had lesser mathematical abilities than males. Thus, in our educational practices we have not expected females to have these abilities, and teachers have tended to treat their male and female mathematics students differently. For instance, in a 1987 study, female students in the fourth through seventh grades who ranked high in mathematics were found to be "less likely to be assigned to high-ability groups by their teachers than were males with comparable scores."[50] Suppose that at a later point we tested people on mathematical ability and found a difference between the male and female scores. Would that mean we could justly prefer one group over the other for positions and jobs that required this skill? It would seem that if we wanted the jobs done well, we should do this. But suppose also that these jobs were the highest-paying and had the greatest esteem and power connected with them. Socialization has contributed to people's being more or less well qualified for valued positions like these in society. We should consider whether our social institutions perpetuate socially induced disadvantages. Using the principle of equality, we could rightly criticize such a system of reward for socially developed skills as unfair because it causes certain traits in people and then penalizes them for having those traits!

Relevant Differences

The principle of equality requires more than showing that real differences exist between people, not just socially learned differences, before we are justified in treating them differently. It also requires that the differences be relevant. This is the idea embodied in the BFOQ of the 1964 Civil Rights Act mentioned earlier. For example, if it could be shown that women are by nature better at bricklaying than men, then this would be a "real" difference between them. Although we might then be justified in preferring women for the job of bricklayer, we would not be justified in using this difference to prefer women for the job of airline pilot. On the other hand, if men and women think differently and if certain jobs require these particular thinking skills, then according to the principle of equality we may well prefer those individuals with these skills for the jobs.

The relevance of a talent or characteristic or skill to a job is not an easy matter to determine. For example, is upper body strength an essential skill for the job of firefighter or police officer? Try debating this one with a friend. In answering this question, it would be useful to determine what kinds of things firefighters usually have to do, what their equipment is like, and so forth. Similarly, with the job of police officer we might ask how much physical strength is

required and how important are other physical or psychological skills or traits. And is being an African American, Asian American, or female an essential qualification for a position as university teacher of courses in black studies, Asian studies, or women's studies? It may not be an essential qualification, but some people argue that this does help qualify a person because she or he is more likely to understand the issues and problems with which the course deals. Nevertheless, this view has not gone unchallenged.

In addition to determining what characteristics or skills are relevant to a particular position, we must be able to assess adequately whether particular persons possess these characteristics or skills. Designing tests to assess this presents a difficulty. Prejudice may play a role in such assessments. For instance, how do we know whether someone works well with people or has sufficient knowledge of the issues that ought to be treated in a women's studies course? This raises another issue. Should or must we always test or judge people as individuals, or is it ever permissible to judge an individual as a member of a particular group? The principle of equality seems better designed for evaluating differential group treatment than differential treatment of individuals. This is just one issue that can be raised to challenge the principle of equality.

Challenges to the Principle

The first problem that this principle faces stems from the fact that those group differences that are both real and relevant to some differential treatment are often, if not always, average differences. In other words, a characteristic may be typical of a group of people, but it may not belong to every member of the group. Consider height. Men are typically taller than women. Nevertheless, some women are taller than some men. Even if women were typically more nurturing than men, it would still be likely or at least possible that some men would be more nurturing than some women. Thus, it would seem that we ought to consider what characteristics an individual has rather than what is typical of the group to which he or she belongs. This would only seem to be fair or just. What, then, of the principle of equality as an adequate or usable principle of justice? It would seem to require us to do unfair things—specifically, to treat people as members of a group rather than as individuals.

Are we ever justified in treating someone differently because of her membership in a particular demographic group and because of that group's typical characteristics—even if that person does not possess them? We do this in some cases, and presumably think it is not unjust. Consider our treatment of people as members of an age group, say, for purposes of driving or voting. We have rules that require that a person must be at least fifteen years old to obtain a driver's permit or license. But is it not true that some individuals who are fourteen would be better drivers than some individuals who are eighteen? Yet we judge them on the basis of a group characteristic rather than their individual abilities. Similarly, in the United States, we require that people be eighteen years of age before they can vote. However, some people who are younger than eighteen would be more intelligent voters than some who are older than eighteen. Is it not unjust to treat persons differently simply because of their age group rather than on the basis of their own individual characteristics and abilities?

Consider possibilities for determining when treating people as members of a group is unfair or wrong and when it is justified. Take our two examples. If an individual is well qualified to drive but is not yet fifteen or sixteen, then she has only to wait one year. This causes no great harm to her. Nor is any judgment made about her natural abilities. Even those fifteen and older have to take a test on which they are judged as individuals and not just as members of a group. Furthermore, suppose that we tried to judge people as individuals for the purposes of voting. We would need to develop a test of "intelligent voting ability." Can you imagine what political and social dynamite this testing would be? The cost to our democracy of instituting such a policy would be too great, whereas the cost to the individual to be judged as a member of an age group and wait a couple years to vote is minimal. Thus, this practice does not seem unduly unfair.

However, if real and relevant sex differences existed, and if we treated all members of one sex alike on the basis of some characteristic that was typical of their group rather than on the basis of their

characteristics as individuals, then this would involve both significant costs and significant unfairness. It would be of great social cost to society not to consider applicants or candidates because of their sex; these individuals might otherwise make great contributions to society. In addition, those who are denied consideration could rightly complain that it was unfair to deny them a chance at a position for which they qualified, something that would also affect them their whole lives. Thus, we could argue that the ideal of the principle of equality is generally valid but would need to be supplemented by such considerations concerning when judging a person as a member of a group would be permissible.

The second challenge to the principle of equality, or to its application, can be found in the debates over *preferential treatment* programs. Could not those people who support these programs claim that past discrimination is, in fact, a relevant difference between groups of people and that we would thus be justified in treating people differently on this basis? Preferential treatments would be designed to benefit those who are members of groups that have been discriminated against in the past. We will look shortly at the various forms of affirmative action and the arguments for and against them. It is useful here, however, to note the way in which the principle of equality might be used to justify some of these programs. The claim would be that being a member of a group is a sufficient reason to treat someone in a special way. Would we need to show that every member of that group was in some way harmed or affected by past discrimination? Some individual members of particular groups would not obviously have been harmed by past discrimination. However, we should also be aware of the subtle ways in which group or community membership affects a person and the subtle ways in which she might thus be harmed. On the other hand, the attempt to use the principle of equality to justify preferential treatment of members of certain groups would contradict the aspect of the principle of equality that requires that the differences that justify differential treatment be real—in other words, caused by nature rather than by nurture—as well as significant.

The third problem users of the principle of equality must address concerns the equality–inequality dilemma. We can exemplify this by using sex or gender differences, but the problem could also be applied to cultural differences. Women have sought equality with men in the workplace, in education, and in public life generally. At the same time, they remain the primary child-care providers, which places them at an inevitable disadvantage in terms of advancement in many professions and so forth. Some feminists have argued that the liberal notion of equality can be detrimental to women.[51] Rather than think of women as similar to men, or use only a formal notion of equality devoid of content, some feminists argue for a more concrete notion of a person.[52] Thus, differences between males and females in such areas as parental responsibilities would be relevant to the justness of requirements for professional advancement.

Issues of multiculturalism also could be raised here. Sometimes, a person identifies him- or herself more by ethnic background than by race. "Whereas race is used for socially marking groups based on physical differences, ethnicity allows for a broader range of affiliation, based for example on shared language, shared place of origin, or shared religion."[53] We live in a complex society in which there are many forms of cultural expression and heritage. To what extent should this cultural heritage be acknowledged and encouraged? Sometimes, respect for cultural practices would lead to the condoning of gender inequality and discrimination.[54] Problems about multiculturalism also arise, for example, in education and its content and in debates about how to present history to young children and what to include in literary canons. Obviously, this is an area that raises many issues for heated debate. However, there probably ought to be some balance between equal treatment under the law and basic civility toward all on the one hand, and acknowledging our differences and respecting the contributions that we all make because of the ways in which we differ, on the other hand.

AFFIRMATIVE ACTION AND PREFERENTIAL TREATMENT

Recently, demographics has led to an unusual problem in college and university enrollment figures. Women now earn approximately 56 percent of bachelor's degrees compared to 43 percent thirty years ago.[55] To remedy this problem, some college admissions officers are thinking about instituting programs that would increase undergraduate male enrollments. In effect, these programs would be affirmative action programs that would benefit males. However, when the figures are examined more closely, one finds that the numbers are partially affected by the larger proportion of minority and older women enrollees. For example, African American undergraduates of traditional age are 63 percent female and only 37 percent male. Moreover, the entering class numbers, 51 percent women and 49 percent men, are different than the graduating numbers. This is partly because male college freshmen spend more time exercising, watching TV, or partying than studying. Nevertheless, it is an interesting problem for affirmative action, reversing the usual issues.[56]

As mentioned earlier in the summary of civil rights legislation, the use of the term *affirmative action* and the policy itself originated more than three decades ago. Disputes about the justification of these practices continue, however. The first thing to note about affirmative action is that it comes in many forms. The idea suggested by the term is that to remedy certain injustices we need to do more than follow the negative requirement "Don't discriminate" or "Stop discriminating." The basic argument given for doing something more is usually that the other way will not or has not worked. Psychological reasons may be cited, for example, that discrimination and prejudice are so ingrained in people that they cannot help discriminating and do not even recognize when they are being discriminatory or prejudiced. According to one writer (see the second reading), it is as though we were transported to a land of giants where everything was made for folks their size. They just couldn't see why anyone else had difficulties, assuming instead that we were just inferior or incompetent.[57] Social and political reasons also can be given, for example, that the discrimination is institutionalized. Many rules and practices have a built-in discriminatory impact, such as the discriminatory result of the seniority system. It's like a top that just keeps on spinning, even when we take our hand away.[58] The only way to change things, the argument goes, is to do something more positive.

But what are we to do? There are many possibilities. One is to make a greater positive effort to find qualified persons. Thus, in hiring, a company might place ads in minority newspapers. In college admissions, counselors might be sent to schools with heavy student populations of underrepresented minority groups, or invite the students to campus, or give them special invitations to apply. Once the pool is enlarged, then all in the pool would be judged by the same criteria, and no special preferences would be given on the basis of race or sex.

Other versions of affirmative action involve what have come to be known as *preferences*. Preference or some special favoring or a plus factor could be given to minority group members or women who were equally well qualified with the other finalists to give them some edge. Preference also may be given for minority group members or women who were somewhat less well qualified than other applicants. In either case, it is clear that determining equality of qualification is in itself a problem. One reason for this is that applicants for a position that has several qualifications are usually stronger on some qualifications and weaker on others. Another is the difficulty of deciding just what qualifications are necessary or important for some position. Although those people who support or oppose preferences seem to imply that determining a position is easy, it is not at all that simple.

Other forms of affirmative action also exist. For example, companies or institutions may establish goals and quotas to be achieved for increasing minority or female representation. *Goals* are usually thought of as ideals that we aim for but that we are not absolutely required to reach. Goals can be formulated in terms of percentages or numbers. As of now, for example, U.S. federal contractors and all institutions with fifty or more employees and who receive federal funds of $50,000 or more must adopt affirmative action plans. These plans have sometimes involved setting goals for increasing the number of underrepresented minority members and women so that it might more closely reflect their percentage in the local labor pool. Companies might have specific recruiting plans for reaching their goals. These plans could, but would not necessarily, involve preferential treatments. *Quotas*, in contrast, are usually fixed percentages or numbers that a company intends to

actually reach. Thus, a university or professional school might set aside a fixed number of slots for its incoming first-year class for certain minority group members (note the Bakke and Weber cases mentioned earlier). The institution would fill these positions even if this meant admitting people with lesser overall scores or points in the assessment system.

In summary, the following types of affirmative action can be specified:

1. Enlarging the pool of applicants, then hiring on the basis of competence.
2. Giving preferences among equally qualified applicants.
3. Giving preferences for less-qualified applicants.
4. Setting goals or ideal numbers for which to aim; these goals need not involve preferences.
5. Setting quotas or fixed numbers to actually attain; these quotas usually do involve preferences.

The next question, then, to ask ourselves is, are these practices good or bad, justified or unjustified? All of them, or some of them, or none of them? In any discussion of affirmative action, it is important to specify what kind of practice one favors or opposes. Let us examine the arguments for and against the various types of affirmative action in terms of the reasons given to support them. These again can be easily divided into consequentialist and nonconsequentialist types of arguments.

Consequentialist Considerations

Arguments both for and against various affirmative action programs have relied on consequentialist considerations for their justification. These considerations are broadly utilitarian in nature. The question is whether such programs do more good than harm or more harm than good. Those people who argue in favor of these programs urge the following sorts of considerations: These programs benefit us all. We live in a multiracial society and benefit from mutual respect and harmony. We all bring diverse backgrounds to our employment and educational institutions, and we all benefit from the contributions of people who have a variety of diverse perspectives. Our law schools should have representation from all of the people who need adequate representation in society. We need to break the vicious circle of discrimination, disadvantage, and inequality. Past discrimination has put women and some minority group members at a continuing disadvantage. Unless something is done, they will never be able to compete on an equal basis or have an equal chance or equal opportunity.

Family plays a crucial role in what chances a child has.[59] To put it simply, low family income leads to poorer education for children, which leads to lower-paying jobs, which leads to low family income, and so on and so on. Affirmative action is one way to break the vicious circle of disadvantage. Children need role models to look up to. They need to know that certain types of achievement and participation are possible for them. Otherwise, they will not have hope and not have the opportunity to work to be what they can become. Without affirmative action programs, supporters argue, things are not likely to change. Discrimination is so entrenched that drastic measures are needed to overcome it. The statistics show that while some progress has been made, a great gap continues in the major indicators of success between members of certain minority groups and women and others in the society. And the programs have shown some success. In their 1998 work, *The Shape of the River*, the former presidents of Princeton and Harvard, William G. Bowen and Derek Bok, showed that race-sensitive policies in college admissions have worked.[60] Students admitted under these programs have graduated at good rates and "were just as likely as their white classmates to earn advanced degrees in law, business, or medicine."[61]

Legal challenges to preferential treatment continue to raise problems for affirmative action. In its 1996 decision in *Hopwood* v. *Texas*, a three-judge panel of the U.S. Court of Appeals for the Fifth Circuit struck down an affirmative action program at the University of Texas law school. This program had accepted lower scores on the Law School Admission Test (LSAT) for black and Mexican American applicants. In a parallel development, Proposition 209 in California outlawed racial preferences in the public sector, and in 1995 the board of regents of the University of California (UC) system voted to ban race considerations in admissions. As a result, the number of black applicants who gained admittance

to the UC system dropped 18 percent between the fall of 1997 and the fall of 1998. The number of African Americans admitted to the University of Texas at Austin law school declined 37.6 percent.[62] In 2003, the U.S. Supreme Court ruled in two related cases that the affirmative action program at the law school at the University of Michigan, which used race as one factor to create a more diverse student body in admissions, was constitutional. It also found that the undergraduate program that gave explicit numbers of points to minority members was unconstitutional as a form of quotas outlawed by the 1978 Bakke case.[63]

Those who argue against affirmative action on consequentialist grounds believe that the programs do not work or do more harm than good. They cite statistics to show that these programs have benefited middle-class African Americans, for example, but not the lower class. "The most disadvantaged black people are not in a position to benefit from preferential admission."[64] Unless affirmative action admissions programs are accompanied by other aid, both financial and tutorial, they are often useless or wasted. Some critics point out that lawsuits filed under the 1964 Civil Rights Act have done more than affirmative action to increase the percentage of blacks in various white-collar positions.[65] There is also the likelihood of stigma attached to those who have been admitted or hired through affirmative action programs. This can be debilitating to those who are chosen on this basis. Black neoconservatives, for example, argue that quotas and racially weighted tests "have psychologically handicapped blacks by making them dependent on racial-preference programs rather than their own hard work."[66] Those who oppose affirmative action programs also cite the increased racial tension that they believe results from these programs: in effect, a white male backlash against women and members of minority groups. Recently, some of the same writers who support affirmative action for underrepresented minority groups and women have also made a case for giving special attention to economically disadvantaged students in college and university admissions.[67] They point out that elite universities have only a miniscule percentage of admissions from lower-income families. It also is in the interest not only of fairness (see the following nonconsequentialist arguments) but also of increasing class diversity.

The key to evaluating these consequentialist arguments both for and against affirmative action is to examine the validity of their assessments and predictions. What, in fact, have affirmative action programs for college admissions achieved? Have they achieved little because they benefit those who least need it and might have succeeded without them, or have they actually brought more disadvantaged students into the system and into better and higher-paying jobs, thus helping break the vicious circle? Have other affirmative action programs increased racial harmony by increasing diversity in the workforce and in various communities, or have they only led to increasing racial tensions? These are difficult matters to assess. Here is another place where ethical judgments depend on empirical information drawn from the various sciences or other disciplines. The consequentialist argument for affirmative action programs will succeed if it can be shown that there is no better way to achieve the goods the programs are designed to achieve and that the good done by these affirmative action programs, or at least some of them, outweighs any harm they cause, including some racial tension and misplaced awards. The consequentialist argument against affirmative action programs will succeed if it can be shown that there are better ways to achieve the same good ends or that the harm they create outweighs the good they help achieve.

Nonconsequentialist Considerations

However, not all arguments about affirmative action programs are based on appeals to consequences. Some arguments appeal to considerations of justice. For instance, some people argue for affirmative action programs on the grounds that they provide justice, a way of making compensation for past wrongs done to members of certain groups. People have been harmed and wronged by past discrimination, and we now need to make up for that by benefiting them, by giving them preferential treatment. However, it is difficult to know how preferential treatment can right a past wrong. We may think of it as undoing the past harm done. Then we find that it is often difficult to undo the harm. How does one

really prevent or erase results such as the loss of self-esteem and confidence in the minority child who asks, "Mom, am I as good as the white kid?" or in the little girl who says, "I can't do that; I'm a girl"?[68] This interpretation of making compensation then becomes a matter of producing good consequences or eliminating bad ones. It is a matter of trying to change the results of past wrongs. Thus, if making compensation is to be a nonconsequentialist reason, then it must involve a different sense of righting a wrong, a sense of justice being done in itself whether or not it makes any difference in the outcome.

Some people also argue against affirmative action on grounds of its injustice. They appeal to the principle of equality, arguing that race and sex are irrelevant characteristics. Just as it was wrong in the past to use these characteristics to deny people equal chances, so it is also wrong in the present, even if it is used this time to give them preferences. Race and sex are not differences that should count in treating people differently to deny benefits to some and grant them to others. Preferences for some also mean denial to others. For this reason, preferential treatment programs have sometimes been labeled *reverse discrimination*. Moreover, opponents of affirmative action criticize the use of compensatory justice arguments. In a valid use of the principles of compensatory justice, they might argue, those and only those wronged should be compensated, and those and only those responsible for the wrong should be made to pay. But some programs of affirmative action have actually compensated people regardless of whether they themselves have been harmed by past discriminatory practices. They have also required that some people pay who have not been responsible for the past discrimination. Those who lose out in affirmative action programs, they argue, may not have ever been guilty of discrimination or may not have wronged anyone.

Consider the case of a group of white firefighters in New Haven, CT that went all the way to the U.S. Supreme Court in 2009. That city administered a test to the firefighters which would determine who was promoted. When no black firefighters passed the test, the city simply dropped all of the results. Those white firefighters who had passed complained of reverse discrimination. By a 5–4 ruling the court agreed with them. You be the judge also of whether the city proceeded properly.[69]

The arguments for affirmative action based on considerations of justice will succeed only if those people who make them also can make a case for the justice of the programs, that they do in fact compensate those who have been wronged, even if they have been affected by discrimination in ways that are not immediately obvious, and it is not unjust if other people have to pay. Supporters may cite the fact that those who lose out are not badly harmed—they have other opportunities and are not demeaned by their loss. Though they have not intentionally wronged anyone, they have likely benefited from past discrimination.

The arguments against affirmative action based on considerations of justice will succeed only if they can respond to these claims and make the principle of equality work for their case. They may cite the matter of consistency in applying the principle, for example. But if they rely primarily on the harms done by continuing to use race or sex as a characteristic that grounds differential treatment, then they will be appealing to a consequentialist consideration and must be judged on that basis. To answer this question, the more basic issues of the moral status of considerations of justice would need to be addressed. Justice is treated further in Chapter 14.

In the first reading, Robert Fullinwider discusses whether affirmative action is a justifiable social practice. In his "Letter from the Birmingham Jail" Martin Luther King, Jr. is responding to a group of white ministers who criticized him for breaking the law.

NOTES

1. www.msnbc.msn.com/id/15824096/; http://en.wikipedia.org/wiki/Flying_Imams_controversy.
2. http://www.militantislammonitor.org/article/id/ 2576
3. David Cole and John Marcello, "Symposium: Insight on the News," *Washington Times*, July 19, 1999, p. 24.
4. www.racialprofilinganalysis.neu.edu/; http://www.dallasnews.com/sharedcontent/dws/news/localnews/stories/DN-profiling_21met.ART.State.Edition1.20897ec.html; www.aclu.org/racialjustice/racialprofiling/index.html.
5. Cole and Marcello, op. cit., 24 (fn). It is interesting to note that "in the early 1970s it primarily was white U.S. citizens who controlled cocaine smuggling" into the United States, but in the 1980s Nigerian heroin smugglers "carried the drugs themselves, and then they started recruiting young white females" (ibid.).
6. *The New York Times*, 4/22/2010, p. A16.
7. Randall Kennedy, "Suspect Policy," *New Republic* (Sept. 13 and 20, 1999): 35.
8. Heather MacDonald, "The Myth of Racial Profiling," *City Journal*, *11*, no. 2 (Spring 2001). Found at http://www.city-journal.org/html/11_2_the_myth.html.
9. *Los Angeles Times*, 4/22/2010.
10. Associated Press; *CBS World News*, July 17, 2005.
11. "More Hate Crimes, Attacks on Mosques," *International Indian Express Web*, online, July 12, 2005.
12. Jodi Unruh, "Hate Crimes," KVAL-13 News, July 14, 2005 (online at www.kval.com).
13. Lucy Yang, "Hate Crimes Against Gays Up," WABC News, New York, June 19, 2005.
14. Naush Boghossian and Lisa M. Sodders, "School Hate Crimes Spike," June 2005 (online at www.dailynews.com); L.A. County Commission on Human Relations, "2006 Hate Crime Report" (http://lahuman-relations.org/hatecrime/hatecrimereport.htm); and the California Attorney General's Report 2006 (http://lahumanrelations.org/hatecrime/hatecrimereport.htm).
15. Cathy Lisa Schneider, "Racism, Drug Policy, and AIDS," *Political Science Quarterly*, *113*, no. 3 (Fall 1998): 427.
16. Alberto F. Cabrera, "Campus Racial Climate and the Adjustment of Students to College," *Journal of Higher Education*, *70* (March–April 1999): 134.
17. CNN, May 5, 2009.
18. *San Francisco Chronicle*, April 17, 2004, p. A5.
19. *The New York Times*, April 22, 2004, p. A22.
20. "Media Portrays Most Poor People as Black," Jet, 92 (Sept. 8, 1997): 25.
21. www.infoplease.com/ipa/A0763170.html.
22. "Bar Association Chief Assails Racial Disparity," The New York Times, Aug. 11, 1999, p. A17. Also see http://www.abanet.org/minorities/publications/milesummary.html.
23. Legal Information Institute, "US Code Collection" (found at www4.law.cornell.edu/uscode/42/12101.html).
24. See www4.law.cornell.edu/uscode/29/621.html.
25. James Brooke, "Denver Breaks New Ground on Gay Rights," *The New York Times*, Sept. 18, 1996.

26. "Women in Engineering: A Review of the 2004 Literature." Available from the Society of Women Engineers (www.swe.org).

27. Louis Uchitelle, "Gaining Ground on the Wage Front," *The New York Times*, Dec. 31, 2004, pp. C1–C2.

28. Ibid.

29. Anne Fisher, "After All This Time, Why Don't People Know What Sexual Harassment Means?" *Fortune*, *137*, no. 1 (Jan. 12, 1998): 156. Also see http://www.eeoc.gov/eeoc/statistics/enforcement/sexual_harassment-a.cfm and http://www.eeoc.gov/eeoc/statistics/enforcement/sexual_harassment.cfm.

30. "Harassed or Hazed; Why the Supreme Court Rules that Men Can Sue Men for Sexual Harassment," *Time*, *151*, no. 10 (March 16, 1998): 55.

31. Hans Kudnani, "Europe's Colour-Blind Prejudice," *New Statesman*, *127*, no. 4390 (June 19, 1998): 18.

32. William Keng Mun Lee, "Gender Inequality and Discrimination in Singapore," *Journal of Contemporary Asia*, *28* (Oct. 1998): 484.

33. Barbara Crosette, "UNICEF Opens a Global Drive on Violence Against Women," *The New York Times*, March 9, 2000, p. A6.

34. Ibid.

35. Amnesty International, "Culture of Discrimination: A Fact Sheet on 'Honor' Killings" (online at http://www.amnestyusa.org/violence-against-women/stop-violence-against-women-svaw/honor-killings/page.do?id=1108230).

36. "The Feminization of AIDS," *The New York Times*, Dec. 13, 2004, p. A28; http://www.iwhc.org/index.php?option=content&task=view&id=2472.

37. Erica Goode, "When Women Find Love Is Fatal," *The New York Times*, Feb. 15, 2000, pp. D1, D6. Also see www.endabuse.org/resources/facts.

38. Hanna Rosin and Steven Mufson, "Feminists Join Forces with Right Wing: 'Prostitution' Definition Rejected," *San Francisco Examiner*, Jan. 16, 2000, p. A8.

39. Linda Greenhouse, "University of Michigan Ruling Endorses the Value of Campus Diversity," *The New York Times*, June 24, 2003, pp. A1, A25.

40. This aspect of the bill confirmed the "disparate impact" notion of the 1971 U.S. Supreme Court ruling in *Griggs* v. *Duke Power Company*, which required companies to revise their business practices that perpetuated past discrimination. This was weakened by the Court's 1989 ruling in *Wards Cove Packing Co.* v. *Antonio*, which, among other things, put the burden of proof on the employee to show that the company did not have a good reason for some discriminatory business practice.

41. We also could cite legislation aimed against discrimination on the basis of age and the disabled: for example, the Age Discrimination Act (1967) and the Americans with Disabilities Act (1991).

42. R. C. Lewontin, "Race: Temporary Views on Human Variation," *Encyclopedia Americana* (online at http://ea.grolier.com). Also see R. C. Lewontin, *Human Diversity* (New York: W. H. Freeman, 1982).

43. Ibid.

44. Carolyn Abraham, "Race," *The Globe and Mail*, June 18, 2005, pp. F1, F8.

45. See www.hapmap.org.

46. Bernard Lewis, "The Historical Roots of Racism," *The American Scholar*, *67*, no. 1 (Winter 1998): 17A.

47. See Mary Ann Warren, "Secondary Sexism and Quota Hiring," *Philosophy and Public Affairs*, *6*, no. 3 (Spring 1977): 240–261.

48. Gina Kolata, "Men and Women Use Brain Differently, Study Discovers," *The New York Times*, Feb. 16, 1995, p. A8.

49. In this regard, the 1993 federal Family and Medical Leave Act allows both men and women to take unpaid leave to take care of a sick child or other close relative without losing their jobs or medical insurance.

50. M. T. Hallinan and A. B. Sorensen, *Sociological Education*, *60*, no. 63 (1987), as reported in Science, 237 (July 24, 1987): 350.

51. *The New York Times*, Feb. 16, 1995, pp. A1, A8.

52. Iris Marion Young, "Polity and Group Difference: A Critique of the Ideal of Universal Citizenship," in Sunstein Cass (Ed.), *Feminism and Political Theory* (Chicago: University of Chicago Press, 1990). Cited in an unpublished manuscript by Jennifer MacKinnon, "Rights and Responsibilities: A Reevaluation of Parental Leave and Child Care in the United States," Spring 1993.

53. Alaka Wali, "Multiculturalism: An Anthropological Perspective," *Report from the Institute for Philosophy and Public Policy*, Spring/Summer 1992, 6–8.

54. Susan Moller Okin, *Is Multiculturalism Bad for Women?* Joshua Cohen, Matthew Howard, and Martha C. Nussbaum (Eds.) (Princeton, NJ: Princeton University Press, 2000).

55. "Should the Lack of Males in College Be a Cause for Concern?" *On Campus*, Dec. 2000–Jan. 2001, p. 4.

56. Ibid.

57. Robert K. Fullinwider, "Affirmative Action and Fairness," *Report from the Institute for Philosophy and Public Policy*, *11*, no. 1 (Winter 1991): 10–13.

58. Ibid.

59. See James Fishkin, Justice, *Equal Opportunity and the Family* (New Haven, CT: Yale University Press, 1983), for documentation and analysis.

60. William G. Bowen and Derek Curtis Bok, *The Shape of the River: Long-Term Consequences of Considering Race in College and University Admissions* (Princeton, NJ: Princeton University Press, 1998).

61. David R. Gergen, "A Study in Black and White: Why Race-Sensitive College Admissions Policies Work," *U.S. News & World Report*, *125*, no. 14 (Oct. 12, 1998): 84.

62. William H. Gray III, "In the Best Interest of America, Affirmative Action in Higher Education Is a Must," *The Black Collegian*, *29*, no. 2 (Feb. 1999): 144.

63. www.npr.org/news/specials/michigan/; www.wsws .org/articles/2003/jun2003/affi-j25.shtml.

64. Stephen Carter, *Reflections of an Affirmative Action Baby* (New York: Basic Books, 1991).

65. Professor Jonathan Leonard, cited in the *San Francisco Examiner*, Sept. 29, 1991.

66. *Time* (May 27, 1991): 23.

67. Amy Argetsinger, "Princeton's Former President Challenges 'Bastions of Privilege'" *San Francisco Chronicle*, April 17, 2004, p. A5.

68. A parent's report.

69. CNN.com, June 29, 2009.

R E A D I N G
Affirmative Action and Fairness
ROBERT K. FULLINWIDER

Study Questions

1. How did the issue of quotas arise in the case of *Weber* v. *Kaiser Aluminum* and George H. W. Bush's veto of the 1990 Civil Rights Act?

2. How did William Bradford Reynolds describe the differences between equality of opportunity and equality of results?

3. According to Fullinwider, why did twenty years of federal judges' decisions support programs of affirmative action?

4. Why does he believe that good intentions not to discriminate are not enough to eliminate discrimination?

5. What did the *Griggs* v. *Duke Power Company* decision require of businesses?

6. How does the question about whether discrimination is "shallow" or "deep," "transparent" or "opaque" play a role in Fullinwider's argument?

7. For what purpose does he use the analogy of the land of the Giants?

Robert K. Fullinwider, "Affirmative Action and Fairness," from the *Report from the Institute for Philosophy and Public Policy*, vol. 11, no. 1 (Winter 1991): 10–13. © 1991 by the Institute for Philosophy and Public Policy. Reprinted by permission.

BEGIN BY talking about four white men: David Duke, Brian Weber, William Bradford Reynolds, and George Bush.

A former Klansman, a former leader of a white supremacist party, a purveyor of neo-Nazi literature, and now a representative in the state legislature, Duke took 40 percent of the vote in the 1990 senatorial primary in Louisiana—40 percent of the vote, 60 percent of the white vote. The main theme of his campaign: the injustice of affirmative action, the need for civil rights for whites. He tapped into something deep. He touched a nerve.

Brian Weber is also from Louisiana. In the 1970s he worked at a Kaiser Company chemical plant. That plant, like industry in general in the South, had a segregated work force. All of its black employees were relegated to a handful of unskilled jobs. There were none in the high-paying craft occupations. Moreover, given the company's rules and practices, little was likely to change. Kaiser hired craft workers by going outside the plant, using a regional labor market in which almost all workers trained in the craft were white. The chemical workers' union and the company agreed to a plan to change things: the company would henceforth train its own craft workers instead of hiring from the outside, and it set up an on-the-job training program, admitting plant workers into the program from two lists—a white list and a black list. For every white worker admitted, one black worker would be admitted—until 30 percent of the craft workers at the plant were black. An explicit racial criterion. A quota.

In Brian Weber's eyes, this was unjustified reverse discrimination. He brought suit in federal court, and in 1979 the Supreme Court found in favor of the company.

There is a real irony in Weber's lawsuit. Weber himself was an unskilled worker at the plant. Had the company maintained its practice of going to outside markets for craft workers, Brian Weber would never have risen very far within the plant. The new program meant that he now had a chance to advance himself; he only had to wait his turn. No matter. The racial preferences in the program touched a nerve. They weren't tolerable. They had to go.

Nor, for George Bush, is the mere threat of preferences in favor of blacks or women acceptable. In October 1990 he vetoed the new Civil Rights Act, which would have clarified certain standards of proof in civil rights lawsuits. His objection was that these standards of proof made it hard for firms to defend themselves against charges of discrimination. Consequently, some firms might be tempted to avoid discrimination charges by using quotas—giving racial or gender preferences to make sure their work forces had the right racial or gender profile. This possibility was enough to cause the president to reject the bill.

WHY QUOTAS ARE ANATHEMA

What is it, though, that makes a program like Kaiser's intolerable? What makes the mere risk of preferences unacceptable? Why is the Q-word anathema? That question brings me to the last man I'll talk about, William Bradford Reynolds. Reynolds headed the Office of Civil Rights in the Department of Justice during the Reagan Administration, and was that administration's leading spokesman on affirmative action and against quotas.

The debate about preferential treatment, he said, is between those (like himself) who believe in *equality of opportunity* and those who believe in *equality of results*. Those who *oppose* preferential treatment believe in individual rights and a colorblind, genderblind society. Those who *support* quotas believe in group rights and dividing up social benefits by race and gender. That's the way Reynolds put it.

Putting the matter this way is politically effective for opponents of affirmative action. Individual rights, equality of opportunity, success through effort and merit, reward because of what you do, not who you are—these values are as American as apple pie. Opposing preferential treatment isn't opposing racial and gender justice; it's just opposing an alien philosophy, an un-American ideology.

There may well be people who support preferential treatment because they believe in equality of results for its own sake, because they believe in group rights, or because they want a society shaped around color and gender. But the federal judges of this country are certainly not among those people, and it is federal courts who for twenty years have created or sustained the various parts of affirmative action, including the occasional use of quotas and preferences. Why have they done this? By their own account, to *prevent* discrimination and *secure* equality of opportunity.

Reynolds says that using racial and sexual preferences to end discrimination is nonsense; the way to end discrimination is not to discriminate in reverse but simply to *stop discriminating*. Exactly—if we can. If we can stop discriminating. That's the rub. And that's the problem courts ran into.

CAN'T WE JUST STOP DISCRIMINATING?

It takes more than good will and good intentions not to discriminate. It takes capability as well, and that may be hard to come by. To see what I'm talking about, let's look back at a company like Kaiser after the Civil Rights Act of 1964 outlawed discrimination in employment. The company may have employed no blacks at all. The sign in the window said: "No blacks apply." Now, how does the company comply with the law and stop discriminating? It takes the sign out of the window and says, "If blacks apply and meet all requirements, we will hire them." And suppose it is sincere. Is that enough?

Look at how other aspects of company policy may work. Suppose the company only advertises its jobs by word of mouth. It posts job openings on the bulletin board and lets the grapevine do the rest. Then few blacks will ever hear of openings since all the workers are white—a fact reflecting, of course, the company's past discrimination. A company policy not itself designed to keep blacks out nevertheless does exactly that. Or suppose that the company requires each applicant to provide a letter of recommendation from some current or former employee. All the current and former employees are white, so this policy, too, is going to exclude blacks. Taking the sign out of the window changes nothing at all.

This is what courts encountered when they began adjudicating civil rights cases in the 1960s. Because the system of discrimination has been so thorough and in place for so long, it was like the child's spinning top, which keeps on spinning even after you take your hand away. Ordinary business practices let a firm's prior discrimination keep reproducing itself—and that reproduction, whether intended or not, is *itself* discrimination. So concluded a unanimous Supreme Court in the landmark 1971 case *Griggs* v. *Duke Power Company*. In order to comply with the law, businesses must look at all parts of their operations—job classifications, work rules, seniority systems, physical organization, recruitment and retention policies, everything—and revise, where possible, those elements that reproduce past discrimination. That's the core idea of affirmative action, as it was born in the early 1970s from the experience of courts trying to assure nondiscrimination and equal opportunity, and as extended through federal rules to all recipients of government contracts and funds.

Make a plan (these rules say) that establishes a system for monitoring your workplace and operations; that changes procedures and operations where you see they may have discriminatory impact; and that predicts what your work force would look like were you successfully nondiscriminating, so you will have some measure of the success or failure of your efforts.

Those are the basic elements of affirmative action. They are surely reasonable. Even William Bradford

Reynolds accepted most of this. Why is there ever a need for more? Why is there ever a need actually to impose racial or gender quotas? Or to risk their being adopted by firms?

Because sometimes it takes strong measures for us to see how to do what is needed to secure the reality of equal opportunity, not just its form. If we've built a whole world around discrimination, then many of the ways the world discriminates may not be visible to us even when we go looking. We may not be able to see all the ways our business practices exclude women and blacks from the workplace or detract from their performance there until the workplace is actually changed by having women and blacks in it. And one quick way of changing the composition of the workplace is through quotas.

Courts have sometimes—not often—resorted to quotas when they were convinced that an institution was simply not capable of identifying and changing all the features of its practices that discriminate. Often the quotas have been imposed on companies or municipal agencies whose own histories showed them completely unwilling to make anything but token changes. But sometimes they've been imposed where the sheer inertial weight of company culture and organization convinced the court that the company would never be able to find "qualified" minorities or women, no matter how hard it tried. The culture itself had to be changed by putting minorities and women in roles from which they had been excluded.

Here is where the real issue lies. It is about the nature and sweep of discrimination. Do we think discrimination is a relatively *shallow* or a very *deep* phenomenon? Do we think discrimination is *transparent* or *opaque*? The answer need not be a flat yes or no. Perhaps in some places discrimination is shallow, in some places deep; in some circumstances transparent, in others opaque. If discrimination is shallow and transparent, then modest affirmative action should be enough to cure it: we look for, find, and eliminate practices that are reproducing the effects of past discrimination. But if discrimination is deep and opaque, then we may not be able to find it even when we look, and more robust forms of affirmative action may be necessary. We may need rather sharp assistance to see the way our practices work to exclude and oppress. We may need to be shocked or shaken out of our old habits, to have our consciousness raised.

This, I think, is the heart of the controversy about affirmative action. The difference is not that some people want equal opportunity and some want equality of results, that some believe in individual rights and some believe in group entitlements. The difference is that some think discrimination is always transparent and shallow while others think it is—sometimes, at least, in some sectors or institutions—deep, enduring, and opaque.

THE LAND OF THE GIANTS

To drive home this point about the opacity of discrimination and how it can subvert good will and good intentions, I ask you to go through some thought experiments with me. Start with a simple fantasy. Imagine we were suddenly all transported to the land of the Giants. They would be puzzled and wonder what in the world to make of us; and in short order they would probably conclude that, though we were like them in many ways, still we were quite incapable, incompetent, *inferior* creatures—for although we have our charming side, we really can't manage to do well even the simplest tasks in Giant Land. We just don't measure up. Perhaps it's just our nature to be helpless, the Giants conclude. We must have been some unfortunate quirk in God's creation.

But we would know that the problem does not lie in us, it lies in the fact that everything in Giant Land is built to the scale of Giants. That world is built for Giants and of course we don't do well in that world—but give us back the world built for us and see what we can do! We can even outperform Giants!

What's my point? It's that the Giants see *their* world as *the* world. They just naturally measure us against it, so they see the problem to be in us.

This is just fantasy, you say, and besides, the Giants wouldn't have been so dense. If you think not, then turn to a second example—a real one.

Twenty-five years ago, we tended to think that people in wheelchairs couldn't do much. It was a shame they were in wheelchairs—it wasn't their fault—but it meant that they were incapable of doing what most of the rest of us did. They were very limited in their mobility, thus not qualified for most jobs. And so they were excluded. Left out. Omitted.

Why did we think that? Not because we disliked people in wheelchairs. It was because, when they had trouble performing operations we do easily, we naturally attributed the trouble to *them*—to *their* condition—because we just took the world as it was for granted. And how was that world? It was a world of *curbs*. Curbs everywhere.

Now, curbs are not supplied by nature. The world of curbs was made—made by and for us, the walking, running, jumping types. It took federal law that mandated tearing up the sidewalks at nearly every intersection in this country to jar us into realizing that many of the problems people in wheelchairs faced lay not in them but in the fact that we had *made* a world that excluded them, and then, like the Giants, had assumed *that* world was *the* world.

UNAVOIDABLE UNFAIRNESS

The world of Giants—the world of curbs—the world of whites and men: imagine, if you will, a world built over a long time by and for men, by and for whites. In that world there would be a thousand and one impediments to women and blacks working effectively and successfully. That world and its institutions would be suffused through and through with inhospitality to blacks and women—just as Giant Land was inhospitable to us little people, and Curb World was inhospitable to wheelchair people. Imagine that world—or do you have to imagine it? That's the world we still live in, isn't it?

Isn't it plausible that strong measures may be needed to change it? Are those strong measures, if they involve racial or gender preferences, unfair to white men? Of course they are. Well, doesn't that settle the matter? It would if we could always be fair without sometimes being unfair. Does that sound puzzling?

Think a moment. What are our options? Consider the civil rights bill George Bush vetoed. . . . If we set high burdens of proof on businesses, some of them may resort to quotas—and *that's* unfair discrimination. But if we don't set high standards, some businesses won't make the necessary effort to change practices that still hinder blacks and women—and that's unfair discrimination. Sometimes we may be faced only with the choice of risking unfairness in one direction or risking it in another. Sometimes we may have no choice except to impose one unfairness or allow another to persist. Then what do we do?

President Bush vetoed the civil rights bill because it created the risk of quotas. Does he believe, then, that vetoing it creates no risks that some blacks and women will continue to be discriminated against, or is the unspoken premise this: that the risk of victimization is tolerable if the victims are not white men?

R E A D I N G
Letter from a Birmingham Jail
MARTIN LUTHER KING, JR.

Study Questions

1. How does King differentiate between just and unjust laws?
2. How does he argue that segregation laws are unjust?
3. How does he argue that in some cases civil disobedience is morally required?
4. How does non-violence play a role in King's argument?
5. How does he criticize white moderates?

My Dear Fellow Clergymen,

While confine here in the Birmingham city jail, I came across your recent statement calling our present activities "unwise and untimely." Seldom, if ever, do I pause to answer criticism of my work and ideas. If I sought to answer all of the criticisms that cross my desk, my secretaries would be engaged in little else in the course of the day, and I would have no time for constructive work. But since I feel that you are men of genuine good will and your criticisms are sincerely set forth, I would like to answer your statement in what I hope will be patient and reasonable terms. . . . ?

. . . . I am in Birmingham because injustice is here. Just as the eighth-century prophets left their little villages and carried their "thus saith the Lord" far beyond the boundaries of their hometowns; and just as the Apostle Paul left his little village of Tarsus and carried the gospel of Jesus Christ to practically every hamlet and city of the Graeco-Roman world, I too am compelled to carry the gospel of freedom beyond my particular hometown. Like Paul, I must constantly respond to the Macedonian call for aid.

Moreover, I am cognizant of the interrelatedness of all communities and states. I cannot sit idly by in Atlanta and not be concerned about what happens in Birmingham. Injustice anywhere is a threat to justice everywhere. We are caught in an inescapable network of mutuality, tied in a single garment of destiny. Never again can we afford to live with the narrow, provincial "outside agitator" idea. Anyone who lives in the United States can never be considered an outsider anywhere in this country.

You deplore the demonstrations that are presently taking place in Birmingham. But I am sorry that your statement did not express a similar concern for the conditions that brought the demonstrations into being. I am sure that each of you would want to go beyond the superficial social analyst who looks merely at effects, and does not grapple with underlying causes. I would not hesitate to say that it is unfortunate that so-called demonstrations are taking place in Birmingham at this time, but I would say in more emphatic terms that it is even more unfortunate that the white power structure of this city left the Negro community with no other alternative.

In any nonviolent campaign there are four basic steps: (1) collection of the facts to determine whether injustices are alive, (2) negotiation, (3) self-purification, and (4) direct action. We have gone through all of these steps in Birmingham. There can be no gainsaying of the fact that racial injustice engulfs this community. . . .

You express a great deal of anxiety over our willingness to break laws. This is certainly a legitimate concern. Since we so diligently urge people to obey the Supreme Court's decision of 1954 outlawing segregation in the public schools, it is rather strange and paradoxical to find us consciously breaking laws. One may well ask, "How can you advocate breaking some laws and obeying others?" The answer is found in the

"Letter from Birmingham Jail" In *I Have a Dream: Writings and Speeches that Changed the World*, ed. J. M. Washington. San Francisco: Harper San Francisco, 1992. Reprinted by arrangement with the The Heirs to the Estate of Martin Luther King, Jr, c/o Writers House as agent for the proprietor. Copyright 1963, renewed 1991 by Corretta Scott King.

fact that there are two types of laws: there are *just* and there are *unjust* laws. I would agree with Saint Augustine that "An unjust law is no law at all."

Now what is the difference between the two? How does one determine when a law is just or unjust? A just law is a man-made code that squares with the moral law or the law of God. An unjust law is a code that is out of harmony with the moral law. To put it in the terms of Saint Thomas Aquinas, an unjust law is a human law that is not rooted in eternal and natural law. Any law that uplifts human personality is just. Any law that degrades human personality is unjust. All segregation statutes are unjust because segregation distorts the soul and damages the personality. It gives the segregator a false sense of superiority, and the segregated a false sense of inferiority. To use the words of Martin Buber, the great Jewish philosopher, segregation substitutes an "I-it" relationship for the "I-thou" relationship, and ends up relegating persons to the status of things. So segregation is not only politically, economically and sociologically unsound, but it is morally wrong and sinful. Paul Tillich has said that sin is separation. Isn't segregation an existential expression of man's tragic separation, an expression of his awful estrangement, his terrible sinfulness? So I can urge men to disobey segregation ordinances because they are morally wrong.

Let us turn to a more concrete example of just and unjust laws. An unjust law is a code that a majority inflicts on a minority that is not binding on itself. This is difference made legal. On the other hand a just law is a code that a majority compels a minority to follow that it is willing to follow itself. This is sameness made legal.

Let me give another explanation. An unjust law is a code inflicted upon a minority which that minority had no part in enacting or creating because they did not have the unhampered right to vote. Who can say that the legislature of Alabama which set up the segregation laws was democratically elected? Throughout the state of Alabama all types of conniving methods are used to prevent Negroes from becoming registered voters and there are some counties without a single Negro registered to vote despite the fact that the Negro constitutes a majority of the population. Can any law set up in such a state be considered democratically structured?

These are just a few examples of unjust and just laws. There are some instances when a law is just on

its face and unjust in its application. For instance, I was arrested Friday on a charge of parading without a permit. Now there is nothing wrong with an ordinance which requires a permit for a parade, but when the ordinance is used to preserve segregation and to deny citizens the First Amendment privilege of peaceful assembly and peaceful protest, then it becomes unjust.

I hope you can see the distinction I am trying to point out. In no sense do I advocate evading or defying the law as the rabid segregationist would do. This would lead to anarchy. One who breaks an unjust law must do it *openly, lovingly* (not hatefully as the white mothers did in New Orleans when they were seen on television screaming, "nigger, nigger, nigger"), and with a willingness to accept the penalty. I submit that an individual who breaks a law that conscience tells him is unjust, and willingly accepts the penalty by staying in jail to arouse the conscience of the community over its injustice, is in reality expressing the very highest respect for law.

Of course, there is nothing new about this kind of civil disobedience. It was seen sublimely the refusal of Shadrach, Meshach and Abednego to obey the laws of Nebuchadnezzar because a higher moral law was involved. It was practiced superbly by the early Christians who were willing to face hungry lions and the excruciating pain of chopping blocks, before submitting to certain unjust laws of the Roman Empire. To a degree academic freedom is a reality today because Socrates practiced civil disobedience.

We can never forget that everything Hitler did in Germany was "legal" and everything the Hungarian freedom fighters did in Hungary was "illegal." It was "illegal" to aid and comfort a Jew in Hitler's Germany. But I am sure that if I had lived in Germany during that time I would have aided and comforted my Jewish brothers even though it was illegal. If I lived in a Communist country today where certain principles dear to the Christian faith are suppressed, I believe I would openly advocate disobeying these anti-religious laws. I must make two honest confessions to you, my Christian and Jewish brothers. First, I must confess that over the last few years I have been gravely disappointed with the white moderate. I have almost reached the regrettable conclusion that the Negro's great stumbling block in the stride toward freedom is not the White Citizens Counciler or the Ku Klux Klanner, but the white moderate who is more devoted to "order" than to justice; who prefers a negative peace which is the absence of tension to a positive peace which is the presence of justice; who constantly says, "I agree with you in the goal you seek, but I can't agree with your methods of direct action"; who paternalistically feels that he can set the timetable for another man's freedom; who lives by the myth of time and who constantly advised the Negro to wait until a "more convenient season." Shallow understanding from people of good will is more frustrating than absolute misunderstanding from people of ill will. Lukewarm acceptance is much more bewildering than outright rejection.

I had hoped that the white moderate would understand that law and order exist for the purpose of establishing justice, and that when they fail to do this they become dangerously structured dams that block the flow of social progress. I had hope a white moderate would understand that the present tension of the South is merely a necessary phase of the transition from an obnoxious negative peace, where the Negro passively accepted his unjust plight, to a substance-filled positive peace, where all men will respect the dignity and worth of human personality. Actually, we who engage in non-violent direct action are not the creators of tension. We merely bring to the surface the hidden tension that is already alive. We bring it out in the open where it can be seen and dealt with. Like a boil that can never be cured as long as it is covered up but must be opened with all its pus-flowing ugliness to the natural medicines of air and light, injustice must likewise be exposed, with all of the tension its exposing creates, to the light of human conscience and the air of national opinion before it can be cured.

In your statement you asserted that our actions, even though peaceful, must be condemned because they precipitate violence. But can this assertion be logically made? Isn't this like condemning the robbed man because his possession of money precipitated the evil act of robbery? Isn't this like condemning Socrates because his unswerving commitment to truth and his philosophical delvings precipitated the misguided popular mind to make him drink the hemlock? Isn't this like condemning Jesus because His unique God-consciousness and never-ceasing devotion to his will precipitated the evil act of crucifixion? We must come to see, as federal courts have consistently affirmed, that it is immoral to urge an individual to withdraw

his efforts to gain his basic constitutional rights because the quest precipitates violence. Society must protect the robbed and punish the robber. . . .

There was a time when the church was very powerful. It was during that period when the early Christians rejoiced when they were deemed worthy to suffer for what they believed. In those days the church was not merely a thermometer that recorded the ideas and principles of popular opinion; it was a thermostat that transformed the mores of society. Wherever the early Christians entered a town the power structure got disturbed and immediately sought to convict them for being "disturbers of the peace" and "outside agitators." But they went on with the conviction that they were "a colony of heaven," and had to obey God rather than man. They were small in number but big in commitment. They were too God-intoxicated to be "astronomically intimated." They brought an end to such ancient evils as infanticide and gladiatorial contest.

Things are different now. The contemporary church is often a weak, ineffectual voice with an uncertain sound. It is so often the arch-supporter of the status quo. Far from being disturbed by the presence of the church, the power structure of the average community is consoled by the church's silent and often vocal sanction of things as they are.

But the judgment of God is upon the church as never before. If the church of today does not recapture the sacrificial spirit of the early church, it will lose its authentic ring, forfeit the loyalty of millions, and be dismissed as an irrelevant social club with no meaning for the twentieth century. I am meeting young people every day whose disappointment with the church has risen to outright disgust.

Maybe again, I have been too optimistic. Is organized religion too inextricably bound to the status quo to save our nation and the world? Maybe I must turn my faith to the inner spiritual church, the church within the church, as the true *ecclesia* and the hope of the world. But again I am thankful to God that some noble souls from the ranks of organized religion have broken loose from the paralyzing chains of conformity and joined us as active partners in the struggle for freedom. They have left their secure congregations and walked the streets of Albany, Georgia, with us. They have gone through the highways of the South on tortuous rides for freedom. Yes, they have gone to jail with us. Some have been kicked out of their churches, and lost support of their bishops and fellow ministers. But they have gone with the faith that right defeated is stronger than evil triumphant. These men have been the leaven in the lump of the race. Their witness has been the spiritual salt that has preserved the true meaning of the gospel in these troubled times. They have carved a tunnel of hope through the dark mountain of disappointment.

I hope the church as a whole will meet the challenge of this decisive hour. But even if the church does not come to the aid of justice, I have no despair about the future. I have no fear about the outcome of our struggle in Birmingham, even if our motives are presently misunderstood. We will reach the goal of freedom in Birmingham and all over the nation,

because the goal of America is freedom. Abused and scorned through we may be, our destiny is tied up with the destiny of America. Before the Pilgrims lauded at Plymouth we were here. Before the pen of Jefferson etched across the pages of history the majestic words of the Declaration of Independence, we were here. For more than two centuries our foreparents labored in this country without wages; they made cotton king; and they built the homes of their masters in the midst of brutal injustice and shameful humiliation—and yet out of a bottomless vitality they continued to thrive and develop. If the inexpressible cruelties of slavery could not stop us, the opposition we now face will surely fail. We will win our freedom because the sacred heritage of our nation aid the eternal will of God are embodied in our echoing demands.

REVIEW EXERCISES

1. In the history of affirmative action and civil rights legislation:
   a. When were the terms *preferential treatment* and *affirmative action* first used?
   b. What is the difference between the Equal Pay Act and Title VII of the 1964 Civil Rights Act?
   c. Has the U.S. Supreme Court ever forbidden the use of racial quotas? Approved them?
2. What is meant by *racism*? *sexism*? Are there any other similar "ism"s?
3. Explain the five different elements of the principle of equality as it was given here.
4. What is the difference between individual, group, and average differences? How are these an issue in the application of the principle of equality?
5. What is "affirmative action," and why does it have this name? Give five different types of affirmative action. Which of them involve or may involve giving preferential treatment?
6. Summarize the consequentialist arguments for and against affirmative action.
7. Summarize the nonconsequentialist arguments for and against affirmative action.

DISCUSSION CASES

1. Preferences in Hiring. XYZ University has an opening in its philosophy department. Currently, the full-time faculty in this department is all-male. The department has received 200 applications for this position. It has been advised by the dean that because half the student body is female, the department should seek a woman to fill this position. The school is also under affirmative action guidelines because it receives federal funding for some of

its programs. The faculty members have agreed to consider seriously the several applications from females that they have received. The qualifications for the position, the field of specialization, have been advertised. But there are several other ways in which the position is open. The list has been narrowed to the ten top candidates, two of whom are women. All ten are well qualified in their own ways. The department is split on what to do. Some members believe that because all ten are well qualified, they should choose one of the two women. The other members believe that the most qualified of the final group do not include the two women.

What do you think the department should do? Why?

2. Campus Diversity. During the last couple of decades, colleges and universities have tried to increase their numbers of minority students by various forms of affirmative action. At Campus X, this has led to no small amount of dissension. Some students complain that the policy of accepting students with lower SAT and other scores just because of their race or minority status is unfair. Others believe that the diversity that results from such policies is good for everyone because we should learn to live together and a university campus should be a place to do this. Still, there is some question even among members of this group as to how well the integration is working. Furthermore, a different type of problem has recently surfaced. Because Asian Americans were represented in numbers greater than their percentage of the population, some universities were restricting the percentage they would accept even when their scores were higher than others they did accept. Also, in some cases where affirmative action has been eliminated,

the number of minority members accepted into certain medical and law schools has plummeted, and many people find this alarming.

Do you think that diversity ought to be a goal of campus admissions? Or do you believe that only academic qualifications ought to count? Why?

3. Racial Profiling. The U.S. Border Patrol has been accused of using racial profiling in its decisions about whom to select for questioning in border regions. People who "look Mexican" have been stopped and questioned under suspicion of being illegal immigrants. Border Patrol agents say that this is justified because a high percentage of Latinos in border areas are in the United States illegally. Latinos who are U.S. citizens say that they are repeatedly stopped just because of their race and appearance, and they resent this. Do you believe that using race in such decisions is a justifiable law-enforcement tactic or is it unjust discrimination? Is the use of race as one element in deciding whom to stop or question ever justified? What if there are sociological data to show that a high percentage of people of some racial or ethnic group account for an unusually high percentage of those who are responsible for a certain type of crime? How do we weigh the costs of such profiling to social harmony and to those individuals wrongly accused?

YOU MAKE THE DECISION

Apply the theories and issues discussed in this chapter by accessing this animated simulation on the Ethics Resource Center.

Use the passkey that accompanies your book to gain access. If you do not have a passkey, visit cengagebrain.com to purchase instant access to additional study material.

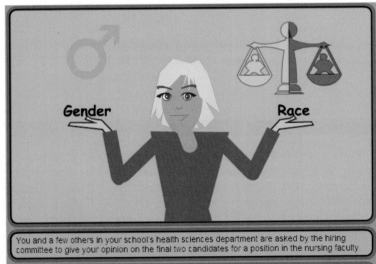

Gender   Race

You and a few others in your school's health sciences department are asked by the hiring committee to give your opinion on the final two candidates for a position in the nursing faculty

Ethics Module 13 : Equality and Discrimination   ◀◀ ▶ ▶▶   UNMUTE ◀

© Cengage Learning

14

Economic Justice

PERHAPS YOU have heard something like the following dialogue. It might be carried on between a student majoring in business and another majoring in philosophy. Here we will call them Betty Business Major and Phil Philosophy Major.

Betty: I think that people have a right to make and keep as much money as they can as long as they do not infringe on others' rights. Thus, we should not be taxing the rich to give to the poor.

Phil: Is it fair that some people are born with a silver spoon in their mouths and others are not? The poor often have not had a chance to get ahead. Society owes them that much. They are people just like everyone else.

Betty: But how could we guarantee that they will not waste what we give them? In any case, it is just not right to take the money of those who have worked hard for it and redistribute it. They who earned it deserve to keep it.

Phil: Why do they deserve to keep what they have earned? If they are in the position that they are in because of the good education and good example provided by their parents, how do they themselves deserve what they can get with that?

Betty: In any case, if we take what such people have earned, whether they deserve it or not, they will have no incentive to work. Profits are what make the economy of a nation grow.

Phil: And why is that so? Does this imply that the only reason people work is for their own self-interest?

That sounds like good old capitalism to me, as your idol Adam Smith would have it. But is a capitalistic system a just economic system?

Betty: Justice does not seem to me to require that everyone have equal amounts of wealth. If justice is fairness, as some of your philosophers say, it is only fair and therefore just that people get out of the system what they put into it. And, besides, there are other values. We value freedom, too, don't we? People ought to be free to work and keep what they earn.

At least we can agree on one thing, that something ought to be done about the latest corporate scandals. There is too much corporate greed and corruption. If there is not sufficient transparency in corporate business practices, then investors will not be able to make wise decisions and inefficiency will taint and harm the system.

Phil: It is also unfair for corporate executives to greedily take more than their honest share of a company's profits. It is the little guy and gal who are saving for their kids' college education or retirement that get hurt the most from such schemes.

The issues touched on in this conversation belong to a group of issues that fall under the topic of what has been called *economic justice*. There are other issues as well. For example, do people have a right to a job and good wages? Is welfare aid to the poor a matter of charity or justice? Is an economic system that requires a pool of unemployed workers a just system? Is it fair to tax the rich more heavily than the middle class?

INCOME INEQUALITY

In 2007, Alan Greenspan, the former chair of the board of governors of the Federal Reserve, noted: "Income inequality is where the capitalist system is most vulnerable. You can't have the capitalist system if an increasing number of people think it is unjust."[1]

The gap between the rich and poor in the United States, for example, has been widening for some time. In recent years, the gap has been the widest since our government began to keep records on it in 1947. In 2006, the richest 20 percent of households saw their share of national income at 49.6 percent, up from 43.6 percent in 1975. Also, those in the lowest 20 percent got just 3.3 percent, a fall from 4.3 percent.[2] "The wealthiest 10 percent of Americans—those making more than $138,000 each year—earned 11.4 times the roughly $12,000 made by those living near or below the poverty line in 2008."[3] And in another startling matter, "the richest one percent of U.S. households now owns 34.3 percent of the nation's private wealth, more than the combined wealth of the bottom 90 percent."[4]

The income of all women compared to men has improved over the years, but in 2007 it was still only 80 percent of what men made. Furthermore, the wage gap "cuts across a wide spectrum of occupations." See chapter 12 for more data on the wage gap.[5] This income gap is partly a result of the fact that more women leave work to care for children and elderly parents, and they are more likely to work part-time. When they work at jobs with similar skills, women who have never had children earn close to 98 percent of what men do.[6]

Race is also a factor in income. In 2004, for example, black men earned only 74.5 percent and Hispanic men only 63.2 percent of what white men earned.

The income gap narrows somewhat when taxes and welfare income are factored in. The gap partly results from an influx of immigrants who have, on average, lower levels of education than native-born Americans.[7] More recently, with the slowing of the economy and fewer jobs available, the gap between rich and poor will probably continue or widen.

Most people find such inequality unsettling. This is particularly true when they compare the huge salaries

Former CEOs of the American International Group (AIG) testifying before Congress. The company played a major role in the 2008 financial collapse and received $170 billion in federal bail-out money. A scandal later erupted over huge bonuses the company continued to pay its executives.

and bonuses of top corporate executives to the incomes of ordinary workers. In January 2010, the nation's biggest banks paid out huge bonuses of millions or billions of dollars in spite of the recession. This was at the same time that many Americans were out of jobs or feeling the hardships of the recession.[8] In 1894, the income of industrialist John D. Rockefeller was $1.25 million. This was some 7,000 times the average national income. In 2004, "the average CEO of a major company received $9.84 million in total compensation. This was an increase of 12 percent over the previous year. Compare this with the average pay of nonsupervisory workers of $27,485, an increase of 2.2 percent over the previous year."[9] And in 2006, James Simon, a hedge-fund manager, made $1.7 billion. This was more than 38,000 times the average national income for that year.[10] In 1980, corporate executives of large companies earned forty-five times more than nonsupervisory workers, but by 2000 the pay of the executives was 458 times that of ordinary workers.[11] Such great differences seem neither fair nor just.

Health Care

In one important area, income inequities are matched by inequities in health care. A family's savings can be wiped out with a major health problem when the family has no health insurance. Hopefully this will change with the 2010 health care reform bill that promised to expand health insurance coverage to many of the tens of millions of uninsured Americans.

Although genes and lifestyle certainly play their roles in a person's health, poverty does so as well. Strangely, perhaps, but poor people are more likely to be obese than those who are economically better off. If you have little to spend on food and want to get the most calories for your dollar, you will find these foods in the center section of your local supermarket. Notice that the healthy fruits and vegetables and the meat sections are located on the periphery. In the center of the store are processed foods that have little nutritional value, such as cookies, chips, and sodas. Orange juice and carrots may be better for you, but they cost more.[12]

Justice, Charity, and Efficiency

It is important to distinguish justice from certain other moral notions. For example, justice is not the same as charity. It is one thing to say that a community, like a family, will help its poorer members when they are in need out of concern for their welfare. But is helping people in need ever a matter of justice? If we say that it is, then we imply that it is not morally optional. We can think of *justice* here as the giving of what is rightly due, and *charity* as what is above and beyond the requirements of justice. Furthermore, justice is not the only relevant moral issue in economic matters. *Efficiency* and *liberty* are also moral values that play a role in discussions on ethics and economics. When we say that a particular economic system is efficient, we generally mean that it produces a maximum amount of desired goods and services, or the most value for the least cost. Thus, some people say that a free-market economy is a good economic system because it is the most efficient type of system, the one best able to create wealth. But it is quite another question to ask

whether such a system is also a *just* system. Nevertheless, efficiency is important, and so too is freedom or liberty. If we could have the most just and perhaps even the most efficient economic system in the world, then would it be worth it if we were not also free to make our own decisions about many things, including how to earn a living and what to do with our money?

In this chapter, we will be discussing what is generally termed *distributive justice*. Distributive justice has to do with how goods are allocated among persons—for example, who and how many people have what percentage of the goods or wealth in a society. Thus, suppose that in some society 5 percent of the people possessed 90 percent of the wealth, and the other 95 percent of the people possessed the other 10 percent of the wealth. Asking whether this arrangement would be just is raising a question of distributive justice. Now how would we go about answering this question? It does seem that this particular distribution of wealth is quite unbalanced. But must a distribution be equal for it to be just? To answer this question, we can examine two quite different ways of approaching distributive justice. One is what we can call a *process view*, and the other is an *end-state view*.

PROCESS DISTRIBUTIVE JUSTICE

According to some philosophers, any economic distribution (or any system that allows a particular economic distribution) is just if the process by which it comes about is itself just. Some call this *procedural justice*. For example, if the wealthiest 5 percent of the people got their 90 percent of the wealth fairly—they competed for jobs, they were honest, they did not take what was not theirs—then what they earned would be rightly theirs. In contrast, if the wealthy obtained their wealth through force or fraud, then their having such wealth would be unfair because they took it unfairly. But there would be nothing unfair or unjust about the uneven distribution in itself. (See the reading selection by Robert Nozick for an example of elements of this view.) We might suspect that because talent is more evenly distributed, there is something suspicious about this uneven distribution of wealth. We might suspect that coercion or unjust taking or unfair competition or dishonesty was involved. Now some people are wealthy because of good luck and fortune, and others are poor because of bad economic luck. However, in this view, those who keep money that through luck or good fortune falls to them from the sky, so to speak, are not being unjust in keeping it even when others are poor.

END-STATE DISTRIBUTIVE JUSTICE

Other philosophers believe that the process by which people attain wealth is not the only consideration relevant to determining the justice of an economic distribution. They believe that we also should look at the way things turn out, the end state, or the resulting distribution of wealth in a society, and ask about its fairness. Suppose that the lucky people possessed the 95 percent of the wealth through inheritance, for example. Would it be fair for them to have so much wealth when others in the society are extremely poor? How would we usually judge whether such an arrangement is fair? We would look to see if there is some good reason why the wealthy are wealthy. Did they work hard for it? Did they make important social contributions? These might be nonarbitrary or good reasons for the wealthy to possess their wealth rightly or justly. However, if they are wealthy while others are poor because they, unlike the others, were born of a certain favored race or sex or eye color or height, then we might be inclined to say that it is not fair for them to have more. What reasons, then, justify differences in wealth?

Several different views exist on this issue. Radical egalitarians deny that there is any good reason why some people should possess greater wealth than others. Their reasons for this view vary. They might stress that human beings are essentially alike as human and that this is more important than any differentiating factors about them, including their talents and what they do with them. They might use religious or semireligious reasons such as that the Earth is given to all of us equally and thus we all have an equal right to the goods derived from it.

Even egalitarians, however, must decide what it is that they believe should be equal. Should there be equality of wealth and income or equality of satisfaction or welfare, for example? These are not the same. Some people have little wealth or income but nevertheless are quite satisfied, while others who have great wealth or income are quite dissatisfied. Some have champagne tastes, and others are satisfied with beer!

On the other hand, at least some basic differences between people should make a difference in what distribution of goods is thought to be just. For example, some people simply have different needs than others. People are not identical physically, and some of us need more food and different kinds of health care than others. Karl Marx's "To each according to his need" captures something of this variant of egalitarianism.[13] Nevertheless, why only this particular differentiating factor—need—should justify differences in wealth is puzzling. In fact, we generally would tend to pick out others as well—differences in merit, achievement, effort, or contribution.

Suppose, for example, that Jim uses his talent and education and produces a new electronic device that allows people to transfer their thoughts to a computer directly. This device would alleviate the need to type or write the thoughts—at least, initially. Surely, people would value this device, and Jim would probably make a great deal of money from his invention. Would not Jim have a right to or *merit* this money? Would it not be fair that he had this money and others who did not come up with such a device had less? It would seem so. But let us think about why we might say so. Is it because Jim had an innate or *native talent* that others did not have? Then through no fault of their own, those without the talent would have less. Jim would have had nothing to do with his having been born with this talent and thus becoming wealthy.

Perhaps it is because Jim not only had the talent but also used it. He put a great deal of *effort* into it. He studied electronics and brain anatomy for many years, and spent years working on the invention in his garage. His own effort, time, and study were his own contribution. Would this be a good reason to say that he deserved the wealth that he earned from it? This might seem reasonable, if we did not also know that his particular education and his motivation also might have been in some ways gifts of his circumstance and family upbringing. Furthermore, effort alone would not be a good reason for monetary reward, or else John, who took three weeks to make a pair of shoes, should be paid more than Jeff, who did them up in three hours. This would be similar to the student who asks for a higher grade because of all the effort and time he spent on study for the course, when the result was actually more consistent with the lower grade.

Finally, perhaps Jim should have the rewards of his invention because of the nature of his *contribution*, because of the product he made and its value to people. Again, this argument seems at first reasonable, and yet there are also fairness problems here. Suppose that he had produced this invention before there were computers. The invention would be wonderful but not valued by people because they could not use it. Or suppose that others at the same time produced similar inventions. Then this happenstance would also lessen the value of the product and its monetary reward. He could rightly say that it was unfair that he did not reap a great reward from his invention just because he happened to be born at the wrong time or finished his invention a little late. This may be just bad luck. But is it also unfair? Furthermore, it is often difficult to know how to value particular contributions to a jointly produced product or result. How do we measure and compare the value of the contributions of the person with the idea, the money, the risk takers, and so forth so that we can know what portion of the profits are rightly due them? Marxists are well known for their claim that the people who own the factories or have put up the money for a venture profit from the workers' labor unfairly or out of proportion to their own contribution.

It may not be possible to give a nonproblematic basis for judging when an unequal distribution of wealth in a society is fair by appealing to considerations of merit, achievement, effort, or contribution. However, perhaps some combination of process and end-state views and some combination of factors as

grounds for distribution can be found. At least this discussion will provide a basis for critically evaluating simple solutions.

EQUAL OPPORTUNITY

Another viewpoint on economic justice does not fit easily under the category of process or end-state views. In this view, the key to whether an unequal distribution of wealth in a society is just is whether people have a fair chance to attain those positions of greater income or wealth—that is, equality of wealth is not required, only equal opportunity to attain it. The notion of equal opportunity is symbolized by the Statue of Liberty in New York Harbor. It sits on Liberty Island, where, historically, new immigrants to the United States were processed. The statue symbolizes the idea of hope—namely, that in this country all people have a chance to make a good life for themselves provided they work hard. But just what is involved in the notion of equal opportunity, and is it a realizable goal or ideal? Literally, it involves both opportunities and some sort of equality of chances to attain them. An opportunity is a chance to attain some benefit or goods. People have equal chances to attain these goods first of all when there are no barriers to prevent them from attaining them. Opportunities can still be said to be equal if barriers exist as long as they affect everyone equally. Clearly, if racism or prejudice prevents some people from having the same chances as others to attain valued goals or positions in a society, then there is not equal opportunity for those who are its victims. For example, if women have twice the family responsibilities as men, then will they have effective equal opportunity to compete professionally?

According to James Fishkin, if there is equal opportunity in my society, "I should not be able to enter a hospital ward of healthy newborn babies and, on the basis of class, race, sex, or other arbitrary native characteristics, predict the eventual positions in society of those children."[14] However, knowing what we do about families and education and the real-life prospects of children, we know how difficult this ideal would be to realize. In reality, children do not start life with equal chances. Advantaged families give many educational, motivational, and experiential advantages to their children that children of disadvantaged families do not have, and this makes their opportunities effectively unequal. Schooling greatly affects equal opportunity, and money spent for a school—teachers, facilities, and books—can make a big difference in the kind of education provided. However, funding per pupil on schooling in this country varies considerably according to locale. Some states spend more per student on the average than others: For example, for the 2004 school year, New Jersey spent $12,981 per pupil and New York $12,930 per pupil, while Mississippi spent $6,237, Oklahoma $6,176, and Idaho $6,028.[15]

One version of equal opportunity is a starting-gate theory. It assumes that if people had equal starts, then they would have equal chances. Bernard Williams provides an example.[16] In his imaginary society, a class of skillful warriors has for generations held all of the highest positions and passed them on to their offspring. At some point, the warriors decide to let all people compete for membership in their class. The children of the warrior class are much stronger and better nourished than other children who, not surprisingly, fail to gain entrance to the warrior class. Would these children have had effective equality of opportunity to gain entrance to the warrior class and its benefits? Even if the competition was formally fair, the outside children were handicapped and had no real chance of winning. But how could initial starting points then be equalized? Perhaps by providing special aids or help to the other children to prepare them for the competition. Applying this example to our real-world situation would mean that a society should give special aid to the children of disadvantaged families if it wants to ensure equal opportunity. According to James Fishkin, however, to do this effectively would require serious infringements on family autonomy. For it would mean not only helping disadvantaged children but also preventing wealthier parents from giving special advantages to their children. Moreover, people have different natural talents and abilities, and those who have abilities that are more socially valued will likely have greater opportunities. Does this mean, then, that the idea of equal opportunity is

unrealizable? It may mean that our efforts to increase equality of opportunity must be balanced with the pursuit of other values such as family autonomy and efficiency.

Still, some philosophers have other questions about the ideal of equal opportunity. Some point out that the whole emphasis on equality is misplaced and distracts us from what is really important. Rather than focus on the fact that some have more than others, according to Harry Frankfurt, it would be better to focus on whether people have enough. We care not that one billionaire makes a few million more than another, but it is important that people have what they need so they can do what they want to in life. All too often, this is not the case. Frankfurt calls his position the "doctrine of sufficiency."[17]

Although the doctrine of equal opportunity is appealing because it implies equal rewards for equal performance and doors open to all, still other people object to the notion of meritocracy on which it is based. According to John Schaar, it is based on notions of natural if not social aristocracy.[18] Those of us who do not have the natural talent of an Einstein, a Lance Armstrong, a Roger Federer, or an Alex Rodriguez, given that we value such talent, will not have the same chances to succeed and prosper as those of us with such talents. We can enter the race, but we delude ourselves if we think that we have a real chance to win it. Schaar believes that stress on equal opportunity thus contributes to the gap between rich and poor. He also argues that equal opportunity threatens the very notion of equality and democracy. It is based on the notion of a marketplace in which we, as atomic individuals, compete against our fellows. As such, it threatens human solidarity. It does so even more if it is accompanied by a tendency to think that those who win are in some way more valuable as persons.[19] There is also something essential to notions of justice that people should not be penalized for something for which they are not responsible. Thus, it would seem unjust or unfair for those who, through no fault of their own, cannot compete or cannot compete well in the market, to suffer—for example, the physically or mentally ill, or the physically or mentally handicapped.[20]

POLITICAL AND ECONOMIC THEORIES

Within discussions of economic justice, people often make use of certain terms and refer to certain theories. Key among them are *libertarianism, capitalism, socialism, liberalism*, and *communitarianism*. To more fully understand the central issues of economic justice, it would be helpful to take a closer look at these terms and theories. They do not divide along the same lines, but we can nevertheless discuss them together. In fact, some of the theories—capitalism and socialism, for example—can be differentiated from one another not only by basic definitions but also by the different emphases they place on the values of liberty, efficiency, and justice. They also are differentiated by how they favor or disfavor process or end-state views of distributive justice. These values and these views of distributive justice will become clearer if we examine these theories briefly.

Libertarianism

Libertarianism is a political theory about both the importance of liberty in human life and the role of government. (See the discussion of negative rights below in the comparison between libertarianism and socialism.) Although a political party goes under this name and draws on the theory of libertarianism, we will examine the theory itself. Libertarians believe that we are free when we are not constrained or restrained by other people. Sometimes, this type of liberty is referred to as a basic right to noninterference. Thus, if you stand in the doorway and block my exit, you are violating my liberty to go where I wish. However, if I fall and break my leg and am unable to exit the door, then my liberty rights are violated by no one. The doorway is open and unblocked, and I am free to go out. I cannot go out simply because of my injury.

According to libertarianism, government has but a minimal function: an administrative function. It should provide an orderly place where people can go about their business. It does have an obligation to ensure that people's liberty rights are not violated, that people do not block freeways (if not doorways), and so forth. However, it has no obligation to see that my broken leg is repaired so that I can walk

where I please. In particular, it has no business taking money from you to pay for my leg repair or any other good that I might like to have or even need. This may be a matter of charity or something that charities should address, but it is not a matter of social justice or obligation.

Libertarians would be more likely to support a process view of distributive justice than an end-state view. Any economic arrangement would be just so long as it resulted from a fair process of competition, and so long as people did not take what is not theirs or get their wealth by fraudulent or coercive means. Libertarians do not believe, however, that governments should be concerned with end-state considerations. They should not try to even out any imbalance between rich and poor that might result from a fair process. They should not be involved in any redistribution of wealth. Libertarianism is a theory about the importance of liberty, of rights to noninterference by others, and of the proper role of government. Libertarians also have generally supported capitalist free-market economies, so brief comments about this type of economic system and its supporting values are appropriate here.

The reading in this chapter by Robert Nozick illustrates many aspects of the libertarian theory. For example, he argues that people ought to be free to exchange or transfer to others what they have not acquired unjustly, so long as they do so in ways that are not wrong. In this he also differs from the end-state views described here that he refers to as "patterned" or "current time-slice principles of justice." Following other libertarians, he thinks of taxation of earnings to achieve even good ends as "on a par with forced labor." You can reflect further on these views as you study this selection.

Capitalism

Capitalism is an economic system in which individuals or business corporations (not the government, or community, or state) own and control much or most of the country's capital. Capital is the wealth or raw materials, factories, and so forth that are used to produce more wealth. Capitalism is also usually associated with a free-enterprise system, an economic system that allows people freedom to set prices and determine production, and to make their own choices about how to earn and spend their incomes. Sometimes this is also referred to as a *market economy*, in which people are motivated by profit and engage in competition, and in which value is a function of supply and demand.

Certain philosophical values and beliefs also undergird this system. Among these can be a libertarian philosophy that stresses the importance of liberty and limited government. Certain beliefs about the nature of human motivation also are implicit—for example, that people are motivated by self-interest. Some people argue that capitalism and a free-market economy constitute the best economic system because it is the most efficient one, producing greater wealth for more people than any other system. People produce more and better, they say, when something is in it for them or their families, or when what they are working for is their own. Moreover, we will usually make only what people want, and we know what people want by what they are willing to buy. So people make their mousetraps and their mind-reading computers, and we reward them for giving us what we want by buying their products. Exemplifying this outlook is the view of economist Milton Friedman that the purpose of a business is to maximize profits, "to use its resources and engage in activities designed to increase its profits. . . ."[21] It is a further point, however, to assert that people have a right in justice to the fruits of their labors. Although libertarian and other supporters of capitalism will stress process views of justice, when end-state criteria for distributive justice are given, they most often are *meritocratic criteria*—people are judged to deserve what they merit or earn.

Socialism

Socialism is an economic system, a political movement, and a social theory. It holds that government should own and control most of a nation's resources. According to this theory, there should be public ownership of land, factories, and other means of production. Socialists criticize capitalism because of its necessary unemployment and poverty, unpredictable business cycles, and inevitable conflicts between workers and owners of the means of production. Rather than allow the few to profit often at the expense of the many, socialism holds that government should engage in planning and adjust production to the needs of all of the people. Justice is stressed over efficiency, but central planning is thought to contribute to efficiency as well as justice. Socialism generally is concerned with end-state justice and is egalitarian in orientation, allowing only for obvious differences among people in terms of their different needs. It holds that it is not only external constraints that limit people's liberty. True liberty or freedom also requires freedom from other internal constraints. Among those constraints are the lack of the satisfaction of basic needs, poor education, and poor health care. These needs must be addressed by government. As with all labels, the term *socialism* simplifies. Thus, there are also different kinds or levels of socialism. Some are highly centralized and rely on a command economy. At the other end are versions that stress the need for government to cushion the economy in times of slump, for example, by manipulating interest rates and monetary policy.

One key distinction between a libertarian and a socialist conception of justice is that the former recognizes only *negative rights* and the latter stresses *positive rights*.[22] Negative rights are rights not to be harmed in some way. Because libertarians take liberty as a primary value, they stress the negative right of people not to have their liberty restricted by others. These are rights of noninterference. In the economic area, they support economic liberties that create wealth, and they believe that people should be able to dispose of their wealth as they choose. For the libertarian, government's role is to protect negative rights, not positive rights. Contrary to this view, socialists believe that government should not only protect people's negative rights not to be interfered with but also attend to their positive rights to be given basic necessities. Consequently, a right to life must not only involve a right not to be killed but also a right to what is necessary to live—namely, food, clothing, and shelter. Positive rights to be helped or benefited are sometimes called "welfare rights." Those who favor such a concept of rights may ask what a right to life would amount to if one did not have the means to live. Positive economic rights would be rights to basic economic subsistence. Those who favor positive rights would allow for a variety of ways to provide for this from outright grants to incentives of various sorts.

None of these three systems is problem-free. Socialism, at least in recent times, often has not lived up to the ideals of its supporters. Central planning systems have failed as societies become more complex and participate in international economic systems. Socialist societies have tended in some cases to become authoritarian, because it is difficult to get voluntary consent to centrally decided plans for production and other policies. Basic necessities may be provided for all, but their quality has often turned out to be low.

Capitalism and a free-market economy also are open to moral criticism. Many people, through no fault of their own, cannot or do not compete well and fall through the cracks. Unemployment is a natural part of the system, but it is also debilitating. Of what use is the liberty to vote or travel if one cannot take advantage of this freedom? Where, some people ask, is the concern for the basic equality of persons or the common good?

Libertarianism has been criticized for failing to notice that society provides the means by which individuals seek their own good—for example, by means of transportation and communication. It fails to notice that state action is needed to protect liberty rights and rights to security, property, and litigation. It must at least admit social welfare in terms of publicly funded compulsory primary education.[23] It also may be criticized for ignoring the effects of individuals' initial life circumstance on their equal chances to compete fairly for society's goods.

Let us consider whether a mixed form of political and economic system might be better. We shall call it "modern liberalism," even though the term *liberalism* has meant many things to many people. One reason for using this name is that it is typically applied to the views of one philosopher who exemplified it and whose philosophy we shall also treat here: John Rawls.

Modern Liberalism

Modern liberalism follows in the footsteps of the classical liberalism of John Stuart Mill, John Locke, and Adam Smith with their stress on liberty rights.

However, it also stresses the primacy of justice. Suppose we were to attempt to combine the positive elements of libertarianism, capitalism, and socialism. What would we pull from each? Liberty, or the ability to be free from unjust constraint by others, the primary value stressed by libertarianism, would be one value to preserve. However, we may want to support a fuller notion of liberty that also recognizes the power of internal constraints. We also might want to recognize both positive and negative rights and hold that government ought to play some role in supporting the former as well as the latter. Stress on this combination of elements characterizes modern liberalism.

In writing the American Declaration of Independence, Thomas Jefferson had prepared initial drafts. In one of these, when writing about the purpose of government and the inalienable rights to life, liberty, and happiness, he wrote, "in order to *secure these ends* governments are instituted among men." In the final draft, the phrase is "in order to secure these rights governments are instituted among men."[24] In some ways, these two versions of the purpose of government, according to Jefferson, parallel the two versions of determining when a distribution of wealth is just—the end-state view and a stress on positive rights ("to secure these ends"), and the process view and a focus on negative rights of noninterference ("to secure these rights"). Whichever we believe to be more important will determine what view we have of the role of government in securing economic justice.

We would want our economic system to be efficient as well as just. Thus, our system would probably allow capitalist incentives and inequalities of wealth. However, if we value positive rights, then we also would be concerned about the least advantaged members of the society. Companies and corporations would be regarded as guests in society, because they benefit from the society as well as contribute to it. They could be thought to owe something in return to the community—as a matter of justice and not just as something in their own best interest. It is also true that the economic productivity and efficiency of a society depend on human development and communication and transportation systems. Public investment in education, health, roads, technology, and research and development pay off for companies in the long run.[25]

John Rawls's Theory of Justice

Among the most discussed works on justice of the last two decades is John Rawls's 1971 book, *A Theory of Justice*.[26] In summarizing the basic ideas in this book, we can review elements of the theories discussed earlier.

According to Rawls, justice is the first virtue of social institutions as truth is of scientific systems. It is most important for scientific systems to be true or well supported. They may be elegant or interesting or in line with our other beliefs, but that is not the primary requirement for their acceptance. Something similar would be the case for social and economic institutions. We would want them to be efficient, but it would be even more important that they be just. But what is justice, and how do we know whether an economic system is just? Rawls sought to develop a set of principles or guidelines that we could apply to our institutions, enabling us to judge whether they are just or unjust. But how could we derive, or where could we find, valid principles of justice?

Rawls used an imaginary device called the *original position*. He said that if we could imagine people in some initial fair situation and determine what they would accept as principles of justice, then these principles would be valid ones. In other words, we would first have our imaginary people so situated or described that they could choose fairly. We then would ask what they would be likely to accept. To make their choice situation fair, we would have to eliminate all bias from their choosing. Suppose that we were those people in the imaginary original position. If I knew that I was a college professor and was setting up principles to govern my society, then I would be likely to set them up so that college professors would do very well. If I knew that I had a particular talent for music or sports, for example, I might be likely to bias the principles in favor of people with these talents, and so on. To eliminate such bias, then, the people in the original position must not be

able to know biasing things about themselves. They must not know their age, sex, race, talents, and so on. They must, as he says, choose from behind what he calls a "veil of ignorance."

If people could choose under such conditions, then what principles of justice would they choose? We need not think of these people as selfless. They want what all people want of the basic goods of life. And as persons, their liberty is especially important to them. If they also chose rationally, rather than out of spite or envy, then what would they choose? Rawls believes that they would choose two principles; the first has to do with their political liberties, and the second concerns economic arrangements. Although he varies the wording of the principles, according to a more developed version they are as follows:

1. Each person is to have an equal right to the most extensive total system of equal basic liberties compatible with a similar system of liberty for all.
2. Social and economic inequalities are to be arranged so that they are
   a. to the greatest benefit of the least advantaged . . . , and
   b. attached to offices and positions open to all under conditions of fair equality of opportunity.[27]

Rawls believes that if people were considering an imaginary society in which to live and for which they were choosing principles of justice, and if they did not know who they would be in the society, they would require that there be *equality of liberties*—that is, they would not be willing to be the people who had less freedom than others. They would want as much say about matters in their society that affect them as any other people. This is because of the importance of liberty to all people as people. When it comes to wealth, however, Rawls believes that these people would *accept unequal wealth* provided certain conditions were met. They would be willing that some would be richer and some would be not so rich provided that the not so rich are better off than they otherwise would be if all had equal amounts of wealth.

Wealth Levels	Society A	Society B	Society C
High income	100,000	700	100
Medium income	700	400	100
Low income	50	200	100

You can test yourself to see if your choices coincide with Rawls's belief about people accepting unequal wealth. The table above shows the number of people at three different wealth levels (high, medium, and low) in three societies. If you had to choose, to which society would you want to belong?

If you chose Society A, then you are a risk taker. According to Rawls, you do not know what your chances are of being in any of the three positions in the society. You do not know whether your chances of being in the highest group are near zero or whether your chances of being in the lowest group are very good. Your best bet when you do not know what your chances are, and you do want the goods that these numbers represent, is to choose Society B: No matter what position you are in, you will do better than any position in Society C. And because you do not know what your chances are of being in the lowest group, even if you were in the lowest position in Society B, you would be better off than in the lowest position in either A or C. This is a *maximin* strategy: In choosing under uncertainty, you choose that option with the best worst or minimum position.

Now what is the relevance of this to Rawls's second principle of justice and his method of deriving it? It is this: When the people in the original position choose, they do not know who they are, and so they will not bias the outcome in their favor. They do not know in what position they will be in the society for which they are developing principles. Thus, they will look out for the bottom position in that society. They will think to themselves that if they were in that lowest position in their society, then they would accept that some people are more wealthy than they, provided that they themselves also were thereby better off. Thus, the first part of the second principle of justice, which addresses the improvement of the least advantaged, is formulated as it is.

Another reason why Rawls believes there must be some special concern in justice to provide for the least advantaged is what he calls the "redress of nature." Nature, so to speak, is arbitrary in doling out initial starting points in life. Some people start off quite well, and others are less fortunate. Justice opposes arbitrariness. If inequalities are to be just, then there must be some good reason for them. But there seemingly is no good reason why some are born wealthy and some poor. If some are born into unfortunate circumstances, it is through no fault of their own but merely because of the arbitrariness of the circumstances of their birth. Justice requires that something be done about this. Thus, again justice requires some special concern about the lot of the least advantaged, and this is part of the requirement for a just society that has inequality of wealth.

The second part of the second principle is an equal opportunity principle. For the institutions in a society that allow inequality of income and wealth to be just, that society must provide equal opportunity for those with the interest and talent to attain the positions to which the greater wealth is attached. As noted in our earlier discussion about equal opportunity, there remain problems with the justness of reward on the basis of talent itself, if naturally endowed talent is arbitrary. However, to do otherwise and require equal opportunity for all no matter what their talents would violate the demands of efficiency and most probably would not be something that people in the original position would accept.

In a more recent work, *Political Liberalism*, Rawls points out that his two principles of justice would not necessarily be those chosen by any persons whatsoever. They are, rather, the principles most likely to be accepted by people who are brought up in the traditions and institutions of a modern democratic society.[28] Modern democratic societies are pluralistic—that is, their people will have many different and irreconcilable sets of moral and religious beliefs. How, then, would they ever agree on substantive matters of justice? Consider what goes on during presidential elections in the United States. People have and manifest extremely strong and diverse political and moral beliefs, yet as members of a modern democratic society they will also share certain political values. One is that for a political system to be legitimate it must have rules that determine a system of fair cooperation for mutual advantage by members who are regarded as free and equal persons. This conception is modeled by the original position, which gives us the two principles of justice: The first specifies that people have equal political liberties, and the second lays down conditions for unequal distribution of wealth—namely, principles of equal opportunity and the improvement of the least advantaged. A free-market system must be limited by the concerns of justice, which is the primary virtue of social institutions.[29]

Communitarianism

The liberalism described above is based on the notion of free and equal persons who agree to certain things. It is also premised on the fact that in modern societies people have sharply different moral and religious views—that is, an irremediable pluralism. Thus, the only way that they can agree is by thinking of themselves as persons who want whatever persons want and who do not bias the rules of society in their own favor. Some recent writers object to what they believe are the universalist and atomistic conceptions of such theories. Rather, they believe, people are by nature social and naturally tend to belong to communities. Rather than focusing on individuals or the community of all members of the human race, they stress the importance of belonging to families, cities, nations, religious communities, neighborhood associations, political parties, and groups supporting particular causes. Their views on what justice requires are then influenced by the views of the groups to which they belong. It is a matter of tradition and culture.

One problem with these views, voiced even by those supporting them, is that we can think of societies with views of justice that we believe are just wrong: those supporting slavery, for example, or condoning forced marriages. Both sides of this issue have modified their view. Liberals, such as Rawls, have more recently attempted to make more room for social consensus, and communitarians have attempted to find ways to avoid a seeming ethical relativism according to which whatever society approves is right.

The readings in this chapter are selections from John Rawls's *Theory of Justice*, Robert Nozick's *Anarchy, State, and Utopia*, and Amartya Sen's *The Idea of Justice*. As you will see, Rawls's views are in stark contrast to those of Nozick's and his entitlement theory of justice, and the reading by Amartya Sen offers a somewhat different view of the idea of justice from that of John Rawls.

NOTES

1. www.demos.org/inequality/; http://www.demos.org/inequality/quotes.cfm.
2. Michael Cox and Richard Alm, "You Are What You Spend," *The New York Times*, February 10, 2008.
3. http://www.msnbc.msn.com/id/33066877/.
4. www.demos.org/inequality/numbers.cfm.
5. www.infoplease.com/ipa/A0763170.html.
6. "The Wage Gap Myth," National Center for Policy Analysis, April 12, 2002 (at www.ncpa.org/pub/ba/ba392).
7. Michael J. Mandel, "The Rich Get Richer, and That's O.K.," *Business Week*, no. 3796 (Aug. 26, 2002): 88.
8. washingtonpost.com, January 15, 2010.
9. See "2004 Trends in CEO Pay"; www.aflcio.org/corporateamerica/paywatch/pay/.
10. Paul Krugman, *The New York Times*, April 27, 2007.
11. Paul Krugman, "Crony Capitalism, U.S.A.," *The Great Unraveling: Losing Our Way in the New Century* (New York: Norton, 2003), 108.
12. *New York Times Magazine*, April 22, 2007, pp. 15–18.
13. We associate the saying "From each according to his ability, to each according to his need" with Karl Marx, but it actually originated with the "early French socialists of the Utopian school, and was officially adopted by German socialists in the Gotha Program of 1875." Nicholas Rescher, *Distributive Justice* (Indianapolis, IN: Bobbs-Merrill, 1966), 73–83.

14. James Fishkin, *Justice, Equal Opportunity, and the Family* (New Haven, CT: Yale University Press, 1983), 4.

15. "National Spending Per Student Rises to $8,287." *Report of the U.S. Census Bureau*, April 3, 2006 (http://www.census.gov/newsroom/releases/archives/economic_surveys/cb06-53.html).

16. Bernard Williams, "The Idea of Equality," in Peter Laslett and W. G. Runciman (Eds.), *Philosophy, Politics and Society* (second series) (Oxford: Basil Blackwell, 1962), 110–131.

17. Harry Frankfurt, "Equality as a Moral Ideal," *Ethics*, 98 (1987): 21–43.

18. John H. Schaar, "Equality of Opportunity, and Beyond," in J. Chapman and R. Pennock (Eds.), *NOMO SIX: Equality*, (New York: Atherton Press, 1967).

19. Ibid.

20. See Thomas Nagel, "Justice," in *What Does It All Mean: A Very Short Introduction to Philosophy* (New York: Oxford University Press, 1987), 76–86.

21. Milton Friedman, *Capitalism and Freedom* (Chicago: University of Chicago Press, 1982), 133.

22. This distinction has been stressed by Philippa Foot in her article, "Killing and Letting Die," in Jay Garfield (Ed.), *Abortion: Moral and Legal Perspectives* (Amherst: University of Massachusetts Press, 1984), 178–185. This distinction is the subject of some debate among recent moral philosophers.

23. Stephen Holmes, "Welfare and the Liberal Conscience," *Report from the Institute for Philosophy and Public Policy*, *15*, no. 1 (Winter 1995): 1–6.

24. Morton White, *The Philosophy of the American Revolution* (New York: Oxford University Press, 1978), 161.

25. Robert B. Reich, "The Other Surplus Option," *The New York Times*, July 11, 1999, p. A23.

26. John Rawls, *A Theory of Justice* (Cambridge, MA: Harvard University Press, 1971).

27. Ibid., 302.

28. John Rawls, *Political Liberalism* (New York: Columbia University Press, 1993). This work is a collection of some of Rawls's essays and lectures over the preceding two decades, together with an overview introduction and several new essays.

29. Rawls, "The Primacy of the Right Over the Good," in *Political Liberalism*.

READING

Justice as Fairness

JOHN RAWLS

Study Questions

1. What does Rawls mean when he states that justice is the first virtue of social institutions?

2. How does Rawls describe the social contract idea that he intends to use to develop his theory of justice?

3. How does he describe what he calls "the original position" and the "veil of ignorance" from behind which people in the original position must choose?

4. How is the original position supposed to correspond to the notion of justice as fairness?

5. What are the people in the original position supposed to choose?

6. What does their choice from this situation have to do with the voluntary cooperation of individuals in a society?

7. What two principles does Rawls believe the people in the original position would choose? Compare his first statement with the formulation later in this reading.

8. According to these principles, can the good of some or of the majority justify the hardship of a minority?

9. What are some advantages of contract language for a theory of justice, according to Rawls?

10. What is Rawls's justification for the "veil of ignorance"?

11. What does Rawls mean when he states that our principles must be made to match our considered convictions about justice and vice versa, going back and forth between these two until we achieve a reflective equilibrium?

12. In his final formulation of the principles in this reading, what does Rawls mean by "equal liberties"? What does the second principle require? What are the primary goods to which it refers?

13. Do the principles allow that liberties be curtailed for the sake of economic gains?

14. How do the principles illustrate a tendency toward equality? Explain this in regard to the principle of "redress."

THE ROLE OF JUSTICE

Justice is the first virtue of social institutions, as truth is of systems of thought. A theory however elegant and economical must be rejected or revised if it is untrue; likewise laws and institutions no matter how efficient and well-arranged must be reformed or abolished if they are unjust. Each person possesses an inviolability founded on justice that even the welfare of society as a whole cannot override. For this reason justice denies that the loss of freedom for some is made right by a greater good shared by others. It does not allow that the sacrifices imposed on a few are outweighed by the larger sum of advantages enjoyed by many. Therefore in a just society the liberties of equal citizenship are taken as settled; the rights secured by justice are not subject to political bargaining or to the calculus of social interests. The only thing that permits us to acquiesce in an erroneous theory is the lack of a better one; analogously, an injustice is tolerable only when it is necessary to avoid an even greater injustice. Being first virtues of human activities, truth and justice are uncompromising.

These propositions seem to express our intuitive conviction of the primacy of justice. No doubt they are expressed too strongly. In any event I wish to inquire whether these contentions or others similar to them are sound, and if so how they can be accounted for. To this end it is necessary to work out a theory of justice in the light of which these assertions can be interpreted and assessed. . . .

THE MAIN IDEA OF THE THEORY OF JUSTICE

My aim is to present a conception of justice which generalizes and carries to a higher level of abstraction the familiar theory of the social contract as found, say, in Locke, Rousseau, and Kant.[1] In order to do this we are not to think of the original contract as one to enter a particular society or to set up a particular form of government. Rather, the guiding idea is that the principles of justice for the basic structure of society are the object of the original agreement.

They are the principles that free and rational persons concerned to further their own interests would accept in an initial position of equality as defining the fundamental terms of their association. These principles are to regulate all further agreements; they specify the kinds of social cooperation that can be entered into and the forms of government that can be established. This way of regarding the principles of justice I shall call justice as fairness. . . .

In justice as fairness the original position of equality corresponds to the state of nature in the traditional theory of the social contract. This original position is not, of course, thought of as an actual historical state of affairs, much less as a primitive condition of culture. It is understood as a purely hypothetical situation characterized so as to lead to a certain conception of justice.[2] Among the essential features of this situation is that no one knows his place in society, his class position or social status, nor does any one know his fortune in the distribution of natural assets and abilities, his intelligence, strength, and the like. I shall even assume that the parties do not know their conceptions of the good or their special psychological propensities. The principles of justice are chosen behind a veil of ignorance. This ensures that no one is advantaged or disadvantaged in the choice of principles by the outcome of natural chance or the contingency of social circumstances. Since all are similarly situated and no one is able to design principles to favor his particular condition, the principles of justice are the result of a fair agreement or bargain. For given the circumstances of the original position, the symmetry of everyone's relations to each other, this initial situation is fair between individuals as moral persons, that is, as rational beings with their own ends and capable, I shall assume, of a sense of justice. The original position is, one might say, the appropriate initial status quo, and thus the fundamental agreements reached in it are fair. This explains the propriety of the name "justice as fairness": it conveys the idea that the principles of justice are agreed to in an initial situation that is fair. The name does not mean that the concepts of justice and fairness are the same, any more than the phrase "poetry as metaphor" means that the concepts of poetry and metaphor are the same. . . .

In working out the conception of justice as fairness one main task clearly is to determine which principles of justice would be chosen in the original position. To do this we must describe this situation in some detail and formulate with care the problem of choice which it presents. . . . It may be observed, however, that once the principles of justice are thought of as arising from an original agreement in a situation of equality, it is an open question whether the principle of utility would be acknowledged. Offhand it hardly seems likely that persons who view themselves as equals, entitled to press their claims upon one another, would agree to a principle which may require lesser life prospects for some simply for the sake of a greater sum of advantages enjoyed by others. Since each desires to protect his interests, his capacity to advance his conception of the good, no one has a reason to acquiesce in an enduring loss for himself in order to bring about a greater net balance of satisfaction. In the absence of strong and lasting benevolent impulses, a rational man would not accept a basic structure merely because it maximized the algebraic sum of advantages irrespective of its permanent effects on his own basic rights and interests. Thus it seems that the principle of utility is incompatible with the conception of social cooperation among equals for mutual advantage. It appears to be inconsistent with the idea of reciprocity implicit in the notion of a well-ordered society. Or, at any rate, so I shall argue.

I shall maintain instead that the persons in the initial situation would choose two rather different principles: the first requires equality in the assignment of basic rights and duties, while the second holds that social and economic inequalities, for example inequalities of wealth and authority, are just only if they result in compensating benefits for everyone, and in particular for the least advantaged members of society. These principles rule out justifying institutions on the grounds that the hardships of some are offset by a greater good in the aggregate. It may be expedient but it is not just that some should have less in order that others may prosper. But there is no injustice in the greater benefits earned by a few provided that the situation of persons not so fortunate is thereby improved. The intuitive idea is that since everyone's well-being depends upon a scheme of cooperation without which no one could have a satisfactory life, the division of advantages should be such as to draw forth the willing cooperation of everyone taking part in it, including those less well situated. Yet this can be expected only if reasonable terms are proposed. The two principles mentioned seem to be a fair agreement on the basis of which those better endowed, or more fortunate in their social position, neither of which we can be said to deserve, could expect the willing cooperation of others when some workable scheme is a necessary condition of the welfare of all.[3] Once we decide to look for a conception of justice that nullifies the accidents of natural endowment and the contingencies of social circumstance as counters in quest for political and economic advantage, we are led to these principles. They express the result of leaving aside those aspects of the social world that seem arbitrary from a moral point of view. . . .

THE ORIGINAL POSITION AND JUSTIFICATION

. . . One should not be misled, then, by the somewhat unusual conditions which characterize the original position. The idea here is simply to make vivid to ourselves the restrictions that it seems reasonable to impose on arguments for principles of justice, and therefore on these principles themselves. Thus it seems reasonable and generally acceptable that no one should be advantaged or disadvantaged by natural fortune or social circumstances in the choice of principles. It also seems widely agreed that it should be impossible to tailor principles to the circumstances of one's own case. We should insure further that particular inclinations and aspirations, and persons' conceptions of their good do not affect the principles adopted.

The aim is to rule out those principles that it would be rational to propose for acceptance, however little the chance of success, only if one knew certain things that are irrelevant from the standpoint of justice. For example, if a man knew that he was wealthy, he might find it rational to advance the principle that various taxes for welfare measures be counted unjust; if he knew that he was poor, he would most likely propose the contrary principle. To represent the desired restrictions one imagines a situation in which everyone is deprived of this sort of information. One excludes the knowledge of those contingencies which sets men at odds and allows them to be guided by their prejudices. In this manner the veil of ignorance is arrived at in a natural way. This concept should cause no difficulty if we keep in mind the constraints on arguments that it is meant to express. At any time we can enter the original position, so to speak, simply by following a certain procedure, namely, by arguing for principles of justice in accordance with these restrictions.

It seems reasonable to suppose that the parties in the original position are equal. That is, all have the same rights in the procedure for choosing principles; each can make proposals, submit reasons for their acceptance, and so on. Obviously the purpose of these conditions is to represent equality between human beings as moral persons, as creatures having a conception of their good and capable of a sense of justice. The basis of equality is taken to be similarity in these two respects. Systems of ends are not ranked in value; and each man is presumed to have the requisite ability to understand and to act upon whatever principles are adopted. Together with the veil of ignorance, these conditions define the principles of justice as those which rational persons concerned to advance their interests would consent to as equals when none are known to be advantaged or disadvantaged by social and natural contingencies.

There is, however, another side to justifying a particular description of the original position. This is to see if the principles which would be chosen match our considered convictions of justice or extend them in an acceptable way. We can note whether applying these principles would lead us to make the same judgments about the basic structure of society which we now make intuitively and in which we have the greatest confidence; or whether, in cases where our present judgments are in doubt and given with hesitation, these principles offer a resolution which we can affirm on reflection. There are questions which we feel sure must be answered in a certain way. For example, we are confident that religious intolerance and racial discrimination are unjust. We think that we have examined these things with care and have reached what we believe is an impartial judgment not likely to be distorted by an excessive attention to our own interests. These convictions are provisional

fixed points which we presume any conception of justice must fit. But we have much less assurance as to what is the correct distribution of wealth and authority. Here we may be looking for a way to remove our doubts. We can check an interpretation of the initial situation, then, by the capacity of its principles to accommodate our firmest convictions and to provide guidance where guidance is needed.

In searching for the most favored description of this situation we work from both ends. We begin by describing it so that it represents generally shared and preferably weak conditions. We then see if these conditions are strong enough to yield a significant set of principles. If not, we look for further premises equally reasonable. But if so, and these principles match our considered convictions of justice, then so far well and good. But presumably there will be discrepancies. In this case we have a choice. We can either modify the account of the initial situation or we can revise our existing judgments, for even the judgments we take provisionally as fixed points are liable to revision. By going back and forth, sometimes altering the conditions of the contractual circumstances, at others withdrawing our judgments and conforming them to principle, I assume that eventually we shall find a description of the initial situation that both expresses reasonable conditions and yields principles which match our considered judgments duly pruned and adjusted. This state of affairs I refer to as reflective equilibrium.[4] It is an equilibrium because at last our principles and judgments coincide; and it is reflective since we know to what principles our judgments conform and the premises of their derivation. At the moment everything is in order. But this equilibrium is not necessarily stable. It is liable to be upset by further examination of the conditions which should be imposed on the contractual situation and by particular cases which may lead us to revise our judgments. Yet for the time being we have done what we can to render coherent and to justify our convictions of social justice. We have reached a conception of the original position. . . .

A final comment. We shall want to say that certain principles of justice are justified because they would be agreed to in an initial situation of equality. I have emphasized that this original position is purely hypothetical. It is natural to ask why, if this agreement is never actually entered into, we should take any interest in these principles, moral or otherwise. The answer is that the conditions embodied in the description of the original position are ones that we do in fact accept. Or if we do not, then perhaps we can be persuaded to do so by philosophical reflection. Each aspect of the contractual situation can be given supporting grounds. Thus what we shall do is collect together into one conception a number of conditions on principles that we are ready upon due consideration to recognize as reasonable. These constraints express what we are prepared to regard as limits on fair terms of social cooperation. One way to look at the idea of the original position, therefore, is to see it as an expository device which sums up the meaning of these conditions and helps us to extract their consequences. On the other hand, this conception is also an intuitive notion that suggests its own elaboration, so that led on by it we are drawn to define more clearly the standpoint from which we can best interpret moral relationships. We need a conception that enables us to envision our objective from afar: the intuitive notion of the original position is to do this for us. . . .[5]

TWO PRINCIPLES OF JUSTICE

I shall now state in a provisional form the two principles of justice that I believe would be chosen in the original position. In this section I wish to make only the most general comments, and therefore the first formulation of these principles is tentative. As we go on I shall run through several formulations and approximate step by step the final statement to be given much later. I believe that doing this allows the exposition to proceed in a natural way.

The first statement of the two principles reads as follows.

> First: each person is to have an equal right to the most extensive basic liberty compatible with a similar liberty for others.
> Second: social and economic inequalities are to be arranged so that they are both (a) reasonably expected to be to everyone's advantage, and (b) attached to positions and offices open to all. . . .

By way of general comment, these principles primarily apply, as I have said, to the basic structure of society. They are to govern the assignment of rights and duties and to regulate the distribution of social and economic advantages. As their formulation suggests, these principles presuppose that the social structure can be divided into two more or less distinct parts, the first principle applying to the one, the second to the other. They distinguish between those aspects of the social system that define and secure the equal liberties of citizenship and those that specify and establish social and economic inequalities. The basic liberties of citizens are, roughly speaking, political liberty (the right to vote and to be eligible for public office) together with freedom of speech and assembly; liberty of conscience and freedom of thought; freedom of the person along with the right to hold (personal) property; and freedom from arbitrary arrest and seizure as defined by the concept of the rule of law. These liberties are all required to be equal by the first principle, since citizens of a just society are to have the same basic rights.

The second principle applies, in the first approximation, to the distribution of income and wealth and to the design of organizations that make use of differences in authority and responsibility, or chains of command. While the distribution of wealth and income need not be equal, it must be to everyone's advantage, and at the same time, positions of authority and offices of command must be accessible to all. One applies the second principle by holding positions open, and then, subject to this constraint, arranges social and economic inequalities so that everyone benefits.

These principles are to be arranged in a serial order with the first principle prior to the second. This ordering means that a departure from the institutions of equal liberty required by the first principle cannot be justified by, or compensated for, by greater social and economic advantages. The distribution of wealth and income, and the hierarchies of authority, must be consistent with both the liberties of equal citizenship and equality of opportunity.

It is clear that these principles are rather specific in their content, and their acceptance rests on certain assumptions that I must eventually try to explain and justify. A theory of justice depends upon a theory of society in ways that will become evident as we proceed. For the present, it should be observed that the two principles (this holds for all formulations) are a special case of a more general conception of justice that can be expressed as follows.

> All social values—liberty and opportunity, income and wealth, and the bases of self-respect—are to be distributed equally unless an unequal distribution of any, or all, of these values is to everyone's advantage.

Injustice, then, is simply inequalities that are not to the benefit of all. Of course, this conception is extremely vague and requires interpretation.

As a first step, suppose that the basic structure of society distributes certain primary goods, that is, things that every rational man is presumed to want. These goods normally have a use whatever a person's rational plan of life. For simplicity, assume that the chief primary goods at the disposition of society are rights and liberties, powers and opportunities, income and wealth. . . . There the primary good of self-respect has a central place. These are the social primary goods. Other primary goods such as health and vigor, intelligence and imagination, are natural goods; although their possession is influenced by the basic structure, they are not so directly under its control. Imagine, then, a hypothetical initial arrangement in which all the social primary goods are equally distributed: everyone has similar rights and duties, and income and wealth are evenly shared. This state of affairs provides a benchmark for judging improvements. If certain inequalities of wealth and organizational powers would make everyone better off than in this hypothetical starting situation, then they accord with the general conception.

Now it is possible, at least theoretically, that by giving up some of their fundamental liberties men are sufficiently compensated by the resulting social and economic gains. The general conception of justice imposes no restrictions on what sort of inequalities are permissible; it only requires that everyone's position be improved. We need not suppose anything so drastic as consenting to a condition of slavery. Imagine instead that men forego certain political rights when the economic returns are significant and their capacity to influence the course of

policy by the exercise of these rights would be marginal in any case. It is this kind of exchange which the two principles as stated rule out; being arranged in serial order they do not permit exchanges between basic liberties and economic and social gains. The serial ordering of principles expresses an underlying preference among primary social goods. When this preference is rational so likewise is the choice of these principles in this order. . . .

THE TENDENCY TO EQUALITY

I wish to conclude this discussion of the two principles by explaining the sense in which they express an egalitarian conception of justice. Also I should like to forestall the objection to the principle of fair opportunity that it leads to a callous meritocratic society. In order to prepare the way for doing this, I note several aspects of the conception of justice that I have set out.

First we may observe that the difference principle gives some weight to the considerations singled out by the principle of redress. This is the principle that undeserved inequalities call for redress; and since inequalities of birth and natural endowment are undeserved, these inequalities are to be somehow compensated for.[6] Thus the principle holds that in order to treat all persons equally, to provide genuine equality of opportunity, society must give more attention to those with fewer native assets and to those born into the less favorable social positions. The idea is to redress the bias of contingencies in the direction of equality. In pursuit of this principle greater resources might be spent on the education of the less rather than the more intelligent, at least over a certain time of life, say the earlier years of school.

Now the principle of redress has not to my knowledge been proposed as the sole criterion of justice, as the single aim of the social order. It is plausible as most such principles are only as a prima facie principle, one that is to be weighed in the balance with others. For example, we are to weigh it against the principle to improve the average standard of life, or to advance the common good.[7] But whatever other principles we hold, the claims of redress are to be taken into account. It is thought to represent one of the elements in our conception of justice. Now the difference principle is not of course the principle of redress. It does not require society to try to even out handicaps as if all were expected to compete on a fair basis in the same race. But the difference principle would allocate resources in education, say, so as to improve the long-term expectation of the least favored. If this end is attained by giving more attention to the better endowed, it is permissible; otherwise not. And in making this decision, the value of education should not be assessed only in terms of economic efficiency and social welfare. Equally if not more important is the role of education in enabling a person to enjoy the culture of his society and to take part in its affairs, and in this way to provide for each individual a secure sense of his own worth.

Thus although the difference principle is not the same as that of redress, it does achieve some of the intent of the latter principle. It transforms the aims of the basic structure so that the total scheme of institutions no longer emphasizes social efficiency and technocratic values. We see then that the difference principle represents, in effect, an agreement to regard the distribution of natural talents as a common asset and to share in the benefits of this distribution whatever it turns out to be. Those who have been favored by nature, whoever they are, may gain from their good fortune only on terms that improve the situation of those who have lost out. The naturally advantaged are not to gain merely because they are more gifted, but only to cover the costs of training and education and for using their endowments in ways that help the less fortunate as well. No one deserves his greater natural capacity nor merits a more favorable starting place in society. But it does not follow that one should eliminate these distinctions. There is another way to deal with them. The basic structure can be arranged so that these contingencies work for the good of the least fortunate. Thus we are led to the difference principle if we wish to set up the social system so that no one gains or loses from his arbitrary place in the distribution of natural assets or his initial position in society without giving or receiving compensating advantages in return. . . .

NOTES*

1. As the text suggests, I shall regard Locke's *Second Treatise of Government*, Rousseau's *The Social Contract*, and Kant's ethical works beginning with *The Foundations of the Metaphysics of Morals* as definitive of the contract tradition. For all of its greatness, Hobbes's *Leviathan* raises special problems. A general historical survey is provided by J. W. Gough, *The Social Contract*, 2nd ed. (Oxford, The Clarendon Press, 1957), and Otto Gierke, *Natural Law and the Theory of Society*, trans. with an introduction by Ernest Barker (Cambridge, The University Press, 1934). A presentation of the contract view as primarily an ethical theory is to be found in G. R. Grice, *The Grounds of Moral Judgment* (Cambridge, The University Press, 1967). See also §19, note 30.

2. Kant is clear that the original agreement is hypothetical. See *The Metaphysics of Morals*, pt. I (Rechtslehre), especially §§47, 52; and pt. II of the essay "Concerning the Common Saying: This May Be True in Theory but It Does Not Apply in Practice," in *Kant's Political Writings*, ed. Hans Reiss and trans. by H. B. Nisbet (Cambridge, The University Press, 1970), pp. 73–87. See Georges Vlachos, *La Pensée politique de Kant* (Paris, Presses Universitaires de France, 1962), pp. 326–335; and J. G. Murphy, *Kant: The Philosophy of Right* (London, Macmillan, 1970), pp. 109–112, 133–136, for a further discussion.

3. For the formulation of this intuitive idea I am indebted to Allan Gibbard.

4. The process of mutual adjustment of principles and considered judgments is not peculiar to moral philosophy. See Nelson Goodman, *Fact, Fiction, and Forecast* (Cambridge, Mass., Harvard University Press, 1955), pp. 65–68, for parallel remarks concerning the justification of the principles of deductive and inductive inference.

5. Henri Poincaré remarks: "Il nous faut une faculté qui nous fasse voir le but de loin, et, cette faculté, c'est l'intuition." *La Valeur de la science* (Paris, Flammarion, 1909), p. 27.

6. See Herbert Spiegelberg, "A Defense of Human Equality," *Philosophical Review*, vol. 53 (1944), pp. 101, 113–123; and D. D. Raphael, "Justice and Liberty," *Proceedings of the Aristotelian Society*, vol. 51 (1950–1951), pp. 187f.

7. See, for example, Spiegelberg, pp. 120f.

---

*Some of the notes have been deleted and the remaining ones renumbered.—ED.

READING
Distributive Justice
ROBERT NOZICK

Study Questions

1. According to Nozick, why can the term *distributive justice* be misleading? What term does Nozick propose to use instead?
2. What does Nozick mean by the principle of justice in acquisition? In addition to the acquisition of holdings, how can one also transfer holdings?
3. According to Nozick, under what conditions would a person be justly entitled to something?
4. What are some impermissible methods of coming to possess or hold things?
5. According to Nozick, what questions does past injustice raise for current holders? How would the principle of rectification apply here?
6. What is the difference between Nozick's historical account of justice and a current time-slice view? Why does he believe the latter view does not give the whole story about what is and is not just?
7. What does Nozick mean by a *patterned* principle of distribution? Give some examples. Are his own principles patterned? Explain.
8. According to Nozick, how does liberty upset patterns of distribution? How does the Wilt Chamberlain example demonstrate this? How does this contention thwart patterned principles?
9. For what reason does Nozick discuss families in this context?
10. What does Nozick think of taxation of earnings from labor and the use of this money to benefit the poor?

THE TERM "distributive justice" is not a neutral one. Hearing the term "distribution," most people presume that some thing or mechanism uses some principle or criterion to give out a supply of things. Into this process of distributing shares some error may have crept. So it is an open question, at least, whether *re*distribution should take place; whether we should do again what has already been done once, though poorly. However, we are not in the position of children who have been given portions of pie by

Robert Nozick, "Distributive Justice," *Anarchy, State, and Utopia*, pp. 149–157, 161–163, 167–169. Copyright © 1977 Basic Books, Inc. Reprinted by permission of Basic Books, a member of the Perseus Books Group.

someone who now makes last minute adjustments to rectify careless cutting. There is no *central* distribution, no person or group entitled to control all the resources, jointly deciding how they are to be doled out. What each person gets, he gets from others who give to him in exchange for something, or as a gift. In a free society, diverse persons control different resources, and new holdings arise out of the voluntary exchanges and actions of persons. There is no more a distributing or distribution of shares than there is a distributing of mates in a society in which persons choose whom they shall marry. The total result is the product of many individual decisions which the different individuals involved are entitled to make. Some uses of the term "distribution," it is true, do not imply a previous distributing appropriately judged by some criterion (for example, "probability distribution"); nevertheless, despite the title of this chapter, it would be best to use a terminology that clearly is neutral. We shall speak of people's holdings; a principle of justice in holdings describes (part of) what justice tells us (requires) about holdings. I shall state first what I take to be the correct view about justice in holdings, and then turn to the discussion of alternate views.[1]

SECTION 1 THE ENTITLEMENT THEORY

The subject of justice in holdings consists of three major topics. The first is the *original acquisition of holdings*, the appropriation of unheld things. This includes the issues of how unheld things may come to be held, the process, or processes, by which unheld things may come to be held, the things that may come to be held by these processes, the extent of what comes to be held by a particular process, and so on. We shall refer to the complicated truth about this topic, which we shall not formulate here, as the principle of justice in acquisition. The second topic concerns the *transfer of holdings* from one person to another. By what processes may a person transfer holdings to another? How may a person acquire a holding from another who holds it? Under this topic come general descriptions of voluntary exchange, and gift and (on the other hand) fraud, as well as reference to particular conventional details fixed upon in a given society. The complicated truth about this subject (with placeholders for conventional details) we shall call the principle of justice in transfer. (And we shall suppose it also includes principles governing how a person may divest himself of a holding, passing it into an unheld state.)

If the world were wholly just, the following inductive definition would exhaustively cover the subject of justice in holdings.

1. A person who acquires a holding in accordance with the principle of justice in acquisition is entitled to that holding.
2. A person who acquires a holding in accordance with the principle of justice in transfer, from someone else entitled to the holding, is entitled to the holding.
3. No one is entitled to a holding except by (repeated) application of 1 and 2.

The complete principle of distributive justice would say simply that a distribution is just if everyone is entitled to the holdings they possess under the distribution.

A distribution is just if it arises from another just distribution by legitimate means. The legitimate means of moving from one distribution to another are specified by the principle of justice in transfer. The legitimate first "moves" are specified by the principle of justice in acquisition.[2] Whatever arises from a just situation by just steps is itself just. The means of change specified by the principle of justice in transfer preserve justice. As correct rules of inference are truth-preserving, and any conclusion deduced via repeated application of such rules from only true premises is itself true, so the means of transition from one situation to another specified by the principle of justice in transfer are justice-preserving, and any situation actually arising from repeated transitions in accordance with the principle from a just situation is itself just. The parallel between justice-preserving transformations and truth-preserving transformations illuminates where it fails as well as where it holds. That a conclusion could have been deduced by truth-preserving means from premises that are true suffices to show its truth. That from a just situation a situation *could* have arisen via justice-preserving means does *not* suffice to show its justice. The fact that a thief's victims voluntarily *could* have presented him with gifts does not entitle the thief to his ill-gotten gains. Justice in holdings is historical; it depends upon what actually has happened. We shall return to this point later.

Not all actual situations are generated in accordance with the two principles of justice in holdings: the principle of justice in acquisition and the principle of justice in transfer. Some people steal from others, or defraud them, or enslave them, seizing their product and preventing them from living as they choose, or forcibly exclude others from competing in exchanges. None of these are permissible modes of transition from one situation to another. And some persons acquire holdings by means not sanctioned by the principle of justice in acquisition. The existence of past injustice (previous violations of the first two principles of justice in holdings) raises the third major topic under justice in holdings: the rectification of injustice in holdings. If past injustice has shaped present holdings in various ways, some identifiable and some not, what now, if anything, ought to be done to rectify these injustices? What obligations do the performers of injustice have toward those whose position is worse than it would have been had the injustice not been done? Or, than it would have been had compensation been paid promptly? How, if at all, do things change if the beneficiaries and those made worse off are not the direct parties in the act of injustice, but, for example, their descendants? Is an injustice done to someone whose holding was itself based upon an unrectified injustice? How far back must one go in wiping clean the historical slate of injustices? What may victims of injustice permissibly do in order to rectify the injustices being done to them, including the many injustices done by persons acting through their government? I do not know of a thorough or theoretically sophisticated treatment of such issues.[3] Idealizing greatly, let us suppose theoretical investigation will produce a principle of rectification. This principle uses historical information about previous situations and injustices done in them (as defined by the first two principles of justice and rights against interference), and information about the actual course of events that flowed from these injustices, until the present, and it yields a description (or descriptions) of holdings in the society. The principle of rectification presumably will make use of its best estimate of subjunctive information about what would have occurred (or a probability distribution over what might have occurred, using the expected value) if the injustice had not taken place. If the actual description of holdings turns out not to be one of the descriptions yielded by the principle, then one of the descriptions yielded must be realized.[4]

The general outlines of the theory of justice in holdings are that the holdings of a person are just if he is entitled to them by the principles of justice in acquisition and transfer, or by the principle of rectification of injustice (as specified by the first two principles). If each person's holdings are just, then the total set (distribution) of holdings is just. To turn these general outlines into a specific theory we would have to specify the details of each of the three principles of justice in holdings: the principle of acquisition of holdings, the principle of transfer of holdings, and the principle of rectification of violations of the first two principles. I shall not attempt that task here. (Locke's principle of justice in acquisition is discussed below.)

Historical Principles and End-Result Principles

The general outlines of the entitlement theory illuminate the nature and defects of other conceptions of distributive justice. The entitlement theory of justice in distribution is *historical*; whether a distribution is just depends upon how it came about. In contrast, *current time-slice principles* of justice hold that the justice of a distribution is determined by how things are distributed (who has what) as judged by some *structural* principle(s) of just distribution. A utilitarian who judges between any two distributions by seeing which has the greater sum of utility and, if the sums tie, applies some fixed equality criterion to choose the more equal distribution, would hold a current time-slice principle of justice. As would someone who had a fixed schedule of trade-offs between the sum of happiness and equality. According to a current time-slice principle, all that needs to be looked at, in judging the justice of a

distribution, is who ends up with what; in comparing any two distributions one need look only at the matrix presenting the distributions. No further information need be fed into a principle of justice. It is a consequence of such principles of justice that any two structurally identical distributions are equally just. (Two distributions are structurally identical if they present the same profile, but perhaps have different persons occupying the particular slots. My having ten and your having five, and my having five and your having ten are structurally identical distributions.) Welfare economics is the theory of current time-slice principles of justice. The subject is conceived as operating on matrices representing only current information about distribution. This, as well as some of the usual conditions (for example, the choice of distribution is invariant under relabeling of columns), guarantees that welfare economics will be a current time-slice theory, with all of its inadequacies.

Most persons do not accept current time-slice principles as constituting the whole story about distributive shares. They think it relevant in assessing the justice of a situation to consider not only the distribution it embodies, but also how that distribution came about. If some persons are in prison for murder or war crimes, we do not say that to assess the justice of the distribution in the society we must look only at what this person has, and that person has, and that person has, . . . at the current time. We think it relevant to ask whether someone did something so that he *deserved* to be punished, deserved to have a lower share. Most will agree to the relevance of further information with regard to punishments and penalties. Consider also desired things. One traditional socialist view is that workers are entitled to the product and full fruits of their labor; they have earned it; a distribution is unjust if it does not give the workers what they are entitled to. Such entitlements are based upon some past history. No socialist holding this view would find it comforting to be told that because the actual distribution *A* happens to coincide structurally with the one he desires *D*, *A* therefore is no less just than *D*; it differs only in that the "parasitic" owners of capital receive under *A* what the workers are entitled to under *D*, and the workers receive under *A* what the owners are entitled to under D, namely very little. This socialist rightly, in my view, holds onto the notions of earning, producing, entitlement, desert, and so forth, and he rejects current time-slice principles that look only to the structure of the resulting set of holdings. (The set of holdings resulting from what? Isn't it implausible that how holdings are produced and come to exist has no effect at all on who should hold what?) His mistake lies in his view of what entitlements arise out of what sorts of productive processes.

We construe the position we discuss too narrowly by speaking of *current* time-slice principles. Nothing is changed if structural principles operate upon a time sequence of current time-slice profiles and, for example, give someone more now to counterbalance the less he has had earlier. A utilitarian or an egalitarian or any mixture of the two over time will inherit the difficulties of his more myopic comrades. He is not helped by the fact that *some* of the information others consider relevant in assessing a distribution is reflected, unrecoverably, in past matrices. Henceforth, we shall refer to such unhistorical principles of distributive justice, including the current time-slice principles, as *end-result principles* or *end-state principles*.

In contrast to end-result principles of justice, *historical principles* of justice hold that past circumstances or actions of people can create differential entitlements or differential deserts to things. An injustice can be worked by moving from one distribution to another structurally identical one, for the second, in profile the same, may violate people's entitlements or deserts; it may not fit the actual history.

Patterning

The entitlement principles of justice in holdings that we have sketched are historical principles of justice. To better understand their precise character, we shall distinguish them from another subclass of the historical principles. Consider, as an example, the principle of distribution according to moral merit. This principle requires that total distributive shares vary directly with moral merit; no person should have a greater share than anyone whose moral merit is greater. (If moral merit could be not merely ordered but measured on an interval or ratio scale, stronger principles could be formulated.) Or consider the principle that results by substituting "usefulness to society" for

"moral merit" in the previous principle. Or instead of "distribute according to moral merit," or "distribute according to usefulness to society," we might consider "distribute according to the weighted sum of moral merit, usefulness to society, and need," with the weights of the different dimensions equal. Let us call a principle of distribution *patterned* if it specifies that a distribution is to vary along with some natural dimension, weighted sum of natural dimensions, or lexicographic ordering of natural dimensions. And let us say a distribution is patterned if it accords with some patterned principle. (I speak of natural dimensions, admittedly without a general criterion for them, because for any set of holdings some artificial dimensions could be gimmicked up to vary along with the distribution of the set.) The principle of distribution in accordance with moral merit is a patterned historical principle, which specifies a patterned distribution. "Distribute according to I.Q." is a patterned principle that looks to information not contained in distributional matrices. It is not historical, however, in that it does not look to any past actions creating differential entitlements to evaluate a distribution; it requires only distributional matrices whose columns are labeled by I.Q. scores. The distribution in a society, however, may be composed of such simple patterned distributions, without itself being simply patterned. Different sectors may operate different patterns, or some combination of patterns may operate in different proportions across a society. A distribution composed in this manner, from a small number of patterned distributions, we also shall term "patterned." And we extend the use of "pattern" to include the overall designs put forth by combinations of end-state principles.

Almost every suggested principle of distributive justice is patterned: to each according to his moral merit, or needs, or marginal product, or how hard he tries, or the weighted sum of the foregoing, and so on. The principle of entitlement we have sketched is *not* patterned.[5] There is no one natural dimension or weighted sum or combination of a small number of natural dimensions that yields the distributions generated in accordance with the principle of entitlement. The set of holdings that results when some persons receive their marginal products, others win at gambling, others receive a share of their mate's income, others receive gifts from foundations, others receive interest on loans, others receive gifts from admirers, others receive returns on investment, others make for themselves much of what they have, others find things, and so on, will not be patterned. Heavy strands of patterns will run through it; significant portions of the variance in holdings will be accounted for by pattern-variables. If most people most of the time choose to transfer some of their entitlements to others only in exchange for something from them, then a large part of what many people hold will vary with what they held that others wanted. More details are provided by the theory of marginal productivity. But gifts to relatives, charitable donations, bequests to children, and the like, are not best conceived, in the first instance, in this manner. Ignoring the strands of pattern, let us suppose for the moment that a distribution actually arrived at by the operation of the principle of entitlement is random with respect to any pattern. Though the resulting set of holdings will be unpatterned, it will not be incomprehensible, for it can be seen as arising from the operation of a small number of principles. . . .

Now suppose that Wilt Chamberlain is greatly in demand by basketball teams, being a great gate attraction. (Also suppose contracts run only for a year, with players being free agents.) He signs the following sort of contract with a team: In each home game, twenty-five cents from the price of each ticket of admission goes to him. (We ignore the question of whether he is "gouging" the owners, letting them look out for themselves.) The season starts, and people cheerfully attend his team's games; they buy their tickets, each time dropping a separate twenty-five cents of their admission price into a special box with Chamberlain's name on it. They are excited about seeing him play; it is worth the total admission price to them. Let us suppose that in one season one million persons attend his home games, and Wilt Chamberlain winds up with $250,000, a much larger sum than the average income and larger even than anyone else has. Is he entitled to this income? Is this new distribution $D2$, unjust? If so, why? There is *no* question about whether each of the people was entitled to the control over the resources they held in $D1$; because that was the distribution (your favorite) that (for the purposes of argument) we assumed was

acceptable. Each of these persons *chose* to give twenty-five cents of their money to Chamberlain. They could have spent it on going to the movies, or on candy bars, or on copies of *Dissent* magazine, or of *Monthly Review*. But they all, at least one million of them, converged on giving it to Wilt Chamberlain in exchange for watching him play basketball. If $D1$ was a just distribution, and people voluntarily moved from it to $D2$, transferring parts of their shares they were given under $D1$ (what was it for if not to do something with?), isn't $D2$ also just? If the people were entitled to dispose of the resources to which they were entitled (under $D1$), didn't this include their being entitled to give it to, or exchange it with, Wilt Chamberlain? Can anyone else complain on grounds of justice? Each other person already has his legitimate share under $D1$. Under $D1$, there is nothing that anyone has that anyone else has a claim of justice against. After someone transfers something to Wilt Chamberlain, third parties *still* have their legitimate shares; *their* shares are not changed. By what process could such a transfer among two persons give rise to a legitimate claim of distributive justice on a portion of what was transferred, by a third party who had no claim of justice on any holding of the others *before* the transfer?[6] To cut off objections irrelevant here, we might imagine the exchanges occurring in a socialist society, after hours. After playing whatever basketball he does in his daily work, or doing whatever other daily work he does, Wilt Chamberlain decides to put in *overtime* to earn additional money. (First his work quota is set; he works time over that.) Or imagine it is a skilled juggler people like to see, who puts on shows after hours.

Why might someone work overtime in a society in which it is assumed their needs are satisfied? Perhaps because they care about things other than needs. I like to write in books that I read, and to have easy access to books for browsing at odd hours. It would be very pleasant and convenient to have the resources of Widener Library in my back yard. No society, I assume, will provide such resources close to each person who would like them as part of his regular allotment (under $D1$). Thus, persons either must do without some extra things that they want, or be allowed to do something extra to get some of these things. On what basis could the inequalities that would eventuate be forbidden? Notice also that small factories would spring up in a socialist society, unless forbidden. I melt down some of my personal possessions (under $D1$) and build a machine out of the material. I offer you, and others, a philosophy lecture once a week in exchange for your cranking the handle on my machine, whose products I exchange for yet other things, and so on. (The raw materials used by the machine are given to me by others who possess them under $D1$, in exchange for hearing lectures.) Each person might participate to gain things over and above their allotment under $D1$. Some persons even might want to leave their job in socialist industry and work full time in this private sector. I shall say something more about these issues in the next chapter. Here I wish merely to note how private property even in means of production would occur in a socialist society that did not forbid people to use as they wished some of the resources they are given under the socialist distribution $D1$.[7] The socialist society would have to forbid capitalist acts between consenting adults.

The general point illustrated by the Wilt Chamberlain example and the example of the entrepreneur in a socialist society is that no end-state principle or distributional patterned principle of justice can be continuously realized without continuous interference with people's lives. Any favored pattern would be transformed into one unfavored by the principle, by people choosing to act in various ways; for example, by people exchanging goods and services with other people, or giving things to other people, things the transferrers are entitled to under the favored distributional pattern. To maintain a pattern one must either continually interfere to stop people from transferring resources as they wish to, or continually (or periodically) interfere to take from some persons resources that others for some reason chose to transfer to them. (But if some time limit is to be set on how long people may keep resources others voluntarily transfer to them, why let them keep these resources for *any* period of time? Why not have immediate confiscation?) It might be objected that all persons voluntarily will choose to refrain from actions which would upset the pattern.

Redistribution and Property Rights

Apparently, patterned principles allow people to choose to expend upon themselves, but not upon others, those resources they are entitled to (or rather, receive) under some favored distributional pattern $D1$. For if each of several persons chooses to expend some of his $D1$ resources upon one other person, then that other person will receive more than his $D1$ share, disturbing the favored distributional pattern. Maintaining a distributional pattern is individualism with a vengeance! Patterned distributional principles do not give people what entitlement principles do, only better distributed. For they do not give the right to choose what to do with what one has; they do not give the right to choose to pursue an end involving (intrinsically, or as a means) the enhancement of another's position. To such views, families are disturbing; for within a family occur transfers that upset the favored distributional pattern. Either families themselves become units to which distribution takes place, the column occupiers (on what rationale?), or loving behavior is forbidden. We should note in passing the ambivalent position of radicals toward the family. Its loving relationships are seen as a model to be emulated and extended across the whole society, at the same time that it is denounced as a suffocating institution to be broken and condemned as a focus of parochial concerns that interfere with achieving radical goals. Need we say that it is not appropriate to enforce across the wider society the relationships of love and care appropriate within a family, relationships which are voluntarily undertaken?[8] Incidentally, love is an interesting instance of another relationship that is historical, in that (like justice) it depends upon what actually occurred. An adult may come to love another because of the other's characteristics; but it is the other person, and not the characteristics, that is loved.[9] The love is not transferrable to someone else with the same characteristics, even to one who "scores" higher for these characteristics. And the love endures through changes of the characteristics that gave rise to it. One loves the particular person one actually encountered. Why love is historical, attaching to persons in this way and not to characteristics, is an interesting and puzzling question.

Proponents of patterned principles of distributive justice focus upon criteria for determining who is to receive holdings; they consider the reasons for which someone should have something, and also the total picture of holdings. Whether or not it is better to give than to receive, proponents of patterned principles ignore giving altogether. In considering the distribution of goods, income, and so forth, their theories are theories of recipient justice; they completely ignore any right a person might have to give something to someone. Even in exchanges where each party is simultaneously giver and recipient, patterned principles of justice focus only upon the recipient role and its supposed rights. Thus discussions tend to focus on whether people (should) have a right to inherit, rather than on whether people (should) have a right to bequeath or on whether persons who have a right to hold also have a right to choose that others hold in their place. I lack a good explanation of why the usual theories of distributive justice are so recipient oriented; ignoring givers and transferrers and their rights is of a piece with ignoring producers and their entitlements. But why is it *all* ignored?

Patterned principles of distributive justice necessitate *re*distributive activities. The likelihood is small that any actual freely-arrived-at set of holdings fits a given pattern; and the likelihood is nil that it will continue to fit the pattern as people exchange and give. From the point of view of an entitlement theory, redistribution is a serious matter indeed, involving, as it does, the violation of people's rights. (An exception is those takings that fall under the principle of the rectification of injustices.) From other points of view, also, it is serious.

Taxation of earnings from labor is on a par with forced labor.[10] Some persons find this claim obviously true: taking the earnings of *n* hours labor is like taking *n* hours from the person; it is like forcing the person to work *n* hours for another's purpose. Others find the claim absurd. But even these, *if* they object to forced labor, would oppose forcing unemployed hippies to work for the benefit of the needy.[11] And they would also object to forcing each person to work five extra hours each week for the benefit of the needy. But a system that takes five hours' wages in taxes does not seem to them like one that forces someone to work five hours, since it offers the person

forced a wider range of choice in activities than does taxation in kind with the particular labor specified. (But we can imagine a gradation of systems of forced labor, from one that specifies a particular activity, to one that gives a choice among two activities, to . . . ; and so on up.) Furthermore, people envisage a system with something like a proportional tax on everything above the amount necessary for basic needs. Some think this does not force someone to work extra hours, since there is no fixed number of extra hours he is forced to work, and since he can avoid the tax entirely by earning only enough to cover his basic needs. This is a very uncharacteristic view of forcing for those who *also* think people are forced to do something *whenever* the alternatives they face are considerably worse. However, *neither* view is correct. The fact that others intentionally intervene, in violation of a side constraint against aggression, to threaten force to limit the alternatives, in this case to paying taxes or (presumably the worse alternative) bare subsistence, makes the taxation system one of forced labor and distinguishes it from other cases of limited choices which are not forcings.[12]

NOTES*

1. The reader who has looked ahead and seen that the second part of this chapter discusses Rawls' theory mistakenly may think that every remark or argument in the first part against alternative theories of justice is meant to apply to, or anticipate, a criticism of Rawls' theory. This is not so; there are other theories also worth criticizing.

2. Applications of the principle of justice in acquisition may also occur as part of the move from one distribution to another. You may find an unheld thing now and appropriate it. Acquisitions also are to be understood as included when, to simplify, I speak only of transitions by transfers.

3. See, however, the useful book by Boris Bittker, *The Case for Black Reparations* (New York: Random House, 1973).

4. If the principle of rectification of violations of the first two principles yields more than one description of holdings, then some choice must be made as to which of these is to be realized. Perhaps the sort of

---

*Notes have been reordered and renumbered.

considerations about distributive justice and equality that I argue against play a legitimate role in this subsidiary choice. Similarly, there may be room for such considerations in deciding which otherwise arbitrary features a statute will embody, when such features are unavoidable because other considerations do not specify a precise line; yet a line must be drawn.

5. One might try to squeeze a patterned conception of distributive justice into the framework of the entitlement conception, by formulating a gimmicky obligatory "principle of transfer" that would lead to the pattern. For example, the principle that if one has more than the mean income one must transfer everything one holds above the mean to persons below the mean so as to bring them up to (but not over) the mean. We can formulate a criterion for a "principle of transfer" to rule out such obligatory transfers, or we can say that no correct principle of transfer, no principle of transfer in a free society will be like this. The former is probably the better course, though the latter also is true.

   Alternatively, one might think to make the entitlement conception instantiate a pattern, by using matrix entries that express the relative strength of a person's entitlement as measured by some real-valued function. But even if the limitation to natural dimensions failed to exclude this function, the resulting edifice would not capture our system of entitlements to *particular* things.

6. Might not a transfer have instrumental effects on a third party, changing his feasible options? (But what if the two parties to the transfer independently had used their holdings in this fashion?) I discuss this question below, but note here that this question concedes the point for distributions of ultimate intrinsic noninstrumental goods (pure utility experiences, so to speak) that are transferrable. It also might be objected that the transfer might make a third party more envious because it worsens his position relative to someone else. I find it incomprehensible how this can be thought to involve a claim of justice. . . .

   Here . . . a theory which incorporates elements of pure procedural justice might find what I say acceptable, *if* kept in its proper place; that is, if background institutions exist to ensure the satisfaction of certain conditions on distributive shares. But if these institutions are not themselves the sum or invisible-hand result of people's voluntary (nonaggressive) actions, the constraints they impose require justification. At no point does *our* argument assume any background institutions more

extensive than those of the minimal night-watchman state, a state limited to protecting persons against murder, assault, theft, fraud, and so forth.

7. See the selection from John Henry MacKay's novel, *The Anarchists*, reprinted in Leonard Krimmerman and Lewis Perry, eds., *Patterns of Anarchy* (New York: Doubleday Anchor Books, 1966), in which an individualist anarchist presses upon a communist anarchist the following question: "Would you, in the system of society which you call 'free Communism' prevent individuals from exchanging their labor among themselves by means of their own medium of exchange? And further: Would you prevent them from occupying land for the purpose of personal use?" The novel continues: "[the] question was not to be escaped. If he answered 'Yes!' he admitted that society had the right of control over the individual and threw overboard the autonomy of the individual which he had always zealously defended; if on the other hand, he answered 'No!' he admitted the right of private property which he had just denied so emphatically . . . . Then he answered 'In Anarchy any number of men must have the right of forming a voluntary association, and so realizing their ideas in practice. Nor can I understand how any one could justly be driven from the land and house which he uses and occupies . . . every serious man must declare himself: for Socialism, and thereby for force and against liberty, or for Anarchism, and thereby for liberty and against force.'" In contrast, we find Noam Chomsky writing, "Any consistent anarchist must oppose private ownership of the means of production," "the consistent anarchist then . . . will be a socialist . . . of a particular sort." Introduction to Daniel Guerin, *Anarchism: From Theory to Practice* (New York: Monthly Review Press, 1970), pages xiii, sv.

8. One indication of the stringency of Rawls' difference principle, which we attend to in the second part of this chapter, is its inappropriateness as a governing principle even within a family of individuals who love one another. Should a family devote its resources to maximizing the position of its least well off and least talented child, holding back the other children or using resources for their education and development only if they will follow a policy through their lifetimes of maximizing the position of their least fortunate sibling? Surely not. How then can this even be considered as the appropriate policy for enforcement in the wider society? (I discuss below what I think would be Rawls' reply: that some principles apply at the macro level which do not apply to micro-situations.)

9. See Gregory Vlastos, "The Individual as an Object of Love in Plato" in his *Platonic Studies* (Princeton: Princeton University Press, 1973), pp. 3–34.

10. I am unsure as to whether the arguments I present below show that such taxation merely is forced labor; so that "is on a par with" means "is one kind of." Or alternatively, whether the arguments emphasize the great similarities between such taxation and forced labor, to show it is plausible and illuminating to view such taxation in the light of forced labor. This latter approach would remind one of how John Wisdom conceives of the claims of metaphysicians.

11. Nothing hangs on the fact that here and elsewhere I speak loosely of *needs*, since I go on, each time, to reject the criterion of justice which includes it. If, however, something did depend upon the notion, one would want to examine it more carefully. For a skeptical view, see Kenneth Minogue, *The Liberal Mind* (New York: Random House, 1963), pp. 103–112.

12. Further details which this statement should include are contained in my essay "Coercion," in *Philosophy, Science, and Method*, ed. S. Morgenbesser, P. Suppes, and M. White (New York: St. Martin, 1969).

READING
The Idea of Justice
AMARTYA SEN

Study Questions

1. What are the two basic approaches to understanding justice that Sen describes?
2. Which is his own approach?
3. With what questions does each approach start?
4. How does Sen describe John Rawls's approach? Does he agree with Rawls that there is "a unique set of principles of justice"?
5. How does Sen describe the problem of the three children and the flute?
6. Which theorists does he think would tend to agree with each of the children?
7. What point does Sen want to make with this example?

THE ENLIGHTENMENT AND A BASIC DIVERGENCE

. . . Even though the subject of social justice has been discussed over the ages, the discipline received an especially strong boost during the European Enlightenment in the eighteenth and nineteenth centuries, encouraged by the political climate of change and also by the social and economic transformation taking place then in Europe and America. There are two basic, and divergent, lines of reasoning

Reprinted by permission of the publisher from *The Idea of Justice* by Amartya Sen, pp. 1–5, Cambridge, Mass.: The Belknap Press of Harvard University Press, Copyright © 2009 by Amartya Sen.

about justice among leading philosophers associated with the radical thought of that period. The distinction between the two approaches has received far less attention than, I believe, it richly deserves. I will begin with this dichotomy since that will help to locate the particular understanding of the theory of justice that I am trying to present in this work.

One approach, led by the work of Thomas Hobbes in the seventeenth century, and followed in different ways by such outstanding thinkers as Jean-Jacques Rousseau, concentrated on identifying just institutional arrangements for a society. This approach, which can be called 'transcendental institutionalism', has two distinct features. First, it concentrates its attention on what it identifies as perfect justice, rather than on relative comparison of justice and injustice. It tries only to identify social characteristics that cannot be transcended in terms of justice, and its focus is thus not on comparing feasible societies, all of which may fall short of the ideals of perfection. The inquiry is aimed at identifying the nature of the 'the just', rather than finding some criteria for an alternative being 'less unjust' than another.

Second, in searching for perfection, transcendental institutionalism concentrates primarily on getting the institutions right, and it is not directly focused on the actual societies that would ultimately emerge. The nature of the society that would result from any given set of institutions must, of course, depend also on non-institutional features, such as actual behaviours of people and their social interactions. In elaborating the likely consequences of the institutions, if and when a transcendental institutionalist theory goes into commenting on them, some specific behavioural assumptions are made that help the working of the chosen institutions.

Both these features relate to the 'contractarian' mode of thinking that Thomas Hobbes had initiated, and which was further pursued by John Locke, Jean-Jacques Rousseau and Immanuel Kant.[1] A hypothetical 'social contract' that is assumed to be chosen is clearly concerned with an ideal alternative to the chaos that might otherwise characterize a society, and the contracts that were prominently discussed by the authors dealt primarily with the choice of institutions. The overall result was to develop theories of justice that focused on transcendental identification of the ideal institutions.

It is important, however, to note here that transcendental institutionalists in search of perfectly just institutions have sometimes also presented deeply illuminating analyses of moral or political imperatives regarding socially appropriate behaviour. This applies particularly to Immanuel Kant and John Rawls, both of whom have participated in transcendental institutional investigation, but have also provided far-reaching analyses of the requirements of behavioural norms. Even though they have focused on institutional choices, their analyses can be seen, more broadly, as 'arrangement-focused' approaches to justice, with the arrangements including right behaviour by all as well as right institutions. There is, obviously, a radical contrast between an arrangement-focused conception of justice and a realization-focused understanding: the latter must, for example, concentrate on the actual behaviour of people, rather than presuming compliance by all with ideal behaviour.

In contrast with transcendental institutionalism, a number of other Enlightenment theorists took a variety of comparative approaches that were concerned with the social realizations (resulting from actual institutions, actual behaviour and other influences). Different versions of such comparative thinking can be found, for example, in the works of Adam Smith,

the Marquis de Condorcet, Jeremy Bentham, Mary Wollstonecraft, Karl Marx, John Stuart Mill, among a number of other leaders of innovative thought in the eighteenth and nineteenth centuries. Even though these authors, with their very different ideas of the demands of justice, proposed quite distinct ways of making social comparisons, it can be said, at the risk of only a slight exaggeration, that they were all involved in comparisons of societies that already existed or could feasibly emerge, rather than confining their analyses to transcendental searches for a perfectly just society. Those focusing on realization-focused comparisons were often interested primarily in the removal of manifest injustice from the world that they saw. . . .

THE POINT OF DEPARTURE

In contrast with most modern theories of justice, which concentrate on the 'just society', this book is an attempt to investigate realization-based comparisons that focus on the advancement or retreat of justice. It is, in this respect, not in line with the strong and more philosophically celebrated tradition of transcendental institutionalism that emerged in the Enlightenment period (led by Hobbes and developed by Locke, Rousseau and Kant, among others), but more in the 'other' tradition that also took shape in about the same period or just after (pursued in various ways by Smith, Condorcet, Wollstonecraft, Bentham, Marx, Mill, among others). The fact that I share a point of departure with these diverse thinkers does not, of course, indicate that I agree with their substantive theories (that should be obvious enough, since they themselves differed so much from each other), and going beyond the shared point of departure, we have to look also at some points of eventual arrival. . . .

Importance must be attached to the starting point, in particular the selection of some questions to be answered (for example, 'how would justice be advanced?'), rather than others (for example, 'what would be perfectly just institutions?'). This departure has the dual effect, first, of taking the comparative rather than the transcendental route, and second, of focusing on actual realizations in the societies involved, rather than only on institutions and rules. Given the present balance of emphases in contemporary political philosophy, this will require a radical change in the formulation of the theory of justice.

Why do we need such a dual departure? I begin with transcendentalism. I see two problems here. First, there may be no reasoned agreement at all, even under strict conditions of impartiality and open-minded scrutiny (for example, as identified by Rawls in his 'original position') on the nature of the 'just society': this is the issue of the *feasibility* of finding an agreed transcendental solution. Second, an exercise of practical reason that involves an actual choice demands a framework for comparison of justice for choosing among the feasible alternatives and not an identification of a possibly unavailable perfect situation that could not be transcended: this is the issue of the *redundancy* of the search for a transcendental solution. . . .

FEASIBILITY OF A UNIQUE TRANSCENDENTAL AGREEMENT

There can be serious differences between competing principles of justice that survive critical scrutiny and can have claims to impartiality. This problem is serious enough, for example, for John Rawls's assumption that there will be a unanimous choice of a unique set of 'two principles of justice' in a hypothetical situation of primordial equality (he calls it 'the original position'), where people's vested interests are not known to the people themselves. This presumes that there is basically only one kind of impartial argument, satisfying the demands of fairness, shorn of vested interests. This, I would argue, may be a mistake.

There can be differences, for example, in the exact comparative weights to be given to distributional equality, on the one hand, and overall or aggregate enhancement, on the other. In his transcendental identification, John Rawls pinpoints one such formula (the lexicographic maxim rule. . . among many that are available, without convincing arguments that would eliminate all other alternatives that might compete with Rawls's very special formula for impartial attention. There can be many other reasoned differences involving the particular formulae on which Rawls concentrates in his two principles of justice, without showing us why other alternatives would not continue to command attention in the impartial atmosphere of his original position.

If a diagnosis of perfectly just social arrangements is incurably problematic, then the entire strategy of transcendental institutionalism is deeply impaired, even if every conceivable alternative in the world were available. For example, the two principles of justice in John Rawls's classic investigation of 'justice as fairness'. . . are precisely about perfectly just institutions in a world where all alternatives are available. However, what we do not know is whether the plurality of reasons for justice would allow one unique set of principles of justice to emerge in the original position. The elaborate exploration of Rawlsian social justice, which proceeds step by step from the identification and establishment of just institutions, would then get stuck at the very base.

In his later writings, Rawls makes some concessions to the recognition that 'citizens will of course differ as to which conceptions of political justice they think most reasonable'. Indeed, he goes on to say in *The Law of Peoples* (1999):

> The content of public reason is given by a family of political conceptions of justice, and not by a single one. There are many liberalisms and related views, and therefore many forms of public reason specified by a family of reasonable political conceptions. Of these, justice as fairness, whatever its merits, is but one.[2]

It is not, however, clear how Rawls would deal with the far-reaching implications of this concession. The specific institutions, firmly chosen for the basic structure of society, would demand one specific resolution of the principles of justice, in the way Rawls had outlined in his early works, including *The Theory of Justice* (1971). Once the claim to uniqueness of the Rawlsian principles of justice is dropped (the case for which is outlined in Rawls's later works), the institutional programme would clearly have serious indeterminacy, and Rawls does not tell us much about how a particular set of institutions would be chosen on the basis of a set of competing principles of justice that would demand different institutional combinations for the basic structure of the society. Rawls could, of course, resolve that problem by abandoning the transcendental institutionalism of his earlier work (particularly of *The Theory of Justice*), and this would be the move that would appeal most to this particular author. But I am afraid I am not able to claim that this was the direction in which Rawls himself was definitely heading, even though some of his later works raise that question forcefully.

THREE CHILDREN AND A FLUTE: AN ILLUSTRATION

At the heart of the particular problem of a unique impartial resolution of the perfectly just society is the possible sustainability of plural and competing reasons for justice, all of which have claims to impartiality and which nevertheless differ from—and rival—each other. Let me illustrate the problem with an example in which you have to decide which of three children—Anne, Bob and Carla—should get a flute about which they are quarrelling. Anne claims the flute on the ground that she is the only one of the three who knows how to play it (the others do not deny this), and that it would be quite unjust to deny the flute to the only one who can actually play it. If that is all you knew, the case for giving the flute to the first child would be strong.

In an alternative scenario, it is Bob who speaks up, and defends his case for having the flute by pointing out that he is the only one among the three who is so poor that he has no toys of his own. The flute would give him something to play with (the other two concede that they are richer and well supplied with engaging amenities). If you had heard only Bob and none of the others, the case for giving it to him would be strong.

In another alternative scenario, it is Carla who speaks up and points out that she has been working diligently for many months to make the flute with her own labour (the others confirm this), and just when she had finished her work, 'just then', she complains, 'these expropriators came along to try to grab the flute away from me'. If Carla's statement is all you had heard, you might be inclined to give flute to her in recognition of her understandable claim to something she has made herself.

Having heard all three and their different lines of reasoning, there is a difficult decision that you have to make. Theorists of different persuasions, such as utilitarians, or economic egalitarians, or no-nonsense libertarians, may each take the view that there is a straightforward just resolution staring at us here, and there is no difficulty in spotting it. But almost certainly they would respectively see totally different resolutions as being obviously right. Bob, the poorest, would tend to get fairly straightforward support the

economic egalitarian if he is committed to reducing gaps in economic means of people. On the other hand, Carla, the maker of the flute, would receive immediate sympathy from the libertarian. The utilitarian hedonist may face the hardest challenge, but he would certainly tend to give weight, more than the libertarian or the economic egalitarian, to the fact that Anne's pleasure is likely to be stronger because she is the only one who can play the flute (there is also the general dictum of 'waste not, want not'). Nevertheless, the utilitarian should also recognize that Bob's relative deprivation could make his incremental gain in happiness from getting the flute that much larger. Carla's 'right' to get what she has made may not resonate immediately with the utilitarian, but deeper utilitarian reflection would nevertheless tend to take some note of the requirements of work incentives in creating a society in which utility generation is sustained and encouraged through letting people keep what they have produced with their own effort.

The libertarian's support for giving the flute to Carla will not be conditional in the way it is bound to be for the utilitarian on the working of incentive effects, since a libertarian would take direct note of a person's right to have what people have produced themselves. The idea of the right to the fruits of one's labour can unite right-wing libertarians and left-wing Marxists (no matter how uncomfortable each might be in the company of the other).

The general point here is that it is not easy to brush aside as foundationless any of the claims based respectively on the pursuit of human fulfilment, or removal of poverty, or entitlement to enjoy the products of one's own labour. The different resolutions all have serious arguments in support of them, and we may not be able to identify, without some arbitrariness, any of the alternative arguments as being the one that must invariably prevail.

I also want to draw attention here to the fairly obvious fact that the differences between the three children's justificatory arguments do not represent divergences about what constitutes individual advantage (getting the flute is taken to be advantageous by each of the children and is accommodated by each of the respective arguments), but about the principles that should govern the allocation of resources in general. They are about how social arrangements should be made and what social institutions should be chosen, and through that, about what social realizations would come about. It is not simply that the vested interests of the three children differ (though of course they do), but that the three arguments each point to a different type of impartial and non-arbitrary reason.

This applies not only to the discipline of fairness in the Rawlsian original position, but also to other demands of impartiality, for example Thomas Scanlon's requirement that our principles satisfy 'what others could not reasonably reject'.[3] As was mentioned earlier, theorists of different persuasions, such as utilitarians, or economic egalitarians, or labour right theorists, or no-nonsense libertarians, may each take the view that there is one straightforward just resolution that is easily detected, but they would each argue for totally different resolutions as

being obviously right. There may not indeed exist any identifiable perfectly just social arrangement on which impartial agreement would emerge. . . .

NOTES

1. See Thomas Hobbes, *Leviathan*, edited by Richard Tuck (Cambridge: Cambridge University Press, 1991); John Locke, *Two Treatises of Government*, edited by Peter Laslett (Cambridge: Cambridge University Press, 1988); Jean-Jacques Rousseau, *The Social Contract*, translated by Maurice Cranston (Harmondsworth: Penguin, 1968); Immanuel Kant, *Principles of the Metaphysics of Ethics*, translated by T. K. Abbott, 3rd edn (London: Longmans, 1907).
2. See John Rawls, *The Law of Peoples* (Cambridge, MA: Harvard University Press, 1999), pp.137, 141.
3. See Thomas Scanlon, *What We Owe to Each Other* (Cambridge, MA: Harvard University Press, 1998).

REVIEW EXERCISES

1. What is the difference between a *process view* of distributive justice and an *end-state view*?
2. Discuss the meaning and problems associated with using the end-state view criteria of merit, achievement, effort, and contribution.
3. What is the literal meaning of "equal opportunity"? What criterion does Fishkin use for judging whether it exists? What is Bernard Williams' "starting-gate theory" of equal opportunity?
4. Describe some problems raised by philosophers Frankfurt and Schaar regarding equal opportunity.
5. Explain the libertarian position on liberty and the role of government.
6. What are the basic differences between capitalism and socialism as social and economic theories?
7. What is Rawls's "original position," and what role does it play in his derivation of principles of justice?
8. What is Rawls's *maximin* principle, and how is it related to his second principle of justice?
9. How does communitarianism differ from liberalism?

DISCUSSION CASES

1. The Homeless. Joe was laid off two years ago at the auto repair company where he had worked for fifteen years. For the first year he tried to get another job. He read the want ads and left applications at local employment agencies. After that, he gave up. He had little savings and soon had no money for rent. He has been homeless now for a year. He will not live in the shelters because they are crowded, noisy, and unsafe.

As time goes by, he has less and less chance of getting back to where he was before. When he can, he drinks to forget the past and escape from the present. Other people he meets on the streets are mentally retarded or psychologically disturbed. He realizes that the city offers some things to try to help people like him, but there is little money and the numbers of homeless people seem to be growing.

Does society have any responsibility to do anything for people like Joe? Why or why not?

2. Rights to Keep What One Earns. Gene and his co-workers have been talking over lunch about how their taxes have continued to rise. Some complain that the harder they work, the less they are making. Others are upset because their taxes are going to pay for things that they do not believe the government should support with our tax dollars—the arts, for example. "Why should we support museums or the opera when we don't ever go to them?" they argue. These should be matters for charity. They also complain that they work hard but that their income is being used to take care of others who could work but do not.

Are they right? Why?

3. Class Debate on Equal Opportunity. The topic for class debate one day was "equal opportunity." First, students were asked what they thought it meant. What would you say? How important do you think it is and why? A second question concerned whether there was equal opportunity in society today and, if there were areas where changes needed to be made to enhance equal opportunity, what would they be? What do you think?

YOU MAKE THE DECISION

Apply the theories and issues discussed in this chapter by accessing this animated simulation on the Ethics Resource Center.

Use the passkey that accompanies your book to gain access. If you do not have a passkey, visit cengagebrain.com to purchase instant access to additional study material.

© Cengage Learning

—15—
Legal Punishment

YOU MAY remember the case of Jessica Lundsford. On February 23, 2005, she disappeared from her home in Homosassa, Florida. John Couey, a convicted sex offender, was staying with his half-sister in a trailer home nearby. He abducted Jessica during the night and took her to his bedroom where he sexually assaulted her. Three days later, he tied her wrists, put her in a garbage bag, and buried her alive near the house, where she suffocated to death. Couey had a long criminal history; because of this, he became a prime suspect. Within a month, he was arrested and then confessed. Police found Jessica's body in a shallow grave. Couey was tried and found guilty of kidnapping and first-degree murder on March 7, 2007. The jury recommended that he receive the death penalty. Couey died in prison, of natural causes, in 2009.[1]

Here is a very different case. The father of thirteen-year-old Dwayne had been locked up in a maximum security prison since Dwayne was five years old.[2] After Dwayne became increasingly disruptive in school, his mother took him and his siblings to visit his father in prison in Joliet, Illinois, travelling two hundred miles round-trip. Despite a stoic exterior with regard to his father's absence, Dwayne wrote stories about his father and finally broke down sobbing during the prison visit. It is worth remembering that imprisonment affects not only the one imprisoned, but others as well, including children and families. The number of children with fathers in prison had risen to 2.1 million by 2007.

"The United States has by far the world's highest incarceration rate." The prison population in 2009 was 2.3 million, which is 25 percent of the world's prisoners. And that is "756 inmates per 100,000 residents, a rate nearly five times the average worldwide of 158 for every 100,000." We also have more than 5 million people on parole, probation, or some form of supervision. This means about "one in every 31 adults in the United States [is] in prison, in jail, or on supervised release." There are various reasons for this high rate.[3]

The reasons most often cited are mandatory sentences for drug crimes and an increase in the number of so-called three-strikes and truth-in-sentencing laws that lessen the number of prisoners released early.[4] Also given as reasons for such a high rate are "violent crime, harsher sentencing laws, a legacy of racial turmoil," longer sentences, and even democracy. In the United States judges are elected and may "yield to populist demands for tough justice." Additionally there is the "easier availability of guns."[5] As noted, the United States has the highest rate of incarceration of any country in the world, with the next highest rates in Britain, China, France, Japan, and Nigeria.[6] Approximately "40 percent of all felony probationers are rearrested for fresh felonies within three years of being placed under community supervision."[7]

In 2006, the annual cost to incarcerate an inmate was between $24,000 and $40,000. In California the cost was $47,000 per year.[8] When multiplied by the 2.2 million inmates, the annual cost overall is staggering. In California alone, the operating budget for the state prison system is more than $10 billion, and the state plans to "spend $7.4 billion to build 40,000 new prison beds" because its prisons are now so overcrowded. Within five years of 2007, "the prison budget will overtake spending on the state's public universities."[9]

In 2004, almost 60 percent of prisoners were racial or ethnic minorities, some 40 percent black, 35 percent white, 19 percent Hispanic, and 2 percent other.[10] Those imprisoned represented 12.6 percent of all black men ages twenty-five to twenty-nine, 3.6 percent of Hispanic men and 1.7 percent of white men in the same age range.[11] "Black men in their early thirties are imprisoned at seven times the rate of whites in the same age group." While in 2007 African Americans . . . made up about 12 percent of the total U.S. population" they "accounted for 37 percent of those arrested on drug charges, 59 percent of those convicted, and 74 percent of all drug offenders sentenced to prison."[12]

There are also racial disparities in the number of prisoners executed. Since 1976, they have been 56 percent white, 35 percent black, 7 percent Hispanic, and 2 percent other.[13] All high school dropouts are at greater risk for being in prison, but "by the time they reach their mid-thirties, a full 60 percent of black high-school dropouts are now prisoners or ex-cons." Related to the racial disparities of incarceration are political effects. For example, given that many states disallow even ex-felons to vote and that a high percentage of blacks vote Democratic, many Republicans would not be elected to Congress without such laws. In fact, if ex-felons had been able to vote in the 2000 election in Florida and using conservative figures on voting, Al Gore would have carried the state by 30,000 votes and thus the electoral college to become president.[14]

Although many prisoners are incarcerated for having committed violent crimes, more than half are there for nonviolent crimes, many of these for drug-related offenses (although violent crimes can also be the result of attempts to get drug money.) Moreover, it is estimated that some 16 percent of the prison population has some mental illness.

In fact, a report by a Ford Foundation commission, *Confronting Confinement* (June 2006), noted that "America's prisons are dangerously overcrowded, unnecessarily violent, excessively reliant on physical segregation, breeding grounds of infections disease, lacking in meaningful programs for inmates, and staffed by underpaid and undertrained guards in a culture that promotes abuse." One of those accused of abuse at Abu Ghraib prison in Iraq had been a prison guard.[15] When these inmates return to society, they bring the results of such prison conditions with them.

By mid-2010, there had been 1,216 executions in the U.S. since 1976, over half of them since 1999. There were fifty-two people executed in 2009, thirty-seven in 2008, and forty-two in 2007. Nearly half of the 2009 executions (24) came from Texas.[16] All of these executions were carried out by lethal injection. Of those executed in Texas in 2009, fourteen were black, seven Latino, and three white. Twelve states do not have the death penalty, with another five having carried out no executions in the past thirty years, and several more having executed no more than three people.

Between 1977 and 2006, there were 368 executions in Texas, 80 in Oklahoma, 66 in Missouri, 96 in Virginia, and 60 in Florida. The last electrocution took place in Virginia in July 2006, the last death by gas chamber in 1999 in Arizona, the last death by hanging in 1996 in Delaware, and the last death by firing squad in 1996 in Utah (although another firing-squad execution there is scheduled for June 2010).

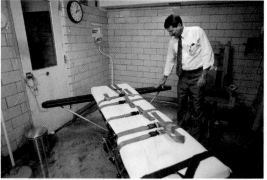

Philip Parker, Warden of the Kentucky State Penitentiary, with the facility's lethal injection table.

AP Photo/Jim Roshan

Five states account for more than two-thirds of executions since 1977.[17]

China executed more people in 2009 "than the rest of the world combined, according to a report published . . . by Amnesty International. Amnesty said there were thousands of Chinese executions in 2009." There were "at least 714 people executed 17 other counties, led by Iran, Iraq, Saudi Arabia, and the United States." The methods included "beheading, stoning, electrocution, hanging, firing squads, and lethal injection." In 2009 Iran alone executed 388 people, "with about a third of the executions coming in the seven weeks of protests and turmoil that followed the country's disputed presidential election in June." In 2009 there were no executions in Europe, though Belarus still has the death penalty. Other countries that carried out executions in 2009 included "Bangladesh, Japan, North Korea, Malaysia, Singapore, Thailand, and Vietnam." In Africa, only Botswana and Sudan carried out executions in 2009.[18]

Capital punishment has a long history in the United States, but by 1966, a large majority of people in the U.S. had come to oppose the death penalty.[19] Not long after this, in 1972, the U.S. Supreme Court revoked it, ruling that the penalty had become too "arbitrary and capricious" and thus violated the federal Constitution's ban on cruel and unusual punishment.[20] By 1976, however, the country's mood had again begun to change, and states had established less arbitrary sentencing guidelines. That year, the high court reinstated the death penalty in *Gregg* v. *Georgia*, arguing that it did not violate the Eighth Amendment's ban on cruel and unusual punishment and thus could be constitutionally applied for convicted murderers. Public support for the death penalty has varied in the decades since. It peaked in the mid-1980s, with as many as 83 percent of Americans supporting it. However, there remain great differences in who receives the death penalty, and it depends often on where one committed the crime and the makeup of the jury. In October 2008, according to Gallup's annual crime survey, 64% of Americans favor the death penalty for someone convicted of murder, while just 30% oppose it.[21] The main public concern seems to be the risk of executing innocent people, primarily because of "revelations of withheld evidence, mistaken eyewitness identification, questionable forensic practices, prosecutorial misconduct, and simple error."[22] Defendants have had poorly trained and poorly paid lawyers—and even lawyers who dozed during their trials. From 1999 to 2002, "24 death row inmates in 14 states [were] given new trials or freed altogether, often on the basis of DNA evidence."[23]

By June, 2010, 254 convicts in the United States had been found to be innocent as a result of DNA testing. These people were exonerated after spending a combined 3,240 years in prison for crimes they did not commit.[24] Some of those released were the result of the work of the Innocence Project, which was started by two attorneys, Barry Scheck and Peter Neufeld. On February 3, 1997, the American Bar Association, the largest and most influential organization of lawyers in the United States, voted for a moratorium on executions until greater fairness in the process could be ensured, especially in the quality of representation that defendants receive.[25]

In three Illinois cases, a Northwestern University journalism teacher and his class reviewed the cases and proved the inmates' innocence. These were three of thirteen people in Illinois who had been scheduled to be executed but had recently been found to be innocent and released. One inmate had been scheduled for execution in just forty-eight hours. On January 31, 2000, the governor of Illinois, George Ryan, ordered that all executions in his state be halted. "Until I can be sure with moral certainty that no innocent man or woman is facing a lethal injection," he said, "no one will meet that fate."[26] Because of these concerns and a review of the cases, on January 11, 2003, Ryan, in one of his last acts as governor, pardoned four inmates and commuted the death sentences of the remaining 167 (163 men and four women).

There also is some evidence of racial bias in death penalty sentencing. Taking Florida as one example, although 12.5 percent of the population is black, 35 percent of those on death row are black. Actually, it is as much the race of the victim as of the defendant that seems to play a key role in sentencing. A Florida commission concluded that "people who kill whites are three to four times more likely to receive the death sentence than people who kill blacks." Of the forty-four Florida executions during the study period, only five of the defendants were executed for killing blacks, despite the fact that nearly half of the state's homicide victims were black.[27]

Moreover, the makeup of the jury is also important. "More than 20% of black defendants who have been executed were convicted by all-white juries." Although there are now more whites on death row than blacks, blacks have a higher rate similar to their presence in the prison population: "80 percent of completed capital cases involve white victims even though nationally only 50 percent of murder victims are white."[28]

Other issues related to the death penalty have recently gained public attention: for example, whether mentally retarded persons or juveniles should be executed. In June 2002, the U.S. Supreme Court ruled that mentally retarded defendants should not be subject to the death penalty. This same court had ruled in 1989 that execution of the retarded was not unconstitutional. However, the majority of justices now stated that because of "evolving standards of decency," they were reversing themselves. This could affect approximately 200 inmates currently on death rows in various states. Obviously, one practical problem that will be faced in such cases is just how to determine when someone is retarded and what degree of mental retardation should count. In March 2005, the U.S. Supreme Court, in a 5–4 vote, ruled that it was cruel and unusual punishment, forbidden by the Constitution, to execute those who were under age 18 when they committed their crimes.[29] The Court had ruled the other way just fifteen years earlier. The key vote was that of Associate Justice Anthony Kennedy, who wrote that he changed his position because of the changing social standards of what counts as cruel and unusual punishment. Adolescents are thought to "lack mature judgment and a full appreciation of the consequences of their actions."[30] The United States had been the only remaining country that executed juveniles.

In 1995, the cost for a sentence of life in prison was estimated to be approximately $800,000

per person, but the cost of a death penalty case is between $2 million and $5 million.[31] In North Carolina, for example, an execution can cost as much as $2.16 million more than the cost of life in prison. In California, it costs $90 million more than life in prison. In Texas, the cost of an appeal of a death sentence is more than $2 million, whereas life in prison would be around $750,000.[32] In 1985, after several years of trying, the Kansas legislature passed a death penalty bill. However, when legislators figured out that it would probably cost the state $10 million in the first year and $50 million by 1990, they repealed the law. Those who protested the death penalty argued that the long appeals process results from strong moral opposition to state-sanctioned killing. Indeed, moral sentiments on this issue are strong on both sides.

To know what to think about cases like this and the various crime statistics, we need to examine some of the reasons that have been given for the practice of legal punishment itself. Only then can we appreciate the nature and strength of the arguments for and against the death penalty.

THE NATURE OF LEGAL PUNISHMENT

The most visible form of legal criminal punishment is imprisonment. However, we also punish with fines, forced work, and corporal punishment, which includes death. What we want to examine here is not *any* sort of punishment, only legal punishment. Eight-year-old Jimmy's parents can punish him with no TV for a week for a failing grade, and I can punish myself for a momentary caloric indulgence. Legal punishment is like parental and self-punishment in that it is designed to "hurt." If something is gladly accepted or enjoyed, then it is not really punishment.

However, legal punishment is distinct from other forms of punishment in several ways. Legal punishment must follow legal rules of some sort. It is authorized by a legal authority and follows a set of rules that establish who is to be punished, how, and by how much. Lynching is not legal punishment. Furthermore, "Every dog gets his first bite," as the old saying goes. You must first commit the crime or be suspected of it. Whatever we say about the justification of detaining people before they commit (or we think they will commit) a crime, it is not punishment. Punishment of any sort presumes someone has done something to merit the penalty. In the case of legal punishment, it is a penalty for doing what the law forbids. Criminal law, by its very nature, must have some sanction, some threat attached to breaking it, or else it loses its force. Without such force, it may be a request, but it is not law.

Thus, we can say that legal punishment is the state's infliction of harm or pain on those who break the law according to a set of legally established rules. But is such a practice justified? What gives a society the right to inflict the pain of punishment on any of its members? In asking this, we are asking a moral and not just a legal question. Is legal punishment of some sort morally justifiable? If so, why?

THE DETERRENCE ARGUMENT

One answer to the question of whether legal punishment is morally justifiable is, "Yes, if (and only if) the punishment could be fashioned to prevent or deter crime." The general idea involved in this first rationale for legal punishment is related to both the *nature of law* and *its purpose*. For a criminal law to be a law and not just a request, sanctions must be attached to it. It must have force behind it. Law has many possible purposes. One purpose is to prevent people from harming others. Our laws presumably are directed to achieving some good. Having penalties as sanctions attached to breaking these laws helps to ensure that the good intended by the laws will be achieved. Of course, not all laws are good laws. However, the idea is that we want not only to have good laws but also to have them enforced in ways that make them effective.

Legal punishment, according to this reasoning, is for the purpose of *preventing* people from breaking the law, *deterring* them from doing so, or both. As such this is a forward-looking consequentialist rationale. Broadly interpreted, the deterrence argument involves these two mechanisms. We can prevent crime by detaining would-be or actual criminals— that is, by simply holding them somewhere so that they cannot do social damage. We also can prevent

crime by means such as increased street lighting, more police officers, and stricter handgun laws. We can deter crime by holding out a punishment as a threat to persuade those who contemplate breaking the law not to do so. If a punishment works as a deterrent, then it works in a particular way—through the would-be lawbreaker's thinking and decision-making processes. One considers the possibility of being punished for doing some contemplated action and concludes that the gain achieved from the act is not worth the price to be paid—namely, the punishment. Then one acts accordingly.

Problematic Aspects

If deterrence works in this way, then we also can notice that it is not likely to work in some cases. It is not likely to deter crimes of passion, in which people are overcome, if you will, by strong emotions. Not only are they not in the mood to calculate the risks versus the benefits, but also they are unlikely to stop themselves from continuing to act as they will. Punishment as a threat is also not likely to work in cases where people do calculate the risks and the benefits and think the benefits are greater than the risks. These would be cases in which the risks of being caught and punished are perceived as small and the reward or benefit is great. The benefit could be financial or the reward of group or gang respect. It also might be the reward of having done what one believed to be right, as in acts of civil disobedience or in support of any cause whether actually good or bad. Although punishment does not deter in some cases, in others presumably people will be motivated by the threat of punishment. A system of legal punishment will be worthwhile if it works for the greater majority, even if not for all, and if there are no bad consequences that outweigh the good ones.

The issue of cost and benefit also helps make another point about the deterrence rationale for legal punishment: Punishment, in this view, is *externally related* to lawbreaking. In other words, it is not essential. If something else works better than punishment, then that other means ought to be used either as a substitution for punishment or in addition to it. Some people argue that punishment itself does not work, but combined with rehabilitation, job training, or psychological counseling, punishment might be effective. However, if a punishment system is not working, then, in this view, it is not morally justifiable, for the whole idea is not to punish for punishment's sake but to achieve the goal of law enforcement. On utilitarian grounds, pain is never good in itself. Thus, if punishment involves suffering, it must be justified. The suffering must be outweighed by the good to be achieved by it.

The deterrence argument has a more serious problem: Some people morally object to using this rationale as the sole grounds for legal punishment. For example, if the whole purpose is to enforce the law, and a particular form of punishment will actually work and work better than other measures to achieve the desired deterrent effect, then it would seem that we ought to use it. Suppose that a community has a particularly vexing problem with graffiti. To clean it up is costing the community scarce resources that could be better spent elsewhere. To get rid of the problem, suppose the community decides to institute a program whereby it would randomly pick up members of particular gangs believed to be responsible for the graffiti and punish these individuals with floggings in the public square. Or suppose that cutting off their hands would work better! We would surely have serious moral objections to this program. One objection would be that these particular individuals may not themselves have been responsible for the defacing. They were just picked at random because of suspicion. Another would be that the punishment seems all out of proportion to the offense. However, in itself (or in principle), on deterrence grounds there would be nothing essentially wrong with this program of law enforcement. It would not be necessary that the individual herself be guilty or that the punishment fit the crime. What would be crucial to determine is whether this punishment worked or worked better than alternative forms.

There is another version of the deterrence argument, and it has to do with how deterrence is supposed to work. According to this view, legal punishment is part of a system of social moral education. A society has a particular set of values. One way in which it can instill these values in its members from their youth is to establish punishments for those who undermine them. If private property is valued, then society should punish those who damage or take others' property. These punishments would then become a deterrent in the sense that they had helped individuals internalize social values, giving them internal prohibitions against violating those values. Key to evaluating this view is to determine whether punishment does work in this fashion. What does punishment teach the young and the rest of us? Does it help us internalize values, and does it motivate us? The way the system is administered also can send a message—and in some cases, it might be the wrong message. For example, if legal punishment is not applied fairly, then the lesson that some might learn may not be the one we would desire.

THE RETRIBUTIVIST ARGUMENT

The second primary rationale for legal punishment is retribution. On the retributivist view, legal punishment is justified as a means of making those who are responsible for a crime or harm pay for it. As such it is a backward-looking argument because it is based on past actions. We can understand the idea embodied in this rationale in several ways. It is an argument that uses the concept of justice. Thus, a proponent might say that because someone caused a great deal of pain or harm to another, it is only just or fair that he suffer similarly or proportionately to the harm or pain he caused the other person. Or we might say that she deserves to suffer because she made her victim suffer. The punishment is only just or a fair recompense. In this view, punishment is *internally related* to the wrongful conduct. One cannot, as in the case of the deterrence argument, say that if something else works better than punishment, then that is what ought to be done. Here the punishing itself is essential for justice to be done.

Let us examine this reasoning a bit further. It is based on a somewhat abstract notion of justice. We punish to right a wrong or restore some original state, or we reset the scales of justice. However, in many cases we cannot really undo the suffering of the victim by making the perpetrator suffer. One can pay back the money or return the property to its original state before it was damaged. But even in these cases, there are other harms that cannot be undone, such as the victim's lost sense of privacy or security. Thus, the erasing, undoing, or righting of the wrong is of some other abstract or metaphysical type. It is difficult to explain, but supporters of this rationale for punishment believe that we do have some intuitive sense of what we mean when we say "justice was done."

According to the retributivist view, payment must be made in some way that is equivalent to the crime or harm done. Writers distinguish two senses of equivalency: an *egalitarian* sense and a *proportional* sense. With egalitarian equivalency, one is required to pay back something identical or almost identical to what was taken. If you make someone suffer two days, then you should suffer two days. However, it would also mean that if you caused someone's arm to be amputated, then your arm should also be cut off. Thus, this version is often given the label *lex talionis*. Translated literally, it means the "law of the talon," of the bird of prey's claw. We also call it the "law of the jungle" or taking "an eye for an eye."

Proportional equivalency holds that what is required in return is not something more or less identical to the harm done or pain caused, but something proportional. In this version, we can think of harms or wrongs as matters of degree—namely, of bad, worse, and worst. Punishments are also scaled from the minimal to the most severe. In this view, punishment must be proportional to the degree of the seriousness of the crime.

Obviously, there are serious problems, both practical and moral, with the *lex talionis* version of the retributivist view. In some cases—for example, in the case of multiple murders—it is not possible to deliver something in like kind, for one cannot kill the murderer more than once. We would presumably also have some moral problems with torturing the torturer or raping the rapist. If one objects to this version of the retributivist view, however, then one would not necessarily have to object to the proportional version.

We also should notice that the retributivist justification of legal punishment does respond to two major problems that the deterrence argument has— that is, it is essential from this point of view that the payment or punishment be just. For it to be just, it must fit both the perpetrator and the crime. First, it must fit the perpetrator in the following ways. Only those who are responsible for a crime should be punished, and only to the degree that they are responsible. It would be important from this perspective that guilt be proved, and that we not single out likely suspects or representatives of a group to make examples of them or use them to intimidate other group members, as in our graffiti example. It also would be important that the punishment fit the person in terms of the degree of his responsibility. This requirement would address the concerns that we have about accomplices to a crime and also about the mental state of the criminal. Diminished mental capacity, mitigating circumstances, and duress, which lessen a person's responsibility, are significant elements of our criminal punishment system.

Second, it is essential in the retributivist view that the punishment fit the crime. Defacing property is not a major wrong or harm and thus should not be punished with amputation of the perpetrator's hand, however well that might work to deter the graffiti artists. This view then requires that we do have a sense of what is more or less serious among crimes and also among punishments so that they can be well matched.

It is because the punishment should fit the crime that many people have problems with the three-strikes laws that several states have passed. These laws provide for life imprisonment for anyone who has a criminal record with two previous convictions for serious crimes and is then found guilty of a third felony. As of the end of 2004, there were "almost 43,000 inmates serving time in prison under the three-strikes law" in California, which is about 26 percent of the total number of prisoners.[33] What has happened, however, is that the third "strike" in some instances has been petty theft. A life sentence looks quite out of proportion to such infractions. On the other side is the consequentialist argument that points out that people who have a history of lawbreaking are removed from society and prevented from continuing in such behavior.

Problematic Aspects

Just as in the case of the deterrence argument, the retributivist argument regarding legal punishment has problems. We have already referred to one: that punishing the perpetrator does not concretely undo the wrong done to the victim. If there is undoing, then it is only in some abstract or perhaps metaphysical sense. Those people who defend this argument would have to explain in what sense the balance is restored or the wrong righted by punishment. However, the retributivist would not have any problem with those who point out that a particular form of punishment does not work. According to a retributivist, this is not the primary reason to punish. Someone should be punished as a way of achieving satisfaction or restitution even if it does the perpetrator or others no good.

A more common objection to the retributivist view is that it amounts to a condoning of revenge. To know whether or not this were true, we would have to clarify what we mean by *revenge*. Suppose we mean that particular people—say, a victim or her family—will get a sense of satisfaction in seeing the wrongdoer punished. But the retributivist view is arguably based on a different sense of justice. According to this view, justice is done when a perpetrator is punished whether or not people feel good about it. However, some may question whether any type of justice exists that is not a matter of providing emotional satisfaction to victims or others who are enraged by a wrong done to them.

Finally, we can wonder whether the retributivist view provides a good basis for a system of legal punishment. Is the primary purpose of such a system to see that justice is done? Do we not have a system of legal punishment to ensure social order and safety? If so, then it would seem that the deterrence argument is the best reason for having any system of legal punishment. One solution to this problem about which justification is better to use for legal punishment is to use both.[34] In designing this system, we can retain consequentialist and thus deterrence and

prevention reasons for having a legal punishment system, and consider first what works to deter and prevent crimes. However, we then can bring in our retributivist concerns to determine who is punished (only those who are guilty and only to the extent that they are guilty) and how much (the punishment fitting the crime). In fashioning the punishment system, however, there may be times when we need to determine which rationale takes precedence. For example, in setting requirements for conviction of guilt, we may need to know how bad it is to punish an innocent person. We may decide to give precedence to the retributivist rationale and then make the requirements for conviction of guilt very strenuous, requiring unanimous jury verdicts and guilt beyond a reasonable doubt. In so doing, we also let some guilty people go free and thus run the risk of lessening the deterrent effect of the punishment system. Or we may decide to give precedence to the deterrence rationale. We thus may weaken the requirements for conviction so that we may catch and punish more guilty people. In doing so, however, we run the risk of also punishing more innocent persons.

PUNISHMENT AND RESPONSIBILITY

A key element of our legal punishment system and practice is the supposed tie between punishment and responsibility. Responsibility is essential for punishment from the retributivist point of view. The retributivist believes it is unjust to punish those who are not responsible for a crime. This also can be supported on deterrence grounds: It probably would work better to punish only those who are responsible, otherwise who would have respect for or obey the law if we could be punished whether or not we obeyed it? Responsibility is essential from the retributivist point of view, but only possibly important from the deterrence point of view.

Thus, our legal punishment system contains defenses that are grounded in the requirement that a person be responsible to be punished. For example, the defense of duress can be viewed this way. If a person were forced to commit a crime, either physically forced or under threat to life, then we would probably say that that person was not responsible. The person may have committed the crime, but that is not enough. We do not have a system of strict liability in which the only issue is whether or not you actually did or caused something.

One of the most problematic defenses in our criminal justice system may well be the insanity defense. It involves a plea and a finding of "not guilty by reason of insanity" or something similar such as "mental defect." This defense has a long history going back at least into the nineteenth century in England with the *M'Naughton Rule* (1843). According to this rule, people are not responsible for their actions if they did not know what they were doing or did not know that it was wrong. This is often referred to as the "right from wrong test." Since that time, other attempts also have been made to list the conditions under which people should not be held responsible for their actions. One example is the "irresistible impulse test." The idea underlying this test for insanity is that sometimes persons are not able to control their conduct and thus act through no fault of their own. Of course, if a person does what he knows will put him in a condition in which he will not be able to control himself and then he unlawfully harms others, then he is held responsible. Thus, the person who drinks and then drives and harms another is held legally liable. However, the person who has some biochemical imbalance that prevents her from controlling her conduct would not be in the same position. In some cases, the insanity defense has been defined in medical terms when the behavior is said to be the result of mental disease. Thus, the *Durham Rule* defines insanity as the "product of mental disease or defect," some sort of abnormal mental condition that affects mental and emotional processes and impairs behavior controls. In our current criminal justice system, mental competence is one requirement for criminal liability. It is called the *mens rea*, or mental element.

Common criticisms of the insanity defense concern our ability to determine whether someone is mentally insane or incompetent. Can't someone feign this? How do psychiatrists or other experts really know whether a person knows what she is doing? However, if we could diagnose these conditions, then a more basic question would still remain—namely, would the conditions diminish or take away responsibility? If so, then would punishment be appropriate? In the extreme case in which a person has a serious brain condition that prevents normal mental function, we assume that this would excuse him from full responsibility. He may, however, be dangerous, and this may be another reason to detain as well as treat him.

Some people have criticized the entire notion of mental illness, especially as it is used in criminal proceedings. They are concerned about the results of a finding such as "not guilty by reason of insanity." For example, it may result in indeterminate sentences for minor crimes, because one must remain in custody in a criminal mental institution until sane. Others find the whole idea wrongheaded and dangerous. For example, one longtime critic of the penal system, Thomas Szasz, held that we have sometimes used this diagnosis of mental illness to categorize and stigmatize people who are simply different.[35] He found this diagnosis often to be a dangerous form of social control.

Some of us also tend to look at some heinous crime and say that "no sane person could have done that!" Or we say that a certain crime was "sick." We use the horror of the crime, its serious wrongness, to conclude that the person committing it must be mentally diseased. One problem with this conclusion is that it implies that the person is not responsible. Are we then implying that no one who does evil things is responsible for what they do? If so, then perhaps they should not be punished. The connection between punishment and responsibility is not only central to our system of legal punishment but also an important element of a morality of legal punishment. In fact, if all acts were determined, in other words they were caused by external or internal influences, and no one of us was responsible for what we do (in the sense that we could have done otherwise), then it would seem that punishment as such (at least in the retributive sense of giving someone what was due them) would never be appropriate.

THE DEATH PENALTY

We now return to a discussion of the death penalty. Throughout history, people have been executed for various, and often political, reasons. Lethal injection, which was first used in Texas in 1982, has been the preferred method more recently. The same two arguments regarding legal punishment—deterrence and retribution—generally are used in arguments about the death penalty. We will return now to these rationales and see what considerations would be relevant to arguments for and against the death penalty.

On Deterrence Grounds

Is the death penalty a deterrent? Does it prevent people from committing certain capital crimes? Consider first the issue of prevention. One would think that at least there is certainty here. If you execute someone, then that person will not commit any future crime—including murders—because he will be dead. However, on a stricter interpretation of the term prevent, this may not necessarily be so.[36] Suppose that we meant that by preventing X from doing Y, we stop X from doing what she would have done—namely, Y. Next, we ask whether by executing a convicted murderer we prevent that person from committing any further murders. The answer is, "Maybe." If that person would have committed another murder, then we have prevented him from doing so. If that person would not have committed another murder, then we would not have prevented him from doing so. In general, by executing all convicted murders we would, strictly speaking, have prevented some of them (those who would have killed again) but not others (those who would not have killed again) from doing so. How many? It is difficult to tell. Those who support the death penalty will insist that it will have been worth it, no matter how small the number of murders being prevented, because the people executed are convicted murderers anyway. The last point must mean that their lives are not worth that much!

What about the deterrence argument for the death penalty? If having the death penalty deters would-be murderers from committing their crimes, then it will have been worth it, according to this rationale. Granted, it would not deter those who kill out of passion or those murders committed by risk takers, but it would deter others. This argument depends on showing that the death penalty is an effective deterrent. There are two kinds of resources to use to make this case. One is to appeal to our own intuitions about the value of our lives—that we would not do what would result in our own death. Threats of being executed would deter us, and thus we think they also would deter others. More likely, however, reasons other than fear of the death penalty restrain most of us from killing others.

The other resource for making the case for the death penalty's deterrent effect is to use empirical studies to make comparisons. For example, we could compare two jurisdictions, say, two states: One has the death penalty, and one does not. If we find that in the state with the death penalty there are fewer murders than in the state without the death penalty, can we assume that the death penalty has made the difference and is thus a deterrent? Not necessarily. Perhaps it was something else about the state with the death penalty that accounted for the lesser incidence of murder. For example, the lower homicide rate could be the result of good economic conditions or a culture that has strong families or religious institutions. Something similar could be true of the state with a higher incidence of homicide. The cause in this case could be factory closings or other poor economic conditions. So, also, if there were a change in one jurisdiction from no death penalty to death penalty (or the opposite), and the statistics regarding homicides also changed, then we might conclude that the causal factor was the change in the death penalty status. But again this is not necessarily so. For example, the murder rate in Canada actually declined after that country abolished the death penalty in 1976.[37] Other studies found no correlation between having or instituting or abolishing the death penalty and the rate of homicide.[38] For example, statistics show that states without the death penalty and with similar demographic profiles do not differ in homicide rates from states with the death penalty. Moreover, since 1976, homicide rates in states that instituted the death penalty have not declined more than in states that did not institute the death penalty. For example, "Massachusetts and Rhode Island, with no death penalty, had homicide rates of 3.7 per 100,000 and 4.2 per 100,000, respectively, from 1977 to 1997, while Connecticut, a death penalty state, had a rate of 4.9 per 100,000."[39] And homicide rates in states with the death penalty have been found to be higher than states without it. The murder rate in states with the death penalty is consistently higher than in the twelve states without the death penalty: in recent years, between 37 percent and 46 percent higher.[40]

To make a good argument for the death penalty on deterrence grounds, a proponent would have to show that it works in this fashion. In addition, the proponent may have to show that the death penalty works better than other alternatives—for example, life in prison without the possibility of parole. If we do not know for sure, then we can ask what are our options. If we have the death penalty and it does not provide an effective deterrent, then we will have executed people for no good purpose. If we do not have the death penalty and it would have been an effective deterrent, then we risk the lives of innocent victims who otherwise would have been saved. Because this is the worse alternative, some argue, we ought to retain the death penalty. Because the deterrence argument broadly construed is a consequentialist argument, using it also should require thinking more generally of costs and benefits. Here the cost of execution could be compared to the cost of life imprisonment.

On Retributivist Grounds

As we have already noted, according to the retributivist argument for legal punishment, we ought to punish people in order to make them pay for the wrong or harm they have done. Those who argue for the death penalty on retributivist grounds must show that it is a fitting punishment and the only or most fitting punishment for certain crimes and criminals. This is not necessarily an argument based on revenge—that the punishment of the wrongdoer gives others satisfaction. It appeals rather to a sense of justice and an abstract righting of wrongs done. Again, there are two different versions of the retributive principle: egalitarian (or *lex talionis*) and proportional. The egalitarian version says that the punishment should equal the crime. An argument for the death penalty would attempt to show that the only fitting punishment for someone who takes a life is that her own life be taken in return. In this view, the value of a life is not equivalent to anything else, thus even life in prison is not sufficient payment for taking a life, though it would also seem that the only crime deserving of the death penalty would be

murder. Note that homicide is not the only crime for which we have assigned the death penalty. We have also done so for treason and rape. Moreover, only some types of murder are thought by proponents of the death penalty to deserve this form of punishment. And as noted in the critique of the *lex talionis* view above, strict equality of punishment would be not only impractical in some cases but also morally problematic.

Perhaps a more acceptable argument could be made on grounds of proportionality. In this view, death is the only fitting punishment for certain crimes. Certain crimes are worse than all others, and these should receive the worst or most severe punishment. Surely, some say, death is a worse punishment than life in prison. However, some people argue that spending one's life in prison is worse. This form of the retributivist principle would not require that the worst crimes receive the worst possible punishment. It only requires that, of the range of acceptable punishments, the worst crimes receive the top punishment on the list. Death by prolonged torture might be the worst punishment, but we probably would not put that at the top of our list. So, also, death could but need not be included on that list.

Using the retributivist rationale, one would need to determine the most serious crimes. Can these be specified and a good reason given as to why they are the worst crimes? Multiple murders would be worse than single ones, presumably. Murder with torture or of certain people also might be found to be among the worst crimes. What about treason? What about huge monetary swindles? What about violation of laws against weapons sales to certain foreign governments? We rate degrees of murder, distinguishing murder in the first degree from murder in the second degree. The first is worse because the person not only deliberately intended to kill the victim but also did so out of malice. These are distinguished from manslaughter, which is killing also, both its voluntary and involuntary forms. The idea supposedly is that the kind of personal and moral involvement makes a difference: The more the person planned with intention and deliberateness, the more truly the person owned the act. The more malicious crime is also thought to be worse. Critics of the death penalty sometimes argue that such rational distinctions are perhaps impossible to make in practice. However, unless it is impossible in principle or by its very nature, supporters could continue to try to refine the current distinctions.

Other Concerns

Not all arguments for and against the death penalty come easily or neatly under the headings of deterrence or retributivist arguments. Some, for example, appeal to the uniqueness of the action by which society deliberately takes the life of a human being. People die all the time. But for some individuals or for the state's representatives deliberately to end the experience and thoughts and feelings of a living human being is the gravest of actions, they argue. As mentioned previously, most Western nations no longer have a death penalty. Some have given it up because they believe it to be uncivilized, brutalizing, degrading, barbarous, and dehumanizing. The one put to death, depending on the form of execution, gasps for air, strains, and shakes uncontrollably. The eyes bulge, the blood vessels expand, and sometimes more than one try is needed to complete the job. In June 1999, for example, 344-pound Allen Lee Davis was executed in Florida's new electric chair. The new chair replaced "Old Sparky," a chair built in 1923 that had ended the lives of 225 convicted murderers. The execution caused blood to appear on Davis's face and shirt. Some believed that this showed that he had suffered. Others said it was simply a nosebleed.[41] On January 7, 2000, the Florida legislature voted to use lethal injections instead of the electric chair in future executions.[42]

Just as the electric chair was thought to be more humane (painless and swift) when Thomas Edison invented it in 1888, so now death by lethal injection is to take the place of electrocution and other less humane methods. Three chemicals are used in this procedure and are injected intravenously. First, an ultrashort-acting barbiturate, usually sodium thiopental, is given. This causes the inmate to become unconscious. Next, a muscle relaxant, either pancuronium bromide or a similar drug, is given to cause paralysis of the muscles, including those responsible for breathing. Finally, potassium chloride, which causes cardiac arrest, is given. If all goes as expected, the inmate falls asleep and does not experience any

pain as death takes place. The entire process can take as short as ten minutes or much longer. Some of the delay is caused by the difficulty the technicians sometimes have in finding an acceptable vein to use. There have been cases of drug users, for example, whose veins were not in good condition or who had to help the technician find a good vein. It is important that it be a vein rather than an artery used because the chemicals go straight to the heart. It is also possible that the person does not remain unconscious or is partially conscious and does experience pain or the feeling of suffocating, but because of the inability to move caused by the second chemical cannot communicate this. Technicians can be more or less capable of giving the drugs correctly and in sufficient amount, though difficult cases seem to be occurring less frequently. Doctors would be more capable but are prohibited by their code of ethics from taking part in executions in this way.[43] There have been thirty-eight botched cases recorded since 1976. In the last few years, half a dozen states have suspended using lethal injection because of concerns about these cases.[44] Clearly, both opponents and supporters of the death penalty may have ammunition for their position in the description of the process of lethal injection as a more humane method of execution.

Other opponents of the death penalty appeal to religious reasons, declaring the wrongness of "playing God." Only God can take a life, they argue. Another argument appeals to the inalienable right to life possessed by all human beings. Critics of this argument assert that those who deliberately kill other human beings forfeit their own right to life. Consider, further, whether a condemned prisoner should have the right to choose his own means of execution. The Utah execution by firing squad mentioned above was the method selected by the condemned man; not long ago, a convicted murderer in Oregon asked to be hanged.[45] Do some forms of execution (the guillotine, for example) violate the Eighth Amendment's ban on cruel and unusual punishment? Should executions become public or videotaped for purposes of information and instruction? When we ask questions such as these, our views on the death penalty and our reasons for supporting or opposing it will be put to the test, which is probably not a bad thing.

Also relevant to a discussion of the morality of legal punishment and the death penalty is the matter of rehabilitation. From a consequentialist perspective, if special programs in prison would help reduce the rate of recidivism or repeat offenders and also help convicted persons lead productive lives when released, then they would be morally recommended. From a nonconsequentialist perspective, there might also be grounds for stressing such programs. One might want to consider whether persons ought to be given a second chance in light of the fact that, given certain circumstances, they might not have been fully responsible for their crimes. On the other hand, those who argue from a consequentialist perspective might in some cases point out that in certain kinds of cases—say, with sexual predators—there is not much likelihood of reform. Or from a nonconsequentialist perspective, some might argue that given the severity of certain crimes, persons deserve the strictest and most severe punishment, not a second chance. As you can see from the discussions in this chapter, matters of legal punishment and the death penalty in particular are complex. Hopefully, the distinctions made in this chapter will help readers make more informed decisions about this subject.

In the readings in this chapter, Ernest van den Haag, a supporter of the death penalty, attempts to answer many of the arguments of those who oppose it, and Hugo Bedau discusses certain factual matters and possible moral principles to help determine the morality of the death penalty.

NOTES

1. http://en.wikipedia.org/wiki/Jessica Lunsford. More can be found on Jessica Lunsford and the law named after her, at http://www.cbsnews.com/stories/2005/03/31/earlyshow/main684190.shtml
2. This short profile of Dwayne appears in Jason Deparle's article in *The New York Review of Books*, April 12, 2007. (www.nybooks.com/articles/20056). More on Dwayne can be found in DeParle's book, *American Dream: Three Women, Ten Kids, and a Nation's Drive to End Welfare* (Viking, 2004).
3. Jim Webb, "Why We Must Fix our Prisons," *San Francisco Chronicle*, March 29, 2009, p. 4.
4. Associated Press, "Nation's Inmate Population Increased 2.3 Percent Last Year," *The New York Times*, April 25, 2005, p. A14.
5. "U.S. Inmate Count Far Exceeds Those of Other Nations," *The New York Times*, April 23, 2008, pp. A1, A14.
6. Siobhan McDonough, "U.S. Prison Population Soars in 2003, '04," April 25, 2005 (at www.news.yahoo.com).
7. John J. Dilulio Jr. and Joseph P. Tierney, "An Easy Ride for Felons on Probation," *The New York Times*, Aug. 29, 2000, p. A27.
8. "Driven to the Fiscal Brink, State Opens Prison Doors, *The New York Times*, March 24, 2010, p. A14.
9. *San Francisco Chronicle*, May 21, 2007, p. A1; www.uscourts.gov/newsroom/incarcerationcosts.html.
10. Fox Butterfield, "Despite Drop in Crime, An Increase in Inmates," *The New York Times*, Nov. 8, 2004, p. A14. Figures are for 2003.
11. *The New York Times*, April 15, 2005, p. A14.
12. Jim Webb, "Why We Must Fix Our Prisons," *San Francisco Chronicle*, March 29, 2009, p. 5.
13. www.deathpenaltyinfo.org/race-death-row-inmates-executed-1976.
14. *New York Review of Books*, April 12, 2007, pp. 33, 36.
15. Ibid., p. 34.
16. John Schwartz, "Death Sentences Dropped, but Executions Rose in '09," *The New York Times*, December 18, 2009, p. A22; Mark McDonald, "China Leads in Executions, Report by Amnesty Finds," *The New York Times*, March 31, 2010, p. A8; www.deathpenaltyinfo.org.
17. www.deathpenaltyinfo.org.
18. Mark McDonald, "China Leads in Executions, Report by Amnesty Finds," *The New York Times* March 31, 2010, p. A8.
19. http://www.deathpenaltyinfo.org/part-i-history-death-penalty#susp.
20. U.S. Supreme Court, *Furman* v. *Georgia*, 1972.
21. http://www.gallup.com/poll/111931/americans-hold-firm-support-death-penalty.aspx.
22. Mike Farrell, "Death Penalty Thrives in Climate of Fear," *San Francisco Chronicle*, Feb. 24, 2002, p. D3.
23. Raymond Bonner, "Still on Death Row, Despite Mounting Doubts," *The New York Times*, July 8, 2002, p. A15.
24. http://www.innocenceproject.org/Content/Facts_on_PostConviction_DNA_Exonerations.php.
25. http://www.abanet.org/moratorium/historypolicy.html
26. Margaret Carlson, "Death, Be Not Proud," *Time* (Feb. 21, 2000): 38.

27. Sara Rimer, "Florida Lawmakers Reject Electric Chair," *The New York Times*, Jan. 7, 2000, p. A14.
28. www.deathpenaltyinfo.org.
29. See, for example, Claudia Wallis, "Too Young to Die," *Time*, March 14, 2005, p. 40.
30. Ibid.
31. Caroline Moorehead, "Tinkering with Death," *World Press Review*, *42*, no. 7 (July 1995): 38–39.
32. http://deathpenaltyinfo.org/costs-death-penalty; C. Hoppe, "Executions Cost Texas Millions," *The Dallas Morning News,* March 8, 1992, 1A.
33. http://www.lao.ca.gov/2005/3_Strikes/3_strikes_102005.htm.
34. See Richard Brandt, *Ethical Theory* (Englewood Cliffs, NJ: Prentice Hall, 1959).
35. Thomas Szasz, *The Myth of Mental Illness* (New York: Harper & Row, 1961).
36. See Hugh Bedau, "Capital Punishment and Retributive Justice," in Tom Regan (Ed.), *Matters of Life and Death* (New York: Random House, 1980), 148–182.
37. It dropped from 3.09 people per 100,000 residents in 1975 to 2.74 per 100,000 in 1983. "Amnesty International and the Death Penalty," Amnesty International USA, *Newsletter* (Spring 1987).
38. See H. Bedau, *The Death Penalty in America* (Chicago: Aldine, 1967), in particular Chapter 6, "The Question of Deterrence."
39. Ford Fessenden, "Deadly Statistics: A Survey of Crime and Punishment," *The New York Times*, Sept. 22, 2000, p. A19.
40. www.deathpenaltyinfo.org; www.truthinjustice.org/922death.htm.
41. "Uproar over Bloody Electrocution," *San Francisco Chronicle*, July 9, 1999, p. A7; "An Execution Causes Bleeding," *The New York Times*, July 8, 1999, p. A10.
42. *The New York Times*, Jan. 7, 2000, p. A14.
43. See Adam Liptak, "Critics Say Execution Drug May Hide Suffering," *The New York Times*, Oct. 7, 2003, pp. A1, A18.
44. *The New York Times*, April 24, 2007, p. A17; www.deathpenaltyinfo.org.
45. I thank one of my reviewers, Wendy Lee-Lampshire of Bloomsburg University, for sharing this fact and calling this problem to my attention.

R E A D I N G
The Ultimate Punishment: A Defense
ERNEST VAN DEN HAAG

Study Questions

1. Why does van den Haag believe that maldistribution of punishment would not in itself make a punishment unjust?
2. What is his reason for holding that the punishment by death of some innocent persons would not in itself be a good reason to abolish the death penalty?
3. Does van den Haag believe that deterrence is the best reason to support the death penalty?
4. If we were not sure or could not prove that the death penalty is a better deterrent than life imprisonment, then would that be a good reason to abolish it, according to van den Haag?
5. Does van den Haag believe that punishment is repayment for the victim's suffering and thus should be equal in kind?
6. What does he mean when he says that the lawbreaker "volunteers" for his punishment?
7. How does van den Haag respond to Associate Justice Brennan's assertions that the death penalty is uncivilized, inhumane, and degrading?

IN AN average year about 20,000 homicides occur in the United States. Fewer than 300 convicted murderers are sentenced to death. But because no more than thirty murderers have been executed in any recent year, most convicts sentenced to death are likely to die of old age.[1] Nonetheless, the death penalty looms large in discussions: it raises important moral questions independent of the number of executions.

Ernest Van Den Haag, "The Ultimate Punishment: A Defense," from *Harvard Law Review 99* (1986) by Harvard Law Review. Some footnotes have been deleted.

The death penalty is our harshest punishment.[2] It is irrevocable: it ends the existence of those punished, instead of temporarily imprisoning them. Further, although not intended to cause physical pain, execution is the only corporal punishment still applied to adults.[3] These singular characteristics contribute to the perennial, impassioned controversy about capital punishment.

I. DISTRIBUTION

Consideration of the justice, morality, or usefulness of capital punishment is often conflated with objections to its alleged discriminatory or capricious distribution among the guilty. Wrongly so. If capital punishment is immoral *in se*, no distribution among the guilty could make it moral. If capital punishment is moral, no distribution would make it immoral. Improper distribution cannot affect the quality of what is distributed, be it punishments or rewards. Discriminatory or capricious distribution thus could not justify abolition of the death penalty. Further, maldistribution inheres no more in capital punishment than in any other punishment.

Maldistribution between the guilty and the innocent is, by definition, unjust. But the injustice does not lie in the nature of the punishment. Because of the finality of the death penalty, the most grievous maldistribution occurs when it is imposed upon the innocent. However, the frequent allegations of discrimination and capriciousness refer to maldistribution among the guilty and not to the punishment of the innocent.

Maldistribution of any punishment among those who deserve it is irrelevant to its justice or morality. Even if poor or black convicts guilty of capital offenses suffer capital punishment, and other convicts equally guilty of the same crimes do not, a more equal distribution, however desirable, would merely be more equal. It would not be more just to the convicts under sentence of death.

Punishments are imposed on persons, not on racial or economic groups. Guilt is personal. The only relevant question is: does the person to be executed deserve the punishment? Whether or not others who deserved the same punishment, whatever their economic or racial group, have avoided execution is irrelevant. If they have, the guilt of the executed convicts would not be diminished, nor would their punishment be less deserved. To put the issue starkly, if the death penalty were imposed on guilty blacks, but not on guilty whites, or, if it were imposed by a lottery among the guilty, this irrationally discriminatory or capricious distribution would neither make the penalty unjust, nor cause anyone to be unjustly punished, despite the undue impunity bestowed on others.[4]

Equality, in short, seems morally less important than justice. And justice is independent of distributional inequalities. The ideal of equal justice demands that justice be equally distributed, not that it be replaced by equality. Justice requires that as many of the guilty as possible be punished, regardless of whether others have avoided punishment. To let these others escape the deserved punishment does not do justice to them, or to society. But it is not unjust to those who could not escape.

These moral considerations are not meant to deny that irrational discrimination, or capriciousness, would be inconsistent with constitutional requirements. But I am satisfied that the Supreme Court has in fact provided for adherence to the constitutional requirement of equality as much as is possible. Some inequality is indeed unavoidable as a practical matter in any system.[5] But, *ultra posse nemo obligatur*. (Nobody is bound beyond ability.)

Recent data reveal little direct racial discrimination in the sentencing of those arrested and convicted of murder.[6] The abrogation of the death penalty for rape has eliminated a major source of racial discrimination. Concededly, some discrimination based on the race of murder victims may exist; yet, this discrimination affects criminal victimizers in an unexpected way. Murderers of whites are thought more likely to be executed than murderers of blacks. Black victims, then, are less fully vindicated than white ones. However, because most black murderers kill blacks, black murderers are spared the death penalty more often than are white murderers. They fare better than most white murderers.[7] The motivation behind unequal distribution of the death penalty may well have been to discriminate against blacks, but the result has favored them. Maldistribution is thus a straw man for empirical as well as analytical reasons.

II. MISCARRIAGES OF JUSTICE

In a recent survey Professors Hugo Adam Bedau and Michael Radelet found that 7,000 persons were executed in the United States between 1900 and 1985 and that 25 were innocent of capital crimes.[8] Among the innocents they list Sacco and Vanzetti as well as Ethel and Julius Rosenberg. Although their data may be questionable, I do not doubt that, over a long enough period, miscarriages of justice will occur even in capital cases.

Despite precautions, nearly all human activities, such as trucking, lighting, or construction, cost the lives of some innocent bystanders. We do not give up these activities, because the advantages, moral or material, outweigh the unintended losses. Analogously, for those who think the death penalty just, miscarriages of justice are offset by the moral benefits and the usefulness of doing justice. For those who think the death penalty unjust even when it does not miscarry, miscarriages can hardly be decisive.

III. DETERRENCE

Despite much recent work, there has been no conclusive statistical demonstration that the death penalty is a better deterrent than are alternative punishments.[9] However, deterrence is less than decisive for either side. Most abolitionists acknowledge that they would continue to favor abolition even if the death penalty were shown to deter more murders than alternatives could deter.[10] Abolitionists appear to value the life of a convicted murderer or, at least, his nonexecution, more highly than they value the lives of the innocent victims who might be spared by deterring prospective murderers.

Deterrence is not altogether decisive for me either. I would favor retention of the death penalty as retribution even if it were shown that the threat of execution could not deter prospective murderers not already deterred by the threat of imprisonment.[11] Still, I believe the death penalty, because of its finality, is more feared than imprisonment, and deters some prospective murderers not deterred by the threat of imprisonment. Sparing the lives of even a few prospective victims by deterring their murderers is more important than preserving the lives of convicted murderers because of the possibility, or even the probability, that executing them would not deter others. Whereas the lives of the victims who might be saved are valuable, that of the murderer has only negative value, because of his crime. Surely the criminal law is meant to protect the lives of potential victims in preference to those of actual murderers.

Murder rates are determined by many factors; neither the severity nor the probability of the threatened sanction is always decisive. However, for the long run, I share the view of Sir James Fitzjames Stephen: "Some men, probably, abstain from murder because they fear that if they committed murder they would be hanged. Hundreds of thousands abstain from it because they regard it with horror. One great reason why they regard it with horror is that murderers are hanged."[12] Penal sanctions are useful in the long run for the formation of the internal restraints so necessary to control crime. The severity and finality of the death penalty is appropriate to the seriousness and the finality of murder.[13]

IV. INCIDENTAL ISSUES: COST, RELATIVE SUFFERING, BRUTALIZATION

Many nondecisive issues are associated with capital punishment. Some believe that the monetary cost of appealing a capital sentence is excessive.[14] Yet most comparisons of the cost of life imprisonment with the cost of execution, apart from their dubious relevance, are flawed at least by the implied assumption that life prisoners will generate no judicial costs during their imprisonment. At any rate, the actual monetary costs are trumped by the importance of doing justice.

Others insist that a person sentenced to death suffers more than his victim suffered, and that this (excess) suffering is undue according to the *lex talionis* (rule of retaliation).[15] We cannot know whether the murderer on death row suffers more than his victim suffered; however, unlike the murderer, the victim deserved none of the suffering inflicted. Further, the limitations of the *lex talionis* were meant to restrain private vengeance, not the social retribution that has taken its place. Punishment—regardless of the motivation—is not intended to revenge, offset, or compensate for the victim's suffering, or to be measured by it. Punishment is to vindicate the law and the social order undermined by the crime. This is why a kidnapper's penal confinement is not limited to the period for which he imprisoned his victim; nor is a burglar's confinement meant merely to offset the suffering or the harm he caused his victim; nor is it meant only to offset the advantage he gained.[16]

Another argument heard at least since Beccaria is that, by killing a murderer, we encourage, endorse, or legitimize unlawful killing. Yet, although all punishments are meant to be unpleasant, it is seldom argued that they legitimize the unlawful imposition of identical unpleasantness. Imprisonment is not thought to legitimize kidnapping; neither are fines thought to legitimize robbery. The difference between murder and execution, or between kidnapping and imprisonment, is that the first is unlawful and undeserved, the second a lawful and deserved punishment for an unlawful act. The physical similarities of the punishment to the crime are irrelevant. The relevant difference is not physical, but social.[17]

V. JUSTICE, EXCESS, DEGRADATION

We threaten punishments in order to deter crime. We impose them not only to make the threats credible but also as retribution (justice) for the crimes that were not deterred. Threats and punishments are necessary to deter and deterrence is a sufficient practical justification for them. Retribution is an independent moral justification.[18] Although penalties can be unwise, repulsive, or inappropriate, and those punished can be pitiable, in a sense the infliction of legal punishment on a guilty person cannot be unjust. By committing the crime, the criminal volunteered to assume the risk of receiving a legal punishment that he could have avoided by not committing the crime. The punishment he suffers is the punishment he voluntarily risked suffering and, therefore, it is no more unjust to him than any other event for which one knowingly volunteers to assume the risk. Thus, the death penalty cannot be unjust to the guilty criminal.[19]

There remain, however, two moral objections. The penalty may be regarded as always excessive as retribution and always morally degrading. To regard the death penalty as always excessive, one must believe that no crime—no matter how heinous—could possibly justify capital punishment. Such a belief can be neither corroborated nor refuted; it is an article of faith.

Alternatively, or concurrently, one may believe that everybody, the murderer no less than the victim, has an imprescriptible (natural?) right to life. The law therefore should not deprive anyone of life. I share Jeremy Bentham's view that any such "natural and imprescriptible rights" are "nonsense upon stilts."[20]

Justice Brennan has insisted that the death penalty is "uncivilized," "inhuman," inconsistent with "human dignity" and with "the sanctity of life,"[21] that it "treats members of the human race as nonhumans, as objects to be toyed with and discarded,"[22] that it is "uniquely degrading to human dignity"[23] and "by its very nature, [involves] a denial of the executed person's humanity."[24] Justice Brennan does not say why he thinks execution "uncivilized." Hitherto most civilizations have had the death penalty, although it has been discarded in Western Europe, where it is currently unfashionable probably because of its abuse by totalitarian regimes.

By "degrading," Justice Brennan seems to mean that execution degrades the executed convicts. Yet philosophers, such as Immanuel Kant and G. W. F. Hegel, have insisted that, when deserved, execution, far from degrading the executed convict, affirms his humanity by affirming his rationality and his responsibility for his actions. They thought that execution, when deserved, is required for the sake of the convict's dignity. (Does not life imprisonment violate human dignity more than execution, by keeping alive a prisoner deprived of all autonomy?)[25]

Common sense indicates that it cannot be death—our common fate—that is inhuman. Therefore, Justice Brennan must mean that death degrades when it comes not as a natural or accidental event, but as a deliberate social imposition. The murderer learns through his punishment that his fellow men have found him unworthy of living; that because he has murdered, he is being expelled from the community of the living. This degradation is self-inflicted. By murdering, the murderer has so dehumanized himself that he cannot remain among the living. The social recognition of his self-degradation is the punitive essence of execution. To believe, as Justice Brennan appears to, that the degradation is inflicted by the execution reverses the direction of causality.

Execution of those who have committed heinous murders may deter only one murder per year. If it does, it seems quite warranted. It is also the only fitting retribution for murder I can think of.

NOTES*

1. Death row as a semipermanent residence is cruel, because convicts are denied the normal amenities of prison life. Thus, unless death row residents are integrated into the prison population, the continuing accumulation of convicts on death row should lead us to accelerate either the rate of executions or the rate of commutations. I find little objection to integration.

2. Some writers, for example, Cesare Bonesana, Marchese di Beccaria, have thought that life imprisonment is more severe. See C. Beccaria, *Dei Delitti e Delle Pene* 62–70 (1764). More recently, Jacques Barzun has expressed this view. See Barzun, "In Favor of Capital Punishment," in *The Death Penalty in America* 154 (H. Bedau ed. 1964). However, the overwhelming majority of both abolitionists and of convicts under death sentence prefer life imprisonment to execution.

3. For a discussion of the sources of opposition to corporal punishment, see E. van den Haag, *Punishing Criminals* 196–206 (1975).

4. Justice Douglas, concurring in *Furman* v. *Georgia*, 408 U.S. 238 (1972), wrote that "a law which . . . reaches that [discriminatory] result in practice has no more sanctity than a law which in terms provides the same." Id. at 256 (Douglas, J., concurring). Indeed, a law legislating this result "in terms" would be inconsistent with the "equal protection of the laws" provided by the fourteenth amendment, as would the discriminatory result reached in practice. But that result could be changed by changing the distributional practice. Thus, Justice Douglas notwithstanding, a discriminatory result does not make the death penalty unconstitutional, unless the penalty ineluctably must produce that result to an unconstitutional degree.

5. The ideal of equality, unlike the ideal of retributive justice (which can be approximated separately in each instance), is clearly unattainable unless all guilty persons are apprehended, and thereafter tried, convicted and sentenced by the same court, at the same time. Unequal justice is the best we can do; it is still better than the injustice, equal or unequal, which occurs if, for the sake of equality, we deliberately allow some who could be punished to escape.

6. See Bureau of Justice Statistics, U.S. Dept. of Justice, Bulletin No. NCJ-98, 399, *Capital Punishment 1984*, p. 9 (1985); Johnson, "The Executioner's Bias," *National Review*, Nov. 15, 1985, at 44.

7. It barely need be said that any discrimination against (for example, black murderers of whites) must also be discrimination for (for example, black murderers of blacks).

8. Bedau and Radelet, *Miscarriages of Justice in Potentially Capital Cases* (1st draft, Oct. 1985) (on file at Harvard Law School Library).

9. For a sample of conflicting views on the subject, see Baldus and Cole, "A Comparison of the Work of Thorsten Sellin and Isaac Ehrlich on the Deterrent Effect of Capital Punishment," *Yale Law Journal* 85 (1975) 170; Bowers and Pierce, "Deterrence or Brutalization: What Is the Effect of Executions?" *Crime and Delinquency* 26 (1980) 453; Bowers and Pierce, "The Illusion of Deterrence in Isaac Ehrlich's Research on Capital Punishment," *Yale Law Journal*, 85 (1975) 18; Ehrlich, "Fear of Deterrence: A Critical Evaluation of the 'Report of the Panel on Research on Deterrent and Incapacitative Effects,'" 6 (1977) 293; Ehrlich, "The Deterrent Effect of Capital Punishment: A Question of Life and Death," *American Economics Review*, 65 (1975) 397, 415–416; Ehrlich and Gibbons, "On the Measurement of the Deterrent Effect of Capital Punishment and the Theory of Deterrence," *Journal of Legal Studies*, 6 (1977) 35.

10. For most abolitionists, the discrimination argument . . . is similarly nondecisive: they would favor abolition even if there could be no racial discrimination.

11. If executions were shown to increase the murder rate in the long run, I would favor abolition. Sparing the innocent victims who would be spared, *ex hypothesi*, by the nonexecution of murderers would be more important to me than the execution, however just, of murderers. But although there is a lively discussion of the subject, no serious evidence exists to support the hypothesis that executions produce a higher murder rate. Cf. Phillips, "The Deterrent Effect of Capital Punishment: New Evidence on an Old Controversy," *American Journal of Sociology*, 86 (1980) 139 (arguing that murder

rates drop immediately after executions of criminals).

12. H. Gross, *A Theory of Criminal Justice*, 489 (1979) (attributing this passage to Sir James Fitzjames Stephen).

13. *Weems* v. *United States*, 217 U.S. 349 (1910), suggests that penalties be proportionate to the seriousness of the crime—a common theme of the criminal law. Murder, therefore, demands more than life imprisonment, if, as I believe, it is a more serious crime than other crimes punished by life imprisonment. In modern times, our sensibility requires that the range of punishments be narrower than the range of crimes—but not so narrow as to exclude the death penalty.

14. Cf. Kaplan, "Administering Capital Punishment," 36 *University of Florida Law Review* 177, 178, 190–191 (1984) (noting the high cost of appealing a capital sentence).

15. For an example of this view, see A. Camus, *Reflections on the Guillotine* 24–30 (1959). On the limitations allegedly imposed by the *lex talionis*, see Reiman, "Justice, Civilization, and the Death Penalty: Answering van den Haag," *Philosophy and Public Affairs*, 14 (1985) 115, 119–134.

16. Thus restitution (a civil liability) cannot satisfy the punitive purpose of penal sanctions, whether the purpose be retributive or deterrent.

17. Some abolitionists challenge: if the death penalty is just and serves as a deterrent, why not televise executions? The answer is simple. The death even of a murderer, however well-deserved, should not serve as public entertainment. It so served in earlier centuries. But in this respect our sensibility has changed for the better, I believe. Further, television unavoidably would trivialize executions, edged in, as they would be, between game shows, situation comedies, and the like. Finally, because televised executions would focus on the physical aspects of the punishment, rather than the nature of the crime and the suffering of the victim, a televised execution would present the murderer as the victim of the state. Far from communicating the moral significance of the execution, television would shift the focus to the pitiable fear of the murderer. We no longer place in cages those

sentenced to imprisonment to expose them to public view. Why should we so expose those sentenced to execution?

18. See van den Haag, "Punishment as a Device for Controlling the Crime Rate," 33 *Rutgers Law Review* (1981) 706, 719 (explaining why the desire for retribution, although independent, would have to be satisfied even if deterrence were the only purpose of punishment).

19. An explicit threat of punitive action is necessary to the justification of any legal punishment: *nulla poena sine lege* (no punishment without [preexisting] law). To be sufficiently justified, the threat must in turn have a rational and legitimate purpose. "Your money or your life" does not qualify; nor does the threat of an unjust law; nor, finally, does a threat that is altogether disproportionate to the importance of its purpose. In short, preannouncement legitimizes the threatened punishment only if the threat is warranted. But this leaves a very wide range of justified threats. Furthermore, the punished person is aware of the penalty for his actions and thus volunteers to take the risk even of an unjust punishment. His victim, however, did not volunteer to risk anything. The question whether any self-inflicted injury—such as a legal punishment—ever can be unjust to a person who knowingly risked it is a matter that requires more analysis than is possible here.

20. *The Works of Jeremy Bentham* (J. Bowring ed. 1972) 105. However, I would be more polite about prescriptible natural rights, which Bentham described as "simple nonsense." Id. (It does not matter whether natural rights are called "moral" or "human" rights as they currently are by most writers.)

21. *The Death Penalty in America* 256–263 (H. Bedau ed., 3d ed. 1982) quoting *Furman* v. *Georgia*, 408 U.S. 238, 286, 305 (1972) (Brennan, J., concurring).

22. Id. at 272–273; see also *Gregg* v. *Georgia*, 428 U.S. 153, 230 (1976) (Brennan, J., dissenting).

23. *Furman* v. *Georgia*, 408 U.S. 238, 291 (1972) (Brennan, J., concurring).

24. Id. at 290.

25. See Barzun, supra [footnote p. 410], passim.

READING
How to Argue About the Death Penalty

HUGO BEDAU

Study Questions

1. What questions of fact does Bedau believe are relevant to judgments about the death penalty? How does he think they can be answered?
2. Does he think that this is all that is relevant to judgments about what to do about the death penalty? Why? If not, what else is relevant, in his view?
3. What two norms does he suggest are needed?
4. Give one of his examples of each.
5. What two relevant social goals does he suggest?
6. What two or three further goals does he suggest?
7. What comments does he make about each of these further goals?
8. What other six principles does he suggest are relevant? Do any of them rule out the death penalty?
9. What further comments does he make specifically about the fifth and sixth principles?
10. What does he believe his examination of the relevant goals and principles has shown?
11. What three considerations does he believe are important for assessing objections to the death penalty?
12. What does our actual practice of the death penalty show?

I

Argument over the death penalty—especially in the United States during the past generation—has been concentrated in large part on trying to answer various disputed questions of fact. Among them two have been salient: Is the death penalty a better deterrent to crime (especially murder) than the alternative of imprisonment? Is the death penalty administered in a discriminatory way, and, in particular, are black or other nonwhite offenders (or offenders whose victim are white) more likely to be tried, convicted, sentenced to death, and executed than whites (or offenders whose victims are nonwhite)? Other questions of fact have also been explored, including these two: What is the risk that an innocent person could actually be executed for a crime he did not commit? What

is the risk that a person convicted of a capital felony but not executed will commit another capital felony?

Varying degrees of effort have been expended in trying to answer these questions. Although I think the current answers are capable of further refinement I also think anyone who studies the evidence today must conclude that the best current answers to these four questions are as follows. (1) There is little or no evidence that the death penalty is a better deterrent to murder than is imprisonment; on the contrary, most evidence shows that these two punishments are about equally (in)effective as deterrents to murder. Furthermore, as long as the death penalty continues to be used relatively rarely, there is no prospect of gaining more decisive evidence on the question. (2) There is evidence that the death penalty has been and continues to be administered, whether intentionally or not in a manner that produces arbitrary and racially discriminatory results in death sentencing. At the very least, this is true in those jurisdictions where the question has been investigated in recent years. (3) It is impossible to calculate the risk that an innocent person will be executed, but the risk is not zero, as the record of convicted, sentenced, and executed innocents shows. (4) Recidivism data show that some murderers have killed after a conviction and prison sentence for murder; so there is a risk that others will do so as well.

Let us assume that my summary of the result of research on these four questions is correct, and that further research will not significantly change these answers. The first thing to notice is that even if everyone agreed on these answers, this would not by itself settle the dispute over whether to keep, expand, reduce, or abolish the death penalty. Knowing these empirical truths about the administration and effects of the death penalty in our society does not entail knowing whether one should support its retention or abolition. This would still be true even if we knew with finality the answers to *all* the factual questions that can be asked about it.

Hugo Bedau, "How to Argue About the Death Penalty," Reprinted from Hugo Adam Bedau (ed.) *The Death Penalty in America.* Copyright © 1982 by Oxford University Press, Inc.

There are two reasons for this. The facts as they currently stand and as seen from the abolitionist perspective do not point strongly and overwhelmingly to the futility of the death penalty or to the harm it does, at least as long as it continues to be used only in the limited and restricted form of the past decade: confined to the crime of murder, with trial courts empowered to exercise "guided discretion" in sentencing, with defense counsel able to introduce anything as mitigating evidence, and with automatic review of both conviction and sentence by some appellate court. Nor do the facts show that the alternative of life imprisonment is on balance a noticeably superior punishment. For example, the evidence of racial discrimination in the administration of the death penalty, while incontestable, may be no worse than the racial discrimination that occurs where lesser crimes and punishments are concerned. No one who has studied the data thinks that the administration of justice for murder approaches the level of racial discrimination reached a generation ago in the South by the administration of justice for rape. Besides, it is always possible to argue that such discrimination is diminishing, or will diminish over time, and that, in any case, since the fault does not lie in the capital statutes themselves—they are color-blind on their face—the remedy does not lie in repealing them.

But the marginal impact of the empirical evidence is not the major factor in explaining why settling disputes over matters of fact does not and cannot settle the larger controversy over the death penalty itself As a matter of sheer logic, it is not possible to deduce a policy conclusion (such as the desirability of abolishing the death penalty) from any set of factual premises, however general and well supported. Any argument intended to recommend continuing or reforming current policy on the death penalty must include among its premises one or more normative propositions. Unless disputants over the death penalty can agree about these normative propositions, their agreement on the general facts will never suffice to resolve their dispute.

II

Accordingly, the course of wisdom for those interested in arguing about the death penalty is to focus attention on the normative propositions crucial to the dispute, in the hope that some headway may be made in narrowing disagreement over their number, content, and weight.

If this is to be done effectively, the context of these norms in general political ideology needs to be fixed. Suffice it to say here that I proceed from within the context of liberal pluralistic constitutional democracy and the conception of punishment appropriate therein.

Logically prior to the idea of punishment is the idea of a crime. What counts as a criminal harm depends in part on our conception of persons as bearers of rights deserving respect and protection. In this setting, liability to punishment and its actual infliction serve the complex function of reinforcing compliance with a set of laws deemed necessary to protect the fundamental equal rights of all members of society. The normative propositions relevant to the death penalty controversy are interwoven with the basic purposes and principles of liberal society, including the recognition and protection of individual rights of life and liberty, and to security of person and property.

These norms can be divided into two groups: those that express relevant and desirable *social goals* or *purposes*, and those that express relevant and respectable *moral principles*. Punishment is thus a practice or institution defined through various policies—such as the death penalty for murder—and intended to be the means or instrument whereby certain social goals are achieved within the constraints imposed by acknowledged moral principles.

Reduction of crime, or at least prevention of an increase in crime, is an example of such a goal. This goal influences the choice of punishments because their impact (hypothesized or verified) on the crime rate. No one, except for purists of a retributive stripe, would dissent from the view that this goal is relevant to the death penalty controversy. Because of its relevance, there is continuing interest in the outcome of research on the differential deterrent efficacy of death versus imprisonment. The only questions normally in dispute are what that research shows (I have summarized it above) and how important this goal is (some regard it as decisive).

Similarly, that no one should be convicted and sentenced to death without a fair trial (i.e., in violation of "due process of law") is a principle of law and morality generally respected. Its general acceptance explains the considerable reformation in the laws governing the death penalty in the United States that have been introduced since 1972 by the Supreme Court. The Court argued that capital trials and death sentencing were in practice unfair (in constitutional jargon, they were in violation of the Eighth and Fourteenth Amendments, which bar "cruel and unusual punishments" and require "equal protection of the laws," respectively). State legislatures and thoughtful observers agreed. Here again the only questions concern how important it is to comply with this principle (some regard it as decisive) and the extent to which the death penalty currently violates it (I have remarked on this point above, too).

The chief use of a moral principle in the present setting is to constrain the methods used in pursuit of policy (as when respect for "due process" rules out curbstone justice as a tactic in crime fighting). However, identifying the relevant goals, acknowledging the force of the relevant principles, and agreeing on the relevant general facts will still not suffice to resolve the dispute The relative importance of achieving a given goal and the relative weight of a given principle remain to be settled, and disagreement over these matters is likely to show up in disagreement over the justification of the death penalty itself.

If this is a correct sketch of the structural character of debate and disagreement over the death penalty, then (as I noted earlier) the best hope for progress may lie in looking more carefully at the nonfactual normative ingredients so far isolated in the dispute. Ideally, we would identify and evaluate the policy goals relevant to punishment generally, as well as the moral principles that constrain the structure and content of the penalty schedule. We would also settle the proper relative weights to attach to these goals and constraints, if not in general, then at least for their application in the present context. Then, with whatever relevant general facts are at our disposal, we would be in a position to draw the appropriate inferences and resolve the entire dispute, confident that we have examined and duly weighed everything that reason and morality can bring to bear on the problem.

As an abstract matter, therefore, the question is whether the set of relevant policies and principles, taken in conjunction with the relevant facts, favors reduction (even complete abolition) of the death penalty, or whether it favors retention (or even extension) of the death penalty. Lurking in the background, of course, is the troubling possibility that the relevant norms and facts underdetermine the resolution of the dispute. But let us not worry about sharks on dry land, not yet.

III

Where choice of punishments is concerned, the relevant social goals, I suggest are few. Two in particular generally commend themselves:

(G 1)   Punishment should contribute to the reduction of crime; accordingly, the punishment for a crime should not be so idle a threat or so slight a deprivation that it has no deterrent or incapacitative effects; and it certainly should not contribute to an increase in crime.

(G 2)   Punishments should be "economical"—they should not waste valuable social resources in futile or unnecessarily costly endeavors.

The instrumental character of these purposes and goals is evident. They reflect the fact that society does not institute and maintain the practice of punishment for its own sake, as though it were a good in itself. Rather, punishment is and is seen to be a means to an end or ends. The justification of a society's punitive policies and practices must therefore involve two steps: first, it must be shown that these ends are desirable; second, it must be shown that the practice of punishment is the best means to these ends. What is true of the justification of punishment generally is true a fortiori of justifying the death penalty.

Endorsement of these two policy goals tends to encourage support for the death penalty. Opponents of capital punishment need not reject these goals, however, and its defenders cannot argue that accepting these goals vindicates their preferred policy. Traditionally, it is true, the death penalty has often been supported on the ground that it provides the best social defense and is extremely cheap to administer. But since the time of Beccaria and Bentham, these empirical claims have been challenged, and rightly so. If support for the death penalty today in a country such as the United States rests on the high priority placed on these goals, then there is much (some would say compelling) evidence to undermine this support. The most that can be said solely by reference to these goals is that recognition of their importance can always be counted on to kindle interest in capital punishment, and to that extent put its opponents on the defensive.

Whether punishment is intended to serve only the two goals so far identified is disputable. An argument can be made that there are two or three further goals:

(G 3) Punishment should rectify the harm and injustice caused by crime.

(G 4) Punishment should serve as a recognized channel for the release of public indignation and anger at the offender.

(G 5) Punishment should make convicted offenders into better persons rather than leave them as they are or make them worse.

Obviously, anyone who accepts the fifth goal must reject the death penalty. I shall not try here to argue the merits of this goal, either in itself or relative to the other goals of punishment. Whatever its merits, this goal is less widely sought than the others, and for that reason alone is less useful in trying to develop rational agreement over the death penalty. Its persuasive power for those not already persuaded against the death penalty on other grounds is likely to be slight to zero. Although I am unwilling to strike it from the list of goals that punishment in general is and should be practiced to achieve, it would be unreasonable to stress its pre-eminence in the present context.

The proposed third goal is open to the objection that rectification of injustice is not really a goal of punishment, even if it is a desirable goal in other settings. (Indeed, it is widely believed that rectification is not a goal of punishment but of noncriminal tort judgments.) But even if it is a goal of punishment generally, it seems irrelevant to the death penalty controversy, because neither death nor imprisonment (as practiced in the United States) rectifies anything. Nonetheless, this goal may be indirectly important for the death penalty controversy. To the extent that one believes punishments ought to serve this goal, and that there is no possible way to rectify the crime of murder, one may come to believe that the fourth goal is of even greater importance than would otherwise be the case. Indeed, striving to achieve this fourth goal and embracing the death penalty as a consequence is quite parallel to striving to achieve the fifth goal and consequently embracing its abolition.

Does this fourth goal have a greater claim on our support than I have allowed is true of the fifth goal, so obviously incompatible with it? Many would say that it does. Some would even argue that it is this goal, not any of the others, that is the paramount purpose of punishment under law. Whatever else punishment does, its threat and infliction are to be seen as the expression of social indignation at deliberate harm to the innocent. Persevering a socially acceptable vehicle for the expression of anger at offenders is absolutely crucial to the health of a just society.

There are in principle three ways to respond to this claim insofar as it is part of an argument for capital punishment. One is to reject it out of hand as a false proposition from start to finish. A second is to concede that the goal of providing a visible and acceptable channel for the emotion of anger is legitimate, but to argue that this goal could at best justify the death penalty only in a very small number of cases (the occasional Adolf Eichmann, for example), since otherwise its importance would be vastly exaggerated. A third response is to concede both the legitimacy and the relative importance of this goal, but to point out that its pursuit, like that of all other goals, is nonetheless constrained by moral principles (yet to be examined), and that once these principles are properly employed, the death penalty ceases to be a permissible method of achieving this goal. I think both the second and third objections are sound, and a few further words here about each are appropriate.

First of all, anger is not the same as resentment or indignation, since the latter feeling or emotion can be aroused only through the perceived violation of some moral principle, whereas the former does not have this constraint. But whether the feeling aroused by a horrible murder is really only anger rather than indignation is just the question whether the principles of morality have been violated or not. Knowing that the accused offender has no legal excuse or justification for his criminal conduct is not enough to warrant the inference that he and his conduct are appropriate objects of our unqualified moral hostility. More about the context of the offense an it causation must be supplied; it may well be that in ordinary criminal cases one rarely or never knows enough to reach such a condemnatory judgment with confidence. Even were this not so, one has no reason to suppose that justified anger at offenders is of overriding importance, and that all countervailing considerations must yield to its pre-eminence. For one thing, the righteous anger needed for that role is simply not available in a pluralistic secular society. Even if it were, we have been assured from biblical times that it passes all too easily into self-righteous and hypocritical repression by some sinners or others.

Quite apart from such objections, there is a certain anomaly even irony, in the defense of the death penalty by appeal to this goal. On the one hand, we are told of the importance of a publicly recognized ritual for extermination of convicted murderers as a necessary vent for otherwise unchanneled disruptive public emotions. On the other hand, our society scrupulously rejects time-honored methods of execution that truly do express hatred and anger at offenders: beheading, crucifixion, dismemberment, and even hanging and the electric chair are disappearing. Execution by lethal injection, increasingly the popular option, hardly seems appropriate as the outlet of choice for such allegedly volatile energies! And is it not ironic that this technique, invented to facilitate life-saving surgery now turns out to be the preferred channel for the expression of moral indignation?

IV

If the purposes or goals of punishment lend a utilitarian quality to the practice of punishment, the moral principles relevant to the death penalty operate as deontological constraints on their pursuit. Stating all and only the principles relevant to the death penalty controversy is not easy, and the list that follows is no more than the latest approximation to the task. . . . With some overlap here and there, these principles are six:

(P 1)   No one should deliberately and intentionally take another's life where there is a feasible alternative.

(P 2)   The more severe a penalty is, the more important it is that it be imposed only on those who truly deserve it.

(P 3)   The more severe a penalty is, the weightier the justification required to warrant its imposition on anyone.

(P 4)   Whatever the criminal offense, the accused and convicted offender does not forfeit all his rights and dignity as a person. Accordingly, there is an upper limit to the severity—cruelty, destructiveness, finality—of permissible punishments, regardless of the offense.

(P 5)   Fairness requires that punishments should be graded in their severity according to the gravity of the offense.

(P 6)   If human lives are to be risked, the risk should fall more heavily on wrong-doers (the guilty) than on others (the innocent).

I cannot argue here for all these principles, but they really need no argument from me. Each is recognized implicitly or explicitly in our practice; each can be seen to constrain our conduct as individuals and as officers in democratic institutions. Outright repudiation or cynical disregard of any of these principles would disqualify one from engaging in serious discourse and debate over punishment in a liberal society. All can be seen as corollaries or theorems of the general proposition that life, limb, and security of person—of *all* persons—are of paramount value. Thus, only minimal interference (in the jargon of the law, "the least restrictive means") is warranted with anyone's life, limb, and security in order to protect the rights of others.

How do these principles direct or advise us in regard to the permissibility or desirability of the death penalty? The first thing to note is that evidently none directly rules it out. I know of no moral principle that is both sufficiently rigid and sufficiently well established for us to point to it and say: "The practice of capital punishment is flatly contradictory to the requirements of this moral principle." (Of course, we could invent a principle that would have this consequence, but that is hardly to the point.) This should not be surprising; few if any of the critics or the defenders of the death penalty have supposed otherwise. Second, several of these principles do reflect the heavy burden that properly falls on anyone who advocates that certain human beings be deliberately killed by others, when those to be killed are not at the time a danger to anyone. For example, whereas the first principle may permit lethal force in self-defense, it directly counsels against the death penalty in *all* cases without exception. The second and third principles emphasize the importance of "due process" and "equal protection" as the finality and incompensability of punishments increase. The fourth principle draws attention to the nature and value of persons, even those convicted of terrible crimes. It reminds us that even if crimes know no upper limit in their wantonness, cruelty, destructiveness, and horror, punishments under law in a civilized society cannot imitate crimes in this regard. Punishment does operate under limits, and these limits are not arbitrary.

The final two principles, however, seem to be exceptions to the generalization that the principles as a group tend to favor punishments other than death. The fifth principle seems to entail that if murder is the gravest crime, then it should receive the severest punishment. This does not of course, *require* a society to invoke the death penalty for murder—unless one accepts *lex talionis* ("a life for a life, an eye for an eye") in a singularly literal-minded manner. Since *lex talionis* is not a sound principle on which to construct the penalty schedule generally, appealing to this interpretation of the fifth principle here simply begs the question. Nevertheless, the principle that punishments should be graded to fit the crime does encourage consideration of the death penalty, especially if it seems that there is no other way to punish murder with the utmost permissible severity.

Of rather more interest is the sixth principle. Some make it the cornerstone of their defense of the death penalty. They argue that it is better to execute all convicted murderers, lest on a future occasion any of them murder again, than it is to execute none of them, thereby averting the risk of executing any who may be innocent A policy of complete abolition—at least in the United States today—would result in thousands of convicted killers (only a few of whom are innocent) being held behind bars for life. This cohort would constitute a permanent risk to the safety of many millions of innocent citizens. The sole gain to counterbalance this risk is the guarantee that no lives (innocent or guilty) will be lost through legal executions. The practice of executions thus protects far more innocent citizens than the same practice puts in jeopardy.

This argument is far less conclusive than it may at first seem. Even if we grant it full weigh, it is simply unreasonable to use it (or any other argument) as a way of dismissing the relevance of principles that counsel a different result, or as a tactic to imply the subordinate importance of those other principles. If used in this manner, the sixth principle would be thoroughly transformed. It has become a disguised version of the first policy goal (viz., Reduce crime!) and in effect would elevate that goal to pre-eminence over every competing and constraining consideration. The argument also fosters the illusion that we can in fact reasonably estimate, if not actually calculate, the number of lives risked by a policy of abolition as opposed to a policy of capital punishment. This is false; we do not and cannot reasonably hope to know what the risk is of convicting the innocent, even if we could estimate the risk of recidivist murder. We therefore cannot really compare the two risks with any precision. Finally, the argument gains whatever strength it appears to have by tacitly ignoring the following dilemma. If the policy of killing the convicted in order to reduce risk to the innocent is to achieve maximum effect, then death must be the *mandatory* penalty for everyone convicted of murder (never mind other crimes). But such a policy cannot really be carried out. It flies in the face of two centuries of political reality, which demonstrates the impossibility of enforcing truly mandatory death penalties for murder and other crimes against the person. The only realistic policy alternative is some version of a *discretionary* death penalty. However, every version of this policy actually tried has proved vulnerable to criticism on grounds of inequity in its administration, as critic after critic has shown. Meanwhile, history tells us that our society is unable to avoid all risk of recidivist murder.

The upshot is that we today run both the risk of executing the innocent and the risk of recidivist murder, even though it is necessary to run only one of these risks.

V

What has our examination of the relevant goals and principles shown about the possibility of resolving the death penalty controversy on rational grounds? First, the death penalty is primarily a means to one or more ends or goals, but it is not the only (and arguably not the best) means to them. Second, several principles of relevance to sound punitive policy in general favor (although they do not demand) abolition of the death penalty. Third, there is no goal or principle that constitutes a conclusive reason favoring either side in the dispute. Unless, of course, some one goal or principle is interpreted or weighted in such a manner (cf. the fifth goal, or the fifth principle). But in that case, one side or the other will refuse to accept it. Finally, the several goals and principles of punishment that have been identified have no obvious rank order or relative weighting. As they stand, these goals and principles do indeed underdetermine the policy dispute over capital punishment. Perhaps such a ranking could be provided by some comprehensive socioethical theory. But the failure of every known such theory to secure general acceptance so far does not bode well for prompt and rational resolution of the controversy along these lines.

Despite the absence of any conclusive reasons or decisive ranking of principles, we may take refuge in the thought . . . that a preponderance of reasons does favor one side rather than the other. Such a preponderance emerges, however, only when the relevant goals and principles of punishment are seen in a certain light, or from a particular angle of vision. Perhaps this amounts to one rather than another weighting of goals and principles but without conscious reliance upon any manifest theory. In any case, I shall mention three such considerations that are important in my assessment of the moral objections to the death penalty.

The first and by far the most important concerns the role and function of power in the hands of government It is in general preferable, *ceteris paribus*,

that such power over individuals should shrink rather than expand. Where such power must be used, then let it be devoted to constructive rather than destructive purposes, thus enhancing the autonomy and liberty of those directly affected. But the death penalty contradicts this concern; it is government power used in a dramatically destructive manner upon individuals in the absence of any compelling social necessity. No wonder it is the ultimate symbol of such power.

Another consideration that shapes my interpretation of the goals and principles of evaluation is an orientation to the *future* rather than to the past. We cannot do anything for the dead victims of crime. (How many of those who oppose the death penalty would continue to do so if, *mirabile dictu*, executing the murderer brought the victim back to life?) But we can—or at least we can try to—do something for the living: we can protect the innocent, prevent illegitimate violence, and help those in despair over their own victimization. None of these constructive tasks involves punishing anyone for expressive, vindictive, or retributive reasons. The more we stress these factors in our choice of punishments, the more we orient our punitive policies toward the past—toward trying to use government power over the lives of a few as a socially approved instrument of moral bookkeeping.

Finally, the death penalty projects a false and misleading picture of man and society. Its professed message for those who support it is this: justice requires killing the convicted murderer. So we focus on the death that all murderers supposedly deserve and overlook our inability to give a rational account of why so few actually get it. Hence, the lesson taught by the practice of capital punishment is really quite different. Far from being a symbol of justice, it is a symbol of brutality and stupidity. Perhaps if we lived in a world of autonomous Kantian moral agents, where all the criminals freely expressed their rational will in the intention to kill others without their consent or desert, then death for the convicted murderer might be just (as even Karl Max was inclined to think). But a closer look at the convicts who actually are on our death rows shows that these killers are a far cry from the rational agents of Kant's metaphysical imagination. We fool ourselves if we think a system of ideal retributive justice designed for such persons is the appropriate model for the penal system in our society.

Have I implicitly conceded that argument over the death penalty is irrational? If I am right that the death penalty controversy does not really turn on controversial social goals or controversial moral principles, any more than it does on disputed general facts, but instead turns on how all three are to be balanced or weighed, does it follow that reason alone cannot resolve the controversy, because reason alone cannot determine which weighting or balancing is the correct one? Or can reason resolve this problem, perhaps by appeal to further theory, theory that would deepen our appreciation of what truly underlies a commitment to liberal institutions and a belief in the possibilities for autonomy of all persons? I think it can—but this is the right place to end the present investigation because we have reached the launching platform for another one.

REVIEW EXERCISES

1. What essential characteristics of legal punishment distinguish it from other types of punishment?
2. What is the difference between the mechanisms of deterrence and prevention? Given their meanings, does the death penalty prevent murders? Deter would-be killers? How?
3. If legal punishment works as a deterrent, then how does it work? For whom would it work? For whom would it not likely work?
4. Summarize the positive aspects of the deterrence view regarding the justification of legal punishment.
5. Explain two moral problems with the deterrence view, using an example comparable to the graffiti example in the text.
6. How does the retributivist view differ from the deterrence view?
7. What is the *lex talionis* version of this view? How does it differ from the proportional view?
8. Discuss the arguments for and against the identification of retributivism with revenge.
9. Why is the notion of responsibility critical to the retributivist view of legal punishment? How does the defense of insanity fit in here?
10. Discuss the use of deterrence arguments for the death penalty. Also summarize opponents' criticisms of these arguments.
11. Discuss the use of retributivist arguments for the death penalty. Summarize also opponents' criticisms of these arguments.

DISCUSSION CASES

1. Imprisonment Numbers. According to figures given in the first part of this chapter, there are currently more than 2 million people in U.S. prisons and jails. This is approximately one person for every 138 residents. These figures are striking. Why do you think the imprisonment rate in this country is so high? Do you think this is an acceptable rate? Why or why not? If not, what do you think should be done about it?

2. Doctors and Execution. When a person is executed, it is the practice that a physician certify that the person executed is dead and when he or she has died. A state medical association has recently objected to the participation of doctors in executions. They assert that doctors take an oath to preserve life and should not be accessories to the taking of life. The state insisted that the doctors certifying death do not participate in the execution.

Should doctors be present at and certify the death of persons executed by the state? Why or why not?

3. Death Penalty Cases. Suppose that you were a member of a congressional or other committee that had as its mandate determining the type of crime that could be considered to be punishable by death. What kinds of cases, if any, would you put on the list? Sexual assault and killing of a minor? Planned killing of a batterer by his (or her) spouse? Persons convicted of war crimes? Mob leaders or others who give an order to kill but who do not carry it out themselves? Killing of a police officer or public figure? Multiple murderers? Others?

Why would you pick out just those crimes on your list as appropriately punished by death or as the worst crimes?

YOU MAKE THE DECISION

Apply the theories and issues discussed in this chapter by accessing this animated simulation on the Ethics Resource Center.

Use the passkey that accompanies your book to gain access. If you do not have a passkey, visit cengagebrain.com to purchase instant access to additional study material.

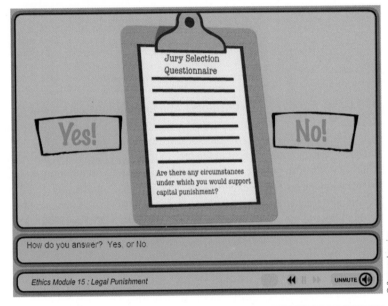

Jury Selection Questionnaire

Are there any circumstances under which you would support capital punishment?

Yes!

No!

How do you answer? Yes, or No.

Ethics Module 15 : Legal Punishment   UNMUTE

© Cengage Learning

—16—
Environmental Ethics

IN JANUARY 2007, 50 feet of Roger Middleton's sugar-beet farm fell into the North Sea. Middleton, who lives on the southeastern coast of England, has also lost 23 acres of potato field to the sea. In this and other sections of the world, coastal erosion is occurring in ways never before experienced. This process has greatly accelerated in recent years and is said to be one effect of global climate change produced by global warming.[1]

The Arctic ice cap is melting and may be gone by 2020, if not earlier. Since the 1970s, the melting has increased dramatically. Unlike in Antarctica, the Arctic ice is only 10 feet thick, and there is no land underneath. This white ice reflects the sun, but as it melts, the dark blue water of the ocean absorbs the solar rays, warming the nearby air in a feedback effect. Moreover, the ice that covers Greenland, the biggest landmass of the Arctic region, has also been melting at an alarming rate and slipping into the sea. According to scientists, "It is shedding 11 cubic miles of ice per year." If this Arctic melting and similar melting and breaking of sections of the Antarctic ice shelves continues, one result will be a serious rise in the height of ocean waters around the world. Although scientists can't predict how much the ocean waters will rise, it could be as much as 20 feet, and low-lying coastal areas will be underwater. This may produce hundreds of millions of environmental refugees. In his slide show, which was made into the award-winning movie *An Inconvenient Truth*, and in the book of the same

name, former Vice President Al Gore shows what would happen to Florida, San Francisco Bay, Amsterdam, and Beijing, among other cities around the world. For example, "In Calcutta and Bangladesh, 60 million people would be displaced." A similar estimate was given by the May 4, 2007 report of the U.N.-sponsored Intergovernmental Panel on Climate Change that was meeting in Brussels. The panel was made up of scientists and government officials from more than one hundred countries.[2]

Other likely effects of the melting of the Arctic ice include changes in the patterns of ocean currents

An ice shelf breaking up in the Antarctic.

that have been stable for the last 10,000 years. The Gulf Stream, for example, pulls warm water north from near the equator and into the north Atlantic where some of it evaporates; as the water evaporates, the ocean becomes saltier and heavier and sinks, cooling and starting a return southern path and then eastward around the globe. Shifts in the Gulf Stream could create unpredictable weather changes.[3]

Unusual weather patterns also include increasing numbers of and strengths of hurricanes and tornados. Think, for example, of the 2005 hurricanes Katrina and Rita in the Gulf of Mexico and the flooding and destruction of vast sections of New Orleans. In 2005, there were twenty-seven hurricanes and tropical storms. The World Meteorological Organization ran out of letters of the alphabet with which to name them all. Thomas Friedman has suggested that we call these weather phenomena "global weirding" instead of global warming. This is "because that is what actually happens as global temperatures rise and the climate changes. The weather gets weird. The hots are expected to get hotter, the wets wetter, the dries drier, and the most violent storms more numerous."[4]

We can see from just these few examples, and others later in this chapter, how our environment affects us and how changes such as global warming can have dramatic and disastrous effects. But just what is meant by the term *environment* and how ought we morally evaluate our actions and why?

THE ENVIRONMENT

Being clear about the terms we use in an ethical debate is one of the first things that can help us. We can start with the meaning of the term *environment*. It comes from *environs*, which means "in circuit" or "turning around in" in Old French.[5] From this comes the common meaning of environment as surroundings; note its spatial meaning as an area. However, we also have come to use the term to refer to what goes on in that space and to all of the climate and other factors that act on living organisms or individuals that inhabit the space. "The environment is what Nature becomes when we view it as a life-support system and as a collection of materials."[6] We can think of the system in a mechanistic fashion—that is, as a collection of materials with various physical and chemical interactions. Or we can think of it in a more organic way, giving attention to the many ways in which the individuals are interdependent in their very nature. From the latter viewpoint, we cannot even think of an individual as an isolated atomic thing, because its environment is a fundamental part of itself. From this point of view, the environment stands in relation to the beings within it—not externally, but internally.

VALUE

You may have seen signs urging us to "Save the Earth." Although we literally cannot kill the planet, we can make it better or worse for us.[7] Most people realize the important effects that their environment has on them. Those things that produce benefit are good or of positive value, and those that cause harm are bad or of negative value. Most of the time it is a mixture of both. Growth is generally good, and poison is bad. But where does this goodness and badness, or positive or negative value, come from? Is it there in the poison or in growth? This is a considerably difficult metaphysical and moral problem. (Refer to the discussion of moral realism in Chapter 2 and the discussion of the reference of the word, "good," in Chapter 1.) Does a thing have value in the same sense that it has hair or weight? This does not seem to be so, because a thing's value does not seem to be something it possesses. When we value something, we have a positive response toward it. However, it may not quite be as some philosophers have said, that things have value only in so far as we do happen to respond positively to them—that is, prefer or desire them. Rather, we want to know whether we *should* value them or value them highly. Is there something about the things that we value, some attributes that they have, for example, that are the legitimate basis for our valuing them? Although we will not go further into a discussion of the nature and basis of value here, we can be aware of the problems involved in trying to give an account of it. We also should be aware that the notion of value and its basis plays a key role in discussions of environmental ethics, as we shall see.

One distinction about value plays a particularly significant role in environmental ethics: that between intrinsic and instrumental value. Things have *intrinsic value* or worth (sometimes referred to as *inherent value*) when they have value or worth in themselves for some reason. Pleasure, as we saw earlier in Chapter 4, is supposed to be intrinsically valuable: We value it for its own sake and not for what we can get or do with it. Something has *instrumental value* if it is valued because of its usefulness for some other purpose and for someone. Some environmentalists believe that trees, for example, have only instrumental and not intrinsic value. They think that trees are valuable because of their usefulness to us. Other environmentalists believe that plants and ecosystems have value in themselves in some sense, as we shall note later in this chapter.

Another term sometimes used in discussions in environmental ethics is *prima facie* value, which literally means "at first glance" or "at first sight." Something has *prima facie* value if it has the kind of value that can be overcome by other interests or values. For example, we might say that economic interests of one group are to be given weight and thus have *prima facie* value, but they may be overridden by stronger interests of another group or by greater values such as human health. (For more on *prima facie* value, see the discussion of W.D. Ross in Chapter 5.)

These considerations about the nature and kinds of value play a key role in judging ethical matters that relate to the environment. This is exemplified by two quite different perspectives in environmental ethics. One is *anthropocentrism*, and the other *ecocentrism* or *biocentrism*. We will consider each in turn here.

ANTHROPOCENTRISM

As you may know, the terms *anthropocentrism* and *anthropocentric* refer to a human-centered perspective. A perspective is anthropocentric if it holds that humans alone have *intrinsic worth* or value. According to this perspective, those things are good that promote the interests of human beings. Thus, for example, some people believe that animals are valuable simply in so far as they promote the interests of humans or are useful to us in one or more of a variety of ways. (More discussion of this is found in the following chapter on animal rights.) For

example, animals provide emotional, aesthetic, nutritional, clothing, entertainment, and medical benefits for us. Those people who hold an anthropocentric view also may believe that it is bad to cause animals needless pain, but if this is necessary to ensure some important human good, then it is justified. (See this chapter's reading selection, "People or Penguins," for more on this matter.) Another example is the substance taxol, a synthesized chemical from the bark of the Pacific yew tree that has been found to be promising in the treatment of ovarian and breast cancers. Estuaries, grasslands, and ancient forests also purify our air and clean our water. Nature provides us with our food and shelter and clothing.

According to an anthropocentric perspective, the environment or nature has no value in itself. Its value is measured by how it affects human beings. Wilderness areas are instrumentally valuable to us as sources of recreation and relaxation and for providing some of our physical needs such as lumber for building. Sometimes, anthropocentric values conflict. For instance, we cannot both preserve the trees for their beauty or historical interest and yet also use them for lumber. Therefore, we need to think about the relative value of aesthetic experiences and historical appreciation as compared with cheaper housing and lumbering jobs. What is the value, for example, of being able to reflect on our history and our ancestors? Consider some 2,000-year-old trees. Touching one of these giants today is in some way touching the beginning of the common era. We can think of all of the great moments and events of history that have occurred in the life of this tree and thus appreciate the reality of the events and their connection with us. How would the value of this experience compare with other values? Cost–benefit analyses present one method for making such comparisons.

Cost–Benefit Analysis

Because many environmental issues involve diverse values and competing interests, we can use a technique known as *cost–benefit analysis* to help us think about what is best to do. (Refer to the discussion of this in Chapter 4.) If we have a choice between various actions or policies, then we need to assess and compare the various harms or costs and benefits that each entails in order to know which is the better policy. Using this method, we should choose the alternative that has the greater net balance of *benefits* over harms or *costs*. It is basically a utilitarian form of reasoning. If we clean up the smoke stacks, then emissions are reduced and acid rain and global warming are curtailed—important benefits. However, this also creates costs for the companies, their employees, and those who buy their products or use their services. We want to know whether the benefits will be worth those costs. We also need to assess the relative costs and benefits of other alternatives. For example, the Obama administration has proposed a "stricter standard for smog-causing pollutants." This would be very costly, estimated at $19 to $90 billion a year by 2020. However, the benefits to human health might well outweigh these costs, for example, preventing premature deaths from heart disease and "thousands of cases of bronchitis, asthma and nonfatal heart attacks."[8]

Involved in such analyses are two distinct elements. One is an *assessment*—that is, a determination or description of these factual matters as far as they can be known. What exactly are the likely effects of doing this or that? The other is *evaluation*, the establishment of relative values. In cost–benefit evaluations, the *value* is generally a function of the usefulness to, or effect on, humans. The usual use of cost–benefit analysis is in the overall context of anthropocentrism. Some things we find more useful or valuable to us than others. In addition, if we have a fixed amount of money or resources to expend on some environmental project, then we know that this money or these resources will not be available for work elsewhere or to buy other things. Thus, every expenditure will have a certain *opportunity* cost. In being willing to pay for the environmental project, we will have some sense of its importance in comparison with other things that we will not then be able to do or have. However, if we value something else just as much or more than a slight increase in cleaner air or water, for example, then we will not be willing to pay for the cleaner air or water. (See the discussion of this in terms of the cost of reducing pollution in the article by Baxter in this chapter.)

In making such evaluations, we may know what monetary costs will be added to a particular forest product such as lumber if certain cutting were to be curtailed. However, we are less sure about how we should value the 2,000-year-old tree. How do we measure the historical appreciation or the aesthetic value of the tree or the animals that live in the tree? How do we measure the recreational value of the wilderness? What is beauty or a life worth? The value of these "intangibles" is difficult to measure because measuring implies that we use a standard measure of value. Only if we have such a standard can we compare, say, the value of a breathtaking view to that of a dam about to be built on the site. However, we do sometimes use monetary valuations, even of such intangibles as human lives or life years. For example, in insurance and other contexts, people attempt to give some measure of the value of a life.[9] Doing so is sometimes necessary, but it is obviously also problematic.

Human Environmental Impact

Taking an anthropocentric instrumentalist point of view of the environment also means thinking about the various ways in which the environment affects us. Consider, for example, just the following four environmental problems: global warming, ozone depletion, waste disposal and pollution, and wilderness preservation.

Global Warming The great majority of scientists now agree that our modern industrial society has created a potentially deadly phenomenon known as the *greenhouse effect, global warming,* or *climate change.* The phenomenon is caused by the burning of fossil fuels as the primary energy source for modern societies. The resulting gases—carbon dioxide, methane, fluorocarbons, nitrous oxide, among others—are released into the atmosphere. There these gases combine with water vapor and prevent the sun's infrared rays from radiating back into space. The trapped solar radiation thus contributes to increased air temperature. In this way, the gases function much as do the glass panes of a greenhouse. They will remain in the atmosphere for thirty to one hundred years, and their buildup will continue to increase over time. Automobile exhaust, along with industrial power plants and agricultural operations, produce most of the gases that lead to climate change. Deforestation also contributes to the warming because less carbon dioxide can be absorbed when vegetation has been removed.

Carbon dioxide accounts for 80 percent of greenhouse gas emissions. In addition, "[s]ixty percent of the methane currently in the atmosphere is produced by humans; it comes from landfills, livestock farming, fossil-fuel burning, wastewater treatment, and other industry." Globally, overall greenhouse gas emissions have risen approximately 70 percent since 1970 and are expected to rise another 90 percent by 2030 unless we take measures to reduce them. As of the beginning of 2007, the United States produced more greenhouse gases than any other country—30 percent—compared to 27.7 percent for all of Europe and 2.5 percent and 3.8 percent, respectively, for Africa and Central and South America. The annual amount of carbon emissions per person is higher in the United States—5.5 tons per person—compared to approximately 2.5 per person for Japan and Europe, respectively. In fact, with only 20 percent of the world's population, developed countries account for 60 percent of all carbon emissions. However, as it continues to grow its economy, China is catching up to the United States. In fact, by July 2007, China had surpassed the United States in greenhouse gas emissions.[10] The country is currently building one new coal-fired power plant per day, enough annually to "light all of Britain." China now "uses more coal than the United States, Europe, and Japan combined." However it is also becoming "the world's leading builder of more efficient, less polluting coal power plants." These plants use extremely hot steam, and "turn coal into a gas before burning it."[11] China also has "announced it would devote nearly $31 billion . . . to 'energy conservation and the environment,'" and will "purchase as many as 60,000 hybrid, electric, and fuel-cell vehicles by 2012 for use in 13 major cities."[12]

Although climate changes have occurred throughout the Earth's history, they have usually been gradual. However, this has not always been the case. Sixty-five million years ago, the dinosaurs are thought to have been wiped out by a dramatic and rapid change in climate caused by a giant meteorite that hit the Earth close to the Yucatan peninsula. The meteorite apparently put so much dust into the air "that sunlight was greatly reduced, temperatures plummeted, many plants didn't grow, and the food chain collapsed."[13] Within the time span of human existence, climate changes have occurred over several generations, allowing people to adapt. If these changes occur rapidly, however, such adaptation becomes more difficult. Food supplies, for example, could be severely stressed.[14] The reduced land fertility will also pose a threat to international security. If crop yields decrease and water shortages increase, those peoples and nations that are affected may resort to violence over the shortage of land and water resources. "More than two billion people already live in regions facing a scarcity of water" and soon "the amount of water needed for a rapidly growing population will double." Alternately, these people may migrate to urban slums, increasing overcrowding, poverty, and infrastructure breakdown.[15]

How do we know that present day global warming is not just a part of a natural pattern? Scientists have determined that recent temperatures and the amount of carbon dioxide in the atmosphere increases are dramatically greater than anything in the past. Scientists have drilled deep into the ice and brought up cylinders of ice, ice cores, that have markings like that of tree rings. They can read the age of the sections and analyze the chemicals and air bubbles in them to determine the average temperature of each year and the carbon dioxide content. Samples as old as 600,000 years have been obtained, and from these samples scientists know that the temperature and greenhouse gases have increased dramatically in the past decades. From this they can also predict how these will continue to rise unless the emissions are controlled.[16]

Scientists still disagree, however, on how much the Earth will warm, how fast, and how different regions will be affected. Still, evidence is now accumulating for the acceleration of this effect in receding glaciers and in the spreading of plants and forests farther north and to higher altitudes. Some European butterfly species have moved their habitats from 20 to 150 miles north of their previous ranges, and British birds are laying their eggs earlier in the

Chapter 16 ‹‹ Environmental Ethics **345**

spring. More evidence of global warming has included the nearly complete melting of the glacier on Mount Kilimanjaro in central Africa, thawing of Arctic permafrost, increasing rain in some areas, and increasing drought in others. Again, Al Gore's book and movie provide dramatic pictures of the changes that are taking place elsewhere among the world's glaciers. Glacier National Park has now lost almost all of its glaciers and should probably be renamed. Similar scenes are shown for Perito Moreno Glacier in Patagonia, Argentina; the Columbia Glacier in Prince William Sound in Alaska; and glaciers in Peru, Switzerland, and Italy, among others around the world.[17]

Some people may benefit from, but more are likely to be harmed by, the phenomenon of global warming. However, those who are most responsible for the warming are the least likely to be harmed, and people in developing countries are most likely to be harmed. Moreover, the cost to future generations must also be considered.[18] How much we would be willing to pay to prevent the various possible negative effects on us will depend on how bad we consider these effects to be. Those who calculate the costs and benefits involved in this area also must be able to factor in the uncertainties that are involved.

What can be done about global warming? And is it too late? Scientists generally believe that we still have a little time; according to Jim Hansen at NASA, "we have until 2015 to reverse the flow of carbon into the atmosphere before we cross a threshold and create a different planet."[19]

Among the means of reducing greenhouse gases are better mileage standards for cars and better public transportation. Other methods include alternative sources of power such as wind, solar, and nuclear. Germany, for example, adds 2,000 windmills each year and now has almost 20,000. France generates three-quarters of its electricity by nuclear plants. And there are also alternative biofuels such as biodiesel from vegetable oil and gas with an ethanol additive derived from corn or sugar cane or cellulose. However, people are hesitant to invest in biorefineries until they are more certain that so-called flex-fuel vehicles will be available.[20]

Other people suggest the implementation of a carbon tax that would charge "anyone who burns fossil fuels for the problems that ensue." This tax could be used, for example, to reimburse or give tax credits to homeowners for solar cells or energy-efficient appliances and research for ways to capture carbon dioxide. A small tax could yield some $50 billion for such purposes. Al Gore even proposes that such a tax be used in place of payroll taxes for Social Security and Medicare that is paid by both employers and employees.[21]

Ozone Depletion A second environmental problem about which we have been concerned for some time is *ozone depletion*. In the past twenty years, scientists have detected holes or breaks in the layer of ozone at the upper reaches of the stratosphere. This layer of ozone protects us from the damaging effects of excessive ultraviolet radiation from the sun, which can cause skin cancer and cataracts. The ozone layer holes are caused by chlorine-bearing pollutants such as the chlorofluorocarbons used in fire extinguishers and as refrigerants, cleaning agents, and spray propellants. Carbon dioxide, which causes the greenhouse effect and global warming, also has been found to contribute to ozone depletion.[22] Currently, the largest known hole is above Antarctica, where the ozone levels have declined by one-third in recent years. However, there are suspicions that it has migrated over Australia and led to increased biological abnormalities there. On certain days, Australian school children have been advised to stay inside. "Between 1996 and 2001, the ozone hole over the Antarctic reached more than 9 million square miles . . . roughly three times the size of the United States." Nearly all of the ozone over Antarctica has been destroyed, with the highest level of depletion occurring in October, the Antarctic spring. Lately, scientists have observed that the ozone hole has dwindled and even split into two sections, a phenomenon now puzzling scientists.[23] Scientists also had been predicting openings over areas in the northern hemisphere, where they have recently found a 9 percent to 14 percent decline in ozone levels.[24] The effects are widespread. For example, fish in waters around Great Britain "are suffering sunburn and blisters caused by the thinning ozone layer," and such effects literally threaten the existence of some fish species.[25]

From a cost–benefit perspective, we need to ask whether the cost to us to decrease or eliminate the causes of ozone depletion is worth the savings in lives. Here again we come up against the issue of how to value human life. The greater its value, the more surely we ought to stop using these chemicals, and the harder we ought to work to find alternatives.

Waste Disposal and Pollution A third area of environmental impact on us is *waste disposal* and *pollution*. No one wants the city dump located next to them, yet the tons of garbage that we produce each year must be put somewhere. Industrial waste is washed into our rivers and lakes and blown into our air. It is estimated that one person per hour dies prematurely in California because of air pollution.[26]

As of 2005, the United States had "almost 9,000 curbside pickup programs for garbage and recyclables." However there is still more trash going into dumps and landfills because we are consuming more and throwing away more. Americans produce 236 million tons of garbage in a year. Only about 30 percent of this is recycled or composted. Packaging makes up about a third of an average city's trash. Recycled bottles and cans can be turned into reusable metal and glass as well as roads, bike parts, and carpets.[27] In fact, recycling one aluminum can save enough electricity to run a TV for three hours.[28]

So-called e-waste is also becoming a major problem. This includes outdated cell phones, computers, TVs, and printers. Approximately 50 million tons of this waste is discarded globally per year. Such items contain huge amounts of toxins, "including beryllium in computer motherboards, cadmium in semiconductors, chromium in floppy disks, lead in batteries and computer monitors, and mercury in alkaline batteries and fluorescent lamps." One good sign of progress in dealing with the problem is that environmental groups have persuaded several technology companies, including "Hewlett-Packard, Dell, LG Electronics, Samsung, Sony, Sony Ericsson, and Nokia to eliminate most hazardous materials from their products." This is also a particular problem in developing countries such as India. It is estimated that the United States sends approximately 75 to 80 percent of its older e-machines to India and China because their recycling costs are less than here.[29]

Recycling, in fact, is tackling a wide variety of problems related to waste disposal and pollution. For example, "a team of chemical engineers has taken the first step to turning plant wastes"—or other forms of biomass such as decaying plant and animal matter—"into Earth-friendly hydrogen fuel that one day could keep the lights burning and engines running without depleting diminishing reservoirs of precious natural resources."[30] Recycling programs aim to reduce the amount of aluminum, glass, paper, and plastics that we throw away each year. Again, we need to determine the economic value of health and life to determine what we ought to pay to eliminate or lessen the risks from these sources.

Wilderness Preservation A fourth environmental issue that concerns us is *wilderness preservation*. The United States now has 671 federally designated wilderness areas, but these are being encroached on by mining, mineral leasing, and road building, among other enterprises.[31] The National Forest Service has responsibility for almost 200 million acres of land and the management of more than 150 national forests. Of the 385 units in the U.S. National Park system, among the ten most endangered are Big Bend National Park, Everglades National Park, Glacier National Park, and the Great Smoky Mountains National Park. Almost 10 million people visit this last park annually, despite the fact that "pollution from coal-fired power plants threatens the health of park visitors, plants, and wildlife and diminishes scenic views."[32]

Recovering natural gas, oil, and other forms of energy from roadless areas in national forests is a hotly argued topic. On one side of the argument are those who say such efforts will reduce U.S. reliance on foreign energy resources. On the other side are those who argue that such resource extractions would make a minimal contribution, meeting U.S. oil and gas needs for only fifteen days and nine to eleven weeks, respectively.[33]

Forests and wilderness areas are valuable for many reasons. One-fourth of today's medicines, for example, had their origins in rain forests. Forests provide habitats for wildlife, including threatened species. They provide us with leisure and relaxation and with many possibilities for recreational opportunities such as white-water rafting, boating, fishing, hiking, and skiing. They also provide aesthetic and religious experiences and simple communing with the wider world of nature.

International Environmental Conventions Because of widespread concerns about these environmental issues, many meetings and conventions have been held over the past two decades. One example is an Earth Summit, the U.N. Conference on Environment and Development, which was held in Rio de Janeiro, Brazil in 1992. Its two themes symbolized the interrelation between environmental issues and sustainable development. Some 2,400 representatives from nongovernmental organizations and 17,000 people overall attended the summit. At its conclusion, the conference issued a general *Report of the United Nations Conference on Environment and Development*, Agenda 21, the Rio Declaration, the Framework Convention on Climate Change, a Convention on Biological Diversity, and a Statement of Forest Principles. The Framework on Climate Change, for example, went into force in March 1994 and had as its primary objective "stabilization of greenhouse gas concentrations in the atmosphere." The United States, along with many other nations, signed this agreement. The Kyoto Protocol is the principal update to this agreement. It was negotiated in Kyoto, Japan, in 1997. Although the United States helped develop this agreement, Congress refused to pass it and President George W. Bush pulled out of the agreement when he took office in 2001, holding that it was flawed and would hurt the U.S. economy. "The United States (U.S.), although a signatory to the Kyoto Protocol, has neither ratified nor withdrawn from the Protocol. The signature alone is merely symbolic, as the Kyoto Protocol is non-binding on the United States unless ratified."[34] It was ratified eventually by 141 other nations, including Russia, and took effect on February 16, 2005. Key provisions included mandatory restrictions on greenhouse gas emissions to "at least 5 percent below levels measured in 1990" by the year 2012.[35] The proto-

col also allowed the thirty-five industrialized countries that were covered by it to "earn credits toward their treaty targets by investing in emissions clean-ups outside their borders," a so-called cap-and-trade system.[36] Developing countries such as India and China were exempt from the controls so as to give them a better chance to catch up economically with the more developed nations. Although the United States alone among industrialized nations has refused to sign this accord, it accounts for some 36 percent of greenhouse gas emissions; still, U.S. businesses that are international in scope will be subject to the protocol's requirements. Moreover, the United States has made known that it would be willing to return to the elements in the original 1994 agreement as a basis for continuing discussions.

Kyoto was chosen for the signing of the treaty in 1997 because of Japan's deep cultural conservation roots with "its disapproval of waste and excess." However, today many Japanese youth are Americanizing and showing preferences for big gas-guzzling cars and high levels of consumption. The Kyoto Protocol has not quite worked as hoped because countries have not met their goals. Even though the United States never ratified the treaty, many U.S. cities have nonetheless adopted it. Developing countries were not covered, although China, for example, has now become an emissions titan. Under the treaty, the United States was supposed to reduce its emissions 7 percent below 1990 levels by 2012. But by 2004, U.S. emission levels were already 16 percent higher. In 2004, Greece's emissions were 19 percent higher than their target, and Spain is not even close to its target. Only Great Britain and Sweden will likely reach their targets by 2012.[37]

In 2002, another world summit on sustainable development was held in Johannesburg, South Africa. One of the promising developments at this summit was the publication of various joint efforts between nongovernmental organizations concerned about the environment and private industry. For example, Greenpeace joined forces with British Petroleum to try to improve environmental aspects of oil drilling, and the World Wildlife Fund teamed up with the World Bank and Amazon River basin nations to protect that valuable environment.[38]

What is the extent of our obligation to preserve these forests and wilderness areas, especially in light of the fact that the preservation often has a negative effect on other human interests such as the ability of many people to make a living?

From December 7–19, 2009, 111 countries and the European Union met in Copenhagen, Denmark, for a climate change conference. Although there was no legally binding agreement, 75 of the nations, which account for 80 percent of global greenhouse gas emissions, did sign pledges of various sorts to reduce these emissions by certain dates. President Barack Obama called it "a meaningful and unprecedented breakthrough . . . [in which] all major economies have come together to accept their responsibility to take action to confront the threat of climate change."[39]

ECOCENTRISM

According to the anthropocentric perspective, environmental concerns ought to be directed to the betterment of people, who alone have intrinsic value. In contrast with this view is one that is generally called an *ecocentric* (or *biocentric*) perspective. It holds that it is not just humans that have intrinsic worth or value. There are variations within this perspective, with some theorists holding that individual life forms have such intrinsic worth and others stressing that it is whole systems or ecosystems that have such value. The ethical questions then become matters of determining what is in the best interests of these life forms or what furthers or contributes to, or is a satisfactory fit with, some ecosystem.

Ecocentrists are critical of anthropocentrists. Why, they ask, do only humans have intrinsic value and everything else only use value? Some fault the Judeo-Christian tradition for this view. In particular, they single out the biblical mandate to "subdue" the Earth and "have dominion over the fish of the sea and over the birds of the air and every living thing that moves upon the Earth" as being responsible for this instrumentalist view of nature and other living things.[40] Others argue that anthropocentrism is reductionistic. All of nature, according to this view, is reduced to the level of "thinghood." The seventeenth-century French philosopher René Descartes is sometimes cited as a source of this reductionist point of view because of his belief that the essential element of humanity is the ability to think ("I think, therefore I am," etc.) and his belief that animals are mere biological machines.[41] Evolutionary accounts also sometimes depict humans at the pinnacle of evolution or the highest or last link in some great chain of being. We can ask ourselves whether we place too high a value on human beings and their powers of reason and intelligence. "Knowledge is power" is a modern notion. One source of this view was *The New Organon* by the early modern philosopher Francis Bacon.[42] Ecocentrists criticize the view that we ought to seek to understand nature so that we can have power over it because it implies that our primary relation to nature is one of domination.

Ecocentrists hold that we ought rather to regard nature with admiration and respect, because of their view that nature and natural beings have intrinsic value. Let us return to our example of the 2,000-year-old trees. You may have seen or viewed pictures of trees large enough for tunnels to be cut through which cars can be driven. In the 1880s, such a tunnel was cut through one such tree, a giant sequoia, near Wawona on the south end of what is now Yosemite National Park. Tourists enjoyed driving through the tunnel. However, some people claimed that this was a mutilation of and an insult to this majestic tree. They claimed that the tree itself had a kind of integrity, intrinsic value, and dignity that should not be invaded lightly. Another way to put it would be to say that the tree itself had moral standing.[43] What we do to the tree itself matters morally, they insisted.

On what account could trees be thought to have this kind of moral standing? All organisms, it might be argued, are self-maintaining systems:

> They grow and are irritable in response to stimuli. They reproduce. . . . They resist dying. They post a careful if also semipermeable boundary between themselves and the rest of nature; they assimilate environmental materials to their own needs. They gain and maintain internal order against the disordering tendencies of external nature. They keep winding up, recomposing themselves, while inanimate things run down, erode, and decompose.[44]

Because they are organized systems or integrated living wholes, they are thought to have intrinsic value and even moral standing. The value may be only *prima facie*, but nevertheless they have their own value in themselves and are not just to be valued in terms of their usefulness to people. According to this perspective, the giant sequoias of Wawona should not just be thought of in terms of their tourist value. There are things that can be good and bad for the trees themselves. The tunnel in the Wawona tree, for example, eventually weakened the tree, and it fell over in a snowstorm in 1968. Although trees are not *moral agents* who act responsibly for reasons, according to this general view they can still be thought of as moral patients. A *moral patient* is any being for which what we do to it matters in itself. A moral patient is any being toward whom we can have *direct duties* rather than simply *indirect duties*. We ought to behave in a certain way toward the tree for its sake and not just indirectly for the sake of how it will eventually affect us. There are things that are in the best interests of trees, even if the trees take no conscious interest in them. (See further discussion of this in the treatment of "rights" in the following chapter.)

In addition to those ecocentrists who argue that all life forms have intrinsic value are others who stress the value of ecosystems. An *ecosystem* is a whole of interacting and interdependent parts within a circumscribed locale. "Ecosystems are a continuum of variation, a patchy mosaic with fuzzy edges. Some interactions are persistent, others occasional."[45] They are loosely structured wholes. The boundary changes and some members come and go. Sometimes there is competition within the whole. Sometimes there is symbiosis. The need to survive pushes various creatures to be creative in their struggle for an adaptive fit. There is a unity to the whole, but it is loose and decentralized. Why is this unity to be thought of as having value in itself? One answer is provided by Aldo Leopold. In the 1940s, he wrote in his famous essay "The Land Ethic" that we should think about the land as "a fountain of energy flowing through a circuit of soils, plants, and animals."[46] Look at any section of life on our planet and you will find a system of life, intricately interwoven and interdependent elements that function as a whole. It forms a *biotic pyramid* with myriad smaller organisms at the bottom and gradually fewer and more complex organisms at the top. Plants depend on the Earth, insects depend on the plants, and other animals depend on the insects. Leopold did not think it amiss to speak about the whole system as being healthy or unhealthy. If the soil is washed away or abnormally flooded, then the whole system suffers or is sick. In this system, individual organisms feed off one another. Some elements come and others go. It is the whole that continues. Leopold also believed that a particular type of ethics follows from this view of nature—a biocentric or ecocentric ethics. He believed that "a thing is right when it tends to preserve the integrity, stability, and beauty of the biotic community. It is wrong when it tends to do otherwise."[47] The system has a certain *integrity* because it is a unity of interdependent elements that combine to make a whole with a unique character. It has a certain *stability*, not in that it does not change, but that it changes only gradually. Finally, it has a particular *beauty*. Here beauty is a matter of harmony, well-ordered form, or unity in diversity.[48] When envisioned on a larger scale, the entire Earth system may then be regarded as one system with a certain integrity, stability, and beauty. Morality becomes a matter of preserving this system or doing only what befits it.

The kind of regard for nature that is manifest in biocentric views is not limited to contemporary philosophers. *Native American* views on nature provide a fertile source of biocentric thinking. For example, Eagle Man, an Oglala Sioux writer, speaks of the unity of all living things. All come from tiny seeds and so all are brothers and sisters. The seeds come from Mother Earth and depend on her for sustenance. We owe her respect for she comes from the "Great Spirit Above."[49] Also certain forms of *romanticism* have long regarded nature in a different way than that found in dominant Western perspectives. Such were the views of transcendentalists Ralph Waldo Emerson and Henry Thoreau. *Transcendentalism* was a movement of romantic idealism that arose in the United States in the mid-nineteenth century. Rather than regarding nature as foreign or alien, Emerson and Thoreau thought of it as a friend or kindred spirit. In fact, nature for them symbolized spirit. Thus, a rock is a sign of endurance and a snake of cunning. The rock and the snake can symbolize spirit because nature itself is full of spirit. As a result of this viewpoint, Thoreau went to Walden Pond to live life to its fullest and commune with nature. He wanted to know its moods and all its phenomena. Although he and Emerson read the lessons of nature, they also read their Eastern texts. Some have characterized aspects of their nature theory as *idealism*, the view that all is ideas or spirit; or as *pantheism*, the doctrine that holds that all is God.

John Muir, the prophet of Yosemite and founder of the Sierra Club, once urged Emerson to spend more time with him. He wrote to Emerson:

> I invite you to join me in a month's worship with Nature in the high temples of the great Sierra Crown beyond our holy Yosemite. It will cost you nothing save the time and very little of that for you will be mostly in eternity. . . . In the name of a hundred cascades that barbarous visitors never see . . . in the name of all the rocks and of this whole spiritual atmosphere.[50]

Such romantic idealistic views provide a stark contrast to anthropocentric views of a reductionist type. However, they also raise many questions. For example, we can ask the transcendentalist how nature can be spirit or god in more than a metaphorical sense. And we can ask followers of Aldo Leopold the following question: Why is the way things are or have become good? Nature can be cruel, at least from the point of view of certain animals and even from our own viewpoint as we suffer the damaging results of typhoons or volcanic eruptions. And, more abstractly, on what basis can we argue that whatever exists is good?

DEEP ECOLOGY

Another variation within ecocentrism is the deep ecology movement. Members of this movement wish to distinguish themselves from establishment environmentalism, which they call "shallow ecology" and which is basically anthropomorphic. The term *deep ecology* was first used by Arne Naess, a Norwegian philosopher and environmentalist.[51] Deep ecologists take a holistic view of nature and believe that we should look more deeply to find the *root causes* of environmental degradation. The idea is that our environmental problems are deeply rooted in the Western psyche, and radical changes of viewpoint are necessary if we are to solve these problems.

Western *reductionism*, *individualism*, and *consumerism* are said to be the causes of our environmental problems. The solution is to rethink and reformulate certain metaphysical beliefs about whether all reality is reducible to atoms in motion. It is also to rethink what it is to be an individual. Are individual beings merely many separate independent beings? Or are they interrelated parts of a whole? According to those who hold this perspective, solving our environmental problems also requires a change in our views about what is a good quality of life. The good life, they assert, is not one that stresses the possession of things and the search for satisfaction of wants and desires.

In addition to describing the radical changes in our basic outlook on life that we need to make, the deep ecologist platform also holds that any intrusion into nature to change it requires justification. If we intervene to change nature, then we must show that a vital need of ours is at stake.[52] We should not intervene lightly not only because we are not sure of the results of our action, which will be possibly far-reaching and harmful, but also because nature *as it is* is regarded as good and right and well balanced. This platform also includes the belief that the flourishing of nonhuman life requires a "substantial decrease in the human population."[53] (See the reading selection from Devall and Sessions in this chapter.) In a more recent collection of writings on deep ecology, George Sessions argues that the Earth's wild ecosystems have intrinsic value and a right to exist on their own as well as instrumental value for our own well-being. He argues that "humanity must drastically scale down its industrial activities on Earth, change its consumption lifestyles, stabilize" and "reduce the size of the human population by humane means."[54] The members of the deep ecology movement have been quite politically active. Their creed contains the belief that people are responsible for the Earth. Beliefs such as this often provide a basis for the tactics of groups such as Earth First! Its tactics have included various forms of "ecosabotage"—for example, spiking trees to prevent logging and cutting power lines.[55]

Both the tactics and the views that underlie them have been criticized. The tactics have been labeled by some as "ecoterrorism."[56] The view that all incursions into nature can be justified only by our vital needs seems to run counter to our intuitions, for the implication is that we must not build the golf course or the house patio because these would change the Earth and vegetation, and the need to play golf or sit on a patio are hardly vital. Others might have difficulty with the implication that nature and other natural things have as much value as people and thus people's interests should not take precedence over the good of nature. The view that nature itself has a "good of its own" or that the whole system has value in itself is also problematic for many people. However, at the least, deep ecologists have provided a valuable service by calling our attention to the possible deep philosophical roots and causes of some of our environmental problems.

ECOFEMINISM

A new variant of ecological ethics put forth some twenty years ago by some feminists is called *ecofeminism* or *ecological feminism*.[57] It may be seen as part of a broader movement that locates the source of environmental problems not in metaphysical or worldviews, as deep ecologists do, but in social practices. *Social ecology*, as this wider movement is called, holds that we should look to particular social patterns and structures to discover what is wrong with our relationship to the environment. Ecofeminists believe that the problem lies in a male-centered view of nature—that is, one of human domination over nature. According to Karen Warren, ecofeminism is "the position that there are important connections . . . between the domination of women and the domination of nature, an understanding of which is crucial to both feminism and environmental ethics."[58] Note here that deep ecologists and ecofeminists do not generally get along well with one another. The deep ecologists criticize ecofeminists for concentrating insufficiently on the environment, and ecofeminists accuse deep ecologists of the very male-centered view that they believe is the source of our environmental problems.[59] However, a variety of ecofeminist views are espoused by diverse groups of feminists.[60]

One version acknowledges the ways in which women differ from men and rejoices in it. This view is espoused by those who hold that because of their female experience or nature women tend to value relationships and the concrete individual. They stress caring and emotion, and they seek to replace conflict and assertion of rights with cooperation and community. These are traits that can and should carry over into our relationship to nature, they believe. Rather than use nature in an instrumentalist fashion, they urge, we should cooperate with nature. We should manifest a caring and benevolent regard for nature just as for other human beings. One version of this view would have us think of nature itself as in some way divine. Rather than think of God as a distant creator who transcends nature, these religiously oriented ecofeminists think of God as a being within nature. Some also refer to this god as Mother Nature or Gaia, after the name of the Greek goddess.[61]

Another version of ecofeminism rejects the dualism that its adherents find in the above position. They hold that this position promotes the devaluing and domination of both women and nature. Rather than divide reality into contrasting elements—the active and passive, the rational and emotional, the dominant and subservient—they encourage us to recognize the diversity within nature and among people. They would similarly support a variety of ways of relating to nature. Thus, they believe that even though science that proceeds from a male orientation of control over nature has made advances and continues to do so, its very orientation misses important aspects of nature. If instead we also have a feeling for nature and a listening attitude, then we might be better able to know what actually is there. They also believe that we humans should see ourselves as part of the community of nature, not as distinct nonnatural beings functioning in a world that is thought to be alien to us.

It is sometimes difficult to know just what, in particular, are the practical upshots of ecocentrism, ecological feminism, and deep ecology. Yet the following sentiment is indicative of a view that might make a difference: "On behalf of the tiny beings that are yet to arrive on Earth, but whose genes are here now, let's try a little CPR for the Earth—conservation, protection, and restoration. And a little tender loving care for the only bit of the universe we know to be blessed with life."[62]

As noted previously, some anthropocentrists contend that they also believe in a wise use of nature, one that does not destroy the very nature that we value and on which we depend. On the other hand, it may well be that if we care for and about nature, then our treatment of it will be better in some important ways.

SUSTAINABLE DEVELOPMENT

The preservation of the environment is also a global issue. Although many problems are specific to certain areas of the world, others are shared in common. When we think of the developing world, for example, we find that attention to the environment is not the first concern. Many people who work for the development of poor nations even view the environmentalist movement as an example of Western elitism.[63] For example, only such environmental elitists, they suggest, can afford to preserve unchanged an environment or wilderness that the poor need to use and change in order to survive. Yet others see the two concerns, development and environment, as closely intertwined and capable of moving forward together. What is needed, they say, is not development that ignores environmental concerns, but "sustainable development." For example, Gus Speth, president of World Resources Institute, writes, "It is . . . clear that development and economic reforms will have no lasting success unless they are suffused with concern for ecological stability and wise management of resources."[64] The idea is that if the forests in an area are depleted or the land is ruined by unwise or short-sighted overuse, then the people living there will not have what they need to continue to develop; that is, development will not be sustainable. We can learn about the disastrous consequences of environmental degradation and unsustainable development from "collapsed" or failed societies such as that on Easter Island and the Maya in the Yucatan.[65] However, poverty also causes environmental problems as people destroy forests for fuel, for example. Pricing policies as well as weak agrarian reforms and mismanagement and intergroup conflict are among the other factors that contribute to "the vicious downward spiral of poverty and environmental degradation. The poor have been exploited, shifted, and marginalized to the extent that they often have no choice but to participate in the denigration of resources, with full knowledge that they are mortgaging their own future."[66] Sustainable development also is connected with issues of biodiversity. For example, the introduction of technological advances into developing nations can reduce the variety of plants that local cultures independently manage for their own development. External and centralized control of what is planted and of the seeds used may sometimes work against rather than for development.[67] On a positive note, Jessica Tuchman Mathews suggests that we can have development without environmental destruction, but we need to "change the means of production, developing technologies that will enable us to meet human needs without destroying the [E]arth."[68]

In the readings in this chapter, William Baxter gives an anthropocentric environmentalist ethics, Bill Devall and George Sessions explain the key elements of deep ecology, and Ramachandra Guha raises questions about deep ecology from the perspective of the developing world and Indian and German environmentalism.

NOTES

1. Elizabeth Rosenthal, "As the Climate Changes, Bits of England's Coast Crumble," *The New York Times*, May 4, 2007, p. A4.
2. Al Gore, *An Inconvenient Truth* (New York: Rodale, 2006), 194–209; Andrew Revkin, "Climate Panel Reaches Consensus on the Need to Reduce Harmful Emissions," *The New York Times*, May 4, 2007, p. A6; Tim Appenzeller, "The Big Thaw," *National Geographic*, June 2007.
3. Gore, op. cit., pp. 148–151.
4. Thomas Friedman, "Global Weirding is Here," *The New York Times*, February 17, 2010, p. A23.
5. Ernest Weekley, *An Etymological Dictionary of Modern English* (New York: Dover, 1967), 516, 518.
6. Mark Sagoff, "Population, Nature, and the Environment," *Report from the Institute for Philosophy and Public Policy, 13*, no. 4 (Fall 1993): 10.
7. "How to Save the Earth," *Time Magazine*, Special Report (Aug. 26, 2002): A1–A62.

8. John M. Broder, "E.P.A. Seeks Tighter Rules to Cut Down Air Pollution," *The New York Times*, January 8, 2010, pp. A1 and A3.

9. Safety regulation needs to make use of such monetary equivalencies, for how else do we decide how safe is safe enough? There is no such thing as perfect safety, for that would mean no risk. Thus, we end up judging that we ought to pay so much to make things just so much safer but no more. The implication is that the increased life years or value of the lives to be saved by stricter regulation is of so much but no more than this much value. See Barbara MacKinnon, "Pricing Human Life," *Science, Technology and Human Values* (Spring 1986): 29–39.

10. Michele Murzak, "Teaching Science and Global Warming," Yale National Initiative to Strengthen Teaching in Public Schools; Andrew C. Revkin, "Climate Panel Reaches Consensus on the Need to Reduce Harmful Emissions," *The New York Times*, May 4, 2007, p. A4; Jane Kay, "Report Predicts Climate Calamity," *The New York Times*, May 9, 2007, pp. C1, C5; David Perlman, "Increase in Carbon Emissions Seen Tripling Since '90s," *San Francisco Chronicle*, May 22, 2007, p. A3; Gore, op. cit., p. 253; Robert Collier, "Warming Strikes a Note in China," *San Francisco Chronicle*, July 8, 2007, p. A4.

11. Keith Bradsher, "Clean Power That Reaps a Whirlwind," *The New York Times,* May 9, 2007 (http://www.nytimes.com/2007/05/09/business/09carbon.html); Keith Bradsher, "China Far Outpaces U.S. in Building Cleaner Coal Fired Plants," *The New York Times*, May 11, 2009, pp. A1 and A3.

12. Michael Standaert, "China Turns to Clean Tech to Stimulate its Economy," *San Francisco Chronicle*, May 10, 2009, p. A21.

13. See http://unfccc.int/essential_background/feeling_the_heat/items/2917.php

14. Kendrick Taylor, "Rapid Climate Change," *American Scientist, 87* (July–Aug. 1999): 320–327.

15. Thomas Homer-Dixon, "Terror in the Weather Forecast," *The New York Times*, April 24, 2007, p. A25; Celia W. Dugger, "Need for Water Could Double in 50 Years, U.N. Study Finds," *The New York Times*, Aug. 22, 2006, p. A12; Jane Kay, "Report Predicts Climate Calamity," *San Francisco Chronicle*, May 7, 2007, p. A1.

16. Gore, op. cit., pp. 60–67.

17. Ibid., pp. 42–59; Appenzeller, p. 60.

18. Bob Herbert, "Rising Tides," *The New York Times*, Feb. 22, 2001, p. A29.

19. Bill McKibben, "How Close to Catastrophe?" *The New York Review of Books*, Nov. 16, 2006, pp. 23–25.

20. Jim Suhr, "Ethanol Enjoying a Booming Renaissance," *San Francisco Chronicle*, May 6, 2007, p. D4; Bill McKibben, "How Close to Catastrophe?" *The New York Review of Books*, Nov. 16, 2006, pp. 23–25.

21. Michael Riordan, "Time for a Carbon Tax?" *San Francisco Chronicle*, March 23, 2007, p. B11.

22. Taylor, "Rapid Climate Change," *Science* (Nov. 24, 1992): B8.

23. By September 2002, the hole seemed to have shrunk to approximately 6 million square miles. Richard Stenger, "Antarctic Ozone Hole Splits in Two," *CNN Report*, Oct. 1, 2002 (see www.cnn.com/2002/TECH/space/09/30/ozone.holes/).

24. *Science* (April 23, 1993): 490–491.

25. "Study: Fish Suffer Ozone Hole Sunburn," *San Francisco Sunday Examiner and Chronicle*, Nov. 12, 2000, p. A20.

26. *Cal Pirg*, 13, no. 2 (Summer 1997): 1.

27. *Sierra Club Magazine*, Nov.–Dec. 2005, pp. 42–47.

28. The History Channel, *Modern Marvels*, April 25, 2007.

29. Anuj Chopra, "Developing Countries Are Awash in E-Waste," *San Francisco Chronicle*, March 30, 2007, pp. A1, A19.

30. "Chemists Try to Turn Plant Waste to Fuel," *UPI Science News*, Aug. 28, 2002 (http://www.upi.com/Science_News/2002/08/28/Chemists-try-to-turn-plant-waste-to-fuel/UPI-80751030559050/)

31. Joseph R. des Jardins, *Environmental Ethics* (Belmont, CA: Wadsworth, 1993), 48.

32. "Ten Most Endangered," National Parks Conservation Association (http://www.npca.org/media_center/press_releases/2003/page-27599890.html).

33. Pete Morton, Chris Weller, and Janice Thomson, "Energy and Western Wildlands, A GIS Analysis of Economically Recoverable Oil and Gas," *Newsroom, The Wilderness Society Special Report* (www.wilderness.org/newsroom/report_energy 101402.htm).

34. http://en.wikipedia.org/wiki/Kyoto_Protocol#United_States

35. Larry Rohter and Andrew C. Revkin, "Cheers, and Concern, for New Climate Pact," *The New York Times*, Dec. 13, 2004, p. A6.

36. Ibid.

37. Joe Nation, "Coordinate Carbon Trading Markets," *San Francisco Chronicle*, March 23, 2007, p. B11; Robert Collier, "Japan Hot and Cold on Warming," *San Francisco Chronicle*, April 16, 2006, pp. A1, A8.

38. Andrew C. Revkin, "Small World After All: At Summit, Ecologists and Corporations Unite in Opposition to Global Warming," *The New York Times*, Sept. 5, 2002, p. A8.

39. http://unfccc.int/home/items/5262.php; http://www.whitehouse.gov/blog/2009/12/18/a-meaningful-and-unprecedented-breakthrough-here-copenhagen.

40. Genesis 1: 26–29. Others will cite St. Francis of Assisi as an example of the Christian with a respectful regard for nature.

41. René Descartes, *Meditations on First Philosophy*. However, it might be pointed out that for Descartes this was not so much a metaphysical point as an epistemological one; that is, he was concerned with finding some sure starting point for knowledge and found at least that he was sure that he was thinking even when he was doubting the existence of everything else.

42. Francis Bacon, *Novum Organum*, Thomas Fowler (Ed.) (Oxford, 1889).

43. See Christopher Stone, *Do Trees Have Standing? Toward Legal Rights for Natural Objects* (Los Altos, CA: William Kaufmann, 1974).

44. Holmes Rolston III, *Environmental Ethics: Duties to and Values in the Natural World* (Philadelphia: Temple University Press, 1988), 97.

45. Ibid., 169.

46. Aldo Leopold, "The Land Ethic," in *Sand County Almanac* (New York: Oxford University Press, 1949).

47. Ibid., 262.

48. See John Hospers, *Understanding the Arts* (Englewood Cliffs, NJ: Prentice Hall, 1982).

49. Eagle Man, "We are All Related," from Ed McGaa, *Mother Earth Spirituality: Native American Paths to Healing Ourselves and Our World* (San Francisco: Harper & Row, 1990), 203–209.

50. Quoted in the *San Francisco Examiner*, May 1, 1988, p. E5.

51. Arne Naess, *Ecology, Community, and Lifestyle*, David Rothenberg (Trans.) (Cambridge, UK: Cambridge University Press, 1989).

52. Paul Taylor, *Respect for Nature* (Princeton, NJ: Princeton University Press, 1986).

53. Naess, Ecology, *Community, and Lifestyle*, op. cit.

54. George Sessions (Ed.), *Deep Ecology for the 21st Century: Readings on the Philosophy and Practice of the New Environmentalism* (Boston: Shambhala Publications, 1995), xxi.

55. On the tactics of ecosabotage, see Bill Devall, *Simple in Means, Rich in Ends: Practicing Deep Ecology* (Layton, UT: Gibbs Smith, 1988).

56. See Michael Martin, "Ecosabotage and Civil Disobedience," *Environmental Ethics, 12* (Winter 1990): 291–310.

57. According to Joseph des Jardins, the term ecofeminism was first used by Françoise d'Eaubonne in 1974 in her work *Le Feminisme ou la Mort* (Paris: Pierre Horay, 1974). See des Jardins, *Environmental Ethics*, op. cit., 249.

58. Karen J. Warren, "The Power and Promise of Ecological Feminism," *Environmental Ethics, 9* (Spring 1987): 3–20.

59. I thank an anonymous reviewer for this point.

60. See the distinctions made by Allison Jaggar between liberal (egalitarian) feminism, Marxist feminism, socialist feminism, and radical feminism. *Feminist Politics and Human Nature* (Totowa, NJ: Rowman & Allanheld, 1983).

61. See Carol Christ, *Laughter of Aphrodite: Reflections on a Journey to the Goddess* (San Francisco: Harper & Row, 1987).

62. David R. Brower, "Step Up the Battle on Earth's Behalf," *San Francisco Chronicle*, Aug. 18, 1993, p. A15.

63. See Ramachandra Guha, "Radical American Environmentalism and Wilderness Preservation: A Third World Critique," in *Environmental Ethics, 11* (Spring 1989): 71–83.

64. James Gustave Speth, "Resources and Security: Perspectives from the Global 2000 Report," *World Future Society Bulletin* (1981): 1–4.

65. Jared Diamond, *Collapse* (New York: Viking Press, 2005).

66. R. Paul Shaw, World Bank official, as quoted in Mark Sagoff, "Population, Nature, and the Environment," *Report from the Institute for Philosophy and Public Policy, 13*, no. 4 (Fall 1993): 8.

67. See Vandana Shiva, "Biotechnological Development and the Conservation of Biodiversity," in Vandana Shiva and Ingunn Moser (Eds.), *Biopolitics: A Feminist and Ecological Reader on Biotechnology* (London: Zed Books, 1995), 193–213.

68. As quoted in Sagoff, "Population," 9; from Jessica Tuchman Mathews, "Redefining Security," *Foreign Affairs* (Spring 1989).

R E A D I N G
People or Penguins: The Case for Optimal Pollution

WILLIAM F. BAXTER

Study Questions

1. Why does Baxter believe that we should have clear goals in mind in order to answer moral questions about the environment and about pollution in particular?
2. What are the four criteria or goals that he suggests? In what ways are these people-oriented criteria?
3. Does he believe that people-oriented criteria will necessarily be bad for the penguins or other elements of our environment?
4. What are his objections to giving penguins, for example, a greater value than their usefulness to humans gives them?
5. What problem does he raise for the belief that we ought to "respect the balance of nature"?
6. Why does he believe that there is no right level of pollution?
7. What is the difference, according to Baxter, between resources and costs? How are they related? Why does the cost of building a dam or controlling pollution involve trade-offs?

I START WITH the modest proposition that, in dealing with pollution, or indeed with any problem, it is helpful to know what one is attempting to accomplish. Agreement on how and whether to pursue a particular objective, such as pollution control, is not possible unless some more general objective has been identified and stated with reasonable precision. We talk loosely of having clean air and water, of preserving our wilderness areas, and so forth. But none of these is a sufficiently general objective: each is more accurately viewed as a means rather than as an end.

With regard to clean air, for example, one may ask, "how clean?" and "what does clean mean?" It is even reasonable to ask, "why have clear air?" Each of these questions is an implicit demand that a more general community goal be stated—a goal sufficiently general in its scope and enjoying sufficiently general assent among the community of actors that such "why" questions no longer seem admissible with respect to that goal.

If, for example, one states as a goal the proposition that "every person should be free to do whatever he wishes in contexts where his actions do not interfere with the interests of other human beings," the speaker is unlikely to be met with a response of "why." The goal may be criticized as uncertain in its implications or difficult to implement, but it is so basic a tenet of our civilization—it reflects a cultural value so broadly shared, at least in the abstract—that the question "why" is seen as impertinent or imponderable or both.

I do not mean to suggest that everyone would agree with the "spheres of freedom" objective just stated. Still less do I mean to suggest that a society could subscribe to four or five such general objectives that would be adequate in their coverage to serve as testing criteria by which all other disagreements might be measured. One difficulty in the attempt to construct such a list is that each new goal added will conflict, in certain applications, with each prior goal listed; and thus each goal serves as a limited qualification on prior goals.

Without any expectation of obtaining unanimous consent to them, let me set forth four goals that I generally use as ultimate testing criteria in attempting to frame solutions to problems of human organization. My position regarding pollution stems from these four criteria. If the criteria appeal to you and any part of what appears hereafter does not, our disagreement will have a helpful focus: which of us is correct, analytically, in supposing that his position on pollution would better serve these general goals. If the criteria do not seem acceptable to you, then it is to be expected that our more particular judgments will differ, and the task will then be yours to identify the basic set of criteria upon which your particular judgments rest.

My criteria are as follows:

1. The spheres of freedom criterion stated above.
2. Waste is a bad thing. The dominant feature of human existence is scarcity—our available resources, our aggregate labors, and our skill in

employing both have always been, and will continue for some time to be, inadequate to yield to every man all the tangible and intangible satisfactions he would like to have. Hence, none of those resources, or labors, or skills, should be wasted—that is, employed so as to yield less than they might yield in human satisfactions.

3. Every human being should be regarded as an end rather than as a means to be used for the betterment of another. Each should be afforded dignity and regarded as having an absolute claim to an evenhanded application of such rules as the community may adopt for its governance.

4. Both the incentive and the opportunity to improve his share of satisfactions should be preserved to every individual. Preservation of incentive is dictated by the "no-waste" criterion and enjoins against the continuous, totally egalitarian redistribution of satisfactions, or wealth; but subject to that constraint, everyone should receive, by continuous redistribution if necessary, some minimal share of aggregate wealth so as to avoid a level of privation from which the opportunity to improve his situation becomes illusory.

The relationship of these highly general goals to the more specific environmental issues at hand may not be readily apparent, and I am not yet ready to demonstrate their pervasive implications. But let me give one indication of their implications. Recently scientists have informed us that use of DDT in food production is causing damage to the penguin population. For the present purposes let us accept that assertion as an indisputable scientific fact. The scientific fact is often asserted as if the correct implication—that we must stop agricultural use of DDT—followed from the mere statement of the fact of penguin damage. But plainly it does not follow if my criteria are employed.

My criteria are oriented to people, not penguins. Damage to penguins, or sugar pines, or geological marvels is, without more, simply irrelevant. One must go further, by my criteria, and say: Penguins are important because people enjoy seeing them walk about rocks; and furthermore, the well-being of people would be less impaired by halting use of DDT than by giving up penguins. In short, my observations about

environmental problems will be people-oriented, as are my criteria. I have no interest in preserving penguins for their own sake.

It may be said by way of objection to this position, that it is very selfish of people to act as if each person represented one unit of importance and nothing else was of any importance. It is undeniably selfish. Nevertheless I think it is the only tenable starting place for analysis for several reasons. First, no other position corresponds to the way most people really think and act—i.e., corresponds to reality.

Second, this attitude does not portend any massive destruction of nonhuman flora and fauna, for people depend on them in many obvious ways, and they will be preserved because and to the degree that humans do depend on them.

Third, what is good for humans is, in many respects, good for penguins and pine trees—clean air for example. So that humans are, in these respects, surrogates for plant and animal life.

Fourth, I do not know how we could administer any other system. Our decisions are either private or collective. Insofar as Mr. Jones is free to act privately, he may give such preferences as he wishes to other forms of life: he may feed birds in winter and do with less himself, and he may even decline to resist an advancing polar bear on the ground that the bear's appetite is more important than those portions of himself that the bear may choose to eat. In short my basic premise does not rule out private altruism to competing life-forms. It does rule out, however, Mr. Jones's inclination to feed Mr. Smith to the bear, however hungry the bear, however despicable Mr. Smith.

Insofar as we act collectively on the other hand, only humans can be afforded an opportunity to participate in the collective decisions. Penguins cannot vote now and are unlikely subjects for the franchise—pine trees more unlikely still. Again each individual is free to cast his vote so as to benefit sugar pines if that is his inclination. But many of the more extreme assertions that one hears from some conservationists amount to tacit assertions that they are specially appointed representatives of sugar pines, and hence that their preferences should be weighted more heavily than the preferences of other humans who do not enjoy equal rapport with "nature." The simplistic assertion that agricultural use of DDT must stop at once because it is harmful to penguins is of that type.

Fifth, if polar bears or pine trees or penguins, like men, are to be regarded as ends rather than means, if they are to count in our calculus of social organization, someone must tell me how much each one counts, and someone must tell me how these life-forms are to be permitted to express their preferences, for I do not know either answer. If the answer is that certain people are to hold their proxies, then I want to know how those proxy-holders are to be selected: self-appointment does not seem workable to me.

Sixth, and by way of summary of all the foregoing, let me point out that the set of environmental issues under discussion—although they raise very complex technical questions of how to achieve any objective—ultimately raise a normative question: what *ought* we to do. Questions of *ought* are unique to the human mind and world—they are meaningless as applied to a nonhuman situation.

I reject the proposition that we *ought* to respect the "balance of nature" or to "preserve the environment" unless the reason for doing so, express or implied, is the benefit of man.

I reject the idea that there is a "right" or "morally correct" state of nature to which we should return. The word "nature" has no normative connotation. Was it "right" or "wrong" for the earth's crust to heave in contortion and create mountains and seas? Was it "right" for the first amphibian to crawl up out of the primordial ooze? Was it "wrong" for plants to reproduce themselves and alter the atmospheric composition in favor of oxygen? For animals to alter the atmosphere in favor of carbon dioxide both by breathing oxygen and eating plants? No answers can be given to these questions because they are meaningless questions.

All this may seem obvious to the point of being tedious, but much of the present controversy over environment and pollution rests on tacit normative assumptions about just such non-normative phenomena: that it is "wrong" to impair penguins with DDT, but not to slaughter cattle for prime rib roasts. That it is wrong to kill stands of sugar pines with industrial fumes, but not to cut sugar pines and build housing for the poor. Every man is entitled to his own preferred definition of Walden Pond, but there is no definition that has any moral superiority over another, except by reference to the selfish needs of the human race.

From the fact that there is no normative definition of the natural state, it follows that there is no normative definition of clean air or pure water—hence no definition of polluted air—or of pollution—except by reference to the needs of man. The "right" composition of the atmosphere is one which has some dust in it and some lead in it and some hydrogen sulfide in it—just those amounts that attend a sensibly organized society thoughtfully and knowledgeably pursuing the greatest possible satisfaction for its human members.

The first and most fundamental step toward solution of our environmental problems is a clear recognition that our objective is not pure air or water but rather some optimal state of pollution. That step immediately suggests the question: How do we define and attain the level of pollution that will yield the maximum possible amount of human satisfaction?

Low levels of pollution contribute to human satisfaction but so do food and shelter and education and music. To attain ever lower levels of pollution, we must pay the cost of having less of these other things. I contrast that view of the cost of pollution control with the more popular statement that pollution control will "cost" very large numbers of dollars. The popular statement is true in some senses, false in others; sorting out the true and false senses is of some importance. The first step in that sorting process is to achieve a clear understanding of the difference between dollars and resources. Resources are the wealth of our nation; dollars are merely claim checks upon those resources. Resources are of vital importance; dollars are comparatively trivial.

Four categories of resources are sufficient for our purposes: At any given time a nation, or a planet if you prefer, has a stock of labor, of technological skill, of capital goods, and of natural resources (such as mineral deposits, timber, water, land, etc.). These resources can be used in various combinations to yield goods and services of all kinds—in some limited quantity. The quantity will be larger if they are combined efficiently, smaller if combined inefficiently. But in either event the resource stock is limited, the goods and services that they can be made to yield are limited; even the most efficient use of them will yield less than our population, in the aggregate, would like to have.

If one considers building a new dam, it is appropriate to say that it will be costly in the sense that it will require x hours of labor, y tons of steel and concrete, and z amount of capital goods. If these resources are devoted to the dam, then they cannot be used to build hospitals, fishing rods, schools, or electric can openers. That is the meaningful sense in which the dam is costly.

Quite apart from the very important question of how wisely we can combine our resources to produce goods and services, is the very different question of how they get distributed—who gets how many goods? Dollars constitute the claim checks which are distributed among people and which control their share of national output. Dollars are nearly valueless pieces of paper except to the extent that they do represent claim checks to some fraction of the output of goods and services. Viewed as claim checks, all the dollars outstanding during any period of time are worth, in the aggregate, the goods and services that are available to be claimed with them during that period—neither more nor less.

It is far easier to increase the supply of dollars than to increase the production of goods and services—printing dollars is easy. But printing more dollars doesn't help because each dollar then simply becomes a claim to fewer goods, i.e., becomes worth less.

The point is this: many people fall into error upon hearing the statement that the decision to build a dam, or to clean up a river, will cost $X million. It is regrettably easy to say: "It's only money. This is a wealthy country, and we have lots of money." But you cannot build a dam or clean a river with $X million—unless you also have a match, you can't even make a fire. One builds a dam or cleans a river by diverting labor and steel and trucks and factories from making one kind of goods to making another. The cost in dollars is merely a shorthand way of describing the extent of the diversion necessary. If we build a dam for $X million, then we must recognize that we will have $X million less housing and food

and medical care and electric can openers as a result.

Similarly, the costs of controlling pollution are best expressed in terms of the other goods we will have to give up to do the job. This is not to say the job should not be done. Badly as we need more housing, more medical care, more can openers, and more symphony orchestras, we could do with somewhat less of them, in my judgment at least, in exchange for somewhat cleaner air and rivers. But that is the nature of the trade-off, and analysis of the problem is advanced if that unpleasant reality is kept in mind. Once the trade-off relationship is clearly perceived, it is possible to state in a very general way what the optimal level of pollution is. I would state it as follows:

People enjoy watching penguins. They enjoy relatively clean air and smog-free vistas. Their health is improved by relatively clean water and air. Each of these benefits is a type of good or service. As a society we would be well advised to give up one washing machine if the resources that would have gone into that washing machine can yield greater human satisfaction when diverted into pollution control. We should give up one hospital if the resources thereby freed would yield more human satisfaction when devoted to elimination of noise in our cities. And so on, trade-off by trade-off, we should divert our productive capacities from the production of existing goods and services to the production of a cleaner, quieter, more pastoral nation up to—and no further than—the point at which we value more highly the next washing machine or hospital that we would have to do without than we value the next unit of environmental improvement that the diverted resources would create.

Now this proposition seems to me unassailable but so general and abstract as to be unhelpful—at least unadministerable in the form stated. It assumes we can measure in some way the incremental units of human satisfaction yielded by very different types of goods. . . . But I insist that the proposition stated describes the result for which we should be striving—and again, that it is always useful to know what your target is even if your weapons are too crude to score a bull's eye.

R E A D I N G
Deep Ecology

BILL DEVALL AND GEORGE SESSIONS

Study Questions

1. How do the authors describe mainstream environmentalism?
2. How do Devall and Sessions describe the alternative presented by deep ecology?
3. What do they mean by the term *ecological consciousness*?
4. How is this exemplified in Taoism, according to the authors?
5. What was the origin of the term *deep ecology*, and what are the two words in it supposed to signify?
6. How do the authors contrast the view of deep ecology with what they describe as the dominant worldview?
7. Describe the two ultimate norms or intuitions that they believe characterize deep ecology.
8. Explain briefly each of the eight basic principles of the platform of the deep ecology movement.

1. REFORM ENVIRONMENTALISM

Environmentalism is frequently seen as the attempt to work only within the confines of conventional political processes of industrialized nations to alleviate or mitigate some of the worst forms of air and water pollution, destruction of indigenous wildlife, and some of the most short-sighted development schemes.

One scenario for the environmental movement is to continue with attempts at reforming some natural resource policies. For example, ecoactivists can appeal administrative decisions to lease massive areas of public domain lands in the United States for mineral development, or oil and gas development. They can comment on draft Environmental Impact Reports; appeal to politicians to protect the scenic values of the nation; and call attention to the massive problems of toxic wastes, air and water pollution, and soil erosion. These political and educational activities call to the need for healthy ecosystems.

Bill Devall and George Sessions, *Deep Ecology: Living as If Nature Mattered*, pp. 2, 7–11, 65–73. Peregrine, 1985. Copyright © 1985 by Gibbs Smith, Publisher. Reproduced by permission.

However, environmentalism in this scenario tends to be very technical and oriented only to short-term public policy issues of resource allocation. Attempts are made to reform only some of the worst land use practices without challenging, questioning or changing the basic assumptions of economic growth and development. Environmentalists who follow this scenario will easily be labeled as "just another special issues group." In order to play the game of politics, they will be required to compromise on every piece of legislation in which they are interested.[1]

Generally, this business-as-usual scenario builds on legislative achievements such as the National Environmental Policy Act (NEPA) and the Endangered Species Act in the United States, and reform legislation on pollution and other environmental issues enacted in most industrialized nations.

This work is valuable. The building of proposed dams, for example, can be stopped by using economic arguments to show their economic liabilities. However, this approach has certain costs. One perceptive critic of this approach, Peter Berg, directs an organization seeking decentralist, local approaches to environmental problems. He says this approach "is like running a battlefield aid station in a war against a killing machine that operates beyond reach and that shifts its ground after each seeming defeat."[2] Reformist activists often feel trapped in the very political system they criticize. If they don't use the language of resource economists—language which converts ecology into "input-output models," forests into "commodity production systems," and which uses the metaphor of human economy in referring to Nature—then they are labeled as sentimental, irrational, or unrealistic.

Murray Bookchin, author of *The Ecology of Freedom* (1982) and *Post-Scarcity Anarchism* (1970), says the choice is clear. The environmental/ecology movement can "become institutionalized as an appendage of the very system whose structure and methods it professes to oppose," or it can follow the minority tradition. The minority tradition focuses on personal growth within a small community and selects a path to cultivating ecological consciousness while protecting the ecological integrity of the place.[3]

II. DEEP ECOLOGY AND CULTIVATING ECOLOGICAL CONSCIOUSNESS

In contrast to the preceding scenarios, deep ecology presents a powerful alternative.

Deep ecology is emerging as a way of developing a new balance and harmony between individuals, communities and all of Nature. It can potentially satisfy our deepest yearnings: faith and trust in our most basic intuitions; courage to take direct action; joyous confidence to dance with the sensuous harmonies discovered through spontaneous, playful intercourse with the rhythms of our bodies, the rhythms of flowing water, changes in the weather and seasons, and the overall processes of life on Earth. We invite you to explore the vision that deep ecology offers.

The deep ecology movement involves working on ourselves, what poet-philosopher Gary Snyder calls "the real work," the work of really looking at ourselves, of becoming more real.

This is the work we call cultivating ecological consciousness. This process involves becoming more aware of the actuality of rocks, wolves, trees, and rivers—the cultivation of the insight that everything is connected. Cultivating ecological consciousness is a process of learning to appreciate silence and solitude and rediscovering how to listen. It is learning how to be more receptive, trusting, holistic in perception, and is grounded in a vision of nonexploitive science and technology.

This process involves being honest with ourselves and seeking clarity in our intuitions, then acting from clear principles. It results in taking charge of our actions, taking responsibility, practicing self-discipline and working honestly within our community. It is simple but not easy work. Henry David Thoreau, nineteenth-century naturalist and writer, admonishes us, "Let your life be a friction against the machine."

Cultivating ecological consciousness is correlated with the cultivation of conscience. Cultural historian Theodore Roszak suggests in *Person/Planet* (1978),

"Conscience and consciousness, how instructive the overlapping similarity of those two words is. From the new consciousness we are gaining of ourselves as persons perhaps we will yet create a new conscience, one whose ethical sensitivity is at least tuned to a significant good, a significant evil."[4]

We believe that humans have a vital need to cultivate ecological consciousness and that this need is related to the needs of the planet. At the same time, humans need direct contact with untrammeled wilderness, places undomesticated for narrow human purposes.

Many people sense the needs of the planet and the need for wilderness preservation. But they often feel depressed or angry, impotent and under stress. They feel they must rely on "the other guy," the "experts." Even in the environmental movement, many people feel that only the professional staff of these organizations can make decisions because they are experts on some technical scientific matters or experts on the complex, convoluted political process. But we need not be technical experts in order to cultivate ecological consciousness. Cultivating ecological consciousness, as Thoreau said, requires that "we front up to the facts and determine to live our lives deliberately, or not at all." We believe that people can clarify their own intuitions, and act from deep principles.

Deep ecology is a process of ever-deeper questioning of ourselves, the assumptions of the dominant worldview in our culture, and the meaning and truth of our reality. We cannot change consciousness by only listening to others, we must involve ourselves. We must take direct action.

Organizations which work only in a conventional way on political issues and only in conventional politics will more or less unavoidably neglect the deepest philosophical-spiritual issues. But late industrial society is at a turning point, and the social and personal changes which are necessary may be aided by the flow of history.

One hopeful political movement with deep ecology as a base is the West German Green political party. They have as their slogan, "We are neither left nor right, we are in front." Green politics in West Germany, and to some extent in Great Britain, Belgium and Australia in the 1980s, goes beyond the conventional, liberal definition of a party, combining personal work (that is, work on clarifying one's own character) and political activism. In West Germany, especially, the Green party has sought a coalition with antinuclear weapons protesters, feminists, human rights advocates and environmentalists concerned with acid rain and other pollution in Europe.[5] Ecology is the first pillar of the German Greens' platform.

In Australia, the Greens are the most important political movement in the nation. In national and state elections in the early 1980s they were a deciding factor in electing Labor Party governments dedicated to some of the planks of the Green platform, including preserving wilderness national parks and rain forests.

The Greens present a promising political strategy because they encourage the cultivation of personal ecological consciousness as well as address issues of public policy. If the Greens propagate the biocentric perspective—the inherent worth of other species besides humans—then they can help change the current view which says we should use Nature only to serve narrow human interests. . . .

Alan Watts, who worked diligently to bring Eastern traditions to Western minds, used a very ancient image for this process, "invitation to the dance," and suggests that "the ways of liberation make it very clear that life is not going anywhere, because it is already there. In other words, it is playing, and those who do not play with it, have simply missed the point."[6]

Watts draws upon the Taoist sages, Sufi stories, Zen, and the psychology of Carl Jung to demonstrate the process of spontaneous understanding. It is recognized, however, that to say "you must be spontaneous" is to continue the massive double-bind that grips consciousness in the modern ethos.

The trick is to trick ourselves into reenchantment. As Watts says, "In the life of spontaneity, human consciousness shifts from the attitude of strained, willful attention to *koan*, the attitude of open attention or contemplation." This is a key element in developing ecological consciousness. This attitude forms the basis of a more "feminine" and receptive approach to love, an attitude which for that very reason is more considerate of women.[7]

In some Eastern traditions, the student is presented with a *koan*, a simple story or statement which may sound paradoxical or nonsensical on the surface but as the student turns and turns it in his or her mind, authentic understanding emerges. This direct action of turning and turning, seeing from different perspectives and from different depths, is required for the cultivation of consciousness. The *koan*-like phrase for deep ecology, suggested by prominent Norwegian philosopher Arne Naess, is: "simple in means, rich in ends."

Cultivating ecological consciousness based on this phrase requires the interior work of which we have been speaking, but also a radically different tempo of external actions, at least radically different from that experienced by millions and millions of people living "life in the fast lane" in contemporary metropolises. As Theodore Roszak concludes, "Things move slower; they stabilize at a simpler level. But none of this is experienced as a loss or a sacrifice. Instead, it is seen as a liberation from waste and busywork, from excessive appetite and anxious competition that allows one to get on with the essential business of life, which is to work out one's salvation with diligence."[8]

But I believe nevertheless that you will not have to remain without a solution if you will hold to objects that are similar to those from which my eyes now draw refreshment. If you will cling to Nature, to the simple in Nature, to the little things that hardly anyone sees, and that can so unexpectedly become big and beyond measuring; if you have this love of inconsiderable things and seek quite simply, as one who serves, to win the confidence of what seems poor: then everything will become easier, more coherent and somehow more conciliatory for you, not in your intellect, perhaps, which lags marveling behind, but in your inmost consciousness, waking and cognizance. . . . Be patient toward all that is unsolved in your heart and to try to love the *questions themselves* like locked rooms and like books that are written in a very foreign tongue. Do not now seek the answers, which cannot be given you because you would not be able to live them. And the point is, to live everything. Live the questions now. Perhaps you will then gradually, without noticing it, live along some distant day into the answer.

—Rainer Maria Rilke, *Letters to a Young Poet* (1963)

Quiet people, those working on the "real work," quite literally turn down the volume of noise in their lives. Gary Snyder suggests that, "The real work is what we really do. And what our lives are. And if we can live the work we have to do, knowing that we are real, and that the world is real, then it becomes right. And that's the real work: to make the world as real as it is and to find ourselves as real as we are within it."[9]

Engaging in this process, Arne Naess concludes, people ". . . will necessarily come to the conclusion that it is not lack of energy consumption that makes them unhappy."[10]

One metaphor for what we are talking about is found in the Eastern Taoist image, the *organic* self. Taoism tells us there is a way of unfolding which is inherent in all things. In the natural social order, people refrain from dominating others. Indeed, the ironic truth is that the more one attempts to control other people and control nonhuman Nature, the more disorder results, and the greater the degree of chaos. For the Taoist, spontaneity is not the opposite of order but identical with it because it flows from the unfolding of the inherent order. Life is not narrow, mean, brutish, and destructive. People do not engage in the seemingly inevitable conflict over scarce material goods. People have fewer desires and simple pleasures. In Taoism, the law is not required for justice; rather, the community of persons working for universal self-realization follows the flow of energy.[11]

To study the Way is to study the self.
To study the self is to forget the self.
To forget the self is to be enlightened by all things.
To be enlightened by all things is to remove the barriers between one's self and others.
—Dogen

As with many other Eastern traditions, the Taoist way of life is based on compassion, respect, and love for all things. This compassion arises from self-love, but self as part of the larger *Self*, not egotistical self-love.

DEEP ECOLOGY

The term *deep ecology* was coined by Arne Naess in his 1973 article, "The Shallow and the Deep, Long-Range Ecology Movements."[12] Naess was attempting to describe the deeper, more spiritual approach to Nature exemplified in the writings of Aldo Leopold and Rachel Carson. He thought that this deeper approach resulted from a more sensitive openness to ourselves and nonhuman life around us. The essence of deep ecology is to keep asking more searching questions about human life, society, and Nature as in the Western philosophical tradition of Socrates. As examples of this deep questioning, Naess points out "that we ask why and how, where others do not. For instance ecology as a science does not ask what kind of a society would be the best for maintaining a particular ecosystem—that is considered a question for value theory, for politics, for ethics." Thus deep ecology goes beyond the so-called factual scientific level to the level of self and Earth wisdom.

Deep ecology goes beyond a limited piecemeal shallow approach to environmental problems and attempts to articulate a comprehensive religious and philosophical worldview. The foundations of deep ecology are the basic intuitions and experiencing of ourselves and Nature which comprise ecological consciousness. Certain outlooks on politics and public policy flow naturally from this consciousness. And in the context of this book, we discuss the minority tradition as the type of community most conducive both to cultivating ecological consciousness and to asking the basic questions of values and ethics addressed in these pages.

Many of these questions are perennial philosophical and religious questions faced by humans in all cultures over the ages. What does it mean to be a unique human individual? How can the individual self maintain and increase its uniqueness while also being an inseparable aspect of the whole system wherein there are no sharp breaks between self and the *other*? An ecological perspective, in this deeper sense, results in what Theodore Roszak calls "an awakening of wholes greater than the sum of their parts. In spirit, the discipline is contemplative and therapeutic."[13]

Ecological consciousness and deep ecology are in sharp contrast with the dominant worldview of technocratic-industrial societies which regards humans as isolated and fundamentally separate from the rest of Nature, as superior to, and in charge of, the rest of creation. But the view of humans as separate and superior to the rest of Nature is only part of larger cultural patterns. For thousands of years, Western culture has become increasingly obsessed with the idea of *dominance*: with dominance of humans over nonhuman Nature, masculine over the feminine, wealthy and powerful over the poor, with the dominance of the West over non-Western cultures. Deep ecological consciousness allows us to see through these erroneous and dangerous illusions.

For deep ecology, the study of our place in the Earth household includes the study of ourselves as part of the organic whole. Going beyond a narrowly materialist scientific understanding of reality, the spiritual and the material aspects of reality fuse together. While the leading intellectuals of the dominant worldview have tended to view religion as "just superstition," and have looked upon ancient spiritual practice and enlightenment, such as found in Zen Buddhism, as essentially subjective, the search for deep ecological consciousness is the search for a more objective consciousness and state of being through an active deep questioning and meditative process and way of life.

Many people have asked these deeper questions and cultivated ecological consciousness within the context of different spiritual traditions—Christianity, Taoism, Buddhism, and Native American rituals, for example. While differing greatly in other regards, many in these traditions agree with the basic principles of deep ecology.

Warwick Fox, an Australian philosopher, has succinctly expressed the central intuition of deep ecology: "It is the idea that we can make no firm ontological divide in the field of existence: That there is no bifurcation in reality between the human and the non-human realms . . . to the extent that we perceive boundaries, we fall short of deep ecological consciousness."[14]

From this most basic insight or characteristic of deep ecological consciousness, Arne Naess has developed two ultimate norms or intuitions which are themselves not derivable from other principles or intuitions. They are arrived at by the deep questioning process and reveal the importance of moving to the philosophical and religious level of wisdom. They cannot be validated, of course, by the methodology of modern science based on its usual mechanistic assumptions and its very narrow defi-nition of data. These ultimate norms are *self-realization* and *biocentric equality*.

I. SELF-REALIZATION

In keeping with the spiritual traditions of many of the world's religions, the deep ecology norm of self-realization goes beyond the modern Western self which

is defined as an isolated ego striving primarily for hedonistic gratification or for a narrow sense of individual salvation in this life or the next. This socially programmed sense of the narrow self or social self dislocates us, and leaves us prey to whatever fad or fashion is prevalent in our society or social reference group. We are thus robbed of beginning the search for our unique spiritual/biological personhood. Spiritual growth, or unfolding, begins when we cease to understand or see ourselves as isolated and narrow competing egos and begin to identify with other humans from our family and friends to, eventually, our species. But the deep ecology sense of self requires a further maturity and growth, an identification which goes beyond humanity to include the nonhuman world. We must see beyond our narrow contemporary cultural assumptions and values, and the conventional wisdom of our time and place, and this is best achieved by the meditative deep questioning process. Only in this way can we hope to attain full mature personhood and uniqueness.

A nurturing nondominating society can help in the "real work" of becoming a whole person. The "real work" can be summarized symbolically as the realization of "self-in-Self" where "Self" stands for organic wholeness. This process of the full unfolding of the self can also be summarized by the phrase, "No one is saved until we are all saved," where the phrase "one" includes not only me, an individual human, but all humans, whales, grizzly bears, whole rain forest ecosystems, mountains and rivers, the tiniest microbes in the soil, and so on.

II. BIOCENTRIC EQUALITY

The intuition of biocentric equality is that all things in the biosphere have an equal right to live and blossom and to reach their own individual forms of unfolding and self-realization within the larger Self-realization. This basic intuition is that all organisms and entities in the ecosphere, as parts of the interrelated whole, are equal in intrinsic worth. Naess suggests that biocentric equality as an intuition is true in principle, although in the process of living, all species use each other as food, shelter, etc. Mutual predation is a biological fact of life, and many of the world's religions have struggled with the spiritual implications of this. Some animal liberationists who attempt to side-step this problem by advocating vegetarianism are forced to say that the entire plant kingdom including rain forests have no right to their own existence. This evasion flies in the face of the basic intuition of equality.[15] Aldo Leopold expressed this intuition when he said humans are "plain citizens" of the biotic community, not lord and master over all other species.

Biocentric equality is intimately related to the all-inclusive Self-realization in the sense that if we harm the rest of Nature then we are harming ourselves. There are no boundaries and everything is interrelated. But insofar as we perceive things as individual organisms or entities, the insight draws us to respect all human and nonhuman individuals in their own right as parts of the whole without feeling the need to set up hierarchies of species with humans at the top.

The practical implications of this intuition or norm suggest that we should live with minimum rather than maximum impact on other species and on the Earth in general. Thus we see another aspect of our guiding principle: "simple in means, rich in ends." . . .

A fuller discussion of the biocentric norm as it unfolds itself in practice begins with the realization that we, as individual humans, and as communities of humans, have vital needs which go beyond such basics as food, water, and shelter to include love, play, creative expression, intimate relationships with a particular landscape (or Nature taken in its entirety) as well as intimate relationships with other humans, and the vital need for spiritual growth, for becoming a mature human being.

Our vital material needs are probably more simple than many realize. In technocratic-industrial societies there is overwhelming propaganda and advertising which encourages false needs and destructive desires designed to foster increased production and consumption of goods. Most of this actually diverts us from facing reality in an objective way and from beginning the "real work" of spiritual growth and maturity.

Many people who do not see themselves as supporters of deep ecology nevertheless recognize an overriding vital human need for a healthy and high-quality natural environment for humans, if not for all life, with minimum intrusion of toxic waste, nuclear radiation from human enterprises, minimum acid rain and smog, and enough free flowing wilderness so humans can get in touch with their sources, the natural rhythms and the flow of time and place.

Drawing from the minority tradition and from the wisdom of many who have offered the insight of interconnectedness, we recognize that deep ecologists can offer suggestions for gaining maturity and encouraging the processes of harmony with Nature, but that there is no grand solution which is guaranteed to save us from ourselves.

The ultimate norms of deep ecology suggest a view of the nature of reality and our place as an individual (many in the one) in the larger scheme of things. They cannot be fully grasped intellectually but are ultimately experiential. . . .

As a brief summary of our position thus far, Figure 1 summarizes the contrast between the dominant worldview and deep ecology.

Dominant Worldview	Deep Ecology
• Dominance over Nature	• Harmony with Nature
• Natural environment as resource for humans	• All nature has intrinsic worth/biospecies equality
• Material/economic growth for growing human population	• Elegantly simple material needs (material goals serving the larger goal of self-realization)
• Belief in ample resource reserves	• Earth "supplies" limited
• High technological progress and solutions	• Appropriate technology; nondominating science
• Consumerism	• Doing with enough/recycling
• National/centralized community	• Minority tradition/bioregion

Figure 1

III. BASIC PRINCIPLES OF DEEP ECOLOGY

In April 1984, during the advent of spring and John Muir's birthday, George Sessions and Arne Naess summarized fifteen years of thinking on the principles of deep ecology while camping in Death Valley, California. In this great and special place, they articulated these principles in a literal, somewhat neutral way, hoping that they would be understood and accepted by persons coming from different philosophical and religious positions.

Readers are encouraged to elaborate their own versions of deep ecology, clarify key concepts and think through the consequences of acting from these principles.

Basic Principles

1. The well-being and flourishing of human and nonhuman Life on Earth have value in themselves (synonyms: intrinsic value, inherent value). These values are independent of the usefulness of the nonhuman world for human purposes.
2. Richness and diversity of life forms contribute to the realization of these values and are also values in themselves.
3. Humans have no right to reduce this richness and diversity except to satisfy *vital* needs.
4. The flourishing of human life and cultures is compatible with a substantial decrease of the human population. The flourishing of nonhuman life requires such a decrease.
5. Present human interference with the nonhuman world is excessive, and the situation is rapidly worsening.
6. Policies must therefore be changed. These policies affect basic economic, technological, and ideological structures. The resulting state of affairs will be deeply different from the present.
7. The ideological change is mainly that of appreciating *life quality* (dwelling in situations of inherent value) rather than adhering to an increasingly higher standard of living. There will be a profound awareness of the difference between the big and the great.
8. Those who subscribe to the foregoing points have an obligation directly or indirectly to try to implement the necessary changes.

Naess and Sessions Provide Comments on the Basic Principles

RE (1). This formulation refers to the biosphere, or more accurately, to the ecosphere as a whole. This includes individuals, species, populations, habitat, as well as human and nonhuman cultures. From our current knowledge of all-pervasive intimate relationships, this implies a fundamental deep concern and respect. Ecological processes of the planet should, on the whole, remain intact. "The world environment should remain 'natural'" (Gary Snyder).

The term "life" is used here in a more comprehensive nontechnical way to refer also to what biologists classify as "nonliving"; rivers (watersheds), landscapes, ecosystems. For supporters of deep ecology, slogans such as "Let the river live" illustrate this broader usage so common in most cultures.

Inherent value as used in (1) is common in deep ecology literature ("The presence of inherent value in a natural object is independent of any awareness, interest, or appreciation of it by a conscious being.")[16]

RE (2). More technically, this is a formulation concerning diversity and complexity. From an ecological standpoint, complexity and symbiosis are conditions for maximizing diversity. So-called simple, lower, or primitive species of plants and animals contribute essentially to the richness and diversity of life. They have value in themselves and are not merely steps toward the so-called higher or rational life forms. The second principle presupposes that life itself, as a process over evolutionary time, implies an increase of diversity and richness. The refusal to acknowledge that some life forms have greater or lesser intrinsic value than others (see points 1 and 2) runs counter to the formulations of some ecological philosophers and New Age writers.

Complexity, as referred to here, is different from complication. Urban life may be more complicated than life in a natural setting without being more complex in the sense of multifaceted quality.

RE (3). The term "vital need" is left deliberately vague to allow for considerable latitude in judgment. Differences in climate and related factors, together with differences in the structures of societies as they now exist, need to be considered (for some Eskimos, snowmobiles are necessary today to satisfy vital needs).

People in the materially richest countries cannot be expected to reduce their excessive interference with the nonhuman world to a moderate level overnight. The stabilization and reduction of the human population will take time. Interim strategies need to be developed. But this in no way excuses the present complacency—the extreme seriousness of our current situation must first be realized. But the longer we wait the more drastic will be the measures needed. Until deep changes are made, substantial decreases in richness and diversity are liable to occur: the rate of extinction of species will be ten to one hundred times greater than any other period of earth history.

RE (4). The United Nations Fund for Population Activities in their State of World Population Report (1984) said that high human population growth rates (over 2.0 percent annum) in many developing countries "were diminishing the quality of life for many millions of people." During the decade 1974–1984, the world population grew by nearly 800 million—more than the size of India. "And we will be adding about one Bangladesh (population 93 million) per annum between now and the year 2000."

The report noted that "The growth rate of the human population has declined for the first time in human history. But at the same time, the number of people being added to the human population is bigger than at any time in history because the population base is larger."

Most of the nations in the developing world (including India and China) have as their official government policy the goal of reducing the rate of human population increase, but there are debates over the types of measures to take (contraception, abortion, etc.) consistent with human rights and feasibility.

The report concludes that if all governments set specific population targets as public policy to help alleviate poverty and advance the quality of life, the current situation could be improved.

As many ecologists have pointed out, it is also absolutely crucial to curb population growth in the so-called developed (i.e., overdeveloped) industrial societies. Given the tremendous rate of consumption and waste production of individuals in these societies, they represent a much greater threat and impact on the biosphere per capita than individuals in Second and Third World countries.

RE (5). This formulation is mild. For a realistic assessment of the situation, see the unabbreviated version of the I.U.C.N.'s *World Conservation Strategy*. There are other works to be highly recommended, such as Gerald Barney's *Global 2000 Report to the President of the United States*.

The slogan of "noninterference" does not imply that humans should not modify some ecosystems as do other species. Humans have modified the earth and will probably continue to do so. At issue is the nature and extent of such interference.

The fight to preserve and extend areas of wilderness or near-wilderness should continue and should focus on the general ecological functions of these areas (one such function: large wilderness areas are required in the biosphere to allow for continued evolutionary speciation of animals and plants). Most present designated wilderness areas and game preserves are not large enough to allow for such speciation.

RE (6). Economic growth as conceived and implemented today by the industrial states is incompatible with (1)–(5). There is only a faint resemblance between ideal sustainable forms of economic growth and present policies of the industrial societies. And "sustainable" still means "sustainable in relation to humans."

Present ideology tends to value things because they are scarce and because they have a commodity value. There is prestige in vast consumption and waste (to mention only several relevant factors).

Whereas "self-determination," "local community," and "think globally, act locally," will remain key terms in the ecology of human societies, nevertheless the implementation of deep changes requires increasingly global action—action across borders.

Governments in Third World countries (with the exception of Costa Rica and a few others) are uninterested in deep ecological issues. When the governments of industrial societies try to promote ecological measures through Third World governments, practically nothing is accomplished (e.g., with problems of desertification). Given this situation, support for the global action through nongovernmental international organizations becomes increasingly important. Many of these organizations are able to act globally "from grassroots to grassroots," thus avoiding negative governmental interference.

Cultural diversity today requires advanced technology, that is, techniques that advance the basic goals of each culture. So-called soft, intermediate, and alternative technologies are steps in this direction.

RE (7). Some economists criticize the term "quality of life" because it is supposed to be vague. But on closer inspection, what they consider to be vague is actually the nonquantitative nature of the term. One cannot quantify adequately what is important for the quality of life as discussed here, and there is no need to do so.

RE (8). There is ample room for different opinions about priorities: what should be done first, what next? What is most urgent? What is clearly necessary as opposed to what is highly desirable but not absolutely pressing?

NOTES

1. The most informative recent book on reformist environmentalism in the context of British society is Philip Lowe and Jane Goyder's *Environmental Groups in Politics* (London: George Allen, 1983).
   Sociological explanations of the environmental movement in North America are found in Craig R. Humphrey and Frederick R. Butell's *Environment, Energy and Society* (Belmont, CA: Wadsworth, 1983); Allan Schnaiberg's *The Environment: From Surplus to Scarcity* (New York: Oxford, 1980); Lester Milbrath's *Environmentalists* (Albany: State University of New York Press, 1984); "Sociology of the Environment," *Sociological Inquiry 53* (Spring 1983); Jonathon Porritt, *Green: The Politics of Ecology Explained* (New York: Basil Blackwell, 1985).

2. Peter Berg, editorial, *Raise the Stakes* (Fall 1983).

3. Murray Bookchin, "Open Letter to the Ecology Movement," *Rain* (April 1980), as well as other publications.

4. Theodore Roszak, *Person/Planet* (Garden City, NY: Doubleday, 1978), p. 99.

5. Fritjof Capra and Charlene Spretnak, *Green Politics* (New York: E.P. Dutton, 1984).

6. Alan Watts, *Psychotherapy East and West* (New York: Vintage, 1975), p. 184.

7. ——. *Nature, Man and Woman* (New York: Vintage, 1970), p. 178.

8. Roszak, p. 296.

9. Gary Snyder, *The Real Work* (New York: New Directions, 1980), p. 81.

10. Stephen Bodian, "Simple in Means, Rich in Ends: A Conversation with Arne Naess," *Ten Directions* (California: Institute for Transcultural Studies, Zen Center of Los Angeles, Summer/Fall 1982).

11. Po-Keung Ip, "Taoism and the Foundations of Environmental Ethics," *Environmental Ethics 5* (Winter 1983), pp. 335–344.

12. Arne Naess, "The Shallow and The Deep, Long-Range Ecology Movements: A Summary," *Inquiry 16* (Oslo, 1973), pp. 95–100.

13. Theodore Roszak, *Where the Wasteland Ends* (New York: Anchor, 1972).

14. Warwick Fox, "Deep Ecology: A New Philosophy of Our Time?" *The Ecologist*, v. 14, 506, 1984, pp. 194–200. Arne Naess replies, "Intuition, Intrinsic Value and Deep Ecology," *The Ecologist*, v. 14, 5–6, 1984, pp. 201–204.

15. Tom Regan, *The Case for Animal Rights* (New York: Random House, 1983). For excellent critiques of the animal rights movement, see John Rodman, "The Liberation of Nature?" *Inquiry 20* (Oslo, 1977). J. Baird Callicott, "Animal Liberation," *Environmental Ethics 2*, 4 (1980); see also John Rodman, "Four Forms of Ecological Consciousness Reconsidered" in T. Attig and D. Scherer (Eds.), *Ethics and the Environment* (Englewood Cliffs, NJ: Prentice Hall, 1983).

16. Tom Regan, "The Nature and Possibility of an Environmental Ethic," *Environmental Ethics 3* (1981), pp. 19–34.

READING
Radical American Environmentalism and Wilderness Preservation: A Third World Critique

RAMACHANDRA GUHA

Study Questions

1. What four characteristics of deep ecology does Guha list?
2. What are his criticisms of the four?
3. Why does he think the emphasis on wilderness preservation is harmful?
4. What problems does he have with the invocation of eastern religions?
5. How is deep ecology related to consumerism?
6. How do the Indian environmental views and the German green movements better reflect a good environmentalism, according to Guha?
7. How does he believe that elements of deep ecology favor the rich and urban elite in the third world?
8. What point does he want to make with the reference to J. K. Galbraith?

The respected radical journalist Kirkpatrick Sale recently celebrated "the passion of a new and growing movement that has become disenchanted with the environmental establishment and has in recent years mounted a serious and sweeping attack on it—style, substance, systems, sensibilities and all."[1] The vision of those whom Sale calls the "New Ecologists"—and what I refer to in this article as deep ecology—is a compelling one. Decrying the narrowly economic goals of mainstream environmentalism, this new movement aims at nothing less than a philosophical and cultural revolution in human attitudes toward nature. In contrast to the conventional lobbying efforts of environmental professionals based in Washington, it proposes a militant defence of "Mother Earth," an unflinching opposition to human attacks on undisturbed wilderness. With their goals ranging from the spiritual to the political, the adherents of deep ecology span a wide spectrum of the American environmental movement. . . .

In this article I develop a critique of deep ecology from the perspective of a sympathetic outsider. . . . I

Ramachandra Guha, "Radical American Environmentalism and Wilderness Preservation: A Third World Critique," *Environmental Ethics* 11 (Spring 1989), pp. 71–83. Reproduced by permission of the publisher and the author.

speak admittedly as a partisan, but of the environmental movement in India, a country with an ecological diversity comparable to the U.S., but with a radically dissimilar cultural and social history. . . . Specifically, I examine the cultural rootedness of a philosophy that likes to present itself in universalistic terms. I make two main arguments: first, that deep ecology is uniquely American, and despite superficial similarities in rhetorical style, the social and political goals of radical environmentalism in other cultural contexts (e.g., West Germany and India) are quite different; second, that the social consequences of putting deep ecology into practice on a worldwide basis (what its practitioners are aiming for) are very grave indeed.

THE TENETS OF DEEP ECOLOGY

. . . Adherents of the deep ecological perspective in [America], while arguing intensely among themselves over its political and philosophical implications, share some fundamental premises about human-nature interactions. As I see it, the defining characteristics of deep ecology are fourfold:

First, deep ecology argues that the environmental movement must shift from an "anthropocentric" to a "biocentric" perspective. In many respects, an acceptance of the primacy of this distinction constitutes the litmus test of deep ecology. A considerable effort is expended by deep ecologists in showing that the dominant motif in Western philosophy has been anthropocentric—i.e., the belief that man and his works are the center of the universe—and conversely, in identifying those lonely thinkers (Leopold, Thoreau, Muir, Aldous Huxley, Santayana, etc.) who, in assigning man a more humble place in the natural order, anticipated deep ecological thinking. In the political realm, meanwhile, establishment environmentalism (shallow ecology) is chided for casting its arguments in human-centered terms. Preserving nature, the deep ecologists say, has an intrinsic worth quite apart from any benefits preservation may convey to future human generations.

The anthropocentric-biocentric distinction is accepted as axiomatic by deep ecologists, it structures their discourse, and much of the present discussions remains mired within it.

The second characteristic of deep ecology is its focus on the preservation of unspoilt wilderness—and the restoration of degraded areas to a more pristine condition—to the relative (and sometimes absolute) neglect of other issues on the environmental agenda. . . . Morally, [this] is an imperative that follows from the biocentric perspective; other species of plants and animals, and nature itself, have an intrinsic right to exist. . . . The preservation of wilderness also turns on a scientific argument—viz., the value of biological diversity in stabilizing ecological regimes and in retaining a gene pool for future generations. Truly radical policy proposals have been put forward by deep ecologists on the basis of these arguments. The influential poet Gary Snyder, for example, would like to see a 90 percent reduction in human populations to allow a restoration of pristine environments, while others have argued forcefully that a large portion of the globe must be immediately cordoned off from human beings.

Third, there is a widespread invocation of Eastern spiritual traditions as forerunners of deep ecology. Deep ecology, it is suggested, was practiced both by major religious traditions and at a more popular level by "primal" peoples in non-Western settings. This complements the search for an authentic lineage in Western thought. At one level, the task is to recover those dissenting voices within the Judeo-Christian tradition; at another, to suggest that religious traditions in other cultures are, in contrast, dominantly if not exclusively "biocentric" in their orientation. This coupling of (ancient) Eastern and (modern) ecological wisdom seemingly helps consolidate the claim that deep ecology is a philosophy of universal significance.

Fourth, deep ecologists, whatever their internal differences, share the belief that they are the "leading edge" of the environmental movement. As the polarity of the shallow/deep and anthropocentric/biocentric distinctions makes clear, they see themselves as the spiritual, philosophical, and political vanguard of American and world environmentalism.

TOWARD A CRITIQUE

Although I analyze each of these tenets independently, it is important to recognize, as deep ecologists are fond of remarking in reference to nature, the interconnectedness and unity of these individual themes.

1. Insofar as it has begun to act as a check on man's arrogance and ecological hubris, the transition from an anthropocentric (human-centered) to a biocentric (humans as only one element in the ecosystem) view in both religious and scientific traditions is only to be welcomed. What is unacceptable are the radical conclusions drawn by deep ecology, in particular, that intervention in nature should be guided primarily by the need to preserve biotic integrity rather than by the needs of humans. The latter for deep ecologists is anthropocentric, the former biocentric. This dichotomy is, however, of very little use in understanding the dynamics of environmental degradation. The two fundamental ecological problems facing the globe are (i) overconsumption by the industrialized world and by urban elites in the Third World and (ii) growing militarization, both in a short-term sense (i.e., ongoing regional wars) and in a long-term sense (i.e., the arms race and the prospect of nuclear annihilation). Neither of these problems has any tangible connection to the anthropocentric-biocentric distinction. Indeed, the agents of these processes would barely comprehend this philosophical dichotomy. The proximate causes of the ecologically wasteful characteristics of industrial society and of militarization are far more mundane: at an aggregate level, the dialectic of economic and political structures, and at a micro-level, the life-style choices of individuals. These causes cannot be reduced, whatever the level of analysis, to a deeper anthropocentric attitude toward nature; on the contrary, by constituting a grave threat to human survival, the ecological degradation they cause does not even serve the best interests of human beings! If my identification of the major dangers to the integrity of the natural world is correct, invoking the bogy of anthropocentricism is at best irrelevant and at worst a dangerous obfuscation.

2. If the above dichotomy is irrelevant, the emphasis on wilderness is positively harmful when applied to the Third World. If in the U.S. the preservationist/utilitarian division is seen as mirroring the conflict

between "people" and "interests," in countries such as India the situation is very nearly the reverse. Because India is a long settled and densely populated country in which agrarian populations have a finely balanced relationship with nature, the setting aside of wilderness areas has resulted in a direct transfer of resources from the poor to the rich. Thus, Project Tiger, a network of parks hailed by the international conservation community as an outstanding success, sharply posits the interests of the tiger against those of poor peasants living in and around the reserve. The designation of tiger reserves was made possible only by the physical displacement of existing villages and their inhabitants; their management requires the continuing exclusion of peasants and livestock. The initial impetus for setting up parks for the tiger and other large mammals such as the rhinoceros and elephant came from two social groups, first, a class of ex-hunters turned conservationists belonging mostly to the declining Indian feudal elite and second, representatives of international agencies, such as the World Wildlife Fund (WWF) and the International Union for the Conservation of Nature and Natural Resources (IUCN), seeking to transplant the American system of national parks onto Indian soil. In no case have the needs of the local population been taken into account, and as in many parts of Africa, the designated wildlands are managed primarily for the benefit of rich tourists. Until very recently, wildlands preservation has been identified with environmentalism by the state and the conservation elite; in consequence, environmental problems that impinge far more directly on the lives of the poor—e.g., fuel, fodder, water shortages, soil erosion, and air and water pollution—have not been adequately addressed.

Deep ecology provides, perhaps unwittingly, a justification for the continuation of such narrow and inequitable conservation practices under a newly acquired radical guise. Increasingly, the international conservation elite is using the philosophical, moral, and scientific arguments used by deep ecologists in advancing their wilderness crusade. A striking but by no means atypical example is the recent plea by a prominent American biologist for the takeover of large portions of the globe by the author and his scientific colleagues. Writing in a prestigious scientific forum, the *Annual*

Review of Ecology and Systematics, Daniel Janzen argues that only biologists have the competence to decide how the tropical landscape should be used. . . . Janzen exhorts his colleagues to advance their territorial claims on the tropical world more forcefully, warning that the very existence of these areas is at stake: "if biologists want a tropics in which to biologize, they are going to have to buy it with care, energy, effort, strategy, tactics, time, and cash."[2]

This frankly imperialist manifesto highlights the multiple dangers of the preoccupation with wilderness preservation that is characteristic of deep ecology. As I have suggested, it seriously compounds the neglect by the American movement of far more pressing environmental problems within the Third World. But perhaps more importantly, and in a more insidious fashion, it also provides an impetus to the imperialist yearning of Western biologists and their financial sponsors, organizations such as the WWF and IUCN. The wholesale transfer of a movement culturally rooted in American conservation history can only result in the social uprooting of human populations in other parts of the globe.

3. I come now to the persistent invocation of Eastern philosophies as antecedent in point of time but convergent in their structure with deep ecology. Complex and internally differentiated religious traditions—Hinduism, Buddhism, and Taoism—are lumped together as holding a view of nature believed to be quintessentially biocentric. Individual philosophers such as the Taoist Lao Tzu are identified as being forerunners of deep ecology. Even an intensely political, pragmatic, and Christian-influenced thinker such as Gandhi has been accorded a wholly undeserved place in the deep ecological pantheon. Thus the Zen teacher Robert Aitken Roshi makes the strange claim that Gandhi's thought was not human-centered and that he practiced an embryonic form of deep ecology which is "traditionally Eastern and is found with differing emphasis in Hinduism, Taoism and in Theravada and Mahayana Buddhism."[3] Moving away from the realm of high philosophy and scriptural religion, deep ecologists make the further claim that at the level of material and spiritual practice "primal" peoples subordinated themselves to the integrity of the biotic universe they inhabited.

I have indicated that this appropriation of Eastern traditions is in part dictated by the need to construct an authentic lineage and in part a desire to present deep ecology as a universalistic philosophy. . . . As it stands, [this reading] does considerable violence to the historical record. Throughout most recorded history the characteristic form of human activity in the "East" has been a finely tuned but nonetheless conscious and dynamic manipulation of nature. Although mystics such as Lao Tzu did reflect on the spiritual essence of human relations with nature, it must be recognized that such ascetics and their reflections were supported by a society of cultivators whose relationship with nature was a far more *active* one. Many agricultural communities do have a sophisticated knowledge of the natural environment that may equal (and sometimes surpass) codified "scientific" knowledge; yet, the elaboration of such traditional ecological knowledge (in both material and spiritual contexts) can hardly be said to rest on a mystical affinity with nature of a deep ecological kind. . . .

In a brilliant article, the Chicago historian Ronald Inden points out that this romantic and essentially positive view of the East is a mirror image of the scientific and essentially pejorative view normally upheld by Western scholars of the Orient. In either case, the East constitutes the Other, a body wholly separate and alien from the West; it is defined by a uniquely spiritual and nonrational "essence," even if this essence is valorized quite differently by the two schools. Eastern man exhibits a spiritual dependence with respect to nature—on the one hand, this is symptomatic of his prescientific and backward self, on the other, of his ecological wisdom and deep ecological consciousness. Both views are monolithic, simplistic, and have the characteristic effect—intended in one case, perhaps unintended in the other—of denying agency and reason to the East and making it the privileged orbit of Western thinkers. . . .

4. How radical, finally, are the deep ecologists? . . . To my mind, deep ecology is best viewed as a radical trend within the wilderness preservation movement. Although advancing philosophical rather than aesthetic arguments and encouraging political militancy rather than negotiation, its practical emphasis—viz., preservation of unspoilt nature—is virtually identical. For the mainstream movement, the function of wilderness is to provide a temporary antidote to modern civilization. As a special institution within an industrialized society, the national park "provides an opportunity for respite, contrast, contemplation, and affirmation of values for those who live most of their lives in the workaday world."[4] Indeed, the rapid increase in visitations to the national parks in postwar America is a direct consequence of economic expansion. . . .

Here, the enjoyment of nature is an integral part of the consumer society. The private automobile (and the life style it has spawned) is in many respects the ultimate ecological villain, and an untouched wilderness the prototype of ecological harmony; yet, for most Americans it is perfectly consistent to drive a thousand miles to spend a holiday in a national park. They possess a vast, beautiful, and sparsely populated continent and are also able to draw upon the natural resources of large portions of the globe by virtue of their economic and political dominance. In consequence, America can simultaneously enjoy the material benefits of an expanding economy and the aesthetic benefits of unspoilt nature. The two poles of "wilderness" and "civilization" mutually coexist in an internally coherent whole, and philosophers of both poles are assigned a prominent place in this culture. Paradoxically as it may seem, it is no accident that Star Wars technology and deep ecology both find their fullest expression in that leading sector of Western civilization, California.

Deep ecology runs parallel to the consumer society without seriously questioning its ecological and socio-political basis. . . . The archetypal concerns of radical environmentalists in other cultural contexts are in fact quite different. The German Greens, for example, have elaborated a devastating critique of industrial society which turns on the acceptance of environmental limits to growth. Pointing to the intimate links between industrialization, militarization, and conquest, the Greens argue that economic growth in the West has historically rested on the economic and ecological exploitation of the Third World.

[Hence] the roots of global ecological problems lie in the disproportionate share of resources consumed by the industrialized countries as a whole *and* the urban elite within the Third World. Since it is impossible to reproduce an industrial monoculture worldwide, the ecological movement in the West must begin by cleaning up its own act. . . . The expansionist character of modern Western man will have to give way to an ethic of renunciation and self-limitation, in which spiritual and communal values play an increasing role in sustaining social life. . . .

Many elements of the Green program find a strong resonance in countries such as India, where a history of Western colonialism and industrial development has benefited only a tiny elite while exacting tremendous social and environmental costs. The ecological battles presently being fought in India have as their epicenter the conflict over nature between the subsistence and largely rural sector and the vastly more powerful commercial-industrial sector. Perhaps the most celebrated of these battles concerns the Chipko (Hug the Tree) movement, a peasant movement against deforestation in the Himalayan foothills. Chipko is only one of several movements that have sharply questioned the nonsustainable demand being placed on the land and vegetative base by urban centers and industry. These include opposition to large dams by displaced peasants, the conflict between small artisan fishing and large-scale trawler fishing for export, the countrywide movements against commercial forest operations, and opposition to industrial pollution among downstream agricultural and fishing communities.

Two features distinguish these environmental movements from their Western counterparts. First, for the sections of society most critically affected by environmental degradation—poor and landless peasants, women, and tribals—it is a question of sheer survival, not of enhancing the quality of life. Second, and as a consequence, the environmental solutions they articulate deeply involve questions of equity as well as economic and political redistribution. Highlighting these differences, a leading Indian environmentalist stresses that "environmental protection per se is of least concern to most of these groups. Their main concern is about the use of the environment and who should benefit from it." They seek to wrest control of nature away from the state and the industrial sector and place it in the hands of rural communities who live within that environment but are increasingly denied access to it. These communities have far more basic needs, their demands on the environment are far less intense, and they can draw upon a reservoir of cooperative social institutions and

local ecological knowledge in managing the "commons"—forests, grasslands, and the waters—on a sustainable basis. If colonial and capitalist expansion has both accentuated social inequalities and signaled a precipitous fall in ecological wisdom, an alternate ecology must rest on an alternate society and polity as well.

This brief overview of German and Indian environmentalism has some major implications for deep ecology. Both German and Indian environmental traditions allow for a greater integration of ecological concerns with livelihood and work. They also place a greater emphasis on equity and social justice (both within individual countries and on a global scale) on the grounds that in the absence of social regeneration environmental regeneration has very little chance of succeeding, Finally, and perhaps most significantly, they have escaped the preoccupation with wilderness preservation so characteristic of American cultural and environmental history.

A HOMILY

In 1958, the economist J. K. Galbraith referred to overconsumption as the unasked question of the American conservation movement. There is a marked selectivity, he wrote, "in the conservationist's approach to materials consumption. If we are concerned about our great appetite for materials, it is plausible to seek to increase the supply, to decrease waste, to make better use of the stocks available, and to develop substitutes. But what of the appetite itself? Surely this is the ultimate source of the problem. If it continues its geometric course, will it not one day have to be restrained? Yet in the literature of the resource problem this is the forbidden question. Over it hangs a nearly total silence."[5]

The consumer economy and society have expanded tremendously in the three decades since Galbraith penned these words; yet his criticisms are nearly as valid today. I have said "nearly," for there are some hopeful signs. Within the environmental movement several dispersed groups are working to develop ecologically benign technologies and to encourage less wasteful life styles. Moreover, outside the self-defined boundaries of American environmentalism, opposition to the permanent war economy is being carried on by a peace movement that has a distinguished history and impeccable moral and political credentials . . . A truly radical ecology in the American context ought to work toward a synthesis of the appropriate technology, alternate life style, and peace movements. By making the (largely spurious) anthropocentric-biocentric distinction central to the debate, deep ecologists may have appropriated the moral high ground, but they are at the same time doing a serious disservice to American and global environmentalism.

NOTES

1. Kirkpatrick Sale, "The Forest for the Trees: Can Today's Environmentalists Tell the Difference," *Mother Jones* 11, No.8 (November 1986): 26.

2. Daniel Janzen, "The Future of Tropical Ecology," *Annual Review of Ecology and Systematics* 17 (1986): 305–306; emphasis added.

3. Robert Aitken Roshi, "Gandhi, Dogen, and Deep Ecology," reprinted as appendix C in Bill Devall and George Sessions, *Deep Ecology: Living as if Nature Mattered* (Salt Lake City: Peregrine Smith Books, 1985).

4. Joseph Sax, *Mountains Without Handrails: Reflections on the National Parks* (Ann Arbor: University of Michigan Press, 1980), 42.

5. John Kenneth Galbraith, "How Much Should a Country Consume?" in Henry Jarrett, ed., *Perspectives on Conservation* (Baltimore: Johns Hopkins Press, 1958), pp. 91–92.

REVIEW EXERCISES

1. What is meant by the term *environment*?
2. Why is the notion of *value* problematic?
3. What are the differences among intrinsic, instrumental, and *prima facie* values? Give an example of each.
4. What is anthropocentrism? How is it different from ecocentrism?
5. How do cost–benefit analyses function in environmental arguments? Give an example of an environmental problem today and how a cost–benefit analysis would be used to analyze it.
6. Describe two different types of ecocentrism.
7. What is Aldo Leopold's basic principle for determining what is right and wrong in environmental matters?
8. What is deep ecology? According to this view, what are the root causes of our environmental problems?
9. Summarize the different ecofeminist views described in this chapter.
10. What is "sustainable development" and why do developmentalists support it?

DISCUSSION CASES

1. The Greenhouse Effect. People disagree about the greenhouse effect. A minority believes that no actual warming trend has or will occur because of the release of greenhouse gases into the atmosphere. Others point out that there have been periods of warming and cooling throughout the Earth's history. Several bills are pending before the U.S. Congress that will restrict the amount of greenhouse gases that may be released into the atmosphere. Such legislation, if passed, would affect car manufacturers, coal-burning manufacturing plants, and the makers of aerosol sprays, cleaning solvents, and refrigerators.

As a member of Congress, would you vote for or against the bills? Why?

2. Preserving the Trees. XYZ Timber Company has been logging forests in the Pacific Northwest for decades. It has done moderately well in replanting where trees have been cut, but it has been cutting in areas where some trees are hundreds of years old. Now the company plans to build roads into a similar area of the forest and cut down similar groups of trees. An environmental group, "Trees First," is determined to prevent this. Its members have blocked the roads that have been put in by the timber company and also engaged in the practice known as *tree spiking*. In this practice, iron spikes are driven into trees to discourage the use of power saws. Loggers are outraged, because this makes cutting in such areas extremely dangerous. When their saws hit these spikes, they become uncontrollable, and loggers have been seriously injured. Forest rangers have been marking trees found to be spiked and noted that some spikes are in so far that they are not visible. They will be grown over and thus present a hidden danger for years to come. People from Trees First insist that this is the only way to prevent the shortsighted destruction of the forests.

Who is right? Why?

3. Asphalt Yard. Bill Homeowner has grown weary of keeping the vegetation on his property under control. Thus, he decides to simply pave over the whole of it.

Even if Bill had a legal right to do this to his property, would there be anything ethically objectionable about it? Why or why not?

4. Sustainable Development. What would you say to the people of the Amazon River basin region who burn the forest so that they can have land to farm to make a living for themselves and their families? The burning and the deforestation have negative worldwide effects. The people point out that North Americans already have destroyed much of their own forests and become prosperous, so is it fair that we now criticize them? We even may be contributing to the loss of the rain forest because we buy mahogany furniture that comes from trees grown there. What should be done?

YOU MAKE THE DECISION

Apply the theories and issues discussed in this chapter by accessing this animated simulation on the Ethics Resource Center.

Use the passkey that accompanies your book to gain access. If you do not have a passkey, visit cengagebrain.com to purchase instant access to additional study material.

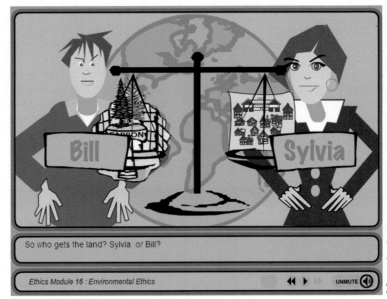

So who gets the land? Sylvia, or Bill?

Ethics Module 16 : Environmental Ethics

◀◀ ▶ ▶▶   UNMUTE ◀◉

© Cengage Learning

-17-
Animal Rights

I N MAY 2007, two humpback whales, a mother and her calf, became stranded up the Sacramento River in fresh water. They were migrating from Mexico to Alaska when they made a wrong turn and swam under the Golden Gate Bridge, into San Francisco Bay, and then up the Sacramento River to the Sacramento delta, some 90 miles from the Pacific Ocean. They caused quite a spectacle as sightseers lined the banks of the river to catch a glimpse of them. They were given the names of Delta, after the delta, and Dawn. After two weeks hanging around the port of Sacramento, they suddenly turned around and swam south some 20 miles. Then they hesitated to swim under a bridge that spanned the river. The Coast Guard had tried several means to encourage them to continue back to the ocean, including banging on underwater pipes, herding them with boats, playing killer whale sounds, and using a fire hose to create bubbles in the water. Still nothing seemed to be working. Thousands of people had sent e-mails and made phone calls to government agencies with suggestions of their own on how to get the whales to move on. Among their suggestions were using trained dolphins and dumping some of their favorite fish food downstream. People were becoming worried about these creatures because they had signs of injuries on their skin. Fortunately, the whales soon swam back into the Pacific Ocean.[1]

Why do people care about such creatures? And should they be spending so much time and effort

The humpback whale Delta breaches in the Sacramento River above Antioch, California.

Aaron Kehoe/UPI/Landov

when there are so many other needs of people to be served?

Every year, millions of Americans go hunting. Sometimes they are successful and sometimes not. However, part of their pleasure comes from just the uncertainty and skills involved. Recently, a new type of hunt has arisen, a hunt that is "rigged." For profit, companies have established areas and procedures in which animals are confined in certain ways and hunters have a much better chance of a kill or trophy. These companies obtain their animals from exotic animal auctions—for example, "zebras, camels, ostriches, kangaroos, and lion cubs."[2] Many hunters and hunters' groups as well as animal lovers have denounced these practices, which are, however, supported by the National Rifle Association. Critics believe that these practices are not only bad sport, but cruel. Although there are no federal laws prohibiting canned hunts, 20 states have now passed laws against them.[3]

In 1921, an Ontario doctor and his assistant severed the connection between the pancreases and digestive systems of dogs in order to find the substance that controlled diabetes. In so doing, they isolated insulin and thus opened the possibility for treating the millions of people who have that disease.[4] Today, laboratory researchers are using leopard frogs to test the pain-killing capacity of morphine, codeine, and Demerol. Japanese medaka fish are being used as a model to determine the cancer-causing properties of substances that are released into rivers and lakes. And research using the giant Israeli scorpion is determining whether a protein in its venom can help the 24,000 Americans who die each year from tumors called *gliomas*.[5]

The number of animals used in research and experimentation each year varies according to the source of the information and the category. "The Animal Welfare Act requires laboratories to report the number of animals used in experiments but it does not cover mice, rats, and birds (used in some 80 to 95 percent of all experiments)."[6] Nevertheless, estimates suggest that some 15 million animals in total are used in animal experiments each year in the United States. Worldwide, the estimate is between 60 million and 70 million used each year.[7] The number peaked in 1970 and has decreased ever since because of "higher standards of animal welfare, scientific advances, and stricter controls."[8] Still, in 2002, according to one accounting, 77,091 cats, 96,061 primates, 77,906 dogs, 304,039 guinea pigs, 312,630 rabbits, and 193,115 hamsters were used for research and experimentation in the United States alone.[9] All of these examples raise a basic question: Are we justified in using nonhuman animals for research that may help us humans, or is this wrongful and cruel treatment of other sentient beings?

U.S. laws that protect animals include the Marine Mammal Protection Act of 1972, which "establishes a moratorium on the taking and importation of marine mammals, including parts and products." The Department of the Interior is charged with enforcing the management and protection of sea otters, walruses, polar bears, dugong, and manatees.[10] The 1973 Endangered Species Act protects animals whose continued existence is threatened and whom the secretaries of the interior or commerce place on a list of endangered species.

International efforts to protect animal species are also under way. For example, international conferences such as the U.N. Convention on International Trade in Endangered Species, held in November 2002, in Santiago, Chile, try to address the problem. Among the issues that were to be decided at this particular conference were whether certain African nations should be allowed to sell ivory from their stockpiles. The United States, however, would continue to prohibit imports of ivory because elephants are protected in this country by not only the Endangered Species Act but also the by African Elephant Conservation Act.[11]

Although we would like to do things to help our fellow humans, we also care about the proper treatment of animals. However, we are less sure about what this requires of us and why. We are uncertain because we are often unclear about our ultimate reasons for what we think we can rightly do to animals. We relate to and depend on our nonhuman counterparts in many ways. They are pets and provide some of us with companionship and comfort. Many people enjoy watching them in our zoos and circuses. Others find sport in the racing of animals or in the display of riding skills. Animals are used for work, for example, in herding sheep and cattle. Some people find pleasure and others economic interest or necessity in the hunting and trapping of animals. Animals are sources of food (such as meat, fish, milk, eggs, and cheese, not to mention shark fin soup, fois gras, and whale meat sushi) and clothing (leather, fur, and wool). Animals are used in experiments to test not only the safety and effectiveness of medical drugs and devices but also the possible side effects of cosmetics. They provide us with medicinal aids such as hormones, blood-clotting factors, and treatments for diseases such as diabetes. "In fact, about forty percent of all prescriptions written today are composed from the natural compounds of different species."[12] Threats to the health of animal species can also warn us about possible dangers to human health. Nonhuman animals are also of obvious commercial benefit—as jobs and income come from fishing and tourism, for example. Recently, ecotourism, in which people travel to learn and appreciate and photograph animals in their natural habitats, has become quite popular. Animals are also sources of wonderment because of their variety, beauty, and strength. However, nonhuman animals are also sentient creatures. They can feel pleasure and pain just as we do and can at times seem almost human in their perceptions of and reactions to us. Thus, we can rightly ask whether we are justified in treating them in all of the ways we do.

SENTIENCE

According to some philosophers, sentience is the key to the ethical status of animals. In thinking about that status, some philosophers look to the utilitarian Jeremy Bentham, who wrote that to know the ethical status of animals, we need not ask if they can speak, but only whether or not they can suffer.[13] Besides feeling pleasure and pain, many higher animals probably also experience other types of emotions such as fear and anger. Unlike the philosopher Descartes, we do not think that animals are machines devoid of an inner sense or consciousness. Because of their sentience, we have laws that protect animals from cruelty. What counts as cruelty, however, will be disputed. Whether caging certain animals, for example, is cruel is a matter about which many people will disagree.

People also disagree about the reasons why we ought not to be cruel to animals. Some believe that a major reason is the effects on those who are cruel. If one is cruel to a sentient animal, then is he or she more likely to be cruel to people as well? The effects on the character of the person who is cruel to animals will also be negative. Moreover, those who witness cruelty to animals may be affected by it. They will themselves feel bad at seeing an animal suffer. Consider animals used for entertainment, as in circuses, rodeos, and zoos. "Not only are elephants, bears, tigers, and other animals abused by trainers, they suffer from extreme lonliness, boredom, and frustration from being locked in tiny cages month after month."[14]

However, unless one believes that only human suffering can be bad, then the reason most people would tend to give for the injunction to not to be cruel to animals is because the suffering of the animals is bad for them. Whether or not something is cruel to an animal might be determined by the extent of the pain the animal experiences, as when we speak of cruelty in terms of causing "unnecessary" pain. Not all pain is bad, even for us. It often tells us of some health problem that can be fixed. The badness of suffering also may be only *prima facie* bad. (See the discussion of this in the previous chapter.) The suffering may be worth it—that is, overcome by the good end to be achieved by it. Doing difficult things is sometimes painful, but we think it is sometimes worth the pain. In these cases, we experience not only the pain but also the benefit. In the case of animals, however, they would experience the pain of, say, an experiment performed on them while we would reap the benefit. Is this is ever justified? This is a central question for those who are concerned with our treatment of animals. Although we address the issue of animal experimentation below, it is well to consider in the first place whether and why the paining of animals is in itself a bad thing. We will also have to acknowledge that animals have different capacities to feel pain. Those with more developed and complex nervous systems and brains will likely have more capacity to feel pain as well as pleasure of various sorts.

One further comment on the issue of animal pain and pleasure is the following. In the wild, it is a fact of life that animals feed on and cause pain to one another. Predation prevails. Carnivores kill for food. The fawn is eaten by the cougar. Natural processes such as floods, fires, droughts, and volcanic eruptions also contribute to animal suffering and death. If animal suffering is important, then are we ethically obligated to lessen it in cases where we could do so? For example, in 1986 the Hubbard Glacier in Alaska began to move, and in a few weeks it had sealed off a particular fjord. Porpoises and harbor seals were trapped inside by the closure. Some people wanted to rescue the animals, while others held that this was a natural event that should be allowed to run its course.[15]

We tend to think that we are generally more bound not to *cause pain* or harm than we are to relieve it.

In special cases, admittedly, there may seem to be no difference where we are bound by some duty or relation to *relieve pain* or prevent the harm. A lifeguard may have an obligation to rescue a drowning swimmer that the ordinary bystander does not. A parent has more obligation to prevent harm to his or her child than a stranger does. In the case of nonhuman animals, would we say the same? Do we also feel constrained to prevent the pain and death to animals in the wild? In general, it would seem that although we may choose to do so out of sympathy, we may not be obligated to do so. At least the obligation to *prevent the harm* seems lesser in stringency than the obligation not to *cause* a similar harm. If there is this moral difference between preventing and causing harm, then we could not argue that because we can allow the animals in the wild to die or suffer pain from natural processes, we thus also may cause a similar pain or harm to them. However, we also may be inclined to think that just because nature is cruel does not give us the right to be so.

ANIMAL RIGHTS

It is one thing to say that the suffering of a nonhuman animal, just as the suffering of us humans, is a *bad* thing in itself. It is another to say that we or the nonhuman animals have a *right* not to be caused to suffer or feel pain. To know what to say about the question of animal rights, we need to think a little about what a right is or what it means to have a right. A *right* (as opposed to something being right instead of wrong) is generally defined as a strong and *legitimate claim* that can be made by a claimant against someone. Thus, if I claim a right to freedom of speech, I am asserting my legitimate claim against anyone who would prevent me from speaking out. (See the further discussion of negative and positive rights in Chapter 14.) A person can claim a right to have or be given something (a positive right) as well as not to be prevented from doing something (a negative type). I can claim the bicycle because it is mine. This would also mean that others have a duty not to take the bicycle from me. So also, if I have a right to health care, others may have a duty to provide it. Sometimes, it is a contractual or other relation that is

the reason why someone has a right to something. Thus, persons may come to have a right to care from a hospital because of a contractual relation they just have established, while a young child has a right to care from her parents because of the natural or legal relationship. We claim some rights as *legal rights*, because they are claims that the law recognizes and enforces. However, we also hold that there are *moral rights*—in other words, things we can rightly claim even if the law does not give its support to the claim. (Recall the discussion of natural rights in Chapter 7.)

Just who can legitimately claim a moral right to something, and on what grounds? One might think that to be the kind of being who can have rights, one must *be able to claim them*. If this were so, then the cat who is left money in a will would not have a right to it. But then neither would the infant who inherits the money. We think we speak correctly when we say that the infant has a right to care from its parents even if the infant does not recognize this right and cannot claim it. *Future generations* do not even exist, and yet some believe that they have at least contingent rights (rights if they come to exist) that we not leave them a garbage-heap world depleted of natural resources.[16] Or one might think that only *moral agents* have rights. According to this view, only if one is a full member of the moral community with duties and responsibilities does one have rights. On the other hand, it is not unreasonable to think that this is too stringent a requirement. Perhaps it is sufficient for one to be a *moral patient* in order to be the type of being who can have rights. In other words, if one is the kind of being to whom what we do matters morally in itself, then one is the kind of being who can have rights. If this is the case and if (as we considered in the previous chapter) some trees can be thought to be moral patients, then they also would be rightly said to have rights. If this does not seem to be correct, then what other reasons should be given for why a being might have rights?

We could argue that it is just because they can feel pain that sentient beings have a *right not to suffer,* or at least not to suffer needlessly. This would mean that others have a *duty* with regard to this claim. However, we may have duties not to cause pain needlessly to animals even if they had no right not to be treated in ways that cause them pain. We have many duties to do or not do this or that which are not directly a matter of respecting anyone's rights. For example, I may have a duty not to destroy a famous building—but not because the building has a *right to exist*. Thus, from the fact that we have duties to animals, for example, not to make them suffer needlessly, we cannot necessarily conclude that they have rights. If we want to argue for this view, then we would need to make a clearer connection between duties and rights or to show why some particular duties also imply rights. Not all duties are a function of rights, as I might have a duty to develop my talents even though no one has a right that I do so. However, having a right seems to entail that someone has a duty to protect that right.

Some philosophers have pointed to the fact that animals have *interests* as a basis for asserting that they have rights. Having an interest in something is to have a consciousness of that thing and to want it. A being who has such a capacity is thus a being who can have rights, according to this position. Thus, Joel Feinberg says that it is because nonhuman animals have "conscious wishes, desires, and hopes; . . . urges and impulses," they are the kind of beings who can have rights.[17] It is these psychological capacities that give these animals the status that makes them capable of having rights to certain treatment, according to this view. Tom Regan argues that the reason nonhuman animals have rights just as we do is because they are what he calls the "subject of a life."[18] The idea is similar to Feinberg's in that it is the fact that animals have an inner life, which includes conscious desires and wants, that is the basis for their status as rights possessors. Nonhuman animals differ among themselves in their capacity to have these various psychic experiences, and it probably parallels the development and complexity of their nervous system. A dog may be able to experience fear, but most probably the flea on its ear does not. This difference would be a problem for these writers only in practice where we would have to determine the character of a particular animal's inner

life. The more serious challenge for them is to support the view itself that these inner psychic states are the basis for animal rights.

Peter Singer has made one of the stronger cases for the view that animals' interests are the basis for their having rights and rights that are equal to those of humans. (His article in this chapter gives the essence of this argument.) Animals may have different interests than we do, but that does not mean that their interests are to be taken more lightly. According to Singer, not to respect the interests of animals is *speciesism*.[19] This is, he believes, an objectionable attitude similar to racism or sexism—objectionable because it treats animals badly simply because they are members of a different species and gives preference to members of our own species simply because we are human beings. But on what grounds is this objectionable? According to Singer, having interests is connected to the ability to feel pleasure and pain, because the pleasure is derived from the satisfaction of an interest. Animals are different from plants in this regard. Plants have things that are *in their interest* even though they do not *have interests*. Because the interests of animals are similar to ours, they ought to be given equal weight, according to Singer. This does not mean that they have a right to whatever we have a right to. It would make no sense to say that a pig or horse has a right to vote, because it has no interest in voting. However, according to Singer, it would make sense to say that they had a right not to suffer or not to suffer needlessly or not to be used for no good purpose.

Others argue that animals need not be treated as equal to humans and that their interests ought not to be given equal weight with ours. It is because of the difference in species' *abilities* and *potentialities* that animals are a lesser form of being, according to this view. (See the article included here by Bonnie Steinbock for an example of this view.) This does not mean, however, that their interests ought to be disregarded. It may mean that peripheral interests of human beings should not override more serious interests of animals. It is one thing to say that animals may be used if necessary for experiments that will save the lives of human beings and quite another to say that they may be harmed for the testing of cosmetics or clothing that is not important for human life. Whether this position would provide a sufficient basis for vegetarianism would then depend on the importance of animal protein, for example, and whether animals could be raised humanely for food.

We have considered various reasons that have been given for why we ought to treat animals in certain ways and not others. One is their sentience. They can feel pleasure and pain. If pain is bad, then we ought not to cause it unless some greater good or duty pushes us to do so. Using this alone as a basis for treatment of animals would not show that we should never use animals for food or clothing or even as subjects of experimentation. In fact, some people have pointed out that by growing animals for food and clothing, we produce animals that otherwise would never have been born to have a sentient life and feel pleasures. Unless the processes involve a greater amount of pain than pleasure, they argue, we have done them a favor by our animal farming practices.

ANIMAL EXPERIMENTATION

The same reasoning might be given for using animals in experimentation. If we actually grow certain animals to provide subjects for experimental laboratories, then they will have been given a life and experiences that they otherwise would not have had. However, there are several "ifs" in this scenario. One is whether the raising or use of the animals does, in fact, involve a great deal of pain—such that it would be better for them if they had not been born.

The practice of using nonhuman animals for research or experimental purposes has a history going back some 2,000 years. In the third century b.c. in Alexandria, Egypt, animals were used to study bodily functions.[20] Aristotle cut open animals to learn about their structure and development. The Roman physician Galen used certain animals to show that veins do not carry air but blood. And in 1622, Harvey used animals to exhibit the circulation of the blood. Animals were used in 1846 to show the effects of anesthesia and in 1878 to demonstrate the relationship between bacteria and disease.[21] In the twentieth century, research with animals made many advances in medicine possible, from cures for infectious diseases and the development

of immunization techniques and antibiotics to the development of surgical procedures. For example, in the development of a vaccine for polio, hundreds of primates were sacrificed. As a result of these experiments, polio is now almost eradicated. In 1952, there were 58,000 cases of this crippling disease in the United States, and in 1984 there were just four. There are now few if any reported cases.[22] AIDS researchers are now using monkeys to test vaccines against HIV. In 2000, "researchers at the University of Massachusetts Medical School [took] immature cells from the spinal cords of adult rats, induced them to grow, and then implanted them in the gap of the severed spinal cords of paralyzed rats."[23] The rats soon were able to move, stand, and walk. This research has given hope to the 300,000 to 500,000 people in the United States and more around the world who suffer from spinal-cord damage. It is part of a growing field of tissue engineering in which scientists grow living tissue to use for replacement parts for the human body.

Other promising research creates transgenic animals to use as drug-producing machines. For example, scientists have spliced human genes into the DNA of goats, sheep, and pigs. These mammals then secrete therapeutic proteins in their milk. Among these therapeutics are those designed to treat hemophilia and cystic fibrosis.[24]

Opposition to these practices dates from at least the nineteenth century and the antivivisectionists who campaigned against all use of animals in experimentation. Currently, the animal rights movement has gained prominence and strength. In 1876, the British Parliament passed the first animal welfare act, the Cruelty to Animals Act. This was followed in the United States in 1966 by the Animal Welfare Act. In a 1976 amendment, however, Congress exempted rats, mice, birds, horses, and farm animals, probably because of problems with enforcement and funding.[25] In 2000, the U.S. Department of Agriculture responded to a lawsuit brought by an animal rights group by agreeing to include rats, mice, and birds in the list of animals protected by this act, a change that laboratories lobbied against as potentially costing them $80 million to $280 million annually to implement.[26] However, in an appropriations bill for 2002 passed by Congress and signed by the president, the designation of animals to be protected by this act was not changed.[27] The law now applies only to warm-blooded animals, restricting it to cats, dogs, monkeys, hamsters, rabbits, and guinea pigs. In the past few years, 23 million rats, mice, and birds were used annually in U.S. labs. They accounted for 85 to 95 percent of all laboratory experimental animals: for example, so-called knockout mice, in which one or more genes are removed to determine what the mice cannot do without those genes. The act requires certain physical and psychological treatments of laboratory animals, including temperature, ventilation, and space requirements. Dogs are required to be properly exercised, and primates cannot be caused undue psychological stress—for example, humans are not allowed to stare at them because primates see this as challenge behavior. Under these provisions, "[m]onkeys are caged, but they have televisions and can be seen enjoying episodes of 'Star Trek.'"[28]

Various institutions have adopted their own "institutional animal care and use committees." Johns Hopkins University, for example, now has its own Center for Alternatives to Animal Testing. The work of the Humane Society is well known, as is that of the Society for the Prevention of Cruelty to Animals and People for the Ethical Treatment of Animals (PETA). Some groups pursue their goals aggressively, conducting "animal rescues." For example, in 1989, the Animal Liberation Front released more than 1,200 laboratory animals (some of which had been infected with *Cryptosporidium*, a bacterium that could harm infants and people with weak immune systems). In 1987, an animal research lab being constructed at the University of California at Davis was burned, causing $3 million in damages.[29]

One issue in all of this is whether the use of animals was ever really *necessary* to effect the medical advances we have made. Animal rights activists argue that other sources of information can be used, including population studies or epidemiology, monitoring of human patients and development of databases, noninvasive medical imaging devices, autopsies, tissue and cell cultures, in vitro tests, and mathematical models.[30] Activists also argue that the use of animals as experimental subjects sometimes actually delayed the use of effective treatment. One example cited in this regard is the development of

penicillin for bacterial infection. When Alexander Fleming used it on infected rabbits, it proved ineffective and thus he put it aside for a decade, not knowing that rabbits excrete penicillin in their urine.[31] It is also true that not only do nonhuman animals vary in their response to particular drugs, but also individual humans do. What works on some individuals does not work on others because of a variety of possible factors, including genetic predisposition. Activists argue that those who hold that we can use animals in experimentation are inconsistent because they want to say both that animals are different from humans and so can be used and at the same time that they are sufficiently like humans so what is learned in the research will apply to us.

Others answer this criticism by pointing out that mice, although quite different from humans, make very good models for the study of human genes simply because we share so many genes with them.[32] Furthermore, they contend, cell and computer studies are insufficient. If we went directly from these cell or computer studies to use in humans, we would put humans at risk. This was the case in the use of the drug thalidomide in the 1950s, a situation in which insufficient animal studies resulted in the deformation of many babies who were born to women who used this drug to lessen nausea during pregnancy.

Whether using animals was necessary for various medical advances or whether other kinds of studies could have been substituted is an empirical matter. We need to turn to the history of medicine to help us determine this. However, most probably some animal research is redundant or other methods could serve just as well. For example, we should probably rely more on human epidemiological studies such as the Framingham Heart Study, in which 5,000 adults were followed over fifty years and much was learned about the effect of cholesterol, diet, and exercise on heart health.[33]

A second concern about the use of nonhuman animals involves the extent to which *pain* is inflicted on these experimental subjects. "In 1984, the Department of Agriculture reported that 61% of research animals were not subjected to painful procedures and another 31% received anesthesia or pain-relieving drugs."[34] The rest did experience pain, but this was sometimes a necessary part of the experiment, such as in pain studies whose purpose is to find better ways to relieve pain in humans. Those who oppose animal research cite their own examples of cruelty to animal subjects. It is not just physical pain to which they point, but, for example, the psychological pain of being caged as in the case of primates. Because of their concern and political action, government restrictions and guidelines for animal research have been strengthened.[35]

There are three positions on the use of nonhuman animals in research. One opposes all use of animals. At the other end of the spectrum is the position that nonhuman animals have no rights or moral standing and thus can be used as we choose. In the middle is the belief that animals have some moral status and thus limits and restrictions should be placed on conducting research with these creatures. We already have discussed the problems regarding the basis for attributing moral status or rights to nonhuman animals, a matter that is crucial to determining what we want to say about animal experimentation. However, it is also useful to consider some of the other arguments used in this debate.

Even those who support animal rights sometimes agree that the uses of animals in experimentation can be ethically supported if they "serve important and worthwhile purposes."[36] They may be justified if they do, in fact, help us develop significant medical advances if the information cannot be obtained in any other way, and if the experiments are conducted with as little discomfort for the animals as possible. What we would want to say about other less vital purposes for using animals is still open. The use of nonhuman animals for food, entertainment, clothing, and the other purposes listed at the beginning of this chapter will probably need to be considered, each on its own terms. However, whatever we want to say about these practices, we will need to be as clear as we can about the other matters discussed in this chapter, matters about the nature and basis of moral standing and moral rights.

ENDANGERED SPECIES

"An endangered species is a population of organisms which is at risk of becoming extinct because it is either few in numbers, or threatened by changing environmental or predation parameters. . . . The International Union for Conservation of Nature (IUCN) . . . calculated the percentage of endangered species as 40 percent of all organisms" in 2006.[37] This included "one in three amphibians and almost half of all freshwater turtles . . . on top of the one in eight birds and one in four mammals . . . in jeopardy."[38] More than one-third of U.S. fish species are currently in trouble.[39] As of 2007, it was estimated that one of every six mammals in Europe was threatened with extinction. One example is the Iberian Lynx. "Not since the time of the sabertooth has a feline species gone extinct. Earth's most endangered cat could be next."[40]

On the other hand, there has been some good news. After many years of efforts at conservation, "the mountain gorillas in Eastern Africa are showing a slow but steady comeback," according to the World Wildlife Fund (WWF), the global conservation organization.[41]

Some of the successes come from the fact that there are more than 3,500 protected areas in the world, including wildlife refuges and reserves. These areas include parks and other reserves. This is approximately 2 million square miles, or 3 percent of our total land area.[42]

The grey wolf was considered to be endangered. Due to similar efforts they were reintroduced into Yellowstone National Park. Now they are flourishing. However, this also creates problems for ranchers in the area as the wolves kill sheep and cattle.[43]

Destruction of animal habitat may be the most potent threat to animal species. Although animals can often adapt to gradual changes in their environment, rapid change often makes such adjustment impossible. Many human activities cause such rapid change. Another cause is the introduction of non-native species into an environment, thus upsetting a delicate ecological balance. Overexploitation is also a source of extinction—for example, whaling and overfishing.[44] According to the WWF, dolphins and porpoises rank high on the list of endangered species that need immediate action.[45] One of the main remediable causes is bycatch, or accidental entrapment in fishing nets intended to catch other fish. The nets are typically gillnets, which because they are difficult for dolphins and porpoises to see, trap them underwater, and prevent them from reaching the surface to breathe. "This is the greatest threat globally to whales, dolphins, and porpoises. In 2003, researchers estimated that more than 300,000 (of these) cetaceans are killed in fishing gear each year in the world's oceans."[46] Especially affected are "harbor porpoises in the Black Sea . . . Atlantic humpback dolphins off the coast of West Africa, and franciscana dolphins in South America."[47] Worldwide, more than 1,000 animal species are now considered to be endangered.[48] The *Global 2000 Report* asserted that within a few decades we will lose up to 20 percent of the species that now exist if nothing is done to change the current trend.[49] Other people contest these figures and projections. For example, they claim that these estimates are extreme and far exceed any known loss of species.[50] They also point out that species have been lost naturally without human intervention. However, throughout evolution the species that have been lost have been replaced at a higher rate than they have disappeared and thus we have the wondrous diversity that we now see. The rate of replacement now may not be able to keep up because of the accelerated time scale of loss.

Although we do need to get our facts straight about the loss of species, we also need to ask ourselves why the loss of species matters. In the first place, we should distinguish the position that holds that *individual animals* have rights or a particular moral status from that position which holds that it is *animal species* that we ought to protect, not individual animals. We generally believe that we have good *anthropocentric reasons* for preserving animal as well as plant species. We have aesthetic interests in the variety of different life forms. Bird watchers know the thrill of being able to observe some rare species. The unusual and variety itself are objects of wonder. We also have nutritional and health interests in preserving species. They may now seem useless, but we do not know what unknown future threat may lead us to find in them the food or medicine we need. Loss of species leaves us genetically poorer and vulnerable. We also have educational interests in preserving species. They tell us about ourselves, our history, and how our systems work or could work. "Destroying species is like tearing pages out of an unread book, written in a language humans hardly know how to read, about the place where they live."[51] If we destroy the mouse lemur, for

example, we destroy the modern animal that is closest to the primates from which our own human line evolved.[52] From other species we can learn about the evolution of the senses of sight and hearing.

However, when we ask whether animal species have *moral standing* or *intrinsic value* or even *rights*, we run into matters that are puzzling. An animal species is not an individual. It is a collection and in itself cannot have the kind of interests or desires that may be the basis for the rights or moral standing of individual animals. Thus, according to philosopher Nicholas Rescher, "moral obligation is . . . always interest-oriented. But only individuals can be said to have interests; one only has moral obligations to particular individuals or particular groups thereof."[53] If we can have duties to a group of individuals and a species is a group, then we may have duties to species. Still, this does not imply that the species has rights.

However, some people challenge the notion of a *species* as the *group* of the individuals that make it up. Consider just what we might mean by a "species." Is it not a *concept* constructed by us as a way of grouping and comparing organisms? Charles Darwin wrote, "I look at the term species, as one arbitrarily given for the sake of convenience to a set of individuals closely resembling each other."[54] If a species is but a term or *class* or *category*, then it does not actually exist. If it does not exist, then how could it be said to have rights? However, consider the following possibility, suggested by environmental ethicist Holmes Rolston. "A species is a living historical form (Latin *species*), propagated in individual organisms, that flows dynamically over generations."[55] As such, species are units of evolution that exist in time and space. According to Rolston, "a species is a coherent, ongoing form of life expressed in organisms, encoded in gene flow, and shaped by the environment."[56] If we think of species in this way, it may be intelligible to speak of our having duties to an animal species. What it would amount to is our respecting "dynamic life forms preserved in historical lines, vital informational processes that persist generically over millions of years, overleaping short-lived individuals."[57] Our duties then would be to a dynamic continuum, a living environmental process, a "lifeline." According to this view, species are like stories and thus, "To kill a species is to shut down a unique story." Or, finally, as Rolston writes, "A duty to a species is more like being responsible to a cause than to a person. It is commitment to an *idea* (Greek, *idea*, 'form,' sometimes a synonym for the Latin *species*)."[58] Although his explanation of the nature of species and his arguments for the view that we have duties to them are often metaphorical ("story," "lifeline"), his reasoning is nevertheless intriguing. It also raises real metaphysical questions about the reality status of an idea. At the least, he gives us cause to rethink the view that only individuals are the kinds of beings toward whom we can have duties, and even possibly also the kinds of beings who can have rights.

Those who support animal rights as the rights of individual animals to certain treatment do not always agree in concrete cases with those who believe that it is species that ought to be protected and not individual animals. Suppose, for example, that a certain population of deer is threatened because its numbers have outstripped the food supply and the deer are starving to death. In some such cases, wildlife officials have sought to thin herds by selective killing or limited hunting. It is thought to be for the sake of the herd that some are killed. Animal rights activists are generally horrified at this policy and argue that ways should be found to save all of the deer. Those who seek to protect species of animals might not object if the practice of thinning will, in fact, serve that goal. We can see that these two groups might be at odds with one another.[59]

In this chapter, we have raised many questions about the moral status of animals. The discussion of rights and duties and their grounding may seem abstract, but they do form a basis for thinking about and deciding for ourselves what we think are our obligations to and regarding nonhuman animals. In the readings in this chapter, Peter Singer and Bonnie Steinbock debate whether nonhuman animals ought to be treated equally in some way with humans.

NOTES

1. Glen Martin and Marisa Lagos, "Latest Whale Rescue Tactic: Underwater Bubble Streams," *San Francisco Chronicle*, May 25, 2007, p. B4; Glen Martin and Tom Chorneau, "Hundreds Offer Ideas for Helping Lost Whales," *San Francisco Chronicle*, May 26, 2007, pp. A1, A9.
2. Wayne Pacelle, "Stacking the Hunt," *The New York Times*, Dec. 9, 2003, p. A29.
3. http://en.wikipedia.org/wiki/siki/Canned_hunt.
4. John F. Lauerman, "Animal Research," *Harvard Magazine* (Jan.–Feb. 1999), pp. 49–57.
5. Ulysses Torassa, "Research Doctors Get Clues from Animals," *San Francisco Chronicle*, Jan. 24, 1999, p. A4.
6. http://www.peta.org/actioncenter/testing.asp.
7. www.hsus.org.
8. www.rds-online.org.uk.
9. www.all-creatures.org.
10. www.endangeredspecie.com/protect.htm.
11. http://www.commondreams.org/headlines02/1112-07.htm.
12. www.endangeredspecie.com/Why_Save_.htm.
13. Jeremy Bentham, *Introduction to the Principles of Morals and Legislation* (1789), Chapter 17.
14. http://www.peta.org/actioncenter/entertainment.asp.
15. Reported by Holmes Rolston III in *Environmental Ethics: Duties to and Values in the Natural World* (Philadelphia: Temple University Press, 1988), 50.
16. Joel Feinberg, "The Rights of Animals and Unborn Generations," in Tom Regan and Peter Singer (Eds.), *Animal Rights and Human Obligations* (Englewood Cliffs, NJ: Prentice Hall, 1976), pp. 190–196.
17. Ibid.
18. Tom Regan, *The Case for Animal Rights* (Berkeley: University of California Press, 1983).
19. Peter Singer, *Animal Liberation: A New Ethic for Our Treatment of Animals* (New York: Random House, 1975). Singer was not the first to use the term speciesism. Ryder also used it in his work *Victims of Science* (London: Davis-Poynter, 1975).
20. Jerod M. Loeb, William R. Hendee, Steven J. Smith, and M. Roy Schwarz, "Human vs. Animal Rights: In Defense of Animal Research," *Journal of the American Medical Association*, 262, no. 19 (Nov. 17, 1989), pp. 2716–2720.
21. Ibid.
22. Ibid.; see also www.who.int/immunization_monitoring/en/globalsummary/timeseries/tsincidencepol.htm.
23. Holcomb B. Noble, "Rat Studies Raise Hope of Conquering Paralysis," *The New York Times*, Jan. 25, 2000, p. D7.
24. Tom Abate, "Biotech Firms Transforming Animals into Drug-Producing Machines," *San Francisco Chronicle*, Jan. 25, 2000, p. B1.
25. Lauerman, "Animal Research." op. cit., p. 51.

26. http://www.the-scientist.com/news/20010716/03/
27. http://www.avma.org/onlnews/javma/jun02/020615a.asp.
28. Nicholas Wade, "Lab Rats, Mice Gain Federal Protection," *The New York Times*, Oct. 15, 2000.
29. Lauerman, "Animal Research." op. cit.
30. www.mrmcmed.org/crit3.html.
31. See Americans for Medical Advancement (http://www.curedisease.com/historical-breakthroughs.html).
32. Lauerman, "Animal Research." op. cit.
33. Ibid.
34. This is a continuation of the estimate for 1980, as given by Peter Singer in "Animals and the Value of Life," in T. Regan (Ed.), *Matters of Life and Death: New Introductory Essays in Moral Philosophy*, 2d ed. (New York: Random House, 1980, 1986), 339.
35. See, for example, the *U.S. National Institutes of Health's Guide for the Care and Use of Laboratory Animals*, rev. ed. (1985).
36. Singer, "Animals and the Value of Life," p. 374.
37. http://en.wikipedia.org/wiki/Endangered_species.
38. www.iucn.org.
39. www.iucn.org/; www.endangeredspecie.com/Interesting_Facts.htm.
40. "A Lifeline for the Iberian Lynx," *National Geographic*, May, 2010, p. 134
41. www.worldwildlife.org/news.
42. www.endangeredspecie.com/Interesting_Facts.htm.
43. Douglas H. Chadwick, "Wolf Wars," *National Geographic*, March 2010, pp. 34-55.
44. www.endangeredspecie.com/causes_of_endangerment.htm.
45. www.worldwildlife.org/news.
46. Ibid.
47. Ibid.
48. www.endangeredspecie.com/Interesting_Facts.htm.
49. Council on Environmental Quality and the Department of State, *The Global 2000 Report to the President* (Washington, DC: U.S. Government Printing Office, 1980): 1, 37; 2, 327–333.
50. See, for example, Julian L. Simon and Aaron Wildavsky, "Facts, Not Species, Are Periled," *The New York Times*, May 13, 1993, p. A15.
51. Rolston, *Environmental Ethics*, op. cit. 129.
52. Ibid.
53. Nicholas Rescher, "Why Save Endangered Species?" in *Unpopular Essays on Technological Progress* (Pittsburgh: University of Pittsburgh Press, 1980), 83. A similar point is made by Tom Regan, *The Case for Animal Rights* (Berkeley: University of California Press, 1983), 359, and Joel Feinberg, "Rights of Animals and Unborn Generations," op. cit., pp. 55–56.
54. Charles Darwin, *The Origin of Species* (Baltimore, MD: Penguin, 1968): 108.
55. Holmes Rolston III, op. cit., p. 135.
56. Ibid., 136.
57. Ibid., 137.
58. Ibid., 145.
59. In fact, one supporter of animal rights has referred to holistic views of the value of animals as "environmental fascism." Tom Regan, *The Case for Animal Rights* (Berkeley: University of California Press, 1983), pp. 361–362.

R E A D I N G
All Animals Are Equal

PETER SINGER

Study Questions

1. What argument against women's rights did Thomas Taylor give?
2. Why does Singer believe that the response to this argument, which stresses the similarity between women and men, does not go far enough?
3. Does equal consideration imply identical treatment? Why or why not, according to Singer?
4. Why does Singer believe it would be wrong to tie equal treatment to the factual equality of those to be treated equally? What principle does he propose instead?
5. What is *speciesism*? According to Singer, how does it parallel racism and sexism?
6. Why does Singer propose that all who can suffer, as Bentham said, ought to have their interests taken into consideration?
7. Why does Singer prefer the principle of equal consideration of interests to concerns about whether or not certain beings have rights?

8. Does Singer believe that there should be no experiments involving animals? Explain.

9. Why does Singer ask whether we would be willing to experiment on brain-damaged orphan children in order to save many other people? Does he believe that this would ever be justified?

"ANIMAL LIBERATION" may sound more like a parody of other liberation movements than a serious objective. The idea of "The Rights of Animals" actually was once used to parody the case for women's rights. When Mary Wollstonecraft, a forerunner of today's feminists, published her *Vindication of the Rights of Woman* in 1792, her views were widely regarded as absurd, and before long an anonymous publication appeared entitled *A Vindication of the Rights of Brutes*. The author of this satirical work (now known to have been Thomas Taylor, a distinguished Cambridge philosopher) tried to refute Mary Wollstonecraft's arguments by showing that they could be carried one stage further. If the argument for equality was sound when applied to women, why should it not be applied to dogs, cats, and horses? The reasoning seemed to hold for these "brutes" too; yet to hold that brutes had rights was manifestly absurd. Therefore the reasoning by which this conclusion had been reached must be unsound, and if unsound when applied to brutes, it must also be unsound when applied to women, since the very same arguments had been used in each case.

In order to explain the basis of the case for the equality of animals, it will be helpful to start with an examination of the case for the equality of women. Let us assume that we wish to defend the case for women's rights against the attack by Thomas Taylor. How should we reply?

One way in which we might reply is by saying that the case for equality between men and women cannot validly be extended to nonhuman animals. Women have a right to vote, for instance, because they are just as capable of making rational decisions about the future as men are; dogs, on the other hand, are incapable of understanding the significance of voting, so they cannot have the right to

vote. There are many other obvious ways in which men and women resemble each other closely, while humans and animals differ greatly. So, it might be said, men and women are similar beings and should have similar rights, while humans and nonhumans are different and should not have equal rights.

The reasoning behind this reply to Taylor's analogy is correct up to a point, but it does not go far enough. There are obviously important differences between humans and other animals, and these differences must give rise to some differences in the rights that each have. Recognizing this evident fact, however, is no barrier to the case for extending the basic principle of equality to nonhuman animals. The differences that exist between men and women are equally undeniable, and the supporters of Women's Liberation are aware that these differences may give rise to different rights. Many feminists hold that women have the right to an abortion on request. It does not follow that since these same feminists are campaigning for equality between men and women they must support the right of men to have abortions too. Since a man cannot have an abortion, it is meaningless to talk of his right to have one. Since dogs can't vote, it is meaningless to talk of their right to vote. There is no reason why either Women's Liberation or Animal Liberation should get involved in such nonsense. The extension of the basic principle of equality from one group to another does not imply that we must treat both groups in exactly the same way, or grant exactly the same rights to both groups. Whether we should do so will depend on the nature of the members of the two groups. The basic principle of equality does not require equal or identical treatment; it requires equal consideration. Equal consideration for different beings may lead to different treatment and different rights.

So there is a different way of replying to Taylor's attempt to parody the case for women's rights, a way that does not deny the obvious differences between human beings and nonhumans but goes more deeply into the question of equality and concludes by finding nothing absurd in the idea that the basic principle of equality applies to so-called brutes. At this point such a conclusion may appear odd; but if we examine more deeply the basis on which our opposition to discrimination on grounds of race or

Peter Singer, *Animal Liberation*, New York Review, 2nd edition 1990: 1–9, 36–37, 40, 81–83, 85–86. Reprinted with permission of the author.

sex ultimately rests, we will see that we would be on shaky ground if we were to demand equality for blacks, women, and other groups of oppressed humans while denying equal consideration to nonhumans. To make this clear we need to see, first, exactly why racism and sexism are wrong. When we say that all human beings, whatever their race, creed, or sex, are equal, what is it that we are asserting? Those who wish to defend hierarchical, inegalitarian societies have often pointed out that by whatever test we choose it simply is not true that all humans are equal. Like it or not we must face the fact that humans come in different shapes and sizes; they come with different moral capacities, different intellectual abilities, different amounts of benevolent feeling and sensitivity to the needs of others, different abilities to communicate effectively, and different capacities to experience pleasure and pain. In short, if the demand for equality were based on the actual equality of all human beings, we would have to stop demanding equality.

Still, one might cling to the view that the demand for equality among human beings is based on the actual equality of the different races and sexes. Although, it may be said, humans differ as individuals, there are no differences between the races and sexes as such. From the mere fact that a person is black or a woman we cannot infer anything about that person's intellectual or moral capacities. This, it may be said, is why racism and sexism are wrong. The white racist claims that whites are superior to blacks, but this is false; although there are differences among individuals, some blacks are superior to some whites in all of the capacities and abilities that could conceivably be relevant. The opponent of sexism would say the same: a person's sex is no guide to his or her abilities, and this is why it is unjustifiable to discriminate on the basis of sex.

The existence of individual variations that cut across the lines of race or sex, however, provides us with no defense at all against a more sophisticated opponent of equality, one who proposes that, say, the interests of all those with IQ scores below 100 be given less consideration than the interests of those with ratings over 100. Perhaps those scoring below the mark would, in this society, be made the slaves of those scoring higher. Would a hierarchical society of this sort really be so much better than one based on race or sex? I think not. But if we tie the moral principle of equality to the factual equality of the different races or sexes, taken as a whole, our opposition to racism and sexism does not provide us with any basis for objecting to this kind of inegalitarianism.

There is a second important reason why we ought not to base our opposition to racism and sexism on any kind of factual equality, even the limited kind that asserts that variations in capacities and abilities are spread evenly among the different races and between the sexes: we can have no absolute guarantee that these capacities and abilities really are distributed evenly, without regard to race or sex, among human beings. So far as actual abilities are concerned there do seem to be certain measurable differences both among races and between sexes. These differences do not, of course, appear in every case, but only when averages are taken. More important still, we do not yet know how many of these differences are really due to the different genetic endowments of the different races and sexes, and how many are due to poor schools, poor housing, and other factors that are the result of past and continuing discrimination. Perhaps all of the important differences will eventually prove to be environmental rather than genetic. Anyone opposed to racism and sexism will certainly hope that this will be so, for it will make the task of ending discrimination a lot easier; nevertheless, it would be dangerous to rest the case against racism and sexism on the belief that all significant differences are environmental in origin. The opponent of, say, racism who takes this line will be unable to avoid conceding that if differences in ability did after all prove to have some genetic connection with race, racism would in some way be defensible.

Fortunately there is no need to pin the case for equality to one particular outcome of a scientific investigation. The appropriate response to those who claim to have found evidence of genetically based differences in ability among the races or between the sexes is not to stick to the belief that the genetic explanation must be wrong, whatever evidence to the contrary may turn up; instead we should make it quite clear that the claim to equality does not depend on intelligence, moral capacity, physical strength, or similar matters of fact. Equality is a moral idea, not an assertion of fact. There is no logically compelling reason for assuming that a factual difference in ability between two people justifies any difference in the amount of consideration we give to their needs and interests. The principle of the equality of human beings is not a description of an alleged actual equality among humans: it is a prescription of how we should treat human beings.

Jeremy Bentham, the founder of the reforming utilitarian school of moral philosophy, incorporated the essential basis of moral equality into his system of ethics by means of the formula: "Each to count for one and none for more than one." In other words, the interests of every being affected by an action are to be taken into account and given the same weight as the like interests of any other being. A later utilitarian, Henry Sidgwick, put the point in this way: "The good of any one individual is of no more importance, from the point of view (if I may say so) of the Universe, than the good of any other." More recently the leading figures in contemporary moral philosophy have shown a great deal of agreement in specifying as a fundamental pre-supposition of their moral theories some similar requirement that works to give everyone's interests equal consideration—although these writers generally cannot agree on how this requirement is best formulated.[1]

It is an implication of this principle of equality that our concern for others and our readiness to consider their interests ought not to depend on what they are like or on what abilities they may possess. Precisely what our concern or consideration requires us to do may vary according to the characteristics of those affected by what we do: concern for the well-being of children growing up in America would require that we teach them to read; concern for the well-being of pigs may require no more than that we leave them with other pigs in a place where there is adequate food and room to run freely. But the basic element—the taking into account of the interests of the being, whatever those interests may be—must, according to the principle of equality, be extended to all beings, black or white, masculine or feminine, human or nonhuman.

Thomas Jefferson, who was responsible for writing the principle of the equality of men into the American Declaration of Independence, saw this point. It led him to oppose slavery even though he was unable to free himself fully from his slaveholding background. He wrote in a letter to the author of a book that emphasized the notable intellectual achievements of Negroes in order to refute the then common view that they had limited intellectual capacities:

> Be assured that no person living wishes more sincerely than I do, to see a complete refutation of the doubts I myself have entertained and expressed on the grade of understanding allotted to them by nature, and to find that they are on a par with ourselves . . . but whatever be their degree of talent it is no measure of their rights. Because Sir Isaac Newton was superior to others in understanding, he was not therefore lord of the property or persons of others.[2]

Similarly, when in the 1850s the call for women's rights was raised in the United States, a remarkable black feminist named Sojourner Truth made the same point in more robust terms at a feminist convention:

> They talk about this thing in the head; what do they call it? ["Intellect," whispered someone nearby.] That's it. What's that got to do with women's rights or Negroes' rights? If my cup won't hold but a pint and yours holds a quart, wouldn't you be mean not to let me have my little half-measure full?[3]

It is on this basis that the case against racism and the case against sexism must both ultimately rest; and it is in accordance with this principle that the attitude that we may call "speciesism," by analogy with racism, must also be condemned. Speciesism—the word is not an attractive one, but I can think of no better term—is prejudice or attitude of bias in favor of the interests of members of one's own species and against those of members of other species. It should be obvious that the fundamental objections to racism and sexism made by Thomas Jefferson and Sojourner Truth apply equally to speciesism. If possessing a higher degree of intelligence does not entitle one human to use another for his or her own ends, how can it entitle humans to exploit nonhumans for the same purpose?[4]

Many philosophers and other writers have proposed the principle of equal consideration of interests, in some form or other, as a basic moral principle;

but not many of them have recognized that this principle applies to members of other species as well as to our own. Jeremy Bentham was one of the few who did realize this. In a forward-looking passage written at a time when black slaves had been freed by the French but in the British dominions were still being treated in the way we now treat animals, Bentham wrote:

> The day may come when the rest of the animal creation may acquire those rights which never could have been withholden from them but by the hand of tyranny. The French have already discovered that the blackness of the skin is no reason why a human being should be abandoned without redress to the caprice of a tormentor. It may one day come to be recognized that the number of the legs, the villosity of the skin, or the termination of the os sacrum are reasons equally insufficient for abandoning a sensitive being to the same fate. What else is it that should trace the insuperable line? Is it the faculty of reason, or perhaps the faculty of discourse? But a full-grown horse or dog is beyond comparison a more rational, as well as a more conversable animal, than an infant of a day or a week or even a month, old. But suppose they were otherwise, what would it avail? The question is not, Can they *reason*? nor Can they *talk*? but, Can they *suffer*?[5]

In this passage Bentham points to the capacity for suffering as the vital characteristic that gives a being the right to equal consideration. The capacity for suffering—or more strictly, for suffering and/or enjoyment or happiness—is not just another characteristic like the capacity for language or higher mathematics. Bentham is not saying that those who try to mark "the insuperable line" that determines whether the interests of a being should be considered happen to have chosen the wrong characteristic. By saying that we must consider the interests of all beings with the capacity for suffering or enjoyment Bentham does not arbitrarily exclude from consideration any interests at all—as those who draw the line with reference to the possession of reason or language do. The capacity for suffering and enjoyment is a prerequisite for having interests at all, a condition that must be satisfied before we can speak of interests in a meaningful way. It would be nonsense to say that it was not in the interests of a stone to be kicked along the road by a schoolboy. A stone does not

have interests because it cannot suffer. Nothing that we can do to it could possibly make any difference to its welfare. The capacity for suffering and enjoyment is, however, not only necessary, but also sufficient for us to say that a being has interests—at an absolute minimum, an interest in not suffering. A mouse, for example, does have an interest in not being kicked along the road, because it will suffer if it is.

Although Bentham speaks of "rights" in the passage I have quoted, the argument is really about equality rather than about rights. Indeed, in a different passage, Bentham famously described "natural rights" as "nonsense" and "natural and imprescriptable rights" as "nonsense upon stilts." He talked of moral rights as a shorthand way of referring to protections that people and animals morally ought to have; but the real weight of the moral argument does not rest on the assertion of the existence of the right, for this in turn has to be justified on the basis of the possibilities for suffering and happiness. In this way we can argue for equality for animals without getting embroiled in philosophical controversies about the ultimate nature of rights.

In misguided attempts to refute the arguments of this book, some philosophers have gone to much trouble developing arguments to show that animals do not have rights.[6] They have claimed that to have rights a being must be autonomous, or must be a member of a community, or must have the ability to respect the rights of others, or must possess a sense of justice. These claims are irrelevant to the case for Animal Liberation. The language of rights is a convenient political shorthand. It is even more valuable in the era of thirty-second TV news clips than it was in Bentham's day; but in the argument for a radical change in our attitude to animals, it is in no way necessary.

If a being suffers there can be no moral justification for refusing to take that suffering into consideration. No matter what the nature of the being, the principle of equality requires that its suffering be counted equally with the like suffering—insofar as rough comparisons can be made—of any other being. If a being is not capable of suffering, or of experiencing enjoyment or happiness, there is nothing to be taken into account. So the limit of sentience (using the term as a convenient if not strictly accurate shorthand for the capacity to suffer and/or experience enjoyment) is the only defensible boundary of concern for the interests of others. To mark this boundary by some other characteristic like intelligence or rationality would be to mark it in an arbitrary manner. Why not choose some other characteristic, like skin color?

Racists violate the principle of equality by giving greater weight to the interests of members of their own race when there is a clash between their interests and the interests of those of another race. Sexists violate the principle of equality by favoring the interests of their own sex. Similarly, speciesists allow the interests of their own species to override the greater interests of members of other species. The pattern is identical in each case.

ANIMALS AND RESEARCH

Most human beings are speciesists. . . . Ordinary human beings—not a few exceptionally cruel or heartless humans, but the overwhelming majority of humans—take an active part in, acquiesce in, and allow their taxes to pay for practices that require the sacrifice of the most important interests of members of other species in order to promote the most trivial interests of our own species. . . .

The practice of experimenting on nonhuman animals as it exists today throughout the world reveals the consequences of speciesism. Many experiments inflict severe pain without the remotest prospect of significant benefits for human beings or any other animals. Such experiments are not isolated instances, but part of a major industry. In Britain, where experimenters are required to report the number of "scientific procedures" performed on animals, official government figures show that 3.5 million scientific procedures were performed on animals in 1988.[7] In the United States there are no figures of comparable accuracy. Under the Animal Welfare Act, the U.S. secretary of agriculture publishes a report listing the number of animals used by facilities registered with it, but this is incomplete in many ways. It does not include rats, mice, birds, reptiles, frogs, or domestic farm animals used in secondary schools; and it does not include experiments performed by facilities that do not transport animals interstate or receive grants or contracts from the federal government.

In 1986 the U.S. Congress Office of Technology Assessment (OTA) published a report entitled "Alternatives to Animal Use in Research, Testing and Education." The OTA researchers attempted to determine the number of animals used in experimentation in the U.S. and reported that "estimates of the animals used in the United States each year range from 10 million to upwards of 100 million." They concluded that the estimates were unreliable but their best guess was "at least 17 million to 22 million."[8]

This is an extremely conservative estimate. In testimony before Congress in 1966, the Laboratory Animal Breeders Association estimated that the number of mice, rats, guinea pigs, hamsters, and rabbits used for experimental purposes in 1965 was around 60 million.[9] In 1984 Dr. Andrew Rowan of Tufts University School of Veterinary Medicine estimated that approximately 71 million animals are used each year. In 1985 Rowan revised his estimates to distinguish between the number of animals produced, acquired, and actually used. This yielded an estimate of between 25 and 35 million animals used in experiments each year.[10] (This figure omits animals who die in shipping or are killed before the experiment begins.) A stock market analysis of just one major supplier of animals to laboratories, the Charles River Breeding Laboratory, stated that this company alone produced 22 million laboratory animals annually.[11]

The 1988 report issued by the Department of Agriculture listed 140,471 dogs, 42,271 cats, 51,641 primates, 431,254 rabbits, and 178,249 "wild animals": a total of 1,635,288 used in experimentation. Remember that this report does not bother to count rats and mice, and covers at most an estimated 10 percent of the total number of animals used. Of the nearly 1.6 million animals reported by the Department of Agriculture to have been used for experimental purposes, over 90,000 are reported to have experienced "unrelieved pain or distress." Again, this is probably at most 10 percent of the total number of animals suffering unrelieved pain and distress—and if experimenters are less concerned about causing unrelieved pain to rats and mice than they are to dogs, cats, and primates, it could be an even smaller proportion.

Other developed nations all use larger numbers of animals. In Japan, for example, a very incomplete survey published in 1988 produced a total in excess of eight million.[12] . . .

Among the tens of millions of experiments performed, only a few can possibly be regarded as contributing to important medical research. Huge numbers of animals are used in university departments such as forestry and psychology; many more are used for commercial purposes, to test new cosmetics, shampoos, food coloring agents, and other inessential items. All this can happen only because of our prejudice against taking seriously the suffering of a being who is not a member of our own species. Typically, defenders of experiments on animals do not deny that animals suffer. They cannot deny the animals' suffering, because they need to stress the similarities between humans and other animals in order to claim that their experiments may have some relevance for human purposes. The experimenter who forces rats to choose between starvation and electric shock to see if they develop ulcers (which they do) does so because the rat has a nervous system very similar to human beings', and presumably feels an electric shock in a similar way.

There has been opposition to experimenting on animals for a long time. This opposition has made little headway because experimenters, backed by commercial firms that profit by supplying laboratory animals and equipment, have been able to convince legislators and the public that opposition comes from uninformed fanatics who consider the interests of animals more important than the interests of human beings. But to be opposed to what is going on now it is not necessary to insist that all animal experiments stop immediately. All we need to say is that experiments serving no direct and urgent purpose should stop immediately, and in the remaining fields of research, we should whenever possible, seek to replace experiments that involve animals with alternative methods that do not. . . .

When are experiments on animals justifiable? Upon learning of the nature of many of the experiments carried out, some people react by saying that all experiments on animals should be prohibited immediately. But if we make our demands absolute as this, the experimenters have a ready reply: Would

we be prepared to let thousands of humans die if they could be saved by a single experiment on a single animal?

This question is, of course, purely hypothetical. There has never been and never could be a single experiment that saved thousands of lives. The way to reply to this hypothetical question is to pose another: Would the experimenters be prepared to carry out their experiment on a human orphan under six months old if that were the only way to save thousands of lives?

If the experimenters would not be prepared to use a human infant then their readiness to use nonhuman animals reveals an unjustifiable form of discrimination on the basis of species, since adult apes, monkeys, dogs, cats, rats, and other animals are more aware of what is happening to them, more self-directing, and, so far as we can tell, at least as sensitive to pain as a human infant. (I have specified that the human infant be an orphan, to avoid the complications of the feelings of parents. Specifying the case in this way is, if anything, overgenerous to those defending the use of nonhuman animals in experiments, since mammals intended for experimental use are usually separated from their mothers at an early age, when the separation causes distress for both mother and young.)

So far as we know, human infants possess no morally relevant characteristic to a higher degree than adult nonhuman animals, unless we are to count the infants' potential as a characteristic that makes it wrong to experiment on them. Whether this characteristic should count is controversial—if we count it, we shall have to condemn abortion along with the experiments on infants, since the potential of the infant and the fetus is the same. To avoid the complexities of this issue, however, we can alter our original question a little and assume that the infant is one with irreversible brain damage so severe as to rule out any mental development beyond the level of a six-month-old infant. There are, unfortunately, many such human beings, locked away in special wards throughout the country, some of them long since abandoned by their parents and other relatives, and, sadly, sometimes unloved by anyone else. Despite their mental deficiencies, the anatomy and physiology of these infants are in nearly all respects identical with those of normal humans. If, therefore, we were to force-feed them with large quantities of floor polish or drip concentrated solutions of cosmetics into their eyes [as has been done in experiments using animals], we would have a much more reliable indication of the safety of these products for humans than we now get by attempting to extrapolate the results of tests on a variety of other species. . . .

So whenever experimenters claim that their experiments are important enough to justify the use of animals, we should ask them whether they would be prepared to use a brain-damaged human being at a similar mental level to the animals they are planning to use. I cannot imagine that anyone would seriously propose carrying out the experiments described in this [article] on brain-damaged human beings. Occasionally it has become known that medical experiments have been performed on human beings without their consent; one case did concern institutionalized intellectually disabled children, who were given hepatitis. When such harmful experiments on human beings become known, they usually lead to an outcry against the experimenters, and rightly so. They are, very often, a further example of the arrogance of the research worker who justifies everything on the grounds of increasing knowledge. But if the experimenter claims that the experiment is important enough to justify inflicting suffering on animals, why is it not important enough to justify inflicting suffering on humans at the same mental level? What difference is there between the two? Only that one is a member of our species and the other is not? But to appeal to that difference is to reveal a bias no more defensible than racism or any other form of arbitrary discrimination. . . .

We have still not answered the question of when an experiment might be justifiable. It will not do to say "Never!" Putting morality in such black-and-white terms is appealing, because it eliminates the need to think about particular cases; but in extreme circumstances, such absolutist answers always break down. Torturing a human being is almost always wrong, but it is not absolutely wrong. If torture were the only way in which we could discover the location of a nuclear bomb hidden in a New York City basement and timed to go off within the hour, then torture would be justifiable. Similarly, if a single

experiment could cure a disease like leukemia, that experiment would be justifiable. But in actual life the benefits are always more remote, and more often than not they are nonexistent. So how do we decide when an experiment is justifiable?

We have seen that experimenters reveal a bias in favor of their own species whenever they carry out experiments on nonhumans for purposes that they would not think justified them in using human beings, even brain-damaged ones. This principle gives us a guide toward an answer to our question. Since a speciesist bias, like a racist bias, is unjustifiable, an experiment cannot be justifiable unless the experiment is so important that the use of a brain-damaged human would also be justifiable.

This is not an absolutist principle. I do not believe that it could never be justifiable to experiment on a brain-damaged human. If it really were possible to save several lives by an experiment that would take just one life, and there were no other way those lives could be saved, it would be right to do the experiment. But this would be an extremely rare case. Admittedly, as with any dividing line, there would be a gray area where it was difficult to decide if an experiment could be justified. But we need not get distracted by such considerations now. . . . We are in the midst of an emergency in which appalling suffering is being inflicted on millions of animals for purposes that on any impartial view are obviously inadequate to justify the suffering. When we have ceased to carry out all those experiments, then there will be time enough to discuss what to do about the remaining ones which are claimed to be essential to save lives or prevent greater suffering. . . .

NOTES

1. For Bentham's moral philosophy, see his *Introduction to the Principle of Morals and Legislation*, and for Sidgwick's see *The Methods of Ethics*, 1907 (the passage is quoted from the seventh edition; reprint, London: Macmillan, 1963), p. 382. As examples of leading contemporary moral philosophers who incorporate a requirement of equal consideration of interests, see R. M. Hare, *Freedom and Reason* (New York: Oxford University Press, 1963), and John Rawls, *A Theory of Justice* (Cambridge, MA: Harvard University Press, Belknap Press, 1972). For a brief

account of the essential agreement on this issue between these and other positions, see R. M. Hare, "Rules of War and Moral Reasoning," *Philosophy and Public Affairs* 1(2) (1972).
2. Letter to Henry Gregoire, February 25, 1809.
3. Reminiscences by Francis D. Gage, from Susan B. Anthony, *The History of Woman Suffrage*, vol. 1; the passage is to be found in the extract in Leslie Tanner (Ed.), *Voices From Women's Liberation* (New York: Signet, 1970).
4. I owe the term "speciesism" to Richard Ryder. It has become accepted in general use since the first edition of this book, and now appears in *The Oxford English Dictionary*, 2nd ed. (Oxford, UK: Clarendon Press, 1989).
5. Introduction to the *Principles of Morals and Legislation*, chapter 17.
6. See M. Levin, "Animal Rights Evaluated," *Humanist* 37, 1415 (July/August 1977); M. A. Fox, "Animal Liberation: A Critique," *Ethics* 88, 134–138 (1978); C. Perry and G. E. Jones, "On Animal Rights," *International Journal of Applied Philosophy* 1, 39–57 (1982).
7. *Statistics of Scientific Procedures on Living Animals*, Great Britain, 1988, Command Paper 743 (London: Her Majesty's Stationery Office, 1989).
8. U.S. Congress Office of Technology Assessment, *Alternatives to Animal Use in Research, Testing and Education* (Washington, D.C.: Government Printing Office, 1986), p. 64.
9. Hearings before the Subcommittee on Livestock and Feed Grains of the Committee on Agriculture, U.S. House of Representatives, 1966, p. 63.
10. See A. Rowan, *Of Mice, Models and Men* (Albany: State University of New York Press, 1984), p. 71; his later revision is in a personal communication to the Office of Technology Assessment; see *Alternatives to Animal Use in Research, Testing and Education*, p. 56.
11. OTA, *Alternatives to Animal Use in Research, Testing and Education*, p. 56.
12. *Experimental Animals* 37, 105 (1988).

R E A D I N G
Speciesism and the Idea of Equality
BONNIE STEINBOCK

Study Questions

1. What is the basic question that the moral philosopher asks about how we treat members of species other than our own?
2. Distinguish racism and sexism from speciesism. Do they have any common characteristics?
3. Why does Bernard Williams believe that all persons should be treated equally? Is this similar to or different from the view of Wasserstrom?
4. Does Steinbock believe that the issue of equality depends on what we say about the rights of human beings or others? Explain.
5. What counterintuitive conclusions flow from treating the suffering or interests of humans and other animals equally? What is the value of our moral feelings on this issue?
6. What three aspects or characteristics of human beings give them special moral worth or a privileged position in the moral community?
7. Why is experimentation on animals justifiable when it benefits humans?
8. Why do we regard human suffering as worse than comparable animal suffering?
9. What is the significance of the fact that we would be horrified to experiment on a severely mentally retarded human being in a way that we would not be if we used a more intelligent pig?

M OST OF us believe that we are entitled to treat members of other species in ways which would be considered wrong if inflicted on members of our own species. We kill them for food, keep them confined, use them in painful experiments. The moral philosopher has to ask what relevant difference justifies this difference in treatment. A look at this question will lead us to reexamine the distinctions which we have assumed make a moral difference.

Bonnie Steinbock, "Speciesism and the Idea of Equality" from *Philosophy*, vol. 53, no. 204 (April 1978): 247–256. 1978 Cambridge University Press. Reprinted with the permission of Cambridge University Press.

It has been suggested by Peter Singer[1] that our current attitudes are "speciesist," a word intended to make one think of "racist" or "sexist." The idea is that membership in a species is in itself not relevant to moral treatment, and that much of our behavior and attitudes towards nonhuman animals is based simply on this irrelevant fact.

There is, however, an important difference between racism or sexism and "speciesism." We do not subject animals to different moral treatment simply because they have fur and feathers, but because they are in fact different from human beings in ways that could be morally relevant. It is false that women are incapable of being benefited by education, and therefore that claim cannot serve to justify preventing them from attending school. But this is not false of cows and dogs, even chimpanzees. Intelligence is thought to be a morally relevant capacity because of its relation to the capacity for moral responsibility.

What is Singer's response? He agrees that nonhuman animals lack certain capacities that human animals possess, and that this may justify different treatment. But it does not justify giving less consideration to their needs and interests. According to Singer, the moral mistake which the racist or sexist makes is not essentially the factual error of thinking that blacks or women are inferior to white men. For even if there were no factual error, even if it were true that blacks and women are less intelligent and responsible than whites and men, this would not justify giving less consideration to their needs and interests. It is important to note that the term "speciesism" is in one way like, and in another way unlike, the terms "racism" and "sexism." What the term "speciesism" has in common with these terms is the reference to focusing on a characteristic which is, in itself, irrelevant to moral treatment. And it is worth reminding us of this. But Singer's real aim is to bring us to a new understanding of the idea of equality. The question is, on what do claims to equality rest? The demand for human equality is a demand that the interests of all human beings be considered equally, unless there is a moral justification for not doing so. But why should the interests of all human beings be considered equally? In order to answer this question, we have to give some sense to the phrase,

"All men (human beings) are created equal." Human beings are manifestly not equal, differing greatly in intelligence, virtue and capacities. In virtue of what can the claim to equality be made?

It is Singer's contention that claims to equality do not rest on factual equality. Not only do human beings differ in their capacities, but it might even turn out that intelligence, the capacity for virtue, etc., are not distributed evenly among the races and sexes.

> The appropriate response to those who claim to have found evidence of genetically based differences in ability between the races or sexes is not to stick to the belief that the genetic explanation must be wrong, whatever evidence to the contrary may turn up; instead we should make it quite clear that the claim to equality does not depend on intelligence, moral capacity, physical strength, or similar matters of fact. Equality is a moral ideal, not a simple assertion of fact. There is no logically compelling reason for assuming that a factual difference in ability between two people justifies any difference in the amount of consideration we give to satisfying their needs and interests. The principle of equality of human beings is not a description of an alleged actual equality among humans: it is a prescription of how we should treat humans.[2]

Insofar as the subject is human equality, Singer's view is supported by other philosophers. Bernard Williams, for example, is concerned to show that demands for equality cannot rest on factual equality among people, for no such equality exists.[3] The only respect in which all men are equal, according to Williams, is that they are all equally men. This seems to be a platitude, but Williams denies that it is trivial. Membership in the species *Homo sapiens* in itself has no special moral significance, but rather the fact that all men are human serves as a reminder that being human involves the possession of characteristics that are morally relevant. But on what characteristics does Williams focus? Aside from the desire for self-respect (which I will discuss later), Williams is not concerned with uniquely human capacities. Rather, he focuses on the capacity to feel pain and the capacity to feel affection. It is in virtue of these capacities, it seems, that the idea of equality is to be justified.

Apparently Richard Wasserstrom has the same idea as he sets out the racist's "logical and moral mistakes" in "Rights, Human Rights and Racial Discrimination."[4] The racist fails to acknowledge that the black person is as capable of suffering as the white person. According to Wasserstrom, the reason why a person is said to have a right not to be made to suffer acute physical pain is that we all do in fact value freedom from such pain. Therefore, if anyone has a right to be free from suffering acute physical pain, everyone has this right, for there is no possible basis of discrimination. Wasserstrom says, "For, if all persons do have equal capacities of these sorts and if the existence of these capacities is the reason for ascribing these rights to anyone, then all persons ought to have the right to claim equality of treatment in respect to the possession and exercise of these rights."[5] The basis of equality, for Wasserstrom as for Williams, lies not in some uniquely human capacity, but rather in the fact that all human beings are alike in their capacity to suffer. Writers on equality have focused on this capacity, I think, because it functions as some sort of lowest common denominator, so that whatever the other capacities of a human being, he is entitled to equal consideration because, like everyone else, he is capable of suffering.

If the capacity to suffer is the reason for ascribing a right to freedom from acute pain, or a right to well being, then it certainly looks as though these rights must be extended to animals as well. This is the conclusion Singer arrives at. The demand for human equality rests on the equal capacity of all human beings to suffer and to enjoy well being. But if this is the basis of the demand for equality, then this demand must include all beings which have an equal capacity to suffer and enjoy well being. That is why Singer places at the basis of the demand for equality, not intelligence or reason, but sentience. And equality will mean, not equality of treatment, but "equal consideration of interests." The equal consideration of interests will often mean quite different treatment, depending on the nature of the entity being considered. (It would be as absurd to talk of a dog's right to vote, Singer says, as to talk of a man's right to have an abortion.)

It might be thought that the issue of equality depends on a discussion of rights. According to this line of thought, animals do not merit equal consideration of interests because, unlike human beings,

they do not, or cannot, have rights. But I am not going to discuss rights, important as the issue is. The fact that an entity does not have rights does not necessarily imply that its interests are going to count for less than the interests of entities which are right-bearers. According to the view of rights held by H. L. A. Hart and S. I. Benn, infants do not have rights, nor do the mentally defective, nor do the insane, in so far as they all lack certain minimal conceptual capabilities for having rights.[6] Yet it certainly does not seem that either Hart or Benn would agree that therefore their interests are to be counted for less, or that it is morally permissible to treat them in ways in which it would not be permissible to treat right-bearers. It seems to mean only that we must give different sorts of reasons for our obligations to take into consideration the interests of those who do not have rights.

We have reasons concerning the treatment of other people which are clearly independent of the notion of rights. We would say that it is wrong to punch someone because doing that infringes his rights. But we could also say that it is wrong because doing that hurts him, and that is, ordinarily, enough of a reason not to do it. Now this particular reason extends not only to human beings, but to all sentient creatures. One has a *prima facie* reason not to pull the cat's tail (whether or not the cat has rights) because it hurts the cat. And this is the only thing, normally, which is relevant in this case. The fact that the cat is not a "rational being," that it is not capable of moral responsibility, that it cannot make free choices or shape its life—all of these differences from us have nothing to do with the justifiability of pulling its tail. Does this show that rationality and the rest of it are irrelevant to moral treatment?

I hope to show that this is not the case. But first I want to point out that the issue is not one of cruelty to animals. We all agree that cruelty is wrong, whether perpetrated on a moral or nonmoral, rational or nonrational agent. Cruelty is defined as the infliction of unnecessary pain or suffering. What is to count as necessary or unnecessary is determined, in part, by the nature of the end pursued. Torturing an animal is cruel, because although the pain is logically necessary for the action to be torture, the end (deriving enjoyment from seeing the animal suffer) is monstrous. Allowing animals to suffer from neglect or for the sake of large profits may also be thought to be unnecessary and therefore cruel. But there may be some ends, which are very good (such as the advancement of medical knowledge), which can be accomplished by subjecting animals to pain in experiments. Although most people would agree that the pain inflicted on animals used in medical research ought to be kept to a minimum, they would consider pain that cannot be eliminated "necessary" and therefore not cruel. It would probably not be so regarded if the subjects were nonvoluntary human beings. Necessity, then, is defined in terms of human benefit, but this is just what is being called into question. The topic of cruelty to animals, while important from a practical viewpoint, because much of our present treatment of animals involves the infliction of suffering for no good reason, is not very interesting philosophically. What is philosophically interesting is whether we are justified in having different standards of necessity for human suffering and for animal suffering.

Singer says, quite rightly I think, "If a being suffers, there can be no moral justification for refusing to take that suffering into consideration."[7] But he thinks that the principle of equality requires that, no matter what the nature of the being, its suffering be counted equally with the like suffering of any other being. In other words sentience does not simply provide us with reasons for acting; it is the only relevant consideration for equal consideration of interests. It is this view that I wish to challenge.

I want to challenge it partly because it has such counter-intuitive results. It means, for example, that feeding starving children before feeding starving dogs is just like a Catholic charity's feeding hungry Catholics before feeding hungry non-Catholics. It is simply a matter of taking care of one's own, something which is usually morally permissible. But whereas we would admire the Catholic agency which did not discriminate, but fed all children, first come, first served, we would feel quite differently about someone who has this policy for dogs and children. Nor is this, it seems to me, simply a matter of sentimental preference for our own species. I might feel much more love for my dog than for a strange child—and yet I might feel morally obliged to feed the child before I fed my dog. If I gave in to the feelings of love and fed my dog and let the child go hungry, I would probably feel guilty. This is not to say that we can simply rely on such feelings. Huck Finn felt guilty at helping Jim escape, which he viewed as stealing from a woman who had never done him any harm. But while the existence of such feelings does not settle the morality of an issue, it is not clear to me that they can be explained away. In any event, their existence can serve as a motivation for trying to find a rational justification for considering human interests above nonhuman ones.

However, it does seem to me that this requires a justification. Until now, common sense (and academic philosophy) have seen no such need. Benn says, "No one claims equal consideration for all mammals—human beings count, mice do not, though it would not be easy to say why not. . . . Although we hesitate to inflict unnecessary pain on sentient creatures, such as mice or dogs, we are quite sure that we do not need to show good reasons for putting human interests before theirs."[8]

I think we do have to justify counting our interests more heavily than those of animals. But how? Singer is right, I think, to point out that it will not do to refer vaguely to the greater value of human life, to human worth and dignity:

> Faced with a situation in which they see a need for some basis for the moral gulf that is commonly thought to separate humans and animals, but can find no concrete difference that will do this without undermining the equality of humans, philosophers tend to waffle. They resort to high-sounding phrases like 'the intrinsic dignity of the human individual.' They talk of 'the intrinsic worth of all men' as if men had some worth that other beings do not have or they say that human beings, and only human beings, are 'ends in themselves,' while 'everything other than a person can only have value for a person.' . . . Why should we not attribute 'intrinsic dignity' or 'intrinsic worth' to ourselves? Why should we not say that we are the only things in the universe that have intrinsic value? Our fellow human beings are unlikely to reject the accolades we so generously bestow upon them, and those to whom we deny the honor are unable to object.[9]

Singer is right to be skeptical of terms like "intrinsic dignity" and "intrinsic worth." These phrases are no substitute for a moral argument. But they may point to one. In trying to understand what is meant by these phrases, we may find a difference or differences between human beings and nonhuman animals that will justify different treatment while not undermining claims for human equality. While we are not compelled to discriminate among people because of different capacities, if we can find a significant difference in capacities between human and nonhuman animals, this could serve to justify regarding human interests as primary. It is not arbitrary or smug, I think, to maintain that human beings have a different moral status from members of other species because of certain capacities which are characteristic of being human. We may not all be equal in these capacities, but all human beings possess them to some measure, and nonhuman animals do not. For example, human beings are normally held to be responsible for what they do. In recognizing that someone is responsible for his or her actions, you accord that person a respect which is reserved for those possessed of moral autonomy, or capable of achieving such autonomy. Secondly, human beings can be expected to reciprocate in a way that nonhuman animals cannot. Nonhuman animals cannot be motivated by altruistic or moral reasons; they cannot treat you fairly or unfairly. This does not rule out the possibility of an animal being motivated by sympathy or pity. It does rule out altruistic motivation in the sense of motivation due to the recognition that the needs and interests of others provide one with certain reasons for acting.[10] Human beings are capable of altruistic motivation in this sense. We are sometimes motivated simply by the recognition that someone else is in pain, and that pain is a bad thing, no matter who suffers it. It is this sort of reason that I claim cannot motivate an animal or any entity not possessed of fairly abstract concepts. (If some nonhuman animals do possess the requisite concepts—perhaps chimpanzees who have learned a language—they might well be capable of altruistic motivation.) This means that our moral dealings with animals are necessarily much more limited than our dealings with other human beings. If rats invade

our houses, carrying disease and biting our children, we cannot reason with them, hoping to persuade them of the injustice they do us. We can only attempt to get rid of them. And it is this that makes it reasonable for us to accord them a separate and not equal moral status, even though their capacity to suffer provides us with some reason to kill them painlessly, if this can be done without too much sacrifice of human interests. Thirdly, as Williams points out, there is the "desire for self-respect": "a certain human desire to be identified with what one is doing, to be able to realize purposes of one's own, and not to be the instrument of another's will unless one has willingly accepted such a role."[11] Some animals may have some form of this desire, and to the extent that they do, we ought to consider their interest in freedom and self-determination. (Such considerations might affect our attitudes toward zoos and circuses.) But the desire for self-respect per se requires the intellectual capacities of human beings, and this desire provides us with special reasons not to treat human beings in certain ways. It is an affront to the dignity of a human being to be a slave (even if a well-treated one); this cannot be true for a horse or a cow. To point this out is of course only to say that the justification for the treatment of an entity will depend on the sort of entity in question. In our treatment of other entities, we must consider the desire for autonomy, dignity and respect, but only where such a desire exists. Recognition of different desires and interests will often require different treatment, a point Singer himself makes.

But is the issue simply one of different desires and interests justifying and requiring different treatment? I would like to make a stronger claim, namely, that certain capacities, which seem to be unique to human beings, entitle their possessors to a privileged position in the moral community. Both rats and human beings dislike pain, and so we have a *prima facie* reason not to inflict pain on either. But if we can free human beings from crippling diseases, pain and death through experimentation which involves making animals suffer, and if this is the only way to achieve such results, then I think that such experimentation is justified because human lives are more valuable than animals' lives. And this is because of certain capacities and abilities that normal human beings have which animals apparently do not, and which human beings cannot exercise if they are devastated by pain or disease.

My point is not that the lack of the sorts of capacities I have been discussing gives us a justification for treating animals just as we like, but rather that it is these differences between human beings and nonhuman animals which provide a rational basis for different moral treatment and consideration. Singer focuses on sentience alone as the basis of equality, but we can justify the belief that human beings have a moral worth that nonhuman animals do not, in virtue of specific capacities, and without resorting to "high-sounding phrases."

Singer thinks that intelligence, the capacity for moral responsibility, for virtue, etc., are irrelevant to equality, because we would not accept a hierarchy based on intelligence any more than one based on race. We do not think that those with greater capacities ought to have their interests weighed more heavily than those with lesser capacities, and this, he thinks, shows that differences in such capacities are irrelevant to equality. But it does not show this at all. Kevin Donaghy argues (rightly, I think) that what entitles us human beings to a privileged position in the moral community is a certain minimal level of intelligence, which is a prerequisite for morally relevant capacities.[12] The fact that we would reject a hierarchical society based on degree of intelligence does not show that a minimal level of intelligence cannot be used as a cut-off point, justifying giving greater consideration to the interests of those entities which meet this standard.

Interestingly enough, Singer concedes the rationality of valuing the lives of normal human beings over the lives of nonhuman animals.[13] We are not required to value equally the life of a normal human being and the life of an animal, he thinks, but only their suffering. But I doubt that the value of an entity's life can be separated from the value of its suffering in this way. If we value the lives of human beings more than the lives of animals, this is because we value certain capacities that human beings have

and animals do not. But freedom from suffering is, in general, a minimal condition for exercising these capacities, for living a fully human life. So, valuing human life more involves regarding human interests as counting for more. That is why we regard human suffering as more deplorable than comparable animal suffering.

But there is one point of Singer's which I have not yet met. Some human beings (if only a very few) are less intelligent than some nonhuman animals. Some have less capacity for moral choice and responsibility. What status in the moral community are these members of our species to occupy? Are their interests to be considered equally with ours? Is experimenting on them permissible where such experiments are painful or injurious, but somehow necessary for human well being? If it is certain of our capacities which entitle us to a privileged position, it looks as if those lacking those capacities are not entitled to a privileged position. To think it is justifiable to experiment on an adult chimpanzee but not on a severely mentally incapacitated human being seems to be focusing on membership in a species where that has no moral relevance. (It is being "speciesist" in a perfectly reasonable use of the word.) How are we to meet this challenge?

Donaghy is untroubled by this objection. He says that it is fully in accord with his intuitions, that he regards the killing of a normally intelligent human being as far more serious than the killing of a person so severely limited that he lacked the intellectual capacities of an adult pig. But this parry really misses the point. The question is whether Donaghy thinks that the killing of a human being so severely limited that he lacked the intellectual capacities of an adult pig would be less serious than the killing of that pig. If superior intelligence is what justifies privileged status in the moral community, then the pig who is smarter than a human being ought to have superior moral status. And I doubt that this is fully in accord with Donaghy's intuitions.

I doubt that anyone will be able to come up with a concrete and morally relevant difference that would justify, say, using a chimpanzee in an experiment rather than a human being with less capacity for reasoning, moral responsibility, etc. Should we then experiment on the severely retarded? Utilitarian considerations aside (the difficulty of comparing intelligence between species, for example), we feel a special obligation to care for the handicapped members of our own species, who cannot survive in this world without such care. Nonhuman animals manage very well, despite their "lower intelligence" and lesser capacities; most of them do not require special care from us. This does not, of course, justify experimenting on them. However, to subject to experimentation those people who depend on us seems even worse than subjecting members of other species to it. In addition, when we consider the severely retarded, we think, "That could be me." It makes sense to think that one might have been born retarded, but not to think that one might have been born a monkey. And so, although one can imagine oneself in the monkey's place, one feels a closer identification with the severely retarded human being. Here we are getting away from such things as "morally relevant differences" and are talking about something much more difficult to articulate, namely, the role of feelings and sentiment in moral thinking. We would be horrified by the use of the retarded in medical research. But what are we to make of this horror? Has it moral significance or is it "mere" sentiment, of no more import than the sentiment of whites against blacks? It is terribly difficult to know how to evaluate such feelings.[14] I am not going to say more about this, because I think that the treatment of severely incapacitated human beings does not pose an insurmountable objection to the privileged status principle. I am willing to admit that my horror at the thought of experiments being performed on severely mentally incapacitated human beings in cases in which I would find it justifiable and preferable to perform the same experiments on nonhuman animals (capable of similar suffering) may not be a moral emotion. But it is certainly not wrong of us to extend special care to members of our own species, motivated by feelings of sympathy, protectiveness, etc. If this is speciesism, it is stripped of its tone of

moral condemnation. It is not racist to provide special care to members of your own race; it is racist to fall below your moral obligation to a person because of his or her race. I have been arguing that we are morally obliged to consider the interests of all sentient creatures, but not to consider those interests equally with human interests. Nevertheless, even this recognition will mean some radical changes in our attitude toward and treatment of other species.[15]

NOTES

1. Peter Singer, *Animal Liberation* (A New York Review Book, 1975).
2. Singer, 5.
3. Bernard Williams, "The Idea of Equality," in Laslett and Runciman (Eds.), *Philosophy, Politics and Society* (Second Series), (Blackwell, 1962), 110–131, reprinted in Feinberg (Ed.), *Moral Concepts* (Oxford, 1970), 153–171.
4. Richard Wasserstrom, "Rights, Human Rights, and Racial Discrimination," *Journal of Philosophy* 61, No. 20 (1964), reprinted in A. I. Melden (Ed.), *Human Rights* (Wadsworth, 1970), 96–110.
5. Ibid., 106.
6. H. L. A. Hart, "Are There Any Natural Rights?," *Philosophical Review* 64 (1955), and S. I. Benn, "Abortion, Infanticide, and Respect for Persons," in Feinberg (Ed.), *The Problem of Abortion* (Wadsworth, 1973), 92–104.
7. Singer, 9.
8. Benn, "Equality, Moral and Social," *The Encyclopedia of Philosophy* 3, 40.
9. Singer, 266–267.
10. This conception of altruistic motivation comes from Thomas Nagel's *The Possibility of Altruism* (Oxford, 1970).
11. Williams, op. cit., 157.
12. Kevin Donaghy, "Singer on Speciesism," *Philosophic Exchange* (Summer 1974).
13. Singer, 22.
14. We run into the same problem when discussing abortion. Of what significance are our feelings toward the unborn when discussing its status? Is it relevant or irrelevant that it looks like a human being?

15. I would like to acknowledge the help of, and offer thanks to, Professor Richard Arneson of the University of California, San Diego; Professor Sidney Gendin of Eastern Michigan University; and Professor Peter Singer of Monash University, all of whom read and commented on earlier drafts of this paper.

REVIEW EXERCISES

1. List ten different ways in which we use nonhuman animals.
2. How is *cruelty* defined in terms of sentience?
3. How can the distinction between causing and allowing harm or pain be used to criticize the view that we can cause pain to animals because this is part of nature—that is, something that happens in the wild?
4. What is the meaning of the term *rights*?
5. For a being to be the kind of thing that can have rights, is it necessary that it be able to claim them? That it be a moral agent? Why or why not?
6. What do those who use the fact that animals have interests as a basis for their having rights mean by this?

7. Describe the issues involved in the debate over whether nonhuman animals' interests ought to be treated equally with those of humans.
8. List some anthropocentric reasons for preserving animal species.
9. What problems does the meaning of a "species" raise for deciding whether animal species have moral standing of some sort?
10. What reasons do supporters give for using nonhuman animals in experimental research? What reasons for opposing it do their opponents give? In particular, discuss the issues of pain and necessity.

DISCUSSION CASES

1. Animal Experimentation. Consider the experiments mentioned in this chapter in which nonhuman animals are used: dogs in early insulin discovery, frogs for testing pain relievers, fish for determining cancer-causing substances in lakes and rivers, monkeys for finding a vaccine for HIV, and various animals to show that veins do not carry air but blood, to test the effects of anesthesia, and to find a vaccine for polio. What do you think of using animals for experiments such as these? Do you agree with those who say that other methods should always be used even if we would then have to do without some life-enhancing or lifesaving knowledge or therapies? Would you distinguish between larger animals and mice and rats and fish? What are your primary reasons for believing as you do?

2. People Versus the Gorilla. Of the approximately 250 remaining mountain gorillas, some 150 are located in the 30,000-acre Parc des Volcans in the small African country of Rwanda. Rwanda has the highest population density in Africa. Most people live on small farms. To this population, the park represents survival land for farming. Eliminating the park could support 36,000 people on subsistence farms.

Should the park be maintained as a way to preserve the gorillas or should it be given to the people for their survival? Why?

3. What Is a Panther Worth? The Florida panther is an endangered species. Not long ago, one of these animals was hit by a car and seriously injured. He was taken to the state university veterinary medical school where steel plates were inserted in both legs, his right foot was rebuilt, and he had other expensive treatment. The Florida legislature was considering a proposal to spend $27 million to build forty bridges that would allow panthers to move about without the threat of other car injuries and death. Those who support the measure point out that the Florida panther is unique and can survive only in swamp land near the Everglades.

Should the state spend this amount of money to save the Florida panther from extinction? Why or why not?

YOU MAKE THE DECISION

Apply the theories and issues discussed in this chapter by accessing this animated simulation on the Ethics Resource Center.

Use the passkey that accompanies your book to gain access. If you do not have a passkey, visit cengagebrain.com to purchase instant access to additional study material.

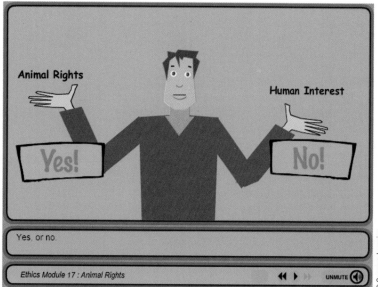

Animal Rights

Human Interest

Yes!

No!

Yes, or no.

Ethics Module 17 : Animal Rights   UNMUTE

18

Stem Cell Research, Cloning, and Genetic Engineering

GENETICS HAS come a long way since the Austrian monk Gregor Mendel's experiments with peas in the 1860s demonstrated that certain "hereditary factors" underlay the transmission of traits. Progress has accelerated since 1953, when biologists James Watson and Francis Crick determined the molecular structure of DNA, the basis of genetic information. The Human Genome Project, which mapped the entire human genome and was completed in 2000, promises even more wondrous things to come.

However, these scientific advances and their possibilities for human use have also been accompanied by serious ethical questions. This chapter will examine several of these questions as they relate to five central areas: stem cell research, human cloning, genetic engineering, genetically modified plants and animals, and genetic screening.

STEM CELL RESEARCH

In recent years, several public figures have made public appeals for the funding of stem cell research with its potential for treating or curing certain serious diseases. For example, Mary Tyler Moore, who has type I (insulin-dependent) diabetes and chairs the Juvenile Diabetes Foundation, brought children with this condition to testify in hearings before Congress. These children are not able to produce enough insulin to change nutrients into the energy needed for life; they must monitor their blood sugar and be injected with the needed amount of manufactured human insulin every day. Nancy and Ron Reagan

also support stem cell research and have spoken publicly about their hopes that this research can lead to cures for Alzheimer's disease, which afflicted the late President Ronald Reagan and currently 4.5 million other Americans. Actor Michael J. Fox has also promoted this research as a possible cure for the Parkinson's disease with which he is afflicted. Before he died, *Superman* star Christopher Reeve also lobbied for this research as a possible treatment for spinal cord injuries such as his.

Stem cell research is part of the field of *regenerative medicine*. The hope of its supporters is that efforts here can lead to the production of new cells, tissues, and organs that can be used to treat disease or injury. Certain stem cell therapies have been around for some time. One example is the transplantation of the stem cells present in bone marrow to treat certain forms of leukemia. Another more recent example is the extraction from cadavers of certain parts of the human pancreas for an experimental treatment of diabetes.[1]

What are stem cells, and how are they supposed to play a role in such efforts? Stem cells are found in the early embryo and in other parts of the human body that are not yet, or not yet fully, differentiated. In other words, they have not yet developed into specific skin, muscle, or other types of body cells and tissues. Embryonic stem cells are the fifty to one hundred cells that make up the inner mass of cells of the *blastocyst* (the rest form the outer shell that becomes the *placenta*) that exists in the first week of

Leslie E Kossoff/AFP/Getty Images

Actor and director Christopher Reeve testifying before Congress about potential stem cell treatments.

embryonic development. These cells are undifferentiated for a short period of time—approximately five to seven days after fertilization. They can be removed and placed in a culture where they will continue to divide. They are the cells from which all of the body's organs develop and thus are called *pluripotent*. However, once removed in this manner, they can no longer develop into a fetus.

In the case of these embryonic stem cells (ES cells), researchers hope to be able to learn how to control the process of their differentiation so as to be able to provoke them to become, for example, the insulin-producing beta cells of the pancreas (thus effecting the cure of diabetes) or neurons for the treatment of spinal cord injuries. Stem cells themselves cannot be directly implanted into the pancreas, however, because they can cause cancerous tumors to develop. Thus, it is necessary first to direct them into becoming the specialized cells that are needed.

On April 2, 2007, medical researchers from Britain reported that they had "grown human heart valve tissue from stem cells." If this is true, the replacement tissue generated could perhaps someday be used for heart disease patients.[2]

There are many practical problems with this process, among which are developing more efficient ways to obtain these cells, determining how to get them directed into such specialization, and controlling this process. Some researchers have pointed out that in the case of some diseases such as Lou Gehrig's disease (amyotrophic lateral sclerosis, or ALS) and other autoimmune diseases, replacing the damaged cells may not help the patient because it is "the cellular environment" that is the problem, and the newly added cells could be damaged as well. The source of the problem with the environment might need first to be addressed.[3]

Just as problematic are the ethical problems that are raised by ES cell research. Among the central ethical issues is the moral status of the early embryo. Those who believe that a human being exists from the time of conception also hold that the blastocyst, although a ball of cells smaller than a grain of sand, has full moral status. As such, they believe it wrong to use these embryos, even to save another life. (See Chapter 11 on abortion for the arguments regarding the moral status of the embryo.) Supporters, however, point out that leftover embryos now stored in fertility clinics (approximately half a million are now frozen in the United States) could be used because they are often otherwise destroyed, and using these embryos could do some good.

Legal and Ethical Issues

Legislative bodies around the world are grappling with the questions regarding the legal regulation or prohibition of stem cell research. As of 2001—by presidential directive of George W. Bush—only those ES cell lines that were already established could be used for research that was funded by the U.S. federal government. At that time, it was thought that some sixty or so viable cell lines would be available. However, as of mid-2005, only fifteen to twenty of these cell lines existed, and these had been largely contaminated with, for example, the mouse feeder cells on which they had been cultured. Worldwide, fewer than 150 lines have been created. In the United States, currently there are no laws prohibiting such research, though most has been conducted through private or state funding. One such example is California's Institute of Regenerative Medicine, for which voters approved $3 billion in funds for startup work. As of March 2007, this institute had decided to fund several groups after an extensive peer review process.[4] Scientists are concerned that the United States may lose its leadership role in this science to other countries. On April 11, 2007, the U.S. Senate passed the Human Cloning Ban and Stem Cell Research Protection Act of 2007; the House of Representatives then passed the bill by a wide margin. As the title indicates, although the ban on cloning human beings continues, the act holds that the federal government should provide funds for stem cell research. The Senate vote was sixty-three to thirty-four, with three more senators abstaining but in support. Nevertheless, the vote in favor was one vote short of that required to override an expected presidential veto. In June 2007, George W. Bush vetoed the bill as he had done the previous year.[5] In March, 2009, President Obama expanded the number of stem cell lines for use by thirteen new lines, and allowed federal grant money to be used for research on these lines.[6]

To overcome certain ethical concerns about the moral status of the early embryo, some people have suggested that adult stem cells be used. These exist in bone marrow and purportedly in other parts of the body such as the brain, skin, fat, and muscle.[7] The use of these cells seems to work in some cases. For example, "German doctors reported having repaired a large gap in a young girl's skull using a combination of bone graft and stem cells derived from her own fatty tissue."[8] Adult stem cells have also been used to treat heart failure patients, either by forming new heart muscle cells or by stimulating their production.[9] These adult stem cells may be part of the body's natural "repair mechanism."[10] However, at most, adult stem cells can be used to produce or spur the development of only a limited number of types of related tissues. They are *multipotent* rather than pluripotent. Moreover, they do not seem to be as vigorous as the ES cells. Recently, researchers have found evidence that stem cells might be present and obtainable from amniotic fluid. It would be a plentiful source and not as problematic as those obtained

from embryos. Although they have elements in common with embryonic stem cells, though, it is again not clear yet whether these amniotic stem cells would have the same potency as those taken from embryos.[11] Various groups in 2007 demonstrated that induced pluripotent stem cells could be made from mouse skin. These cells were found to be "indeed equivalent to ES cells, at least in mice. . . . [I]n November [2007] . . . two teams repeated the feat in human cells."[12]

Another line of research is inspired by the newt, a small amphibian. If it loses a limb, the newt can regenerate a new one. The idea would be to see whether certain already differentiated body cells could be reprogrammed in such a way that they could be de-differentiated—in other words, they might be brought back to a state closer to that of ES cells. Even further, this type of research might lead to a better understanding of the body's "innate capacity for regeneration" such as in wound healing.[13]

To supply ethical guidelines for stem-cell research, the National Academy of Sciences (NAS) has proposed a set of such recommendations for voluntary use by researchers. This set is modeled on the type of self-regulation that scientists proposed for recombinant DNA research in 1975, guidelines later adopted by the National Institutes of Health (NIH). These guidelines are particularly relevant for stem cell research in which the tissues and organs that might be developed would need to be tested first in animals. This may lead to the creation of *chimeras*, animals with some human cells or organs. This research is for medical purposes, not to produce the centaur and mermaids of mythology. In fact, doctors are already using pig heart valves that have some human cells to treat heart patients. While recommending that such testing be allowed, the NAS also recommended that (1) chimeraic animals not be allowed to mate because, if the cells invaded the sperm and eggs, this could lead to a human being conceived; (2) human stem cells not be allowed to become part or all of an animal's brain and not be injected into other primates; (3) the embryo should not be allowed to develop for more than fourteen days; and (4) women who donate eggs not be paid in order to avoid financial inducement.[14]

In 2007, a task force of the International Society for Stem Cell Research published its own guidelines for embryonic stem cell research. These guidelines were developed by ethicists and scientists and legal experts from fourteen countries. They are much like those of the National Academy of Sciences in the United States and do allow some research on chimeraic animals—those that could carry human gametes—but only if such research passes the review of an oversight committee. They also sought to justify the fourteen-day limit for embryo development, arguing that it is not until this point in the development of a "primitive streak" that the embryo "has begun to initiate organogenesis."[15]

HUMAN CLONING

A separate but possibly related issue is human cloning. There are basically two kinds of human cloning: therapeutic and reproductive. These should be treated separately.

Therapeutic Cloning

Therapeutic cloning is the use of cloning for medical purposes. It is possible to use this type of cloning in conjunction with stem cell therapy. The reason is that even if it were possible to direct embryonic stem cells to make tissue needed to treat a disease or injury, this tissue would be subject to immunological rejection by a patient's body. In this type of cloning, the nucleus of a somatic or bodily cell of a person, such as a skin cell, is inserted into an unfertilized egg that has had its own nucleus removed. The egg would then be stimulated and develop into an embryo. The stem cells in this blastocyst would be genetically identical to the person whose skin cell it was. The tissue would not then be rejected as foreign.

The ethical issues raised by this type of cloning mirror those of stem cell research and therapy as discussed above. However, additional ethical questions and concerns are raised by reproductive cloning.

Reproductive Cloning

A clone can be thought of as an individual or as a group of individuals who are genetically identical. Identical twins are such clones. Since the birth of Dolly the sheep at the Roslin Institute near Edinburgh, Scotland, in March 1996, people have wondered whether it also would be possible to produce humans by cloning. Dolly was a clone, a genetic "copy," of a six-year-old ewe. She was created by inserting the nucleus of a cell from the udder of this ewe into a sheep egg from which the nucleus had been removed. After being stimulated to grow, the egg was implanted into the uterus of another sheep from which Dolly was born. Because Dolly was a mammal like us, people concluded that it might be possible to clone human beings as well. Moreover, Dolly was produced from a somatic cell of an adult sheep with already-determined characteristics. Because the cells of an adult are already differentiated—that is, they have taken on specialized roles—scientists had previously assumed that cloning from such cells would not be possible. Now, it seemed, producing an identical, although younger, twin of an already existing human being might be possible.

The type of cloning described above is called *somatic cell nuclear transfer* (SCNT) because it transfers the nucleus of a somatic or bodily cell into an egg whose own nucleus has been removed. Cloning can also be done through a *fission* process, or cutting of an early embryo. Through this method it may be possible to make identical human twins or triplets from one embryo.

The potential for human cloning can be surmised from the progress of animal cloning. In just the past two decades, many higher mammals have been produced through cloning, including cows, sheep, goats, mice, pigs, rabbits, and a cat named "CC" for "carbon copy" or "copy cat." CC was produced in a project funded by an Arizona millionaire, John Sperling, who wanted to clone his pet dog, Missy, who had died. The company he and his team of scientists established, Genetic Savings and Clone, was based in Sausalito, California, and Texas A&M University at College Station, Texas.[16] In 2004, it was charging $50,000 for a cloned cat and $295 to $1,395 to store genetic material from a cat. Two kittens, Tabouli and Baba Ganoush, who were cloned from the same female Bengal tiger cat, were displayed at the annual cat show at Madison Square

Garden in October 2004. According to the owners, the kittens have personality similarities as well as differences.[17] Genetic Savings and Clone shut down in 2006.[18] However, Sperling established a new company, BioArts, in 2007. He then again attempted to clone the dog, Missy, using samples he had saved and frozen. She was "three quarters border collie and one quarter husky." This time he was successful and produced three clones, Mira, Chin-Gu, and Sarang, all born in February 2008. He said that "cloning techniques had become more efficient over the years" such that "1 percent to 4 percent of embryo transfers now result in a puppy."[19] Cloned animals have themselves produced offspring in the natural way. Dolly had six seemingly normal lambs. Several generations of mice have also been produced through SCNT. Clones have been derived not only from udder cells but also from cells from embryos and fetuses, as well as from mice tails and cumulus cells.

On February 25, 2005, a cloned foal stallion of a prize race horse was born in Cremona, Italy. The owners reported that the foal would be used primarily for breeding and, as of 2007, he appeared to be well and ready for that purpose.[20]

However, animal cloning has not always been efficient or safe. In the case of Dolly, for example, 277 eggs were used but only one lamb was produced. Moreover, cloned animals also have exhibited various abnormalities. In one study, all twelve cloned mice died between one and two years of age. Six of the cloned mice had pneumonia, four had serious liver damage, and one had leukemia and lung cancer. Dolly may have had arthritis, although this contention has been disputed. Some theorists suggest that this may be because she was cloned from the cell of an already aged adult sheep. In February 2003, Dolly was euthanized because she had developed an infectious and terminal lung disease. (However, see the discussion of this in the reading in this chapter by Macintosh.)

In terms of human reproduction, cloning would be directed to the development of a new human being who would be the identical twin of the person whose cell was used in the process. On the one hand, reproductive cloning may be thought of as one of several reproductive technologies that have been developed in recent decades. Among these are artificial insemination, in vitro fertilization with its resulting "test-tube babies," donated and frozen embryos and eggs, and the use of surrogate mothers.

Although these other methods of reproduction have been widely accepted, there is almost universal objection to reproductive cloning, even among those countries that allow and support stem cell research or therapeutic cloning. Some countries, such as the United Kingdom, have laws prohibiting reproductive cloning while still actively supporting therapeutic cloning. Japan, China, Singapore, and South Korea have similar laws. However, Germany, Austria, France, and The Netherlands have banned both types of cloning. Countries in South America, the Middle East, and Africa also have a diversity of regulation. In the United States, bills to regulate or prohibit human cloning have been proposed, but none has yet passed both houses of Congress. One reason is the failure to agree on whether to make a distinction between the two types of cloning. Ethical questions are central to reproductive cloning, and thus our focus here is on that form.

Ethical Issues

Although much of the reaction to cloning humans has been the product of both hype and fear, serious ethical questions also have been raised. One of the most serious concerns is that cloning might lead to harm to a child produced in this way, just as it has in some cases of animal cloning. For this reason alone, caution is advised. Some people have pointed out, though, that fertility clinics have had broad experience in growing human embryos, and thus cloning humans might be less risky than cloning animals. However, objections are also based on other considerations.

One ethical objection to human cloning is that it would amount to "playing God." The idea is that only God can and should create a human life. This role is specifically reserved to God, so we take on a role we should not play when we try to do it ourselves. Those who hold this view might use religious reasons and sources to support it. Although this looks like a religious position, it is not necessarily so. For example, it might mean that the coming to be of a new person is a *creation*, not a making or production. A creation is the bringing into being of a human being, a mysterious thing and something that we should regard with awe. When we take on the role of producing a human being, as in cloning, we become makers or manipulators of a product that we control and over which we take power. Another version of this objection stresses the significance of nature and the natural. In producing a human being through cloning, we go against human nature. In humans, as in all higher animals, reproduction is sexual, not asexual. Cloning, however, is asexual reproduction. Leon Kass is one of the strongest proponents of this view. (See the reading selection by him in this chapter). He alleges that in cloning someone, we would wrongly seek to escape the bounds and dictates of our sexual nature. According to another criticism of the "playing God" concept, attempting to clone a human being demonstrates *hubris* in that we think we are wise enough to know what we are doing when we are not. When we deal with human beings, we should be particularly careful. Above all, we should avoid doing what unknowingly may turn out to be seriously harmful for the individuals produced as well as for future generations.

Those who defend human cloning respond to this sort of objection by asking how this is any different from other ways we interfere with or change nature—in medicine, for example. Others argue that God gave us brains to use, and we honor God in using them especially for the benefit of humans and society. Critics also point out that in using technology to assist reproduction, we do not necessarily lose our awe in the face of the coming into being of a unique new being, albeit it happens with our help.

A second objection to the very idea of cloning a human being is that the person cloned would not be a *unique individual*. He or she would be the genetic copy of the person from whom the somatic cell was transferred. He or she would be the equivalent of an identical twin of this person, although years younger. Moreover, because our dignity and worth are attached to our uniqueness as individuals, cloned individuals would lose the something that is the basis of the special value we believe persons to have. Critics point out the difficulties that clones might have in maintaining their individuality would be similar to the difficulties that identical twins sometimes have. Sometimes they are dressed alike, and

often they are expected to act alike. The implication is that they do not have the freedom or ability to develop their own individual personalities. This objection is sometimes expressed as the view that a cloned human being would not have a soul, that he or she would be a hollow shell of a person. The idea is that if we take on the role of producing a human being through cloning, then we prevent God from placing a soul in that person.

One response to this objection points out how different the cloned individual would be from the original individual. Identical twins are more like each other than a clone would be to the one cloned. This is because the twins shared the same nuclear environment as well as the same uterus. Clones would have different mitochondria, the genes in the cytoplasm surrounding the renucleated cell that play a role in development. Clones would develop in different uteruses and be raised in different circumstances and environments. Studies of plants and animals give dramatic evidence of how great a difference the environment makes. The genotype does not fully determine the phenotype—that is, the genes' actual physical manifestations. CC, the cloned cat mentioned previously, does not quite look like its mother, Rainbow, a calico tricolored female. They have different coat patterns because genes are not the only things that control coat color. Just one year later, the visual difference was even more clear. CC also has a different personality. "Rainbow is reserved. CC is curious and playful. Rainbow is chunky. CC is sleek."[21] Although genes do matter, and thus there would be similarities between the clone and the one cloned, they would not be identical. On the matter of soul, critics wonder why could God not give each person, identical twin or clone, an individual soul because any living human being, cloned or not, would be a distinct being and so would have a human psyche or soul.

A third objection to human cloning is that any person has a *right to an open future* but that a cloned human being would not. He or she would be expected to be like the originating person and thus would not be free to develop as he or she chose. The person of whom someone was a clone would be there as the model of what he or she would be expected to be. Even if people tried not to have such expectations for the one cloned, they would be hard-pressed not to do so. Critics of this argument may admit that there might be some inclination to have certain expectations for the clone, but, they argue, this undue influence is a possibility in the case of all parents and children, and thus a possibility that is not limited to clones. Parents decide on what schools to send their children to and what sports or activities they will promote. The temptation or inclination may be there to unduly influence their children, but it is incumbent on parents to control it.

Related to the previous objection is one that holds that cloned children or persons would tend to be *exploited*. If one looks at many of the reasons given for cloning a person, the objection goes, they tend to be cases in which the cloning is for the sake of others. For example, the cloned child could be a donor for someone else. We might make clones who are of a certain sort that could be used for doing menial work or fighting wars. We might want to clone certain valued individuals, stars of the screen or athletics. In all of these cases, the clones would neither be valued for their own selves nor respected as unique persons. They would be valued for what they can bring to others. Kant is cited as the source of the moral principle that persons ought not simply be used but ought to be treated as ends in themselves.

Critics could agree with Kant but still disagree that a cloned human being would be any more likely than anyone else to be used by others for their own purposes only. Just because a child was conceived to provide bone marrow for a sick sibling would not prevent her from also being loved for her own sake. Furthermore, the idea that we would allow anyone to clone a whole group of individuals and imprison them while training them to be workers or soldiers is not living in the present world in which there are rightly legal protections against such treatment of children or other individuals. So, also, critics may contend, the possibility that some group might take over society and create a "brave new world" in which children were produced only through cloning is far-fetched and nothing more than fiction.

Some people believe that if human cloning were a reality, then it would only add to the *confusion within families* that is already generated by the use of other reproductive technologies. When donated eggs and surrogate mothers are used, the genetic parents are different from the gestational parents and the rearing parents, and conflicts have arisen regarding who the "real" parents are. Cloning, objectors contend, would create even more of a problem, adding to this confusion the blurring of lines between generations. The mother's child could be her twin or a twin of her own mother or father. What would happen to the traditional relationships with the members of the other side of the family, grandparents, aunts, and uncles? Or what will be the relationship of the husband to the child who is the twin of the mother or the wife to the child who is the twin of her husband?

Critics of these arguments respond that, although there is a traditional type of family that, in fact, varies from culture to culture, today there are also many different kinds of nontraditional families. Among these are single-parent households, adopted families, blended families, and lesbian and gay families. It is not the type of family that makes for a good loving household, the argument goes, but the amount of love and care that exists in one.

A final objection to human cloning goes something as follows: Sometimes we have a *gut reaction* to something we regard as abhorrent. This objection is sometimes called the "yuck" objection. We are offended by the very thought of it. We cannot always give reasons for this reaction, yet we instinctively know that what we abhor is wrong. Many people seem to react to human cloning in this way. The idea of someone making a copy of themselves or many copies of a famous star is simply bizarre, revolting, and repulsive, and these emotional reactions let us know that there is something quite wrong with it, even if we cannot explain fully what it is.

Any adequate response to this argument would entail an analysis of how ethical reasoning works when it works well. Emotional reactions or moral intuitions may indeed play a role in moral reasoning. However, most philosophers would agree that adequate moral reasoning should not rely on intuition or emotion alone. Reflections about why one might rightly have such gut reactions are in order. People have been known to have negative gut reactions to things that, in fact, are no longer regarded as wrong—interracial marriage, for example. It is incumbent on those who assert that something is wrong, most philosophers believe, that they provide rational arguments and well-supported reasons to justify these beliefs and emotional reactions.

Ethical objections to human cloning (whether reproductive or therapeutic) and stem cell research also often revolve around the treatment of embryos. Some of the same arguments regarding abortion are raised regarding these practices. One novel idea is to mix together embryos from fertility clinics. In some cases, the mixture would contain both male and female embryos. They would have virtually no chance of developing into a human being, and yet they would still produce stem cells. Thus, destroying them might not be objectionable.[22] It may also be possible to produce sources of stem cells from a human egg alone through parthenogenesis. Eggs do not halve their genetic total until late in their maturation cycle. Before that, they have a full set of genes. If they could be activated before this time and stimulated to grow, there might not be the same objection to using eggs as there has been to using early embryos made from combining sperm and egg.[23] The move to prohibit destroying new embryos but permit the use of already existing stem cell lines has proved to be problematic because these lines have been found to be limited in number and poor in quality.[24]

As we have seen, concerns about the protection of embryos have frequently prompted government to restrict or prohibit their use in research, as in therapeutic or reproductive cloning. Of particular concern has been the production of embryos for the express purpose of harvesting their stem cells, thus destroying them. No such restrictions have been placed on research using private funding, and thus several nongovernment labs have proceeded with such work. In early 1999, the legal counsel of the Department of Health and Human Services ruled that it is within the legal guidelines to fund human stem cell research if the cells are obtained from private funds. Later, the members of the National Bioethics Advisory Commission (NBAC)—fifteen geneticists, ethicists, and others appointed by President Clinton in 1996— voted against making a distinction between producing and deriving the cells and simply using them. One suggestion was to use germline cells of fetuses that are already dead as a result of legal abortion.

However, these cells may not be identical to stem cells derived from embryos, and deriving stem cells from this source is difficult. The National Bioethics Advisory Commission's charter expired in 2001. In its place was established the President's Council on Bioethics. This commission reported its conclusions on human cloning in July 2002, and recommended a four-year moratorium on all types of human cloning. In 2009, President Barack Obama replaced the Council with the Presidential Commission for the Study of Bioethical Issues, to be chaired by philosopher Amy Gutmann and focused on specific policy recommendations.[25] This Commission has yet to issue a recommendation on cloning. As of 2008, fifteen states had banned cloning in one form or another, but California has reversed an earlier moratorium. In September 2002, the state's governor signed into law a bill that "explicitly allows research on stem cells from fetal and embryonic tissue."[26] The state also plans to fund such research.

Some critics of state cloning laws argue that it is too difficult to ban one type of cloning without the other. For example, if reproductive cloning were prohibited but research or therapeutic cloning were allowed, then how would one know whether cloned embryos were being used in fertility clinics? It would be impossible to distinguish them from ordinary ones. Furthermore, if there are no federal funds provided for research cloning, then there also will be no oversight. We will not know what was going on behind closed doors. Scientists also point out how essential federal research funds have been for new developments. Just how the public will continue to respond to these possibilities remains to be seen. However, we can and do generally believe it appropriate to regulate scientific research and industrial applications in other areas, and we may well consider such regulations appropriate for human cloning also. For example, regulations regarding consent, the protection of experimental subjects and children, and the delineation of family responsibilities are just some of the matters that may be appropriately regulated. Other ethical issues are raised by the use of *surrogate mothers* and *prenatal embryo transfer* and are related to social matters such as the nature of parentage and to concerns about the dangers of commercialization and the buying and selling of babies.[27]

GENETIC ENGINEERING

Developments in modern genetics also have presented us with new ethical problems. The Human Genome Project, an effort to map the entire human genome, was completed in the summer of 2000 and its results first published in early 2001. The map was expected to contain 100,000 genes, but scientists now believe that only 20,000 human genes exist. Humans have roughly the same number of genes as other animals, but scientists found that "we have only 300 unique genes in the human (genome) that are not in the mouse," for example.[28] However, although humans have approximately the same number of genes as a spotted green puffer fish, it is surmised that human capacity comes from "a small set of regulatory genes that control the activity of all the other genes." These would be different in the puffer fish.[29]

Two entities had competed in this race to map the entire human genome. One was a public consortium of university centers in the United States, Great Britain, and Japan. It made its findings publicly available. It used the genome from a mosaic of different individuals. The other research was done by Celera Genomics, a private company run by Dr. Craig Venter. It used a "shotgun" strategy. Its genetic source material came from Venter and four others. Celera also proposed to make its results available to the public after they have been analyzed—that is, to tell where the genes lay in the entire DNA sequence. On September 4, 2007, Dr. Venter published his entire genetic sequence.[30] To have one's complete genome sequenced in this way, the cost is still quite high, as much as $350,000. However, a few companies have begun charging much less, from $1000 to $2500, for a genetic screening of roughly 20 medical conditions. These companies include 23 and Me, Navigenics, and deCODE genetics. You simply send them a saliva or cheek swab and they "match the results with the latest publications on traits, common diseases, and ancestry."[31]

Such projects have also attempted to determine what role the various hereditary elements, including the genes, play. In this effort, one focus has been on individual differences. The human genome, "a string of 3 billion chemical letters that spell out every inherited trait," is almost identical in all humans: 99.99 percent. But some differences, so-called genetic misspellings that are referred to as *single nucleotide polymorphisms* (SNPs or "snips"), can be used to identify genetic diseases. The SNPs give base variations that contribute to individual differences in appearance and health, among other things. Scientists will look for differences, for example, by taking DNA samples of 500 people with diabetes and a similar number from people without the disease and then look for DNA patterns.[32] The SNPs also influence how people react differently to medications. Some people can eat high-calorie and high-fat foods and still not put on weight while others are just the opposite. Some have high risks of heart disease, whereas others do not. With genetic discoveries based on the Human Genome Project and more recent efforts, one hope is that diets will be able to be tailored to individual human genetic makeups.

On October 30, 2002, "a $100 million project to develop a new kind of map of the human genome was announced." The group behind the effort is an international consortium of government representatives from Japan, China, and Canada, and the Wellcome Trust of London. The U.S. NIH is investing $39 million in the project. The "goal is to hasten discovery of the variant genes thought to underlie common human diseases like diabetes, asthma, and cancer."[33] Scientists have used the Human Genome Project map as a master reference and compare individual genomes to it. They are attempting to locate the genes that cause various diseases. Some diseases are caused by single genes, such as that producing cystic fibrosis, but others are thought to be caused by several genes acting together. Other genes might be discovered that relate to certain beneficial human traits. For example, some scientists are working on locating what they call a "skinny gene." Using mice from whom a single gene has been removed, scientists at Deltagen, a company in Redwood City, California, have been able to produce mice that remain slim no matter how much they are fed.[34] According to geneticist David Botstein, the impact of the Human Genome Project on medicine "should exceed that 100 years ago of X-rays, which gave doctors their first view inside the intact, living body."[35] Currently, "gene therapies are being developed that would block myostatin in humans," something directed to the treatment of muscular dystrophy and frailty in older persons. Myostatin curbs the growth of muscles. However, this also has wider applications. For example, a breed of cattle called Belgian Blue has been developed that has huge muscles and very little fat.[36] This may also cause concern about use of such techniques by athletes, who could pump up without much effort. Moreover, "gene therapy leaves no trace in the blood or urine," which would make drug testing of athletes, which is already problematic, even more difficult. Other gene therapies, including so-called gene doping, have been and are being developed that could cause the human body to produce extra red blood cells. Persons with this natural abnormality have often been exceptional athletes, including a gold medalist in cross-country skiing.[37]

Ethical Issues

Before new developments in genetics can be transformed into practical benefits, studies using human subjects often must be done. Since the Nuremberg trials and the resulting code for ethical experimentation, informed consent has been a requirement for the conduct of research that involves human subjects. Consider a study designed to determine the possible benefits of an experimental treatment for Parkinson's disease.[38] This frightening disease afflicts 1.5 million people in the United States as well as many others around the world. Its sufferers first experience weakness and then slurred speech, uncontrollable tremors, and eventually death. The cause of the disease is not entirely known, and there is no cure yet. What is known is that the disease works by destroying a small section of the brain, the substantia nigra, which controls movement. One new hope for treatment of Parkinson's disease uses the transplanted brain cells from aborted six- to eight-week-old fetuses.[39] Are the patients in this trial and others that involve genetic engineering likely to be able to give the requisite kind of informed consent to guarantee that the experiment is ethically acceptable? Consider the actual case. The potential participants already have experienced some symptoms of the disease. Here is a treatment that promises to help them. They are informed that the study is a randomized clinical trial and that if they agree to

participate they may or may not get the experimental treatment. If they are randomized to the control group rather than the treatment group, then they will go through the same procedure including having holes drilled in their skull and tubes passed into their brain, but they will not actually be receiving anything that will benefit them. In fact, like those in the treatment group, they will be subject to the usual risk of brain damage and stroke that accompanies the procedure.

What kind of thought process would such persons be likely to undergo in deciding whether to participate in this trial? Is informed and free consent likely? Would they really be aware of the various details of the procedure? Would they really understand their chances of being in the treatment group? Would they be influenced, if not coerced, into joining the study because of the nature of their disease and great need? Would they also have to be willing to undergo this risky procedure solely for the sake of the knowledge that might be gained from the study and not for their own immediate benefit? In other words, would they have to be willing to be used as guinea pigs? It is possible that the conditions of genuine informed and free consent would be met. However, it is also likely that these conditions could not be met, because the patients either would not understand what was involved or would be somehow coerced into participation.

As in the testing of many new medical therapies, modern scientific methodology demands that studies be controlled and randomized; otherwise, the information derived could be unreliable. However, to do this particular study we seem required to violate one demand for an ethical experiment that uses human subjects—namely, that the participants' consent be informed and uncoerced. What we have here is an example of one of the many ethical dilemmas that we face today because we live in a world in which modern science and technology are pervasive. We use knowledge gained by science to help us, but we are also subject to the demands of science. Modern technologies provide us with many goods and opportunities, yet in giving us more choices they also present us with more difficult ethical decisions. These problems have no easy solutions. Another ethical question that scientists sometimes face is whether one should let ethical concerns determine whether to carry on some research. An example of failing to heed such ethical concerns is the Tuskegee syphilis study discussed in Chapter 5. Is knowing always a good, and thus should the science that helps us know what is the case always be pursued? Those who analyze the ethics of research using human subjects continue to debate the issues surrounding the informed consent requirement. In the end, this requires that people not be used or that they not be used for goals and purposes to which they do not consent or make their own. You may recognize this as a requirement of Kant's moral philosophy and can refer to the discussion of its basis in Chapter 5. In this chapter, we will suggest ways to analyze a few other problems that modern science and technology now pose.

The possibility of gene therapy for example, presents us with new ethical problems. If it were possible to use these methods to activate, replace, or change malfunctioning genes, then this would be of great benefit for the many people who suffer from genetic diseases. Using genetic techniques to provide human blood-clotting factor for hemophiliacs, manufactured human insulin for diabetics, human growth hormone for those who need it, and better pain relievers for everyone is surely desirable and ethically defensible. However, use of the technology also raises ethical concerns. Among these questions are those related to the risks that exist for those who undergo experimental genetic therapies. We also should be concerned about the access to these procedures, so that it is not just those who are already well off who benefit from them. The biotechnology industry continues to grow. Should information and products of great medical benefit be able to be kept secret and patented by their developers? For example, the company Myriad Genetics found a gene linked with breast cancer, and attempted to patent the gene.[40] In another example, therapeutic techniques now allow the alteration of genes in sperm, that affect not the individual himself but his offspring and thus alter human lineage.[41] It is one thing to do this in the interest of preventing genetic disease in one's offspring, but it is quite another to add new genetically based capabilities to one's children or to the human race.

Although many of these capabilities are still only a distant possibility, they give us cause for concern, not the least of which is whether we are wise enough to do more good than harm with these methods. Two of the National Bioethics Advisory Commission's major topics of discussion were the rights of human research subjects and the use of genetic information. You can continue to follow news accounts of the new reproductive and genetic technologies as well as the reports of committees such as the Presidential Commission for the Study of Bioethical Issues. As you do, you should be more aware of the variety of ethical issues that they involve or address. The issues are complex, but the first step in responding to them is to recognize them.

GENETICALLY MODIFIED PLANTS AND ANIMALS

You may be aware of protests against genetically modified food, sometimes called "Frankenfood." That nickname comes from Mary Shelley's novel about Dr. Frankenstein, who creates a monster that cannot be controlled. Critics fear the same for food that has been genetically modified or tampered with. What are they talking about? These are crops that have been genetically modified to include desired traits such as drought tolerance or lowered freezing level. Although some of these traits could be established through traditional breeding methods, some could not. Genetic mechanisms both speed up the process and give more control over it.

In 2004, the National Academy of Sciences determined that "genetically engineered crops do not pose health risks that cannot also arise from crops created by other techniques, including conventional breeding."[42] It is not the method of production that should be of concern, the NAS argued, but the resulting product. Nevertheless, there is much that the general public does not understand about so-called genetically modified food.

Strictly speaking, genetic engineering involves inserting a specific gene from one organism into another—and the function of the gene is known. On the other hand, "nearly every food we eat has been genetically modified" in the broader sense in that plants have been cross-bred for centuries.[43]

Cross-breeding "involves the mixing of thousands of genes, most unknown."[44] In some cases, mutations are now caused by "bombarding seeds with chemicals or radiation" and seeing what comes of it. For example, lettuce, beans, and grapefruit have been so modified.[45]

Over time, U.S. farms have gradually increased the amount of crops that have been genetically engineered. In 2002, one-third of the corn grown in the United States was genetically engineered. Farmers now grow "more than 79 million acres of genetically engineered corn and soybeans, the nation's two most widely planted commodities."[46] Of the cotton crop, 71 percent is also gene-altered. "Nearly two-thirds of the products on American supermarket shelves are estimated to contain genetically altered crops."[47] These crops are easier and cheaper to grow and can provide more food from less land. They need fewer chemicals in the way of insect repellants, herbicides, and fertilizers because they are "engineered to be toxic to insect pests or to be resistant to a popular weed killer."[48] For example, the insertion of *Bacillus thuringiensis* (B.t.) genes into corn enables it to resist the corn borer. Environmentally damaging herbicides can then be reduced. New strains of rice may also help solve the world famine problem. So-called "golden rice" can also help lessen vitamin A deficiency in poor countries because it contains greater amounts of the vitamin than other rice strains. (Vitamin A deficiency causes blindness and other infections among the world's poorest children.) "Edible vaccines in tomatoes and potatoes" would make them more easily available to people than injectable ones.[49] Moreover, genetically modified foods can also lead to "more healthful foods, a cleaner environment, and a worldwide ability to produce more food on less land—using less water, fewer chemicals, and less money."[50] This is especially important for areas in the world—for example, many African countries—where famine and malnutrition are serious problems. For example, opposition to genetically modified food has led Uganda to prohibit efforts to develop a fungus-resistant banana, even though this fungus has seriously damaged its banana crop, one of its most important.[51]

At the same time, protests against genetically-modified foods have grown, especially in Europe and Japan, but also in the United States. Some of the criticism is probably based on ungrounded fears. On the other hand, some hazards may be real. Herbicide-resistant crops may help create "super-weeds." Neighboring crops may be contaminated with foreign genes. New forms of insects that are resistant to the inbred herbicides may develop. Crop antibiotic resistance may transfer to humans.[52] It may well be possible to reduce some of these risks, for example, by creating sterile plants—that is, plants that do not produce pollen, which could be a means of contamination. So far, many of the cited possible risks have not materialized, but this does not prove such risks do not exist.

Ethical Issues

Much of the debate about genetically modified food and crops has been a matter of comparing benefits and risks. As described in Chapter 4, cost–benefit analysis first involves estimating risks and benefits—an empirical matter—and then a comparative evaluation in which one tries to determine the various values to show whether the positive values outweigh the negative consequences. Longer and healthier lives for more people weigh on the positive side, and risks to longevity and health weigh on the negative side. There is also the problem of how to count speculative and unknown risks and who should prove what. If we are risk-averse and come down on the side of conservatism, then we may avoid unknown risks but also eliminate possible benefits, including that of saving lives.

A different ethical issue that concerns some people is the whole idea of interfering with nature. Are there not natural species of plants as well as animals that we should respect and not manipulate? One problem with this line of criticism is that it is difficult to distinguish good forms of manipulating nature from unacceptable ones. Those who object on these grounds may point out that cross-species transfers are what is objectionable. One problem with this objection is that similar transfers have occurred in nature—from basic plant genetics to the long-term patterns of evolution.

Genetically modified animals may present some of the same ethical problems, for there are benefits and risks to be compared and also transfers among species. Some of the benefits from genetic modifications can be seen in animals such as goats, rabbits, and cows, which may be modified to include pharmaceuticals in their milk. PPL Therapeutics in the United Kingdom, for example, has been "experimenting with transgenic sheep's milk to produce protein drugs for cystic fibrosis and hemophilia."[53] Other species may be modified to produce more meat or meat with less fat or to have better resistance to disease. Still, in other cases, these practices promote economic efficiency. Genetically modified animals may also benefit us in other ways. For example, pigs have been created with human genes. The reason for this is that pig organs are similar to human organs and, if modified with human genes, may be transplanted into humans without immune rejection. This is called *xenotransplantation*. Cloned animals also present a kind of case of genetically modified animal. In the process of cloning, genes may be inserted or removed. One company has cloned five pigs—Millie, Christa, Alexis, Carrel, and Dotcom—with human genes as a prelude to use for transplants.[54]

Genetically modified (GM) animals are used in research. (See, for example, the knockout mice example from the previous chapter.) But they also might provide "better yields of meat, eggs, and milk."[55] Still, they may also pose risks. For example, some critics worry that farm-raised and genetically altered salmon, if released into the wild, might harm other species of fish.[56] There is uneasiness, too, about combining elements of different species because it transgresses natural boundaries. The same responses to these ethical problems here can be given as in the case of plants, however. In addition, the "yuck" objection is sometimes also raised in this context. For example, just the thought of having a pig heart or lung within one's own body might provoke this reaction in some people. The same response regarding the objection to human cloning noted earlier in this chapter may also be given here. Among the ethical issues that apply to animals but not plants is their ethical or humane treatment. This may involve not only the engineering of them but also their suffering and death—as in the case of pigs whose organs would be transplanted or mice who would be given a human cancer. (See the previous chapter on animal rights for more on this problem.)

GENETIC SCREENING

Advances in genetics have also made possible a new type of screening procedure. Insurers and prospective employers may now or soon have access to individual genetic information and be able to use that information to their own advantage—but not necessarily to the advantage of the person being screened. Although the procedures may be new, the ethical issues are similar to those raised by other types of screening, including drug screening.

If you are on the job in your office, should your employer be able to monitor your behavior with cameras, microphones, and access to your computer and other files? It may well be in the best interest of your employer to make sure that you are using your time well for the benefit of the company. However, you may want and expect a certain amount of privacy, even at work. Privacy is also at risk on the Internet. Many people are very concerned about giving out personal information over the web and want to be assured that they will have control over how their personal information is used.[57]

"In a typical five-day stay at a teaching hospital, as many as 150 people—from nursing staff to X-ray technicians to billing clerks—have legitimate access to a single patient's records."[58] Increasingly, more of the things that we used to take as guaranteed areas of privacy are no longer so. Thus, we need to consider whether this should be the case. We think that people generally have a right to privacy, but we are less sure what this means and what kinds of practices would violate privacy. Suppose, for example, that a technology existed that could read a person's mind and the condition of various parts of her body, could hear and see what goes on in one's home—his bedroom or bathroom—and could record all of these in a data bank that would be accessible to a variety of interested parties. What, if anything, would be wrong with this?[59] One of the things that we find problematic about others having access to this knowledge is that they would have access to matters that we would not want anyone else to know. According to Thomas Scanlon, this is what the right to privacy is—a right "to be free from certain intrusions."[60] Some things, we say, are just nobody else's business.

The Value of Privacy

If this definition of privacy seems reasonable, then we can ask why we would not want certain intrusions like those in the hypothetical example. Many reasons have been suggested, and you may sympathize with some more than others. Four are provided here. The first concerns the kinds of feelings that one would have about certain things being known or observed— one's thoughts, bathroom behavior, or sexual fantasies, for example. It may well be that one should not feel emotions like shame or unease at such things being known. Perhaps we have these feelings simply as a result of social expectation. Nevertheless, many of us do have these *negative feelings*.

A second reason why we might want certain things kept to ourselves is our desire to control information about us and to let it be known only to those to whom we choose to reveal it. Such control is part of our ability to own our own lives. We speak of it as a form of *autonomy* or self-rule. In fact, the loss of control over some of these more personal aspects of our lives is a threat to our very selfhood, some say. For example, in his study of what he calls "total institutions" such as prisons and mental hospitals, Erving Goffman described the way that depriving a person of privacy is a way of *mortifying* (literally killing) the self.[61] Having a zone of privacy around us that we control helps us define ourselves and mark us off from others and our environment. This reason for the value of privacy is related to both the third and fourth reasons.

Third, privacy helps in the formation and continuation of *personal relations*. We are more intimate with friends than with strangers, and even more so with lovers than with mere acquaintances. Those things about ourselves that we confide in with those closest to us are an essential part of those relationships. According to Charles Fried, "privacy is the necessary context for relationships which we would hardly be human if we had to do without—the relationships of love, friendship, and trust."[62] Sexual intimacies are thus appropriate in the context of a loving relationship because they are privacy sharings that also help to establish and further that relationship.

Fourth, we want to keep certain things private because of the risk that the knowledge might be used against us to cause us harm. *Screening* procedures in particular come to mind here. Drug screening, HIV testing, or genetic disease scans all make information available to others that could result in social detriment. For example, we could be harmed in our employment or our ability to obtain insurance. The problem of *data banks* is also at issue here. Our medical records, records of psychiatric sessions, histories of employment, and so forth could be used legitimately by certain people. However, they also may be misused by those who have no business having access to them. In a particularly problematic case, the managed care company that was paying for the psychological counseling of one patient asked to inspect his confidential files. The psychologist was concerned. "The audit occurred, they rifled through my files," he said, and "made copies and went. But it changed things. He (the patient) became more concerned about what he was saying. . . . A few visits later he stopped coming."[63] Another case is also illustrative of the harm that can be caused by the invasion of privacy. In 1992, someone obtained a copy of the hospital records of a person running for Congress and sent them anonymously to the press. *The New York Post* published the material, including notes about this person's attempt to kill herself with sleeping pills and vodka. In spite of this, the candidate won the election; still, she successfully sued the hospital for invasion of privacy.[64]

Screening and Conflicts of Interest

It is with this fourth reason in particular that the matter of possible *conflict of interest* arises. An employer may have a legitimate interest in having a drug-free workplace, for example. It has a valid economic interest, for one's employees may not be able to do an effective job if they have drug-use problems. Passengers on public transportation may also have a legitimate interest in seeing that those who build and operate the bus, train, or plane are able to function well and safely. Airline passengers may have an interest in having other passengers and their bags scanned to prevent dangerous materials from being carried on board. It is not clear in whose interest is the drug screening of athletes. In professional athletics, it may be the economic interests of the owners, and in collegiate athletics and nonprofessional competitions such as the Olympics it may be for the sake of the fairness of the competition as well as the health of the athletes themselves.

In cases of conflicts of interest generally, and in the cases given here, we want to know on which side the interest is stronger. In the case of *drug testing* of airline pilots, the safety of the passengers seems clearly to outweigh any interest the pilots might have in retaining their privacy. In the case of employee drug use, it is not so clear that employers' economic interests outweigh the employees' privacy interests. In these cases, one might well argue that unless there is observable evidence of inefficiency, drug testing should not be done, especially mandatory random drug testing. In the case of *genetic screening* by life or health insurance providers, the answer also seems less clear. If a person has a genetic defect that will cause a disease that will affect his life expectancy, is his interest in keeping this information secret more important than the financial interests of the insurer knowing that information? A person's ability to obtain life insurance will affect payments to others on his or her death. In the case of health insurance coverage where not socially mandated or funded, the weight might well be balanced in favor of the person because having access to health care plays such a major role in a person's health. In fact, some state legislatures have moved to prevent health insurers from penalizing individuals who are "genetically predisposed to certain diseases."[65] In arguing for these laws, supporters insisted that they were designed to prevent "genetic discrimination." The phrase is apt in the sense that it seeks to prevent people from being singled out and penalized for things that are not in their power to control—their genes. Currently, the "Genetic Information Nondiscrimination Act . . . makes it illegal for insurers and employers to discriminate against people with genetic markers for diseases like cancer, Alzheimer's disease, and diabetes." This act took full effect on Nov. 21, 2009.[66]

In the case of *AIDS screening*, consequentialist arguments might make the most sense. We would thus ask whether mandatory testing would really produce more harm than good or more good than harm overall. Would mandatory screening lead fewer people to come forth voluntarily? What of the mandatory screening of physicians, dentists, and their patients? Some people argue that "mandatory testing of health workers for the AIDS virus . . . would be costly, disruptive, a violation of doctors' right to privacy, and the ruination of some careers."[67] The well-known case of a Florida dentist infecting a patient who later died caused quite a bit of alarm. However, in one study of patients of a surgeon who died of AIDS, 1,652 of his total of 1,896 patients were found and only one, an intravenous drug user, had AIDS.[68] The risk also goes the other way, with patients infecting health care workers. In 1990, the U.S. Centers for Disease Control and Prevention reported that 5,819 of the 153,000 reported cases of AIDS, or 4 percent, involved health care workers. This included 637 physicians, 42 surgeons, 156 dentists and hygienists, and 1,199 nurses.[69] It is not known whether any of these had other risk factors, but it does raise serious concern for health care workers.

In the case of airport *security screening*, a "backscatter" machine has been developed that can see through a person's clothing—that is, down to the skin—so that security personnel can determine better than with metal detectors whether a person is carrying a concealed item that could pose a danger to others.[70] Will people mind this invasion of their privacy? They may sometimes appear almost nude to the screeners. Or would the better detection achieved by this method be worth the kind of invasion of privacy that is involved? (See chapter 1 for more on this issue and an image from such a scanner.)

This as well as other screening procedures can be evaluated in several ways. However, one of the most reasonable is to compare the interests of the various parties involved in order to determine whether the interest in privacy on the part of the ones screened is stronger or more important morally than the interests of those who wish or need the information produced by the screening. Whether the privacy interest is stronger will depend on the reasons why we might think privacy is important or valuable.

With every new scientific advance and development come new ethical problems, for there are new questions about what we ought and ought not to do. The areas treated in this chapter that are based on scientific advances in genetics are no different. As new genetic information comes along, further ethical questions will need to be addressed. However, from the suggestions given for thinking ethically about the problems addressed here, hopefully a basis has been provided for future discussions as well.

In the readings in this chapter, the Leon Kass essay reflects the views of a geneticist and physician who is deeply concerned about one of these new developments, human cloning. On the other side is Kerry Lynn Macintosh, who believes that, with care, technologies such as human cloning are not as problematic as often thought.

NOTES

1. *Scientific American* (July 2005): A6–A27.
2. "British Researchers Grow Heart Tissue from Stem Cells," Agence France Presse, Yahoo News, April 2, 2007; "British Team Grows Human Heart Valve from Stem Cells," *The Guardian*, April 2, 2007 (at http://www.guardian.co.uk/science/2007/apr/02/stemcells.genetics).
3. Carl T. Hall, "Stem Cell Research Opens New Doors," *San Francisco Chronicle*, April 16, 2007, pp. A1, A9.
4. Carl T. Hall, "Stem Cell Grants Come with Dash of Criticism," *San Francisco Chronicle*, March 31, 2007, pp. B1–B2.
5. http://en.wikipedia.org/wiki/Stem_cell_controversy.
6. Nicholas Wade, "13 New Stem Cell lines Open to research," *The New York Times*, Dec. 2, 2009, p. A25.
7. *Scientific American*, op. cit., pp. A12–A13.
8. Ibid., p. A13.
9. *The Johns Hopkins Medical Letter* (Nov. 2003), pp. 1, 2, 7.
10. *The New York Times*, Aug. 24, 2004, p. D1.
11. Carl T. Hall, "Amniotic Fluid a Promising Stem Cell Source, *San Francisco Chronicle*, Jan. 8, 2007, pp. A1, A6.
12. "Breakthrough of the Year: The Runners-Up," *Science*, December 21, 2007, p. 1844.

13. *Scientific American*, op. cit., p. A14.
14. *The New York Times*, April 27, 2005, pp. A1, A16.
15. George Q. Daley et al., "The ISSCR Guidelines for Human Embryonic Stem Cell Research," *Science*, vol. 315, February 2, 2007, pp. 603–604.
16. Jason Thompson, "Here, Kitty, Kitty, Kitty, Kitty!" *San Francisco Chronicle*, Feb. 24, 2002, p. D6. The project had a Web site (www.missyplicity.com).
17. *The New York Times*, Oct. 8, 2004, p. A24.
18. Peter Fimrite, "Pet-Cloning Business Closes—Not 'Commercially Viable.'" *San Francisco Chronicle*, Oct. 11, 2006, p. B9.
19. James Barron, "Biotech Company to Auction Chances to Clone a Dog," *The New York Times*, May 21, 2008, p. A17.
20. Yahoo News, April 14, 2005; www.cryozootech.com/index.php?m=the_horses&d=pieraz_st_en&l=en.
21. "Copied Cat Hardly Resembles Original," CNN.com, Jan. 21, 2003. It is also interesting to note that CC has since given birth to normal, healthy kittens that were naturally fathered; see http://en.wikipedia.org/wiki/CC_%28cat%29.
22. Gina Kolata, "Hybrid Embryo Mixture May Offer New Source of Stem Cells for Study," *The New York Times*, June 5, 2002, p. D3.
23. Jose B. Cibel et al., "The First Human Cloned Embryo," *Scientific American* (Jan. 2002): 44–51.
24. Gina Kolata, "Researchers Say Embryos in Labs Aren't Available," *The New York Times*, Aug. 26, 2002, p. A1; Marjorie Miller, "New Breed of Cloned Pigs—Organs Wanted for Humans," *San Francisco Chronicle*, March 15, 2000, p. A3.
25. http://en.wikipedia.org/wiki/The_President's_Council_on_Bioethics.
26. http://www.ncsl.org/issuesresearch/health/human-cloninglaws/tabid/14284/default.aspx; "California Law Permits Stem Cell Research," *The New York Times*, Sept. 23, 2002, p. A18.
27. The procedure known as embryo transfer involves flushing the embryo out of the uterus and implanting it in the uterus of another female. Sometimes this is done when a woman is able to carry a fetus but not able to conceive because of damaged or missing ovaries. A man can provide the sperm for artificial insemination of a surrogate. The procedure then transfers the fetus to her uterus, and she undergoes a normal pregnancy and birth.
28. Tom Abate, "Genome Discovery Shocks Scientists," *San Francisco Chronicle*, Feb. 11, 2001, p. A1.
29. *The New York Times*, Oct. 21, 2004, p. A23.

30. http://en.wikipedia.org/wiki/Human_Genome_ Project#Whose_genome_was_sequenced.3F.

31. "Breakthrough of the Year: The Runners-Up," *Science*, Dec. 21, 2007, p. 1843.

32. Tom Abate, "Proofreading the Human Genome," *San Francisco Chronicle*, Oct. 7, 2002, p. E1; Nicholas Wade, "Gene-Mappers Take New Aim at Diseases," *The New York Times*, Oct. 30, 2002, p. A21.

33. Wade, "Gene-Mappers."

34. "Decoding the Mouse," San Francisco Chronicle, Feb. 24, 2002, p. G2.

35. Nicholas Wade, "On Road to Human Genome, a Milestone in the Fruit Fly," *The New York Times*, March 24, 2000, p. A19.

36. To see a photo of the Belgian Blues go to www.ansi. okstate.edu/breeds/cattle/belgianblue.

37. *The New York Times*, Aug. 25, 2004, p. A23.

38. See Barbara MacKinnon, "How Important Is Consent for Controlled Clinical Trials?" *Cambridge Quarterly of Healthcare Ethics*, 5, no. 2 (Spring 1996): 221–227.

39. We will bracket the issue of using aborted fetuses in research for the purpose of focusing on the other aspects of this study.

40. Reported in *The New York Times*, May 21, 1996.

41. *The New York Times*, Nov. 22, 1994, p. A1.

42. *The New York Times*, July 28, 2004, p. A13.

43. *The New York Times*, Jan. 11, 2005, p. D7.

44. *The New York Times*, July 28, 2004, p. A13.

45. *The New York Times*, Jan. 11, 2005, p. D7.

46. Philip Brasher, "Plowing Ahead with Biotech Crops," *San Francisco Chronicle*, March 30, 2002, p. A4.

47. Carey Goldberg, "1,500 March in Boston to Protest Biotech Food," *The New York Times*, March 27, 2000, p. A14.

48. Brasher, op cit.

49. See http://www.csa.com/discoveryguides/gmfood/ overview.php.

50. *The New York Times*, Jan. 1, 2005, p. D7.

51. Ibid.

52. See www.genewatch.org.

53. Tom Abate, "Biotech Firms Transforming Animals into Drug-Producing Machines," *San Francisco Chronicle*, Jan. 17, 2000, p. B1.

54. Gina Kolata, "Company Says It Cloned Pig in Effort to Aid Transplants," *The New York Times*, March 15, 2000, p. A21; and Marjorie Miller, "New Breed of Cloned Pigs—Organs Wanted for Humans," *San Francisco Chronicle*, March 15, 2000, p. A3.

55. www.ornl.gov/sci/techresources/Human_Genome/ elsi/gmfood.shtml.

56. See www.greennature.com.

57. "Privacy in the Online World," *The New York Times*, March 23, 2000, p. A12.

58. "Who's Looking at Your Files?" *Time* (May 6, 1996): 60–62.

59. This is modeled after a "thought experiment" by Richard Wasserstrom in "Privacy," *Today's Moral Problems*, 2d ed. (New York: Macmillan, 1979), pp. 392–408.

60. Thomas Scanlon, "Thomson on Privacy," in *Philosophy and Public Affairs*, *4*, no. 4 (Summer 1975): 295–333. This volume also contains other essays on privacy, including one by Judith Jarvis Thomson on which this article comments. W. A. Parent offers another definition of privacy as "the condition of not having undocumented personal knowledge about one possessed by others." W. A. Parent, "Privacy, Morality, and the Law," *Philosophy and Public Affairs*, *12*, no. 4 (Fall 1983): 269–288.

61. Erving Goffman, *Asylums* (Garden City, NY: Anchor Books, 1961).

62. Charles Fried, *An Anatomy of Values: Problems of Personal and Social Choice* (Cambridge, MA: Harvard University Press, 1970), p. 142.

63. "Questions of Privacy Roil Arena of Psychotherapy," *The New York Times*, May 22, 1996, p. A1.

64. "Who's Looking at Your Files?" op. cit.

65. "Bill in New Jersey Would Limit Use of Genetic Tests by Insurers," *The New York Times*, June 18, 1996, p. A1.

66. Tracey Neithercott "A Victory for Your Genes," *Diabetes Forecast*, August, 2008, p. 35.

67. *The New York Times*, Dec. 27, 1990, pp. A1, A15.

68. Ibid.

69. Ibid.

70. www.usatoday.com/travel/news/2005-05-15-airport-xray-bottomstrip_x.htm; http://en.wikipedia. org/wiki/Backscatter_X-ray.

R E A D I N G
The Wisdom of Repugnance

LEON R. KASS

Study Questions

1. What were the unusual conditions of Dolly the sheep's birth?
2. What does Kass mean by "the inherent procreative teleology of sexuality itself"?
3. According to Kass, how would cloning be a kind of narcissistic self-creation?
4. By what aspects of human cloning does Kass believe people are repelled?
5. How would Kass respond to those who say that emotional repugnance is not an argument?
6. What aspects of human cloning does Kass find morally repugnant?
7. According to Kass, in what three contexts is cloning usually discussed? Explain each.
8. What does Kass find objectionable about applying each context to the matter of human cloning?
9. What do biological truths about human generation and the human condition tell us about our common humanity and our genetic individuality, according to Kass?
10. Why does he believe that asexual reproduction is a radical departure from the natural human way of reproducing?
11. To what three kinds of concerns and objections does Kass believe that human cloning is thus vulnerable?
12. What does Kass mean by saying that the "soul-elevating power of sexuality, is at bottom, rooted in its strange connection to mortality"?

OUR HABIT of delighting in news of scientific and technological breakthroughs has been sorely challenged by the birth announcement of a sheep named Dolly. Though Dolly shares with previous sheep the "softest clothing, woolly, bright," William Blake's question, "Little Lamb, who made thee?" has for her a radically different answer: Dolly was, quite literally, made. She is the work not of nature or nature's God but of man, an Englishman, Ian Wilmut, and his fellow scientists. What is more, Dolly came

Leon R. Kass, "The Wisdom of Repugnance," from *The Ethics of Human Cloning* (Washington, D.C.: AEI Press, 1998), pp. 3–4, 8–10, 17–31. Reprinted by permission of AEI Press.

into being not only asexually—ironically, just like "He [who] calls Himself a Lamb"—but also as the genetically identical copy (and the perfect incarnation of the form or blueprint) of a mature ewe, of whom she is a clone. This long-awaited yet not quite expected success in cloning a mammal raised immediately the prospect—and the specter—of cloning human beings: "I a child and Thou a lamb," despite our differences, have always been equal candidates for creative making, only now, by means of cloning, we may both spring from the hand of man playing at being God.

After an initial flurry of expert comment and public consternation, with opinion polls showing overwhelming opposition to cloning human beings, President Clinton ordered a ban on all federal support for human cloning research (even though none was being supported) and charged the National Bioethics Advisory Commission to report in ninety days on the ethics of human cloning research. The commission (an eighteen-member panel, evenly balanced between scientists and nonscientists, appointed by the president and reporting to the National Science and Technology Council) invited testimony from scientists, religious thinkers, and bioethicists, as well as from the general public. In its report, issued in June 1997, the commission concluded that attempting to clone a human being was "at this time . . . morally unacceptable," recommended continuing the president's moratorium on the use of federal funds to support cloning of humans, and called for federal legislation to prohibit anyone from attempting (during the next three to five years) to create a child through cloning. . . .

Cloning turns out to be the perfect embodiment of the ruling opinions of our new age. Thanks to the sexual revolution, we are able to deny in practice, and increasingly in thought, the inherent procreative teleology of sexuality itself. But, if sex has no intrinsic connection to generating babies, babies need have no necessary connection to sex. . . . If male and female are not normatively complementary and generatively significant, babies need not come from male and female complementarity. Thanks to the prominence and the acceptability of divorce and out-of-wedlock births, stable, monogamous marriage as the ideal home for procreation is no longer the agreed-upon cultural norm. For that new dispensation, the clone is the ideal emblem: the ultimate "single-parent child."

Thanks to our belief that all children should be *wanted* children (the more high-minded principle we use to justify contraception and abortion), sooner or later only those children who fulfill our wants will be fully acceptable. Through cloning, we can work our wants and wills on the very identity of our children, exercising control as never before. Thanks to modern notions of individualism and the rate of cultural change, we see ourselves not as linked to ancestors and defined by traditions, but as projects for our own self-creation, not only as self-made men but also man-made selves; and self-cloning is simply an extension of such rootless and narcissistic self–re-creation.

Unwilling to acknowledge our debt to the past and unwilling to embrace the uncertainties and the limitations of the future, we have a false relation to both: cloning personifies our desire fully to control the future, while being subject to no controls ourselves. Enchanted and enslaved by the glamour of technology, we have lost our awe and wonder before the deep mysteries of nature and of life. We cheerfully take our own beginnings in our hands and, like the last man, we blink. . . .

THE WISDOM OF REPUGNANCE

Offensive, grotesque, revolting, repugnant, and *repulsive*—those are the words most commonly heard regarding the prospect of human cloning. Such reactions come both from the man or woman in the street and from the intellectuals, from believers and atheists, from humanists and scientists. Even Dolly's creator has said he "would find it offensive" to clone a human being.

People are repelled by many aspects of human cloning. They recoil from the prospect of mass production of human beings, with large clones of look-alikes, compromised in their individuality; the idea of father-son or mother-daughter twins; the bizarre

prospects of a woman's giving birth to and rearing a genetic copy of herself, her spouse, or even her deceased father or mother; the grotesqueness of conceiving a child as an exact replacement for another who has died; the utilitarian creation of embryonic genetic duplicates of oneself, to be frozen away or created when necessary, in case of need for homologous tissues or organs for transplantation; the narcissism of those who would clone themselves and the arrogance of others who think they know who deserves to be cloned or which genotype any child-to-be should be thrilled to receive; the Frankensteinian hubris to create human life and increasingly to control its destiny; many playing God. Almost no one finds any of the suggested reasons for human cloning compelling; almost everyone anticipates its possible misuses and abuses. Moreover, many people feel oppressed by the sense that there is probably nothing we can do to prevent it from happening. That makes the prospect all the more revolting.

Revulsion is not an argument; and some of yesterday's repugnances are today calmly accepted—though, one must add, not always for the better. In crucial cases, however, repugnance is the emotional expression of deep wisdom, beyond reason's power fully to articulate it. Can anyone really give an argument fully adequate to the horror which is father-daughter incest (even with consent), or having sex with animals, or mutilating a corpse, or eating human flesh, or raping or murdering another human being? Would anybody's failure to give full rational justification for his revulsion at those practices make that revulsion ethically suspect? Not at all. On the contrary, we are suspicious of those who think that they can rationalize away our horror, say, by trying to explain the enormity of incest with arguments only about the genetic risks of inbreeding.

The repugnance at human cloning belongs in that category. We are repelled by the prospect of cloning human beings not because of the strangeness or novelty of the undertaking, but because we intuit and feel, immediately and without argument, the violation of things that we rightfully hold dear. Repugnance, here as elsewhere, revolts against the excesses of human willfulness, warning us not to transgress what is unspeakably profound. Indeed, in this age in which everything is held to be permissible so long as it is freely done, in which our given human nature no longer commands respect, in which our bodies are regarded as mere instruments of our autonomous rational wills, repugnance may be the only voice left that speaks up to defend the central core of our humanity. Shallow are the souls that have forgotten how to shudder.

The goods protected by repugnance are generally overlooked by our customary ways of approaching all new biomedical technologies. The way we evaluate cloning ethically will in fact be shaped by how we characterize it descriptively, by the context into which we place it, and by the perspective from which we view it. The first task for ethics is proper description. And here is where our failure begins.

Typically, cloning is discussed in one or more of three familiar contexts, which one might call the technological, the liberal, and the meliorist. Under the first, cloning will be seen as an extension of existing techniques for assisting reproduction and determining the genetic makeup of children. Like them, cloning is to be regarded as a neutral technique, with no inherent meaning or goodness, but subject to multiple uses, some good, some bad. The morality of cloning thus depends absolutely on the goodness or badness of the motives and intentions of the cloners. As one bioethicist defender of cloning puts it, "The ethics must be judged [only] by the way the parents nurture and rear their resulting child and whether they bestow the same love and affection on a child brought into existence by a technique of assisted reproduction as they would on a child born in the usual way."

The liberal (or libertarian or liberationist) perspective sets cloning in the context of rights, freedoms, and personal empowerment. Cloning is just a new option for exercising an individual's right to reproduce or to have the kind of child that he wants. Alternatively, cloning enhances our liberation (especially women's liberation) from the confines of nature, the vagaries of chance, or the necessity for sexual mating. Indeed, it liberates women from the need for men altogether, for the process requires only eggs, nuclei, and (for the time being) uteri—plus, of course, a healthy dose of our (allegedly "masculine") manipulative science that likes to do all those things to mother nature and nature's

mothers. For those who hold this outlook, the only moral restraints on cloning are adequately informed consent and the avoidance of bodily harm. If no one is cloned without her consent, and if the clonant is not physically damaged, then the liberal conditions for licit, hence moral, conduct are met. Worries that go beyond violating the will or maiming the body are dismissed as "symbolic"—which is to say, unreal.

The meliorist perspective embraces valetudinarians and also eugenicists. The latter were formerly more vocal in those discussions, but they are now generally happy to see their goals advanced under the less threatening banners of freedom and technological growth. These people see in cloning a new prospect for improving human beings—minimally, by ensuring the perpetuation of healthy individuals by avoiding the risks of genetic disease inherent in the lottery of sex, and maximally, by producing "optimum babies," preserving outstanding genetic material, and (with the help of soon-to-come techniques for precise genetic engineering) enhancing inborn human capacities on many fronts, Here the morality of cloning as a means is justified solely by the excellence of the end, that is, by the outstanding traits of individuals cloned—beauty, or brawn, or brains.

These three approaches, all quintessentially American and all perfectly fine in their places, are sorely wanting as approaches to human procreation. It is, to say the least, grossly distorting to view the wondrous mysteries of birth, renewal, and individuality, and the deep meaning of parent-child relations, largely through the lens of our reductive science and its potent technologies. Similarly, considering reproduction (and the intimate relations of family life!) primarily under the political-legal, adversarial, and individualistic notion of rights can only undermine the private yet fundamentally social, cooperative, and duty-laden character of child-bearing, child-rearing, and their bond to the covenant of marriage. Seeking to escape entirely from nature (to satisfy a natural desire or a natural right to reproduce!) is self-contradictory in theory and self-alienating in practice. For we are erotic beings only because we are embodied beings and not merely intellects and wills unfortunately imprisoned in our bodies. And, though health and fitness are clearly great goods, there is something deeply disquieting in looking on our prospective children as artful products perfectible by genetic engineering, increasingly held to our willfully imposed designs, specifications, and margins of tolerable error.

The technical, liberal, and meliorist approaches all ignore the deeper anthropological, social, and, indeed, ontological meanings of bringing forth a new life. To this more fitting and profound point of view cloning shows itself to be a major violation of our given nature as embodied, gendered, and engendering beings—and of the social relations built on this natural ground. Once this perspective is recognized, the ethical judgment on cloning can no longer be reduced to a matter of motives and intentions, rights and freedoms, benefits and harms, or even means and ends. It must be regarded primarily as a matter of meaning: Is cloning a fulfillment of human begetting and belonging? Or is cloning rather, as I contend, their pollution and perversion? To pollution and perversion the fitting response can only be horror and revulsion; and, conversely, generalized horror and revulsion are prima facie evidence of foulness and violation. The burden of moral argument must fall entirely on those who want to declare the widespread repugnances of humankind to be mere timidity or superstition.

Yet repugnance need not stand naked before the bar of reason. The wisdom of our horror at human cloning can be partially articulated, even if this is finally one of those instances about which the heart has its reasons that reason cannot entirely know.

THE PROFUNDITY OF SEX

To see cloning in its proper context, we must begin not, as I did before, with laboratory technique, but with the anthropology—natural and social—of sexual reproduction.

Sexual reproduction—by which I mean the generation of new life from (exactly) two complementary elements, one female, one male, (usually) through coitus—is established (if that is the right term) not by human decision, culture, or tradition, but by nature; it is the natural way of all mammalian reproduction. By nature, each child has two complementary biological progenitors. Each child thus stems from and unites exactly two lineages. In natural generation, moreover, the precise genetic constitution of the resulting offspring is determined by a combination of nature and chance, not by human design: each human child shares the common natural human species genotype, each child is genetically (equally) kin to each (both) parent(s), yet each child is also genetically unique.

Those biological truths about our origins foretell deep truths about our identity and about our human condition altogether. Every one of us is at once equally human, equally enmeshed in a particular familial nexus of origin, and equally individuated in our trajectory from birth to death—and, if all goes well, equally capable (despite our mortality) of participating, with a complementary other, in the very same renewal of such human possibility through procreation. Though less momentous than our common humanity, our genetic individuality is not humanly trivial. It shows itself forth in our distinctive appearance through which we are everywhere recognized; it is revealed in our "signature" marks of fingerprints and our self-recognizing immune system; it symbolizes and foreshadows exactly the unique, never-to-be-repeated character of each human life.

Human societies virtually everywhere have structured child-rearing responsibilities and systems of identity and relationship on the bases of those deep natural facts of begetting. The mysterious yet ubiquitous "love of one's own" is everywhere culturally exploited, to make sure that children are not just produced but well cared for and to create for everyone clear ties of meaning, belonging, and obligation. But it is wrong to treat such naturally rooted social practices as mere cultural constructs (like left- or right-driving, or like burying or cremating the dead) that we can alter with little human cost. What would kinship be without its clear natural grounding? And what would identity be without kinship? We must resist those who have begun to refer to sexual reproduction as the "traditional method of reproduction," who would have us regard as merely traditional, and by implication arbitrary, what is in truth not only natural but most certainly profound.

Asexual reproduction, which produces "single-parent" offspring, is a radical departure from the natural human way, confounding all normal understandings of father, mother, sibling, and grandparent and all moral relations tied thereto. It becomes even more of a radical departure when the resulting offspring is a clone derived not from an embryo, but from a mature adult to whom the clone would be an identical twin; and when the process occurs not by natural accident (as in natural twinning), but by deliberate human design and manipulation; and when the child's (or children's) genetic constitution is preselected by the parent(s) (or scientists). Accordingly, as we shall see, cloning is vulnerable to three kinds of concerns and objections, related to these three points: cloning threatens confusion of identity and individuality, even in small-scale cloning; cloning represents a giant step (though not the first one) toward transforming procreation into manufacture, that is, toward the increasing depersonalization of the process of generation and, increasingly, toward the "production" of human children as artifacts, products of human will and design (what others have called the problem of "commodification" of new life); and cloning—like other forms of eugenic engineering of the next generation—represents a form of despotism of the cloners over the cloned, and thus (even in benevolent cases) represents a blatant violation of the inner meaning of parent-child relations, of what it means to have a child, of what it means to say yes to our own demise and "replacement."

Before turning to those specific ethical objections, let me test my claim of the profundity of the natural way by taking up a challenge recently posed by a friend. What if the given natural human way of reproduction were asexual, and we now had to deal with a new technological innovation—artificially induced sexual dimorphism and the fusing of complementary gametes—whose inventors argued that sexual reproduction promised all sorts of advantages, including hybrid vigor and the creation of greatly increased individuality? Would one then be forced to defend natural asexuality because it was natural? Could one claim that it carried deep human meaning?

The response to that challenge broaches the ontological meaning of sexual reproduction. For it is impossible, I submit, for there to have been human life—or even higher forms of animal life—in the absence of sexuality and sexual reproduction. We find asexual reproduction only in the lowest forms of life: bacteria, algae, fungi, some lower invertebrates. Sexuality brings with it a new and enriched relationship to the world. Only sexual animals can seek and find complementary others with whom to pursue a goal that transcends their own existence. For a sexual being, the world is no longer an indifferent and largely homogeneous *otherness*, in part edible, in part dangerous. It also contains some very special and related and complementary beings, of the same kind but of opposite sex, toward whom one reaches out with special interest and intensity. In higher birds and mammals, the outward gaze keeps a lookout not only for food and predators, but also for prospective mates; the beholding of the many-splendored world is suffused with desire for union—the animal antecedent of human eros and the germ of sociality. Not by accident is the human animal both the sexiest animal—whose females do not go into heat but are receptive throughout the estrous cycle and whose males must therefore have greater sexual appetite and energy to reproduce successfully—and also the most aspiring, the most social, the most open, and the most intelligent animal.

The soul-elevating power of sexuality is, at bottom, rooted in its strange connection to mortality, which it simultaneously accepts and tries to overcome. Asexual reproduction may be seen as a continuation of the activity of self-preservation. When an organism buds or divides to become two, the original being is (doubly) preserved, and nothing dies. Sexuality, by contrast, means perishability and serves replacement; the two that come together to generate one soon will die. Sexual desire, in human beings as in animals, thus serves an end that is partially hidden from, and finally at odds with, the self-serving individual. Whether we know it or not, when we are sexually active we are voting with our genitalia for our own demise. The salmon swimming upstream to spawn and die tell the universal story: sex is bound up with death, to which it holds a partial answer in procreation.

The salmon and the other animals evince that truth blindly. Only the human being can understand what it means. As we learn so powerfully from the story of the Garden of Eden, our humanization is coincident with sexual self-consciousness, with the recognition of our sexual nakedness and all that it implies: shame at our needy incompleteness, unruly self-division, and finitude; awe before the eternal; hope in the self-transcending possibilities of children and a relationship to the divine. In the sexually self-conscious animal, sexual desire can become eros, lust can become love. Sexual desire humanly regarded is thus sublimated into erotic longing for wholeness, completion, and immortality, which drives us knowingly into the embrace and its generative fruit—as well as into all the higher human possibilities of deed, speech, and song.

Through children, a good common to both husband and wife, male and female achieve some genuine unification (beyond the mere sexual "union," which fails to do so). The two become one through sharing generous (not needy) love for that third being as good. Flesh of their flesh, the child is the parents' own commingled being externalized and given a separate and persisting existence. Unification is enhanced also by their commingled work of rearing. Providing an opening to the future beyond the grave, carrying not only our seed but also our names, our ways, and our hopes that they will surpass us in goodness and happiness, children are a testament to the possibility of transcendence. Gender duality and sexual desire, which first draws our love upward and outside ourselves, finally provide for the partial overcoming of the confinement and limitation of perishable embodiment altogether.

Human procreation, in sum, is not simply an activity of our rational wills. It is a more complete activity precisely because it engages us bodily, erotically, and spiritually as well as rationally. There is wisdom in the mystery of nature that has joined the pleasure of sex, the inarticulate longing for union, the communication of the loving embrace, and the deep-seated and only partly articulate desire for children in the very activity by which we continue the chain of human existence and participate in the renewal of human possibility. Whether or not we know it, the severing of procreation from sex, love, and intimacy is inherently dehumanizing, no matter how good the product. . . .

R E A D I N G
Illegal Beings: Human Clones and the Law
KERRY LYNN MACINTOSH

Study Questions

1. According to Macintosh, does biology determine what is "natural"? Why or why not?
2. How does she compare human cloning with in vitro fertilization (IVF) in this regard?
3. How then does she believe we determine what is natural and unnatural with regard to reproductive methods?
4. What does the fact that cloning is asexual reproduction have to do with this?
5. How does using the term *unnatural* become a damaging stereotype, according to Macintosh? And how does it become a moral term?
6. In what sense might cloning be thought of as a lesser form of reproduction?
7. What portion of fertilized eggs or embryos never make it to birth? What lesson does Macintosh believe we should learn from this fact?
8. Why does Macintosh cite the many steps that are involved in cloning?
9. Describe the problem of "shortened telomeres," which are possibly associated with cloning, and with the case of Dolly the sheep in particular. What does Macintosh think we can conclude from these facts?
10. How does Macintosh believe the media has contributed to inaccuracies about and exaggerated safety concerns over cloning?
11. How does she believe certain restrictive cloning laws prevent access to the truth about the prospects of cloning?

FROM THE leftist point of view, human reproductive cloning is morally wrong because it is a kind of technological rape of Mother Nature. That which is "natural" is good; that which is "unnatural" is bad.

One immediate problem with this argument concerns the concepts of "natural" and "unnatural." Although these terms may seem simple to apply, they are not. Biology does not determine what is "natural"—cultural and moral values, which change over time, do.

For example, one might wonder why some people oppose human reproductive cloning on the grounds that it is unnatural when they calmly accept in vitro fertilization (IVF) and related assisted reproductive technologies. For the uninitiated, here is a brief description of an IVF cycle: an infertile woman takes powerful drugs to stimulate the production of multiple eggs; a doctor punches a large needle through her vaginal wall to siphon the eggs out of her ovaries; the eggs are then mixed with ejaculated sperm in a dish; if any eggs are fertilized, the embryos are grown in the laboratory until they are developed enough to be transferred back into her uterus through a catheter.[1] If sperm quality is poor, fertilization may be accomplished through a process know as intracytoplasmic sperm injection (ICSI) in which a technician forcibly injects individual sperm into individual eggs.[2]

When IVF was new, back in 1978, the world was horrified by it. According to polls, 85 percent of the public thought it should be banned.[3] Scientists, doctors, and philosophers decried the practice, asserting that "test-tube babies" would be physically deformed and psychologically impaired.[4] Political activists complained that scientists were meddling with nature.[5] But after healthy babies were born, the firestorm died down.[6] Today, 25 years later, IVF has led to the birth of over one million babies worldwide.[7] IVF has become commonplace and has enriched the lives of many individuals and families. Certain religions still hold that assisted reproductive technologies are contrary to the will of God,[8] but one seldom hears complaints about how unnatural it is.

From this history, it appears that what we consider to be natural depends on how experienced and comfortable we are with a reproductive method rather than on how similar that method is to sexual intercourse. Human reproductive cloning seems strange now because it is new; however, if society

stood aside and allowed cloning to develop without legal interference, it could seem entirely natural within a few decades.

Nevertheless, opponents insist that human reproductive cloning is much stranger than IVF and other assisted reproductive technologies. This is because cloning makes *asexual* reproduction possible for mammals. The California Advisory Committee on Human Cloning duly noted this fact:

> Certainly, cloning could be considered "unnatural" as it relies on human intervention in a "natural process." It clearly runs counter to a normally functioning natural environment, at least for mammals. It does not provide for the random combination of genetic material from eggs and sperm that is the essence of sexual reproduction. In addition, it could theoretically render males reproductively obsolete.[9]

Asexual reproduction, however, is not as contrary to nature as opponents assert. Scientists believe that *all* life on Earth evolved from simple one-celled organisms that reproduced asexually by cell division.[10] Many organisms, ranging from bacteria[11] to worms[12] to the trees in an aspen forest (which are clones propagated from a single seedling)[13] continue to reproduce asexually today. Thus, asexual reproduction is entirely natural for much of Earth life; it simply is not the way that humans have reproduced up until now. The truly stunning thing about the science of cloning is its unexpected revelation of a basic truth: even humans and other mammals retain, in every cell of their bodies, the ability to reproduce asexually just as their distant evolutionary ancestors once did. Human reproductive cloning may require a greater level of technological intervention than does IVF, but this is a difference of degree rather than one of fundamental character.

What it boils down to is this: Different people have different ideas about how far humanity should go in using technology to expand our *inborn* capabilities. Novel reproductive technologies, like cloning, tend to draw the most disapproval. If a person believes that cloning goes too far, he or she might use the word "unnatural" as a concise way of expressing that moral judgment.

Unfortunately, the use of this particular shorthand to express a complex moral judgment has strong

Kerry Lynn Macintosh, *Illegal Beings, Human Clones and the Law* (New York: Cambridge University Press, 2005, pp. 12–15, 49–51, 61–63, 68–69). Reprinted with the permission of Cambridge University Press.

implications for human clones. If the technology of human reproductive cloning is unnatural, it follows that human clones must also be unnatural. This is a damaging stereotype.

Moreover, the dictionary defines the word "unnatural" as including the following concepts: "abnormal," "strange," "artificial," and "evil."[14] These related meanings encourage the public to view human clones as abnormal, strange, artificial, and evil.

Nor do the stereotypes stop there. Simple organisms reproduce asexually; traditionally, humans and other mammals have not. Thus, some people may infer that sexual reproduction goes along with a higher level of evolution.[15] The argument that cloning is unnatural because it is asexual reproduction implies a hierarchy of reproductive origin in which human clones rank alongside bacteria and worms in quality and importance.

It might be argued that, once cloned babies are born and everyone sees how cute they are, such stereotypes will wither away. After all, that is what happened when the public saw photographs of adorable "test-tube babies" and forgot about its fears.[16] The unfortunate difference is that IVF was never outlawed, but cloning already has been. As a result, fewer cute babies will be born; those that are born are likely to go underground along with their frightened parents. The anticloning laws themselves will make it harder for society to develop experience with human reproductive cloning and thus harder for society to accept cloning as a natural process.[17] . . .

When it comes to cloning, it is important to distinguish adult cell experiments from fetal and embryonic cell experiments whenever possible. Many embryos and fetuses do not implant, or they miscarry; often, this is because the gamble of sexual reproduction has produced an inadequate genome. For example, in human reproduction, up to 75 percent of embryos conceived through sexual intercourse never make it to birth; most do not implant in the uterus and are spontaneously aborted.[18] Thus, when cloning from nuclear DNA harvested from embryos and fetuses, one might expect a fairly significant number of failures to occur simply because the selected genomes are inadequate. By contrast, nuclear DNA taken from an adult animal already has proven its ability to generate a healthy term birth (of

that adult). What this means is that one must be cautious in extrapolating from experiments that involve cloning from embryonic and fetal cells. Dr. Wilmut's efforts to clone sheep from embryonic and fetal cells may not predict success in adult cell cloning, but they do not necessarily predict failure either.

A second possible reason for the misreporting of the Dolly experiment has to do with expectations. If a person views cloning as a Frankenstein horror, a spit in the face of God, or a rape of nature, then he or she might logically expect disastrous results such as miscarriages and deaths. This expectation has led not only to mistakes in the original reporting of the scientific data but also to the endless reiteration of those mistakes. Reporters and policymakers have not corrected the errors because the errors do not look like errors to them. Instead, they have repeated the errors over and over. This constant repetition has cloaked the myth of the 277 "attempts" with the mantle of an irrefutable truth.

Too often, reporters and lawmakers rely on the Dolly experiment (undertaken back in 1996) as if it were the only one. Cloning is a science, and science constantly changes. Recent publications more accurately state the current success rates for animal cloning.

In November 2001, scientists at Advanced Cell Technology (ACT) summarized their work with cows cloned from fetal cells.[19] In this work, the scientists transferred a total of 496 blastocysts into 247 surrogate cows.[20] Of these, 110 became pregnant, but 80 had miscarriages. (This was a miscarriage rate of 73 percent compared with a 7–24-percent miscarriage rate for cow pregnancies derived from in vitro fertilization.)[21] Thirty fetuses developed to term, but six calves died shortly after birth. The remaining 24 cloned calves grew into a vigorous and healthy adulthood.[22] In terms of the percentage of healthy births to embryos transferred, this represented a success rate of about 5 percent; or, to put it negatively, a failure rate of about 95 percent. Most failures (386 out of 496) involved embryos that were transferred but did not implant in the womb.

Similarly, in January 2002, a team of Japanese researchers working with mice reported that about 2.8 percent of blastocysts cloned from adult and fetal cells developed to term after transfer into surrogate mice. Of the newborn pups, 92.9 percent were healthy.[23] In terms of the percentage of healthy births to embryos transferred, this was a success rate of 2–3 percent or, to put it negatively, a failure rate of about 97–98 percent.

In 2002, the National Academies published a report on cloning, which included a table summarizing success and failure rates in other animal cloning experiments, most of which were conducted before 2001. In reviewing those experiments that involved cloning from adult cells, one finds the same basic pattern. The percentage of live births to embryos transferred ranged from 0.32 to 11 percent.[24] The vast majority of cloning failures (from about 83 to 99 percent) involved embryos that never developed to the point of transfer or never produced a pregnancy.[25] Once a pregnancy was established, the miscarriage rate ranged widely from zero (the Dolly experiment) to a high of 94 percent.[26] Although the vast majority of newborns survived, some died of causes that might or might not have been related to cloning.[27]

The low success rates in animal cloning raise several questions. Why do more embryos not implant? Why do some pregnancies miscarry? Why do some newborn animals die shortly after birth?

Today, it is not possible to answer these questions definitively. Cloning involves many steps as follows:

› Eggs must be removebld from the bodies of females and matured in the laboratory.
› Technicians must take the original maternal chromosomes out of the eggs.
› Donor cells must be selected (by type and individually) and removed from the adult to be cloned.
› The donor cells must be brought to a state of rest.
› The chromosomes must be extracted from the quiescent donor cells.
› Those chromosomes must be introduced into the eggs.
› The reconstituted eggs must be induced through electricity or chemicals to start dividing.
› The resulting embryos must be cultured, and
› The embryos must be transferred into the uteri of surrogate mothers.[28]

Errors or suboptimal procedures in any of these steps could lead to failures. Cloning, however, is a new science that will continue to advance so long as experimentation is allowed to continue. Most experiments that have been published so far report the experiences of scientists who are cloning for the first or second time.[29] Comparing the results of their own early experiments with those of others, scientists have the chance to generate hypotheses about which methodologies and protocols work and which do not. Scientists can test those hypotheses through more research, which ultimately can lead to the development of an effective and safe technology.

Given that cloning technology is a work in progress, any assessment of its efficiency is likely to become dated within a short time. This fact weights against the enactment of laws that impose flat bans on the ground that human reproductive cloning is inefficient. . . .

From the time her birth was announced, some critics speculated that [Dolly] was older than her chronological age.[30] Once again, to explain this charge, I must provide a brief explanation of the relevant biology.

Telomeres are repetitive DNA sequences that protect chromosome tips.[31] As an animal gets older, its telomeres tend to get shorter. Scientists believe this happens because telomeres wear down over the course of repeated cell divisions. At some point, the telomeres shrink to nothing and the cell dies.[32]

Dolly was cloned from nuclear DNA taken from a 6-year-old donor sheep. If Dolly inherited that sheep's shortened telomeres, her lifespan could be shortened, too. She might look like a lamb, but at the DNA level, she would be the equivalent of a 6-year-old sheep.[33]

In 1999, the worst of these fears was seemingly confirmed. Dr. Wilmut and his associates published a letter in Nature magazine stating that they had measured Dolly's telomeres and found them to be about 20 percent shorter than those of other sheep her own age.[34] The scientists admitted that this difference could be within the range of natural variation in the telomere lengths of sheep.[35] The scientists did not mention a second weakness in their findings: telomeres are so small that measuring their length is difficult. The difference between the length of Dolly's telomeres and "normal" telomeres was within the range of experimental error.[36]

On the basis of these data, the scientists speculated that Dolly's telomeres were shorter because she had been cloned from a 6-year-old sheep (whose telomeres were already shortened consistent with her age) and also because the donor cells had been cultured for a period of time before cloning.[37] The scientists conceded, however, that they did not know whether the shorter telomeres indicated that Dolly was physiologically older than her chronological age—particularly given that veterinary examinations had confirmed that she was healthy and typical for a sheep of her breed.[38]

Despite the tentative nature of these findings, the media quickly picked up on the most sensationalistic aspects of the research.[39] Most reports emphasized the scary idea that clones were prematurely aged without mentioning the important qualifications that the scientists had placed on their data and its interpretation.[40]

Meanwhile, researchers at Advanced Cell Technology studied the telomeres of several cows that had been cloned from cells that were nearing the end of their life spans. In 2000, they reported that the resulting cattle had telomeres that were significantly longer than those of regular cows of the same age.[41]

In another experiment that same year, Japanese researchers succeeded in the reiterative cloning of mice. In other words, they cloned mouse pups from other cloned mice out to six generations. Their paper, "Cloning of Mice to Six Generations," reported that the mice showed no outward signs of premature aging. Telomeres were not shortened; rather, they had increased slightly in length.[42]

In 2001, Dr. Rudolph Jaenisch reported that telomere length adjustment was faithfully accomplished following nuclear transfer and would not be expected to impair survival of cloned animals.[43]

Policymakers resisted this good news. Although the National Academies admitted that the possibility of shortened telomeres was not a major concern,[44] the California Advisory Committee on Human Cloning asserted that the question of telomere shortening and consequent premature aging remained unresolved on the basis of the Dolly study. The committee

acknowledged that scientists had succeeded in the reiterative cloning of mice but did not note that lengthened telomeres and normal behavior had been observed in the mice. Instead, it observed that the reiterative cloning "might suggest that telomere shortening will not be a problem, but the normal lifespan of a mouse is only two years, and the scientists did encounter progressive difficulty in creating clones with each succeeding generation."[45] The committee did not report that lengthened telomeres had also been observed in cloned cattle.[46]

Unfortunately, the charge that Dolly was old beyond her years persisted. When she developed arthritis in her left hip and knee at age 5½ years, many people speculated that cloning was to blame.[47] However, Dr. Wilmut was more cautious. He pointed out that the arthritis could have developed because Dolly stood on her hind legs to greet the many admiring tourists who came to see her.[48] Also, 5½ is relatively old for a sheep; joint disease is sometimes seen in sheep that age.[49]

On February 14, 2003, Dolly was put to sleep at the age of 6 years. At the time, she was suffering from a contagious lung disease that was spreading among the sheep at the Roslin Institute.[50] According to Dr. Wilmut, her illness and death probably had nothing to do with the fact she was a clone. Sheep that live indoors (as Dolly did for security reasons) are prone to developing lung infections of this kind.[51] Nevertheless, many news reports strongly implied that Dolly had died from premature aging by reminding readers about her arthritis and allegedly shortened telomeres.[52]

While the media and policymakers cling to the telomere scare, good news continues to roll in on the scientific front. In 2004, Japanese researchers reported that they had cloned two generations of offspring from a stud bull. Significantly, their data showed that both generations seemed healthy and had normal telomere lengths.[53]

Now that several research teams have demonstrated that telomeres in cloned animals are normal, the telomere scare should be over. However, the way in which the media reported Dolly's death shows that the scare has enormous staying power. . . .

To some readers, the fact that some scientists, the media, and policymakers have done all they can to accentuate the safety hazards of cloning may seem unremarkable and even commendable. Given the risks, it may seem that it pays to err on the side of caution—at least for now. After all, can we not count on science to set the record straight eventually? Surely, experiments will continue. Time will determine which safety theories are correct and which are not.

Every public policy, however, including caution, has its dangers. . . . I have argued that the safety arguments unfairly stereotype an entire category of human being. This is a significant cost that deserves to be recognized in the cloning debate.

Moreover, it is naive to believe that we can count on science to set the record straight and debunk the stereotypes. For one thing, some theories may not be accurate and yet may be inherently hard to disprove. The hypothesis that cloned animals are flawed at the epigenetic level cleverly asserts its own defense: even if scientists measure the physical attributes of cloned animals and find them to be normal, the measurements cannot disprove the hypothesis because epigenetic flaws are difficult to detect and may not produce negative effects for years.

For another thing, most people are not scientists and do not grasp the distinction between hypothesis and scientific fact. Thus, if the media or policymakers embrace certain scientific theories prematurely, or present those theories one-sidedly, it may become difficult to dislodge those theories from the imagination of the public later on. For example, people continue to believe that cloning produces prematurely aged animals despite scientific evidence to the contrary. This belief may linger because most people are not educated or interested in science and pay attention only to the most widely reported and sensationalistic science stories. Or, perhaps the belief lingers because premature aging is consistent with other notions such as the idea that cloning is a sin of pride destined to produce shoddy products or that a clone is a duplicate that continues the lifespan of the original animal. In either case, the end result is that, even after scientific theories are proven wrong, they may live on for years, decades, or even centuries in the public mind.

Finally, there is no guarantee that scientists in the United States will have the freedom they need to conduct the experiments that *could* set the record

straight. Exaggerated safety arguments have been used to justify the enactment of flat bans on human cloning (including research cloning). These laws threaten to stop the very research that is necessary to find out what the truth is. If we enact inflexible laws today, we will reap what we sow tomorrow in the form of scientific ignorance, and the perpetuation of harmful stereotypes about the health of human clones.

NOTES*

1. See generally Sherman J. Silber, *How to Get Pregnant with the New Technology* 288–319 (1991).
2. See The National Academies, *Scientific and Medical Aspects of Human Cloning*, 63 (2002).
3. See Mark D. Eibert, "Human Cloning: Myths, Medical Benefits and Constitutional Rights." 53 *Hastings L. J.* 1097, 1102 (2002).
4. See Gregory E. Pence, *Who's Afraid of Human Cloning?* 26–27 (1998).
5. Silber, op. cit. 268.
6. See Eibert, op. cit. 1103.
7. See "Test Tube Babies, 25 Years Later" at <http://www.cnn.com/2003/HEALTH/parenting/07/25/wf.anniversary/index.html> (July 25, 2003): Patricia Reaney. "Test Tube Babies Celebrate 25 Years of IVF" at <http://uk.news.yahoo.com/030725/80/e4wm8.html> (July 25, 2003).
8. See NBAC Report: California Advisory Committee on Human Cloning. Cloning Californians? Report of the California Advisory Committee on Human Cloning, 31 (2002) (hereinafter California Report); see also National Bioethics Advisory Commission, Cloning Human Beings, Report and Recommendations of the National Bioethics Advisory Commission 44–45 (1997).
9. California Report, op. cit. 31 (emphasis added).
10. See Stanley N. Salthe, *Evolutionary Biology* 57 (1972).
11. Lee Silver, "Public Policy Crafted in Response to Public Ignorance is Bad Public Policy," 53 *Hastings L. J.* 1039 (2002).
12. See *The Columbia Encyclopedia* 112–13 (Paul Lagasse ed., 6th ed. 2000).
13. Dale L. Bartos, *Landscape Dynamics of Aspen and Conifer Forests*, USDA Forest Service Prog. RMRS-P18 at 5 (2001).

_____

*Notes have been renumbered and edited as necessary.—ED.

14. See *Webster's New World Dictionary of The American Language* 1594 (college ed. 1968).

15. Erasmus Darwin, the grandfather of Charles Darwin, was one of the first to assert this point of view. See Anne K. Mellor, *Mary Shelley, Her Life, Her Fiction, Her Monsters* 97–98 (1989 ed.). Professor Mellor has argued that the novel *Frankenstein* draws upon this view in portraying the creation of life through scientific means as a violation of the canons of nature. See id. at 101.

16. See Eibert, op. cit. 1103.

17. For a fuller development of the argument that anti-cloning laws could perpetuate stereotypes by restricting information about human clones, see Chapter 9, infra. *Remaking Eden: Cloning and Beyond in a Brave New World*. New York: Avon Books, Inc., 1997.

18. See Steven Pinkner, *The Blank Slate* 225 (2002): Silver, *Remarking Eden: Cloning and Beyond in a Brave New World*. New York: Avon Books, Inc., 1997, p. 103.

19. Robert P. Lanza et al., "Cloned Cattle Can Be Healthy and Normal," 294 *Sci.* 1893 (2001) (hereinafter Lanza, "Cloned Cattle"). This work was a follow-up on two experiments that Advanced Cell Technology had conducted earlier. See Robert P. Lanza et al., "Extension of Cell Life-Span and Telomere Length in Animals Cloned from Senescent Somatic Cell," 288 *Sci.* 665 (2000) (hereinafter Lanza, "Telomere Length"): Jose B. Cibelli et al., "Cloned Transgenic Calves Produced from Nonquiescent Fetal Fibroblasts," 280 *Sci.* 1256 (1998).

20. See Lanza, "Cloned Cattle," 1893.

21. Ibid.

22. Ibid.

23. See Kimono Inoue et al., "Faithful Expression of Imprinted Genes in Cloned Mice," 295 *Sci.* 297 (2002).

  A recent experiment involving cats hints that better success rates are possible. First, researchers made 188 attempts to transfer the nuclei of adult fibroblast cells from oral mucosa into eggs. This resulted in 82 cloned embryos, all of which were transferred into 7 surrogate mother cats. There was one pregnancy, but the fetus stopped developing and was surgically removed. See Tae Young Shin et al., "A Cat Cloned by Nuclear Transplantation," 415 *Nature* 859 (2002). Despite this discouraging early failure, the researchers did not give up. They transferred three embryos cloned from cumulus cells and two embryos derived from fibroblast cells into a surrogate queen. One of the three cumulus cell embryos developed to term and was born as a healthy, normal kitten. See ibid. Thus, in terms of live births to embryos transferred, the second stage of the experiment had a 20-percent success rate.

24. See The National Academies, *Scientific and Medical Aspects of Human Cloning* 2 (2002). (Hereinafter NAS Report)

25. For adult cell experiments, the yield of fetuses from embryos produced ranged from 0.36 to 16.7 percent; that lowest percentage is from the Dolly experiment. See ibid. (comparing Table 1, column 3 [number of embryos produced] to Table 1, column five [number of fetuses after embryo transfer]).

26. See ibid., Table 1, column 6.

27. The NAS Report provides the percentage of offspring alive or healthy at the time of its publication. This percentage ranged from 100 percent (the Dolly experiment and several others) to 0 percent (a lone experiment in which the only calf died). See ibid. at Table 1, column 10. The mouse data likely understate success because mice have short life spans and may have died from natural causes before publication.

28. See Jose B. Cibelli et al., "The Health Profile of Cloned Animals," 20 *Nature Biotechnology* 13 (2002) (hereinafter Cibelli, "Health Profile").

29. Ibid.

30. See Kolata, *Clone: The Road to Dolly and the Path Ahead*. New York: William Morrow, 1999, p. 240; NBAC Report, 24. Interestingly, the National Bioethics Advisory Commission speculated that the process of cloning would reset telomere length, which is a speculation that later turned out to be correct.

31. See Kolata, *Clone*, 240.

32. Ibid.

33. Ibid.

34. Paul G. Shiels et al., "Analysis of Telomere Lengths in Cloned Sheep," 399 *Nature* 316, 317 (1999). The paper also documented the telomere length of two other cloned sheep. One had been cloned from an embryo cell, and another had been cloned from a fetal cell. These sheep showed telomere shortening of approximately 9 to 15 percent.

35. Ibid.

36. Gina Kolata, "Cloned Sheep Showing Signs of Old Cells, Report Says," *N.Y. Times*, May 27, 1999, at A19 (hereinafter Kolata, "Old Cells").

37. See Shiels, op. cit. 317.

38. Ibid.

39. See Rick Weiss, "Dolly: 'A Sheep in Lamb's Clothing,'" *Wash. Post*, May 27, 1999 A01.

40. See e.g., ibid. but see Kolata. "Old Cells," op. cit. (explaining that the measured difference in telomere length could be within the range of natural variation among sheep.)

41. See, e.g., Lanza, "Telomere Length."

42. Teruhiko Wakayama et al., "Cloning of Mice to Six generations," 407 *Nature* 318 (2000).

43. See W. M. Rideout, III, et al., "Nuclear Cloning and Epigenetic Reprogramming of the Genome," 293 Sci, 1095 (2001).

44. See NAS Report, op. cit. 48.

45. See California Report op. cit., 10.

46. See Lanza, "Telomere Length."

47. See Rick Weiss, "Middle-Aged Dolly Develops Arthritis, Questions on Clone's Aging Raised," Wash. Post, Jan. 5, 2002, at A03.

48. Ibid.

49. Ibid; Gina Kolata, "First Manual Clone Dies; Dolly Made Science History," *N.Y. Times*, Feb. 15, 2003, at A4 (hereinafter Kolata, "Clone Dies").

50. See Ulysses Torassa, "Dolly Euthanized for Lung Disease, *S.F. Chron.*, Feb. 15, 2003, at A2.

51. See Kolata, "Clone Dies."

52. See, e.g., "First Cloned Sheep Dolly Dies at 6," at <http:// www.cnn.com/2003/WORLD/europe/02/14/cloned dolly dies/index.html> (Feb. 14, 2003).

53. Chikara Kubota et al. "Serial Bull Cloning by Somatic Cell Nuclear Transfer." *Nature Biotechnology* advance online publication, May 23, 2004 (doi: 10.1038/nbt975), at <http://www.crb.uconn.edu/webupdate.files/recline-nt-final0604.pdf.>

REVIEW EXERCISES

1. What is cloning through somatic cell nuclear transfer?

2. What has been accomplished with animal cloning through this technique?

3. How might stem cells play a role in human cloning in the future?

4. Summarize the arguments for and against human cloning based on the idea that it would be "playing God."

5. Summarize the arguments that are based on possible threats that cloning might pose to individuality.

6. What is meant by a "right to an open future"? What might human cloning have to do with it?

7. Summarize the arguments regarding human cloning related to exploitation, confusion of families, and the so-called yuck factor.

8. What is the Human Genome Project and what did it produce?

9. What are the primary ethical concerns related to experimental genetic therapies?

10. What ethical issues have been raised regarding the production and use of genetically modified plants and crops?

11. What ethical concerns do people raise about genetically modified animals?

12. Discuss the value of privacy and how it relates to genetic and other types of screening.

DISCUSSION CASES

1. Human Cloning. Suppose this technique for producing children were perfected. If you were to choose to have children, would you consider using this technique? What if there was a chance that you otherwise might pass on a genetic disease to your children? Would there be any circumstance in which you would consider human cloning?

2. Food Labeling. Jane belongs to a group that is concerned about genetically altered food. The group is pushing to have information about genetic modifications in foods and ingredients listed on the labels along with nutritional information so those who object to such modifications can make informed choices about what to buy for themselves and their families. The food industry believes that this would be costly to do and raise the price of these products for all, including those who do not object. The industry wonders what else might logically also be required to be listed on labels—where the food was produced, what pesticides were used, and so forth. Do you agree with Jane's group? Why or why not?

3. Genetic Screening. Suppose you are living twenty-five years from now. Suppose that among the advancements in genetics is the ability to screen individuals for particular genetically caused or influenced disorders and conditions. Would you want to have such information? What kinds of information would you want to access? Would there be any information that you would not want to know? How much would you be willing to pay for such a screen? Do you think society should pay for anyone's screening? Why or why not?

YOU MAKE THE DECISION

Apply the theories and issues discussed in this chapter by accessing this animated simulation on the Ethics Resource Center.

Use the passkey that accompanies your book to gain access. If you do not have a passkey, visit cengagebrain.com to purchase instant access to additional study material.

© Cengage Learning

19

Violence, Terrorism, and War

O N THE morning of April 16, 2007, student Cho Seung-Hui entered Norris Hall at Virginia Tech in Blacksburg, Virginia, bolted the doors shut from the inside, and proceeded to go first to a German classroom where he slowly and deliberately shot the instructor and then as many students as he thought still alive. Next he proceeded to a French class where he did the same. Finally, he entered an engineering class and again shot the teacher and students. In all, he killed thirty people before turning the gun on himself as police were closing in. Earlier in the day, he had killed two more students in a dormitory. Cho was a loner who would rarely respond to the initiatives of others. One of his teachers was worried about his behavior and some of his violent writings. He was a troubled young man who was angry and felt marginalized, a fact which became clear from videos sent to NBC News that he made of himself before the shootings. He was going to make people pay for the perceived slights he felt. He had been recommended for psychiatric care after being judged to be a danger to himself or others. It is not clear whether he was treated. However, because he had not been committed, he was able to legally purchase two guns in Virginia in the months before the killing spree. He had seemingly been preparing for this rampage for months or longer. He was unlike some other serial killers who seem to enjoy the killings that take place over many years. Such school killings are, in fact, rare, although shocking. "Mass killings are less than one-quarter of 1% of U.S. homicides."[1]

Among the questions we ask about various forms and examples of violence is, why? What was behind these events and actions? What can be done to decrease or prevent such violence? There are also moral questions that can be addressed. Put simply, is violence, or terrorism, or war ever justified? If so, why and under what conditions? If not, why not? This chapter is meant to address these questions.

VIOLENCE

Worldwide, violence claims the lives of between one and two million people each year. "Each year in the United States, more than 50,000 people die from acts of violence, including more than 32,000 deaths from suicide and 18,000 deaths from homicide."[2] According to a report by the World Health Organization, 14 percent of all deaths for American males in 2001 resulted from violence, and 7 percent for females. Men were responsible for more than three-quarters of all homicides, with males aged fifteen to twenty-nine having the highest rates.[3]

According to the lobbying group Handgun Control, "more Americans were killed with guns in the 18-year period between 1979 and 1997 (651,697) than were killed in battle in all wars since 1775 (650,858)."[4] In the United States in 2006, "there were 30,896 deaths from firearms."[5] Although exact numbers are difficult to come by, one can assume that this number remains much the same. Arguments about the contribution of gun availability to violent gun deaths often depend on empirical claims that are difficult to verify. Supporters of gun ownership most often appeal to particular interpretations of the Second Amendment to the U.S. Constitution and its stipulations about the "right to bear arms." Critics of such claims point out that this had to do with the need at the time for an armed militia as an internal protective force and that the same conditions no longer apply.

Violence is generally thought of as the use of physical force to cause injury to another or others. Physical assaults, shooting, and bombing are examples. However, we would not say that someone who pushed another out of the way of an oncoming car had been violent or acted violently. This is because violence also implies infringement of another in some way. It also has the sense of something intense or extreme. A small injury to another may not be considered an act of violence. Whether some sports— for example, football—can be considered violent games is something to think about.

Those who study the issue seek to understand the incidence and causes of violence. Violence has also been found to be correlated with income, and the majority of violent deaths are recorded in poor countries. In the United States, there is also more violent crime in low-income neighborhoods. Homicide rates have been correlated with economic downturns as well. Also, children and young adults who commit violent crimes are often found to have been subject to violence in their homes growing up.

On the other hand, studies have also shown that violence may be linked to violence in the media. According to some social scientists, movies today may provoke and play a causal role in violence, and many believe that the rash of school shootings as well as other random attacks can be linked to children and young people watching violent acts in movies and TV shows. This is particularly true, they claim, for children, who are more vulnerable to such influence and are less able to distinguish fiction from reality. No one study proves this conclusively, but hundreds of studies show a high probability of this connection.[6] One study showed that "children who watched more violence behaved more aggressively the next year than those who watched less violence on television, and more aggressively than would

have been expected based on how they had behaved the previous year."[7] Even after the killings at Virginia Tech, Canadian-based Lionsgate Studios released *Hostel: Part II*—about the torture killing of college students—less than two months later. Another movie example is *Scream*, which "opens with a scene in which a teenage girl is forced to watch her jock boyfriend tortured and then disemboweled by two fellow students . . . the killers stab and torture the girl, then cut her throat and hang her body from a tree so that Mom can discover it when she drives up."[8] Characters joke about the murders. They take it as great fun. In *Natural Born Killers*, killing is also treated as a personal thrill. *Pulp Fiction*, *Seven*, and *The Basketball Diaries* (and you may be able to think of others) also involve random killing in grotesque ways, with whimpering and pleading victims, some of them high-school classmates. These movies make big money for their producers—whether Disney, Miramax, or Time-Warner, for example—because the teens to whom they appeal make up a large segment of today's movie audience. Prime-time TV network shows "now average up to five violent acts per hour," and "the typical American boy or girl . . . will observe a stunning 40,000 dramatizations of killing by age 18."[9]

Just as many people are concerned about violence in movies, they also wonder about the effects of violent video games. In 2005, the California legislature voted to ban the sale or rental of violent video games to minors. Now the U.S. Supreme Court has agreed to review this law.[10] For example, the two teen killers at Columbine High School in 1999 were addicted to the game *Doom*. In a video they made themselves, the two even compared *Doom's* shotguns with their own.[11] Whether this game actually influenced their killing spree is controversial. Some research shows a low correlation between such game violence and aggressive behavior. The violence is too unreal, some researchers suggest. Others believe that it could be one factor in many that influence such behavior, especially if the violence is intense and realistic. The Entertainment Software Rating Board gives ratings to video and computer games from "Suitable for Children" to "For Adults Only." Among the terms used to describe the content is "intense violence," which is defined as "graphic and realistic-looking depictions of physical conflict. May involve extreme and/or realistic blood, gore, weapons, and depictions of human injury or death."[12] Such games could function as a release, provide simple fantasy experiences, or be incitements to commit certain aggressive acts.

Among the ethical questions related to these matters are the nature of the responsibility of corporations such as those that benefit financially from violent TV, movies, and video games. Even if there are no legal limits on graphic violence, is there not some moral responsibility to limit gratuitous depictions, especially knowing the good probability of some negative effects? Another moral question concerns freedom of speech. One of the points of free speech proponents is that being able to air different views does make a difference in what people believe and do. If this is so, then one cannot simultaneously support free speech and claim that such speech does not really affect people's behavior, as an excuse for producing profitable but potentially harmful entertainment.

We can use the same ethical theories and perspectives to evaluate violence that we have used for other issues in this text. For example, consequentialists such as utilitarians would want to weigh the harms caused by the violence with the supposed good, in at least some cases, to be produced by that violence. For example, one may be justified in killing an intruder who is threatening your life. However, killing any number of innocent people for your own profit would not be justified. Nonconsequentialists such as Kant would want to evaluate the violence from a perspective of using persons or doing something that involves something irrational, such as saying that my killing is permissible but others in similar situations are not. We can also see how violence would be judged by looking at two particular kinds of violence: terrorism and war.

TERRORISM

Although there had been both warnings of terrorist attacks on Americans and American interests and some incidents in the preceding decade, nothing compared with the September 11, 2001 attacks on the twin towers of the World Trade Center in New York and the Pentagon in Washington, D.C., in

which nearly 3,000 people were killed. Since then, there have been several more attempts at large-scale terrorist attacks in the United States. People worry about attacks on water supplies, transportation systems, computer systems, and fuel depots. Individual suicide attacks in Iraq, Israel, India, and other countries have targeted civilians in crowded markets, shopping malls, and buses. While the total number of worldwide terrorist attacks decreased by 20 percent from 2007 to 2008, the incidence of such attacks rose sharply in Afghanistan and Pakistan, where they have more than quadrupled since 2006. The situation has shifted dramatically from 2005–2006, when one-half of the 20,000 terrorist-caused fatalities worldwide were in Iraq.[13] In most of these countries, terrorists use weapons and materials such as unexploded ordinance and other explosives that are widely available. They do not need complicated or high-tech mechanisms to cause serious damage and widespread fear. Terrorists can be domestic or international. If international, they can be state-sponsored or members of loosely affiliated groups.

Before considering the ethical questions concerning whether terrorism or terrorist attacks are ever morally justified and why or why not, we should first clarify for ourselves what is meant by *terrorism*. After this, we can also understand it better by considering particular kinds of terrorism.

There are many different definitions of terrorism. When determining what is to count as terrorism, it may be said that one person's terrorist is another person's freedom fighter. The term's first known use

Iraqi policemen carry a wounded colleague away from a car bomb attack in Baghdad, Iraq.

was during the French Revolution for those who, like Maximilien Robespierre, used violence *on behalf* of a state. Only later was the term used to categorize violence *against* a state. The U.S. Department of State uses the following definition: "The term 'terrorism' means premeditated, politically motivated violence perpetrated against noncombatant targets by subnational groups or clandestine agents, usually intended to influence an audience." The U.S. Department of Defense defines terrorism as "the calculated use of violence or the threat of violence to inculcate fear; intended to coerce or to intimidate governments or societies in the pursuit of goals that are generally political, religious, or ideological."[14] By combining these definitions, we see that terrorism is, first of all, a particular kind of violence with particular aims and goals. The more immediate goal is to create fear. This is why civilians simply going about their daily routines are targeted at random. The more distant goals vary. In some cases, terrorists may use such violence to achieve some political goal such as independence. In Iraq, for example, it may be intended to intimidate political or ethnic opponents or to cause the American forces to leave. Web sites used by terrorist groups also speak of wanting to rid the Arab world of Western infidels. They may see their way of life and values as threatened. They may feel that they are serving the will of God. According to Thomas Friedman, one reason why so many young Sunni Muslim men are willing to blow themselves up is that, although they believe that Islam is a superior monotheistic religion, "its decision to ban the reform and reinterpretation of Islam since the [twelfth] century has choked the spirit of innovation out of Muslim lands" and left them less economically developed and less powerful. One way to assert their worth is to fight Western decadence and the presence of foreigners in their land by becoming suicide bombers.[15] Most suicide bombers are young and thus probably more idealistic and easily influenced and manipulated. Furthermore, they seem to lack any ability to empathize with the innocent victims of their attacks. Many of the hundreds of web sites devoted to some of these causes include graphic videos of beheadings and bombings to the accompaniment of spirited music, often giving the violence a religious blessing. It has also been determined that those behind these sites use them to contact users they think may be possible recruits.[16]

It has also been suggested that fundamentalist preaching and religious schools such as the madrassas play a key role in recruiting young people to the cause. However, those who have investigated the background of known terrorists find that most of them are at least middle class and most often well educated. Of seventy-five terrorists involved in prominent anti-Western attacks over the past two decades, 53 percent had "either attended college or had received a college degree . . . [whereas] only 52 percent of Americans have been to college."[17] Some terrorists are more rational in their goals than others, in having sufficient historical and political sense to know what will and will not work. In other cases, it seems that there is no realistic calculation of what the results of terrorist actions are likely to be.

What moves other terrorists, according to this analysis, are certain aspects of their personalities. Some are unhappy with their life prospects. They find meaning in belonging to and being accepted by their group. They find it difficult to see things from the perspective of their victims or to think of them as real individuals. They think they themselves cannot be wrong. They demonize entire nations and peoples, thus helping to make them acceptable targets.

A third motivating factor for some terrorists is said to be certain cultural beliefs that are difficult for others to appreciate. Willingness to be a martyr for the cause and regarding their actions as divinely sanctioned are two such culturally influenced traits. Some see outsiders as threatening to their way of life and values. They feel they have no other way to influence the state of affairs than to resort to terrorism.[18] As of 2006, the U.S. State Department's list of "Foreign Terrorist Organizations" numbered forty two. However, of these "only a half-dozen—all of them branches, offshoots, or ideological allies of al-Qaeda—have ever attacked the United states, or even indicated a readiness to do so." Among the others are the Revolutionary Armed Forces of Columbia (FARC) and the Liberation Tigers of Tamil Eelam (LITTE) in Sri Lanka, Hamas, and Hezbollah.[19]

Another analysis of al-Qaeda in particular likens its motives to those of leftist Western groups over the years. It sees this group not simply as a product of Islamic fundamentalism but also as having a "global revolutionary, anti-Western perspective that echoed the anti-imperialism of the older Arab and European new left and even today's anti-globalization movement."[20] It should be noted that "there is no special link between Islam and terrorism. Most major religions have produced some form of terrorism, and many terrorist groups have professed atheism."[21] The solution, according to some analysts, is to integrate these individuals into Western society and to help remove social and economic obstacles to such integration.

Ethical Issues

We should first of all grant that some uses of the term *terrorism* are evaluative in nature. In other words, in these cases one uses the term if one wants to say that something is bad. If we want to be able to make moral assessments of terrorism, and if we do not want to settle its moral status before we start our evaluation, then we should narrow and stabilize the definition so that we will know what we are about to judge.

What kind of ethical justification could be given in support of terrorism? The reasoning that supports terrorism is most often basically consequentialist and utilitarian. The end is thought to justify these means. If one supported this type of reasoning, then one would want to know whether, in fact, the benefits or good of the end or cause was such that it outweighed the harm and suffering caused by the means. One also could do empirical studies to see whether these means when used actually have produced the desired effects. Did the Oklahoma City bombing lessen the power of such federal agencies as the FBI or the Department of Treasury's Bureau of Alcohol, Tobacco, Firearms, and Explosives? Did the Unabomber stop the progress of technology? Did the bombing of American embassies weaken the position of the United States in the world? Did the September 11 attacks bring down the U.S. government or change its international behavior?

One also might question the very notion that violence can achieve a peaceable good end. Does not violence instead beget violence, some ask? Similar questions are asked by pacifists (see below). Or one can question the consequentialist nature of this type of reasoning. Are there not other ethical imperatives to consider? One long-standing element of international law and the just war theory (discussed below) is the inviolability of civilians or noncombatants. Sometimes, the reasoning behind this has been to avoid the inefficient use of power and resources and concentrate force on subduing the opposite military power rather than unarmed nonmilitary personnel. At other times, a nonconsequentialist element becomes part of the ethical arguments. Although self-defense of some sort might be a basis for using violence against another, those who are not attacking but are simply going about the business of life cannot be used by others no matter how good the latter's cause. Thus the Geneva Conventions, including the fourth (adopted on August 12, 1949—more than sixty years ago), enunciated principles to protect civilian populations from the worst effects of war. For example, they hold that civilians not be the direct objects of attack. Where the attack of civilians has occurred, the offenders often are accused of "war crimes" and sometimes subject to international arrest and prosecution (see the discussion below).

Another ethical issue that arises in discussions of terrorism has to do with the means used to combat it. A much debated means is the U.S.A. Patriot Act. The full title of this act is "Uniting and Strengthening America by Providing Appropriate Tools Required to Intercept and Obstruct Terrorism Act of 2001." It was introduced less than a week after the September 11 attacks, hastily considered by Congress, and signed into law by President George W. Bush on October 26, 2001. The purpose of the act was to strengthen the country's defenses against terrorism. It amended several laws in a way that expanded and strengthened the government's surveillance and investigative powers by increasing its ability to "monitor private communications and access personal information."[22] Whereas the government was previously required to show probable cause of the commission of a crime in order to obtain a court order for such surveillance, this is no longer the case in many instances. For example, it is now easier for the government to obtain "roving wiretaps" when suspects switch phone numbers. A suspect's business, medical, educational, and library records may be accessed. Critics worry about the effect the act may have on civil liberties and privacy rights. The ethical issue may be formulated in terms of a balancing act: How important are the provisions of the law, what risk does it curtail, and how important are the privacy and liberty rights that might be compromised? The same issue arose earlier in this text in relation to genetic screening, and one can consider some of the ethical arguments by reviewing that section.

Another means used is video surveillance. For example, London has an extensive system of video surveillance—closed-circuit television (CCTV)—on its subways and throughout much of the city, which seems to have led to the identification of the bombers involved in the July 7, 2005 terror attacks. San Francisco has CCTV cameras installed on all of its subway station platforms. In New York City, the placement and use of cameras is sporadic. Only in some cases in the United States are the videos recorded and stored. However, new electronic surveillance technology has made it easier to store and retrieve such images, which are also much more clear and detailed.[23] The ethical issue here is also one of balancing—whether the increase in safety provided by these systems is worth the reduction in privacy.

PACIFISM

Pacifism is the view that the use of force, including lethal force, is morally objectionable. It is the opposite of militarism, or the view that the use of force, especially military force, is noble and just. In his essay "The Moral Equivalent of War," American pragmatist philosopher William James knew that fighting a war required the virtues of heroism, self-sacrifice, and loyalty.[24] Yet he called for a substitute for war, something that could develop those same virtues without the destruction of armed conflict. He envisioned something like today's California Conservation Corps, in which groups of people work to clear brush and clean up the environment. Not all pacifists oppose the use of all types of force. After all, there are nonphysical means of exerting force. One

can think of there being degrees of pacifism—that is, in terms of the degree and type of force thought acceptable. Some pacifists also support the use of physical and even lethal physical force when it is necessary, such as to defend oneself. The question, then, is whether such lethal means are ever justified to defend others or a nation.

The reasons given in support of pacifism vary. Some people believe that nonviolent means to achieve some good end are preferable to violent means because they work better. You will recognize this consequentialist form of reasoning. Violence does more harm than good, they argue, because it can only beget violence. How can we determine whether or not this is true? We can look to see whether historical examples support the generalization. We also can inquire whether this may result from something in human nature—that we are prone to violence and easily imitate the violent behavior of others, for example. Our judgments will then depend on adequate factual assessments. However, nonconsequentialist reasons are also given in support of pacifism—for example, that to kill another is wrong in itself. The reasons for this must be presented, and any exceptions to the rule must be discussed. Pacifists must address the criticism that it seems inconsistent to hold that life is of the highest value and yet not be willing to use force to defend it.

Intermediate between the more extreme versions of some forms of pacifism and militarism is a range of positions according to which the use of force, including military force, is sometimes justified. The problem is to circumscribe when it is and is not morally permissible to use force—even lethal force. Some people who have been long known for their opposition to war, for example, have relented when faced with situations such as those in Somalia, Bosnia, Kosovo, and Darfur. "Moral isolation is simply not a defensible position for those opposed to war," according to longtime pacifist William Sloane Coffin, Jr.[25] Massive famine caused by civil war and "ethnic cleansing" are likely candidates for military intervention if this is the only way to eliminate them, some argue. Nevertheless, national boundaries and the national right to self-determination also cannot be ignored, so not every seeming injustice may rightly be a candidate for military intervention. Political philosopher Michael Walzer puts it this way: "I think of this in terms of the old international law doctrine of humanitarian intervention. . . . It was always held that in cases of massacre on the other side of the border, you have a right, and maybe an obligation, to go in and stop it if you can."[26] People have certain fundamental rights that states may not override. To what extent, and when, are others obligated to protect these rights?

In a speech to the U.S. Military Academy at West Point on January 5, 1992, President George H. W. Bush put forth the following criteria: "Using military force makes sense as a policy where the stakes warrant, where and when force can be effective, where its application can be limited in scope and time, and where the potential benefits justify the potential costs and sacrifice."[27] These criteria are not new. They have traditionally been part of international law. They are also part of what is known as just war theory. Because these principles are still used in the discussions and debates about justified military intervention, it would be well to briefly summarize them here. Some people have preferred the use of the phrase "justified war" instead of "just war" because they believe that in just war theory there is a presumption against the use of military force that must be overcome.

JUST WAR THEORY

As of June 2010, 4,394 U.S. soldiers had died in Iraq and 1,098 in Afghanistan.[28] The numbers of Iraqis killed since the U.S. invasion varies widely, with estimates as low as 23,000 and and as high as 655,000— in a study by the British medical journal, *The Lancet*. The latter figure would amount to 2.5 percent of the population. Moreover, an estimated 2 million to 4 million Iraqis have fled to Syria and Jordan, and many have been displaced but remain in the country. When one considers not only the deaths and displacements caused by and in war but also the destruction of cities and property, one can rightly ask whether war can ever be justified.[29]

Just war theory has a long history. Its origins can be traced to the writings of St. Augustine, the Bishop of Hippo in North Africa, in approximately 400 A.D.

Augustine was concerned about how to reconcile traditional Christian views about the immorality of violence with the necessity of defending the Roman Empire from invading forces.[30] He asked what one should do if one sees an individual attacking an innocent, defenseless victim. His response was that one should intervene and do whatever is necessary (but only so much as was necessary) to protect the victim, even up to the point of killing the aggressor. Further developments of the theory were provided by Thomas Aquinas, the practices of medieval chivalry, and jurists such as Hugo Grotius. In modern times, the theory was given additional detail by the Hague and Geneva Conventions. The first Geneva Conventions were written in 1864 "at the urging of Henri Dunant, founder of the Red Cross, to establish a code for the care and treatment of the sick, wounded, and dead in wartime."[31]

There is general agreement that just war theory includes two basic areas: principles that would have to be satisfied for a nation to be justified in using military force, or initiating a war, and principles governing the conduct of the military action or war itself. These have been given the Latin names of *jus ad bellum* (the justness of going to war) and *jus in bello* (justness in war).

Jus ad Bellum

Just Cause The first principle that provides a condition for going to war is the *just cause principle*. To use force against another nation, there must be a serious reason to justify it. In the preceding Bush quotation, the phrase is "when the stakes warrant it." Although according to the just war theory there must be a just cause, the theory itself does not specify what is to count as a just cause. Defense of one's territory against an invader would seem to be such a cause. However, there may also be other reasons. For example, righting a wrong may be insufficient cause and helping the world's downtrodden too vague, but intervening to prevent another nation from committing genocide on its own people may be a sufficient justification (assuming the other principles are also met). Other causes may sound familiar but may be questionable as justification, including preventing the spread of communism, ridding another country of a despotic and possibly dangerous leader, preventing a nation from obtaining and possibly using nuclear weapons, and protecting the world's oil supply. These may be cases of self-defense, using a broad definition of what is in a nation's vital interest and thus can be defended, but the connection and the seriousness of the circumstances would need to be demonstrated.

Among other related issues is that of preventive and preemptive strikes. A *preventive strike*, as Israel used in 1981 when its air force blew up an Iraqi nuclear reactor that could have been employed to make nuclear weapons materials, seeks to prevent some future harm. Just war theory does not in itself seem to help determine whether this type of strike or attack is ever justifiable, although common sense and notions of proportionality may sometimes support it (see below). However, the theory may provide some help with regard to *preemptive strikes*. Say that another nation is about to invade one's territory. Defense against such aggression would seem to be a just response. However, must one wait until the attacker steps across the border or sends planes in order to respond? One would think not. The principle of "only if attacked first" may be too strict. However, the farther one gets from this scenario, the more problematic the justification of preemptive strikes becomes. For example, "They are only now drawing up plans to attack but have not yet even assembled their forces." One might even not be sure that they will put their plans into action. This is not to say that even though remote in connection, such justifications have not been used in recent wars.[32]

The question is more complicated when, for example, there is the possibility of an Israeli or U.S. attack on Iran to prevent it from developing nuclear weapons. Even if it were possible, the benefit–harm comparison might well show that the harm done by the attack would outweigh any prevention of possible development.[33]

Proportionality   Not only must the cause be just, according to the theory, but also the probable good to be produced by the intervention must outweigh the likely evil that the war or use of force will cause. This is the second principle, the *proportionality principle*. It requires that, before engaging in such action, we consider the probable costs and benefits and compare them with the probable costs and benefits of doing something else or of doing nothing. Involved in this utilitarian calculation are two elements: One assesses the likely costs and benefits, and the other weighs their relative value. The first requires historical and empirical information, whereas the second involves ethical evaluations. In making such evaluations, we might well compare lives that are likely to be saved with lives lost, for example. But how do we compare the value of freedom and self-determination, or a way of life with the value of a life itself? (Refer to the discussion of cost–benefit analysis in Chapter 4.)

Last Resort   A third requirement for justly initiating a war or military intervention is the *last resort principle*. The idea is that military interventions are extremely costly in terms of suffering, loss of life, and other destruction, so other means must be considered first. They need not all be tried first, for some will be judged useless beforehand. However, this principle may well require that some other means be attempted, at least those that are judged to have a chance of achieving the goal specified by the just cause. Negotiations, threats, and boycotts are such means. When is enough enough? When have these measures been given sufficient trial? There is always something more that could be tried. This is a matter of prudential judgment and therefore always uncertain.[34]

Right Intention   A fourth principle in the jus ad bellum part of the just war theory is the *right intention principle*. It requires that the intervention be always directed to the goal set by the cause and to the eventual goal of peace. Thus, wars fought to satisfy hatreds or to punish others are unjustified. However, this principle also requires that what is done during the conduct of the war is necessary and that it not unnecessarily make peace harder to attain. There should be no gratuitous cruelty, for example. This moves us into discussion of the conduct of a war, the second area covered by the principles of just war theory.[35]

Jus in Bello

Proportionality   Even if a war were fought for a just cause, with the prospect of achieving more good than harm, as a last resort only, and with the proper intention, it still would not be fully just if it were not conducted justly or in accordance with certain principles or moral guidelines. The jus in bello part of the just war theory consists of two principles. The first is a *principle of proportionality*. In the conduct of the conflict, this principle requires that to meet the various limited objectives, no more force than necessary be used, and that the force or means used be proportionate to the importance of the particular objective for the cause as a whole.

Discrimination   The second principle is that of *discrimination*. This prohibits direct intentional attacks on noncombatants and nonmilitary targets. The principle has two basic elements. One directs us to focus on the issue of what are and are not military targets, and the other on who is and is not a combatant. Are roads and bridges and hospitals that are used in the war effort of the other side to be considered military targets? The general consensus is that the roads and bridges are targets if they contribute directly and in significant ways to the military effort, but that hospitals are not legitimate targets. The principle to be used in making this distinction is the same for the people as for the things. Those people who contribute directly are combatants, and those who do not are not combatants. Obviously, there are gray areas in the middle. One writer suggests that persons who are engaged in doing what they do for persons as persons are noncombatants, while those who perform their functions specifically for the war effort are combatants.[36] Thus, those who grow and provide food would be noncombatants, whereas those who make or transport the military equipment would be combatants.

Note, too, that although we also hear the term *innocent civilians* in such discussions, it is noncombatants who are supposed to be out of the fight and not people who are judged on some grounds to be innocent. Soldiers fighting unwillingly might be thought to be innocent but are nevertheless combatants. Those behind the lines spending time verbally supporting the cause are not totally innocent, yet they are noncombatants. The danger of using the term *innocents* in place of *noncombatants* is that it also allows some to say that no one living in a certain country is immune because they are all supporters of their country and so not innocent. However, this is contrary to the traditional understanding of the principle of discrimination.

The reason why the terms *combatant* and *noncombatant* are preferable is also related to the second aspect of the principle of discrimination—namely, that noncombatants not be the subject of direct attack. Combatants are not immune because they are a threat. Thus, when someone is not or is no longer a threat, as when they have surrendered or are incapacitated by injury, then they are not to be regarded as legitimate targets. This principle does not require that for a war to be conducted justly no noncombatants be injured or killed, but that they not be the direct targets of attack. Although directly targeting and killing civilians may have a positive effect on a desired outcome, this would nevertheless not be justified according to this principle. It is not a consequentialist principle. The end does not justify the use of this type of means. This principle may be grounded in the more basic *principle of double effect*, which we discussed in Chapter 10. If this is true, then the other aspect of the principle of double effect would be relevant; that is, not only must the civilians not be directly targeted, but also the number of them likely to be injured when a target is attacked must not be disproportionately great compared to the significance of the target.

According to just war theory, then, for a war or military intervention to be justified, certain conditions for going to war must be satisfied, and the conduct in the war must follow certain principles or moral guidelines. We could say that if any of the principles are violated, that a war is unjust, or we could say that it was unjust in this regard but not in some other aspects. Some of just war theory has become part of national and international law, including the U.S. Army Rules for Land Warfare and the U.N. Charter. However, some of its principles also appeal to common human reason. As such, you too can judge whether these are valid or reasonable qualifications and whether they can play a useful role in debates about justified use of military force.

NON-TRADITIONAL MILITARY CONFLICTS

When one considers the history of wars and the tradition of just war theory, it can seem inappropriate or metaphorical to speak of a "war on terrorism." Today when so-called terrorists are not part of any recognized state, the weapons and rules of war often do not apply. One might use military force against supposed terrorists, but that does not necessarily constitute a "war on terrorism."

Many conflicts now are not typical of traditional war, with armies fighting each other. It is difficult to say whether the conflict in Afghanistan is such. But there are non-traditional elements involved. For example, the Taliban are not part of a conventional army in military dress, and many seem motivated by local or tribal grievances. Similarly, much of the recent focus among U.S. and NATO commanders has been on non-military activites such as building up the infrastructure, setting up schools, and trying to reform a frequently corrupt Afghan political establishment. Thus traditional just war theory may not fully apply to this type of conflict.

WEAPONS OF MASS DESTRUCTION

Between 2001 and 2008, the total arms sales by the United States worldwide was $154.882 billion, or 41 percent of total sales. As such the United States was the biggest arms dealer during that period. Second was Russia, with 17 percent of the total, France with 8 percent of the total, and The United Kingdom with 7 percent of the total.[37] These figures reflect sales of conventional weapons. The so-called weapons of mass destruction are a different issue. This category usually includes biological, chemical, and nuclear weapons. Biological weapons are living microorganisms that can be used as weapons to maim, incapacitate, and kill. Among these weapons is anthrax, which infects either the skin or the lungs. Breathing only a small amount of anthrax causes death in 80 to 90 percent of cases. Smallpox, cholera, and bubonic or pneumonic plague are other biological agents that might be used. Genetic engineering may also be used to make more virulent strains. There have been no proven usages of biological weapons in modern wars, although movies such as *The Paradise Virus* and *Outbreak* have dramatized the possibilities. One hundred sixty-three states have ratified the Biological Weapons Convention (1975), which prohibits the production, stockpiling, and use of such agents as weapons.

Chemical weapons include blister agents such as mustard gas, which is relatively easy and cheap to produce. It produces painful blisters and incapacitates rather than kills. Iraq is said to have used mustard gas in its 1980 to 1988 war with Iran as well as some type of chemical weapon on the Kurdish inhabitants of Halabja in 1988. Through low-level repeated airdrops, as many as 5,000 defenseless people in that town were killed. Phosgene is a choking agent, and hydrogen cyanide "prevents transfer of oxygen to the tissues." Large quantities of the latter, however, would be needed to produce significant effects.[38] Hydrogen cyanide is a deadly poison gas, as is evidenced by its use in executions in the gas chamber. Sarin is called a nerve "gas," but it is actually a liquid. It affects the central nervous system and is highly toxic. In 1995, the Japanese cult group Aum Shinrikyo used many containers of sarin in the Tokyo subway. It sickened thousands and killed twelve people. Chemical weapons were also used somewhat extensively in both world wars. For example, in World War I, the Germans used mustard gas and chlorine, and the French used phosgene. Although it might not be usually classified as the use of a chemical weapon, in 1945 American B-29 bombers "dropped 1665 tons of napalm-filled bombs on Tokyo, leaving almost nothing standing over 16 square miles." One hundred thousand people were killed in this raid, not from napalm directly but from the fires that it caused.[39] One hundred and eighty-eight nations are party to the Chemical Weapons Convention (1994). Because such weapons can be made by private groups in small labs, however, verifying international compliance with the convention is highly problematic. Furthermore, Angola, Egypt, Syria, Somalia, and North Korea have refused to sign the convention, some arguing that they should do this only if all weapons of mass destruction were banned, implying nuclear as well.[40]

Nuclear weapons, including both fission and fusion bombs, are the most deadly because of not only their powerful explosiveness but also their radiation and lingering genetic damage. The effects were well demonstrated by the U.S. bombings of Hiroshima and Nagasaki in August 1945. It is estimated that more than 100,000 people died and another 95,000 were injured. There have been many nuclear weapons treaties—for example, the Nuclear Non-Proliferation Treaty (1968), the Strategic Arms Limitation Treaties (SALT I in 1972 and SALT II in 1993), and the Strategic Offensive Reductions Treaty (2002). Nations known to have nuclear weapons now include China, France, India, Israel, North Korea, Pakistan, Russia, the United Kingdom, and the United States. Although the parties to the 1968 agreement promised to pursue negotiations in good faith and move to a future treaty on general and complete disarmament, none of them has made real efforts in this regard. On the other hand, there has been some progress made regarding the agreement to reduce their stockpiles and the numbers of deployed warheads in the 2002 treaty.[41] On April 8, 2010, in a New START treaty, President Barack Obama and Russian President Dmitry Medvedev agreed to cut their nuclear warheads "to 1550 each over seven years, down about a third from the current ceiling of 2200."[42]

There is still a worrisome global black market in nuclear materials and know-how. These weapons are difficult but not impossible to make. A. Q. Kahn, a nuclear scientist who helped develop Pakistan's nuclear program, is thought to have sold such materials and information to Libya, Iran, and North Korea. Although Russia agreed to secure its tactical nuclear weapons, many of which were poorly guarded, some are small enough that they could be "carried by one person, put in the back of a truck, and blow up a large part of a city."[43]

In calling these agents *weapons of mass destruction*, we imply that they are of a different order of magnitude than the usual means of modern warfare. It is clear why nuclear weapons are labeled in this way, but it is not so clear why the others are. Even when used somewhat extensively in World War I, "fewer than 1 percent of battle deaths" during that war were caused by gas, and only "2 percent of those gassed during the war died, compared with 24 percent of those struck by bullets, artillery shells, or shrapnel."[44] For gas to work well, there can be no wind or sun, and it must be delivered by an aircraft flying at very low altitude. If delivered by bombs, the weapons would be incinerated before they could become effective. Today's gas masks and antibiotics and other preventives and treatments lessen the lethality of such

weapons even more. In 1971, smallpox accidentally got loose in Kazakhstan but killed only three people; and in 1979, a large amount of anthrax was released through the explosion of a Soviet plant, but only sixty-eight people were killed.[45] Nevertheless, the anthrax scare of 2001 in the United States showed that even small amounts can be deadly.

Is the use of biological, chemical, or nuclear weapons unethical, and if so, why? It would at least seem that their use would violate the discrimination and proportionality principles of just war theory. It would be difficult to target them only at those who are directly involved in the fighting and not also involve a disproportionate number of civilians. One wonders, however, whether ordinary bombs and bullets that explode and kill many more people than biological or chemical weapons are less objectionable. Nevertheless, people seem to fear biological and chemical weapons more than conventional weapons. Possibly it is the thought of being killed by something invisible that makes them so feared and is behind the desire to call them weapons of mass destruction, with the implication that they are morally abhorrent.

WAR CRIMES AND UNIVERSAL HUMAN RIGHTS

Many of the elements of the laws of war and the nature of war crimes have been developed in the various declarations of the Geneva Conventions. The first convention was formulated in 1864 "to protect the sick and wounded in war time."[46] It was inspired by the founder of the Red Cross, Henri Dunant, and this organization has continued to play a role in its enforcement since then. Other treaties were passed in 1899, 1907, and 1925 relating to the use of poison gas and biological warfare. The convention of 1929 concerned the treatment of prisoners of war and the wounded, while the four agreements of 1949 sought to include protection for sailors and civilians and covered civil wars. A key provision of these conventions was the distinction between *combatants* and *civilians*. Important here was the requirement for combatants to wear uniforms so that they could be distinguished from civilians. The Geneva Conventions and two 1977 "protocols" also determined that "mercenaries," or fighters who do not belong to any state, are not protected by the Geneva Convention.[47] Those who violate these conventions and protocols may be held guilty of "war crimes." However, other treaties apply more widely than the Geneva Conventions. For example, the U.N. Convention Against Torture, which was ratified by the United States, requires that all signatory nations "prevent in any territory under its jurisdiction . . . cruel, inhuman, or degrading treatment."[48] In addition, the U.S. Uniform Code of Military Justice makes "cruelty, oppression, or maltreatment of prisoners a crime."[49]

War crimes are often equated with "crimes against humanity." The idea is akin to notions espoused by natural law and natural rights theories discussed in Chapter 7. Certain things are violations of the natural value and dignity of persons, and all those who consider them should know this no matter what their own society's views or the orders they receive. Thus, those in 1995 who separated the unarmed civilian men from the women and children in Kosovo and who marched them to the river and shot them, as well as those who moved people by force from their homes and burned the buildings because they wanted to "cleanse" the province from members of that ethnic group, should have known that this was wrong. When called explicitly a "war crime," the implication is also that there are rules of war that have been adopted by the international community over the decades. As noted already, among these is the immunity of civilians or noncombatants during war. Some of these rules were put in place after World War II with its great civilian death toll and the bombings of the cities of London, Dresden, Hiroshima, and Nagasaki. It is also to point out how a number of modern-day practices violate these rules. Among the examples are using civilians as a cover for rebel operations or as human shields against air attacks, as well as terrorist attacks and ethnic cleansing. From 2001 to 2003, high-ranking members of the Serbian Yugoslav government and military, most notably Slobodan Milosevic, were put on trial for war crimes at the International Criminal Tribunal in the Hague. Among the crimes of which they were accused were forced expulsions of ethnic Albanians, mass executions and burials of civilians, and sexual assault.

There is an ongoing debate about whether the so-called detainees at the U.S. base in Guantanamo Bay, Cuba are protected by the Geneva Conventions and whether they are to be considered prisoners of war with the rights guaranteed by these conventions. The denomination of *enemy combatant* is meant to distinguish such prisoners from those covered by these international conventions. Rights to a fair hearing and the ability to be represented by legal counsel to challenge their detention are among the concerns of rights activists. According to Global Rights, an international group, "enemy combatant is an invented classification that is not recognized in international law."[50] Moreover, the Geneva Conventions as well as some other U.S. laws require the humane treatment of prisoners as noted above. Questions have been raised about possible abuses of these detainees as well as others, most notably in the Abu Ghraib prisoner abuse scandals in Iraq that began in 2004.

In an opening address to the U.N. General Assembly on September 20, 1999, Secretary General Kofi Annan said, "nothing in the (U.N.) Charter precludes a recognition that there are rights beyond borders."[51] Although it would be better if a country itself took care to prevent human rights abuses of its citizens, sometimes this does not happen. What, then, is the responsibility of the international community? There is first the question of intervention, whether it can be effective given the conditions; if so, then what kind would be most effective? There is also the question of whether there are other bases for selective international concern about human rights abuses. The lack of intervention to prevent genocide in Rwanda is often cited here as well as the conflict in the Darfur region of Sudan. Others point out that it is too often after the fact of the abuse that international interest is aroused, rather than earlier, when other means than military intervention have prevented it. Among these means are the curbing of the supply of weapons and alleviation of extreme poverty, which is perhaps the main cause of conflict.

There are many politically unstable countries around the world today. According to Robert Kaplan, a correspondent for *The Atlantic Monthly* and author of *The Ends of the Earth*, "More and more it is population growth that threatens stability in the third world."[52] Currently more than 6 billion people live on Earth. The proportion of poor people to middle-class people in the third world is growing because their birthrate is higher. Such growth and urban over-crowding makes it difficult for countries to build stable civic institutions and to develop decent standards of living.[53] Combine this with ethnic diversity and mistrust and the availability of weapons, and we have a recipe for military conflict. Issues of war and peace are altogether bound up, then, with economic matters.

Furthermore, economist Amartya Sen argues that when people have a say in their government, policies of abuse will not endure. "In any country with a democratic form of government and a relatively free press," he notes, "no substantial famine has ever occurred. People will not stand for it."[54] Among the notions on which the U.N. Declaration of Human Rights is based is that people ought to be able to choose the life that they wish to lead. In fact, this is the ideal of most democratic forms of government. This view is not necessarily an imposition from above of Western ways. Rights movements such as Poland's Solidarity and the National Conference on Soviet Jewry, as well as women's groups in some Muslim countries, are examples of bottom-up efforts to establish human rights. In 1990s Afghanistan, for example, the ruling fundamentalist Taliban regime imposed strict prohibitions on women's place in society, but the women did not want to abandon their hard-won freedoms and continued to press for better access to education and health care. What is seemingly needed is an agreement that, although individual nations remain a pillar of the international community, there is a responsibility to intervene that lies somewhere between the extremes of a broad license by which the United States, the United Nations, or NATO becomes the world police force and a narrow interpretation where the rest of the world stands by while observing terror, ethnic cleansing, and serious violations of human rights.

It has been more than fifty years since the signing of the Universal Declaration of Human Rights. It was Eleanor Roosevelt who, in her apartment in February 1947, first brought together a committee to draft a human rights document.[55] The final document simply declared that there were universal human rights and then described them. It did not give reasons why we possess these rights. It could not do so because those drafting and signing it had different views on this. For some, it was the dignity given to

humans by a divine creator God. For others, it was a recognition of the common humanity that we share and a sympathy for the plight of others like ourselves as well as the ability to imagine the pain or degradation of other human beings and to empathize with them. As a declaration, it appealed to the conscience of peoples and nations, but it included no enforcement agency. In fact, the notion of a world tribunal to punish human rights violations is today a controversial idea, one that the United States, for example, opposes. Nongovernmental organizations are said to be the primary enforcers of the rights specified in the declaration: groups such as Amnesty International and Human Rights Watch, which publicize information on known violations and thus appeal to the moral conscience of state and non-state actors.

Sometimes there is conflict over the primacy of different kinds of human rights. Some believe that political rights are primary—for example, the rights to freedoms of speech, the press, and movement. Others believe that social and economic rights—such as the rights to food, shelter, education, and health care—are more basic. Those who support the latter often insist that the former emphasis is too individualistic. However, it may well be that they each depend on the another. The United Nations has established a Commission on Human Rights to investigate rights abuses. The members meet every year for six weeks to name and thus shame violators. However, more recently the members themselves come from nations that clearly violate the rights of their own citizens—for example, Burma, China, Cuba, Libya, and North Korea—and thus the group has lost some of its power to exercise influence on behalf of human rights. Efforts have been made in recent years to address this problem.[56]

TORTURE

One of the issues related to human rights and non-traditional conflicts is that of torture. First of all, it is not entirely clear what is to count as torture. During the George W. Bush administration the office of legal council in the justice department issued a number of memos suggesting that certain methods of trying to extract information from prisoners suspected of terrorism were not torture. The author of a number of these was a lawyer named John Yoo. According to

Yoo's memo, "inflicting physical pain does not count as torture unless the interrogator specifically intends the pain to reach the level associated with organ failure or death." This definition was supposedly to avoid the Geneva Agreements that forbid torture. Among the means used was the now infamous "waterboarding," and stress methods, sleep deprivation, and the use of loud music. The administration claimed that these tactics were justified since 9/11 to prevent future terrorist attacks. Critics complained loudly that this was not consistent with what the Geneva Conventions held and contrary to American values.[57]

In the reading selections in this chapter, Jean Bethke Elshtain discusses the issue of terrorism, and Michael Walzer evaluates some elements of the just war theory.

NOTES

1. Nancy Gibbs, "Darkness Falls: One Troubled Student Rains Down Death on a Quiet Campus," and Jeffrey Keuger, "Why They Kill," *Time*, April 30, 2007, pp. 36–59.
2. www.hss.state.ak.us/dph/ipems/AKVDRS/assets/ NVDRS-17States.pdf.
3. Sheryl Gay Stolberg, "War, Murder and Suicide: A Year's Toll Is 1.6 Million," *The New York Times*, Oct. 3, 2002, p. A12.
4. Bob Herbert, "The N.R.A.'s Campaign," *The New York Times*, March 16, 2000, p. A31.
5. http://library.med.utah.edu/WebPath/TUTORIAL/ GUNS/GUNSTAT.html.
6. Lawrie Mifflin, "Evidence Strong for Media Role in Violence," *The New York Times*, May 9, 1999, p. A3.
7. Ibid.
8. Gregg Easterbrook, "Watch and Learn. Yes, the Media Do Make Us More Violent," *New Republic* (May 17, 1999): 22–25.
9. Ibid.
10. http://lakeconews.com/content/view/13669/928/.
11. http://doom.wikia.com/wiki/Columbine_High_School_massacre.
12. www.esrb.org.
13. http://www.cnn.com/2009/WORLD/asiapcf/04/ 30/terrorism.report; http://www.state.gov/documents/ organization/122599.pdf; http://www.monstersand- critics.com/news/usa/news/article_1298539.php/ Terrorist_attacks_worldwide_rose_sharply_in_2006.
14. Alan B. Krueger and Jitka Maleckova, "Does Poverty Cause Terrorism?" *The New Republic* (June 24, 2002): 27. See also Robert K. Fullinwider, "Terrorism, Innocence, and War," *Philosophy and Public Policy Quarterly*, *21*, no. 4 (Fall 2001): 9–16; and http://www.nationalserviceresources.org/ node/17538.
15. Thomas L. Friedman, "A Poverty of Dignity and a Wealth of Rage," *The New York Times*, July 15, 2005, p. A21.
16. Jonathan Curiel, "Terror.com," *San Francisco Chronicle*, July 10, 2005, pp. A1, A11.
17. Peter Bergen and Swati Pandey, "The Madrassa Myth," *The New York Times*, June 14, 2005, p. A19.
18. Ibid.
19. Max Rodenbeck, "How Terrible Is It?" *The New York Review of Books*, Nov. 30, 2006, p. 33.
20. John B. Judis, "Paris Diarist," *New Republic* (Oct. 7, 2002): 42.
21. Max Rodenbeck, "How Terrible Is It?" *The New York Review of Books*, Nov. 30, 2006, p. 35.
22. www.epic.org/privacy/terrorism/usapatriot.
23. Sewell Chan, "U.S. Transit Agencies Turn to Cameras in Terror Fight, but Systems Vary in Effectiveness," *The New York Times*, July 14, 2005, p. A13.
24. William James, "The Moral Equivalent of War," *Popular Science Monthly* (Oct. 1910).
25. Quoted in Peter Steinfels, "Reshaping Pacifism to Fight Anguish in Reshaped World," The New York Times, Dec. 21, 1992, p. A1.
26. Ibid.
27. *The New York Times*, Jan. 6, 1993, p. A5.
28. http://projects.washingtonpost.com/fallen/.
29. Sarah Boseley, "655,000 Iraqis Killed Since Invasion," *The Guardian*, Oct. 11, 2006 (online at www.guardian.co.uk/Iraq/Story/0,,1892888,00.html).
30. Robert W. Tucker, *The Just War* (Baltimore: Johns Hopkins University Press, 1960), 1.
31. "Swiss Call Meeting on How to Apply Historic War Rules," *San Francisco Chronicle*, Oct. 6, 2002, p. A15.
32. Max Boot, "Who Says We Never Strike First?" *The New York Times*, Oct. 4, 2002, p. A29. See also the review of Boot's book, *The Savage Wars of Peace: Small Wars and the Rise of American Power* (New York: Basic Books, 2002), as well as a review of it by Brian Urguhard, "Is There a Case for Little Wars?" *New York Review of Books*, 49, no. 15 (Oct. 10, 2002): 10–13.
33. John Green, "Just How Should We Decide to Strike First?" (a review of *Preemption: The Knife that Cuts Both Ways* by Alan Dershowitz), *San Francisco Chronicle*, March 5, 2006, p. M3.

34. We might consider this particular principle as what is called a regulative rather than a substantive principle. Instead of telling us when something is enough or the last thing we should try, it can be used to prod us to go somewhat further than we otherwise would.

35. Some versions of the just war theory also note that for a war to be just it must be declared by a competent authority. This was to distinguish not only just wars from battles between individuals but also civil wars and insurrections. These would need to be argued for on other grounds. This principle also would direct the discussion of the justness of a war of nations to whether the proper national authorities had declared the war—with all of the constitutional issues, for example, that this raises.

36. James Childress, "Just-War Theories," *Theological Studies* (1978), 427–445.

37. www.globalissues.org/article/74/the-arms-trade-is-big-business.

38. www.fas.org/nuke/intro/cw/intro.htm.

39. Howard W. French, "100,000 People Perished, but Who Remembers?" *The New York Times*, March 14, 2002, p. A4.

40. Daniel J. Kevles, "The Poor Man's Atomic Bomb," *New York Review of Books*, April 12, 2007, pp. 60–63; http://treaties.un.org.

41. *Time* (Aug. 1, 2005): 38–39.

42. http://abcnews.go.com/US/wireStory?id=10317355.

43. Ibid.; www.ppionline.org/ppi_ci.cfm?knlgAreaID=124& subsecID=160&contentID=1316.

44. Gregg Easterbrook, "Term Limits, The Meaninglessness of 'WMD'" *New Republic* (Oct. 7, 2002): 23.

45. Ibid.

46. http://www.spj.org/gc-history.asp.

47. http://www.icrc.org/ihl.nsf/full/470?opendocument.

48. Anthony Lewis, "Guantanamo's Long Shadow," *The New York Times*, June 21, 2005, p. A23.

49. Ibid.

50. Linda Greenhouse, "Top Court Pits Detainee Rights Against Presidential Powers," *San Francisco Chronicle*, April 18, 2004, p. A10.

51. Barbara Crosette, "U.N. Chief Issues a Call to Speed Interventions and Halt Civil Wars," *The New York Times*, Sept. 21, 1999, p. A1.

52. Robert D. Kaplan, "Weakness in Numbers," *The New York Times*, Oct. 18, 1999, p. A27. Also see Kaplan, *The Ends of the Earth* (New York: Random House, 1996).

53. Ibid.

54. Michael Ignatieff, "Human Rights: The Midlife Crisis," *New York Review of Books,* May 20, 1999, pp. 58–62.

55. Ibid.

56. See Joseph Loconte, "Morality for Sale," *The New York Times*, April 1, 2004, p. A27.

57. David Luban, "The Defense of Torture," *The New York Review of Books*, March 15, 2007, pp. 37–40.

R E A D I N G
What Is a Terrorist?

JEAN BETHKE ELSHTAIN

Study Questions

1. What does the author mean when she says that "a terrorist is one who sows terror"?

2. What questions does she believe we should ask in order to know whether one is aptly called a terrorist according to her definition?

3. Why does she hold that "there is a nihilistic edge to terrorism"?

4. What comparison is made between training teachings and videos of the U.S. military and those described for certain terrorist groups?

5. Why does she assert that certain extremists hate us not for what we do but for what we are?

6. Does she imply that U.S. foreign policy should not be criticized? Does she believe doing so will solve the problem?

THIS LINE of reasoning pertains directly to how we talk about *terror* and *terrorists*. Just as the words *martyr* and *martyrdom* are distorted, whether in the Western or the Islamic tradition, when applied not to

From Jean Bethke Elshtain, *Just War Against Terror: The Burden of American Power in a Violent World.* New York: Basic Books, 2003, pp. 118–123. Copyright © 2004 by Jean Bethke Elshtain. Reprinted by permission of Basic Books, a member of the Perseus Books Group.

those prepared to die as witnesses to their faith but instead to those who commit suicide while killing as many civilians as possible, so *terrorist* is twisted beyond recognition if it is used to designate anyone anywhere fighting for a cause.

Terrorists are those who kill people they consider their "objective enemy," no matter what those people may or may not have done, *Terrorist* and *terrorism* entered ordinary language to designate a specific phenomenon: killing directed against all ideological enemies indiscriminately and outside the context of a war between combatants. According to the logic of terrorism, enemies can legitimately be killed no matter what they are doing, where they are, or how old they are.

The word *terror* first entered the political vocabulary of the West during the French Revolution. Those who guillotined thousands in the Place de la Concorde in Paris were pleased to speak of revolutionary terror as a form of justice.[1] Since the era of the French Revolution, a complex, subtle, and generally accepted international language has emerged to make critical distinctions between different kinds of violent acts. Combatants are distinguished from noncombatants. A massacre is different from a battle. An ambush is different from a firefight. When Americans look back with sadness and even shame at the Vietnam War, it is horrors like the My Lai *massacre* they have in mind. Those who called the slaughter of more than four hundred unarmed men, women, and children a *battle* were regarded as having taken leave of their senses, perhaps because they were so determined to justify anything that Americans did in the Vietnam War that they had lost their moral moorings.[2]

A terrorist is one who sows terror. Terror subjects its victims or would-be victims to paralyzing fear. In the words of the political theorist Michael Walzer, terrorism's "purpose is to destroy the morale of a nation or a class, to undercut its solidarity, its method is the random murder of innocent people. Randomness is the crucial feature of terrorist activity. If one wishes fear to spread and intensify over time, it is not desirable to kill specific people identified in some particular way with a regime, a party, or a policy. Death must come by chance."[3] Terrorism is "the random murder of innocent people." The reference is not to

moral innocence, for none among us are innocent in that way, but to our inability to defend ourselves from murderous attacks as we go to work, take a trip, shop, or ride a bus. In other words, civilians are not combatants.

Terrorists are not interested in the subtleties of diplomacy or in compromise solutions. They have taken leave of politics. Sometimes elements of movements that resort to terrorism—say, the Irish Republican Army—may also develop a political arm and begin negotiating a political solution. No political solution is possible, however, when the terrorism is aimed at the destruction of innocent civilians—when that itself is the goal.

THE IMPORTANCE OF MAKING THE RIGHT DISTINCTIONS

The designation of terrorism becomes contested because terrorists and their apologists would prefer not to be depicted accurately. It is important to distinguish between two cases here. In some hotly contested political situations, it may be in the interest of one side to try to label its opponents as "terrorists" rather than "combatants" or "soldiers" or "fighters." We must ask who such men (and women) are attacking. Do they target soldiers at outposts or in the field? Do they try to disable military equipment, killing soldiers in the process? As they carry out such operations, are they open to negotiation and diplomacy at the same time? If so, it seems reasonable to resist any blanket label of "terrorism" for what they are up to.

In a situation in which noncombatants are *deliberately* targeted and the murder of the maximum number of noncombatants is the *explicit* aim, using terms like "fighter" or "soldier" or "noble warrior" is not only beside the point but pernicious. Such language collapses the distance between those who plant bombs in cafés or fly civilian aircraft into office buildings and those who fight other combatants, taking the risks attendant upon military forms of fighting. There is a nihilistic edge to terrorism: It aims to destroy, most often in the service of wild and utopian goals that make no sense at all in the usual political ways.

The distinction between terrorism, domestic criminality, and what we might call "normal" or "legitimate" war is vital to observe. It helps us to assess what is happening when force is used. This distinction, marked in historic moral and political discourses about war and in the norms of international law, seems lost on those who call the attacks of September 11 acts of "mass murder" rather than terrorism and an act of war under international law, and who go on to claim that the United States has also engaged in "mass murder" in its legally authorized counteroffensive that removed the Taliban and disrupted the Al Qaeda network and its terrorist training camps in Afghanistan. This argument perpetuates a moral equivalence that amounts to the "pile of garbage" that Stephen Carter noted.[4] If we could not distinguish between an accidental death resulting from a car accident and an intentional murder, our criminal justice system would fall apart.

And if we cannot distinguish the killing of combatants from the intended targeting of peaceable civilians and the deliberate and indiscriminate sowing of terror among civilians, we live in a world of moral nihilism. In such a world, everything reduces to the same shade of gray and we cannot make distinctions that help us take our political and moral bearings. The victims of September 11 deserve more from us.

THE IMPORTANCE OF DISTINCTIONS TO DEMOCRATIC ARGUMENT

A robust politics of democratic argument turns on making the right distinctions. America's war against terrorism would collapse into a horror were we to fail to distinguish between combatants and noncombatants in our response. It is thus both strange and disheartening to read the words of those distinction-obliterators for whom, crudely, a dead body is a dead body and never mind how it got that way. Many of these same individuals would, of course, protest vehemently, and correctly, were commentators, critics, and political actors to fail to distinguish between the great world religion that is Islam and the terrorists who perpetrated the events of September 11. One cannot have it both ways, however, by insisting on the distinctions one likes and heaping scorn on those that put pressure on one's own ideological and political commitments.

For example, those of us who locate ourselves within a tradition that insists on critically assessing the policies of our own government, past and present, by deploying criteria that help us to determine whether a resort to war is or is not justified, cannot simply abandon those criteria when we feel like it. This tradition—called "just war"—requires that we apply distinctions and limitations to our own side as well as to the other side in conflict. . . . [I]t is important to emphasize that if the United States was training its combatants to be terrorists rather than soldiers fighting under strict rules of engagement, the just war analyst would have to say so and in no uncertain terms. Those of us who have studied this matter in detail, however, know that a basic norm of U.S. military training is the combatant-noncombatant distinction—the principle of discrimination. We know that American soldiers are trained to refuse to obey illegal orders under the code of restraints called the "laws of war," derived in large measure from the historic evolution of the just war tradition and its spin-offs as encoded in international conventions and arrangements.

U.S. military training films include generous helpings of "what went wrong" in various operations. "Wrong" refers not only to U.S. military losses but also to operations that led to the unintentional loss of civilian life. These films ask: How can such losses be prevented in the future in a theater of war? No one is encouraged, or even allowed, to call the killing of civilians "God's will" or, even worse, an act carried out in God's name.

Consider, by contrast, a training video now being used to recruit Islamist radicals. An analyst for the British newspaper *The Observer*, which obtained a copy of this training video, found it "worse than anything expected." It emanated from the Groupe Salafiste pour Predication et Combat (Salafist Group for Preaching and Fighting, or GSPC), "the most radical of Islamic terrorist groups who have been fighting the Algerian government for more than ten years."[5] This film has been screened in various sites but is routine fare in a particular mosque in Finsbury Park, North London, where young men who come for spiritual guidance are subjected to a course in radical terror instead. (This is the mosque through which Richard Reed, the would-be "shoe-bomber," passed and where Zacarias Moussaoui, the so-called twentieth hijacker, used to worship.)

The video shows enemies being decapitated with knives after they are disarmed—something strictly forbidden by the laws of war. The film's narrator intones: "You have to kill in the name of Allah until you are killed. Then you will win your place forever in Paradise. The whole Islamic world should rise up to fight all the sick unbelievers. The flag of Jihad will be forever held high. Our enemies are fighting in the name of Satan. You are fighting in the name of God."

The viewer is subjected to "excited shouting as the militants notice that one soldier is still alive. 'He is moving, he is moving,' calls out a fighter. A militant calmly bends down and runs a knife across the wounded conscript's throat. The image of the blood pumping from his severed carotid artery is shown five times during the video." Another scene shows "ordinary young men doing their national service" being killed. These Algerian soldiers are tarred with the same brush as all "enemies of Islam," including the "Jews and the Christians."[6] Some, reading this description, will say, "But this is extreme." Yes, it is. That is the point. Terrorism is extremism. And Islamist fundamentalism is an extreme repudiation of modernity itself—another reason why it is impossible to negotiate and split the differences between its adherents and those immersed in the Western politics of negotiation and compromise.

Without in any way claiming that there is something intrinsic to Islam that "makes it hostile to modernity," Francis Fukayama, writing in Newsweek, takes note of the basic facts as gleaned from the first-person accounts, the reports, the fatwas, and the manuals of Islamist extremists:

These groups celebrated September 11 because it humbled a society that they believed was at its base corrupt. This corruption was not just a matter of sexual permissiveness, homosexuality and women's rights as they exist in the West, but stemmed in their view from secularism itself. What they hate is that the state in Western societies should be dedicated to religious tolerance and pluralism, rather than trying to serve religious truth. . . . So this is not simply a "war" against terrorists, as the American government understandably portrays it. Nor, as many Muslims argue, is the real issue American foreign policy in Palestine or toward Iraq. Unfortunately, the basic conflict we face is much broader.[7]

This brand of Islamist ideology is promoted in textbooks, "including one mandated for use in Saudi tenth-grade classes" that declares it compulsory for Muslims "to consider the infidels their enemies."[8] That is why I argue that such persons hate us for *what we are and what we represent and not for anything in particular that we have done*. How could we respond to their demands? By refusing to educate girls and women? By repealing the franchise? By establishing a theocracy run by radicals? As an editorial in *The Economist* insists, "Militant Islam despises the West not for what it does but for what it is."[9]

To be sure, there are those who oppose. U.S. foreign policy in specific ways and say so, often vehemently. That is different from promoting indiscriminate slaughter. One can argue with such critics. One may even come to agree with them on some points. But one fights back against those who have declared you a mortal enemy unfit to share our beautiful earth. The terrorist commits himself to violence *without limits*. Those fighting under a set of established restraints fight back by observing limits, most importantly between combatants and noncombatants. It is reasonable to argue that certain changes in U.S. foreign policy *might* reduce the attraction of radical Islamism to many young men. It is unreasonable to assume that changes in U.S. foreign policy would disarm radical Islamism.

NOTES

1. That terrorism, past and present, has always had its apologists says nothing about how one accurately defines the phenomenon.
2. To be sure, it would only be fair to point out that the Vietnam War was a terrible one in part because it was often difficult to distinguish combatants from noncombatants (although one is obliged to try), and because noncombatants often harbored combatants who lay in wait to ambush American soldiers. The soldiers at My Lai were inflamed, having just lost comrades. But none of that exculpates or justifies what happened. Massacre it was. Anyone who claimed a glorious victory over these villagers and belittled their suffering would rightly be regarded as morally reprehensible.
3. Michael Walzer, *Just and Unjust Wars* (New York: Basic Books, 1977), p. 197.
4. On some international debates about terrorism, see Todd S. Purdum, "What Do You Mean 'Terrorist'?" *New York Times*, April 7, 2002, sect. 4, pp. 1, 5.

5. Jason Burke, "You Have to Kill in the Name of Allah Until You Are Killed," *The Observer*, January 27, 2002, pp. 6–7.
6. Ibid.
7. Francis Fukayama, "Their Target: The Modern World," *Newsweek*, December 17, 2001.
8. Ibid.
9. "The Need to Speak Up," *The Economist*, October 13, 2001, p. 14. It is also important to note that

"the laws of jihad categorically preclude wanton and indiscriminate slaughter. . . . What the classical jurists of Islam never remotely considered is the kind of unprovoked, mass slaughter of uninvolved civil populations that we saw in New York. . . . For this there is no precedent and no authority in Islam." Bernard Lewis, "Jihad vs. Crusade," *Wall Street Journal*, September 27, 2001, p. A18.

R E A D I N G
The Triumph of Just War Theory (and the Dangers of Success)
MICHAEL WALZER

Study Questions

1. What was the original function of just war theory with which Walzer agrees?
2. In what sense was the theory "an argument of the religious center," according to Walzer, and how did the faculty of the University of Salamanca in 1520 exemplify this position?
3. What role did "the national interest" play in the new realism of the 1950s and 1960s, according to Walzer?
4. What elements of a common moral language that became part of the academic and military arguments about war does Walzer believe we learned from certain moralizing about the Vietnam War?
5. In addition to the "Vietnam syndrome," what lesson does Walzer believe we learned from this war?
6. While noting objections to certain strategies of the Gulf War, in what way does Walzer believe it included a compromise? Why did this compromise come about?
7. According to Walzer, in what way has moral theory about just war triumphed?
8. What two responses to this position does Walzer describe, and what are his criticisms of each?
9. Why does Walzer call the just war theory a "doctrine of radical responsibility"?

SOME POLITICAL theories die and go to heaven; some, I hope, die and go to hell. But some have a long life in this world, a history most often of service to the powers-that-be, but also, sometimes, an oppositionist history. The theory of just war began in the service of the powers. At least that is how I interpret

Michael Walzer, "The Triumph of Just War Theory (and the Dangers of Success)," *Social Research* (Winter 2002): 925–933. Reprinted by permission of *Social Research*.

Augustine's achievement: he replaced the radical refusal of Christian pacifists with the active ministry of the Christian soldier. Now pious Christians could fight on behalf of the worldly city, for the sake of imperial peace (in this case, literally, *pax Romana*); but they had to fight justly, only for the sake of peace, and always, Augustine insisted, with a downcast demeanor, without anger or lust.[1] Seen from the perspective of primitive Christianity, this account of just war was simply an excuse, a way of making war morally and religiously possible. And that was indeed the function of the theory. But its defenders would have said, and I am inclined to agree, that it made war possible in a world where war was, sometimes, necessary.

From the beginning, the theory had a critical edge: soldiers (or, at least, their officers) were supposed to refuse to fight in wars of conquest and to oppose or abstain from the standard military practices of rape and pillage after the battle was won. But just war was a worldly theory, in every sense of that term, and it continued to serve worldly interests against Christian radicalism. It is important to note, though, that Christian radicalism had more than one version: it could be expressed in a pacifist rejection of war, but it could also be expressed in war itself, in the religiously driven crusade. Augustine opposed the first of these; the medieval scholastics, following in Aquinas's footsteps, set themselves against the second. The classic statement is Vitoria's: "Difference of religion cannot be a cause of just war." For centuries, from the time of the Crusades to the religious wars of the Reformation years, many of the priests and preachers of Christian Europe, many lords and barons (and even a few kings), had been committed to the legitimacy of using military force against unbelievers: they had their own version of *jihad*. Vitoria claimed, by contrast, that "the sole and only just cause for waging war is when harm has been inflicted."[2] Just war was an argument of the religious center against pacifists, on the one side, and holy warriors, on the other, and because of its enemies (and even though its proponents were theologians), it took shape as a secular theory—which is simply another way of describing its worldliness.

So the rulers of this world embraced the theory, and did not fight a single war without describing it, or hiring intellectuals to describe it, as a war for peace and justice. Most often, of course, this description was hypocritical: the tribute that vice pays to virtue. But the need to pay the tribute opens those who pay it to the criticism of the virtuous—that is, of the brave and virtuous, of whom there have been only a few (but one could also say: at least a few). I will cite one heroic moment, from the history of the academic world: sometime around 1520, the faculty of the University of Salamanca met in solemn assembly and voted that the Spanish conquest of Central America was a violation of natural law and an unjust war.[3] I have not been able to learn anything about the subsequent fate of the good professors. Certainly, there were not many moments like that one, but what happened at Salamanca suggests that just war never lost its critical edge. The theory provided worldly reasons for going to war, but the reasons were limited—and they had to be worldly. Converting the Aztecs to Christianity was not a just cause; nor was seizing the gold of the Americas or enslaving its inhabitants.

Writers like Grotius and Pufendorf incorporated just war theory into international law, but the rise of the modern state and the legal (and philosophical) acceptance of state sovereignty pushed the theory into the background. Now the political foreground was occupied by people we can think of as Machiavellian princes, hard men (and sometimes women), driven by "reason of state," who did what (they said) they had to do. Worldly prudence triumphed over worldly justice; realism over what was increasingly disparaged as naive idealism. The princes of the world continued to defend their wars, using the language of international law, which was also, at least in part, the language of just war. But the defenses were marginal to the enterprise, and I suspect that it was the least important of the state's intellectuals who put them forward. States claimed a right to fight whenever their rulers deemed it necessary, and the rulers took sovereignty to mean that no one could judge their decisions. They not only fought when they wanted; they fought how they wanted, returning to the old Roman maxim that held war to be a lawless activity: *inter arma silent leges*—which, again, was taken to mean that there was no law above or beyond the decrees of the state; conventional restraints on the conduct of war could always be overridden for the sake of victory.[4] Arguments about justice were treated as a kind of moralizing, inappropriate to the anarchic conditions of international society. For this world, just war was not worldly enough.

In the 1950s and early 1960s, when I was in graduate school, realism was the reigning doctrine in the field of "international relations." The standard reference was not to justice but to interest. Moral argument was against the rules of the discipline as it was commonly practiced, although a few writers defended interest as the new morality.[5] There were many political scientists in those years who preened themselves as modern Machiavellis and dreamed of whispering in the ear of the prince; and a certain number of them, enough to stimulate the ambition of the others, actually got to whisper. They practiced being cool and tough-minded; they taught the princes, who did not always need to be taught, how to get results through the calculated application of force. Results were understood in terms of "the national interest," which was the objectively determined sum of power and wealth here and now plus the probability of future power and wealth. More of both was almost always taken to be better; only a few writers argued for the acceptance of prudential limits; moral limits were, as I remember those years, never discussed. Just war theory was relegated to religion departments, theological seminaries, and a few Catholic universities. And even in those places, isolated as they were from the political world, the theory was pressed toward realist positions; perhaps for the sake of self-preservation, its advocates surrendered something of its critical edge.

Vietnam changed all this, although it took a while for the change to register at the theoretical level.

What happened first occurred in the realm of practice. The war became a subject of political debate; it was widely opposed, mostly by people on the left. These were people heavily influenced by Marxism; they also spoke a language of interest; they shared with the princes and professors of American politics a disdain for moralizing. And yet the experience of the war pressed them toward moral argument. Of course, the war in their eyes was radically imprudent; it could not be won; its costs, even if Americans thought only of themselves, were much too high; it was an imperialist adventure unwise even for the imperialists; it set the United States against the cause of national liberation, which would alienate it from the Third World (and significant parts of the First). But these claims failed utterly to express the feelings of most of the war's opponents, feelings that had to do with the systematic exposure of Vietnamese civilians to the violence of American war-making. Almost against its will, the left fell into morality. All of us in the antiwar camp suddenly began talking the language of just war—though we did not know that that was what we were doing.

It may seem odd to recall the '60s in this way, since today the left seems all too quick to make moral arguments, even absolutist moral arguments. But this description of the contemporary left seems to me mistaken. A certain kind of politicized, instrumental, and highly selective moralizing is indeed increasingly common among leftist writers, but this is not serious moral argument. It is not what we learned, or ought to have learned, from the Vietnam years. What happened then was that people on the left, and many others too, looked for a common moral language. And what was most available was the language of just war. We were, all of us, a bit rusty, unaccustomed to speaking in public about morality. The realist ascendancy had robbed us of the very words that we needed, which we slowly reclaimed: aggression intervention, just cause, self-defense, noncombatant immunity, proportionality, prisoners of war, civilians, double effect, terrorism, war crimes. And we came to understand that these words had meanings. Of course, they could be used instrumentally; that is always true of political and moral terms. But if we attended to their meanings, we found ourselves involved in a discussion that had

its own structure. Like characters in a novel, concepts in a theory shape the narrative or the argument in which they figure.

Once the war was over, just war became an academic subject; now political scientists and philosophers discovered the theory; it was written about in the journals and taught in the universities—and also in the (American) military academies and war colleges. A small group of Vietnam veterans played a major role in making the discipline of morality central to the military curriculum.[6] They had bad memories. They welcomed just war theory precisely because it was in their eyes a critical theory. It is, in fact, doubly critical—of war's occasions and its conduct. I suspect that the veterans were most concerned with the second of these. It is not only that they wanted to avoid anything like the My Lai massacre in future wars; they wanted, like professional soldiers everywhere, to distinguish their profession from mere butchery. And because of their Vietnam experience, they believed that this had to be done systematically; it required not only a code but also a theory. Once upon a time, I suppose, aristocratic honor had grounded the military code; in a more democratic and egalitarian age, the code had to be defended with arguments.

And so we argued. The discussions and debates were wide-ranging even if, once the war was over, they were mostly academic. It is easy to forget how large the academic world is in the United States: there are millions of students and tens of thousands of professors. So a lot of people were involved, future citizens and army officers, and the theory was mostly presented, though this presentation was also disputed, as a manual for wartime criticism. Our cases and examples were drawn from Vietnam and were framed to invite criticism. Here was a war that we should never have fought, and that we fought badly, brutally, as if there were no moral limits. So it became, retrospectively, an occasion for drawing a line—and for committing ourselves to the moral casuistry necessary to determine the precise location of the line. Ever since Pascal's brilliant denunciation, casuistry has had a bad name among moral philosophers; it is commonly taken to be excessively permissive, not so much an application as a relaxation of the moral rules. When we looked back at the Vietnamese cases, however, we were more likely to deny permission than to grant it, insisting again and again that what had been done should not have been done.

But there was another feature of Vietnam that gave the moral critique of the war special force: it was a war that we lost, and the brutality with which we fought the war almost certainly contributed to our defeat. In a war for "hearts and minds," rather than for land and resources, justice turns out to be a key to victory. So just war theory looked once again like the worldly doctrine that it is. And here, I think, is the deepest cause of the theory's contemporary triumph: there are now reasons of state for fighting justly. One might almost say that justice has become a military necessity.

There were probably earlier wars in which the deliberate killing of civilians, and also the common military carelessness about killing civilians, proved to be counterproductive. The Boer war is a likely example. But for us, Vietnam was the first war in which the practical value of *jus in bello* became apparent. To be sure, the "Vietnam syndrome" is generally taken to reflect a different lesson: that we should not fight wars that are unpopular at home and to which we are unwilling to commit the resources necessary for victory. But there was in fact another lesson, connected to but not the same as the "syndrome": that we should not fight wars about whose justice we are doubtful, and that once we are engaged we have to fight justly so as not to antagonize the civilian population, whose political support is necessary to a military victory. In Vietnam, the relevant civilians were the Vietnamese themselves; we lost the war when we lost their "hearts and minds." But this idea about the need for civilian support has turned out to be both variable and expansive: modern warfare requires the support of different civilian populations, extending beyond the population immediately at risk. Still, a moral regard for civilians at risk is critically important in winning wider support for the war . . . for any modern war. I will call this the usefulness of morality. Its wide acknowledgement is something radically new in military history.

Hence the old spectacle of George Bush (the elder), during the Persian Gulf war, talking like a just war theorist.[7] Well, not quite: for Bush's speeches and press conferences displayed an old American tendency, which his son has inherited, to confuse just wars and crusades, as if a war can be just only when

the forces of good are arrayed against the forces of evil. But Bush also seemed to understand—and this was a constant theme of American military spokesmen—that war is properly a war of armies, a combat between combatants, from which the civilian population should be shielded. I do not believe that the bombing of Iraq in 1991 met just war standards; shielding civilians would certainly have excluded the destruction of electricity networks and water purification plants. Urban infrastructure, even if it is necessary to modern war-making, is also necessary to civilian existence in a modern city, and it is morally defined by this second feature.[8] Still, American strategy in the Gulf war was the result of a compromise between what justice would have required and the unrestrained bombing of previous wars; taken overall, targeting was far more limited and selective than it had been, for example, in Korea or Vietnam. The reasons for the limits were complicated: in part, they reflected a commitment to the Iraqi people (which turned out not to be very strong), in the hope that the Iraqis would repudiate the war and overthrow the regime that began it; in part, they reflected the political necessities of the coalition that made the war possible. Those necessities were shaped in turn by the media coverage of the war—that is, by the immediate access of the media to the battle and of people the world over to the media. Bush and his generals believed that these people would not tolerate a slaughter of civilians, and they were probably right (but what it might mean for them not to tolerate something was and is fairly unclear). Hence, although many of the countries whose support was crucial to the war's success were not democracies, bombing policy was dictated in important ways by the demos.

This will continue to be true: the media are omnipresent, and the whole world is watching. War has to be different in these circumstances. But does this mean that it has to be more just or only that it has to look most just, that it has to be described, a little more persuasively than in the past, in the language of justice? The triumph of just war theory is clear enough; it is amazing how readily military spokesmen during the Kosovo and Afghanistan wars used its categories, telling a causal story that justified the war and providing accounts of the battles that emphasized the restraint with which they were being fought. The arguments (and rationalizations) of the past were very different; they commonly came from outside the armed forces—from clerics, lawyers, and professors, not from generals—and they commonly lacked specificity and detail. But what does the use of these categories, these just and moral words, signify?

Perhaps naively, I am inclined to say that justice has become, in all Western countries, one of the tests that any proposed military strategy or tactic has to meet—only one of the tests and not the most important one, but this still gives just war theory a place and standing that it never had before. It is easier now than it ever was to imagine a general saying, "No, we can't do that; it would cause too many civilian deaths; we have to find another way." I am not sure that there are many generals who talk like that, but imagine for a moment that there are; imagine that strategies are evaluated morally as well as militarily; that civilian deaths are minimized; that new technologies are designed to avoid or limit collateral damage, and that these technologies are actually effective in achieving their intended purpose. Moral theory has been incorporated into war-making as a real constraint on when and how wars are fought. This picture is, remember, imaginary, but it is also partly true; and it makes for a far more interesting argument than the more standard claim that the triumph of just war is pure hypocrisy. The triumph is real: what then is left for theorists and philosophers to do?

This question is sufficiently present in our consciousness that one can watch people trying to respond. There are two responses that I want to describe and criticize. The first comes from what might be called the postmodern left, which does not claim that affirmations of justice are hypocritical, since hypocrisy implies standards, but rather that there are no standards, no possible objective use of the categories of just war theory.[9] Politicians and generals who adopt the categories are deluding themselves—though no more so than the theorists who developed the categories in the first place. Maybe new technologies kill fewer people, but there is no point in arguing about who those people are and whether or not killing them is justified. No agreement about justice, or about guilt or innocence, is possible. This view is summed up in a line that speaks to our immediate situation: "One man's terrorist is another man's freedom fighter." On

this view, there is nothing for theorists and philosophers to do but choose sides, and there is no theory or principle that can guide their choice. But this is an impossible position, for it holds that we cannot recognize, condemn, and actively oppose the murder of innocent people.

A second response is to take the moral need to recognize, condemn and oppose very seriously and then to raise the theoretical ante—that is, to strengthen the constraints that justice imposes on warfare. For theorists who pride themselves on living, so to speak, at the critical edge, this is an obvious and understandable response. For many years, we have used the theory of just war to criticize American military actions, and now it has been taken over by the generals and is being used to explain and justify those actions. Obviously, we must resist. The easiest way to resist is to make noncombatant immunity into a stronger and stronger rule, until it is something like an absolute rule: all killing of civilians is (something close to) murder; therefore any war that leads to the killing of civilians is unjust; therefore every war is unjust. So pacifism reemerges from the very heart of the theory that was originally meant to replace it. This is the strategy adopted, most recently, by many opponents of the Afghanistan war. The protest marches on American campuses features banners proclaiming, "Stop the Bombing!" and the argument for stopping was very simple (and obviously true): bombing endangers and kills civilians. The marchers did not seem to feel that anything more had to be said.

Since I believe that was is still, sometimes, necessary, this seems to me a bad argument and, more generally, a bad response to the triumph of just war theory. It sustains the critical role of the theory vis-à-vis war generally, but it denies the theory the critical role it has always claimed, which is internal to the business of war and requires critics to attend closely to what soldiers try to do and what they try not to do. The refusal to make distinctions of this kind, to pay attention to strategic and tactical choices, suggests a doctrine of radical suspicion. This is the radicalism of people who do not expect to exercise power or use force, ever, and who are not prepared to make the judgments that this exercise and use require. By contrast, just war theory, even when it demands a strong critique of particular acts of war, is the doctrine of people who do expect to exercise power and use force. We might think of it as a doctrine of radical responsibility, because it holds political and military leaders responsible, first of all, for the well-being of their own people, but also for the well-being of innocent men and women on the other side. Its proponents set themselves against' those who will not think realistically about the defense of the country they live in and also against those who refuse to recognize the humanity of their opponents. They insist that there are things that it is morally impermissible to do even to the enemy. They also insist, however, that fighting itself cannot be morally impermissible. A just war is meant to be, and has to be, a war that it is possible to fight.

NOTES

1. Augustine's argument on just war can be found in *The Political Writings of St. Augustine*, ed. Henry Paolucci (Chicago: Henry Regnery, 1962), 162–83; modern readers will need a commentary: see Herbert A. Dean, *The Political and Social Ideas of St. Augustine* (New York: Columbia University Press, 1963), 134–71.

2. See Francisco deVitoria, *Political Writings*, ed. Anthony Pagden and Jeremy Lawrance (Cambridge: Cambridge University Press, 1991), 302–4, and for commentary, see James Turner Johnson, *Ideology, Reason, and the Limitation of War: Religious and Secular Concepts*, 1200–1740 (Princeton: Princeton University Press, 1975), 150–71.

3. See James Boswell, *Life of Samuel Johnson LL.D.*, ed. Robert Maynard Hutchins, vol. 44 of *Great*

Books of the Western World (Chicago: Encyclopedia Britannica, 1952), 129, quoting Dr. Johnson: "'I love the University of Salamanca, for when the Spaniards were in doubt as to the lawfulness of conquering America, the University of Salamanca gave it as their opinion that it was not lawful.' He spoke this with great emotion."

4. With some hesitation, I cite my own discussion of military necessity (and the references there to more sympathetic treatments): Michael Walzer, *Just and Unjust Wars* (New York: Basic Books, 1977), 144–51, 239–42, 251–55.

5. The best discussion of the realists is Michael Joseph Smith, *Realist Thought from Weber to Kissinger* (Baton Rouge: Louisiana State University Press, 1986); chapter 6, on Hans Morgenthau, is especially relevant to my argument here.

6. Anthony Hartle is one of those veterans, who eventually wrote his own book on the ethics of war: Anthony E. Hartle, *Moral Issues in Military Decision Making* (Lawrence: University Press of Kansas, 1989).

7. See the documents collected in *The Gulf War: History, Documents, Opinions*, ed. Micah L. Sifry and Christopher Cerf (New York: Times Books, 1991), 197–352, among them Bush's speeches and a wide range of other opinion papers.

8. I made the case against attacks on infrastructural targets immediately after the war (but others made it earlier) in *But Was It Just? Reflections on the Morality of the Persian Gulf War*, ed. David E. DeCosse (New York: Doubleday, 1992), 12–13.

9. Stanley Fish's op-ed piece in *The New York Times* (October 15, 2001) provides an example of the postmodernist argument in its most intelligent version.

REVIEW EXERCISES

1. What is *terrorism*? What motivates various types of terrorists?
2. Discuss the problems involved in defining terrorism.
3. Give a consequentialist argument for the use of terrorism. Give one against it.
4. What is *pacifism*?
5. How would a consequentialist decide whether or not to be a pacifist?
6. How would a nonconsequentialist decide whether to be a pacifist?
7. What is *just war theory*, and how did it come to be developed?
8. List and explain the four basic principles of the jus ad bellum part of just war theory.
9. What is the difference between the proportionality principle as it constitutes part of the jus ad bellum and jus in bello components of just war theory?
10. Explain the two basic elements of the principle of discrimination.
11. What counts as a "war crime" or a "crime against humanity"?
12. How did the U.N. Declaration of Human Rights come about? Why did it not include a rationale?

D I S C U S S I O N   C A S E S

1. Movie and Video Game Violence. Describe the kinds of violence that can be found today in movies. Give examples of particular movies you have seen recently or know about. Do you think that these movies glorify violence? Do you think that these depictions have anything to do with incidents of violence in our society? What about video games? Do you think there should be some sort of legal regulation of this type of entertainment? Why or why not?

2. Terrorism. Do you think that there are any causes or reasons that would justify acts of terrorism? If not, why not? If so, what kinds of terrorist activities do you think would be morally justified?

3. Military Intervention. Suppose you had to write a paper on whether you thought military intervention in some other country was ever justified. What would you write? Do you believe there would ever be any situations under which resort to war would be justified? Knowing the destruction and loss of human life that would be involved, would it still be justified? What if that country's rulers were killing members of certain ethnic groups in their own country? What if they were about to develop weapons of mass destruction? What if their rulers were dangerous madmen? What if they possessed some resource that your country could not do without and could not obtain through trade?

YOU MAKE THE DECISION

Apply the theories and issues discussed in this chapter by accessing this animated simulation on the Ethics Resource Center.

Use the passkey that accompanies your book to gain access. If you do not have a passkey, visit cengagebrain.com to purchase instant access to additional study material.

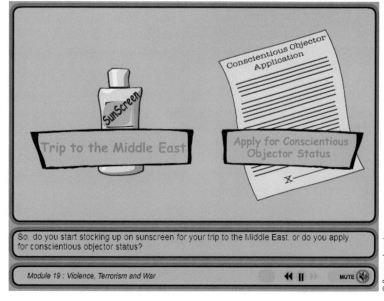

So, do you start stocking up on sunscreen for your trip to the Middle East, or do you apply for conscientious objector status?

Module 19 : Violence, Terrorism and War

20

Global Issues and Globalization

IN APRIL 2010, the world's population was estimated to be between 6,800,000,000 and 6,817,700,000. There are about 134 million new births worldwide each year. China had the most people with about 1,337,210,000. India was second with 1,179,970,000, the United States was third at 309,160,000, and Indonesia was fourth with 231,369,500 people.[1]

The most populous metropolitan areas were Tokyo, Japan, with 32,450,000 people, followed by Seoul, South Korea with 20,550,000 people, then Mexico City with 20,450,000 people, and New York City with 19,750,000 people. Following them were Mumbai, India; Jakarta, Indonesia; Sao Paulo, Brazil; and Delhi, India.[2]

RICH AND POOR NATIONS

We have become accustomed to categorizing nations in terms of their economic status and level of development as rich and poor, more affluent and less affluent, developed and developing, and as first-, second-, third-, and possibly fourth-world nations. Whichever classification system we use, a tremendous gap clearly exists between the level of economic development of those nations at the top and those at the bottom. According to Gustav Speth of the human development program of the United Nations, "an emerging global elite, mostly urban-based and interconnected in a variety of ways, is amassing great wealth and power, while more than half of humanity is left out."[3] A 1999 U.N. study reported that technology and Internet access will intensify this difference.[4]

In 2008, the World Bank estimated that the number of people living in extreme poverty was estimate to be "nearly 1 billion to 1.4 billion. . . . In sub-Saharan Africa, the percentage of people living under $1.25 a day" was 50 percent.[5] *Extreme poverty* means "poverty that kills." People in extreme poverty live on less than $1 a day and thus are "chronically hungry, unable to get health care, lack safe drinking water and sanitation, cannot afford education for their children, and perhaps lack rudimentary shelter . . . and clothing."[6] According to UNICEF, "[o]ver 24,000 children die every day around the world from various causes," including "poverty, hunger, easily preventable diseases and illnesses."[7] The poor are also more likely to die of preventable disease. For example, approximately 3 million in Africa die of malaria each year.[8] Improving economies in East Asia have reduced the extent of poverty there "from 58% in 1981 to 15% in 2001, and in South Asia from 52% to 31%," but "the situation is deeply entrenched in Africa, where almost half of the continent's population lives in extreme poverty." Moreover, this situation in Africa has worsened over the last two decades.[9]

In July 2005, the Group of Eight (G8), or heads of eight industrialized nations, held its annual economic summit meeting in a resort in Gleneagles, Scotland. One purpose of the meeting was to discuss how to address the problem of poverty in Africa. In

Children left homeless by a massive earthquake in Haiti, the poorest country in the Western hemisphere.

the month before this meeting, a series of "Live 8" concerts were held in major cities around the world with the aim of influencing the G8 members to "double aid sent to the world's poorest countries, fully cancel the debt of developing nations, and revise trade laws in favor of African countries."[10] At their meeting, these world leaders agreed to raise the aid to Africa to $34 billion by 2010 (from the current $23 billion annually). Moreover, in May 2005, the world's richest nations "agreed to write off $40 billion in loans owed by the world's 18 poorest countries, all but four of them in Africa."[11] Using GDP (gross domestic product), in 2009 the United States was the world's richest country, with Japan, China, and Germany following.[12] In 2009, the U.S. budget for defense was $680 billion,[13] and it spent 28.7 billion on foreign aid to developing countries. While this total makes the U.S. the world's biggest donor, it represents only 0.20 percent of U.S. income, compared to Sweden and the Netherlands, for example, which gave 1.12 and 0.82 percent of their income respectively, but spent much less on their military.[14]

The 1,011 billionaires in the world control assets larger than the GDP of every country in the world apart from China, Japan, and the United States.[15] As of 1998, "the ratio of average income of the richest countries in the world to that of the poorest ha[d] risen from about 9 to 1 at the end of the nineteenth century to at least 60 to 1." For example, "the average family in the United States is 60 times richer than the average family in Ethiopia."[16]

Mexico is among the countries with the largest gap between the rich and poor—in this case, generally between the industrialized north with its Spanish-speaking Mexicans and the rural south with its 10 million Indians.[17] The wealth and income gap in Latin America continues to be the highest in the world and continues to grow despite democratization. Clearly, the status of nations can change, and the rate of change of nations also varies. Some improve, some remain the same, and some fall backward. And some do so faster than others: A 2005 UN study found living standards in 18 countries to be substantially worse than they were in 1990, with twelve of them in sub-Saharan Africa and most others in former Soviet republics.[18] Currently, the economies of China and India are growing faster than that of the United States. As these nations advance technologically, this rate is expected to slow.[19] Still, in 2004 the per capita income of people in the United States was eight times greater than that of people in China and eleven times greater than people in India. By the year 2050, the Chinese are expected to reach approximately one-half and Indians approximately one-quarter the income level of people in the United States.[20]

Figures on levels of education, longevity, and health in the world's poorest countries are also depressing. As of 2002, more than half of all children in India were malnourished. In Bangladesh, only one-fourth of adult women could read or write and only one-half of all men. Of the poorest fifty countries in the world, twenty-three had lower average incomes in 1999 than in 1990.[21]

The rich and poor nations differ significantly in life expectancy. Countries with the highest life expectancy included Japan at 82.6 years, Iceland with 81.8 years, Switzerland at 81.7 years, and Australia at 81.2 years. Countries with the lowest life expectancy were Swaziland with 39.6 years, Mozambique with 42.1 years, Zambia with 42.4 years, and Sierra Leone with 42.6 years. The United States was 38th highest with 78.2.[22] Around the world, women almost always have higher life expectancies than men, with worldwide averages for males at 62.7 and females at 66 years; men in Russia, however, live 13 fewer years than Russian women.[23] Unfortunately, one main reason for lower life expectancies in many countries is the toll of AIDS. "More than 25 million people have died of AIDS since 1981," and there were also some 33.4 million people in 2008 living with AIDS.[24] According to a report from a July 2002 United Nations AIDS Conference in Barcelona, if current infection rates continue, AIDS "will kill 68 million people in the 45 most affected countries over the next 20 years." This is more than the 55 million that were killed in all of World War II. "In some of these nations, AIDS could kill half of today's new mothers."[25] Famine is also a killer in many poorer nations. It is estimated that the lack of food is the number one cause of death worldwide, with 3.4 million deaths in 2000. "About 170 million children in poor countries are underweight because of lack of food, while more than a billion adults in North America, Europe, and middle-income countries are thought to be obese or overweight."[26]

Causes

The causes of extreme poverty and lack of development in a nation are many and complicated. Among them are said to be geographic isolation, epidemic disease, drought and other natural disasters, lack of clean water, poor soil, poor physical infrastructure, lack of education and a decent health care system, civil war and corruption, and the colonial and trade practices of Western nations.[27]

Colonialism In one view, it is colonialism that has been the cause of poverty in many of the world's poorest countries. Among those who hold this to be the case is Franz Fanon in his work *The Wretched of the Earth*.[28] The idea is that the Western nations stole the riches of their colonies, thus enhancing their own wealth while depressing the wealth of the colonies. According to Fanon, "European opulence has been founded on slavery. The well-being and progress of Europe have been built up with the sweat and the dead bodies of Negroes, Arabs, Indians, and the yellow races."[29] It is true that Western countries took gold from Peru, rubber from Brazil, tea from India, and cocoa from West Africa. However, modern world history is long and complicated and open to different assessments and interpretations. For example, there have been many colonialisms. Before Western colonial rule, there was "the Egyptian empire, the Persian empire, the Macedonian empire, the Islamic empire, the Mongol empire, the Chinese empire, and the Aztec and Inca empires of the Americas."[30] Other writers point out that in at least some of the modern cases it was the Western colonizer nations that first helped their colonies develop these resources—which the colonizers then took.

Farm Subsidies and Other Trade Barriers Subsidies for farms of Western countries have also been blamed by some critics for the poverty in developing countries. For example, "the world's wealthiest nations give more than $300 billion of subsidies to their farmers every year."[31] This makes it extremely difficult for poor farmers in sub-Saharan Africa to compete with their Western counterparts. Moreover, in some cases the subsidies go to the biggest industrialized farms, chiefly in the United States, that produce huge surpluses for export. These subsidies originally were intended to help farmers hurt by the Great Depression. In other countries, subsidies are given to small specialty farms—for example, those in the grape-growing or cheese-producing regions of France. According to a representative of the World Bank, "reducing these subsidies and removing agricultural trade barriers is one of the most important things that rich countries can do for millions of people to escape poverty all over the world."[32] Other people, however, argue that the global market demands such movements of foods. Moreover, they point out that eliminating these subsidies may not help poor farmers or be good for the environment. If it leads to the development of industrialized farms in developing nations, then poor people there who otherwise would have worked small farms will migrate to cities where there is often no work for them. Although "high-tech agriculture wastes fossil fuels, it spares land, by growing more food on less acreage."[33]

Cultural and Historical Reasons Another cause or contributing factor may be thought to be cultural or historical. One area of particular interest today is the Arab world. As of 2002, the combined gross domestic product of all twenty-two Arab nation-states (with a combined population of 280 million people) was less than that of Spain. According to a report from the U.N. Development Program in coordination with the Arab Fund for Economic and Social Development, there are three main reasons why Arab countries have not advanced economically in modern times: "a shortage of freedom to speak, innovate, and affect political life, a shortage of women's rights, and a shortage of quality education."[34] The freedoms at issue are "civil liberties, political rights, a voice for the people, independence of the media, and government accountability." According to the report, these societies are depriving themselves of the political and economic contributions of half of their citizens. It also points out that education is not as it should be. One indication of this is the lack of translated works. Greece translates fives times more than the mere 300 books that are translated each year in all Arab countries combined. Moreover, "investment in research is less than one-seventh the world average; and Internet connectivity is worse than in sub-Saharan Africa." There are still 65 million Arab adults who are illiterate, two-thirds of them women. These conditions contribute to dissatisfaction and instability.[35] However, there have been some recent improvements. For example, in May 2005, Kuwaiti women won the right to vote. Women could already vote in Oman, Bahrain, Qatar, and Iran.

World Bank and IMF Debate also continues about the role in world development played by international financial institutions. The International Monetary Fund (IMF) and World Bank were both established in 1944 to preserve international financial stability. According to Joseph Stiglitz, a Nobel Prize–winning economist, the key to problems in developing nations has been the financial institutions' ideological support of strict capitalism. He writes, "free markets left to their own devices, do not necessarily deliver the positive outcomes claimed for them by textbook economic reasoning that assumes that people have full information, can trade in complete and efficient markets, and can depend on satisfactory legal and other institutions."[36] As a result, some IMF and World Bank policies, for example, have harmed rather than helped the development of third-world countries. High interest rates harmed fledgling companies, trade liberalization policies made poorer countries unable to compete, and liberalization of capital markets enabled larger foreign banks to drive local banks out of business. Privatization of government-owned enterprises without adequate local regulation also contributed to the increasingly desperate situation of some developing countries. According to Stiglitz, these international financial institutions have ignored some of the consequences of their policies because of their almost religious belief in unfettered capitalism. He writes:

> Stabilization is on the agenda; job creation is off. Taxation, and its adverse effects, are on the agenda; land reform is off. There is money to bail out banks but not to pay for improved education and health services, let alone to bail out workers who are thrown out of their jobs as a result of the IMF's macroeconomic mismanagement.[37]

Moreover, not all financial aid given to poor countries actually gets directly to the people. Much of it, for example, covers consultants, administrative costs, and debt relief.

Corruption and Other Political Causes In 2005, African countries such as Ghana, Malawi, Mali, Senegal, and Tanzania were relatively well governed and progressing. Others remained problematic because of continuing civil wars and corrupt and unstable governments. Corruption and mismanagement have contributed not only to the poverty of the people but also to the hesitancy of wealthy countries to give aid. On the other hand, corruption is not the sole cause of poverty. Other societies in Asia, for example, are thought to have "extensive corruption, such as Bangladesh, Indonesia, and Pakistan," and yet they have enjoyed rapid economic growth.[38]

Some Solutions

Developmental economist Jeffrey Sachs has argued that we should focus on five "development interventions": (1) boosting agriculture, with improvements in fertilizers and seeds; (2) improving basic health, in particular through bed nets and medicines for malaria and treatments for AIDS; (3) investing in education, including meals for primary school children; (4) bringing power; and (5) providing clean water and sanitation.[39] Others argue that money is the solution. As a percentage of the U.S. GDP, aid spending "has fallen from nearly 3 percent in 1946" to 0.1 percent in 2001.[40] Those who study the matter differ in their views of whether or how much this aid actually has helped. According to some, "numerous studies have found no real correlation between aid levels and the economic performance of developing countries." For example, China and India receive little assistance in relation to their impressive economic output, and African nations perform most poorly in spite of their receiving the most aid. On the other hand, there are success stories, according to World Bank representatives. Uganda, Mozambique, Vietnam, and Poland "show that aid can help drive economic growth when developing countries have policies in place like open trade, low inflation, and controlled government spending."[41]

Ethical Considerations

A more basic question is whether richer or Western nations have any moral responsibility or obligation to help poorer ones. Here we examine some ethical principles that can be used as a basis for how we might answer this question.

Self-Interest On the one hand, our own interests may dictate that we should do something to lessen

the gap between rich and poor nations and alleviate the conditions of the less fortunate. In terms of trade alone, these nations can contribute much to our economic benefit by the goods they could purchase from us. Moreover, the worldwide problems of migration of desperate people to wealthier countries could be moderated. Furthermore, the present-day problem of terrorism might be dramatically reduced. However, some critics argue that it is not poverty that breeds terrorism but "feelings of indignity and frustration."[42] (See Chapter 19.) One of the consequences of global poverty is stress on the environment. Poor people in the Amazon region, for example, cut down trees to make farms and charcoal to sell. Impoverished people burning wood for cooking and warmth are producing a two-mile-thick blanket of smoke over East Asia. Because we are all affected by damage to the environment, it is in our best interest to find ways to eliminate the poverty that leads to some of this damage. Nevertheless, although there are many self-interested reasons to call for doing something to change things, it is an open question whether these reasons are either practically or ethically sufficient.

Justice On the other hand, it may be that justice requires that we ought to do something about this situation. Justice is not charity. It may well be that *charity* or altruistic concern for the plight of others ought to play a role in our view of ourselves in relation to far-distant peoples. Charity is certainly an ethically important notion, but a more difficult consideration is whether we have any obligation to help those in need in faraway places. Charity, in some sense, is optional. But if we are obligated to help others, then this is not an optional matter. As Kant reminded us, although we may decide not to do what we ought to do, we do not thereby escape the obligation. It is still there. But are we under any obligation to help those faraway persons in need, and why or why not?

Again, justice is not morally optional. It is something whose requirements we are obligated to follow. Recall from Chapter 14 that considerations of justice play a role in evaluating the distribution of goods. In that chapter we discussed this in relation to such a distribution within a society. However, it can also be used to evaluate the distribution of goods in human society as a whole. We can then ask whether or not a particular distribution of goods worldwide is just. As noted in that previous chapter, there are differences of opinion as to how we ought to determine this. One was the process view, according to which any distribution can be said to be just if the process by which it comes to be is just. In other words, if there was no theft or fraud or other immoral activity that led to the way things have turned out, then the resulting arrangement is just. In applying this at the global level, we can ask whether the rich nations are rich at least partly because of wrongful past actions. In this case, the issue of whether colonialization played a role in the poverty of poor nations would be relevant.

The other view was called *end-state justice*. According to this view, the end state, or how things have turned out, is also relevant. Egalitarians will argue that the gap between rich and poor is something wrong in itself because we are all members of the same human family and share the same planet. On the one hand, some argue that it is morally permissible for some to have more and others less if the difference is a function of something like the greater effort or contributions of the richer nations. Thus, they might point to the sacrifice and investment and savings practices of the newly industrialized East Asian nations as justifying their having more. They sacrificed and saved while others did not. On the other hand, if the wealth of some and the poverty of others result instead from luck and fortune, then it does not seem fair that the lucky have so much and the unlucky so little. Is it not luck that one nation has oil and another next to it does not?

Justice is also a matter of *fairness*. For example, people in developing countries in 1992 accounted for only 23 percent of world energy use, even though they had 80 percent of the world's population.[43] Thus people in the developed world with only 20 percent of the world's population accounted for about 75 percent of the world's energy use. We could ask whether this represents a fair share. However, this would seem to imply that there was only a set amount of energy and that each nation should withdraw from it only a fair share based on its population, for example. That there is a fixed amount might be true of nonrenewable energy resources such as

fossil fuels, but not necessarily true of all energy sources. To address this issue more fully would require complex analysis of the very idea of fair shares of world resources and problems of ownership and distribution.

Other people point out that there is a considerable unfairness in some trade practices. Subsidies for exported goods constitute one area of unfairness. The IMF and the World Bank often ask countries to which they give loans and other aid to eliminate subsidies for their exports. However, industrialized countries continue to subsidize their products. For example, James D. Wolfensohn, former World Bank president, has "accused wealthy countries of 'squandering' $1 billion a day on farm subsidies that often have devastating effects on farmers in Latin America and Africa."[44] In 2001, the U.S. Congress passed a bill that authorized more than $100 billion in farm subsidies over eight years. Critics charge that it is hypocritical as well as unfair for wealthy countries to continue such protectionist policies while requiring poor countries to do without. Western cotton subsidies are said to have hurt Brazilian exports and cost that country $640 million in 2001 alone.[45] In mid-2007, Congress was halfway through approving a new farm bill, this time allotting $180 billion for farmers over the next decade. "Although the program began in the 1930s to aid poor family farmers, [now] almost three-quarters of the money goes to the richest 10 percent of American farmers."[46] At the World Summit on Sustainable Development in Johannesburg in the summer of 2002, Oxfam International, a nongovernmental organization devoted to helping poor nations, dumped 9,000 sachets of subsidized European sugar near the meeting site to protest the subsidies on sugar and other major commodities that the organization claims are driving poor farmers out of business.[47] However, other people point out that there are other reasons for declining prices of cotton and other third-world exports. Nevertheless, the moral ideal of fair competition is certainly relevant in such discussions. Just how to make competition fair is a matter for debate, however.

Rights According to some Westerners, political freedoms, civil rights, and labor standards are not separable from economic progress. They stress that prohibitions on child labor, enforcement of women's rights, prevention of deforestation and pollution, and the enhancement of "intellectual property rights, a free press (and), civil liberties" are essential to any secure development.[48] Some Asian leaders who met with Europeans at a 1996 Bangkok conference on trade and economics responded that this was not their way, and that the welfare of society and economic development ought to come first before political rights. They insisted that human rights should temporarily be put on hold for the sake of economic growth. Thus, it would be better, they say, to give a starving person a loaf of bread than a crate on which to stand and speak his mind. But according to Alex Magno, a political scientist at the University of the Philippines, it is not so much an "Asian way" that gives human rights a back seat, but political self-interest on the part of rulers who are spurred on by a growing middle class. The middle class is "not an Islamic or Buddhist or Catholic middle class," but one that "is intoxicated with growth, whose own personal fortunes depend on the GNP [gross national product] rate." Moreover, a group from Forum Asia insisted that the notion of human rights is not strictly a Western import but also their own concern. It points out that the real Western imports are the economic practices of "consumerism, capitalism, investment, (and) industrialization."[49]

This debate raises the following ethical questions: How important are political and civil rights in comparison with a society's economic development? Should one take precedence over the other? You can get further help in thinking about some of these issues by recalling the distinction between positive and negative rights in Chapter 14, as well as the discussion of natural rights in Chapter 7 and the discussions of utilitarianism in Chapter 4. This is also a crucial question asked by Peter Singer in his article on famine in this chapter.

We can make the general issues of aid to poor countries clearer by considering the issue of famine.

Famine Starvation and famine remain problems around the world. Political corruption and mismanagement of resources are often the cause, but so are uncontrollable events such as earthquakes, famines, and floods. What responsibility do those in other countries have to people suffering starvation? According to Peter Singer, giving to victims of famines, for example, is not charity but duty. (See his article in this chapter.) He makes the same argument in his recently published book, *The Life You Can Save: Acting Now to End World Poverty*.[50] In fact, Singer believes that we have an obligation to help those less well off than ourselves to the extent that helping them does not make us less well off than they are, or require us to sacrifice something of comparable value. This is an ethically demanding position. It implies that I must always justify spending money on myself or my family or friends. Whether I am justified in doing so, in this view, depends on whether anything I do for myself or others is of comparable moral importance to the lives of others who are perhaps starving and lacking in basic necessities.

Of the opposite point of view is Garrett Hardin, who believes that we have no such obligation to give because to do so will do no good.[51] For example, famine relief only postpones the inevitable—death and suffering. According to Hardin, this is because overpopulation produced by famine relief will again lead to more famine and death. However, whether his prediction is correct is an empirical matter. In other words, it needs to be verified or supported by observation and historical evidence. For example, will all forms of famine relief, especially when combined with other aid, necessarily do more harm than good as Hardin predicts? Answering such questions is difficult because it requires knowledge of the effects of aid in many different circumstances. It is worthwhile reflecting, however, on the consequentialist nature of these arguments and asking ourselves whether other nonconsequentialist arguments that rely on notions of justice and fairness are at least as important in determining what we ought to think and do in such matters.

GLOBALIZATION

According to Robert Wright, "globalization dates back to prehistory, when the technologically driven expansion of commerce began."[52] The building of roads and inventions such as wheels and boats led to huge changes in transportation, expanded the world, and at the same time made it smaller. Writing was the original innovation of information technology, first used for trade to record debts and make contracts. Later, the great empires and merchant leagues played a key role in increasing globalization. Movable print increased the ability of the common person to learn about others, both to increase understanding and sympathy.[53] On the one hand, this would seem to lead to increased tolerance and respect for human equality. The economic integration of isolated communities often brings with it greater peace and understanding as people of different races and cultures trade and rub shoulders with one another, but it can also be the basis of resentment and antipathy.

One can think of globalization in Thomas Friedman's terms, as the world being made flat. People around the world are now connected in ways unimaginable twenty years ago, and the playing field in which they operate is now more even—provided that they have access to computers, Internet connections, and e-mail. This is partly made possible by the invention of the Web and common Internet protocols that allow people with different systems to still connect with one another and transport data around the Internet. It is also made possible by digitization of words, music, and video, and the ability to carry more signals more reliably over long distances by fiber-optic cable. "We are now connecting all the knowledge centers on the planet together into a single global network."[54]

One example of this availability of knowledge is Wikipedia, the online collaborative encyclopedia. Articles are contributed and edited by viewers. The word wiki comes from the Hawaiian word for "quick." Started only in 2001, within two years it had more than 20,000 articles, and by 2004 it had 250,000 articles in English and 600,000 in other languages. Another example is Google, the online search engine. Its name is the incorrect spelling of googol, or "a play on the word . . . which is sometimes called the largest number and is represented by the numeral 1 followed by 100 zeros."[55]

Outsourcing is one example of how globalization and modern technologies come together and work together. Part of a process—say, one's taxes or call center help—can be farmed out. When you call Dell for help with one of its products, the person answering the phone may be in India, the Philippines, or Panama. One-quarter of a million people in India work in call centers. It makes financial sense for companies such as Dell to hire out this help to India, where the workers at the centers make the equivalent of $200 to $400 a month. Another example of globalization is offshoring. This differs from outsourcing in that rather than taking some specific limited function and hiring it out, one takes the whole factory or operation offshore—for example to Canton, China. Examples might be textiles and auto parts.[56]

One might think that if service and professional jobs and companies go where the lowest priced workers are located, then this would lead to a quick rush to the bottom. However, as will be discussed in the following section on capitalism, this has not happened. In 2003, an information technology company in India "received nearly one million applications from Indian techies for 9,000 software jobs."[57] Although some Americans complain about manufacturing jobs going to Mexico, Mexico itself is reported to have lost some 500,000 such jobs in 2003 to 2004. Many of these jobs have gone to China. Discount stores in Mexico now have significant quantities of shoes, electronics, and clothing labeled "Made in China."[58] Companies use outsourcing for many reasons. One is the lower cost of labor. Another is the quality of education. For example, Toyota recently decided to build a plant to make its small SUV in Toronto rather than in Mississippi, in part because of a desire for a more educated urban workforce. And the educated middle class in India has significantly better mathematics training than do comparable students in the United States.

To know better what to say about globalization, one must first be clear about what the term means. According to one writer, there are at least five different definitions of the term, some of which are overlapping: internationalization, liberalization, universalization, modernization or Westernization, and deterritorialization.[59]

Internationalization According to this version, *globalization* refers to the many types of "cross-border relations between countries." Among these are trade, finance, and communication. From these flow an international interdependence among nations and peoples.

Liberalization   A second meaning focuses on the free and "open, borderless world economy." Trade and foreign exchange, as well as travel barriers, are abolished or reduced, making it possible to participate in the world as a whole.

Universalization   *Globalization* can also refer to the various ways in which a synthesis of cultures has taken place. This covers such things as having a common calendar and similar methods of manufacturing, farming, and means of transportation.

Modernization or Westernization   This is perhaps the most common meaning of *globalization*, namely, the way in which "the social structures of modernity"—capitalism, science, movies, music, and so forth—have spread throughout the world. Among the characteristics of modernity is scientific rational thought. It is the idea that we can know the world as it is and mold it to serve our needs. Technology and technological innovation are among its consequences.

Deterritorialization   A final use of the term *globalization* points out that "social space is no longer wholly mapped in terms of territorial places . . . and borders."[60] Thus, corporations as well as nongovernmental organizations transcend local groupings. World-governing bodies such as the World Trade Organization, the World Court, and the United Nations also exemplify this.

Values

People disagree about the extent of all of these types of globalization. They point out the ways in which local cultures and law still dominate human interactions. There are also critical reactions to these movements. Some people fear the loss of cultural identities and values and so press for their own ways of doing and being. Some worry about Western imperialism and revolt against it.

With any of its meanings, we can ask whether globalization of that sort is a good thing or bad. For example, how has it affected certain things that are thought to be important for human life? Among these are security, justice, and autonomy.[61]

Security   Peace and harmony are thought to be good for humanity and to contribute to security. Has globalization in any of its meanings contributed to peace and harmony or been the cause of conflict and wars? On the one hand, one can find examples of international cooperation. International conferences are held to decide on a global level what to do about global warming or the loss of species or the AIDS epidemic or the condition of women. Some measure of agreement is often reached, and security is enhanced. On the other hand, with the development of modern weaponry, strong and militarily powerful nations can dominate weaker ones, leading to resentment as often as respect. We also have seen the rise of extreme nationalist movements, racism, and terrorism. The extent of the role that globalization has played in these movements, however, is far from clear.

Justice   Justice is giving what is due as well as what is fair. Serving justice is a moral imperative. We can also ask whether globalization has promoted justice. The problem of rich and poor countries and the issue of justice were discussed above and can be reconsidered here. Free trade allows corporations to move their factories anywhere. In some ways, this seems to help the poor who, though they may work in what are labeled "sweat shops," are nevertheless better off there than working in other places or facing their alternatives. Yet the poor are frequently exploited and often work in unsafe and unhealthy circumstances, conditions that should surely be improved.

Autonomy   Finally, if democracy provides a way for people to have a say about what happens to them in their own lives and societies, and if such control over their lives or autonomy is a good, then democracy would seem to be also. However, we can also ask whether globalization has helped spread democracy. One would think that when people see how it works, they would demand democracy. However, powerful interests and fears may and do prevent its development. Local customs and circumstances also influence its forms.

Free-Market Capitalism

There are also other ways to evaluate globalization. Those who hold an economic liberal point of view laud globalization's seeming emphasis on free trade and open markets. Free markets are thought to lead to free minds because they work best in open societies. The idea is that economic liberty will bring with it political liberty and democracy, which are good things. With U.S. jobs fleeing overseas, what happens to the lesser-skilled but higher-paid U.S. workers? If companies grow by these means, then the number of jobs may increase overall. However, they may be at a higher level of skills. Is protectionism then the answer? There are alternatives. For example, instead of lifetime employment for workers, the emphasis might be shifted to providing them with lifetime employability.[62]

Companies may be shamed into being more responsible and providing continuing training for their employees. They may also gain a good name by being good stewards—for example, by ensuring that their outsourced jobs follow fair labor laws and practices and give due regard for the environment. Parents may also need to teach their children to be adaptable and to work harder if they want to succeed. Among the areas of study for which the United States has lately been found wanting are science and engineering. Ways need to be found to encourage and support students to enter these fields, which will be pivotal to the economy of the future. According to Friedman's argument in *The World Is Flat*, globalization is necessarily a free market phenomenon, but will also bring with it peace and human economic fulfillment. Critics, however, point out that the technological advancements that have made the world smaller have not made it flatter. There are still large portions of world populations that are, as earlier described, extremely poor and not benefiting from these advances. Moreover, they argue that globalization characterized by technological advancement is entirely compatible with different types of economic systems, including those of less-than-democratic regimes. With other countries such as China and India becoming more powerful in the globalized world, there is also the continued possibility for conflict as much as for peace. Those who believe in the necessary correlation of technological advances and free-market capitalism do not adequately acknowledge the powerful roles of nationalism and religion in history, according to these critics.[63]

Those who hold a more socialist perspective also believe that it is important to keep a so-called safety net of basic goods for those who are not able to compete well in a capitalistic or free-market system. They often blame certain forms of globalization for their inability to compete and sometimes argue that we ought to return to simpler and more localized ways of living. In the middle are those who believe that market economics and cross-border transfers and trade are good but that they also need to be supplemented by measures that help those who fall behind and restrain powerful corporations. Market capitalism also needs to be adapted to the particular conditions of developing countries.[64]

Modernization

Universalization, modernization, and Westernization are often cited as other aspects of globalization. Western-style clothing, advertising, and products are becoming more and more pervasive. Coca-Cola, McDonald's, and Wal-Mart seem to be everywhere. Can it be that this is because this is what many people around the world admire or want? So-called Western values have also been the cause for antipathy and resentment by people who hold other traditional cultural or religious values. Among the examples cited are the lack of modest dress in women and graphic and sexualized forms of popular entertainment and music. Clearly, there are criticisms to be made of some elements of Western societies that are showing up around the world. On the other hand, we may want to argue that other elements of modern culture ought to become universally accepted. Take, for example, the position of women. Should modern notions of individual rights and freedoms become the norm? There are those who argue against this. They would retain individual cultural and religious practices regarding the position of women. Can we actually judge the practices of another culture? Are one culture and its values as good as any other? This is the issue of ethical relativism discussed in Chapter 2. We surely want to say that if some culture has a practice of enslaving some of its members, this is not morally acceptable. Which elements of globalization are good and bad is not always an easy matter to judge. Hopefully, however, the ethical signposts, values, and principles discussed here and elsewhere in this text can help determine the way we should go in a world that is, in ever-increasing ways, becoming one.

In the readings in this chapter, Peter Singer addresses the issue of our responsibility to victims of famine, Herman Daly critically evaluates some of the consequences of globalization, and Vandana Shiva provides criticisms of a globalized free-market economy.

NOTES

1. http://en.wikipedia.org/wiki/World_population.
2. http://en.wikipedia.org/wiki/List_of_metropolitan_areas_by_population.
3. Quoted by Barbara Crossette in "U.N. Survey Finds World Rich-Poor Gap Widening," *The New York Times*, July 15, 1996, p. A3.
4. Judith Miller, "Globalization Widens Rich–Poor Gap, U.N. Report Says," *The New York Times*, July 13, 1999, p. A8.
5. http://www.un.org/apps/news/story.asp?NewsID=27842&Cr1=world%20bank.
6. *Time*, March 14, 2005, p. 47.
7. http://www.globalissues.org/article/715/todaay-over-24000-children-died-around-the-world.
8. *Time*, March 14, 2005, p. 46.
9. Ibid., p. 47.
10. *San Francisco Chronicle*, July 3, 2005, p. A13.
11. *The New York Times*, July 6, 2005, p. A1.
12. http://en.wikipedia.org/wiki/List_of_countries_by_GDP_nominal.
13. http://en.wikipedia.org/wiki/Military_budget_of_the_United_States.
14. http://www.oecd.org/document/11/0,3343,en_21571361_44315115_44981579_1_1_1_1,00.html; *Time*, op. cit., p. 46.
15. http://www.globalresearch.ca/index.php?context=va&aid=18083.
16. Nancy Birdsall, "Life Is Unfair: Inequality in the World," *Foreign Policy*, *111* (Summer 1998): 76.
17. Anthony DePalma, "Mexico's Serious Divisions Getting Wider and Deeper," *The New York Times*, July 20, 1996, p. A8.
18. http://articles.latimes.com/2005/sep/08/world/fg-develop8.
19. Jeffrey D. Sachs, "Welcome to the Asian Century: By 2050, China and Maybe India Will Overtake the U.S Economy in Size" (http://money.cnn.com/magazines/fortune/fortune_archive/2004/01/12/357912/index.htm).
20. Ibid.
21. Ibid.; Benjamin M. Friedman, "Globalization: Stiglitz's Case," *New York Review of Books*, 49, no. 13 (Aug. 15, 2002). This is a review of *Globalization and Its Discontents* by Joseph F. Stiglitz.
22. http://en.wikipedia.org/wiki/List_of_countries_by_life_expectancy.
23. http://geography.about.com/od/populationgeography/a/lifeexpectancy.htm; http://en.wikipedia.org/wiki/List_of_countries_by_life_expectancy.
24. http://www.avert.org/worldstats.htm.
25. Peter Piot, "In Poor Nations, a New Will to Fight AIDS," *The New York Times*, July 3, 2002, p. A19.
26. "Agency Puts Hunger No.1 on List of World's Top Health Risks," *The New York Times*, Oct. 31, 2002, p. A11.
27. *Time*, op. cit., pp. 46–48.
28. Franz Fanon, *The Wretched of the Earth* (New York: Grove Press, 1968).
29. Quoted in Dinesh D'Souza, "Two Cheers for Colonialism," *San Francisco Chronicle*, July 7, 2002, p. D6.
30. Ibid.
31. *The New York Times*, Sept. 8, 2003, p. A8.
32. Ibid.
33. Ibid., p. A27.
34. Thomas L. Friedman, "Arabs at the Crossroads," *The New York Times*, July 3, 2002, p. A19.
35. Ibid.
36. Summarized in Benjamin M. Friedman, op. cit., p. 48.
37. Ibid., p. 52.
38. *Time*, op. cit. p. 53.
39. Jeffrey Sachs, *The End of Poverty: Economic Possibilities for Our Time* (New York: Penguin Press, 2005); cited in *Time*, op. cit., pp. 50–51.
40. Joseph Kahn and Tim Weiner, "World Leaders Rethinking Strategy on Aid to Poor," *The New York Times*, March 18, 2002, p. A3.
41. Ibid.
42. Alan B. Krueger and Jitka Maleckova, "Does Poverty Cause Terrorism?" *New Republic* (June 24, 2002): 27.
43. David Ordal, "Energy in the Developing World" (April 28, 1999); U.S. Congress Office of Technology Assessment, "Fueling Development," p. 1; Andrew C. Revkin, "Climate Panel Reaches Consensus on the Need to Reduce Harmful Emissions," *The New York Times*, May 4, 2007, p. A4.

44. Edmund L. Andrews, "Rich Nations Criticized for Barriers to Trade," *The New York Times*, Sept. 20, 2002, p. A7.

45. Ibid.

46. www.commondreams.org/views02/0506-09.htm; www.washingtonpost.com/wp-dyn/content/article/2006/07/01/AR2006070100962.html.

47. "Oxfam Dumps Sugar at WSSD," *Oxfam Exchange* (Fall 2002): 3.

48. Seth Mydans, "Do Rights Come First? Asia and Europe Clash," *The New York Times* International, March 1, 1996, p. A6.

49. Ibid.

50. Thomas Nagel, "What Peter Singer Wants of You," *The New York Review of Books*, March 25, 2010, pp. 24–26.

51. Garrett Hardin, "Living on a Lifeboat," *Bioscience* (Oct. 1974).

52. Robert Wright, "Two Years Later, a Thousand Years Ago," *The New York Times*, Op-Ed., Sept. 11, 2003.

53. Ibid.

54. Thomas L. Friedman, *The World Is Flat: A Brief History of the Twenty-First Century* (New York: Farrar, Straus, and Giroux, 2005), 8.

55. Ibid., pp. 94–95, 152. And see www.lrb.co.uk/v28/n02/lanc01_.html.

56. Ibid., pp. 24, 114–115.

57. Thomas L. Friedman, "Small and Smaller," *The New York Times*, March 4, 2004, p. A31.

58. Thomas L. Friedman, "What's That Sound?" *The New York Times*, April 1, 2004, p. A27.

59. Ibid., pp. 15–17.

60. Ibid.

61. Jan Aart Scholte, *Globalization, A Critical Introduction* (New York: St. Martin's Press, 2000), 15–17. Scholte writes of these in terms of security, equity, and democracy.

62. Friedman, op. cit, p. 284.

63. See, for example, John Gray, "The World is Round," *New York Review of Books* (August 11, 2005): pp. 13–15; Thomas L. Friedman, *The World is Flat*, op. cit.

64. This is a version of the category system in Scholte, *Globalization*.

READING
Famine, Affluence, and Morality
PETER SINGER

Study Questions

1. How does Singer use the situation in Bengal in 1971 to exemplify the moral problem he wants to address? (You might think of similar situations existing today.)

2. With what assumption or moral principle does Singer begin his discussion?

3. Explain what he means by his second principle. Does it require us to do good or prevent harm? How far does it require us to go to prevent the harm?

4. Why does he believe that this second principle is quite controversial?

5. Should it make any difference to our moral obligation that others could help those in need and do not?

6. Does Singer believe, then, that there is a significant moral difference between "duty" and "charity"?

7. How does Singer respond to the views of Sidgwick and Urmson that morality must not demand too much of us?

8. What is his response to the criticism that following his principle is impractical? How does he respond to the idea that governments rather than individuals should be the source of relief for the distant poor and starving?

9. What contrast does he make between a strong and a moderate version of how much we ought morally to give to these others in need?

10. What does he conclude about the consumer society and philosophers and philosophy?

A S I WRITE THIS, in November 1971, people are dying in East Bengal from lack of food, shelter, and medical care. The suffering and death that are occurring there now are not inevitable, not unavoidable in any fatalistic sense of the term. Constant poverty, a cyclone, and a civil war have turned at least nine million people into destitute refugees; nevertheless, it is not beyond the capacity of the

Peter Singer, "Famine, Affluence, and Morality," from *Philosophy & Public Affairs*, vol. 1, no. 3 (Spring 1972); 229–243. Copyright © 1972 Wiley Periodicals, Inc. Reproduced by permission of Blackwell Publishing Ltd.

richer nations to give enough assistance to reduce any further suffering to very small proportions. The decisions and actions of human beings can prevent this kind of suffering. Unfortunately, human beings have not made the necessary decisions. At the individual level, people have, with very few exceptions, not responded to the situation in any significant way. Generally speaking, people have not given large sums to relief funds; they have not written to their parliamentary representatives demanding increased government assistance; they have not demonstrated in the streets, held symbolic fasts, or done anything else directed toward providing the refugees with the means to satisfy their essential needs. At the government level, no government has given the sort of massive aid that would enable the refugees to survive for more than a few days. Britain, for instance, has given rather more than most countries. It has, to date, given £14,750,000. For comparative purposes, Britain's share of the nonrecoverable development costs of the Anglo–French Concorde project is already in excess of £275,000,000, and on present estimates will reach £440,000,000. The implication is that the British government values a supersonic transport more than thirty times as highly as it values the lives of the nine million refugees. Australia is another country which, on a per capita basis, is well up in the "aid to Bengal" table. Australia's aid, however, amounts to less than one-twelfth of the cost of Sydney's new opera house. The total amount given, from all sources, now stands at about £65,000,000. The estimated cost of keeping the refugees alive for one year is £464,000,000. Most of the refugees have now been in the camps for more than six months. The World Bank has said that India needs a minimum of £300,000,000 in assistance from other countries before the end of the year. It seems obvious that assistance on this scale is not forthcoming. India will be forced to choose between letting the refugees starve or diverting funds from her own development program, which will mean that more of her own people will starve in the future.[1]

These are the essential facts about the present situation in Bengal. So far as it concerns us here, there is nothing unique about this situation except its magnitude. The Bengal emergency is just the latest and most acute of a series of major emergencies in various parts of the world, arising both from natural and from man-made causes. There are also many parts of the world in which people die from malnutrition and lack of food independent of any special emergency. I take Bengal as my example only because it is the present concern, and because the size of the problem has ensured that it has been given adequate publicity. Neither individuals nor governments can claim to be unaware of what is happening there.

What are the moral implications of a situation like this? In what follows, I shall argue that the way people in relatively affluent countries react to a situation like that in Bengal cannot be justified; indeed, the whole way we look at moral issues—our moral conceptual scheme—needs to be altered, and with it, the way of life that has come to be taken for granted in our society.

In arguing for this conclusion I will not, of course, claim to be morally neutral. I shall, however, try to argue for the moral position that I take, so that anyone who accepts certain assumptions, to be made explicit, will, I hope, accept my conclusion.

I begin with the assumption that suffering and death from lack of food, shelter, and medical care are bad. I think most people will agree about this, although one may reach the same view by different routes. I shall not argue for this view. People can hold all sorts of eccentric positions, and perhaps from some of them it would not follow that death by starvation is in itself bad. It is difficult, perhaps impossible, to refute such positions, and so for brevity I will henceforth take this assumption as accepted. Those who disagree need read no further.

My next point is this: if it is in our power to prevent something bad from happening, without thereby sacrificing anything of comparable moral importance, we ought, morally, to do it. By "without sacrificing anything of comparable moral importance" I mean without causing anything else comparably bad to happen, or doing something that is wrong in itself, or failing to promote some moral good, comparable in significance to the bad thing that we can prevent. This principle seems almost as uncontroversial as the last one. It requires us only to prevent what is bad, and not to promote what is good, and it requires this of us only when we can do it without sacrificing anything that is, from the moral point of view, comparably important. I could even, as far as the application of my argument to the Bengal emergency is concerned, qualify the point so as to make it: if it is in our power to prevent something very bad from happening, without thereby sacrificing anything morally significant, we ought, morally, to do it. An application of this principle would be as follows: if I am walking past a shallow pond and see a child drowning in it, I ought to wade in and pull the child out. This will mean getting my clothes muddy, but this is insignificant, while the death of the child would presumably be a very bad thing.

The uncontroversial appearance of the principle just stated is deceptive. If it were acted upon, even in its qualified form, our lives, our society, and our world would be fundamentally changed. For the principle takes, firstly, no account of proximity or distance. It makes no moral difference whether the person I can help is a neighbor's child ten yards from me or a Bengali whose name I shall never know, ten thousand miles away. Secondly, the principle makes no distinction between cases in which I am the only person who could possibly do anything and cases in which I am just one among millions in the same position.

I do not think I need to say much in defense of the refusal to take proximity and distance into account. The fact that a person is physically near to us, so that we have personal contact with him, may make it more likely that we *shall* assist him, but this does not show that we *ought* to help him rather than another who happens to be further away. If we accept any principle of impartiality, universalizability, equality, or whatever, we cannot discriminate against someone merely because he is far away from us (or we are far away from him). Admittedly, it is possible that we are in a better position to judge what needs to be done to help a person near to us than one far away, and perhaps also to provide the assistance we judge to be necessary. If this were the case, it would be a reason for helping those near to us first. This may once have been a justification for being more concerned with the poor in one's own town than with famine victims in India. Unfortunately for those who like to keep their moral responsibilities limited, instant communication and swift transportation have changed the situation. From the moral point of view, the development of the world into a "global village" has made an important, though still unrecognized, difference to our moral situation.

Expert observers and supervisors, sent out by famine relief organizations or permanently stationed in famine-prone areas, can direct our aid to a refugee in Bengal almost as effectively as we could get it to someone in our own block. There would seem, therefore, to be no possible justification for discriminating on geographical grounds.

There may be a greater need to defend the second implication of my principle—that the fact that there are millions of other people in the same position, in respect to the Bengali refugees, as I am, does not make the situation significantly different from a situation in which I am the only person who can prevent something very bad from occurring. Again, of course, I admit that there is a psychological difference between the cases; one feels less guilty about doing nothing if one can point to others, similarly placed, who have also done nothing. Yet this can make no real difference to our moral obligations.[2] Should I consider that I am less obliged to pull the drowning child out of the pond if on looking around I see other people, no further away than I am, who have also noticed the child but are doing nothing? One has only to ask this question to see the absurdity of the view that numbers lessen obligation. It is a view that is an ideal excuse for inactivity; unfortunately most of the major evils—poverty, overpopulation, pollution—are problems in which everyone is almost equally involved.

The view that numbers do make a difference can be made plausible if stated in this way: if everyone in circumstances like mine gave £5 to the Bengal Relief Fund, there would be enough to provide food, shelter, and medical care for the refugees; there is no reason why I should give more than anyone else in the same circumstances as I am; therefore I have no obligation to give more than £5. Each premise in this argument is true, and the argument looks sound. It may convince us, unless we notice that it is based on a hypothetical premise, although the conclusion is not stated hypothetically. The argument would be sound if the conclusion were: if everyone in circumstances like mine were to give £5, I would have no obligation to give more than £5. If the conclusion were so stated, however, it would be obvious that the argument has no bearing on a situation in which it is not the case that everyone else gives £5. This, of course, is the actual situation. It is more or less certain that not everyone in circumstances like mine will give £5. So there will not be enough to provide the needed food, shelter, and medical care. Therefore by giving more than £5 I will prevent more suffering than I would if I gave just £5.

It might be thought that this argument has an absurd consequence. Since the situation appears to be that very few people are likely to give substantial amounts, it follows that I and everyone else in similar circumstances ought to give as much as possible, that is, at least up to the point at which by giving more one would begin to cause serious suffering for oneself and one's dependents—perhaps even beyond this point to the point of marginal utility, at which by giving more one would cause oneself and one's dependents as much suffering as one would prevent in Bengal. If everyone does this, however, there will be more than can be used for the benefit of the refugees, and some of the sacrifice will have been unnecessary. Thus, if everyone does what he ought to do, the result will not be as good as it would be if everyone did a little less than he ought to do, or if only some do all that they ought to do.

The paradox here arises only if we assume that the actions in question—sending money to the relief funds—are performed more or less simultaneously, and are also unexpected. For if it is to be expected that everyone is going to contribute something, then clearly each is not obliged to give as much as he would have been obliged to had others not been giving too. And if everyone is not acting more or less simultaneously, then those giving later will know how much more is needed, and will have no obligation to give more than is necessary to reach this amount. To say this is not to deny the principle that people in the same circumstances have the same obligations, but to point out that the fact that others have given, or may be expected to give, is a relevant circumstance: those giving after it has become known that many others are giving and those giving before are not in the same circumstances. So the seemingly absurd consequence of the principle I have put forward can occur only if people are in error

about the actual circumstances—that is, if they think they are giving when others are not, but in fact they are giving when others are. The result of everyone doing what he really ought to do cannot be worse than the result of everyone doing less than he ought to do, although the result of everyone doing what he reasonably believes he ought to do could be.

If my argument so far has been sound, neither our distance from a preventable evil nor the number of other people who, in respect to that evil, are in the same situation as we are, lessens our obligation to mitigate or prevent that evil. I shall therefore take as established the principle I asserted earlier. As I have already said, I need to assert it only in its qualified form: if it is in our power to prevent something very bad from happening, without thereby sacrificing anything else morally significant, we ought, morally, to do it.

The outcome of this argument is that our traditional moral categories are upset. The traditional distinction between duty and charity cannot be drawn, or at least, not in the place we normally draw it. Giving money to the Bengal Relief Fund is regarded as an act of charity in our society. The bodies which collect money are known as "charities." These organizations see themselves in this way—if you send them a check, you will be thanked for your "generosity." Because giving money is regarded as an act of charity, it is not thought that there is anything wrong with not giving. The charitable man may be praised, but the man who is not charitable is not condemned. People do not feel in any way ashamed or guilty about spending money on new clothes or a new car instead of giving it to famine relief. (Indeed, the alternative does not occur to them.) This way of looking at the matter cannot be justified. When we buy new clothes not to keep ourselves warm but to look "well-dressed" we are not providing for any important need. We would not be sacrificing anything significant if we were to continue to wear our old clothes, and give the money to famine relief. By doing so, we would be preventing another person from starving. It follows from what I have said earlier that we ought to give money away, rather than spend it on clothes which we do not need to keep us warm. To do so is not charitable, or generous. Nor is it the kind of act which philosophers and theologians have called "supererogatory"—an act which it would be good to do, but not wrong not to do. On the contrary, we ought to give the money away, and it is wrong not to do so.

I am not maintaining that there are no acts which are charitable, or that there are no acts which it would be good to do but not wrong not to do. It may be possible to redraw the distinction between duty and charity in some other place. All I am arguing here is that the present way of drawing the distinction, which makes it an act of charity for a man living at the level of affluence which most people in the "developed nations" enjoy to give money to save someone else from starvation, cannot be supported. It is beyond the scope of my argument to consider whether the distinction should be redrawn or abolished altogether. There would be many other possible ways of drawing the distinction—for instance, one might decide that it is good to make other people as happy as possible, but not wrong not to do so.

Despite the limited nature of the revision in our moral conceptual scheme which I am proposing, the revision would, given the extent of both affluence and famine in the world today, have radical implications. These implications may lead to further objections, distinct from those I have already considered. I shall discuss two of these.

One objection to the position I have taken might be simply that it is too drastic a revision of our moral scheme. People do not ordinarily judge in the way I have suggested they should. Most people reserve their moral condemnation for those who violate some moral norm, such as the norm against taking another person's property. They do not condemn those who indulge in luxury instead of giving to famine relief. But given that I did not set out to present a morally neutral description of the way people make moral judgments, the way people do in fact judge has nothing to do with the validity of my conclusion. My conclusion follows from the principle which I advanced earlier, and unless that principle is rejected, or the arguments shown to be unsound, I think the conclusion must stand, however strange it appears.

It might, nevertheless, be interesting to consider why our society, and most other societies, do judge differently from the way I have suggested they

should. In a well-known article, J. O. Urmson suggests that the imperatives of duty, which tell us what we must do, as distinct from what it would be good to do but not wrong not to do, function so as to prohibit behavior that is intolerable if men are to live together in society.[3] This may explain the origin and continued existence of the present division between acts of duty and acts of charity. Moral attitudes are shaped by the needs of society, and no doubt society needs people who will observe the rules that make social existence tolerable. From the point of view of a particular society, it is essential to prevent violations of norms against killing, stealing, and so on. It is quite inessential, however, to help people outside one's own society.

If this is an explanation of our common distinction between duty and supererogation, however, it is not a justification of it. The moral point of view requires us to look beyond the interests of our own society. Previously, as I have already mentioned, this may hardly have been feasible, but it is quite feasible now. From the moral point of view, the prevention of the starvation of millions of people outside our society must be considered at least as pressing as the upholding of property norms within our society.

It has been argued by some writers, among them Sidgwick and Urmson, that we need to have a basic moral code which is not too far beyond the capacities of the ordinary man, for otherwise there will be a general breakdown of compliance with the moral code. Crudely stated, this argument suggests that if we tell people that they ought to refrain from murder and give everything they do not really need to famine relief, they will do neither, whereas if we tell them that they ought to refrain from murder and that it is good to give to famine relief but not wrong not to do so, they will at least refrain from murder. The issue here is: Where should we draw the line between conduct that is required and conduct that is good although not required, so as to get the best possible result? This would seem to be an empirical question, although a very difficult one. One objection to the Sidgwick–Urmson line of argument is that it takes insufficient account of the effect that moral standards can have on the decisions we make. Given a society in which a wealthy man who gives five percent of his income to famine relief is regarded as most generous, it is not surprising that a proposal that we all ought to give away half our incomes will be thought to be absurdly unrealistic. In a society which held that no man should have more than enough while others have less than they need, such a proposal might seem narrow-minded. What it is possible for a man to do and what he is likely to do are both, I think, very greatly influenced by what people around him are doing and expecting him to do. In any case, the possibility that by spreading the idea that we ought to be doing very much more than we are to relieve famine we shall bring about a general breakdown of moral behavior seems remote. If the stakes are an end to widespread starvation, it is worth the risk. Finally, it should be emphasized that these considerations are relevant only to the issue of what we should require from others, and not to what we ourselves ought to do.

The second objection to my attack on the present distinction between duty and charity is one which has from time to time been made against utilitarianism. It follows from some forms of utilitarian theory that we all ought, morally, to be working full time to increase the balance of happiness over misery. The position I have taken here would not lead to this conclusion in all circumstances, for if there were no bad occurrences that we could prevent without sacrificing something of comparable moral importance, my argument would have no application. Given the present conditions in many parts of the world, however, it does follow from my argument that we ought, morally, to be working full time to relieve great suffering of the sort that occurs as a result of famine or other disasters. Of course, mitigating circumstances can be adduced—for instance, that if we wear ourselves out through overwork, we shall be less effective than we would otherwise have been. Nevertheless, when all considerations of this sort have been taken into account, the conclusion remains: we ought to be preventing as much suffering as we can without sacrificing something else of comparable moral importance. This conclusion is one which we may be reluctant to face. I cannot see, though, why it should be regarded as a criticism of the position for which I have argued, rather than a criticism of our ordinary standards of behavior. Since most people are self-interested to some degree, very few of us are likely to do everything that we ought to do.

It would, however, hardly be honest to take this as evidence that it is not the case that we ought to do it.

It may still be thought that my conclusions are so wildly out of line with what everyone else thinks and has always thought that there must be something wrong with the argument somewhere. In order to show that my conclusions, while certainly contrary to contemporary Western moral standards, would not have seemed so extraordinary at other times and in other places, I would like to quote a passage from a writer not normally thought of as a way-out radical, Thomas Aquinas.

> Now, according to the natural order instituted by divine providence, material goods are provided for the satisfaction of human needs. Therefore the division and appropriation of property, which proceeds from human law, must not hinder the satisfaction of man's necessity from such goods. Equally, whatever a man has in superabundance is owed, of natural right, to the poor for their sustenance. So Ambrosius says, and it is also to be found in the Decretum Gratiani: "The bread which you withhold belongs to the hungry; the clothing you shut away, to the naked; and the money you bury in the earth is the redemption and freedom of the penniless."[4]

I now want to consider a number of points, more practical than philosophical, which are relevant to the application of the moral conclusion we have reached. These points challenge not the idea that we ought to be doing all we can to prevent starvation, but the idea that giving away a great deal of money is the best means to this end.

It is sometimes said that overseas aid should be a government responsibility, and that therefore one ought not to give to privately run charities. Giving privately, it is said, allows the government and the noncontributing members of society to escape their responsibilities.

This argument seems to assume that the more people there are who give to privately organized famine relief funds, the less likely it is that the government will take over full responsibility for such aid. This assumption is unsupported, and does not strike me as at all plausible. The opposite view—that if no one gives voluntarily, a government will assume that its citizens are uninterested in famine relief and would not wish to be forced into giving aid—seems more plausible. In any case, unless there were a definite probability that by refusing to give one would be helping to bring about massive government assistance, people who do refuse to make voluntary contributions are refusing to prevent a certain amount of suffering without being able to point to any tangible beneficial consequence of their refusal. So the onus of showing how their refusal will bring about government action is on those who refuse to give.

I do not, of course, want to dispute the contention that governments of affluent nations should be giving many times the amount of genuine, no-strings-attached aid that they are giving now. I agree, too, that giving privately is not enough, and that we ought to be campaigning actively for entirely new standards for both public and private contributions to famine relief. Indeed, I would sympathize with someone who thought that campaigning was more important than giving oneself, although I doubt whether preaching what one does not practice would be very effective. Unfortunately, for many people the idea that "it's the government's responsibility" is a reason for not giving which does not appear to entail any political action either.

Another, more serious reason for not giving to famine relief funds is that until there is effective population control, relieving famine merely postpones starvation. If we save the Bengal refugees now, others, perhaps the children of these refugees, will face starvation in a few years' time. In support of this, one may cite the now well-known facts about the population explosion and the relatively limited scope for expanded production.

This point, like the previous one, is an argument against relieving suffering that is happening now, because of a belief about what might happen in the future; it is unlike the previous point in that very good evidence can be adduced in support of this belief about the future. I will not go into the evidence here. I accept that the earth cannot support indefinitely a population rising at the present rate. This certainly poses a problem for anyone who thinks it important to prevent famine. Again, however, one could accept the argument without drawing the conclusion that it absolves one from any obligation to do anything to prevent famine. The conclusion that should be drawn is that the best means of preventing famine, in the long run, is population control. It would then follow from the position reached earlier that one ought to be doing all one can to promote population control (unless one held that all forms of population control were wrong in themselves, or would have significantly bad consequences). Since there are organizations working specifically for population control, one would then support them rather than more orthodox methods of preventing famine.

A third point raised by the conclusion reached earlier relates to the question of just how much we all ought to be giving away. One possibility, which has already been mentioned, is that we ought to give until we reach the level of marginal utility—that is, the level at which, by giving more, I would cause as much suffering to myself or my dependents as I would relieve by my gift. This would mean, of course, that one would reduce oneself to very near the material circumstances of the Bengali refugee. It will be recalled that earlier I put forward both a strong and a moderate version of the principle of preventing bad occurrences. The strong version, which required us to prevent bad things from happening unless in doing so we would be sacrificing something of comparable moral significance, does seem to require reducing ourselves to the level of marginal utility. I should also say that the strong version seems to me to be the correct one. I proposed the more moderate version—that we should prevent bad occurrences unless, to do so, we have to sacrifice something morally significant—only in order to show that even on this surely undeniable principle a great change in our way of life is required. On the more moderate principle, it may not follow that we ought to reduce ourselves to the level of marginal utility, for one might hold that to reduce oneself and one's family to this level is to cause something significantly bad to happen. Whether this is so I shall not discuss, since, as I have said, I can see no good reason for holding the moderate version of the principle rather than the strong version. Even if we accepted the principle only in its moderate form, however, it should be clear that we would have to give away enough to ensure that the consumer society, dependent as it is on people spending on trivia rather than giving to famine relief, would slow down and perhaps disappear entirely. There are several reasons why this would be desirable in itself. The value and necessity of economic growth are now being questioned not only by conservationists, but by economists as well.[5]

There is no doubt, too, that the consumer society has had a distorting effect on the goals and purposes of its members. Yet looking at the matter purely from the point of view of overseas aid, there must be a limit to the extent to which we should deliberately slow down our economy; for it might be the case that if we gave away, say, forty percent of our Gross National Product, we would slow down the economy so much that in absolute terms we would be giving less than if we gave twenty-five percent of the much larger GNP than we would have if we limited our contribution to this smaller percentage.

I mention this only as an indication of the sort of factor that one would have to take into account in working out an ideal. Since Western societies generally consider one percent of the GNP an acceptable level for overseas aid, the matter is entirely academic. Nor does it affect the question of how much an individual should give in a society in which very few are giving substantial amounts.

It is sometimes said, though less often now than it used to be, that philosophers have no special role to play in public affairs, since most public issues depend primarily on an assessment of facts. On questions of fact, it is said, philosophers as such have no special expertise, and so it has been possible to engage in philosophy without committing oneself to any position on major public issues. No doubt there are some issues of social policy and foreign policy about which it can truly be said that a really expert assessment of the facts is required before taking sides or acting, but the issue of famine is surely not one of these. The facts about the existence of suffering are beyond dispute. Nor, I think, is it disputed that we can do something about it, either through orthodox methods of famine relief or through population control or both. This is therefore an issue on which philosophers are competent to take a position. The issue is one which faces everyone who has more money than he needs to support himself and his dependents, or who is in a position to take some sort of political action. These categories must include practically every teacher and student of philosophy in the universities of the Western world. If philosophy is to deal with matters that are relevant to both teachers and students, this is an issue that philosophers should discuss.

Discussion, though, is not enough. What is the point of relating philosophy to public (and personal) affairs if we do not take our conclusions seriously? In this instance, taking our conclusion seriously means acting upon it. The philosopher will not find it any easier than anyone else to alter his attitudes and way of life to the extent that, if I am right, is involved in doing everything that we ought to be doing. At the very least, though, one can make a start. The philosopher who does so will have to sacrifice some of the benefits of the consumer society, but he can find compensation in the satisfaction of a way of life in which theory and practice, if not yet in harmony, are at least coming together.

NOTES

1. There was also a third possibility: that India would go to war to enable the refugees to return to their lands. Since I wrote this paper, India has taken this way out. The situation is no longer that described above, but this does not affect my argument, as the next paragraph indicates.

2. In view of the special sense philosophers often give to the term, I should say that I use "obligation" simply as the abstract noun derived from "ought," so that "I have an obligation to" means no more, and no less, than "I ought to." This usage is in accordance with the definition of "ought" given by the *Shorter Oxford English Dictionary*: "the general verb to express duty or obligation." I do not think any issue of substance hangs on the way the term is used; sentences in which I use "obligation" could all be rewritten, although somewhat clumsily, as sentences in which a clause containing "ought" replaces the term "obligation."

3. J. O. Urmson, "Saints and Heroes," in *Essays in Moral Philosophy*, Abraham I. Melden (Ed.) (Seattle and London, 1958), p. 214. For a related but significantly different view see also Henry Sidgwick, *The Methods of Ethics*, 7th ed. (London, 1907), pp. 220–221, 492–493.

4. *Summa Theologica II–II*. Question 66, Article 7, in Aquinas, *Selected Political Writings*, A. P. d'Entreves (Ed.), J. G. Dawson (Trans.) (Oxford, 1948), p. 171.

5. See, for instance, John Kenneth Galbraith, *The New Industrial State* (Boston, 1967); and E. J. Mishan, *The Costs of Economic Growth* (London, 1967).

R E A D I N G
Globalization and Its Discontents
HERMAN E. DALY

Study Questions

1. As Daly uses the terms, what is the difference between *internationalization* and *globalization*?
2. What serious consequences does globalization entail, according to Daly?
3. What are the Bretton Woods institutions, and what were they designed to do?
4. What questions does Daly raise regarding the goals of these institutions?
5. What does Daly mean by "standards-lowering competition" and uncounted social and environmental costs?
6. Why does Daly believe that this competition would result in more inequality between those who supply investment capital and labor or workers?
7. As corporations become larger through mergers, what results does Daly foresee?
8. According to Daly, how does globalization reduce the choices of people about how they make their living and thus their welfare or enjoyment of life?
9. What middle position regarding ownership and patenting of innovative and beneficial discoveries does Daly support?
10. What is the distinction that Daly seems to support in quoting John Maynard Keynes?

EVERY DAY, newspaper articles and television reports insist that those who oppose globalization must be isolationists or—even worse—xenophobes. This judgment is nonsense. The relevant alternative to globalization is internationalization, which is neither isolationist nor xenophobic. Yet it is impossible to recognize the cogency of this alternative if one does not properly distinguish these two terms.

"Internationalization" refers to the increasing importance of relations among nations. Although the

Herman E. Daly, "Globalization and its Discontents," *Philosophy and Public Policy Quarterly*, Vol. 21, Number 2/3 (Spring/Summer 2001), pp. 17–21. Copyright Spring 2001 Institute for Philosophy and Public Policy. Reprinted by permission of the Institute for Philosophy and Public Policy.

This article arose from a discussion given at the Aspen Institute's 50th Anniversary Conference, "Globalization and the Human Condition," held in Aspen, Colorado, on August 20, 2000.

basic unit of community and policy remains the nation, increasingly trade, treaties, alliances, protocols, and other formal agreements and communications are necessary elements for nations to thrive. "Globalization" refers to global economic integration of many formerly national economies into one global economy. Economic integration is made possible by free trade—especially by free capital mobility—and by easy or uncontrolled migration. In contrast to internationalization, which simply recognizes that nations increasingly rely on understandings among one another, globalization is the effective erasure of national boundaries for economic purposes. National boundaries become totally porous with respect to goods and capital, and ever more porous with respect to people, who are simply viewed as cheap labor—or in some cases as cheap human capital.

In short, globalization is the economic integration of the globe. But exactly what is "integration"? The word derives from *integer*, meaning one, complete, or whole. Integration means much more than "interdependence"—it is the act of combining separate although related units into a single whole. Since there can be only one whole, only one unity with reference to which parts are integrated, it follows that global economic integration logically implies national economic *dis*integration—parts are torn out of their national context (disintegrated), in order to be reintegrated into the new whole, the globalized economy.

As the saying goes, to make an omelet you have to break some eggs. The disintegration of the national egg is necessary to integrate the global omelet. But this obvious logic, as well as the cost of disintegration, is frequently met with denial. This article argues that globalization is neither inevitable nor to be embraced, much less celebrated. Acceptance of globalization entails several serious consequences, namely, standards-lowering competition, an increased tolerance of mergers and monopoly power, intense national specialization, and the excessive monopolization of knowledge as "intellectual property." This article discusses these likely consequences, and concludes by advocating the adoption of internationalization, and not globalization.

THE INEVITABILITY OF GLOBALIZATION?

Some accept the inevitability of globalization and encourage others in the faith. With admirable clarity, honesty, and brevity, Renato Ruggiero, former director-general of the World Trade Organization, insists that "We are no longer writing the rules of interaction among separate national economies. We are writing the constitution of a single global economy." His sentiments clearly affirm globalization and reject internationalization as above defined. Further, those who hold Ruggiero's view also subvert the charter of the Bretton Woods institutions. Named after a New Hampshire resort where representatives of forty-four nations met in 1944 to design the world's post-World War II economic order, the institutions conceived at the Bretton Woods International Monetary Conference include the World Bank and the International Monetary Fund. The World Trade Organization evolved later, but functions as a third sister to the World Bank and the International Monetary Fund. The nations at the conference considered proposals by the U.S., U.K., and Canadian governments, and developed the "Bretton Woods system," which established a stable international environment through such policies as fixed exchange rates, currency convertibility, and provision for orderly exchange rate adjustments. The Bretton Woods institutions were designed to facilitate *internationalization*, not *globalization*, a point ignored by director-general Ruggiero.

The World Bank, along with its sister institutions, seems to have lost sight of its mission. After the disruption of its meetings in Washington, D.C. in April 2000, the World Bank sponsored an Internet discussion on globalization. The closest the World Bank came to offering a definition of the subject under discussion was the following: "The most common core sense of economic globalization . . . surely refers to the observation that in recent years a quickly rising share of economic activity in the world seems to be taking place between people who live in different countries (rather than in the same country)." This ambiguous description was not improved upon by Mr. Wolfensohn, President of the World Bank, who told the audience at a subsequent Aspen Institute conference that "Globalization is a practical methodology for empowering the poor to improve their lives." That is neither a definition nor a description—it is a wish. Further, this wish also flies in the face of the real consequences of global economic integration. One could only sympathize with demonstrators protesting Mr. Wolfensohn's speech some fifty yards from the Aspen conference facility. The reaction of the Aspen elite was to accept as truth the title of Mr. Wolfensohn's speech, "Making Globalization Work for the Poor," and then ask in grieved tones, "How could anyone demonstrate against *that*?"

Serious consequences flow from the World Bank's lack of precision in defining globalization but lauding it nonetheless. For one thing, the so-called definition of globalization conflates the concept with that of internationalization. As a result, one cannot reasonably address a crucial question: Should these increasing transactions between people living in different countries take place *across national boundaries* that are economically significant, or *within an integrated world* in which national boundaries are economically meaningless?

The ambiguous understanding of globalization deprives citizens of the opportunity to decide whether they are willing to abandon national monetary and fiscal policy, as well as the minimum wage. One also fails to carefully consider whether economic integration entails political and cultural integration. In short, will political communities and cultural traditions wither away, subsumed under some monolithic economic imperative? Although one might suspect economic integration would lead to political integration, it is hard to decide which would be worse—an economically integrated world *with*, or *without*, political integration. Everyone recognizes the desirability of community for the world as a whole—but one can conceive of two very different models of world community: (1) a federated community of real national communities (internationalization), versus (2) a cosmopolitan direct membership in a single abstract global community (globalization). However, at present our confused conversations about globalization deprive us of the opportunity to reflect deeply on these very different possibilities.

This article has suggested that at present organizations such as the International Monetary Fund and the World Bank (and, by extension, the World Trade Organization) no longer serve the interests of their member nations as defined in their charters. Yet if one asks whose interests are served, we are told they service the interests of the integrated "global economy." If one tries to glimpse a concrete reality behind that grand abstraction, however, one can find no individual workers, peasants, or small businessmen represented, but only giant fictitious individuals, the transnational corporations. In globalization, power is drained away from national communities and local enterprises, and aggregates in transnational corporations.

THE CONSEQUENCES OF GLOBALIZATION

Globalization—the erasure of national boundaries for economic purposes—risks serious consequences. Briefly, they include, first of all, standards-lowering competition to externalize social and environmental costs with the goal of achievement of a competitive advantage. This results, in effect, in a race to the bottom so far as efficiency in cost accounting and equity in income distribution are concerned. Globalization also risks increased tolerance of mergers and monopoly power in domestic markets in order that corporations become big enough to compete internationally. Third, globalization risks more intense national specialization according to the dictates of competitive advantage. Such specialization reduces the range of choice of ways to earn a livelihood, and increases dependence on other countries. Finally, worldwide enforcement of a muddled and self-serving doctrine of "trade-related intellectual property rights is a direct contradiction of the Jeffersonian dictum that "knowledge is the common property of mankind."

Each of these risks of globalization deserves closer scrutiny.

1. Standards-lowering competition. Globalization undercuts the ability of nations to internalize environmental and social costs into prices. Instead, economic integration under free market conditions promotes standards-lowering competition—a race to the bottom, in short. The country that does the poorest job of internalizing all social and environmental costs of production into its prices gets a competitive advantage in international trade. The external social and environmental costs are left to be borne by the population at large. Further, more of world production shifts to countries that do the poorest job of counting costs—a sure recipe for reducing the efficiency of global production. As uncounted, externalized costs increase, the positive correlation between gross domestic product (GDP) growth and welfare disappears, or even becomes negative. We enter a world foreseen by the nineteenth-century social critic John Ruskin, who observed that "that which seems to be wealth is in verity but a gilded index of far-reaching ruin."

Another dimension of the race to the bottom is that globalization fosters increasing inequality in the distribution of income in high-wage countries, such as the U.S. Historically, in the U.S. there has been an implicit social contract established to ameliorate industrial strife between labor and capital. As a consequence, the distribution of income between labor and capital has been considered more equal and just in the U.S. compared to the world as a whole. However, global integration of markets necessarily abrogates that social contract. U.S. wages would fall drastically because labor is relatively more abundant globally than nationally. Further, returns to capital in the U.S. would increase because capital is relatively more scarce globally than nationally. Although one could make the theoretical argument that wages would be *bid up* in the rest of the world, the increase would be so small as to be insignificant. Making such an argument from the relative numbers would be analogous to insisting that, theoretically, when I jump off a ladder gravity not only pulls me to the earth, but also moves the earth towards me. This technical point offers cold comfort to anyone seeking a softer landing.

2. Increased tolerance of mergers and monopoly power. Fostering global competitive advantage is used as an excuse for tolerance of corporate mergers and monopoly in national markets. Chicago School economist and Nobel laureate Ronald Coase, in his classic article on the theory of the firm, suggests that corporate entities are "islands of central planning in a sea of market relationships." The islands of central planning become larger and larger relative to the remaining sea of market relationships as a result of merger. More and more resources are allocated by within-firm central planning, and less by between-firm market relationships. Corporations are the victor, and the market principle is the loser, as governments lose the strength to regulate corporate capital and maintain competitive markets in the public interest. Of the hundred largest economic organizations, fifty-two are corporations and forty-eight are nations. The distribution of income within these centrally-planned corporations has become much more concentrated. The ratio of the salary of the Chief Executive Officer to the average employee has passed 400 (as one would expect, since chief central planners set their own salaries).

3. Intense national specialization. Free trade and free capital mobility increase pressures for specialization in order to gain or maintain a competitive advantage. As a consequence, globalization demands that workers accept an ever-narrowing range of ways to earn a livelihood. In Uruguay, for example, everyone would have to be either a shepherd or a cowboy to conform to the dictates of competitive advantage in the global market. Everything else should be imported in exchange for beef, mutton, wool, and leather. Any Uruguayan who wants to play in a symphony orchestra or be an airline pilot should emigrate.

Of course, most people derive as much satisfaction from how they earn their income as from how they spend it. Narrowing that range of choice is a welfare loss uncounted by trade theorists. Globalization assumes either that emigration and immigration are costless, or that narrowing the range of occupational choice within a nation is costless. Both assumptions are false.

While trade theorists ignore the range of choice in *earning* one's income, they at the same time exaggerate the welfare effects of range of choice in *spending* that income. For example, the U.S. imports Danish butter cookies and Denmark imports U.S. butter cookies. Although the gains from trading such similar commodities cannot be great, trade theorists insist that the welfare of cookie connoisseurs is increased by expanding the range of consumer choice to the limit.

Perhaps, but one wonders whether those gains might be realized more cheaply by simply trading recipes? Although one would think so, *recipes—* trade-related intellectual property rights—are the one thing that free traders really want to protect.

4. Intellectual property rights. Of all things, knowledge is that which should be most freely shared, since in sharing, knowledge is multiplied rather than divided. Yet trade theorists have rejected Thomas Jefferson's dictum that "Knowledge is the common property of mankind" and instead have accepted a muddled doctrine of "trade-related intellectual property rights." This notion of rights grants private corporations monopoly ownership of the very basis of life itself—patents to seeds (including the patent-protecting, life-denying terminator gene) and to knowledge of basic genetic structures.

The argument offered to support this grab is that, without the economic incentive of monopoly ownership, little new knowledge and innovation will be forthcoming. Yet, so far as I know, James Watson and Francis Crick, co-discoverers of the structure of DNA, do not share in the patent royalties reaped by their successors. Nor of course did Gregor Mendel get any royalties—but then he was a monk motivated by mere curiosity about how Creation works!

Once knowledge exists, its proper price is the marginal opportunity cost of sharing it, which is close to zero, since nothing is lost by sharing knowledge. Of course, one does lose the monopoly on that knowledge, but then economists have traditionally argued that monopoly is inefficient as well as unjust because it creates an artificial scarcity of the monopolized item.

Certainly, the cost of production of new knowledge is not zero, even though the cost of sharing it is. This allows biotech corporations to claim that they deserve a fifteen- or twenty-year monopoly for the expenses incurred in research and development. Although corporations deserve to profit from their efforts, they are not entitled to monopolize on Watson and Crick's contribution—without which they could do nothing—or on the contributions of Gregor Mendel and all the great scientists of the past who made fundamental discoveries. As early twentieth-century economist Joseph Schumpeter emphasized, being the first with an innovation already gives one the advantage of novelty, a natural temporary monopoly, which in his view was the major source of profit in a competitive economy.

As the great Swiss, Jean Sismondi, argued over two centuries ago, not all new knowledge is of benefit to humankind. We need a sieve to select beneficial knowledge. Perhaps the worse selective principle is hope for private monetary gain. A much better selective motive for knowledge is a search in hopes of benefit to our fellows. This is not to say that we should abolish all intellectual property rights—that would create more problems than it would solve. But we should certainly begin restricting the domain and length of patent monopolies rather than increasing them so rapidly and recklessly. We should also become much more willing to share knowledge. Shared knowledge increases the productivity of all labor, capital, and resources. Further, international development aid should consist far more of freely-shared knowledge, and far less of foreign investment and interest-bearing loans.

Let me close with my favorite quote from John Maynard Keynes, one of the founders of the recently subverted Bretton Woods institutions:

> I sympathize therefore, with those who would minimize, rather than those who would maximize, economic entanglement between nations. Ideas, knowledge, art, hospitality, travel—these are the things which should of their nature be international. But let goods be homespun whenever it is reasonably and conveniently possible; and, above all, let finance be primarily national.

READING
Principles of Earth Democracy
VANDANA SHIVA

Study Questions

1. What is the point Shiva wants to make with the quote from Chief Seattle?
2. Rather than viewing the planet as private property, what does Shiva suggest?
3. What does she mean in saying that "corporate globalization is based on new enclosures of the commons"?
4. Why does she oppose the privatization of public goods? What does she believe results from it?
5. Why does she call her project "earth democracy"?
6. How does she describe the community she envisions?

EARTH DEMOCRACY is both an ancient worldview and an emergent political movement for peace, justice, and sustainability. Earth Democracy connects the particular to the universal, the diverse to the common, and the local to the global. It incorporates what in India we refer to as *vasudhaiva kutumbkam* (the earth family)—the community of all beings supported by the earth. Native American and indigenous cultures worldwide have understood and experienced life as a continuum between human and nonhuman species and between present, past, and future generations. A 1848 speech attributed to Chief Seattle of the Suquamish tribe captures this continuum.

> How can you buy or sell the sky, the warmth of the land? The idea is strange to us. If we do not own the freshness of the air and the sparkle of the water, how can you buy them?
>
> Every part of this earth is sacred to my people. Every shining pine needle, every sandy shore, every mist in the dark woods, every clearing and humming insect is holy in the memory and experience of my people. The sap which courses through the trees carries the memories of the red man.
>
> This we know; the earth does not belong to man; man belongs to the earth. This we know. All things are connected like the blood which unites our family. All things are connected.

Earth Democracy is the awareness of these connections and of the rights and responsibilities that flow from them. Chief Seattle's protest that "the earth does not belong to man" finds echoes across the world: "Our world is not for sale," "Our water is not for sale," "Our seeds and biodiversity are not for sale." This response to privatization under the insane ideology known as corporate globalization builds

Vandana Shiva, "Principles of Earth Democracy," in *Earth Democracy: Justice, Sustainability, and Peace* (Cambridge, MA: South End Press, 2005), pp. 1–7. Reprinted with permission of South End Press.

Earth Democracy. Corporate globalization sees the world only as something to be owned and the market as only driven by profits. From Bangalore in 1993, when half a million Indian peasants pledged to resist the classification of seeds as private property required by the Trade Related Aspects of Intellectual Property Rights (TRIPS) agreement of the World Trade Organization (WTO) to Seattle in 1999 and Cancún in 2003 when protests stopped the WTO ministerial meetings, the corporate globalization agenda has been responded to creatively, imaginatively, and courageously by millions of people who see and experience the earth as a family and community consisting of all beings and humans of all colors, beliefs, classes, and countries.

In contrast to viewing the planet as private property, movements are defending, on a local and global level, the planet as a commons. In contrast to experiencing the world as a global supermarket, where goods and services are produced with high ecological, social, and economic costs and sold for abysmally low prices, cultures and communities everywhere are resisting the destruction of their biological and cultural diversity, their lives, and their livelihoods. As alternatives to the suicidal, globalized free market economy based on plundering and polluting the earth's vital resources, which displaces millions of farmers, craftspeople, and workers, communities are resolutely defending and evolving living economies that protect life on earth and promote creativity.

Corporate globalization is based on new enclosures of the commons; enclosures which imply exclusions and are based on violence. Instead of a culture of abundance, profit-driven globalization creates cultures of exclusion, dispossession, and scarcity. In fact, globalization's transformation of all beings and re-sources into commodities robs diverse species and people of their rightful share of ecological, cultural, economic, and political space. The "ownership" of the rich is based on the "dispossession" of the poor—it is the common, public resources of the poor which are privatized, and the poor who are disowned economically, politically, and culturally.

Patents on life and the rhetoric of the "ownership society" in which everything—water, biodiversity, cells, genes, animals, plants—is property express a worldview in which life forms have no intrinsic worth, no integrity, and no subjecthood. It is a worldview in which the rights of farmers to seed, of patients to affordable medicine, of producers to a fair share of nature's resources can be freely violated. The rhetoric of the "ownership society" hides the anti-life philosophy of those who, while mouthing pro-life slogans, seek to own, control, and monopolize all of the earth's gifts and all of human creativity. The enclosures of the commons that started in England created millions of disposable people. While these first enclosures stole only land, today all aspects of life are being enclosed—knowledge, culture, water, biodiversity, and public services such as health and education. Commons are the highest expression of economic democracy.

The privatization of public goods and services and the commoditization of the life support systems of the poor is a double theft which robs people of both economic and cultural security. Millions, deprived of a secure living and identity, are driven toward extremist, terrorist, fundamentalist movements. These movements simultaneously identify the other as enemy and construct exclusivist identities to separate themselves from those with whom, in fact, they are ecologically, culturally, and economically connected. This false separation results in antagonistic and cannibalistic behavior. The rise of extremism and terrorism is a response to the enclosures and economic colonization of globalization. Just as cannibalism among factory-farmed animals stops when chicken and pigs are allowed to roam free, terrorism, extremism, ethnic cleansing, and religious intolerance are unnatural conditions caused by globalization and have no place in Earth Democracy.

Enclosures create exclusions, and these exclusions are the hidden cost of corporate globalization. Our movements against the biopiracy of neem, of basmati, of wheat have aimed at and succeeded in reclaiming our collective biological and intellectual heritage as a commons. Movements such as the victorious struggle started by the tribal women of a tiny hamlet called Plachimada in India's Kerala state against one of the world's largest corporations, Coca-Cola, are at the heart of the emerging Earth Democracy.

New intellectual property rights enclose the biological, intellectual, and digital commons.

Privatization encloses the water commons. The enclosure of each common displaces and disenfranchises people which creates scarcity for the many, while generating "growth" for the few. Displacement becomes disposability, and in its most severe form, the induced scarcity becomes a denial of the very right to live. As the use of genetically modified seed and sex-selective abortions spread, large groups of people—especially women and small farmers—are disappearing. The scale and rate of this disappearance is proportional to the "economic growth" driven by the forces of neoliberal corporate globalization. However, these brutal extinctions are not the only trend shaping human history.

On the streets of Seattle and Cancún, in homes and farms across the world, another human future is being born. A future based on inclusion, not exclusion; on nonviolence, not violence; on reclaiming the commons, not their enclosure; on freely sharing the earth's resources, not monopolizing and privatizing them. Instead of being shaped by closed minds behind closed doors, as the hawkish right-wing Project for the New American Century was, the people's project is unfolding in an atmosphere of dialogue and diversity, of pluralism and partnerships, and of sharing and solidarity. I have named this project Earth Democracy. Based on our self-organizing capacities, our earth identities, and our multiplicities and diversity, Earth Democracy's success concerns not just the fate and well-being of all humans, but all beings on the earth. Earth Democracy is not just about the next protest or the next World Social Forum; it is about what we do in between. It addresses the global in our everyday lives, our everyday realities, and creates change globally by making change locally. The changes may appear small, but they are far-reaching in impact—they are about nature's evolution and our human potential; they are about shifting from the vicious cycles of violence in which suicidal cultures, suicidal economies, and the politics of suicide feed on each other to virtuous cycles of creative nonviolence in which living cultures nourish living democracies and living economies.

Earth Democracy is not just a concept, it is shaped by the multiple and diverse practices of people reclaiming their commons, their resources, their livelihoods, their freedoms, their dignity, their identities, and their peace. While these practices, movements, and actions are multifaceted and multiple, I have tried to identify clusters that present the ideas and examples of living democracies, living cultures, and live economies which together build Earth Democracy. Economy, politics, culture are not isolated from each other. The economies through which we produce and exchange goods and services are shaped by cultural values and power arrangements in society. The emergence of living economies, living cultures, and living democracies is, therefore, a synergistic process.

Living economies are processes and spaces where the earth's resources are shared equitably to provide for our food and water needs and to create meaningful livelihoods. Earth Democracy evolves from the consciousness that while we are rooted locally we are also connected to the world as a whole, and, in fact, to the entire universe. We base our globalization on ecological processes and bonds of compassion and solidarity, not the movement of capital and finance or the unnecessary movement of goods and services. A global economy which takes ecological limits into account must necessarily localize production to reduce wasting both natural resources and people. And only economies built on ecological foundations can become living economies that ensure sustainability and prosperity for all. Our economies are not calculated in the short term of corporate quarterly returns or the four- to five-year perspective of politicians. We consider the evolutionary potential of all life on earth and re-embed human welfare in our home, our community, and the earth family. Ecological security is our most basic security; ecological identities are our most fundamental identity. We are the food we eat, the water we drink, the air we breathe. And reclaiming democratic control over our food and water and our ecological survival is the necessary project for our freedom.

Living democracy is the space for reclaiming our fundamental freedoms, defending our basic rights, and exercising our common responsibilities and duties to protect life on earth, defend peace, and promote justice. Corporate globalization promised that free markets would promote democracy. On the contrary, the free markets of global corporations have destroyed democracy at every level. At the most fundamental level, corporate globalization destroys grassroots democracy through the enclosure of the commons. The very rules of globalization, whether imposed by the World Bank and the International Monetary Fund (IMF) or by the WTO, have been written undemocratically, without the participation of the most affected countries and communities. Corporate globalization undermines and subverts national democratic processes by taking economic decisions outside the reach of parliaments and citizens. No matter which government is elected, it is locked into a series of neoliberal reform policies. Corporate globalization is in effect the death of economic democracy. It gives rise to corporate control and economic dictatorship.

When economic dictatorship is grafted onto representative, electoral democracy, a toxic growth of religious fundamentalism and right-wing extremism is the result. Thus, corporate globalization leads not just to the death of democracy, but to the democracy of death, in which exclusion, hate, and fear become the political means to mobilize votes and power.

Earth Democracy enables us to envision and create living democracies. Living democracy enables democratic participation in all matters of life and death—the food we eat or do not have access to; the water we drink or are denied due to privatization or pollution; the air we breathe or are poisoned by. Living democracies are based on the intrinsic worth of all species, all peoples, all cultures; a just and equal sharing of this earth's vital resources; and sharing the decisions about the use of the earth's resources.

Living cultures are spaces in which we shape and live our diverse values, beliefs, practices, and traditions, while fully embracing our common, universal humanity, and our commonality with other species through soil, water, and air. Living cultures are based on nonviolence and compassion, diversity and pluralism, equality and justice, and respect for life in all its diversity.

Living cultures that grow out of living economies have space for diverse species, faiths, genders, and ethnicities. Living cultures grow from the earth, emerging from particular places and spaces while simultaneously connecting all humanity in a planetary consciousness of being members of our earth family. Living cultures are based on multiple and diverse identities. They are based on earth identity as both the concrete reality of our everyday lives— where we work, play, sleep, eat, laugh, or cry—and the processes which connect us globally.

"All things are connected," Chief Seattle tells us. We are connected to the earth locally and globally. Living cultures based on the recovery of our earth identity create the potential for reintegrating human activities into the earth's ecological processes and limits. Remembering we are earth citizens and earth children can help us recover our common humanity and help us transcend the deep divisions of intolerance, hate, and fear that corporate globalization's ruptures, polarization, and enclosures have created.

Ancient concepts of living peacefully as one while evolving in biologically and culturally diverse trajectories cross our interconnected earth family and inspire Earth Democracy. The ancient wisdom and tradition of non-separability and interconnectedness that we revive is evident in quantum theory, the space-time continuum of general relativity, and the self-organized complexity of living organisms.

REVIEW EXERCISES

1. What are some of the current contrasting conditions between rich and poor nations described in the text?
2. What causes do people give for the inequalities?
3. What self-interested reasons can be given for doing something to remedy the situation of poor countries?
4. What is justice, and what role does it play in determining what ought to be done and why?
5. What is the difference between economic and political rights, and how is this distinction related to Eastern and Western perspectives?
6. Describe the ethical problem concerning responsibility for those far and near.
7. Contrast Singer's and Hardin's views on how we ought to deal with famine.
8. Summarize the five different meanings of *globalization* given in the text.
9. Describe some positive and some negative aspects of globalization.

DISCUSSION CASES

1. Job Flight. For some time, companies in the United States and other Western countries have sought to cut costs by moving some manufacturing jobs to countries where labor is cheaper. Often the working conditions are deplorable and workers have fewer protections than in first-world countries. Should these companies have the freedom to do this? Or do these countries have a responsibility to the employees in their own countries?

2. Famine Relief. In a certain African country, the drought has been unusually harsh this year. Many people are starving. The political situation in the country is unstable. Some of the lack of food is the result of government mismanagement. The news media have nevertheless been able to get to the area and broadcast images of people who are clearly malnourished. Do people with so much more have any obligation to help these folks? Why or why not? If we ought to help them, is it a matter of charity or obligation?

3. Global Culture. Sam and Jane have been arguing about the effects of globalization as a form of modernization or Westernization of the world. Sam points out all of globalization's crass and commercialized aspects—including the ubiquitous McDonald's and Levis—that have negative effects on local cultures. Jane argues that Western personal and political freedoms ought to be made universal. With whom do you agree, Sam or Jane? Why?

4. Controlling Global Environmental Threats. Consider the threats to civilization as we know it presented by global warming and newly formed gaps in the protective ozone layer. Consider also the various nations and what each contributes to the threats. Suppose there are no strong international curbs. Each nation, then, must determine its own responsibility for lessening the threats. However, if Nation X lessens its own contribution by controlling emissions and other damaging chemicals, it will be put at a disadvantage economically in comparison with similarly developed nations that do not discipline themselves. It is the problem of the "free rider"—that is, when others do their share, I benefit most by not contributing.

Do problems such as this require some sort of international organizations and agreements, or should each nation or region make its own decisions on such matters?

YOU MAKE THE DECISION

Apply the theories and issues discussed in this chapter by accessing this animated simulation on the Ethics Resource Center.

Use the passkey that accompanies your book to gain access. If you do not have a passkey, visit cengagebrain.com to purchase instant access to additional study material.

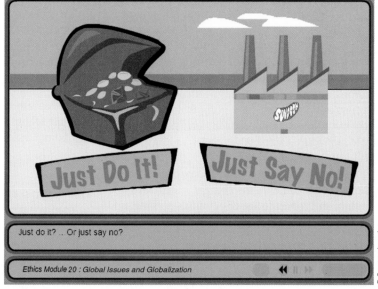

Just do it? .. Or just say no?

Ethics Module 20 : Global Issues and Globalization

© Cengage Learning

Appendix

HOW TO WRITE AN ETHICS PAPER

WRITING a paper does not have to be difficult. It can at least be made easier by following certain procedures. Moreover, you want to do more than write a paper—you want to write a *good* paper. You can do several things to improve your paper, changing it from a thing of rags and patches to a paper of which you can be proud. If it is a good paper, then you also will have learned something from producing it. You will have improved your abilities to understand and communicate, and you will have come to appreciate the matters about which you have written.

Writing philosophy papers, in particular, has a value beyond what one learns about the subject matter. As you know, philosophy is a highly rational discipline. It requires us to be clear, precise, coherent, and logical. Skill in doing this can be improved through practice and care. By trying to make your philosophy paper excel in these aspects, you will build skills that should carry over to other areas of your life. You may find that you are less likely to engage in sloppy and careless thinking, speaking, and writing.

In what follows, I review general procedures for writing papers and then outline elements that are particularly important for writing ethics papers. By following the suggestions given here, you should be able to produce a good ethics paper and further perfect your reasoning skills.

Several elements are basic to any paper. Among these are its content, the content's structure and format, and correct usage of grammar, spelling, and gender-neutral pronouns.

THE CONTENT OF THE PAPER

Your paper's subject matter is partly determined by the course for which it is assigned. Sometimes the topic will be chosen for you. As detailed in Chapter 1 and exemplified throughout this text, if the paper is for an ethics course, then it will deal with matters of right and wrong, good and bad, or just and unjust. It also probably will be given as a certain type of paper: a summary or critical analysis of some article or other writing, an exploration of a thesis or idea, or a research paper (more on this below). At other times, you will choose a topic yourself from a list or be asked to choose something specific from some more general area. You can select something in which you are particularly interested or something you would like to explore. It may be a topic you know something about or one about which you know little but would like to know more. Sometimes you can begin with a tentative list that is the result of brainstorming. Just write down ideas as you think of them. Sometimes you will have to do exploratory reading or library or Internet research to get ideas. In any case, choosing a topic is the first order of business in writing a paper. This is true of papers in general and ethics papers in particular.

THE PAPER'S STRUCTURE

I still recall the good advice of a teacher I had in graduate school. It was two simple bits of advice, but this did not make it less valuable.

1. A paper should have a beginning, a middle, and an end.
2. First you should tell what you are going to do. Then you should do it. Finally, you should tell what you have said or done.

This may seem overly simplistic, but you may be surprised to find out how many papers suffer from not including one or both of these elements. Over the years of writing papers in school and beyond, I have found this simple advice extraordinarily helpful.

You can develop the structure of your paper with an outline. Here is a sample using the advice just discussed.

1. *Beginning paragraph(s)*. Tell what you are going to do or say. Explain what the problem or issue is and how you plan to address it. You should make your reader want to go on. One way to do this is by showing why there is a problem. This can be done by giving contrasting views on something, for example. This is a particularly good way to begin an ethics paper.

2. *Middle Paragraph(s)*. Do what you said you were going to do. This is the bulk of the paper. It will have a few divisions, depending on how you handle your subject matter. (A more detailed outline of an ethics paper is given at the end of this appendix.)

3. *End Paragraph(s)*. Tell what you have done or said or concluded. More often than not, students end their papers without really ending them. Perhaps they are glad to have finished the main part of the paper and then forget to add an ending. Sometimes they really have not come to any conclusion and thus feel unable to write one. The conclusion can be tentative. It can tell what you have learned, for example, or it can tell what questions your study has raised for you.

Some word-processing programs provide an outlining function. These are helpful because they provide templates that allow you to set your main points first and then fill in the details. Parts can be expanded, moved, and reoriented. You can look at your paper as you progress with just the main headings or with as much detail as you like. In this way you can keep your focus on the logic of your presentation. If your word processor provides such a program, then you may want to get acquainted with and use it. Or you might try printing out your draft and marking the different sections by hand, checking it against a separate outline.

Format

How you arrange and present your ideas is also important. Among the elements you should examine

are the following: size, notes, citing Internet sources, and title page and bibliography.

Size This is most often the first, and perhaps the most significant, question asked by students when a paper is assigned: "How long does it have to be?" To pose the question of length in this way may suggest that the student will do no more than the minimum required. Although an excellent paper of the minimum length may fetch a top grade, it is probably a good idea to aim at more than the minimum length. It is also not enough just to know how many pages within a range are expected. If I use a large font, then I will write much less in five pages than if I use a small one. A word-count estimate is more definite. For example, one could be told that the paper should be between eight and ten pages with approximately 250 typed words per page. In some cases, professors have very specific requirements, expecting, for instance, ten pages of Times-style font, point size 12, with one-inch margins all around! You should have definite information as to what is expected in this regard.

Footnotes Does the instructor expect notes or citations? If so, must they be at the bottom of the page or is it permissible to place them at the end of the paper? Is there a specific format that must be followed for these?[1] Failing to document sources that you have used may be a form of *plagiarism*. Plagiarism is not acknowledging the source of ideas you include and attempting to pass them off as your own. This not only is deceitful, but also can even be thought of as a form of stealing. The use of proper citations avoids this.

Footnotes and endnotes have three basic purposes. The first purpose is to give the source of a direct quotation. This gives proper credit to other authors for their ideas and statements. You use quotations to back up or give examples of what you have said. You should always introduce or comment on the quotations that you use. You can introduce a quotation with something like this:

> One example of this position is that of Jack Sprat, who writes in his book, *Why One Should Eat No Fat*, that'. . . .'[1]

This quotation is followed by a footnote marker that would lead to the full citation. Sometimes, you will want to follow a quote with your own interpretation of it, such as "I believe that this means. . . ." In other words, you should always put the quotation in a context.

The second purpose is to give credit for ideas that you have used but summarized or put into your own words. Sometimes students think that the instructor will be less pleased if they are using others' ideas and are tempted to treat them as their own without giving a footnote reference. Actually, these attempts are often suspicious. Thus, the student who says that "Nowhere in his writings does Descartes mention x, y, or z," obviously strains credibility; it is unlikely that the student will have read all of the works of Descartes or know this on his or her own. It is one sign of a good paper if it gives credit for such indirect references. It shows that the student has read the source that is cited and has made an attempt to put it into his or her own words. This is a plus for the paper.

The third purpose of footnotes and endnotes is to give further information or clarification. For example, you might want to say that you mean just *this* in the paper and not *that*. You might also want to say something further about a point in the paper but you don't want to markedly interrupt the current line of thought.

Citing Internet Sources Many students find help for writing papers from the Internet. Some of these sources are more reliable and suitable for your ethics papers than others. InfoTrac, a source available by subscription through some libraries, for example, has many periodicals available online. It has an encyclopedia and many empirically oriented articles. Another recommended gateway site is Voice of the Shuttle: Web Page for Humanities Research, from the University of California at Santa Barbara.[2] Google, Yahoo, and other search engines can be exceptionally helpful if used correctly. Suppose you type in "cloning." You may find a million entries. You may then want to narrow your search by typing "human cloning." Even then you will have many entries to choose from. To be more specific, before typing either of these on Google, you can choose "more," which will give

you various possibilities. You may want to choose "news" for the latest news on your topic or "scholar" for scholarly papers.

You can learn a lot about your topic this way. However, if you include any of the material in your paper, you need to be sure that you credit your source—otherwise you are plagiarizing the material. You should cite your source and use quotation marks when you make a direct quote. But you should also cite it if you are putting the ideas there in your own words (as noted above on the purposes of notes and citations). You may think you will not be found out, but professors now have tools to check suspicious aspects of any paper. Depending on your instructor's directions for your paper, you probably should not limit your research or sources to the Internet, however, especially if you are doing something in-depth or on historical topics such as the philosophy of Kant. You also should be aware that not all Web sites are equally reliable sources of information. According to Jim Kapoun, a reference and instruction librarian, you should base your "Web evaluation on five criteria . . . accuracy, authority, objectivity, currency, and coverage."[3] You should consider who wrote the page, what the author's credentials are, whether the source of publication is a respected institution, whether the presentation is objective or is a mask for advertising, whether it is up-to-date, and whether the article is whole and intact or has elements that you must find elsewhere.

Using and then showing how you used the Internet itself requires some detail and direction. For example, you probably should supply the *uniform resource locator* (URL) of the site you use. Because these frequently change, you also can use the site's author, date you visited, and title. Giving the URL involves giving the whole reference, often enclosed in angle brackets as follows.

<http://www.search.yahoo.com/com/bin/
search?p=justice>

The "http" (hypertext transfer protocol) in the address is the usual method of connecting to information on the World Wide Web (the "www") through linked text and graphics. The rest of the items in the address indicate the path, folders, or directory names that tell where the information can be found. Much of the time, references end with "html," which means "hypertext markup language"; this type of file is still the primary type of document on the Internet.[4]

Title Page and Bibliography   You also will want to know whether your instructor expects a title page, a bibliography, and so forth. A bibliography will be fitting for certain types of papers—namely, research papers—and unnecessary for others. A paper in which you are mainly arguing for a point and developing ideas of your own may not require a bibliography. If a bibliography is required, then just how extensive it should be will depend on the paper's purpose, type, and length.

Grammar, Spelling, and Gender

In many cases, your paper will be graded not only on its content but also on mechanics such as grammar and spelling. It is always advisable to check your paper for grammar before the final version. For example, make sure all of your sentences are complete sentences. In the initial writing or revision, a sentence may lose its verb, the subject and predicate may no longer match, nouns and pronouns may not match, and so forth. You should review the paper to correct such mistakes.

Misspelling often is a sign of carelessness. We know how to spell the words, but we do not always take care to do so. Sometimes we are uncertain and do not take the time to look up the word in a dictionary. In using a word processor, the checking of spelling is made much simpler. However, even here spelling mistakes can be missed. For example, a spell checker cannot tell that you mean to say "to" instead of "too" or that you wanted to write "he" rather than "hell."

Today, we are also much more conscious of gender issues and gender bias than in decades past. In writing your ethics paper, you should be careful to avoid gender bias or sexist assumptions. For example, you should avoid such terms as *mailman* and *policeman*. Acceptable substitutes are *mail carrier* and *police officer*. You also can avoid gender bias by not using traditional gender roles. You might, for instance, speak of the business executive as a "she" and the nurse as a "he."

In times past, it also may have been acceptable to use *he* as a generic pronoun throughout a paper. Today, this is often less acceptable or even unacceptable. It is not always easy to remedy the situation, however, even when one wants to be fair and non-sexist. If one is referring to a particular male or female, then choosing the proper pronoun is easy. But if the reference can be either male or female, then what should one do with the pronouns? One can say "she" or "he" or "he or she." You can also alternate pronouns throughout the paper, sometimes using "he" and sometimes "she." As I have done in this paragraph, you can also use the gender-neutral "you," "one," or "they," "their," or "them" when possible.

TYPES OF ETHICS PAPERS

There are several different types of ethics papers that may be assigned in a philosophy class. You should be clear from the beginning which type you have been assigned or which you intend to pursue if you have a choice. According to one writer, there are five types of philosophy papers:[5]

1. thesis defense papers in which one "state[s] a position and give[s] reasons for believing it is true",[6]
2. a paper that compares and contrasts two viewpoints,
3. an analysis paper in which some particular viewpoint is examined more closely,
4. a paper that summarizes an article or a book, and
5. research papers or surveys on a specific topic.[7]

Our discussion of ethics papers overlaps this five-fold division. The following sections describe three types of ethics papers. Short examples of each can be found at the end of this appendix.

A Historical Approach

If you have already covered at least part of the beginning of this text, you will have some background in the history of ethics. Writings on ethics go back to the time of Plato in the West and earlier in other cultures. Other major figures in the history of Western ethics are Aristotle, Augustine, Aquinas, Locke, Hume, Kant, Marx, Mill, Nietzsche, Kierkegaard, and Sartre, and innumerable philosophers in the twentieth and twenty-first centuries have written and are writing on matters of ethics. If you are interested in exploring the ethical views of any of these philosophers, you can start with a general overview of their philosophies as given in some more general historical commentary on philosophy. *The Encyclopedia of Philosophy* (Macmillan and the Free Press, 1967) or the *Stanford Encyclopedia of Philosophy* (at http://plato.stanford.edu) might be an initial starting point. From this, you can determine whether a philosopher's views interest you, and you can see in general what type of ethical theory he or she espouses.

The main point of a historical exposition is to summarize or analyze a philosopher's views. It involves learning and writing down in some structured way your own understanding of those views. Your own views and interpretive comments can be added either as you go along or in some final paragraphs. You also can add your own critical or evaluative comments (positive or negative or both), possibly saving them for the end of the paper. Alternatively, you might make the paper entirely exposition, without adding your own views or critical comments.

A Problem in Ethical Theory

Another type of ethics paper is one that examines some particular issue in ethical theory. Part I of this text addresses several of these. Among these problems are:

> The Nature of Ethical Reasoning
> An Ethics of Rights Versus an Ethics of Care
> Ethical Relativism
> Moral Realism
> Moral Pluralism
> Ethical Egoism
> Why Be Moral?
> The Nature of a Right
> Charity Versus Obligation
> What Is Justice?
> What Is Virtue?

The point of a paper that treats a matter of ethical theory is to examine the problem itself. One approach is to start with a particular view on the issue, either in general or from some philosopher's point of view,

and then develop it using your own ideas. Another approach is to contrast two views on the issue and then try to show which one is more reasonable, in your opinion. For example, you could give two views on the nature of justice. One might hold that justice requires some kind of equality. Thus, a just punishment is one that fits the crime, or a just distribution of wealth is one that is equal. Then contrast this with another view and follow that with your own comments. For another approach, you might do a general presentation that simply tries to state the gist of the issue or problem and then give your own position on it. To summarize these, you could:

1. State a view, then develop it with your own ideas.
2. Contrast two views on a subject, then say which, if either, you find more persuasive.
3. Explain the problem and present your views on it.

A Contemporary Moral Issue

A third type of ethics paper focuses on some practical moral issue that is currently being debated. Part II of this text presents a selection of such issues. However, in each chapter in Part II, there are several issues from which you could choose. You might, for example, just focus on the issue of active euthanasia or physician-assisted suicide. You might write about the ethical issues that arise in our treatment of endangered species. Both issues are treated as part of chapters in this text. You might want instead to address some ethical issue that is not treated in this text: gun control, for example. However, on this topic as well as the others just mentioned, you should be certain to focus on the specific ethical issues involved if you are to make this an ethics paper.

One useful method of approaching a contemporary moral issue is to distinguish conceptual, factual, and ethical matters. *Conceptual matters* are matters of meaning or definition. *Factual matters* refer to what is the case about something. *Ethical matters* are matters of good and bad, better and worse, and they involve evaluation. Thus, regarding the issue of pornography, we could distinguish conceptual problems related to the attempt to say what it is as well as categorizing various forms of it. Factual matters would include descriptions of the types of pornography available, where they can be found, the numbers of users or viewers, its cost, and so on. The majority of an ethics paper should be the attempt to evaluate it and give reasons for the evaluation. I have tried to exemplify this approach in the chapters throughout Part II of this text.

IS IT AN ETHICS PAPER?

An ethical problem can be approached in different ways. Not all of them are ethical approaches or would make the basis of an ethics paper. Take problems of violence in this country. Many people believe that the United States is too violent. One approach to examining the problem is to focus on questions about the causes of violence. Is it something in our history or our psyche? Do the media cause violence or reflect it or both? To make either of these issues the focus of one's paper, however, is not to do ethics or an ethics paper but a sociological analysis or descriptive account of the situation.

An ethics paper requires that you take a *normative* approach and ask about what is better or worse, right or wrong, good or bad, just or unjust, and so on. (See Chapter 1 on the distinction between a normative and descriptive approach.) Therefore, regarding violence, an ethics paper might begin with a clarification of what is meant by violence and a description of the different kinds of violence. Next, it should become a discussion of what kinds of violence are justified or unjustified, for example. It might address the question of whether social or legal force is justified to diminish violence. This latter discussion could raise issues of the morality of legal force or the importance of individual liberty. In such discussions, one would be doing ethics, because one would be addressing the ethical issues about just and unjust behavior or the moral justification of some practice or the moral value of liberty.

To be sure that your presentation is one that strictly addresses an ethical issue as an ethical problem, make sure you do not appeal primarily to sources who are not authorities on ethical matters. For instance, if you are addressing the issue of gun control, then you should not appeal simply to legal sources such as the U.S. Constitution to back up your ideas. You may appeal to ethical values that are part of the Constitution, such as the value of life or freedom of speech, but then you are using them as ethical values apart from whether or not the law values them. If you are considering whether the law ought to permit active euthanasia or physician-assisted suicide, then you may consider whether having such a law would or would not promote certain ethical values. This would be an approach that could be used in an ethics paper.

STRUCTURING OR ANALYZING AN ETHICAL ARGUMENT

Most ethics papers either present or analyze ethical arguments, so you should consider some of the elements and types of ethical arguments. (Review the sections on ethical reasoning and ethical arguments from Chapter 1.) Among these are the following:

Reasons and Conclusions

It is important to notice and to be clear about what follows from what. Sometimes, key words or phrases will indicate this. For example, consider this statement: "Because X has better results than its alternative Y, we ought thus to adopt X." In this statement, the conclusion is that we ought to adopt some practice. The reason for this is that it has better results than its alternative. The key to knowing what follows from what in this example are the words *thus* and *because*. Being clear about this distinction enables you to make a better argument, for you can then back up your conclusion with other reasons and fill in the conclusions with more details.

Types and Sources of Evidence

As just noted, if you are to make an ethical argument, strictly speaking, you should not appeal to legal sources as such in order to make your case. You also cannot appeal to scientific sources for the ethical values or principles that you want to stress. For instance, although physicians are experts in diagnoses and prognoses, such medical expertise does not make them experts in knowing what kind of life is worthwhile or valuable, or how important are rights or autonomy. So, also, natural scientists can give us valuable information about the results of certain environmental practices, but this information and knowledge does not determine the importance or value of wilderness or endangered species. Sometimes, religious sources or authorities can be used in ethical arguments. When this is acceptable in an ethics or moral philosophy paper, however, it is usually because the values supported by religious sources are ethical values. For example, respect for one's parents might be promoted by a religion, but it also can be reasoned about by those who are not members of that or any religion.

Types of Reasons

As noted throughout this text, one primary distinction in ethical reasoning is the difference between an appeal to the consequences of some action or practice, and a judgment of actions and practices as right or wrong regardless of the consequences. It is important to be clear about which type of reason you or your source uses or critically evaluates.

Consequentialist Reasoning Your argument or the argument that you are summarizing or evaluating may be one that appeals to consequences. For example, you or the argument may assert that if we do such and such it will produce certain bad results. The argument can demonstrate these results by appeal to a scientific or other empirical source. The argument also must show why these results are bad—they may result in loss of life or produce great suffering, for example.

Nonconsequentialist Reasoning If your argument appeals to some basic moral value or what is alleged to be a moral right, then it is nonconsequentialist. For example, it might be based on the idea that we ought to be honest no matter the consequences. It may appeal to certain basic rights that ought to be protected whatever the consequences. To complete the argument or our evaluation of it, we should show or ask what the basis is for this type of assertion. For example, we might want to ask why autonomy is said to be a value or why liberty of action is a moral right.

Other Types of Reasons Consequentialist and nonconsequentialist are not the only types of reasons that can be given. One might say that something is just or unjust because all persons, when they think about it in the proper light, would agree that this is just. This is an appeal to something like common moral rationality or a common moral sense. Although this is problematic, the appeals to other types of reasons are also not without their critics.

Some people believe that persons of good character or virtue or of caring temperaments will best be able to judge what is right. To give a moral reason appealing to this sort of belief will also need some explanation. But it will be a start to notice that this is the type of reason that is being given.

Top-to-Bottom or Bottom-to-Top Reasoning?

Another way to construct or analyze ethical arguments is to decide whether the reasoning moves from top to bottom or from bottom to top.

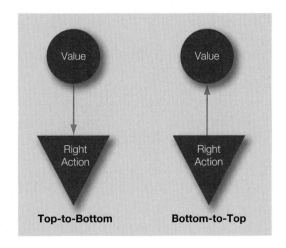

The top-to-bottom argument starts with a particular moral principle or moral value, and then applies the principle to a specific situation. For example, you might do the following:

1. Start with the assertion that happiness is the most important value, or the principle that we always ought to do whatever promotes the greatest amount of happiness (the utilitarian moral principle).
2. Then you would examine which action or practice among those that you are analyzing would promote the most happiness.

The bottom-to-top argument starts with a situation in which we intuitively feel that a certain course of action is right. We take a concrete case and our judgment about it, and then ask what moral value or principle leads us to make this judgement. For example, one might take the following approach:

1. Start with a case in which we believe that if someone is in great danger of drowning and we can save them, then we ought to do so.
2. Then we proceed to ask why we believe that this is so. What value does it promote or what rights or principles? We ask why we believe that we ought to do so. We might conclude that it flows from a moral principle that says that we always ought to help others in great need when we can do so without much cost to ourselves, and that this is a matter of obligation rather than of charity.

Although one can construct an argument that uses one or the other of these types of reasoning, actual moral reasoning often does both. Thus, your ethics paper also could incorporate both types.

Using Analogies

Many writings in ethics today use real or imaginary examples in their arguments. Among the more famous ones are Judith Thomson's violinist analogy (described in Chapter 11 on abortion) and James Rachels's tub example (in the Chapter 10 reading on euthanasia). There are also innumerable lifeboat and trolley examples. The method of arguing by analogy is as follows: If I start with some case and reach a certain moral conclusion about it, and if there is another case that is like it in the relevant respects, then I should conclude the same about it. Consider this example:

If we are dividing a pie and one person is hungrier than another, then that person should get the bigger piece. This is only fair. So, also, then we should say that in society at large the fair distribution of wealth is one in which those people who have greater needs should have a greater share of the wealth.

We can critically evaluate an analogy by considering whether the analogy fits. We ask whether the two situations or scenarios are similar in the relevant respects. Thus, in the previous example we might ask whether being hungrier than another is the same as having greater needs. We might also wonder whether there is anything crucially different between what is fair among individuals in sharing some good and what is fair in society with regard to sharing a nation's wealth. We might say that nothing else matters so much in the pie-sharing situation, but that additional things do matter in the situation of sharing a nation's wealth.

Many other considerations go into making an ethical argument a strong argument. However, these few given here should help you construct and critically analyze ethical arguments, which are the heart of an ethics paper.

SAMPLE ETHICS PAPERS

Here follow three shortened versions or outlines of the three types of ethics papers described. The first gives an outline of a historical ethics paper. The other two give examples of papers that address issues in ethical theory and practice. Although there are a few footnotes and endnotes included in the sample ethics papers, other examples of endnotes can be found throughout this text.

NOTES

1. See, for example, Modern Language Association, *MLA Handbook for Writers of Research Papers*, 7th ed. (New York: The Modern Language Association of America, 2009), for detailed help on forms of citation.
2. Christian Crumlish, *The ABCs of the Internet*, 2d ed. (Alameda, CA: Sybex, 1997).
3. Jim Kapoun, "Questioning Web Authority: How a Librarian Trains Students to Assess Web Page Credibility," *On Campus* (February 2000): 4.
4. See the current edition of the *MLA Handbook, The Chicago Manual of Style,* and other style guides, for more details on proper Internet citations.
5. Zachary Seech, *Writing Philosophy Papers*, 3d ed. (Belmont, CA: Wadsworth, 1997).
6. Ibid., 5.
7. Ibid.

Historical Approach

Kant's Theory of the Good Will

I. The Problem: Is it always good to do what you yourself think is right?

Sometimes people seem to act out of conscience and we like to praise this. However, sometimes they then do things that turn out to hurt others. How can we praise such behavior? Is it enough to have a good intention or a good will?

In this paper I plan to consider this issue from the perspective of the modern philosopher, Immanuel Kant, who is known for his views on the importance of motive in ethics. I will look briefly at who Kant was and then proceed to examine his views on the good will. Finally, I will see whether his views help me to answer the question I have posed in this paper.

II. Kant's Theory of the Good Will

A. Who was Kant?

B. What Kant holds on the good will

1. It is always good

2. To act with a good will is to act out of duty

3. To act with a good will is to act out of respect for the moral law

C. How this position relates to the initial problem

III. In this paper I have described Kant's views on the good will. I have found that, according to Kant, it is always good because the person who acts with a good will acts with the motive to do what morality requires. I then returned to the original questions that I posed to see how Kant answered them.

Finally, in my view Kant does (not) give a reasonable answer to my question, because . . .

A Problem in Ethical Theory

Moral Relativism

Many people today seem to be moral relativists. We tend to believe that what is good for some people is not necessarily also good for others. In some circumstances it seems that it is permissible to lie, and at other times it seems that we ought to tell the truth. On the other hand, we also argue with one another all the time about what actually is right and wrong. We do not seem to always accept the view that there is no better way. Are we then moral relativists or not? What is moral relativism? This paper will address these questions. It will begin with an attempt to determine what ethical relativism is. Then it will look at some of the arguments about whether it is true. Finally it will draw some conclusions about whether we actually do believe in ethical relativism.

What Ethical Relativism Is

According to the philosopher Richard Grace, ethical relativism is a theory which holds that "....."[1] He goes on to explain that.... As I understand it, this would mean....

Two Views of Ethical Relativism

Professor Grace believes that what ethical relativism asserts is not correct. The reasons he gives for his view are....[2]

A contrasting view is held by the philosopher Eleanor Brown. She writes that "....."[3] The reasons that Professor Brown believes that ethical relativism is a valid theory are....

My Views

I believe that Professor Grace has given reasonable arguments against ethical relativism. In particular I agree with his argument that....
My reason for doing so is that this is true to my experience. For example, ...

Notes as Footnotes

---

1. Richard Grace, "What Relativism Is," <u>Journal of Philosophy</u>, vol. 3, no. 2 (June 1987): 5–6.

2. Ibid., 6.

3. Eleanor Brown, Relativism (Cambridge, Mass: Harvard University Press, 1988), 35.

My Conclusions

In this paper, I have looked at two views on ethical relativism, one critical of it and one supporting it. Now that I have become clearer about what relativism is and have looked at opposing views on it, I conclude that it is not a reasonable view. Additionally, I believe that if we understand relativism in the way that these philosophers have explained it, we generally do not behave as though we were ethical relativists. For example, ... On the other hand, there are some things that are still questions in my mind about ethical relativism. Among these are. . . . I look forward sometime to finishing my inquiry into this difficult problem.

Notes as Endnotes

Notes

1. Richard Grace, "What Relativism Is," <u>Journal of Philosophy</u>, vol. 3, no. 2 (June 1987): 5–6.

2. Ibid., 6.

3. Eleanor Brown, <u>Relativism</u> (Cambridge, Mass: Harvard University Press, 1988), 35.

A Contemporary Ethical Issue

The Ethics of Cloning

Just the other day in the newspaper there was a report of a case of the cloning of a human being.[1] According to this report, while we have cloned vegetables and some small animals in the past, there has never before been a published report of a case of a human being being cloned. This case has raised quite a stir. In particular many people have raised ethical questions about this case. There is a diversity of opinion about whether such a practice is right or wrong. In this paper I will examine the ethical debate over the cloning of human beings. I will begin with a description of the process and this case. Next I will summarize the arguments for and against this practice. Finally I will present my own conclusions about the ethics of cloning human beings.

What Is Cloning?

There are two types of cloning.[2] One is. . . . The other is. . . . In this case the second type was used. What these scientists did was. . . .

The Case against Cloning

Many people wonder about the ethics of cloning human beings. Some express fears that it would be abused. For example, Professor . . . is quoted in the news article saying that. . . .[3] The idea seems to be that many people might have themselves cloned so that they could use this clone for organ transplants. Others worry that. . . .

   The arguments of Professor . . . seem reasonable. I especially agree with him that. . . .

The Case in Favor of Cloning

On the other hand, Doctor . . . and others argue that with the right kinds of safeguards the cloning of humans would be just as ethically acceptable as the cloning of carrots. Among the safeguards that they list are. . . .[4]

   One of the problems that I see with this position is. . . .

My Conclusions

In this paper I have found that the project to clone human beings consists in a process of. . . . I have looked at ethical arguments in support of and critical of this procedure when applied to humans. I conclude that while there may be some advantages to be gained from this method of producing babies, what worries me about cloning humans is. . . . I will continue to follow this issue as it develops, for I'm sure that this is not the last time we will hear of the cloning of humans nor the last of the debate about its ethical implications.

Notes

1. <u>The Sue City Daily News</u>, January 17, 1993, C7.

2. Jane Gray, <u>Modern Genetics</u> (New York: The American Press, 1988), 5–10.

3. <u>The Sue City Daily News</u>, C7.

4. See Chapter 4 in Martin Sheen and Sam Spade, <u>Cloning</u> (San Francisco: The Free Press, 1991), 200–248.

Index